Municipal Finances

7.5 X 9.25

Municipal Finances

A Handbook for Local Governments

Catherine Farvacque-Vitkovic and
Mihaly Kopanyi, Editors

THE WORLD BANK
Washington, D.C.

CONTENTS

Chapter 8. Achieving Greater Transparency and Accountability: Measuring Municipal Finances Performance and Paving a Path for Reforms 379
Catherine Farvacque-Vitkovic and Anne Sinet

Boxes

Figures

Maps

Tables

FOREWORD

Municipal Finances, A Handbook for Local Governments takes sides. It takes the side of mayors and municipal managers. Few publications on municipal finance target local-level decision makers and financial staff in such a direct and pragmatic way. This book's content and key messages are geared to respond to daily concerns and issues that cities and municipalities face in the management of their finances. Municipalities have made it clear that they need access to global knowledge and that they are seeking to be part of a larger community of practice. A companion e-learning program ("Municipal Finances—A Learning Program for Local Governments") has also been developed by the same World Bank team. Its online delivery by the World Bank and its partners will help reach out to an even greater number of interested audiences and help create a platform for a larger community of practice.

Municipal Finances, A Handbook for Local Governments takes a position. Much has been learned about what works and what does not, and yet every time we talk about finances or engage in policy discussions or project preparation we tend to reinvent the wheel. Structured around eight chapters, this book reviews lessons learned about intergovernmental relations, metropolitan finance, financial management, revenues management, expenditures management, public assets management, external funding, and municipal finances performance measurement. It spans the arc from decentralization to transparency and accountability and travels the less-charted waters of assets management, creditworthiness, response to financial crisis, reporting mechanisms to various levels of government and civil representation.

Municipal Finances, A Handbook for Local Governments calls for action. Not only does it provide cutting-edge knowledge on many technical issues, it also guides local governments through the maze of existing instruments. In particular, it provides a framework for municipal finances self-assessment to help municipalities evaluate their situations honestly and pragmatically, draw conclusions, and move forward on the path of reforms. In democratic societies, where open government and open data have become accepted norms, an abundance of social media tools is ready to capture citizen voices demanding accountability and transparency from their governments. It is essential that local governments be prepared to present, and articulate as genuinely as possible, their current financial and economic situation, their bottlenecks, and their perspectives for the future.

The world of today will shape the cities of tomorrow, and the cities of today will shape the world of tomorrow. The task of getting municipal finances right is an immediate and urgent goal. We hope that the lessons and propositions outlined in this handbook will be a step in the right direction.

Ede Jorge Ijjasz-Vasquez
Senior Director for Urban,
Rural and Social Development
Global Practice
The World Bank

Abha Joshi-Ghani
Director, Knowledge Exchange and
Learning
The World Bank

ACKNOWLEDGMENTS

First, we would like to thank all the contributing authors of this book, who devoted immeasurable time and energy to this effort. Their diligence and patience toward the editors' numerous requests, queries and revisions and their professional expertise were vital to the success of this endeavor.

We are especially thankful to Christine F. Kessides, Manager, World Bank Institute, and to Abha Joshi-Ghani, Director, World Bank Institute, for their support and guidance. We would like to thank our formal reviewers for their valuable advice and constructive comments, especially Jonas Frank, Matthew Glasser, Tony Levitas, Lili Liu, Gabor Peteri, Hiroaki Suzuki, and Victor Vergara, as well as Stephen Hammer and Sameh Naguib Wahba, World Bank. We also have greatly benefited from numerous conversations with colleagues, peers, regional experts within the World Bank and outside the World Bank. Our engagement with many municipalities and local government practitioners around the globe has provided the fertile ground for learning "from the trenches." There are too many to mention by name.

We have benefited from the professional and technical support of Sabine Palmreuther, Sheila Jaganathan, Maya Brahmam and Chisako Fukuda, World Bank Institute, and of Jeffrey N. Lecksell, Cartographer, World Bank. Sawdatou Wane and Brett Beasley have provided important support.

We also are grateful to the World Bank department of publishing and knowledge, especially Patricia Katayama, Rick Ludwick, and Nora Ridolfi for their professional guidance.

Last but not least, we are grateful to the Austrian government which helped finance some parts of this work under the World Bank-Austria Urban Partnership.

Catherine Farvacque-Vitkovic and Mihaly Kopanyi
Editors

Dedicated to Patrick Farvacque, whose love of mathematics and contribution to municipal finances were an inspiration.

ABOUT THE EDITORS

Catherine Farvacque-Vitkovic has more than 25 years of World Bank experience in many regions of the world and has worked in about 30 countries. As a Lead Urban Development Specialist, she has led the preparation and implementation of a large number of urban development and municipal management projects around the world and has been the recipient of numerous awards for excellence. She is the author or coauthor of several sector studies as well as several books, such as *Crest 1650–1789: La Ville et Son Evolution; Reforming Urban Land Policies and Institutions in Developing Cities/Politiques Foncières des Villes en Développement; The Future of African Cities, Challenges and Opportunities for Urban Development/ L'Avenir Des Villes Africaines, Enjeux et Priorités; Street Addressing and the Management of Cities; Building Local Governments' Capacity; Municipal Self-Assessments, A Handbook for Local Governments* (forth coming). She has a keen interest in translating lessons from experience and cutting-edge know-how into practical knowledge products and is currently leading the development and worldwide delivery of an e-learning curriculum on land management, urban planning and municipal finances.

Mihaly Kopanyi is a municipal finance consultant. Before he retired from the World Bank in 2011, he was a municipal finance adviser and cochair of the Municipal Finance Thematic Group and worked in 30 countries. His core competency areas include intergovernmental finance and financial intermediaries. He has written or edited a dozen books and numerous articles, the latest of which is "Financing Municipalities in Turkey," and the municipal finances e-learning program of the World Bank Institute. He holds a PhD in price policy and a doctor of university degree in logistics. He was a professor and chair of the Microeconomics Department, Budapest University. His postgraduate studies include training at the Wharton School and Stanford University.

KEY CONTRIBUTORS

Mats Andersson specializes in urban development and metropolitan management, municipal finance, project management, institutional development, and related training. His clients include multilateral and bilateral development agencies, financial institutions, governments, and research institutes. From 1994 through 2007 he was an urban management and municipal finance specialist at the World Bank, responsible for project development, lending, and advisory programs in China and Eastern and Central Europe. He has also advised clients in Sweden, Canada, East Africa, and Latin America. Mats holds MBA degrees from Sweden and the United States, and is a Certified Management Consultant (CMC) of the Canadian Association of Management Consultants.

Robert D. Ebel is an international consultant and former Lead Economist with the World Bank Institute (WBI). While at the WBI, he served as the World Bank's technical representative to the Sudan Peace Consultations (2002–05), and for the African Union, a technical resource person at the Inter-Sudanese Peace Consultations on Darfur (2006). From 2006 to 2009, he was Deputy Chief Financial Officer for Revenue Analysis and Chief Economist for the government of Washington, D.C.

Maria E. (Mila) Freire is an international consultant on urban economics and public finance. While at the World Bank, she held several positions, including Senior Advisor to the Sustainable Development Network, Manager of the Urban Program for Latin America, and core member of the *World Development Report 2009, Reshaping Economic Geography*. Her recent publications include *Urban Land Markets* (2009), *Cities and Climate Change—An Urgent Agenda* (2011), and *Financing Slum Upgrading* (2013, Lincoln Institute of Land Reform). Mila holds a PhD in economics from the University of California, Berkeley. She teaches urban economics at The Johns Hopkins University in Baltimore, Md.

Hernando Garzón is an economist. He earned his doctorate at the Maxwell School at Syracuse University (1988) and joined the World Bank as an Inter-Governmental Finance Specialist in 1989. Dr. Garzón is a former staff member of the Bank and currently works as an international consultant. He has worked extensively in fiscal decentralization, intergovernmental finance, urban finance, and municipal development funds. His broad international experience in developing and emerging economies covers 36 countries across all regions. His most recent World Bank publications include "Municipal Finance and Service Provision in West Bank and Gaza" (2010) and "City Finances of Ulaanbaatar" (2013).

Olga Kaganova is Principal Research Scientist at NORC at the university of Chicago and is an internationally recognized expert on government land and asset management, consulting for donor organizations and governments on a wide range of reforms, from national policies to improving the performance of municipal property. She has worked in 30 countries and advised the governments of Chile, the Arab Republic of Egypt, Ethiopia, Kosovo, and Kuwait; the U.S. state of California; and the cities of Bishkek, Cape Town, Moscow, Mecca, Ulaanbaatar, Warsaw, and Laibin. She has published two books and numerous papers and is an adviser for the Canadian National Executive Forum on Public Property and an adjunct professor at Clemson University.

Lance Morrell has more than 35 years of professional experience in financial management in the public and private sectors. After he retired from the World Bank with more than 22 years of project experience in East Asia and Africa, Mr. Morrell founded FEI Consulting, LLC, and continued to work on financial management and institutional strengthening projects throughout the world. Before joining the World Bank, Mr. Morrell served as treasurer and as division controller for major corporations. He is a Certified Public Accountant and a Chartered Global Management Accountant.

Abdu Muwonge is a Senior Economist in the Urban and Water Unit, in the Sustainable Department in the South Asia Region at the World Bank. Before joining the World Bank, he worked at the Economic Policy Research Center (EPRC) in Uganda. He has previously taught undergraduate economics and statistics at Makerere University and Mbarara University of Science and Technology in Uganda. Mr. Muwonge holds a master of arts degree in economics from the University of Dar es Salaam and a master's degree and PhD in public finance from Andrew Young School of Policy Studies, Georgia State University.

Anne Sinet is a lead international specialist in local and municipal government finance and institutional organization in France and developing countries. Her work includes a senior managerial position in the DGCL (French Ministry of the Interior); she was a Senior Associate in three private French consulting firms and has undertaken many consulting assignments for the World Bank, European Union, EIB, ADB, and French Cooperation Agencies. She has been extensively involved in financial and fiscal analyses for local governments in more than 50 countries and is author or coauthor of several handbooks and research-based books.

Rama Krishnan Venkateswaran is a Lead Financial Management Specialist at the World Bank. His extensive experience in municipal finance includes work in Sri Lanka, Bhutan, Nepal, India, Ghana, Uganda, and Swaziland. He has worked with the Cities Alliance Secretariat in the Municipal Finance Task Force. Before the World Bank, Rama worked with the government of India and held senior positions in local governments, including chief administrative officer of a district. Rama has a master's degree in economic policy management, Columbia University, and a master's in accounting, George Washington University. He is a Certified Public Accountant and a Certified Government Financial Manager.

Introduction

Catherine Farvacque-Vitkovic

From Detroit to Lahore, most cities around the world are facing financing challenges. Bankruptcy, budget deficits, financial debacles, unmaintained infrastructure, declining quality of services, entire neighborhoods closing down, increasing urban poverty, and mounting social exclusion are common headlines and are the unfortunate fate of many local governments. Most countries have embarked on a decentralization process, with various degrees of progress and success. It is fair to say that, in most cases, the transfer of responsibilities from the central government to local governments has not been accompanied by the adequate transfer of resources. Among the most important pending issues are the needs to (a) clarify the distribution of responsibilities among the levels of government and (b) strengthen the resource base of local governments. Some reforms attempt to clarify responsibilities without addressing financial issues. Others assign municipal governments new responsibilities that they are ill equipped to manage. At the same time, municipalities are becoming increasingly dependent on intergovernmental transfers, which have been shrinking over time, in part because of the fiscal pressure created by the global economic slowdown.

Today, in most countries, municipal budgets are sufficient to cover cities' operating costs but not to finance much needed capital investments. That will require that cities make more effective use of their own revenues as well as access credit markets. A key issue is how local governments can expand their resource base beyond transfers. Municipal practitioners are keen to use and integrate new financial management ideas and tools to control their costs, identify new revenue sources, and improve local tax collection. In addition, local governments have potential access to large sources of external funding, though they often do not know how to tap them (EU funding for southeastern Europe, for example). Municipalities seek support on how to plan and execute priority investments and prepare fundable projects. For those local governments that are in better financial shape, enhancing their creditworthiness and prudently accessing capital markets offer opportunities for profound change. In all cases, improved governance practices and enhanced accountability mechanisms have become central to sound city government and municipal management.

The World Bank has been involved in a large number of urban and municipal development projects. The 2009 Internal Evaluation (IEG) Report noted that over 190 such projects were implemented since 1998 and found that "among the three dimensions of municipal management – planning, finance, and service provision – finance yielded successful results". It also pointed out that the highest performance was among municipal development projects implemented by the World Bank in Africa and we will review in this book how the introduction of specific tools helped achieve this result. Lessons from the ground show that, although reforms at the macro-level are difficult to achieve, a lot can be done at the local government level when there is political will for greater accountability in the use of public funds and when reforms on revenue generation are clearly connected to visible expenditures/investments in infrastructure and service delivery. This is grounded in the understanding that (a) the strategic management of municipal finances is critical in ensuring long-term sustainability of local services and infrastructure and (b) increased fiscal constraints and pressure from the global financial and economic downturn require increasingly sophisticated responses from local governments in mobilizing and using financial resources.

Against this backdrop, there is both a sense of urgency and a huge opportunity for capacity building programs directed at local governments. Despite the financial pressures weighing on local governments across the globe, there are many good practices which need to be shared and many failures which need to be learned from. This handbook builds on these practices and is designed to help city officials improve their financial management even in the toughest of economic environments.

What to Expect? A Quick Overview of Handbook Objectives and Content

Objective: This handbook is a component of a larger program promoted by the World Bank "Municipal Finances—A Learning Program for Local Governments". It is a companion publication to an e-learning product delivered by the World Bank and other partners. It aims to enhance the knowledge and capacity of local governments. The program adopts local governments' perspective and provides tools and how-to instruments to improve the management and transparency of local finances.

Chapter 1: Intergovernmental Finances in a Decentralized World. Written for municipal finance practitioners and policy makers alike, chapter 1 provides the basic foundation for working through the next seven chapters. It begins with a discussion of why "getting municipal finance right" is key to achieving a nation's broader goals of economic growth, macroeconomic stabilization, and, for some countries, national cohesion among diverse populations. It then summarizes the key considerations of alternative governance structures, as well as fundamental questions related to what role municipalities should play in a country's revenue and expenditure systems. The chapter concludes with an examination of the role of government-to-government grants policy and the tools for ensuring accountability between the various levels of government and between the municipality and its citizens.

Chapter 2: Metropolitan Governance and Finances. This chapter describes how cities tend to grow and the challenges that interdependent local governments in larger metropolitan areas have to deal with. Readers will find an overview of governance models and municipal finance issues in metropolitan cities around the world. On municipal finance, the chapter focuses on those aspects that are unique to municipalities that are part of larger, interdependent agglomerations. The chapter includes several case descriptions.

Chapter 3: Municipal Financial Management. This chapter introduces the basic building blocks of municipal financial management and provides the conceptual foundation for the subsequent chapters on improving expenditure management and performance assessment. The chapter discusses the fundamental concepts of budgeting, accounting, financial reporting, and auditing and their applications in a local government context through case studies and simple problem sets. The objective of the chapter is to enable the reader to develop a good understanding of those critical processes in municipal financial management and link them in a practical way to larger goals of improving local government financial transparency, efficiency, and effectiveness.

Chapter 4: Managing Local Revenues. This chapter reviews the main revenue sources available to local governments, the issues typically associated with such sources, and the key challenges facing city financial officers. It provides a position on what are the most promising sources of revenues. It supports the enhancement of local institutional capacity by highlighting the different roles and responsibilities of a revenue authority, including a description of the main functions of a revenue administration. It discusses the main issues and challenges associated with revenue management functions and offers guidance to practitioners on how to achieve more effective and efficient revenue administration and collection. It illustrates how to conduct revenue trend analysis, including a discussion of different approaches to revenue forecasting. Finally, it addresses the main challenges that the political economy poses for revenue management, describes how to implement revenue mobilization strategies, and examines the impacts of revenue policy.

Chapter 5: Managing Local Expenditures. This chapter introduces concepts designed to strengthen the ability of local government administrators, local government council members, department heads, and finance staff to manage and control expenditures so that local services can be provided efficiently and effectively and the tax burden on citizens can be minimized. By managing and controlling expenditures and developing procedures to monitor and evaluate the results, government officials will be better able to minimize the tax burden on the population while providing desired levels of services.

Chapter 6: Managing Local Assets. This chapter demonstrates why physical assets (land, buildings, infrastructure, etc.) and enterprises are important for local well-being. It provides a framework and a set of practical tools for improving asset management and for linking asset management with financial management. The chapter guides local governments on who should do what and how to begin a long-term improvement program. It suggests ways to find additional savings and generate additional revenues from assets and provides tools for the financial analysis of assets. It elaborates on a number of technical issues because such technical details are critical for successful asset management (e.g., how to improve the attractiveness of municipal land to investors or induce competition in land auctions). Finally, the chapter discusses more advanced instruments of asset management, such as land policies, land-based financing, land asset strategy, public-private partnerships, and special purpose corporations.

Chapter 7: Managing External Resources. This chapter discusses how local governments can access external resources to finance local development programs. It reviews the types of external resources available to local governments—from grants to borrowing and private sector partnerships—discusses how to ensure prudent borrowing, and illustrates the importance of a participatory capital investment program to guide the choice of priority programs and ensure their financing. Case studies are used to illustrate experiences and strategies. By the end of the book, readers will be able to assess which financing alternatives will be more suitable for their local government.

Chapter 8: Achieving Greater Transparency and Accountability: Measuring Municipal Finances Performance and Paving a Path for Reforms. This chapter attempts to define what performance measurement really means. Are we doing the right things? Are we doing things right? First, the chapter focuses on lessons learned from performance measurement practices and experiences in developed countries and assesses how to adapt performance measurement in the context of developing cities. Second, it reviews the four key reporting mechanisms commonly used for measuring municipal finances performance: (a) state supervision, (b) risk analysis by financial partners, (c) internal financial follow-up by municipal staff, (d) reporting to citizens. Third, it also provides step-by-step guidance to complete a Municipal Finances Self-Assessment (MFSA) to (a) assess a city's financial health and (b) identify specific actions to improve financial management practices, mobilization of local revenues, public spending, public assets management and maintenance, investment programming, and access to external funding. By the end of the book, readers will be able to use the MFSA template for their city and apply the findings of assessment in their day-to-day business and in their medium-term reform agenda. For users' convenience, the Excel template can be downloaded at http://siteresources.worldbank.org/EXTURBAN DEVELOPMENT/Resources/MFSA-Template .xlsx.

CHAPTER 1

Intergovernmental Finances in a Decentralized World

Abdu Muwonge and Robert D. Ebel

The *World Development Report, Entering the Twenty-First Century,* reaches the dramatic conclusion that two forces are shaping the world in which development policy will be defined and implemented. The first is *globalization,* the continuing integration of the countries of the world. The second is *localization,* political self-determination and the devolution of finances (World Bank 2000). What is labeled "localization" is often cited as "decentralization"—the sorting out of intergovernmental public sector functions among multiple types of government, central and subnational. Moreover, whereas at first glance the two trends seem countervailing, they are in fact complementary, as they often stem from the same set of external factors.

The underpinnings of the complementarity of globalization and localization are several. For example, advances in information and communications technology are facilitating the spread of global knowledge that allows local groups to bypass central authorities in their search for improved government effectiveness. Also influential is the emergence of local, national, and supranational organizations and institutions, such as civil society and other citizen networks, free trade regimes, *Millennium Development Goal* partnerships, and, in some cases, a common currency.

This chapter is organized in three sections. The first develops the "big picture" of intergovernmental finance by drawing the distinction between political and fiscal decentralization and then proceeds to identify alternative models or variants of decentralized governance. It concludes with a review of what has been learned from recent empirical literature regarding the economic and fiscal results of decentralizing.

The second section takes on the key topic of transfers from central to local governments, their design, uses, and intended outcomes. The chapter concludes with a list of takeaway lessons.

Overview of Intergovernmental Finance

Wherever one looks around the globe, some kind of decentralization is taking place or being discussed. A variety of definitions, rationales, and arrangements are, and can be, encompassed under the very imprecise and awkward term "decentralization." Thus, it is useful to begin by laying out some terminology.

Political Decentralization

Political decentralization refers to arrangements whereby the legal legitimacy of local government is recognized either explicitly in the national constitution or by statutory and administrative decisions. In most countries it involves providing for (a) local elections; (b) a division of spending responsibilities or competencies among types of governments; (c) subnational (e.g., municipal) own-taxing authority; (d) rules and regulations relating to local borrowing and debt management; and (e) a special status for capital cities (Slack and Chattopadhyay 2009). In much of the postsocialist and developing worlds, this process is centrally led and legislated; that is, it is "top-down." Even though the political impetus for decentralizing the central state may reflect a reaction "from below" to long years of extensive central control (Bird, Ebel, and Wallich 1995; Swianiewicz 2006; Regulski 2010), and in some cases even a "reaction from above," as in order to generate trust in a new system of governance, and even though the center has started decentralizing with lower levels (Smoke and Taliercio 2007), it is nevertheless the general case that the central authority manages the decentralization process. This is true even in cases where the political outcome is such that subnational governments are, at least by law, allowed a high degree of political and fiscal authority (boxes 1.1 and 1.2).

Fiscal Decentralization

Whereas the decision to decentralize is political, the economic and financial payoff flows from a well-designed system of *fiscal decentralization*— that is, the intergovernmental sorting out of responsibilities for expenditures and financing among the various types, tiers, or levels of government, in a manner that is in harmony with the political framework.

Questions for Any Intergovernmental Setting

Four fundamental questions must be addressed with respect to fiscal decentralization:

1. Which type or tier of government does what (expenditure assignment)?

2. Which type of government is responsible for obtaining which revenues (revenue assignment)?

3. How can fiscal imbalances between the center and subnational units and across subnational jurisdictions be resolved, when the case for decentralizing spending is almost always greater than that for decentralizing revenue generation (a role for intergovernmental transfers)?

4. How shall the timing of receipts and payment for capital spending be addressed (borrowing and debt)?

This chapter addresses only the third of those four questions, the topic of intergovernmental transfers. The first two questions and the fourth are addressed in subsequent chapters of this book. A brief summary is useful before proceeding to the details of intergovernmental transfers.

Expenditure assignment. The fundamental guideline for which type of government has the responsibility for which spending functions is the *subsidiarity principle,* that is, that public

Box 1.1 Political Economy of Decentralization Reform: Nepal

A country's structure of local governments is a function of several complex factors, including history, politics, economic potential, constitutions, and legislation, among others. Nepal is an example of the complexity of establishing, transitioning to, and managing decentralization processes. Throughout its modern history, Nepal was defined by a unitary system of government. Before 1951, little or no consideration was given to empowering the local governments. But even after a series of political reforms in the 1950s, it was not until the 1980s that some efforts were made to decentralize power. Underlying the present local government system are several pieces of legislation. In the 1950s, two acts had been promulgated establishing local government units: the Municipality Act of 1953 and the Village Act of 1956. Following the country's return to autocratic rule in 1960, those acts were replaced by the Town Panchayat Act of 1962 and the Village Panchayat Act of 1962.

In 1981–82 the Decentralization Act was introduced, and local bodies were given some responsibilities in local-level planning and resource allocation. By 1990, multiparty democracy was restored, and the country's fifth constitution was ratified, which enshrined decentralization as a fundamental element of democracy. In 1991, three acts were passed creating elected local bodies, namely, the District Development Committee Act, the Village Development Committee Act, and the Municipality Act. These laws were criticized as not having provided local governments enough autonomy; local bodies lacked sufficient expenditure and taxing power, and civil society, nongovernmental organizations, disadvantaged groups, and the private sector were not explicitly brought into the local governance structure.

In 1999 Parliament passed the Local Self-Governance Act (LSGA). The LSGA was considered a landmark in Nepal. It laid down the foundations of local self-governance by increasing the devolution of administrative, fiscal, and judicial powers to local bodies. The current assignment of expenditure responsibilities in Nepal is largely based on the LSGA. As of 2011, Nepal's local government structure was divided into 75 districts, 58 municipalities, and 3,913 village development committees (VDCs). These jurisdictions fall into 5 development regions and 14 administrative zones. A VDC consists of 9 wards, and the municipalities consist of from nine to 35 wards. Municipalities and VDCs are directly elected. Officially, all three local bodies are autonomous, so there is no legally mandated hierarchical relationship between them. In practice, district-level governments have some supervisory role over both municipalities and villages, and some resources that fund municipal and village programs are channeled through the districts.

Although the LSGA was intended to be the blueprint for fiscal decentralization, most of the major elements of the act were not actually implemented. Most public services in local areas are provided by line agencies of central government ministries. In some cases, these are deconcentrated to the local area. Local governments provide services, but only in limited amounts. In general, Nepal remains largely centralized, with only about 6 percent of total government expenditures made by local governments.

Source: Sharma and Muwonge 2010.

Box 1.2 Poland: Political Decentralization in a Multitier System

The local government structure in Poland is a result of two waves of decentralization reform. The first wave took place in 1990, when the local government system was introduced on a *gmina* level. Local government reform was one of the main priorities for the first postcommunist government, which was formed in September 1989. Quick but intensive preparations allowed the passage of the new Local Government Law in March 1990, which was followed by local elections in May 1990 and a radical decentralization of financial regulations in January 1991. The 1990 reform introduced elected local government on the *gmina* level only; upper tiers of territorial divisions continued to be managed by the state administration. The second stage of the reform introduced two new tiers of elected subna-

tional governments in 1999: *powiat* (county) and *voivodship* (region).

At present there are three tiers of territorial governments: almost 2,500 municipalities; 315 counties, plus 65 cities with county status; and 16 regions. On both a municipal and a county level, local self-governments are the only form of public administration. Central state functions, such as registration of births and marriages, are delivered by local government as delegated functions financed by specific grants. On a regional level, there is a dual structure—elected self-government and a governor, appointed by the prime minister, with his or her own administrative apparatus. However, functions of self-government and state regional administrations are clearly separated, and there is no hierarchical subordination between them.

Source: Swianiewicz 2006.

responsibilities should generally be exercised by the authorities that are closest to the citizens, and that assigning a responsibility to another authority should be based on considerations of the extent of the task and requirements of efficiency (Oates 1972; Yilmaz, Vaillancourt, and Dafflon 2012; Marcou 2007). Further considerations include the presence of externalities (the spillover of spending activities across legal jurisdictional boundaries), economies of scale (unit cost of production), and capacity to administer and implement the function (among the several good expositions of the expenditure assignment question are Martinez-Vazquez 1999 and Dafflon 2006). In chapter 5 of this book, Morrell and Kopanyi explore expenditure practices for municipalities in detail.

Revenue assignment. One of the guidelines for the implementation of a well-designed system of

fiscal decentralization is that "finance follows function" (Bahl 1999a; Bahl and Martinez-Vazquez 2006; Smoke and Taliercio 2007). After the assignment of expenditure responsibility, the next question is: Which government unit shall levy which revenues? This question of finance is just as important and complex as the spending function. Indeed, a good argument can be made that one does not have a system of fiscal decentralization unless subnational (e.g., local) governments have the autonomy to levy (and, in many cases, collect) their own revenues. To realize the efficiency benefits that will flow from a well-designed system of decentralization, local governments must be able to generate own-source revenues (Jensen 2001; Ebel and Weist 2007). The assignment of revenues to different types of government should not be interpreted to imply that the proceeds from each type of tax should be designated to only one type of government. There is no reason to assign revenues of a given tax or fee to one government, as long as the overlapping use of the tax or fee does not cause unacceptable inequities, economic distortions, or complexities of taxpayer compliance and revenue administration. Such problems can often be avoided by assigning a given tax to more than one type of government (McClure 1999). The robust literature in this regard is discussed and applied to municipalities by Garzón and Freire in chapter 4 (see also Ebel and Taliercio 2005; Bird 2011a; and Smoke 2008).

Intergovernmental transfers. Once one has sorted out the expenditure and revenue assignments among different types of government, it becomes very clear that there is no a priori reason why, for subnational (e.g., municipal) governments, the expenditure sum will equal the potential revenue flow. In almost every case, there will be a financial imbalance between the central and subnational governments (vertical imbalance), as well as among municipal governments (horizontal imbalance). That is the reason why decentralized systems must also establish a system of intergovernmental transfers, almost always from the central to the local authority. The problem of imbalances and how to address them is discussed below.

Borrowing and debt. What about the timing of receipts to pay for capital spending? How is infrastructure such as schools, roads and highways, and water and transportation systems financed? Thus, the fourth issue facing a decentralized society arises—the role of local borrowing and debt management. How can the timing of receipts to local government to pay for capital spending be structured? The Golden Rule of capital finance is that, on both efficiency and equity grounds, the payment for capital goods should be spread over their useful life. It therefore follows that a financing mechanism be established so that the future generations that benefit from today's capital spending for infrastructure will pay for the benefits they derive from using it. Local governments

must be allowed to borrow and take on debt that is financed over time, if their financial situation is in good standing.

There are principles and rules to sort through it all—a process that is studied under the topic of subnational debt management (Canuto and Liu 2013). An important intergovernmental issue arises when local governments that are part of a unitary intergovernmental hierarchy become a source of contingent liabilities. Under these (typical) circumstances, it may become necessary for the central government to impose limits or other controls on local borrowing activity. This and other topics of debt management are discussed by Kaganova and Kopanyi in chapter 6 and by Freire in chapter 7 (for additional material, see Rangarajan and Prasad 2012; Wong 2013; Peteri and Sevinc 2011; and Canuto and Liu 2013; also helpful is the World Bank Thematic Group website on subnational borrowing and debt, www.worldbank.org/subnational).

The Three Ds—Deconcentration, Delegation, and Devolution

The term "fiscal decentralization" encompasses three distinct arrangements or variants, each of which has a place in a country's intergovernmental financial system. The three are deconcentration, devolution, and delegation. An important policy question is which of the three variants can be said to dominate a nation's public finances.

Deconcentration. Deconcentration is sometimes referred to as *administrative decentralization*. It denotes a process whereby regional offices of central ministries are established in local jurisdictions for the purpose of deciding the level and composition of the local goods and services to be provided. Deconcentration *with authority* means that the regional branches of ministries have some ability to make independent decisions, albeit usually within central guidelines. Deconcentration *without authority* occurs when regional offices are created with no independent decision-making authority. In either case, when deconcentrated offices provide services (such as education, health services, water, or transportation), local residents are likely to have little to say regarding the scope or quality of the services and the manner in which they are provided (box 1.3).

Devolution. Devolution is at the other end of the "three-D" line. In devolution, independent local self-governments are established, with responsibility for the delivery of a set of public services and the authority to impose taxes and fees to finance them. Devolved governments have considerable flexibility to select the mix and level of services and in some cases plenary authority to generate their own revenues. With devolution, citizens have the ability to use their local government to express their preferences regarding the mix and level of public services they want (demand), while taking into account their cost (supply). The result of devolution that provides for such local decision making is "better" (more efficient) utilization of limited resources than would occur if the decisions on local tax and spending policies were made in some distant capital. When each locality makes local decisions, the entire society gains financially. In technical jargon, there has been an increase in social welfare. Efficiency or welfare gains from decentralization can be particularly significant in countries with a high degree of economic, demographic, and geographic diversity.

Delegation. The third variant, delegation, is often thought of as an intermediate arrangement between devolution and deconcentration. It can be characterized as a principal-agent relationship between a higher-level government (principal) that assigns a local government (agent) responsibility for supplying certain local functions (e.g., education, water distribution, health clinics), which may or may not be financed by transfers from the principal to the agent. The failure of

Box 1.3 Egypt: Deconcentration with Limited Authority

The Urab Republic of Egypt has five types of local governments: governorate, *markaz*, city, district, and village. It has 26 governorates, headed by governors who are appointed by the president. A governorate is the main service delivery unit in Egypt. It can be simple and completely urban (with no *markaz* or village) or complex, consisting of urban and rural communities. Governorates are deconcentrated local governments, without policy-making power; they simply follow instructions from the center.

The *markaz* is the second-tier local government unit in complex governorates. A *markaz* consists of a capital city, as well as other cities and villages, and functions as the center for the jurisdiction. It is headed by a *markaz* chief, appointed by the prime minister. Each governorate has at least one city. Cities may be divided into districts. A district (*hay*) is the smallest local government unit in urban governorates. Districts are divided into sections (subdistricts) or neighborhoods (*sheyakha*). City and district chiefs are appointed by the minister of local development. The village (*qariya*) is the smallest local government unit in rural governorates. The service responsibilities of villages vary according to their size. Larger villages are part of the local government system and have service responsibilities. Smaller ones, called "satellite" villages, are not considered local government units and have no service delivery responsibilities. They are part of either a village or a *markaz*. The village chief is appointed by the governor.

Source: Amin and Ebel 2006.

the higher, principal authority to pay for the delegated responsibilities—that is, the creation of an *unfunded mandate*—can establish a potentially contentious central-local relationship and may lead to legal battles (if the locality has the legal right to go to court), incentives for local budgeting sleight-of-hand, and even conflict.

When funded, however, delegation may improve efficiency if it allows subnational government units to administer programs of national priority in ways that better reflect local economic, social, and financial circumstances. Under such arrangements the center may—indeed, is likely to—set minimum or standard levels of services. If the detailed, day-to-day decisions on service delivery remain local, however, an opportunity exists for finding new, creative, and perhaps cost-reducing ways to deliver those services. As will be discussed in the following section, the design of intergovernmental fiscal transfers and the degree and nature of central monitoring will influence the balance between central and local decision making in the delegated areas of responsibility.

Unitary, Federal, and Confederal versus Federal Systems

To add to the complexity of just what decentralization entails, there is wide variation in how intergovernmental systems are structured around the world. Three systems of governance can be distinguished: *unitary, federal, and confederal systems*. What adds to the complexity is that in practice each of these systems may be characterized as having various degrees of the three Ds.

Unitary systems. A unitary system is one in which the central government has the constitutionally bestowed authority (in some cases the authority is bestowed by an absolute monarchy or a theocracy) not only to determine what political powers are assigned to its constituent units (subnational governments, including, of course, municipalities), but also whether to create, abolish, or change the boundaries of the subnational

jurisdictions. In such cases, various types of subnational governments, such as municipalities, may exist, but they are not sovereign; rather, they are creatures of the central state.

Examples abound around the world. In Africa, Burkina Faso, Egypt, Ghana, and Uganda are such unitary systems. East Asia and Pacific examples include Thailand, Japan, and the Republic of South Korea. In Europe and Central Asia, the United Kingdom, Ukraine, and all the Central Asian republics are examples. Such systems in Latin America include Colombia and Peru. Examples in the Middle East and North Africa are Egypt, Jordan, Saudi Arabia, and Tunisia. Examples in South Asia include Bangladesh, Sri Lanka, and Bhutan. But to be unitary may not be the same as being centralized. For example, China has been characterized as both federal and decentralized (Wong 2007; Bahl 1999b). Indonesia is a case of a unitary state that has decentralized its fiscal system such that now subnational governments are major deliverers of services, account for one-third of public spending, and manage half of all public investments (Ellis 2010).

Federal systems. Under a *federal* system, public sector decisions are made by different types or tiers of governments that are independent of one another (Griffiths with Nerenberg 2005; Ahmad and Brosio 2006; Boadway and Shah 2009). Though not nearly as numerous as that list of unitary states, there are plenty of examples: in Africa, Ethiopia, Nigeria, and South Sudan; in East Asia and the Pacific, Australia, Malaysia, and the Federated States of Micronesia; in Europe, Austria, Belgium, and Germany; in Latin America, Brazil, Mexico, and Saint Kitts and Nevis; in the Middle East and North Africa, Iraq and the United Arab Emirates; and in South Asia, India, Pakistan, and Nepal. In a federation, some constitutions are quite explicit that there is no hierarchy among certain types of governments (e.g., Pakistan's center vis-à-vis the four provinces; the central government of the United States and the 50 state governments). Others are constitutionally federal but nevertheless more central than decentralized (Ethiopia, Malaysia, Sudan).

Confederation. A confederation is typically a treaty-based system of states in which a weak central government serves as the agent of the member units, usually without significant independent spending and taxing powers (Wallich and Zhang 2013). A few such arrangements have existed over the years (such as Switzerland as Confederation Helvetia, 1815–48). Today's best example is Bosnia and Herzegovina (box 1.4 sheds light on the Bosnia situation). Even in that case, however, the center is gaining more of a fiscal foothold, having been authorized to levy a national value added tax (VAT) as of January 2006.

To Decentralize, or Not?

Three steps help us get at the question of why some states tend to remain centrally controlled, both politically and fiscally, whereas others move ahead with decentralization. The first is to look at the reasons why so many countries continue holding on to centralized public sectors. The second is to examine the arguments, both theoretical and practical, that are conventionally made in support of decentralizing and how the theory of public finance treats the question. The third is to explore the impact of decentralization—that is, the empirical evidence.

Why Tilt to Centralization?

The *World Development Report 1999/2000* (World Bank 2000) observed that many developing countries are still centralized, notwithstanding the identified trend toward localization. Three arguments are offered in support of centralization:

Lack of local capacity. An argument often set forth in developing countries is that local

---

Box 1.4 Bosnia-Herzegovina Confederalism

Under the Dayton-Paris Agreement (1995), the former Yugoslav Republic of Bosnia and Herzegovina now contains two entities: the Federation of Bosnia and Herzegovina and the Republika Srpska. These are de facto separate governments and administrative organs with substantial powers to pass legislation, impose taxes, and otherwise govern. Sarajevo is both the capital of Bosnia and the capital of the federation. Banja-Luka is the capital of Republika Srpska.

The federation contains 10 intermediate-tier units (cantons) and approximately 80 municipalities. The cantons have their own legislatures, their own basic laws and constitutions, and their own governors and ministries. Financial and budgetary matters affecting municipalities in the federation either are delegated to the cantons or are shared by several departments in the federal ministries. The constitution of the Federation of Bosnia and Herzegovina defines the functions of each level of government, including granting to the cantons all powers not expressly granted to the federation, such as land use planning, local business development, and local economic development. The Republika Srpska has a centralized administrative structure and its own ministry of local government to regulate and conduct dialogue with its municipalities (approximately 60, including one independent city, Brcko); the federation does not have such a ministry.

Source: Fox and Wallich 2007.

governments do not have the capacity for self-government. This argument is most often heard when discussion arises as to the merits of granting localities such as municipal governments authority to generate their own revenues or the authority to borrow. In a country with a long tradition of centralization, that local governments lack the capacity to be self-governing is an observation that is likely to be both true and tautology. As local governments in several newly decentralizing countries have demonstrated, developing capacity to govern is a learning-by-doing process (Thomas 2006). To broadly paraphrase Amartya Sen's essay "Democracy as a Universal Value," a country does not have to be deemed "fit" to be decentralized, but rather governments become capable by being decentralized (Sen 1999).

Thus, for example, in the early 1990s under Mayor Gabor Demszky, the Budapest municipality borrowed in the Eurobond market, not because it could not borrow from Hungarian sources but rather to demonstrate that the city was sufficiently creditworthy to do so. As Demszky writes, in 1991 the "sad state of Budapest was a true reflection of forty years of dictatorship," and thus, its "citizens chose to follow another path" (Demszky 2003).

Here it is important to stress two lessons concerning a country's becoming capable of being decentralized. First, to "decentralize the central state" is not about dismantling it. Successful decentralization is just as much about building the capacity of the center to become intergovernmental (Kopanyi et al. 2000; Pallai 2003). Second, successful public sector reform requires much more than focusing on individual (e.g., bureaucratic) capacity; it also requires linking organizational, institutional, and individual capacity to intended development outcomes (Thomas 2006).

Ensuring that central functions are fulfilled. The second argument is that in an established unitary or federal system, the central government can assert its precedence vis-à-vis subnational government because the priorities of the nation-state must come first. Those include providing for the national defense, conducting foreign policy, protecting national borders, and managing macroeconomic stabilization. Such an argument against extensive decentralization is particularly common in low- and middle-income countries that tend not to be economically diversified and that are therefore more exposed to fluctuations in international commodity prices, to natural disasters, and to debt burden costs. The result is that the central government holds tight control of the main tax and borrowing instruments (Tosun and Yilmaz 2010).

Legacy. The argument for the concentration of political and fiscal power in the center is often about the persistence of old methods—"old ways are good ways." This is seen particularly across much of the African continent, where decades of colonialism led to a deeply ingrained tradition of top-down authoritarianism. (Ndegwa 2002; Commins and Ebel 2010). Reflecting on the legacy of colonialism, the *African Charter for Popular Participation in Development and Transformation* (the Arusha Declaration, 1990) characterized Africa as having an "over-centralization of power and impediments to the effective participation of the overwhelming majority ... regarding social, political and economic development."

Of course, Africa is not alone in the "old ways are our ways" approach. Despite a tradition of local self-government in much of Europe, the governance of command and control still characterizes many former Soviet republics, particularly those of Central Asia. The past couple of years have also witnessed a clawback of power by the central government in Hungary (Barati-Stec 2012). In the Middle East, authoritarian control has been maintained by a long-established system of political oligarchy, resulting in what Tosun labels "excessive centralization," a legacy model that is being challenged all over the region. The world waits to see whether the endgame of this challenge will be more of the same or more pluralist and self-governing societies (Tosun 2010; Tosun and Yilmaz 2010).

Why Decentralize?

That much of the world is undergoing some form of decentralization attests to the importance of such a development. At least four factors help explain the trend to decentralization:

The globalization link. The conclusion of the *World Development Report 1999–2000* that the early 21st century trends toward globalization and localization are reinforcing is supported by more recent research. It includes "separation" modeling that finds a "demand by the hinterlands regions for local autonomy, which increases with national income growth, greater relative hinterland population, and increasing national population" (Arzaghi and Henderson 2005), as well as case studies of a growth of citizen organizations that "no longer rely on top-down measures to improve governance" (McNeil and Malena 2010).

That said, not only trends but also cycles apply to countries, regardless of the degree of their economic development (Bird 2011b). Thus, a period of intergovernmental reform may be followed by a political clawback by central authorities of reforms gained in earlier years. Such reversals are likely to happen more quickly and deeply in unitary states than in federal states, the latter of which, if well established, give subnational governments the constitutional powers to raise their own revenue.

Indeed, a cyclical central clawback in unitary states is now occurring. Thus, the 2011 United Cities and Local Governments (UCLG) report on local government in Africa concludes that "fiscal decentralization is suffering from the difficult financial situation in most African countries today" and that "although revenue generation by African countries has been gradually improving since the early 2000s, following four decades of stagnation, the outlook is not bright" (Yatta and Vaillancourt 2010). A similar warning has been made with respect to some recent European decentralizing actions because of "the suddenness and severity" of the fiscal crisis that has interrupted a prolonged period of steady growth in local budget resources (Regulski 2010).

Politics and the "reaction from below." The second explanation goes back to the point above, that although the decision to decentralize is political, once that decision is made it is the economic and fiscal reforms that lead to a change in intergovernmental fiscal arrangements. Focusing on Africa, Latin America, and post-communist Eurasia, Kalandadze and Orenstein (2009) cite 17 cases—not all successful, as yet—of popular, soft electoral revolutions "from below" since 1991.

The economic efficiency argument. For the economist, the chief argument for decentralization concerns improvements in efficiency—that is, the payoff in general "welfare gains" that results from well-designed intergovernmental arrangements (Oates 1972, 1997; Yilmaz, Vaillancourt, and Dafflon 2012). The efficiency argument for decentralized government goes as follows: Due to different preferences for level and mix of local public goods and services across jurisdictions and differences in the local costs of producing and distributing goods and services, the general welfare of the whole society will be enhanced if decisions about which bundle of local goods and services should be provided from locality to locality are made locally (presumably by freely chosen local officials), rather than by a central official (who may make decisions based some set of centrally determined standards or to satisfy bureaucratic incentives).

Consider, for example, a set of local goods and services, such as primary health care and education. Now assume that the costs of producing those services are the same across the country. Communities have different preferences and needs for the mix of the services to be provided. Thus, in apportioning a public budget of a given size, Community Y, with a large young population, can be expected to express a strong preference for schooling, whereas Community E, which has a predominantly aging population, sees a greater need for health clinics. For a given budget, decentralized matching of costs and preferences leads to efficient use of public resources. By not having underutilized health clinics in Y and empty classrooms in E, the society as a whole has a "welfare gain." This "matching principle"—that the provision of public services should be carried out to the extent possible by the type of government that is closest to the people—is reflected in the "subsidiarity principle" of the European Charter of Local Governments (Marcou 2007).

Nation building. In some countries decentralization has been a strategy to promote national cohesion and to defuse tensions if the society is fragmented by ethnicity, religion, language, endowment of natural resources, or other conditions. Several cases have been documented in which a nation-state's practical use of

the principle of subsidiarity has led to greater national cohesion and helped to deflate secessionist tendencies in a particular region. Historical cases include ones in Belgium, Canada, India, Indonesia, Germany, the Russia Federation, Spain, Sudan, and Switzerland. Box 1.5 sheds light on Sudan (see also Bird and Ebel 2007; Bird and Vaillancourt 2010).

In October 2012, the Benigno Aquino–led central government of the Philippines signed a peace agreement with the Moro Islamic Liberation Front (MILF) that is to serve as a framework to end a four-decade-long conflict in the southern Mindanao region. The agreement envisions that by 2015 a new, autonomous local government in the region will have worked with the central government to sort out issues surrounding the sharing of wealth generated from petroleum and mineral mining, with the center still managing matters such as currency, customs, national defense, and foreign policy. As the Sudan peace consultations (2002–05) have demonstrated, it will take time, goodwill, and good politics to make this work. How any opposition to the peace agreement from a rival rebel group, the Moro National Liberation Front (MNLF), will play out remains to be seen, but if the agreement works, it will be because

---

Box 1.5 Nation Building by Means of Decentralization in Sudan and South Sudan

Following the signing of the 2005 Comprehensive Peace Agreement, the government of South Sudan has registered important progress in infrastructure and basic services. However, improving local communities' access to these services is a huge task. Decentralization of authority can be adopted to improve access to basic public services. Decentralization can also help in building national cohesion to hold the state together. In addition, if implemented well, it can enable empowered citizens to hold the local authorities accountable.

Source: Zoellick 2009.

decentralization worked (Bauzon 1999; Wallich, Manasan, and Sehili 2007).

Decentralization—Emerging Lessons and Results

The argument presented above is the answer to the question "Why decentralize?" But does it work? Does decentralization deliver on its theoretical promises? Although measuring decentralization is difficult (Ebel and Yilmaz 2003), the following summarizes what is known empirically about the relationship between decentralized fiscal autonomy and the accomplishment of a nation's broader economic and fiscal objectives:

- *A strong correlation between decentralization and growth* in gross domestic product (GDP) per capita supports the argument that as people become more educated, better informed about their government, and more aware of problems that affect their lives, their desire to bring the control of government functions closer to themselves grows.

- *The dismal macroeconomic record* of centralized command and control in Central and Eastern Europe has been well documented (Bird, Ebel, and Wallich 1995). Conversely, developed countries are associated with mature systems of decentralization and degrees of fiscal autonomy (e.g., Akai and Sakata 2002).

- If, as the theory argues, *decentralization enhances efficiency* in the allocation of public services, that should show up as economic growth. And, indeed, the evidence is supportive. Martinez-Vazquez and McNab (1997) found such a relationship with respect to the revenue side of the budget. Ebel and Yilmaz (2003) reached a similar conclusion, whether the decentralization variable is defined in terms of a narrow or a broad definition of revenues (a broad definition includes unrestricted grants), with respect to the growth rate of real

per capita output. A similar finding with respect to revenue autonomy concludes that "decentralization of expenditures coming with centrally controlled revenues seems to be an obstruction to economic growth" (Meloche, Vaillancourt, and Yilmaz 2004). Imi (2005) concluded that in a mixed pool of developed and transition countries, decentralization "particularly on the expenditure side is instrumental to economic growth."

- On the matter of *macroeconomic stability,* there is evidence that subnational revenue autonomy improves the fiscal position of subnational governments but that reliance on intergovernmental transfers may worsen that fiscal position (Ebel and Yilmaz 2003).

- The findings relating to *the relationship between fiscal decentralization and public sector size* are decidedly mixed, with a study on the United States, which is a mature federation, finding no evidence of a relationship (Oates 1985), and others suggesting that in the postsocialist transition countries, the public sector's expenditure share of national GDP decreases with increased subnational tax autonomy (Ebel and Yilmaz 2003).

Once the definition, the rationale, and the scholarly findings on decentralization results have been presented, one must turn to the hard work of implementing intergovernmental reforms (Kopanyi, El Daher, and Wetzel 2004; Barati-Stec 2012; Martinez-Vazquez and Vaillancourt 2011). A first step entails getting right the responses to the four fundamental questions, set out above, of (1) revenue assignment, (2) expenditure assignment, (3) the design of intergovernmental transfers, and (4) borrowing and debt assignment. The tasks associated with the four fundamentals fall to central finance and planning officials, civil society organizations, and municipal finance practitioners, cooperation among whom is to be desired. Tensions will surely arise among the implementers, but in an open, pluralistic society such tensions can be healthy for the system as a whole (Soros 2006; Eaton, Kaiser, and Smoke 2011; Smoke, 2013).

Intergovernmental Transfers

The next section of this chapter addresses selected issues on the topic of intergovernmental transfers, including the rationale of transfers, their classification among government tiers, the elements of a good and bad transfer design, the institutional setting in that design, fiscal equalization, and practical examples of performance grants and municipal contracts.

Such transfers are a necessary element of any well-decentralized system, as two types of financial imbalances—*vertical* and *horizontal*—will occur and will need to be resolved. "Vertical imbalance" refers to the differences between expenditures and own revenues for different types or levels of government. That difference across governments of the same type or level—municipalities, for example—is referred to as "horizontal imbalance" (Bird, Ebel, and Gianci 2007; Boadway and Shah 2009).

This section addresses the financial aspects of intergovernmental relations that strongly influence the nature, scope, and depth of decentralization. The financial aspects are often measured by (a) the distribution of revenues and expenditures among government tiers: the central government; the middle tier, that is, the state or province; and the local governments (e.g., municipalities); (b) the assignment of public service delivery functions among the tiers; and (c) the "own-source" revenues of the subnational government tiers, meaning the revenues that they may collect or obtain independently and use at their own discretion (Jensen, 2001; Blöchliger and Petzold 2009; Blöchliger and Rabesona 2009).

At lower tiers of government, a revenue deficiency often arises from a mismatch between revenue means and expenditure needs, referred to as a "vertical fiscal gap." A national government may have more revenues than warranted by its direct and indirect spending responsibilities, whereas regional and local governments may have revenues that fall short of their expenditure responsibilities. A vertical fiscal imbalance occurs when such a vertical fiscal gap is not adequately addressed by the reassignment of responsibilities, by fiscal transfers, or by other means. Often central governments in developing countries are assigned the power to collect the most robust revenue streams—such as customs taxes, the value added tax, and personal and corporate income tax. Table 1.1 illustrates a vertical imbalance in Pakistan, where the federal state collects 90 percent of public revenues but spends only 67 percent. In contrast, the subnational levels collect about 10 percent of revenues but account for 33 percent of public expenditures.

Very often the expenditure and revenue assignments in a fiscally decentralized nation produce horizontal fiscal imbalances because of the different fiscal capacities and expenditure needs of subnational governments. As a result, intergovernmental transfers play a crucial role, both vertically (in enabling local governments to perform their assigned responsibilities) and horizontally (in holding interregional disparities to acceptable levels).

Expenditure needs depend on the assignment of functions. Thus, in countries where municipalities have few responsibilities, their expenditure needs are relatively small. For instance, municipalities in Jordan provide mainly solid waste, road, and some administrative services; the

Table 1.1 Vertical Imbalances in Pakistan

	Revenues (%)	Expenditures (%)
National	90.2	67.1
Provincial	4.9	28.8
Local	4.8	4.1
All levels	100	100

Source: Shah 1998.

municipal sector's share of public expenditures is small by international comparison, at less than 5 percent (Dillinger 1994). At the other extreme, when local governments provide most local services, including basic health care, primary education, the social safety net, infrastructure, water, and solid waste disposal, their expenditure needs and share in public expenses are much larger. In Hungary, the local share of public expenditures was about 12 percent in 2012.

Types of Transfers among Government Tiers

Intergovernmental transfers can be broadly classified into two main categories: *general purpose* (also called "unconditional") transfers and *specific purpose* (also called "conditional" or "earmarked") transfers (table 1.2). The source of the transfers, or the "transfer pool," could be the general budget of the central government and may include a share of specific taxes. For instance, in Turkey 11.5 percent of the revenue from the value added tax and from personal and corporate income taxes is channeled to the transfer pool for local governments (Peteri and Sevinc 2011). Box 1.6 shows an example of the various transfers a local government may receive and how they are reported in a typical financial statement.

General Purpose Transfers

General purpose transfers have no conditions attached to the nature of the recipient's spending. Municipalities thus have the freedom to exercise policy discretion on the use of this type of transfer (table 1.2). Sector *block grants* are one form of general purpose transfer. They provide budget support with no terms attached in a broad but specific area of subnational expenditure. In many countries, general purpose transfers are formula based, meaning that they are allocated based on specific factors, such as population and area of jurisdiction as a proxy for service coverage. Examples of countries with unconditional transfers are Germany and South Africa. Recently, international agencies such as the World Bank

have supported local government operations with unconditional transfers in Bangladesh, Ghana, India, Tanzania, Uganda, and other developing countries.

Specific Purpose Transfers

Specific purpose—also called "conditional" or "earmarked"—transfers finance, or provide incentives for governments to undertake, specific programs or activities. These grants may be regular or mandatory in nature, or they may be discretionary or ad hoc. Conditional transfers typically specify the type of expenditures that can be used to finance ("input-based conditionality"). These may be capital expenditures, specific operating expenditures, or both. Conditional transfers may also require attainment of certain results in service delivery ("output-based conditionality"). Input-based conditionality is often intrusive and unproductive, whereas output-based conditionality can advance grantors' objectives while preserving local autonomy.

Conditional transfers may incorporate matching provisions; that is, they may require municipalities to finance a specified percentage of the expenditure using their own resources (table 1.2). Matching requirements can be either open-ended, meaning that the central or other higher-level government matches whatever level of resources the municipality provides, or closed-ended, meaning that the grantor matches municipal funds only up to a prespecified limit. Matching requirements encourage greater scrutiny and local ownership of grant-financed expenditures. Closed-ended matching ensures that the grantor has some control over the costs of the transfer program.

The central government enforces matching payments as a signal of commitment by the municipalities to contribute to the maintenance of established assets. Municipalities may be required to finance a specific expenditure up to a certain level, above which the central or the state government supplies the additional resources

Table 1.2 Classification of Forms of Intergovernmental Transfers

	Conditional			Unconditional
	Open-ended, matching	**Closed-ended, matching**	**Nonmatching**	
Description	Matching: For every Euro (or other currency unit) the subnational government (SNG) receives from the granting (e.g., central) government, the recipient must spend some own funds on the activity to receive the grant. This "match" is typically expressed as a % of the size of the donor grant. With an "open-ended" grant, there is no "cap" on the amount of grant funds. The cost of the grant depends on the amount of funds matched by the recipient.	If the grant is "closed-ended," the donor government sets a ceiling on the amount of funds being transferred.	The donor gives a fixed sum of money with the stipulation that it be spent on a public good. There is no percentage share ("match") required of the recipient.	Provided for equalization purposes or basic functional areas. Funds may be used at the recipient's discretion.
Purpose of grant	Encourage spending on production of good or service having positive social and/or interjurisdictional externalities.		Encourage spending on a national priority sector. Restriction on its use differentiates it from an unconditional grant.	Increases overall capacity to spend. May have specific equalization goal (horizontal imbalance) and/or be a way to correct vertical imbalance.
Illustration	There is no ceiling or cap on the amount of the funds as long as the recipient group (which may be an SNG or a defined group of individuals) meets the conditions (e.g., measure of need) for qualifying to receive the transfer. Thus, the grant becomes an "entitlement." Grants to give people access to safety net, housing, or education services are often structured in this manner.	Most categorical grants (environmental management, housing, substance abuse treatment) have some limit on donor cost (closed-ended). Another example is performance grants (these may be nonmatching).	Community development, job training, transportation. capital grants.	An equalization grant is designed to address the horizontal imbalance of a recipient. Sector "block" grants have a designated purpose, broadly defined. "Sector" refers to a category such as health, education, transportation, water.

(continued next page)

Table 1.2 *(continued)*

	Conditional			Unconditional
	Open-ended, matching	**Closed-ended, matching**	**Nonmatching**	
Effect on governmental spending	The donor government (e.g., center) sets the terms of the match, but the recipient may or may not agree to accept the match. Thus, even though the center greatly influences the potential amount of spending, the actual amount is jointly determined.	The determination of total amount spent is determined jointly by donor and recipient. But this all ends when the donor-determined cap is reached. The cap is a way that the center can control its own budget. That is, at some point the recipient is no longer entitled to the grant.	The donor gives recipient a fixed amount of a grant with stipulation on its use. If the community wanted to consume less of the public good than the grant condition, then the grant affects SNG behavior. Otherwise this looks like an unconditional grant.	The donor will cap the amount of the grant. As long as the community wants to consume at least an amount of the public good equal to the amount of the grant, then the fact that the grant is conditional or unconditional is irrelevant.
Fungibility	Fungibility means that money can be used for more than the designated purpose. Thus, the new money that flows from donor government grants may replace own-recipient spending that would have been spent on the designated activity in the absence of the grant. That is, the grant "frees up" the SNG's other funds that would have been used for the grant-designated purpose in the absence of the grant. One strategy for donor governments to reduce the degree of fungibility is to require a *maintenance-of-effort* pre-donor grant. Recognizing that all grant funds have some degree of fungibility (this is especially true for the unconditional and matching grant), the donor stipulates that the SNG must maintain own-SNG support for a given program equal to that in some previous year. This previous year may be expressed as an absolute funding amount or a percentage of total revenues available to the SNG.			
Other comments	Relative price of public goods declines.	Relative price of public goods declines.	No change in relative prices of public goods in excess of the grant.	No change in relative prices of public versus private goods.

Source: Authors, adapted from Ebel and Peteri 2007.

required. This kind of matching raises an equity issue in that municipalities with ample resources of their own can afford to meet matching requirements and may thus acquire substantial central government transfers. In contrast, poorer municipalities will find it difficult to meet matching requirements to finance certain expenditures, particularly in developing countries.

As is evident from table 1.2, some conditional transfers do not require local matching, but only require that the funds be spent for a particular purpose. These are referred to as "conditional nonmatching transfers." For a given level of assistance, municipalities may prefer unconditional nonmatching transfers, which provide them with maximum flexibility to pursue their own objectives. Because such grants augment resources without influencing spending patterns, they allow municipalities to maximize their own welfare (Shah 2007).

Shared Taxes

A number of policy questions are relevant to the topic of tax sharing between higher levels of government and municipalities.

A basic intergovernmental finance guideline says that finance (revenue assignment and intergovernmental transfers) should follow function (expenditure responsibilities). Ideally, from the viewpoint of accountability, each government unit should be able to raise the revenues it needs to finance its expenditures from its own sources. However, as noted above, except for the most revenue-rich local governments, gaps between expenditures and revenue assignments are likely to occur for many reasons. This gives rise to yet another form of central-to-local transfer, *revenue sharing.*

Shared tax base. Revenue sharing arrangements can be of two types. In the first type, the revenue-generating government (e.g., the center or middle-tier governmental unit) determines the tax base, and the recipient (e.g., municipal) government adds to that its own "surtax," which is an extra local tax applied on the revenue base, using a rate determined by the municipality. In such an arrangement either the local government or, typically, the central authority administers and collects the revenue for all tax base sharing governments. Tax base sharing, in which the central government "vacates" some of the total tax base so as to allow a subnational government the option to determine its own tax rate—often referred to as "tax piggybacking"—is particularly common in North America. The merit of piggybacking is that it preserves local fiscal autonomy while minimizing the cost of local tax administration.

Revenue collection sharing. The second type of arrangement specifies that a proportion of centrally generated revenues be shared between central and subnational governments. The central-subnational tax split may be determined by a constitutional commission, decided on the basis of an agreement between the central and subnational governments, or, more commonly, established by direct parliamentary, statutory action that allows the central government control over the central budget. The structure of such revenue (or, as listed in some statistical reports, "tax" rather than "revenue" sharing) arrangements varies among countries with respect to type of revenue shared, procedures for setting the central-local split, frequency of formula changes, and whether the sharing is based on origin (derivation) or the geographic location or builds in some degree of horizontal equalization (Blöchliger and Rabesona 2009).

Regardless of matters such as the structure and process of sharing centrally levied revenues, as a matter of classification, shared revenue is clearly not "own-local" revenue. For a receipt to be classified as "own source" revenue requires at a minimum, some degree of authority to establish the tax rate or the level of a nontax charge or fee (Jensen 2001). Even with this understanding, readers should be alert to complications in how revenue sharing policies are listed in financial documents. For reporting purposes, "what counts as *tax sharing* in one country may count as an *intergovernmental grant* in another," thereby making "the two sub-central funding arrangements of tax sharing and intergovernmental grants difficult to disentangle" (Blöchliger and Petzold 2009).

As with grants, shared revenues signify a commitment by the central government to address vertical imbalance. Even so, however, the commitment may change over time. In Hungary the personal income tax (PIT) is a centrally collected tax that is partially redistributed to the local level. In 1990, 100 percent of the PIT was redistributed to its origin; by 2006, only 8 percent was redistributed by origin, with another 20 percent to 25 percent distributed by formula to other municipalities. As of 2011, that 8 percent derivation share had been eliminated (Barati-Stec 2012). Sometimes a central, provincial, or, as in

the case of Lima, Peru, even a well-established local government may collect certain taxes on behalf of other governments and return the proceeds to that government after deducting a fee for the cost of collection (Mikesell 2003).

Revenue sharing is a feature in a number of federations, both developed and developing (Rao 2007). Among Organisation for Economic Co-operation and development countries, examples include Austria (where the shares of the personal and corporate income, property, and value added taxes are determined by the national parliament every four years) and Germany, where the revenue split of the central personal and corporate taxes and value added tax is set by the national parliament (the Bundestag representing the central government) with the consent of the state and local governments (Blöchliger and Rabesona 2009). Australia assigns the entire revenue received from the goods and services tax to the states on the basis of an equalization or "relativities" formula. States' equalization payments are reduced by an amount proportional to the share of the goods and services tax they receive. In effect, this arrangement simply ensures a source of equalization payments.

The growing revenue requirements of local governments in newly decentralizing "transition" economies have led to revenue sharing in several postsocialist countries in addition to the case already cited of Hungary (table 1.3). Thus, in the Russian Federation, the central government now shares all of its personal income tax, a portion of the VAT, and a portion of corporate income tax with the *oblasts*. And in Romania local governments have a claim on both profit and dividend taxes levied by the central government on locally owned enterprises. In these economies the central government may reduce its deficit by cutting shares to the local governments when fiscal pressure at the central level increases, as occurred in Hungary.

Another feature of transition economies is that taxes are often shared based on where they are

Table 1.3 Shared Revenues (Taxes) in South East Europe Countries

Country	Tax	Local share percentage
Bulgaria	Personal income	50
Croatia	Personal income	52
	Real estate	60
Macedonia	Personal income	3
Montenegro	Personal income	10
	Real estate	50
	Natural resource	30
Romania	Personal income	77
Slovenia	Personal income	50
Serbia	Personal income	40
	Inheritance	100
	Property transfer	100
Turkey	All national collected taxes	5

Source: NALAS 2008.

derived, in part because of the subnational governments' strong notions of source entitlement and primary claim on tax revenues generated in their jurisdictions. Problems may arise when local governments collect revenues and are required to pass them on to the central government, retaining their shares according to contracted or predetermined ratios.

In Indonesia, although most tax sharing is based primarily on the derivation principle, fishery and property-related taxes use "equal shares" as an added criterion. The 9 percent national share of the property tax is actually a fee to compensate the national tax administration for collecting and administering the tax. It is noteworthy that in apportioning personal income taxes, place of work, rather than the almost universally used place of residence, is the basis. In addition to the sharing arrangements for national revenues, local governments receive shares of the four provincial taxes: the motor vehicle tax (30 percent), the vehicle transfer tax (30 percent), the fuel excise tax (70 percent), and

the groundwater extraction and use tax (70 percent). Their contributions to overall local revenues are relatively small, however. As of 2009, 84.5 percent of oil revenue accrues to the central government and 15.5 percent to subnational governments. For gas revenue, 69.5 percent goes to the center and 30.5 percent to the regions. Subnational governments receive an extra 0.5 percent of both oil and gas revenues, which is earmarked for increasing local spending on primary education. The sharing of oil and gas revenues was introduced to redress complaints by the resource-rich provinces that although they face the development costs and environmental consequences of resource exploitation, the benefits were accruing only to the central government.

Output-Based Transfers

Conditional, nonmatching, output-based transfers may be used if the purpose of the grant is to allow the recipient government to address central spending priorities (e.g., when the center determines that there are net "external" or "spillover" benefits to a multijurisdictional region or the country as a whole) or when accountability for results is an aim. Output-based transfers respect local autonomy and budgetary flexibility, while providing incentives and accountability mechanisms to improve service delivery. Output-based grants may also empower citizens by increasing their knowledge regarding a link between grant financing and service delivery performance (as in Canada and Chile, described below). These transfers impose conditions based on the results to be achieved, while providing flexibility in the design of programs and spending levels to achieve those objectives. Such transfers help restore cities' focus on the results-based chain and the most effective service delivery framework.

To achieve grant objectives, a municipal official examines the results-based chain to determine whether or not program activities are expected to yield the desired results

Figure 1.1 Results Chain in Education

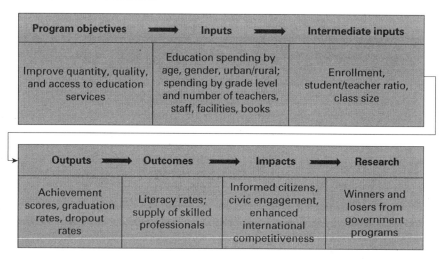

Source: Shah 2007.

(see figure 1.1). To do that requires monitoring program activities and inputs, including intermediate inputs (resources used to produce outputs); outputs (quantity and quality of public goods and services produced and access to them); and outcomes (intermediate- to long-run consequences for consumers and taxpayers of public service provision or progress in achieving program objectives); impact (program goals or long-term consequences of public service provision); and reach (the numbers of people who benefit from, or are hurt by, a program). Such a managerial focus reinforces joint ownership and accountability by the principal and the agent in achieving shared goals by highlighting terms of mutual trust. Thus, internal and external reporting shifts from the traditional focus on inputs to a focus on outputs and outcomes, especially outputs that lead to results.

An example of an output-based grant system is the Canadian health transfer program (Shah 2007). The program has enabled the Canadian provinces to ensure access to high-quality health care for all, regardless of income or place of residence. Other examples include Chile's per pupil grants to all schools, which include a 25 percent additional grant as a salary bonus for teachers in the best-performing schools (Gonzalez 2005); a central grant to municipal governments to subsidize water and sewer use by the poor in Chile (Gomez-Lobo 2001); central per capita transfers for education in Colombia and South Africa; and federal per pupil grants to states for secondary education and to municipalities for primary education in Brazil (Gordon and Vegas 2004).

Institutional Settings in the Design of Transfers

Designing intergovernmental transfers is not a simple task. The central government may choose to take up the transfer design or may delegate it to an independent entity. A separate body may be involved in the design and enforcement of the fiscal arrangements. Such a body may have true decision-making authority or be purely advisory. The fiscal resources of a central budget come from different sources, partly from the taxes on incomes generated in the municipalities. A key question is how to allocate the portion going to the municipalities. It is good practice to transfer resources to municipalities based on a clear formula, as in the examples shown in box 1.7, which summarizes the transfer formulas in South Africa and Saudi Arabia. The South Africa formula is complex and includes general revenue grants, development grants, and an equalization factor for fiscal capacity differences. The Saudi formula allocates only development grants, while taking into account general needs (measured by population and area) and infrastructure needs (measured by cost of and gap in infrastructure).

Box 1.7 Formulas for Fiscal Transfers—South Africa and Saudi Arabia

South Africa uses an equitable share formula to provide transfers from the central government to local governments. The size of the grant is determined as follows:

$$Grant = (BS + D + I - R) \pm C,$$

where BS is the basic services component, D is the development component, I is the institutional support component, R is the revenue-raising capacity correction, and C is a correction and stabilization factor.

The basic services component is to enable municipalities to provide basic services (water, sanitation, electricity, refuse removal, and others), including free basic services to households earning less than R800 (about US$111) a month. (As of April 1, 2006, environmental health care services have been included as a basic service.) Since by its nature environmental health is delivered to everyone in a municipality, this subcomponent is calculated on all households, not only poor ones. For each subsidized basic service, there are two levels of support: a full subsidy for households that actually receive services from the municipality and a partial subsidy for unserviced households, currently set at one-third of the cost of the subsidy to serviced households.

The development component was set at zero when the current formula was introduced on April 1, 2005.

The institutional support component supplements the funding of a municipality for administrative and governance costs. It is important for poor municipalities, which are often unable to raise sufficient revenue to fund the basic costs of administration and governance.

The revenue-raising capacity correction raises additional resources to fund the cost of basic services and administrative infrastructure. The approach uses the relationship between demonstrated revenue-raising capacity by municipalities that report information and objective municipal information from *Statistics South Africa* to proxy revenue-raising capacity for all municipalities.

The government of Saudi Arabia introduced a transfer formula for distributing development grants in 2009, as local governments are supposed to cover their operation expenses from own-source revenues. The adopted formula allocates funds from the development pool such that the grant is based 35 percent on population, 20 percent on area, 10 percent on the Index of Construction Costs, and 35 percent on infrastructure deficit (gap). The formula is more precisely stated as follows:

$$0.35^*(Pop_i/\Sigma Pop) + 0.20^*(Area_i/\Sigma Area) + 0.10^* ICC_i + 0.35^* Infgap_i$$

The formula is clear and simple but requires detailed data to estimate the cost of the construction index and the infrastructure gap.

Sources: Shah 2007; and authors.

Transfer formulas are subjects of both science and politics, as the results of analytic studies are often overruled by political considerations. Thus, some formulas change year by year and end up including a dozen variables (as in Jordan) that often are redundant, inconsistent, and conflicting and undermine the effectiveness of the transfer system.

Common in the design of transfers is the designation of an independent grants commission, an intergovernmental forum, or an intergovernmental-cum-civil-society forum. The grants commission can be permanent, as in Australia or South Africa, or can convene periodically, as in India, where independent grants commissions in the states provide fiscal advice on state-local government relations. Because Indian fiscal commissions are advisory, their recommendations may not always be adopted. In one case, in Kerala, nearly all fiscal commission recommendations have been embraced by the state government (see Shah 2007).

Other countries, such as Canada and Germany, have intergovernmental forums or federal-provincial committees that negotiate the design of the fiscal transfer system. Another option is the use of intergovernmental-cum-civil-society committees, with equal representation from all constituent units, chaired by the federal government, to negotiate changes in federal-provincial and local fiscal relations. In Pakistan, for example, provincial-level finance commissions design and allocate provincial-local fiscal transfers. The provincial finance commission awards in Pakistan are based on a revenue sharing rule between the federal government and the provincial governments. Each province then has the authority to devise a formula for distributing its allocation to the local governments.

In India, the most critical function of the state finance commissions (SFCs) is to determine the fiscal transfer from the state to local bodies in the form of revenue sharing and grants-in-aid. Since the 80th amendment to the constitution, which followed a recommendation by the 10th Finance Commission (1995–2000), a certain percentage of all union taxes has been distributed to the states. Many SFCs have also adopted this system because it allows the local governments automatically to share in the buoyancy of state taxes and levies. Such a system also has built-in transparency, objectivity, and certainty. Local governments can anticipate, at the beginning of each fiscal year, their share in the divisible pool. The system enables local governments to consider the entire economy in creating their own annual budgets, giving them incentives to generate their own revenues and mobilize additional resources.

Fiscal Equalization

As noted above, allocation of expenditure and revenue assignments in a fiscally decentralized nation typically leads to horizontal imbalances because of the different revenue capacities and expenditure needs among subnational governments. Decentralization design also often leads to vertical imbalances in favor of the central government because tax revenue sources are seldom as decentralized as expenditure responsibilities. To overcome these imbalances, as well as to achieve other policy objectives, equalization grants and other intergovernmental transfers have become key elements of intergovernmental finance reform around the world (Martinez-Vasquez 2007).

Equalization can be undertaken to guarantee some basic (minimum) level of local service provision, in conjunction with the broader goal of equalizing fiscal capacity among subnational governments. A key issue is whether a grant actually does *equalize* across municipalities with different economic and financial endowments (fiscal disparities). The central government may not commit to full equalization for several reasons: First, central resources to do so may be inadequate. Second, full equalization might penalize better performers and create incentives for backward local governments toward grant seeking. Third, it may be difficult to develop a formula that truly equalizes across municipalities.

Policy makers in both developed and developing countries face significant challenges with the introduction and reform of equalization grants and other intergovernmental transfers. One of the challenges is a lack of any clear framework, in either the decentralization literature or the recorded details of international practice, in which to consider numerous hard issues. For example, should the capital expenditure needs of subnational governments be considered part of equalization grants? Are independent grants commissions a preferred institutional setup for implementing equalization grants? What is the appropriate relationship between the conditional and unconditional grant elements of the system? Should efforts be made to equalize differences in fiscal capacity, or expenditure needs, or both? And how can those differences be measured with limited data (Vaillancourt 2002; Box and Martinez-Vazquez 2004; Hofman and Guerra 2007). Fiscal capacity equalization, when not done correctly, can create an incentive for regions to act strategically to influence the size of their grants, leading to inefficiencies in the provision of local public goods.

Most East Asian governments care about equitable services to their people and consequently take an interest in the distribution of fiscal resources among the subnational governments that deliver the services. Countries such as Indonesia have included subnational fiscal equity as an explicit goal in the constitution. The constitutions of other countries, such as the Philippines or China, include strong commitments to equal access to services, and the delivery of many of the services is devolved to subnational governments (Hofman and Guerra 2007).

Many of the equalization grant systems in East Asian countries contain desirable features. All base distribution of resources on a formula, and most determine the pool of resources to be distributed based on a formula as well. In some countries, the equalization system takes into account both revenue capacity and expenditure needs, whereas in others (Thailand and the Philippines) only expenditure needs are considered. The size of the distribution pool differs greatly from country to country. Whereas in Indonesia and the Philippines equalization grants make up the largest share of central-local grants, in Thailand and China earmarked grants dominate. In addition to the equalization grant, the distribution of earmarked grants sometimes includes equalizing elements. In other cases, however, those grants are not targeted to poor regions and may even have a counter-equalizing effect.

In Indonesia the equalization grant, called *Dana Alokasi Umum* or DAU, has become a key part of the intergovernmental fiscal system. The funding for the DAU consists of 25 percent of central government revenues after tax sharing with the regions. Ten percent of the DAU goes to the provincial level, which plays a relatively minor role in public services, and 90 percent to the local governments. In the aggregate, this grant finances some 70 percent of local government spending and 50 percent of provincial government spending. The DAU is distributed according to a formula that takes both revenue capacity and expenditure needs into account. Revenue capacity is defined as potential own-source revenues, plus shared tax revenues, plus 75 percent of shared natural resource revenues. Expenditure needs are defined as a function of population, poverty rate, land area, and construction cost index as an indicator of geographical circumstances. In addition to the formula allocation, part of the DAU is distributed based on past spending patterns, by and large to accommodate transitory effects that occurred in the 2001 decentralization. Finally, a lump sum per region is included. The new earmarked grants system, the *Dana Alokasi Khusus* (DAK), is still small compared to the general grants system (about 3 percent of total grants), but it also includes an element of equalization through required counterpart funding: Regions with low fiscal capacity pay the minimum of 10 percent counterpart (matching) funds, whereas those with high fiscal capacity pay up to 50 percent in counterpart funds.

In China, an ad hoc amount is dedicated to transfers to the 16 poorest provinces and distributed on an equalizing basis. Although the 1994 tax sharing reform introduced a formula-based equalization scheme, it is still in a "transitional" status with limited funds. The formula-based scheme relies on variables such as provincial GDP, student-teacher ratios, number of civil servants, and population density. The scheme remains small, and each beneficiary province receives only a fraction of its fiscal needs as determined by the transfer allocation formula. In 2001, the equalization scheme accounted for only 3 percent of total central transfers.

Equalization mechanisms diminish subnational fiscal disparities, but even with such mechanisms, disparities remain. Inequalities may persist for numerous reasons:

- Expenditure needs may vary significantly, for example, because of wide variations in costs among the subnational governments or asymmetry in decentralization; in other words, some regions do better than others.

- Central government emphasis on revenue mobilization. Too much or poorly designed equalization could reduce the incentive for own revenue mobilization, to the detriment of general government's tax take in the economy.

- Inequalities among regions could induce migration to regions with better economic prospects.

- Poor regions may be less capable of handling money than rich ones, or less concerned with poverty alleviation than the center.

- Rich regions are also powerful regions, and they do not like to lose out against the poorer regions. It is hard for the center to tax away and redistribute resources from the rich regions (Hofman and Guerra 2007).

Designing Transfers

Local government financial management is made easier if transfers are designed and implemented effectively and simply, using a basic formula for which data can easily be accessed. The following guidelines will be helpful in designing transfers:

- *Clarity in grant objectives.* Grant objectives should be clear and precise.

- *Autonomy.* Subnational governments should have complete independence and flexibility in setting priorities.

- *Revenue adequacy.* Subnational governments should have adequate revenues to discharge designated responsibilities.

- *Responsiveness.* The grant program should be flexible enough to accommodate unforeseen changes in the fiscal situations of the cities.

- *Equity (fairness).* Allocated funds should vary directly with fiscal need factors and inversely with the tax capacity of each jurisdiction.

- *Predictability.* The grant mechanism should ensure predictability of the total size of the pool and of subnational governments' allocation shares by enabling publication of five-year projections of funds availability.

- *Transparency.* Both the formula and the allocations should be disseminated widely, to achieve as broad a consensus as possible on the objectives and operation of the program.

- *Efficiency.* The grant design should be neutral with respect to subnational governments' choices of resource allocation to different sectors or types of activity.

- *Simplicity.* Grant allocation should be based on objective factors over which individual units have little control. The formula should be easy to understand, so as not to reward grantsmanship.

- *Incentive.* The design should provide incentives for sound fiscal management and discourage inefficient practices.

- *Reach.* All grant-financed programs create winners and losers. Consideration must be given to identifying beneficiaries and those who will be adversely affected to determine the overall usefulness and sustainability of the program.

- *Safeguarding of the grantor's objectives.* The grantor's objectives are best safeguarded by having grant conditions that specify the results to be achieved (output-based grants) and by giving cities flexibility in the use of funds.

- *Affordability.* The grant program must recognize donors' budget constraints.

- *Single focus.* Each grant program should focus on a single objective.

- *Accountability for results.* The grantor or higher-level government must be accountable for the design and operation of the program. The municipality must be accountable to the grantor and to its citizens for financial integrity and results, that is, improvements in service delivery performance.

Bad or Detrimental Design of Transfers

Transfers can be perceived as being ill designed or detrimental based on the following:

- A *dependency syndrome* can be generated when local governments always know that someone else will pick up their tab.

- *Autonomy* in revenue and expenditure decision making can be lost, especially when

transfers are conditional in nature or driven by political patronage.

- *Sustainability* may be lacking when there are no built-in sustainability mechanisms, so that transfers serve short-term purposes and do not contribute to strengthening an intergovernmental fiscal transfer system. That typically is the case with ad hoc transfers that are based on political patronage (e.g., special allocations for each member of the provincial assembly in Pakistan). A related problem occurs when no mechanism is put in place to sustain the operation and maintenance of established investments using such ad hoc transfers.

- *Capacity development* is undermined when transfers are built around top-down systems that do not stimulate local governments to develop compliance systems that they own. Sometimes compliance and administrative requirements are too laborious, and the required data may not be available, contributing to high transaction costs of using the transfers. The problem is compounded when only limited human resources are available to manage huge demands from the top for reporting.

- *"Deficit grants"*—specific transfers to finance municipal government deficits—are very negative and create perverse incentives unless hard conditions are attached.

- *Accountability* is thwarted when transfers are not accompanied by monitoring to ensure that local officials are able to honorably account for the use of transfer funds.

Data Concerns Regarding Fiscal Equalization Transfers

The policy debate on fiscal inequalities, and on intergovernmental fiscal relations more generally, requires more data. Without more sound information on how large inequalities are and how they have evolved over time, a policy debate on what inequalities are acceptable or desirable may be based on soft ground and political will. Most developing countries lack much subnational fiscal data. For levels of government below the first subnational tier, data are even scarcer. Data on differentials for service delivery are also critical for assessing interregional disparities in access to services. To obtain better data requires setting up monitoring systems in government, an undertaking that requires significant resources. Indonesia, for example, has managed to maintain a database of subnational fiscal information at the center that—supported by laws requiring the regions to report—has information on most of its 410 local governments. In China, the needed data exist at the originating level, but the aggregation of information at each level of government implies that the central government has little relevant information on the fiscal situation at subnational levels. For some countries, obtaining better data requires adjustments in accounting systems and budget classifications. Moreover, more policy analysis of the data is needed to inform the policy debate. Ultimately countries should aim to regularly review the results and progress of their intergovernmental fiscal systems, including fiscal disparities and service delivery disparities. For example, following the highly successful example of South Africa, Indonesia has embarked on preparation of intergovernmental fiscal reviews; such reports would allow policy makers to evaluate their intergovernmental fiscal system on a regular basis.

In summary, irrespective of whether more or less fiscal equalization is desirable, significant scope exists for improvement in the design of intergovernmental systems. Most countries need to identify a more comprehensive objective for their equalization system as a whole. The center must determine its equalization objectives and priorities (that is, income levels, fiscal capacity, expenditure needs, per person revenues available) within a viable assessment of the political environment. The objectives pursued by equalization grants are frequently unclear, so that

some embody the features of earmarked grants. A more comprehensive objective would be to aim for each local government to be able to deliver at least a minimum level of public goods and services.

Performance Grants Systems in the Developing World

Local governments receive transfers either as formula-based general purpose grants, or based on criteria such as population, poverty, or remoteness or some form of performance conditions. As discussed above in the section on types of transfers, performance-based transfer systems are used to promote governance and institutional development reforms, including financial management, transparency, and citizen involvement and participation. This section summarizes conditions for obtaining intergovernmental transfers based on various performance criteria.

Access to Performance-Based Grants

Access to some transfers from a higher government tier (central, state, or provincial government) is conditioned on overall performance in areas such as budget execution, revenue mobilization, and service delivery. Such performance-based grants often supplement basic transfers that are allocated to local governments regardless of their effort or improvements. Box 1.8 presents the example of Nepal's Minimum Conditions Performance Measurement (MCPM) system, which provides incentives for improved basic local services. Other similar programs incorporating performance measures financed by the World Bank include the Uganda Local Government Development Program, Kerala Local Government and Service Delivery Project, West Bengal Institutional Strengthening Project, and the Bangladesh Local Governance Support Project.

Transfers that are allocated conditional upon a municipality's performance are underpinned by a logical formula that takes into account factors such as population and area. Typically, the grants are allocated based either on historical

Box 1.8 Minimum Conditions Performance Measurement

The purpose of the Minimum Conditions Performance Measurement system (MCPM) is to augment grant support to local governments nationwide and to introduce incentives for better local performance and compliance with governance standards, based on 35 measured parameters.

These general, unconditional grant funds are to help local self-governments to deliver more public goods and services and respond more effectively to citizens' needs and priorities. Increased block grant transfers are also expected to act as incentives for empowerment, enhancing local citizens' participation in local governance. The minimum conditions (MC) and performance measures (PM) are linked to the development grants to bring about better performance in core areas such as planning, financial management, good governance, and transparency.

The MCs serve as safeguards to ensure that critical functions (e.g., approval of annual budget and program on time) of the local bodies are discharged. The Ministry of Local Development annually adjusts the grants to local bodies based on their scoring in the MCPM assessment. Local bodies that meet the minimum conditions and score high in the performance measures receive additional capital grants, and those that fail the MCs do not.

Source: Government of Nepal.

---

figures or on some simple formula. For example, Nepal's formula is based on population (50 percent), area (10 percent), poverty (25 percent), and tax effort (15 percent). Municipalities still must comply with basic or minimum conditions (MCs) to access their grants. Compliance means access to the transfers, and noncompliance means no access. The MCs include safeguards to bring down fiduciary risks to acceptable levels. For example, a local government may be deemed to qualify for transfers based on clean audits, preparation of regular quarterly financial reports, and evidence of participatory planning.

A major premise of performance-based grants is that they will generate desired behavior on the part of city authorities, who will care about the results. It is important to note that the academic debate as to whether transfers induce improved revenue mobilization remains unsettled. From an operational perspective, however, the process aims to make it plain to city authorities that "there is no free lunch." As noted above, performance grants shift consideration away from only inputs and toward the notion that city authorities are accountable for improvements in outputs, processes, and outcomes. Municipalities are likely to respond to the central government goals by seeking to ensure that they can demonstrate program results, so as to be rewarded with higher subsequent transfers. Hence, well-designed performance-based grants can generate benefits for both the central government and the municipalities. However, several challenges—including data constraints, inadequate capacity at the municipal level, elite capture, corruption, and lack of commitment—can impede the realization of well-intentioned performance-based grants.

Performance Improvement Targets and Indicators

Local governments are often required to demonstrate improvements in public finance management to access performance grants. In some cases other indicators, such as gender, poverty, and environment issues, are also taken into account. The process involves assigning weights and scores to a cluster of indicators that are being considered in a particular environment. For example, in some cases, greater weight may be put on planning and budgeting, and in other cases emphasis may be placed on revenue mobilization. The decision is a conscious one based on the desire to provide incentives to local governments for behavioral change on a particular indicator. The scoring is carried out by a team of professionals (ideally with an independent view), and scores are communicated to the local and central governments in time to allow for decision making for the next cycle of grant allocation. Table 1.4 provides examples of indicators and their corresponding objectives.

Data Considerations

Conceiving and establishing a good transfer system depends on having the necessary fiscal data. A key source of data is typically the municipal budget, which would provide a summary of annual revenue and expenditure patterns. Additional data requirements (quantitative or qualitative) may come into play, such that municipalities would have to demonstrate to the central government achievement of a certain score to obtain the grant. An example is a minimum condition requirement that municipalities hold a participatory planning process, with well-documented minutes of participation, and have a good-quality annual plan that is linked to the five-year development plan. Municipalities would then be scored on this criterion as part of the assessment of whether they qualify for the grant, for example, from a low grade of 1 to a maximum of 10.

Such a combination of qualitative and quantitative data can be used to analyze a variety of public policy matters in the municipality and make informed decisions on revenue and

Table 1.4 Selected Output Indicators Applied to Performance-Based Grants

Area of municipal finance	Objectives	Example of indicators
Planning	• Extending time horizon • Project selection	• 5-year development plan • 3-year rolling capital investment plan
Budgeting	• Timeliness • Credibility	• Submission by agreed date • Variance between midterm budget and actual
Expenditure management	• Efficiency • Timeliness of contract management • Sustainability of operations and maintenance • Control (asset, expenditure authorities)	• Percentage of expenditures done timely • Procurement plans in place by specified date • Created or updated asset registry • Compliance with procurement procedures
Revenue management	• Fiscal effort	• Percentage improvement in revenue collection year on year
Reporting	• Timeliness and accuracy	• Annual financial statement
Oversight and monitoring	• Audit • Disclosures • Citizen satisfaction	• Public display of audit opinion • Resolution of audit queries • Public display of annual financial statement • Evidence that consultative meetings have been held

expenditure management and guide local governments in their investments programming. The discussion by Farvacque-Vitkovic and Sinet in chapter 8 provides advice for local practitioners in collecting and structuring municipal data, financial reports, and performance ratios to fulfill performance criteria (Municipal Finances Self-Assessment—MFSA) and guide local governments in their day to day business and medium-term reform agenda.

Thus, an outcome of performance-based grants—direct or indirect—may be the emergence of a new set of fiscal data at the local government level. Better organizational capabilities are gained along the way, as city officials prepare to access available grants and develop simple formats of fiscal data. Sometimes, local governments do not even recognize that they are building a good, simple fiscal database. In other cases, support may be required to design simple and easy-to-use financial statements, asset registry checklists, and service delivery updates. If those things are done well and captured electronically, local governments will be able to develop a history of records on office and information management (see also chapters 3 and 8). In India (for example, in Kerala, West Bengal, Tamil Nadu, and Karnataka), a series of e-governance initiatives have transformed the way municipalities are capturing key fiscal and service delivery data, thanks in part to the information communication technology revolution in the country.

Distortions in Measuring Performances

Various events and practices can distort efforts to improve local government performance.

Ad hoc transfer mechanisms, which the authors would classify as transfer mechanisms and practices to avoid, are transfers to municipalities that are allocated without a clear central government objective and are not driven by a formula or a clear decision-making process. Often, such transfers are driven by political patronage, and if they coexist with a reasonably good transfer system, the entire system may be subject to distortions and foul play among municipalities. An example is the special allocations that members of the provincial assembly have in Pakistan, the "personal grant envelope." These are funds given to the elected members of provincial and national assemblies to distribute, largely at their own discretion, for projects in their political constituency. Another problem with this type of funding is that it tends to undermine the autonomy of local governments.

Unforeseen events can also cause the central government to release transfers (usually conditional) for a specific purpose. For example, earthquakes, hurricanes, and severe flooding can destroy infrastructure and property and cause deaths in many localities. Today, many local governments are expected to formulate and implement a disaster risk reduction strategy. They have a significant role in providing emergency relief and damage assessment. When a natural disaster occurs, the central government may release transfers in response.

In *natural resource sharing*, a transfer program may be created to compensate some regions and local governments based on resource wealth (or lack thereof). Such a transfer system may be advocated to try to promote equity among the local authorities in a country. A major political debate is going on in this regard in Pakistan because less-urbanized provinces such as Baluchistan, that are blessed with abundant natural resources, receive unfairly small shares of transfers allocated based on population or urbanized area. They argue for a fairer share based on the revenues that originate in their natural resources, but which are often realized by the industrialized provinces that sell the processed products. South Africa has a similar debate with multinational investors (Haysom and Kane 2009).

Municipal Contracts

Municipal contracts are another key performance-based instrument. In a context of increased decentralization and greater involvement of local governments and of communities, the Municipal Contract has emerged as a useful tool to facilitate the selection, implementation and financing of urban services and infrastructure and push the envelope on municipal management reforms. Many countries in Europe have adopted the Municipal Contract approach. In France, municipal contracts were initially introduced on an experimental basis in the 80's. During the 2000's, 247 municipal contracts involving 2,000 municipalities were signed to benefit inter-municipal projects (2 billion euros in investments). The Netherlands adopted the contract formula in its "large city" policy. The UK adopted an original form of partnership policy based on a "strategic local partnership" which brought together local stakeholders (civil society, the private sector, local governments) for the purpose of identifying and financing neighborhood projects. The UK is currently expanding the use of city contracts beyond the initial urban renewal objective. Sweden, Belgium, Germany and Canada have also experimented with various forms of municipal contracts. A municipal contract is usually a consensual and binding, performance-based agreement between a municipality and the central government for a four- or five-year period. It typically includes a priority investment plan, a municipal maintenance plan, and a municipal adjustment or reform program. In North Africa, municipal contracts have also been used in Tunisia and Morocco. In Sub-Sahara Africa, municipal contracts have been widely implemented with the support of the World Bank and AFD in countries such as Senegal, Guinea, Mali, Burkina Faso, Mauritania, Cote d' Ivoire, Niger, Cameroon, Madagascar, Benin, Rwanda, Chad. (Farvacque-Vitkovic and Godin). Box 1.9 summarizes the key objectives and attributes of municipal contracts.

Box 1.9 Objectives of Municipal Contracts

The following are some of the key objectives of municipal contracts:

- To support integrated urban and local development through an increase in urban investments in infrastructure and service delivery and by focusing on improving municipal governance and management.
- To give the municipality greater responsibility in the selection and financing of municipal investments by putting its role on a contractual footing.
- To ensure prioritization of investments and greater visibility and transparency on the use of public funds.
- To ensure strong commitment, through signing of a municipal contract between the central government and the municipal government, based on the provisions of the contract and publicly acknowledged obligations.
- To enhance citizen participation in developing the strategic vision of the municipality for its future growth and development and develop stronger accountability between the municipality and its citizens.
- To define and monitor the implementation of the key components of the Municipal Contract (Municipal Investments Program and Municipal Adjustment Program – including the Municipal Finances Improvement Plan).

Sources: Farvacque-Vitkovic and Godin 1998; Farvacque-Vitkovic, Godin and Sinet 2013; Goudrian 2010.

Box 1.10 The Process of Municipal Contracts

A municipal contract is developed based on an assessment of the municipality's characteristics, particularly urban features and organizational and financial capacities and weaknesses. The assessment leads to a municipal program which includes clear investments priorities (Priority Investments Program) as well as clear capacity development measures (Municipal Adjustment program).

Development of municipal contracts can be divided into four stages:

1. The *diagnostic/audit/self-assessment stage*: This stage includes (1) the completion of a financial and organizational audit/self-assessment which aims to assess a city's financial health and to identify specific actions to improve mobilization of local resources, public spending, public assets management and maintenance, investment programming and access to external financing. The MFSA leads to a very concrete Municipal Finances Improvement Plan; and (2) an Urban Audit which aims to locate, identify and quantify existing gaps in service delivery and infrastructure and which leads to (a) a Priority Investment program and (b) a Municipal Maintenance Program.
2. The *validation/consultation stage* examines the key findings of these assessments/audits. It is a very important stage because it involves a set of consultations with the key stakeholders in order to reach a consensus on a "municipal program" which would consist of (1) a set of very concrete and monitorable capacity development and revenue enhancement measures and (2) a program of investments based on the financial capacity and the priorities of the citizens.
3. The third stage consists of drafting the municipal contract, itself, with a clear set of commitments from the local and central governments in order to close the deal on a financing and technical program. It will specify the content of the priority investment programs (PIPs) and of the Municipal Adjustment/Improvement Program (MAP).
4. The *implementation and monitoring stage* requires a coordinated effort to align the financing with the technical and human resources, as well as the political commitment to implement the contract.

Evidence suggests that municipal contracts have been very effective in supporting local governments, even where decentralization reform has been a difficult process (World Bank 2009). They have enhanced municipalities' financial capacity and contributed to investments in infrastructure and service delivery.

The success or failure of a municipal contract depends on two main factors: the quality of the municipal contract process itself and the political and institutional environment in which it is developed and implemented. The quality of the municipal contract depends on the capacity-building efforts that municipalities engage in to enable better preparation, implementation, monitoring, auditing, and strategic development. The level of political commitment and ownership at the central and local levels, the degree of participation by stakeholders and citizens, and the extent of harmonization and alignment among various donors working in the local government sector are also important influences.

Source: Farvacque-Vitkovic, Godin, Sinet, 2013.

Box 1.11 Municipal Contracts: Some Examples of Best Practice

A recent Independent Evaluation Group (IEG) review points out that by the late 2000s, more than 200 municipalities across French-speaking West Africa were implementing municipal contracts. In the short term, they resulted in increased municipal capacity to invest. Municipal capital investment as a share of current revenues rose from 10 percent to 17 percent over the period 2001–03 (World Bank 2009).

Among the examples of successful municipal contract projects are Senegal I (Urban Development and Decentralization Program), which helped 67 municipalities throughout Senegal strengthen their financial and organizational management and improve implementation of investments in urban infrastructure and services. The project used municipal contracts in which central and local governments agreed to certain benchmarks for municipal reform.

A highly satisfactory project was Benin I (Urban Rehabilitation and Management), which helped improve urban services in the country's two largest cities, Cotonou (population 690,584) and Porto Novo (population 234,168). Confirmed by beneficiary assessments at completion, the success was helped by the introduction of delegated contract management practices. Those practices enabled rapid processing and execution of service contracts with local small and medium-size enterprises, which provided higher-quality, lower-cost urban infrastructure services and left municipal administrations more time to concentrate on their planning and programming tasks.

Ghana also had a string of successful municipal development programs (MDPs). Ghana I brought significant service improvements, notably in solid waste management, to six municipalities. This success was extended to 11 more municipalities by Ghana II. Ghana IV took the model further by investing intensely in financial and technical training for the staffs of 23 municipalities through the national Institute of Local Government Studies, which itself came out of the project considerably strengthened (World Bank 2009).

The Internal Evaluation Group (IEG) of the World Bank found that among the most successful are Benin's First Urban Rehabilitation and Management, Second Decentralized City Management, and the Third Second Decentralized City Management; and Senegal's First Urban Development and Decentralization Program and Second Local Authorities Development Program, under various World Bank projects (World Bank 2009).

Takeaway Messages

Wherever one looks around the globe, a new generation of public policy makers, academics, and civil society activists are discussing the pros and cons of decentralized government. This is true in unitary, federal, and confederal states alike. The character of a "decentralized" system of public sector reform varies from country to country, but there is general agreement that by "decentralization" one is referring to the structure of the relations among different types of government—that is, the sorting out of governmental roles and responsibilities among central and subnational (e.g., municipal) governments. There is also agreement that to be "intergovernmental" requires a financially strong, but reorganized and refocused, central government along with a well-designed and capable system of subnational governments. At present, the public finance literature typically distinguishes two primary forms of a decentralized system: political and fiscal. "Political decentralization" refers to arrangements whereby the legal legitimacy of local government is recognized explicitly in the national constitution or by statutory and administrative decisions. "Fiscal decentralization" is the intergovernmental sorting out of expenditure and financing roles and responsibilities among the various types of governments in a manner that is in harmony with the political framework. For a nation to realize the theory-promised social and economic benefits of an intergovernmental society requires both political and fiscal decentralization.

There are four fundamental questions to be addressed in fiscal decentralization: (1) Which type or tier of government does what (expenditure assignment)? (2) Which type levies which revenues (revenue assignment)? (3) How can "vertical" fiscal imbalances between the center and subnational units and "horizontal" imbalances across subnational jurisdictions be resolved? (4) How shall the timing of receipts be addressed (borrowing and debt)?

"Fiscal decentralization" is also a term encompassing three variants: deconcentration, delegation, and devolution. An important policy question is which of these three variants can be said to dominate a nation's public finances. *Deconcentration* denotes a process whereby regional offices of central ministries and/or of centrally appointed administrative officials are established in local jurisdictions for the purpose of determining the level and composition of the provision of local goods and services. The central authority retains control of the rules for the financing side of the budget equation. Deconcentration "with authority" means that the regional offices are given some flexibility to make "own" local service and tax decisions, but again, subject to central guidelines. Under a system of deconcentration "without authority" the nonelected regional offices and officers have no power to modify centrally mandated rules and regulations. *Delegation* can be characterized as a principal-agent relationship in which higher-level governments (principals) assign local governments (agents) the responsibility for supplying certain local functions. With *devolution*, independent local self-governments are established with the full responsibility for the delivery of a set of public services, along with the authority to impose taxes and fees to finance the services.

Why do some states tend to remain heavily politically and fiscally centrally controlled while others move ahead with decentralization? Three arguments are offered to explain a continuing tilt to centralization. They are (1) the argument that there is a lack of local capacity to govern; (2) ensuring that central functions such as national defense, foreign policy, protecting national borders, and managing macroeconomic stabilization are fulfilled; and (3) legacy—the persistence of old methods—and "old ways are good ways."

That much of the world is undergoing some form of decentralization attests to its importance. There are at least four explanations for this trend: (1) the complementary, indeed reinforcing, nature of the 21st-century trends of globalization and localization; (2) the politics of the "reaction from below" for systems of citizen control over their local government; (3) the economic efficiency and political accountability arguments that there is payoff in terms of general welfare gains that result from well-designed intergovernmental arrangements; and (4) for some nations, decentralization can serve as a strategy for promoting national cohesion to defuse tensions that arise where the society is fragmented by history, ethnicity, religion, language, endowment of natural resources, or other aspect of geography and place.

What are practitioners learning? What does one know about the relationship between decentralized fiscal autonomy and the accomplishment of a nation's broader economic and fiscal objectives? Four lessons are being learned: (1) There is a proven dismal macroeconomic record of centralized command and control; the advanced (e.g., OECD) countries of the world tend to be those that have adopted a system with some degree of local political self-determination and devolution of finances. (2) Consistent with the theory of public finance that argues that decentralization enhances efficiency in the allocation of public services, there is an emerging body of empirical evidence that reveals a positive relationship between a well-designed and implemented system of decentralized government and national economic growth. (3) Case study work attests to the national cohesion outcome for several nation states. (4) Some evidence exists that subnational revenue autonomy improves the macroeconomic stability of the nation state.

Intergovernmental transfers play a key role in the finances of municipalities. How they are designed and implemented is very important in understanding their impacts in a decentralized framework. Designing intergovernmental transfers is not a simple task. The fiscal life of a local government financial manager in a typical working day can be made more effective if transfers are designed and implemented in a formula-driven, transparent, and accountable manner that relies on data that can be readily accessed and understood by donor and recipient alike. The central government may choose to take up the transfer design or may delegate it to an independent entity, which may have the final decision-making authority or be advisory. The four commonly practiced options in the design of transfers include a central legislative or executive authority, an independent grants commission, an intergovernmental forum, and an intergovernmental-cum-civil-society forum.

Intergovernmental transfers can be broadly classified into two main categories: general purpose (also called "unconditional") transfers and specific purpose (also called "conditional" or "earmarked") transfers. General purpose transfers have no conditions ("strings") attached and may be either mandated by the law (e.g., the constitution) or made at central legislative discretion. Unconditional grants may be designed to simultaneously address both vertical (central versus local capacity to generate revenues) and horizontal imbalances (equalization of fiscal capacity disparities among subnational governments). Specific purpose or conditional or earmarked transfers are financing, or intended to provide incentives, for governments to undertake specific programs or activities. Such transfers may incorporate matching provisions by requiring municipalities to finance a specified percentage of expenditures using their own resources. Another important type of transfer is centrally shared revenue, an arrangement in which a portion of the monies (receipts) derived from a national tax, or other, nontax revenue, is transferred to subnational governments. However, depending on the formula for the central-subnational division of receipts, revenue sharing may exacerbate or reduce the horizontal fiscal disparities among subnational governments.

Performance-based transfer systems are intended to promote and create incentives for governance and institutional development reforms, including financial management, transparency, and citizen involvement and participation. Under a system of performance-based transfers, local governments access grants based on some criteria (e.g., population, poverty, remoteness) or some form of performance conditions. However, various events and practices can distort the efforts made toward improving performance-based grants systems of local governments. These include transfers that (a) are arbitrarily allocated without a clear objective or transparent formula; (b) serve as "gap filling" to cover subnational government fund deficits; (c) are intended to address events (e.g., earthquakes, hurricanes, and severe flooding) but which may be conditional for a specific purpose granted for a limited time; and (d) take into account the sharing of natural resource revenues to compensate specific regions and thus local governments for resource wealth (or deficiencies), without paying attention to the performance of local governments.

Municipal contracts are another key performance-based-instrument through which municipalities have been supported to address urbanization challenges. Municipal contracts focus essentially on capacity building and financial and organizational reforms to build municipalities as key institutions to deliver basic services to the citizens.

References

Ahmad, E., and G. Brosio. 2006. *Handbook of Fiscal Federalism*. Cheltenham, U.K.: Edward Elgar.

Akai, Nobu, and Masayo Sakata. 2002. "Fiscal Decentralization Contributes to Economic Growth: Evidence from State-Level Cross Section Data for the United States." *Journal of Urban Economics* 52 (1): 93–108.

Amin, Khalid, and Robert D. Ebel. 2006. "Intergovernmental Relations and Fiscal Decentralization in Egypt." Egypt Public Expenditure Review, Policy Note No. 8, World Bank, Washington, DC.

Arzaghi, Mohammad, and J. Vernon Henderson. 2005. "Why Countries Are Fiscally Decentralizing." *Journal of Public Economics* 89: 1157–89.

Bahl, Roy W. 1999a. "Implementation Rules for Fiscal Decentralization." Georgia State University, Andrew Young School of Public Policy, Atlanta, Georgia, U.S.A., www: asyps .gsu.edu/publications.

———. 1999b. *Fiscal Policy in China: Taxation and Intergovernmental Fiscal Relations*. Ann Arbor: 1990 Institute Press/University of Michigan Press.

Bahl, R., and J. Martinez-Vazquez. 2006. "Sequencing Fiscal Decentralization." World Bank Policy Research Working Paper 3914, World Bank, Washington, DC.

Barati-Stec, Izabella. 2012. *Hungary: An Unfinished Decentralization?* IMFG Papers on Municipal Finance and Governance. Toronto: Munk School of Global Affairs.

Bauzon, Kenneth E. 1999. "The Philippines: The 1996 Peace Agreement Southern Philippines: An Assessment." *Ethnic Studies Report* 17 (2): 253–80.

Bird, Richard M. 2011a. "Subnational Taxation in Developing Countries: A Review of the Literature." *Journal of International Commerce, Economics and Policy* 2 (1): 1–23.

———. 2011b. "Are There Trends in Local Finance? A Cautionary Note on Comparative Studies and Normative Models of Local Government Finance." Institute on Municipal Finance and Governance, Munk School of Global Affairs, University of Toronto.

Bird, Richard M., and Robert D. Ebel. 2007. *Fiscal Fragmentation in Decentralized Countries: Subsidiarity, Solidarity, and Asymmetry*. Cheltenham, U.K. and Northampton, MA: Edward Elgar.

Bird, Richard M., Robert D. Ebel, and Sebastiana Gianci. 2007. "Country Studies: Aspects of the Problem." In *Fiscal Fragmentation in Decentralized Countries: Subsidiarity, Solidarity, and Asymmetry*, edited by Richard M. Bird and Robert D. Ebel. Cheltenham, U.K. and Northampton, MA: Edward Elgar.

Bird, Richard M., Robert D. Ebel, and Christine I. Wallich. 1995. *Decentralization of the Socialist State: Intergovernmental Finance in Transition Economies.* Washington, DC: World Bank.

Bird, Richard M., and François Vaillancourt. 2006. "Perspectives on Fiscal Federalism." WBI Learning Resources Series 35628, World Bank, Washington, DC.

———. 2010. "Is Decentralization 'Glue' or 'Solvent' for National Unity?" Working Paper 10-03, International Studies Program, Andrew Young School of Policy Studies. Atlanta: Georgia State University.

Blöchliger, H., and O. Petzold. 2009. *Finding the Dividing Line between Tax Sharing and Grants: A Statistical Investigation.* OECD Working Paper on Fiscal Federalism No. 10. Paris: Organisation for Economic Co-operation and Development.

Blöchliger, H., and J. Rabesona. 2009. *The Fiscal Autonomy of Sub-Central Governments: An Update.* OECD Working Paper on Fiscal Federalism No. 9. Paris: Organisation for Economic Co-operation and Development.

Boadway, R., and A. Shah, eds. 2009. *Fiscal Federalism.* Cambridge: Cambridge University Press.

Box, Jamie, and Jorge Martinez-Vazquez. 2004. "Designing Intergovernmental Equalization Transfers with Imperfect Data: Concepts, Practices and Lessons." Working Paper 04-12, International Studies Program, Andrew Young School of Policy Studies. Atlanta: Georgia State University. www.aysps.gsu.edu.

Canuto, Otaviano, and Lili Liu, eds. 2013. *Until Debt Do Us Part: Subnational Debt, Insolvency and Markets.* Washington, DC: World Bank.

Commins, Stephen, and Robert D. Ebel. 2010. "Participation and Decentralization in Africa: Revisiting the Arusha Declaration." Consultation for African Civil Society Organizations on Peace Building and State Affairs. Addis Ababa: United Nations Economic Commission for Africa.

Dafflon, Bernard. 2006. "The Assignment of Functions to Decentralized Government: From Theory to Practice." In *Handbook on Federalism,* edited by Ahmad Ehtisham and Giorgio Brosio. Cheltenham, U.K.: Edward Elgar.

Demszky, Gabor. 2003. "Liberalism in Practice" In *The Budapest Model: A Liberal Urban Policy Experiment,* edited by Katalin Pallai. Budapest: Open Society Institute.

Dillinger, William. 1994. "Decentralization and Its implications for Urban Service Delivery." Urban Management Program Notes Series 16, World Bank, Washington, DC.

Eaton, Kent, Kai Kaiser, and Paul Smoke. 2011. *The Political Economy of Decentralization Reforms in Developing Countries: A Development Partner Perspective.* Washington, DC: World Bank.

Ebel, Robert D., and Gabor Peteri. 2007. *The Kosovo Decentralization Briefing Book.* Prishtina: Kosovo Foundation for an Open Society/Soros Foundation. www.lgi.osi.

Ebel, Robert D., and Robert Taliercio. 2005. "Subnational Tax Policy and Administration in Developing Countries." *Tax Notes International* 37 (1): 919–36.

Ebel, Robert D., and Dana Weist. 2007. *Sequencing Subnational Tax Policy and Administration.* World Bank Decentralization Thematic Group. Washington, DC: World Bank.

Ebel, Robert D., and Serdar Yilmaz. 2003. "On the Measurement and Impact of Fiscal Decentralization." In *Public Finance in Developing and Transition Countries: Essays in Honor of Richard M. Bird,* edited by Jorge Martinez-Vazquez and James Alm. Cheltenham, U.K.: Edward Elgar.

Ellis, Peter. 2010. "Indonesia Rising. Policy Priorities for 2010 and Beyond: Completing Decentralization." Policy Note, World Bank, Washington, DC.

Farvacque-Vitkovic, Catherine, and Lucien Godin. 1998. *The Future of African Cities.* Washington, DC: World Bank.

Farvacque-Vitkovic, Catherine, Lucien Godin and Anne Sinet. *Municipal Self-Assessments: A Handbook for Local Governments.* Washington, DC: World Bank (forthcoming).

Fox, William, and Christine Wallich. 2007. "Fiscal Federalism in Bosnia and Herzegovina: Subsidiarity in a Three-Nation State." In *Fiscal Fragmentation in Decentralized Countries: Subsidiarity, Solidarity, and Asymmetry*, edited by Richard M. Bird and Robert D. Ebel, 267–94. Cheltenham, U.K.: Edward Elgar.

Gomez-Lobo, Andres. 2001. "Making Water Affordable." In *Contracting for Public Services*, edited by Penelope Brooke and Suzanne Smith, 23–29. Washington, DC: World Bank.

Gonzalez, Pablo. 2005. "The Financing of Education in Chile." Fund for the Study of Public Policies, University of Chile, Santiago, Chile.

Gordon, Nora, and Emiliana Vegas. 2004. "Education Finance Equalization, Spending, Teacher Quality and Student Outcomes: The Case of Brazil's FUNDEF." Working paper, World Bank, Washington, DC.

Goudriaan, Mirco. 2010. "Effective Aid through Municipal Contracts." Internal working paper, VNG International, The Hague, Netherlands.

Griffiths, Ann L., with Karl Nerenberg, eds. 2005. *Handbook of Federal Countries*. Montreal and Kingston: McGill-Queens University Press.

Haysom, N., and S. Kane. 2009. "Negotiating Natural Resources for Peace. Ownership, Control and Wealth Sharing." Briefing paper, Center for Humanitarian Dialogue, Geneva, Switzerland.

Hofman, Bert, and S. C. Guerra. 2007. "Ensuring Inter-regional Equity and Poverty Reduction." In *Fiscal Equalization*, edited by J. Martinez-Vazquez and B. Searle. New York: Springer.

Imi, A. 2005. "Fiscal Decentralization and Economic Growth Revisited: An Empirical Note." *Journal of Urban Economics* 57: 449–61.

Jensen, Leif. 2001. *Fiscal Design Surveys across Levels of Government*. Tax Policy Studies No. 7. Paris: Organisation for Economic Co-operation and Development.

Kalandadze, K., and M. A. Orenstein. 2009. "Electoral Protests and Democratization: Beyond the Color Revolutions." *Comparative Political Studies* 42 (11): 1403–25.

Kopanyi, Mihaly, Samir El Daher, and Deborah Wetzel. 2004. *Intergovernmental Finance in Hungary: A Decade of Experience, 1990–2000*, edited by Mihaly Kopanyi, Deborah Wetzel, and Samir El Daher. Washington, DC: World Bank.

Kopanyi, Mihaly, Samir El Daher, Deborah Wetzel, Michel Noel, and Anita Papp. 2000. "Modernizing the Subnational Government System." World Bank Discussion Paper No. 417, World Bank, Washington, DC.

Marcou, Gerard. 2007. "Legal Framework and the European Charter of Local Self Government." In *The Kosovo Decentralization Briefing Book*, edited by Robert D. Ebel and Gabor Peteri, 50–59. Prishtina: Kosovo Foundation for an Open Society.

Martinez-Vazquez, Jorge. 1999. "The Assignment of Expenditure Responsibilities." Paper prepared for the core course on Intergovernmental Relations and Local Financial Management, World Bank Institute, Washington, DC.

———. 2007. "Challenges in the Design of Intergovernmental Transfers." In *Fiscal Equalization*, edited by Jorge Martinez-Vazquez and Bob Searle. New York: Springer.

Martinez-Vazquez, Jorge, and Robert Martin McNab. 1997. "Tax Reform in Transition Economies: Experience and Lessons." Working Paper No. 97-6, Andrew Young School of Policy Studies, Georgia State University, Atlanta.

Martinez-Vazquez, Jorge, and François Vaillancourt, eds. 2011. *Decentralization in Developing Countries: Global Perspectives on the Obstacles to Fiscal Devolution*. Northampton, MA: Edward Elgar.

McClure, Charles E., Jr. 1999. "The Tax Assignment Problem: Conceptual and Administrative Considerations in Achieving Subnational Fiscal Autonomy." Paper prepared for the core course on Intergovernmental Relations and Local Financial Management, World Bank Institute, Washington, DC.

McNeil, Mary, and Carmen Malena. 2010. "Social Accountability in Africa." In *Demanding Good*

Governance: Lessons from Social Accountability Initiatives in Africa, edited by Mary McNeil and Carmen Malena, 1–28. Washington, DC: World Bank.

Meloche, J. P., F. Vaillancourt, and S. Yilmaz. 2004. "Decentralization or Fiscal Autonomy? What Does Really Matter? Effects on Growth and Public Sector Size in European Transition Countries." Policy Research Working Paper 3254, World Bank, Washington, DC.

Mikesell, John L. 2003. "International Experiences with Administration of Local Taxes: A Review of Practices and Issues (2003)." Report prepared for the World Bank Thematic Group on Taxation and Tax Policy, World Bank, Washington, DC. www.worldbank.org.

NALAS (Network of Association of Local Authorities of South-East Europe). 2008. Skopje, www.nalas.eu.

Ndegwa, Stephen N. 2002. "Decentralization in Africa: A Stocktaking Survey." Africa Region Working Paper Series No. 40, World Bank, Washington, DC.

Oates, Wallace E. 1972. *Fiscal Federalism.* New York: Harcourt Brace Jovanovich.

———. 1985. "Searching for Leviathan: An Empirical Study." *American Economic Review* 75 (4): 748–57.

———. 1997. "On the Welfare Gains from Fiscal Decentralization." *Journal of Public Finance and Public Choice* 2 (3): 83–92.

Pallai, Katalin. 2003. *The Budapest Model.* Budapest: Open Society Institute. www.lgi.osi.hu.

Peteri, Gabor, and Fikret Sevinc. 2011. "Municipal Revenues and Expenditures in Turkey and in Selected EU Countries." Local Administration Reform Project in Turkey, LAR Phase II. Local Administration Reform Project, Bakanliklar-Ankara.

Rangarajan, C., and Abha Prasad. 2012. "Managing State Debt and Ensuring Solvency: The Indian Experience." Policy Research Working Paper 6039, World Bank, Washington, DC.

Rao, M. Govinda. 2007. "Resolving Fiscal Imbalances." In *Intergovernmental Fiscal Transfers: Principles and Practice,* edited by Robin Boadway and Anwar Shah. Washington, DC: World Bank.

Regulski, Jerzy. 2010. *A Practical Guide to Building Local Government: The Polish Experience.* Budapest: Local Government and Public Service Reform Initiative/Open Society Institute. www.lgi.osi.hu.

Sen, Amartya. 1999. "Democracy As a Universal Value." *Journal of Democracy* 10 (3): 3–17. http://muse.jhu,demo/jod.10.3sen.html.

Shah, A. 2007. "A Practitioner's Guide to Intergovernmental Fiscal Transfers." In *Intergovernmental Fiscal Transfers: Principles and Practice,* edited by R. Boadway and A. Shah. Washington, DC: World Bank.

Shah, Anwar. 1998. "Indonesia and Pakistan: Fiscal Decentralization—An Elusive Goal?" In *Fiscal Decentralization in Developing Countries,* edited by Richard M. Bird and François Vaillancourt. Cambridge: Cambridge University Press.

Sharma, Y., and A. Muwonge. 2010. "An Opportunity to Improve Service Delivery in Nepal through Local Governance." Himalayan Research Papers Archive. Fifth Annual Himalayan Policy Research Conference, Nepal Study Center, University of New Mexico. http://repository.unm.edu/handle/1928/11328.

Slack, Enid, and Rupak Chattopadhyay, eds. 2009. *Finance and Governance of Capital Cities in Federal Systems.* Montreal and Kingston: McGill-Queen's University Press.

Smoke, Paul. 2008. "Local Revenues under Fiscal Decentralization in Developing Countries: Linking Policy Reform, Governance and Capacity." In *Fiscal Decentralization and Land Policies,* edited by Gregory Ingram and Yu-Hung Hong, 33–69. Cambridge, MA: Lincoln Institute Press.

———. 2013. "Why Theory and Practice Are Different: The Gap between Principles and Reality in Subnational Revenue Systems." In *Taxation and Development: The Weakest Link.*

Essays in Honor of Roy Bahl, edited by Richard M. Bird and Jorge Martinez-Vazquez. Cheltenham, U.K.: Edward Elgar.

Smoke, Paul, and Robert R. Taliercio, Jr. 2007. "Aid, Public Finance, and Accountability: Cambodian Dilemmas." In *Peace and the Public Purse,* edited by James K. Boyce and Madalene O'Donnell, 55–84. London: Lynne Rienner.

Soros, George. 2006. *The Age of Fallibility.* Cambridge, MA: Public Affairs Books.

Swianiewicz, Pawel. 2006. "Local Government Organization and Finance: Poland." In *Local Governance in Developing Countries,* edited by Anwar Shah. Washington, DC: World Bank.

Thomas, Vinod. 2006. "Linking Individual, Organizational, and Institutional Capacity Building to Results." WBI Capacity Development Brief 19, World Bank, Washington, DC.

Tosun, Mehmet Serkan. 2010. "Middle East and North Africa." In *Local Government Finance: The Challenges of the 21st Century,* edited by Jorge Martinez-Vazquez and Paul Smoke. Barcelona: United Cities and Local Governments.

Tosun, Mehmet Serkan, and Serdar Yilmaz. 2010. "Centralization, Decentralization and Conflict in the Middle East and North Africa." *Middle East Development Journal* 2 (1): 1–14.

Vaillancourt, François. 2002. "Simulating Intergovernmental Equalization Transfers with Imperfect Data." Proceedings of the Annual Conference, 2001, 57–64, National Tax Association, Washington, DC.

Wallich, Christine, and Qianqian Zhang. 2013. "Bosnia and Herzegovina: Subsidiarity As Conflict Avoidance in a Three Nation State." Paper presented to the Forum on Conflict, Security and Development, May, World Bank, Washington, DC.

Wallich, Christine I., Rosario Manasan, and Saloua Sehili. 2007. "Subsidiarity and Solidarity: Fiscal Decentralization in the Philippines."

In *Fiscal Fragmentation in Decentralized Countries: Subsidiarity, Solidarity, and Asymmetry,* edited by Richard M. Bird and Robert D. Ebel, 363–98. Cheltenham, U.K.: Edward Elgar.

Wong, Christine. 2007. "Ethnic Minority Regions and Fiscal Decentralization in China: The Promises and Reality of Asymmetric Treatment." In *Fiscal Fragmentation in Decentralized Countries: Subsidiarity, Solidarity, and Asymmetry,* edited by Richard M. Bird and Robert D. Ebel, 267–94. Cheltenham, U.K.: Edward Elgar.

———. 2013. "Paying for Urbanization in China: Challenges of Municipal Finance in the 21st Century." In *Financing Metropolitan Governments in Developing Countries,* edited by R. W. Bahl, J. F. Linn, and D. L. Wetzel. Cambridge, MA: Lincoln Institute for Land Policy.

World Bank. 2000. *World Development Report 1999/2000. Entering the 21st Century.* New York: Oxford University Press.

———. 2009. *Improving Municipal Management for Cities to Succeed: An Independent Evaluation Group (IEG) Special Study.* Washington, DC: World Bank.

Yatta, F., and F. Vaillancourt. 2010. "Africa." In *Local Government Finance: The Challenges of the 21st Century,* edited by Jorge Martinez-Vazquez and Paul Smoke. Barcelona: United Cities and Local Governments.

Yilmaz, Serdar, François Vaillancourt, and Bernard Dafflon. 2012. "State and Local Governments: Why They Matter and How to Finance Them." In *The Oxford Handbook of State and Local Government Finance,* edited by Robert D. Ebel and John E. Petersen, 45–82. Oxford and New York: Oxford University Press.

Zoellick, Robert. 2009. "Securing Development." Conference on Passing the Baton, United States Institute of Peace, Washington, DC, January 8.

CHAPTER 2

Metropolitan Governance and Finance

Mats Andersson

Urbanization around the world is creating larger cities and economic areas. More than 3.5 billion people now live in cities and their vicinities. In mid-2012, there were 27 megacities with more than 10 million people, and more than 500 metropolitan areas with over a million (Brinkoff 2012). Cities are growing particularly rapidly in developing countries, some at rates of 3 percent to 5 percent annually. People move to cities for better jobs, better services, or a better business environment; for family reasons; or because of natural disasters or social unrest in their places of origin. With improved transportation, people are also able to commute over longer distances from villages or small towns to larger urban areas. As a result, cities have become economically interdependent with their surrounding settlements and hinterlands, constituting *metropolitan areas*— each a single economy and labor market, a community with common interests, benefiting from some joint actions.

This chapter summarizes the main characteristics of metropolitan areas. It starts by highlighting the socioeconomic factors of urbanization, the ways that cities grow spatially, and the opportunities and challenges of megacities. It summarizes the metropolitan-level governance models applied internationally and describes their municipal finance implications, with examples. A great diversity of metropolitan governance models and modalities and many effective and equitable arrangements exist. Often political circumstances and decisions influence the formation or evolution of governance and finance systems.

Emergence of Metropolitan Areas

Cities have been emerging and growing since known historic times. But also, many large cities have over time become more economically interdependent with their surrounding urban settlements and hinterlands, constituting a *single economy and labor market* that is called a city-region, a metropolitan area, or an extended urban region. The economic links between the core and the periphery may become so close that one part cannot succeed without the other, and thus they behave as a single entity. The term "metropolitan area" is often a loose definition with no clear boundaries. It may be based on labor market (people live in one part of the area and work in another part), a catchment area for amenities and education institutions, or access to key infrastructure, or it may be an area based on a firm's local economic environment. Some definitions of related concepts are shown in box 2.1 for general reference. This chapter defines a metropolitan area as follows:

> An area constituting a single economy and labor market, a community with common interests and joint actions; often including a number of local government jurisdictions.

The radius of such an area is often on the order of 20 to 40 kilometers (km), but is sometimes larger, or the area may be shaped as an urban corridor or "belt" (one jurisdiction after another). Socioeconomic cohesion characterizes the formation and emergence of a metropolitan area. Although the jurisdictional boundaries of local governments tend to have a long history, years of urban growth often change an area's character. Therefore, a metropolitan area usually includes a number of independent local government jurisdictions. Metropolitan areas are often supported with some institutions or arrangements to coordinate their development or some joint functions for more efficient and equitable service provision and cost sharing, in addition to efforts by each individual local government.

Agglomerations of this kind host a quarter of the world's population. Around the world, there are more than 500 metropolitan areas with populations of a million or more (Brinkoff 2012), a total population estimated to be more than 1.6 billion in mid-2012. These agglomerations include a central city and neighboring communities linked to the core by continuous built-up areas or through commuting patterns. An agglomeration is typically named after its central city. Some have more than one central city (such as "the Ruhr" area in Germany).

How Do Cities Grow Spatially?

Cities grow spatially in different ways. Figures 2.1 through 2.4 illustrate four types of spatial growth

Box 2.1 Terms Related to Metropolitan Areas

Urban agglomeration is an extended city or town area comprising the built-up area of a central place (a municipality) and suburbs linked by a continuous urban area.

Conurbation is a more specific term for large urban clusters, where the built-up zones of influence of distinct cities or towns are connected by continuous built-up development (e.g., Essen–Dortmund in the Rhine-Ruhr district in Germany), even in different regions, states, or countries (e.g., Lille–Kortrijk at the border between France and Belgium). Each city or town in a conurbation may nevertheless continue to act as an independent focus for a substantial part of the area.

Metropolis is a very large city or urban area which is a significant economic, political, and cultural center for a country or region and an important hub for regional or international connections and communications. New York City is often cited as the quintessential metropolis.

Source: Wikipedia.

of a city or area. In a *monocentric structure* (figure 2.1), a core city is growing outward from a central core, in more or less concentric circles over time, with decreasing population densities the farther one gets from the center. Sometimes the spatial extension has instead the character of *sprawl* (figure 2.2), with low-density areas expanding in various directions.

A *polycentric structure* (figure 2.3) results from growth that is more a matter of integration of various areas than an outward expansion of a core area. Often a number of urban subcenters exist and grow, and over time they become sufficiently close to a main city, from a transport perspective, to allow significant business interaction and daily commuting. A polycentric structure tends to evolve toward a *multipolar structure* (figure 2.4), which is characterized by a core city and various secondary subcenters, with the areas in between them having become denser in population, forming contiguous urban

settlements. Thus, a metropolitan area may emerge or be formed either through outbound growth of a city or through a gradual expansion and integration of various settlements that at some point form an interdependent, agglomerated metropolitan area.

A metropolitan area sometimes forms a corridor or a "belt" (one jurisdiction after another), for example, because of the topography or the location of key infrastructure (such as an international airport) or a tourist attraction. The metropolitan area of Tbilisi, Georgia, provides a good example (see map B2.2.1). It is a 60-km corridor of four local governments along a valley, with Tbilisi the dominant city. The emergence of this corridor is summarized in box 2.2 and illustrated in the accompanying map.

Informal Settlements
Agglomerations are mixtures of towns, villages, urban and rural areas, forests, riverbeds, and

Figure 2.1   Monocentric Structure

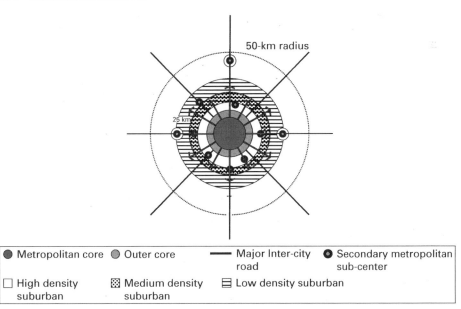

Source: Chreod Ltd.

Figure 2.2   Sprawl

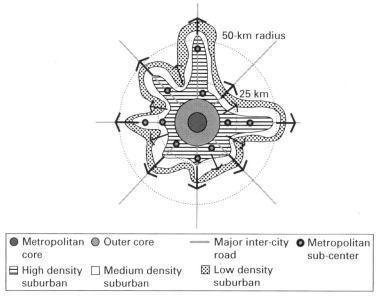

Source: Chreod Ltd.

Figure 2.3   Polycentric Structure

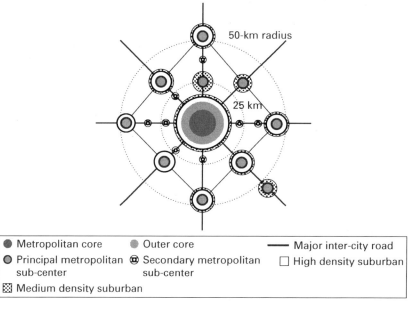

Source: Chreod Ltd.

Figure 2.4   Multipolar Structure

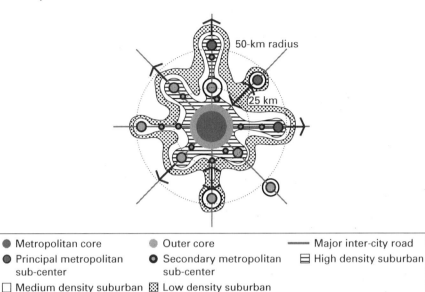

50-km radius

25 km

- ● Metropolitan core
- ● Principal metropolitan sub-center
- ☐ Medium density suburban
- ◍ Outer core
- ◉ Secondary metropolitan sub-center
- ▨ Low density suburban
- ▬▬▬ Major inter-city road
- ⊟ High density suburban

Source: Chreod Ltd.

Box 2.2 The Emergence of the Tbilisi Corridor

The Tbilisi area has grown into an agglomeration, with the local economy and labor market spanning Rustavi city and the Gardabani district and municipality in one direction, and the district and municipality of Mtskheta in the other. These four local governments form the Tbilisi Metropolitan Area (TMA), an area of about 2,600 square kilometers with a population of 1.5 million.

To realize the full potential of the TMA, the Tbilisi city government established the Tbilisi Metropolitan Development Agency (TMDA) in 2009. For some functions, all four municipalities may benefit by joint or coordinated efforts, rather than acting individually or competing with one another.

Tbilisi is the dominant city, but the metropolitan area is more than an extension of Tbilisi. It is a small cluster of jurisdictions with complementary strengths and characteristics. Rustavi and Mtskheta can draw economic strength from their proximity to the much larger city of Tbilisi, and Tbilisi may, over time, benefit from developments in Rustavi, Mtskheta, and Gardabani through reduced congestion. The proximity of the urban areas, with a good road network connecting them, has created a fairly integrated labor market. It is estimated that about 20 percent to 30 percent of Rustavi residents, and more than 40 percent of Mtskheta residents, work in Tbilisi; and that some 10 percent of the residents of Gardabani town

(continued next page)

Box 2.2 *(continued)*

commute to Tbilisi. Certain entities and facilities serve a great part of the area, such as a private water and waste-water company, covering Tbilisi, Rustavi, and Mtskheta, and a new landfill under construction to serve Rustavi and Gardabani.

Map B2.2.1 Tbilisi Metropolitan Area

Source: World Bank.

Source: Tbilisi Local Authority.

state and private lands. That mixture creates opportunities for rural people to move into the urban area for agglomeration benefits, and they often create large informal settlements, mostly on public land. These settlements either are scattered in parts of the city (as in Lahore, Pakistan) or may contain a substantial part of the city's population.[1] Many form in wetlands, riverbeds, or zones exposed to flooding. The term "slums" denotes settlements with overcrowded housing that lack basic infrastructure (road, water, electricity, health and education services), and where most dwellings have no land ownership or formal use permits. Informal settlements are common side effects of agglomeration development that is positive overall, and they create major legal, social, and economic challenges in the developing world.

Megacities

As already stated, in 2012 the world had 27 megacities with populations of 10 million or more

(Brinkoff 2012). Large urban areas offer large local markets (because of lower transport costs) and facilitate economies of scale and industrial diversity (providing innovation incentives). All contribute to job creation and economic development. Agglomeration facilitates economic growth through the sharing of information, labor, and other inputs; specialization and intraindustry trade; and competition. However, megacities also face challenges, including the following:

- Infrastructure and housing shortages (creating large unplanned settlements)

- Severe traffic and housing congestion

- Large informal (household enterprise) sectors in need of support

- Megacity governance and management challenges

- Insufficient access to investment capital.

Responding to Urbanization

Those challenges produce needs for action by local and national governments; for example,

- Increased need for supporting infrastructure (to reduce distances, mitigate congestion, prevent slums, etc.)

- Increased demand for basic services

- Need to mitigate higher costs for firms and residents for land, labor, housing, etc.

- Need to mitigate environmental stress

- Need for a more effective governance structure, with institutions to facilitate the mobility of goods and people, enforce regulations, etc.

- Need for subsidies to reduce social and economic divisions.

Economic densities are very concentrated around the world (map 2.1). Megacity management needs to be somewhat differentiated from

Map 2.1 Economic Densities ("Economic Mountains") in Parts of the World

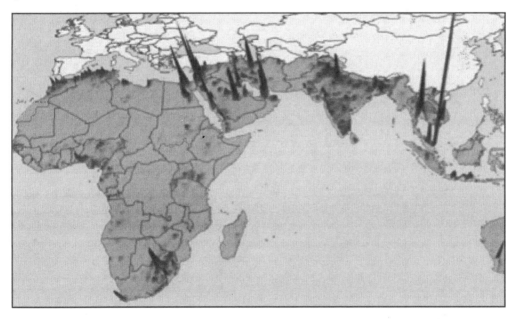

Source: World Bank 2010.

management of other cities. Large urban centers and their development need to be placed in the context of their national economies. Megacities and the productivity of urban centers are increasingly determining national economic growth, as well as the economics of subregions (World Bank 2010). For example, Dar es Salaam's efficiency as a port city has effects on Tanzania and on neighboring countries (Democratic Republic of Congo, Uganda, and Zambia). The connections of cities across countries mean that productivity of each city influences others, forming a cross-border growth pole at a subregional level. The map of East Africa (map 2.2) well illustrates the significance of the large cities in the region.

Although Africa has to date been lagging in terms of urbanization, it is well on its way to becoming a predominantly urban continent. Africa's annual urban population growth averages 4 percent, the fastest in the world. Three of the ten fastest-growing cities in the world are in Africa (Lagos, Nigeria; Dar es Salaam, Tanzania; and Lilongwe, Malawi). It is expected that the urban population will overtake the rural population in this large continent by 2030.

Metropolitan Governance

Metropolitan areas strongly benefit from coordinating or integrating service provision, joint development, and cost sharing, instead of separate individual efforts by each adjacent local government. International experience has shown that in successful metro areas, significant economies of scale have been accomplished in certain service functions. For example, in Paris, London, and Shanghai, the metro administrations address areas that have twice the population of their core city. The concept of *metropolitan area governance* can be defined as follows:

> a set of institutions, rules, and actions that delineate policies and conditions for the life and economy of a metropolitan region.

Metro areas are often characterized by rapid change in density and landscape, evolving mixed land use, speculative real estate markets, a lack of spatial integration of the local economy and infrastructure, and disparities in service provision and administrative capacities. Whereas activities to *retain* existing businesses should normally be left to the lowest level of government serving the business community, *attracting* new firms for job creation and related efforts for economic development are normally best pursued at a broader regional level. The same applies to solid waste disposal or to addressing various environmental challenges, such as air and water quality, whose impacts transcend jurisdictional boundaries. For example, inadequate maintenance of storm drains in one area can cause flooding in other communities (spillover effects). As for police services, crime does not respect jurisdictional boundaries, so coordination is needed. Strong interdependencies also exist in tourism promotion and management. Such spillover effects tend to provide incentives for intergovernmental

Map 2.2 East Africa with Population Density

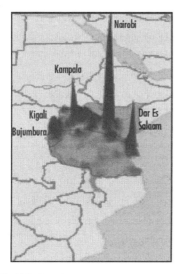

Source: World Bank 2010.

Municipal Finances

dialogue and special arrangements among local governments.

A lack of any (formal or informal) governance arrangement at a metropolitan scale tends to create serious problems and missed opportunities (summarized in box 2.3).

Good Metropolitan Governance

As metropolitan areas emerge and grow, the need for metropolitan-level management—for coordination and joint decisions—increases. The following are examples of cases in which metro-level management is particularly beneficial for the residents and their local governments. Many are driven by financing concerns or opportunities:

- *Pooling financial resources.* When synergy would be achieved through a joint effort by the local governments in the area, by pooling their financial or human resources for a particular purpose, such as promotion of the area, joint procurement, sharing emergency equipment, and so forth

- *Cost sharing.* When the local governments in the area would achieve efficiency (economies of scale) by sharing the costs of delivering a service; for example, a waste disposal facility or coordinated drainage system for the whole area, or a single police force.

- *Spillovers.* When spillovers (also called "externalities") across jurisdictional borders need to be addressed for fairness; for example, in cases of air or water pollution caused by neighboring industrial areas (negative spillover), or when all the tourism attractions are in one area, but visitors stay and spend in another area (positive spillover).

- *Specialized services.* When local governments in the area have a need for specialized services (for example, hazardous waste

---

Box 2.3 Risks and Missed Opportunities Due to Lack of Metropolitan Governance

Some rules are always in place in metropolitan regions, but one can distinguish adequate from inadequate governance. The negative consequences of poor governance, which is characterized by a lack of dialogue and coordination (possibly due to political diversity), include these:

- *Fragmentation.* Provision of some public services (particularly those of common interest, such as bus or other public transport services) may be fragmented, resulting in higher costs and financing challenges for each local government.
- *Free ridership.* For example, if some areas, usually the inner city, are congested, with increasing air pollution, the troubled city may need to fix what is a joint or regional problem from its own resources, without fair contribution by the neighbors, who benefit from the positive effects of the agglomeration but spend their money elsewhere and may even aggravate the troubles of the inner city.
- *Underutilization.* Some land may have limited value locally but potentially a higher value from a regional perspective.
- *Disparities.* Different parts of the metro area may experience differences in the quality and level of amenities and services because income inequality among residents affects the tax base of the various local governments.

disposal) or equipment that would be most effectively met jointly, or by one of the local governments with all others paying for the service

- *Disparity*. When the metropolitan area has significant inequalities (income disparities) among its residents, by subarea or jurisdiction, and that is considered a priority to be addressed.

It is important to recognize, however, that the needs and potential for action for a particular city area depend on a number of local factors, for example:

- National context:

  — The constitution and other laws and regulations of the country

  — The division of responsibilities (functions) among various government levels

  — Relations with higher-level governments, the intergovernmental system

- Local context:

  — The history and culture of the area (e.g., a strong tradition of local autonomy or no such tradition)

  — The importance of easy access by the residents to their local government and ensuring their corresponding accountability

  — Revenue sources available to the local governments.

Fragmented local government structures in metropolitan areas are usually highly dependent on intergovernmental transfers or on spending by higher-tier governments. Metropolitan-wide governance arrangements, on the other hand, allow externalities for many public services to be internalized and a broader range of services to be assigned to the metro-level agencies (Bahl, Linn, and Wetzel 2013).

The local governments in some areas cooperate with one another only when they are required to do so by a higher-tier government or in matters of joint convenience (e.g., to be eligible for some funding). That may or may not create true and lasting metropolitan governance. Cooperation among local governments has sometimes been encouraged by incentives from a provincial or national government. For example, in the United States, it was for many years a prerequisite for obtaining grant funding from the federal government—particularly for road and transit infrastructure and wastewater management—that the local governments show approval of the needs and solutions in a regional plan by a regional entity. Many regional planning councils were created following the availability of EU regional economic development grants (OECD 2006). Other incentives for regional coordination have been created through intergovernmental systems (e.g., in India), through legal frameworks (e.g., Brazil, France, Italy, and Poland), or through financial incentives and political influence (e.g., in the Netherlands).

Metropolitan Governance Models

International experience demonstrates a great diversity of metropolitan models, particularly across North America (Dodge 1996) and Europe (OECD 2006). In East Asia, China, Japan, and the Republic of Korea have consolidated metropolitan governments for their megacities (Yang 2009). Many megacities are in South Asia, but few well-established and functioning approaches exist. While many metropolitan development authorities exist, they tend to focus mostly on investment planning and land development.

Although Latin America is also home to many megacities, the frameworks for metropolitan governance in São Paulo, Mexico City, Buenos Aires, and Rio de Janeiro are lacking or weak. An exception is the metropolitan district of Quito, in Ecuador, which has an elected metropolitan council with broad responsibilities, presided over by an elected metropolitan mayor. Somewhat similar systems exist in Bogotá and Caracas, but they are weaker in practice (Rojas, Cuadrado-Roura, and Fernández Güell 2007). Sub-Saharan Africa is rapidly urbanizing, but most cities lack effective institutions to address subjects at a metropolitan scale. South Africa is an exception, having through amalgamations established eight municipalities, each essentially covering its metropolitan area.

Where institutional arrangements at local levels are lacking or weak, coordination tends to be exercised by national or provincial or state governments (e.g., Lagos state). In Australia public transport and other local functions are managed by the provincial governments (Abbott 2011).

International practices underscore that some formalized governance framework is needed to coordinate local governments across a metropolitan area. Various models have been applied internationally to address that need. Several models may coexist in a single metropolitan area. The approaches listed below will be described further, and variations illustrated through city examples. Subsequent sections will show how cities have addressed finance challenges and how their institutional and financial arrangements have evolved over time.

The main models and approaches to metropolitan governance are the following:

- Cooperation among local governments

  - Case-by-case joint initiatives

  - Contracting among local governments

  - Committees, commissions, working groups, partnerships, consultative platforms, etc.

- Regional authorities (sometimes called "special purpose districts")

  - A metropolitan council of governments (COG)

  - A regional planning authority

  - A regional service delivery authority

  - A regional planning and service delivery authority

- Metropolitan-level government

  - Metropolitan-level local government

  - A regional government established by a higher tier of government (federal, state, or provincial)

- Annexation of territory or amalgamation of local governments.

How Do Stakeholders Select or Change a Model?

The system of local administration has a significant impact on the efficiency and equity of a regional economy. Although there is no single perfect arrangement for local governance—each has advantages and disadvantages—the system of political accountability and responsibility ideally coincides with authority and the revenue base. The emergence of larger metro areas indicates a need for governing fairly large jurisdictional areas, establishing an *authority that coincides with representation.* That means that any entity established to coordinate subordinate localities or service delivery functions should ideally be representative of, and accountable to, the entire jurisdiction and should receive corresponding resources and authority.

The governance structure affects its accessibility to citizens, the degree of public participation in decision making, and the accountability and responsiveness of the governments. The evolving size of an urban area, its economic potential, economies of scale, financing power, accessibility, and easy movement of labor are among the main factors that determine a specific metropolitan governance design. The most appropriate model for a particular area depends on both the national and local contexts. Box 2.4 includes a simple list of

Box 2.4 Questions to Ask When Reviewing the Governance Structure of a Metropolitan Area

The following questions can be used to advance the evolution of the governance structure of a metropolitan area:

- What *problems* of a similar nature exist among the local jurisdictions in the area that need to be, or might most effectively be, addressed jointly? Examples include public transport, the local road network, solid waste disposal, road maintenance, and drainage.
- What *opportunities* exist for the local authorities in the metropolitan area to be stronger and more effective by acting jointly? Examples of such opportunities include city branding, attracting foreign direct investment (FDI), tourism promotion, and some procurements.
- Could the local authorities *save public resources* (gain efficiency) by managing some service delivery jointly rather than individually, for example, through economies of scale, coordination potential, and so forth?
- Could the problems and opportunities be addressed by a *metropolitan agency* or not? Why not? What constraints would exist? If not, how would the problems and opportunities most effectively be addressed? If yes, would such an agency be established and directed by local governments or by a higher-tier government? Would creating it require a lengthy legislative or regulatory process? If so, is it worth it?
- If a *regional development agency* already exists for certain functions, could its

mandate be expanded to address some of the items mentioned or not? What would be the pros and cons?
- Would the various problems and opportunities be better addressed through a *higher-level metropolitan government* for some functions? If so, could the functions of any existing regional agency be incorporated into it or not? Would *amalgamation* of some local authorities be an option to consider?
- How could it be ensured that *citizen accessibility* to the government, and government responsiveness and accountability, would not be weakened in any revised structure?
- If a metropolitan agency exists, what *additional functions* that are currently managed by a higher-tier government could be assigned to it?
- Should *inequality* among the local government areas (in income and service provision) be addressed by the national government via the local governments in the area, or as a metropolitan issue, by the local governments acting jointly?
- Is the *cost sharing* within the metropolitan area fair with regard to spillovers and externalities across the jurisdictions (e.g., air pollution, people living and paying taxes in one jurisdiction but working in another, etc.)? If not, should it be addressed by the national government through the transfer system or as a metropolitan issue, through action by the local governments themselves?

questions to help one analyze metropolitan governance arrangements.

Benefits of Smaller Government Units

Experience in metropolitan areas underscores that good metropolitan governance systems institutionalize an adequate division of labor between the metropolitan-level institutions and the local governments. With few exceptions, local governments remain key governing bodies for most functions, while agreeing to allow a joint metropolitan governing body to perform other functions. Local governments remain critical to ensuring accessibility, responsiveness, and accountability and close and clear links between expenditures and revenues; to allocating resources efficiently; and, last but not least, to ensuring participation by citizens in local decisions. Many believe that even some level of competition among local governments may be healthy in specific areas, as it provides incentives for them to be more efficient.

Metropolitan experiences also suggest that politics, rather than efficiency and equity, often determines the choice of governance structure. Case studies discussed in later sections show that changes in metropolitan governance in London, Toronto, and South Africa were driven substantially by political factors, although economics, finance, and efficiency were also taken into consideration. International experiences suggest that flexibility of governance arrangements over time and across jurisdictions is desirable. As shown in some of the cases described below, some metro areas have applied different models over time.

Table 2.1 summarizes the pros and cons of various governance models, which are discussed in detail in the following sections.

Financing Metropolitan Areas or Functions

The success of metropolitan-area public finances depends to a large extent on how the vertical intergovernmental relations are structured. It depends in particular on whether metropolitan cities will be treated the same as other local governments in the country or be treated differently—for example, a special status for national capital cities or cities with "provincial city" status; whether they have special expenditure assignment and taxing arrangements because of their size; or whether other special arrangements exist under the intergovernmental transfer system. The degree to which the actions of local governments in a metropolitan area will be regulated by higher-tier government ministries is also important, as is the coordination of service delivery in the area by the local governments and higher-tier governments (Bahl, Linn, and Wetzel 2013).

Financial considerations are often among the prime incentives to form special metropolitan arrangements, either through a bottom-up process by the incumbent local governments or as a top-down decision by a higher-level government (provincial or national). The main economic or financial factors include potentials for cost savings by joint initiatives (scale economies); cost sharing in areawide service provision or capital investments; and desire to address fiscal inequality, when significant tax base differences exist among the jurisdictions of a metro area. This section summarizes generic financial aspects applicable to any of the governance models; various financial implications and related solutions in individual cities are included in the case study descriptions below.

Financing Services and Operation

To a large extent it is operational financial factors (operational revenues and expenditures) that motivate metropolitan cooperation and influence its form, depth, and instruments.

Service Cost Sharing

When a public service is managed across a metropolitan area, an equitable cost-sharing arrangement is needed among the local governments—for

Table 2.1 Advantages and Disadvantages of the Various Metropolitan Governance Models

Conceptual model	Pros (advantages)	Cons (disadvantages)
	HORIZONTAL COOPERATION AMONG LOCAL GOVERNMENTS	
Case-by-case joint initiatives (agreements among local authorities).	Useful for areas where limited interdependencies among local governments exist (or a small area with, for example, only two local governments).	Usually limited in scope.
		No commitment to addressing a need on a permanent, ongoing basis.
	Can be an initial phase to gain experience and build trust regarding coordinated joint efforts among the local governments.	
	Possible approach when more permanent and formal arrangements are constrained by politics or prohibited by legal frameworks.	
Contracting among local governments.	One local government can specialize in a particular service or function, for the benefit of all local governments in the area.	The contracting local government still must monitor the quality and coverage of the service provision (contracting out does not mean abdicating responsibility for the service or function).
	Sometimes useful when one of the local governments dominates in terms of human and financial capacity.	Risks: Access by residents to the service provider may be affected; accountability may be weakened or unclear to residents.
Committees, commissions, working groups, partnerships, consultative platforms, etc.	Temporary or permanent bodies for coordination. Often character of networks rather than institutions.[a]	Usually advisory role only.
	Flexible approaches.	

Metropolitan council of governments (COG) and similar arrangements.	A forum for the member local governments to address items of common and regional interest, while maintaining their authority over any decisions through the requirement for endorsement by their respective councils. Can provide flexibility if local governments are allowed to join and exit at any time.	Impact depends on (a) the financial and human resources mobilized or allocated to the COG, and (b) the general coherence among the member local government councils regarding views on metro issues.
Regional planning authority (with or without authority to enforce or implement plans).	Permanent focal point for metropolitan (regional) planning. Specialized, metropolitan-level analytical resources (highlighting spillovers, opportunities for scale economies, inequalities, etc.).	Risk of limited impact if their power is advisory only, without ability to enforce or implement plans. Ability requires significant institutional capacity and resources to be effective.
Regional service delivery authority (as public entity or corporation or a regional utility company).	Achieving economies of scale (efficiencies) for certain services. Engagement by local governments as "owners" of the authority or company because its service provision responsibility is "delegated" to the authority or utility company. If corporatized (utility company), facilitates a transition to private sector service provision or a public-private partnership (PPP) arrangement (as required).	Effectiveness depends on authority to levy user fees, collect contributions from local governments, apply precept powers, or have earmarked transfers or tax authority. Risks: Access by residents may be affected; accountability may be weakened or unclear.
Regional planning and service delivery authority (as public entity or corporation, regional utility company).	Combination of those for regional planning authorities and regional service delivery authorities, noted above.	Combination of those for regional planning authorities and regional service delivery authorities, noted above.

(continued next page)

Table 2.1 *(continued)*

Conceptual model	Pros (advantages)	Cons (disadvantages)
	METROPOLITAN-LEVEL GOVERNMENT	
A higher-level metropolitan local government.	A permanent government structure (directly elected or through lower-level local governments) for certain metro functions. Specialized metropolitan-level resources.	Effectiveness tends to depend on (a) the degree of authority over the lower-level local governments and (b) whether it has mainly planning functions or some service delivery functions as well.
A regional government established by higher-tier government (for a particular metropolitan area).	A permanent government structure (directly elected or appointed by a higher-tier government) for certain metro functions. Specialized metropolitan-level resources. Resourcing directly from the higher-level government.	Risk of limited connection with, and engagement by, the local governments in the area (can sometimes be mitigated with strong local government representation). Access by residents may be affected; accountability may be weakened or unclear.
	ANNEXATION OF TERRITORY OR AMALGAMATION OF LOCAL GOVERNMENTS	
	Creates a jurisdiction that covers a larger portion (or all) of the metropolitan area, which tends to facilitate metropolitan-level coordination, although local administrative offices or sector arrangements may still be needed. Facilitates addressing equalization within the area (one tax base).	With a larger jurisdiction, access by residents to the local government may be affected, and local accountability may be weakened.

a. OECD 2006.
b. Also called a special purpose district; bottom-up, voluntary organizations.

example, for solid waste disposal, drainage network maintenance, sewerage networks and wastewater discharge, and road maintenance. Costs that can be charged based on usage, such as the volume of garbage disposed of from a settlement, should ideally be charged on that basis (such as a tipping fee paid at the landfill). In the case of maintenance of areawide networks, (such as roads, drains, and sewers) however, charges based on network size and use in different local government areas may not always be appropriate or equitable. All transport users in the area benefit from a well-integrated and well-maintained road network, for example. Well-maintained storm drains and sewers have sanitary benefits across the area. Nevertheless, some sections of a network may cost more to maintain than others because of geography (some people live on hills; some on flat land), the locations of pumping stations, and so forth. Agreements need to be reached among the various local constituents as to what is a reasonably fair cost-sharing arrangement. That often becomes a politically charged subject.

Tax Spillovers

In some countries, value added tax (VAT) revenues are shared between the national and the local governments. Cases in which the revenues due local governments are transferred to the jurisdiction where a business enterprise has its headquarters may distort the allocation among local governments. This may particularly affect a metropolitan area if, for example, headquarters are located in the core city but production plants or businesses operate in the suburban areas. In such cases, it is necessary that tax revenues be adjusted either by a higher government (at the transferring level) or locally at the metropolitan level. Box 2.5 summarizes financial considerations for regional cooperation and the establishment of regional entities.

Box 2.5 Common Financial Reasons for Regional Cooperation or Establishing Regional Service Entities

- *Coordinated tax or fee policy agreements* (e.g., harmonized tax base, rate, and administration) between the local governments in the area can prevent tax and fee competition. The area can, for example, have a common business tax, property tax formula, and automobile tax and common fees for various types of permits. (Joint tax policies may or may not support the overall revenue mobilization, however.)
  Example: Marseille, France, uses a joint system for the collection of a business tax, with a common tax rate to avoid some tax competition in the area.
- *A common budget for metropolitan-level initiatives* and services can be based on

an agreed, formula-based contribution by each local government from its general revenues.
  Example: Lyon, France, shares the tax base of its metro area. Part of the local tax revenues of each commune is allocated to a common budget for joint initiatives and expenditures.
- *A tax-sharing system,* to harmonize revenues and expenditures across a region, can address a significant mismatch between social needs and the tax base (for example, the local property tax) in different local government areas.
  Example: In the Twin Cities (Minneapolis and St. Paul, Minnesota), in the United States,

(continued next page)

---

a metro council has expanded access to property taxes in the region to finance its service provision and targeted transportation subsidies.

- *Revenue mobilization* through user charges, property taxes, earmarked taxes (for example, road, payroll, and gas taxes for transportation), or agreed compensation from local governments (direct support subsidies), or authority to capture a revenue stream to local governments. *Example:* Vancouver, Canada, applies a variety of revenue instruments to finance its service delivery.

Ad Hoc Scale Economies

Local governments may act together for a specific purpose to benefit from economies of scale, for example, to purchase equipment at a better price or to contract for a service. Acting jointly can reduce transaction costs and potentially yield a price benefit in such activities as engaging a consulting firm to prepare a metropolitan-level land use plan, promoting an international event, or trying to attract firms to locate in the area. These actions usually require specific negotiations among the local governments to reach a cost-sharing agreement.

Funding a Metropolitan-Level Entity

Any metropolitan-level entity (such as a metropolitan planning or service delivery authority) has to be funded on a sustainable basis. Operating expenditures are usually financed from a combination of sources, such as the following: (a) predefined, agreed-upon contributions from concerned local governments; (b) to the extent possible, user charges for the services that the metropolitan entity is in charge of providing; (c) transfers from higher tiers of government; (d) earmarked taxes; (e) authority to capture a revenue stream to the local governments ("precept power"); (f) direct taxing power (such as a road tax); (g) donations; and (h) other sources, such as fees and direct subsidies, depending on the functions of the entity.

Contracting out certain services may sometimes be an option for more integration. A private service organization may establish larger, coordinated entities through contracts with each local government in the metropolitan area.

Financing Large Infrastructure Projects in a Metropolitan Area

Mobilizing funds for large infrastructure projects that affect (or benefit) several jurisdictions requires special arrangements. Sometimes stakeholders establish a separate entity to implement the project and possibly also to own and operate it, maintaining the created assets over time (e.g., a bridge, a wastewater treatment plant, or a landfill). Alternatively, they might contract with an existing metropolitan (regional) utility company to plan, implement, and manage the project. In either case, the project entity or utility company often borrows (issues debt) to finance the project. Another option is for the respective local governments to borrow individually to contribute to the capital cost of the joint infrastructure investment. The participants must agree on an equitable contribution scheme, proportional to the expected benefits that each will receive, or perhaps using a formula that takes into account numbers of citizens who will benefit.

Examples of Investment Financing

Due to the large size of metropolitan-level investments, frequently a higher-tier government is actively involved, and funding from various stake-holders is needed. Two such examples are described below. In the first, a company named ARPEGIO was established to plan and contract on behalf of regional and metropolitan area local governments in Spain. The second describes a metrowide rail investment with the cooperation of the federal government, a state authority, and two county governments in the United States.

ARPEGIO and the Comunidad Autonoma de Madrid. ARPEGIO, operating under private company law, is owned by the Comunidad Autonoma de Madrid (CAM) in Spain, a regional government which covers more or less the functional area of the Madrid metropolis of 5.2 million people.[2] The responsibilities of CAM include transport and infrastructure, education, health, planning, economic development, environment, culture, and research. The purpose of ARPEGIO is to supply and manage land for all classes of use: industrial, residential, offices, commercial, and public. It is a means for responsive planning and contracting, with capacity to undertake medium- and long-term strategic projects that are not very attractive to the private sector. ARPEGIO puts development land on the market at affordable prices; invests in infrastructure, properties, and amenities; and subsequently manages urban public services in the areas. ARPEGIO is financed by obtaining public lands from the governments at low prices, restructuring and selling them for development, and providing marketing and management services within a framework set by the CAM government (www.arpegio.com).

The Dulles Corridor Metrorail Project. The Dulles Corridor Metrorail line is a 37-km extension of the existing commuter rail system in the greater Washington, D.C., area to Dulles International Airport and important employment centers. The Metropolitan Washington Airports Authority (MWAA) manages the project. Project partners include the Washington Metropolitan Area Transit Authority (WMATA), the state of Virginia, and two counties. When completed, the line will be turned over to WMATA to own and operate. Box 2.6 details the governance and financial arrangements for this metropolitan rail project, highlighting the eagerness of the partners to maximize benefits from joint financing and a clear management arrangement. None of the entities involved would have been able to finance and implement this project as a sole investor and operator.

Leveraging Finance through Public-Private Partnerships

For some local governments, borrowing may not be an option, whether because of national regulations or because they are not creditworthy in the eyes of banks and capital markets. In those cases, public-private partnerships (PPP) offer opportunities to access external financing. The local governments may join forces with private partners for jointly funding and operating service assets, based on agreements to share costs, risks, and the benefits of investment. PPP agreements usually include arrangements for asset ownership, operations, and maintenance. Various approaches to them are explained in chapter 7.

Municipal or Metropolitan Development Fund

Establishing a municipal, metropolitan, or regional development fund for capital investments may also be an option, with contributions from various levels of government, international agencies, and the private sector. About 60 countries (such as Georgia, India, Nepal, Tanzania, and Uganda) have created national funds as part of their intergovernmental system specifically to finance local government development projects. Such financing vehicles usually do not apply exclusively to metropolitan areas but to all urban areas or local governments in the country. However, governments in metropolitan areas are often prime recipients of such funds as loans or grants.

Box 2.6 The Dulles Corridor Metrorail Project

The Dulles Metrorail project is funded by many interested parties, including voluntary taxes by local businesses and landowners, county governments, a state government, and grant funds from the U.S. federal government. Owners of land and commercial property in the area agreed to pay a special tax for the project's first phase (three years before its completion), in the hope that this extension of rail service would bring opportunities for increased density and development, and higher property values.

Phase 2 of the project, with an estimated cost of US$2.7 billion, will be financed by the MWAA, the state of Virginia, and two counties, with loan guarantees but no cash funding by the U.S. government. The parties have signed a cooperation agreement for financing and managing the project.

Funding Breakdown Phase 1 (US$2.6 billion)

	Funding entity	Source
41%	MWAA	Revenues from existing toll road (with toll increases)
10%	State of Virginia	State bonds and other budget sources
15%	County	Special tax on businesses/landowners in the area
34%	U.S. federal government	From fuel tax revenues and economic stimulus funds

Source: www.dullesmetro.com.

Metropolitan Governance Cases

The following sections discuss various metropolitan governance and financing models and cases.

Horizontal Coordination among Local Governments

When special efforts need to be made for local coordination, but the autonomy of the local governments must be preserved, coordination can be achieved through various ad hoc arrangements without any broader or long-term commitment. Models, characteristics, and examples of such horizontal coordination approaches are summarized in table 2.2.

Case-by-Case Joint Initiatives by Local Governments

The local governments in an area may join forces when it clearly benefits all of them and their constituents, compared with acting independently. They typically agree to solve a particular temporary problem, such as managing a flood or coordinating traffic related to a large event. Less common, but equally possible, is pooling their assets to make the area more attractive to a firm considering locating a plant or office, to be a stronger competitor for a regional or international event, to obtain a bank loan on slightly better terms, or to promote tourism and attract visitors to the area.

Contracting among Local Governments

That it has the responsibility to provide a public service does not necessarily mean that a local government has to deliver that service itself. A government can engage with another government in various ways for delivery of a service: (a) a contract between two governments of the same level

Table 2.2 Horizontal Coordination among Local Governments

Models	Characteristics	Examples
Case-by-case joint initiatives	Joint action puts the local governments in a position to achieve economies of scale (e.g., bulk purchasing, firefighting, road maintenance, tourism promotion) or in a stronger position, for example, for attracting a firm or event or promoting tourism. Common financial considerations: • Agreements are usually based on each participating local government's assessment of the cost and benefit to them of the joint activity. • When significant costs are involved, a reasonable cost-sharing formula needs to be agreed on.	City candidates for the Olympic Games or other big events tend to apply on behalf of their metro area.
Contracting among local governments	A local government engages another local (or higher-level) government for the delivery of a service that it is responsible for. Common financial considerations: • The local government contracting out the service or function would determine the cost and benefit of this option, compared to providing the service itself. This is particularly important if significant capital investments are needed, whether in the short or longer term.	Los Angeles County, United States; U.S. Association of Contract Cities; Shanghai, China.
Committees, working groups, consultative platforms, etc.	Temporary or permanent bodies for coordination.	Ruhr, Germany; Turin, Milan, Italy; Paris, France; greater Toronto, Canada.

(one local government performs another local government's service responsibility for a fee or other compensation, or another service); (b) performance by a local government of another level local government's service responsibility for a fee; or (c) performance by a higher-tier government of the responsibility of a local government for a fee. Box 2.7 describes contracting by a number of local governments in the Los Angeles area. In Shanghai, some district and county local governments have contracted a specialized unit at the higher, municipal local government level to arrange funding and manage the implementation of some of their infrastructure projects, benefiting from the higher capacities at the municipal government level.

Although the service contracting approach does not apply specifically to metropolitan areas, but rather to any local government, it is mentioned here because it is a way in which local governments in a metropolitan area can engage in a limited but still beneficial way. It is particularly applicable where an area has one dominating local government, possibly with more human and financial capacity. Positive results of an initial contractual arrangement may pave the way for more advanced and broader models of cooperation such as will be discussed below.

Regional Authorities

A regional authority is an independent legal entity, conceptually a voluntary association or organization established by the member local governments for planning, service delivery, or to make better use of their public resources. Such city-to-city

Box 2.7 The U.S. Association of Contract Cities

Service delivery contracts between two or more local governments can be organized individually or be facilitated by an association of local governments. The U.S. Association of Contract Cities—whose members are mostly in the state of California—promotes and facilitates a market-based approach for particularly small local governments. These governments perform few of their mandated functions themselves. Instead they buy and sell services among partner cities based on specialization. They often involve private firms in a highly competitive environment. Although

the savings from such a contract or cooperative provision of services must be balanced against the costs of coordinating the actions (transaction costs), the program provides organizational flexibility in providing local services, particularly for small local governments that may not have the capacity to carry out certain functions themselves. The Los Angeles, California, area has numerous small local governments. The Los Angeles County government, by far the largest, provides a variety of services to the smaller governments on a contract basis.

Source: www.contractcities.org.

arrangements are sometimes called "special purpose associations" or "special purpose districts" in the United States. The concepts of various such models are summarized in table 2.3.

Two or more local governments may create an association to achieve economies of scale. For example, for waste management they may jointly operate a garbage disposal facility, a landfill, or public transport. Some countries (e.g., Brazil, France, Italy, and Poland) have established a separate legal framework for such arrangements. This approach represents an administrative or political integration, with the member governments represented on the governing board or council of the association. Regional authorities or utility companies can collect contributions from member local governments or levy user fees to pay for the services provided. Some are even authorized to levy taxes.

The local governments in metropolitan areas in North America frequently establish such "special purpose" bodies for particular services. They include school boards, police boards, library boards, conservation authorities, recreation

commissions, health boards, utility commissions (e.g., for a lake or a river basin or watershed), and transit authorities. For services with more spillovers (externalities), such as roads, for which user charges are not feasible or efficient, the metropolitan authorities sometimes have taxing powers. Such service consolidation mechanisms can generate efficiency gains, particularly for smaller local governments in a metro area, allowing them to remain independent.

Box 2.8 summarizes the solid waste disposal system in Shanghai municipality. It is a coordinated operation among nine district governments, which collect about 9 million tons of waste daily and transport it to a large landfill operated through a public-private partnership.

Service delivery contracts are agreed to between the metropolitan authority (utility company) and the participating member governments. In some cases national governments have encouraged establishment of regional authorities through incentives and special legislation. In the United States, it was for many years a prerequisite for obtaining grant funding from the federal

Table 2.3 Types of Regional Authorities

Models	Characteristics	City examples
Metropolitan Council of Governments (COG)	Forum for coordinated efforts by the member local governments. Decisions need endorsement of the respective local government board or council.	São Paulo, Brazil; Bologna, Italy; numerous examples across the United States.
Regional Planning Authority	Responsibility for planning or solving a specific problem, for broad regional planning, or for specific functions; with or without authority to enforce or implement plans.	Many examples of advisory entities exist, but few with decision-making or implementing powers. Portland, United States (in the past, with decision-making power); New York City (operated by an NGO).
Regional Service Delivery Authority	Responsible for delivery of one or more services; maybe called a "special purpose district"; operates as a public entity, a service agency (corporation or cooperative) owned by the member local governments (shareholders or members). Can usually levy user fees and taxes or collect funds from the local governments to pay for the services.	Greater Vancouver Regional Service District (GVRSD), Canada, is a multiservice public corporation; it has significant planning functions but focuses on extensive service delivery responsibilities.
Regional Planning and Service Delivery Authority	Combination forum that plans and delivers one or more services (e.g., a regional transportation or water authority); operates as a public entity, public corporation, regional utility company, or cooperative.	In France, the cities of Lyon and Marseille, some "municipal development agencies" (e.g., in Delhi and Dhaka), and the Lagos Mega-City Development Authority in Nigeria.

government—particularly for roads and transit and wastewater treatment infrastructure—that local governments show approval of the needs and solutions in a regional plan by a regional entity.

Many variations on regional authorities exist. An important common element, in contrast to elected or appointed metropolitan governments, is that member local governments direct the operations through representation on councils or boards. Table 2.4 shows various dimensions characterizing a regional authority.

Metropolitan Councils of Governments

Metropolitan councils of governments represent a bottom-up approach to regionalization that is common in the United States for various purposes. It is so frequently applied that a few national associations of councils of governments (COGs) also exist.[3] The COG is a variation of the regional authority approach, with limited independent decision-making authority so as not to undermine the accountability of each individual local government.

The Metropolitan Washington Council of Governments

The Metropolitan Washington Council of Governments, in the United States, was formed in 1957. It is composed of 21 local governments surrounding Washington, D.C., covering an area of 7,733 square kilometers (km²), with a population of about 4.5 million. It is an independent, nonprofit association financed by contributions from the participating local governments, federal and

Box 2.8 Solid Waste Management in Shanghai Municipality

Shanghai offers an example of how solid waste management can be arranged in a diverse way, seeking the most cost-effective solution for all involved, including using a public-private partnership arrangement. Shanghai municipality is composed of nine core city district governments, seven suburban district governments, and one rural county government. In 2004, a municipal investment and holding company formed a joint venture with an international firm for the construction, operation, and maintenance of a sanitary landfill (for 25 years) to serve the core city districts. Collection and transportation of waste to the landfill are the responsibility of the district governments, some of which contract them out to private firms. The district governments pay a charge based on the volumes disposed of at

the landfill (they collect a limited flat fee from households). Food waste is collected from restaurants separately and charged by volume. The municipal government also operates a centralized hazardous waste facility, serving all the district and county governments, and two incinerator facilities. In addition, a few private recycling facilities exist.

The municipal investment and holding company mobilizes its financing from various sources, including domestic bond issues, and also supports the investment programs of the suburban districts and county if requested. This is an example of how a large metropolitan-level entity can use its financial and human resource strengths to support local governments with less capacity.

Table 2.4 Characteristics of Regional (Metropolitan) Authorities

Dimension	Simple	Advanced
Function	Planning	Planning and service delivery
Scope	Single function	Multiple functions
Degree of authority	Advising or guiding the function(s)	Managing the function(s)
Legal status	Public sector agency	Public sector corporation or utility company
Operational	Nonprofit	For profit (although rare)
Accountability of the council or board	Appointed or elected by the local governments in the area	Elected by residents of the area

state grants, service contracts, and donations from foundations or the private sector (see box 2.9 and table 2.5).

COG policies are set by the local governments through a board of directors. Most COG decisions require endorsement by the respective local government councils. For intermunicipal transport infrastructure (such as the main road network), the Washington COG has some independent decision-making authority based on one vote per member.

São Paulo ABC Region

The São Paulo ABC Region[4] is one of only a few examples of intermunicipal cooperation in Brazil (see box 2.10). A political body made up of representatives from the state government, seven local governments, and civil society has played important roles in economic development for at least part of the area. In addition to the area's local governments, it has the active engagement of civil society and the local private sector.

Box 2.9 The Metropolitan Washington Council of Governments

The Metropolitan Washington Council of Governments (COG) provides a focus for action and develops responses to issues of regional significance in the greater Washington, D.C., area. Its mission is to enhance the quality of life and competitive advantages of the region by providing a forum for consensus building and policy making; implementing intergovernmental policies, plans, and programs; and supporting the region as a source of expert information. COG has committees on transportation, the environment, health and human services, housing and planning, cooperative purchasing, and publications, reflecting its scope and the common goals of its 21 members.

COG recently produced a document titled "Region Forward—A Comprehensive Guide for Regional Planning and Measuring Progress in the 21st Century," which is a new planning guide for environment, housing, transportation, and other regional priorities. It is a voluntary agreement that requests area governments to pledge to advance the goals articulated in the document to their best effort. It accepts the differences among the cities and counties but also interconnections across the region. The targets and indicators set to measure progress judge the region as a whole, rather than measuring individual jurisdictions. Measuring such things as regional green space, affordable housing units, school graduation rates, and financial performance, using targets and indicators, will help to determine if the region as a whole is heading in the right direction.

Source: www.mwcog.org.

Table 2.5   Metropolitan Washington Council of Governments Financial Snapshot 2010

Revenues	US$000	Expenses	US$000
Building rents/interest	1,000.0	Community planning and services	1,095.1
Membership dues	3,223.5	Member services	1,105.7
State grants	4,323.6	Public safety and health	1,883.0
Other grants and fees for services	4,427.4	Environmental programs	5,649.4
Federal grants	14,526.7	Transportation planning and projects	17,768.0
Total	27,501.2	Total	27,501.2

Bologna, Italy

Bologna, Italy, is another city where metro governance has been established on a voluntary basis. In 1994, 48 local governments and the province of Bologna signed a "metropolitan city accord" creating a metro council composed of the mayors in the area and presided over by the provincial president. Each local government is free to withdraw at any time and may participate in all or only some of the council's activities. This is a flexible, low-risk approach for the local governments.

Metropolitan Montreal Community (MMC)

In 2000, the provincial government of Quebec created the Metropolitan Montreal Community (MMC), a metropolitan coordinating body for the greater Montreal area. The MMC board is composed of representatives of the member municipalities. MMC is in charge of planning, funding, and coordinating public transport, waste management, economic development, and social housing. It is headed by an appointed president (currently the mayor of Montreal) and covers an area of 3,838 km^2, with a population of about

Box 2.10 São Paulo ABC Region

Brazil's 1988 constitution increased the autonomy of local governments and delegated responsibility for designing metropolitan structures to the state (provincial) legislatures. The São Paulo metropolitan region includes the City of São Paulo and 38 surrounding municipalities, with a total population of 18 million.

Although there is no institution of metropolitan governance per se for the area, there is an Intermunicipal Consortium of the Greater ABC Region, which comprises seven cities with 2.5 million people (map B2.10.1). These municipalities created the consortium in 1990 to focus primarily on coordinating policies that had spillover effects across municipal boundaries. Issues that the local governments faced forged a regional identity to help local leaders and politicians address economic decline through a number of initiatives.

The purpose of the consortium, made up of representatives from the state government, seven local governments, and civil society, is to promote economic development of the region through consensus and to implement innovative public policies. Although the engagement of concerned mayors weakened in the mid-1990s, the local community undertook several initiatives, including creating a Forum for Issues of Citizenship, an umbrella nongovernmental organization (NGO) with more than 100 NGOs as members, with an emphasis on regional issues. In 1997 a Chamber of the Greater ABC Region was created as a forum for strategic planning, with participation from civil society, the public sector, and the local economy (businesses and labor unions). One of the most important results of the regional planning process articulated through the chamber was the creation in October 1998 of the Regional Development Agency (RDA), with a board of directors composed of private sector members (a controlling 51 percent) and the Intermunicipal Consortium (49 percent). The RDA is now considered the legal branch of the consortium and can sign agreements with external agencies and receive financial resources. Since 1997, many agreements on economic, social, and territorial development have been signed. The RDA is an example of a flexible and pragmatic approach in solving metro problems. Pilot projects have built trust among the participants over time.

Map B2.10.1 São Paulo Metropolitan Region

Source: World Bank.

Sources: See www.agenciagabc.com.br; additional information is available at www.unhabitat.org/downloads/docs/SantoAndredetailedsummary.pdf.

3.5 million. Its budget is mainly funded by contributions from the member municipalities and some grants from the provincial government.

Regional Planning Authorities

A regional planning authority is a formal entity whose purpose is to design regional (metropolitan) strategies or exercise planning and policy development authority on an ongoing basis. Some regional planning authorities have been established with very broad mandates, whereas others have a narrow focus, such as a river basin or watershed commission. Numerous examples of advisory, guiding, and planning entities exist (e.g., for land use), although some are weak because they lack clear authority for decision making or implementation of plans.

Council of Governments, Portland, Oregon

Initially, the COG in Portland, Oregon, was mainly a metropolitan authority for land use management. With that authority, it introduced the concept of a growth boundary for the metro area. Over time it has taken on other functions as well, and eventually it was elevated by the government of the state of Oregon to a higher-level, elected metropolitan government.

Regional Plan Association, New York City Area

New York City is part of a metropolitan area for which most regional planning is done by a nongovernmental organization (NGO), the Regional Plan Association (RPA). Serving the New York–New Jersey–Connecticut metropolitan region, the Regional Plan Association (RPA) covers the largest urban region in the United States, comprising 31 counties. The RPA performs most regional planning functions. It is an independent metropolitan policy, research, and advocacy group supported and partly funded by the municipalities. RPA has three state committees, composed of business leaders, experts, and opinion makers who provide strategic advice to the association's state offices. Guided by the state committees, these offices ensure an on-the-ground presence for the organization in New Jersey and Connecticut and on Long Island. They have a critical part in research, planning, and advocacy for projects in their respective areas. Projects include environmental protection (watershed and green area development); public transport concepts, including reviews of functionality and development of light rail and other systems; highways; and the comprehensive plan for coordinated airport development (more information is available at www.rpa.org).

Metropolitan Planning and Development Agencies

Metropolitan planning and development agencies are legal forms of regional authorities, often combining governing authority and development and service functions. Many larger cities around the world have established a separate agency for planning and development, some with a narrow mandate such as land use planning only, and others with broader development mandates covering the entire metropolitan region. These agencies are founded by local or national governments as self-financing entities and often receive state or municipal land to be developed and sold for housing or business purposes. The following are several examples.

London Development Agency, U.K.

In 1999, the Greater London Authority (GLA) was created, comprising 32 local governments and the Corporation of London. GLA is led by an elected assembly and chaired by the directly elected lord mayor of London. He has the power to direct a "subordinated" local government to reject, but may not direct it to approve, a large development initiative.

Until 2012 the London Development Agency (LDA) was accountable to the GLA assembly, through the lord mayor, for coordinating economic development. It worked in partnership with industry and the public and voluntary sectors. The mayor appointed a 17-member board and the chief executive of the LDA. Table 2.6

Table 2.6 London Development Agency Financial Snapshot 2010–11 (£ millions)

Project delivery	142
Land for 2012 Olympic Games	214
Assembly administration	56
Total net expenditure	412
Government grant	275
Borrowing	111
Capital receipts	44
Total financing	430
Surplus/(deficit)	18

Source: www.lda.gov.uk.

shows a financial snapshot of the LDA for 2010/11. Effective March 2012, the LDA was abolished by the government of the United Kingdom and its functions were incorporated into the GLA.

Dhaka Capital Development Authority, Bangladesh

The greater Dhaka area currently consists of a Dhaka City Corporation and five municipalities (including Dhaka itself), with an estimated population of 15 million people. Its population is anticipated to grow by 3 percent to 4 percent annually. The authority (local name, Rajdhani Unnayan Kartripakkha, or RAJUK) was established in 1987 to develop, improve, extend, and manage the city and the peripheral areas through a process of proper development planning and development control. RAJUK addresses issues related to development policies, projects, and controls and also engages in land acquisitions and disposals. The government of Bangladesh appoints the chairman and five other full-time members to govern the RAJUK (more information is available at www.rajukdhaka.gov.bd).

Delhi Metropolitan Area and Delhi Development Authority, India

The National Capital Territory of Delhi (NCT) is the metropolitan agglomeration around Delhi, home to more than 22 million people. NCT is divided into nine revenue districts, which are further subdivided into 27 *tehsils,* lower-level local

governments. Delhi has been under the effective control of the national government since 1953. Because it is a "Union Territory," the financial transfers provided to the states in India are not available to Delhi. Delhi receives only discretionary grants rather than a share in central taxes. Delhi's major sources of tax revenue are the value added tax or VAT, state excise, stamp and registration fees, and taxes on vehicles. Delhi collected Rs 121.9 billion (about US$ 2.2 billion) in its own taxes in 2008–09 (more information is available at www.delhi.gov.in).

The Delhi Development Authority (DDA) was formed in 1957 to provide and secure the development of Delhi according to an approved plan. The responsibilities of the DDA include preparing master plans, designing and investing in housing, land acquisition and development, greening, sports, biodiversity, urban heritage, constructing highway overpasses, sports facilities, and biodiversity parks. DDA played a major role in developing sport, housing, and transport facilities for the Commonwealth Games in 2011. Its budget at a glance is shown in table 2.7. The DDA is a small entity compared to the overall Delhi budget, but it plays a substantial role in land development and construction of public infrastructure.

Regional Service Delivery Authorities

A regional service delivery authority is an entity established with clear operational authority to deliver certain services to meet regional (metropolitan) needs, based on agreements among the participating local governments. It may be focused on a single service (such as public transport, water supply, or solid waste management) or be a multiservice authority. Its regional planning responsibility (if any) is usually limited to planning for the services for whose delivery it is responsible.

Metro Vancouver/Greater Vancouver Regional Service District, Canada

The Vancouver metropolitan administration is a flexible and demand-driven example of an

Table 2.7 Financial Snapshot of Delhi Development Authority (2010–11 revised estimates)

Revenues	Rs millions	Expenditures	Rs millions
Disposal of land for residential and commercial use	1,036.2	Acquisition of land	246.0
Receipts from shops	93.0	Development of land	1,272.6
Disposal of houses	226.6	Houses and shops	449.3
Government housing services or institutional	10.7	Estate expenditure	250.4
Interest from investments	1,605.0	Development scheme maintenance	226.8
Deposit works (earmarked transfers)	525.6	Deposit works	525.6
Miscellaneous revenue	260.9	Miscellaneous expenditure	255.4
Total	3,232.4		3,226.0

Source: http://dda.org.in.

organization providing different services to member municipalities through individual agreements.

The Metro Vancouver/Greater Vancouver Regional Service District (GVRD) was established in 1965. At first it was a service organization to assume responsibility for regional planning and take over the functions of separate agencies for sewerage service, water supply, health and hospitals, and business development. Functions of managing affordable housing, regional parks, air quality, and emergency response were added later. The organization now also provides various human resource management services to the municipalities on a contract basis. It does not have particularly strong land use planning powers. The GVRD is now a public corporation with a board composed of representatives of the 18 member local governments. It was initially established by the provincial government but has evolved into a corporation governed by the member municipalities. It finances most of its services through user charges, cost recovery, a share of the property tax, and annual contributions from the member local governments (more information is available at www.metrovancouver.org).

Regional Planning and Service Delivery Authorities

Some regional authorities serve substantial functions in both planning and service delivery, and so they combine the two previously described approaches. This is a particularly popular approach in France. The areas and average populations of French local governments (called *communes*) are small by international standards. They therefore make extensive use of cooperative arrangements for service provision. There is a particular legal framework for intermunicipal cooperation called *syndicats intercommunaux* in France. The *syndicats* are similar to cooperatives or federations of local governments formed to carry out single or multiple functions. One local government may be involved in several *syndicats*.

Grand Lyon, France

The Grand Lyon metropolitan government is a *communauté urbaine* ("urban community," or UC) established in 1969, three years after approval of a related national law (see map 2.3). It was established bottom-up, derived from the needs and interests of the participating municipalities. The governments not only coordinate economic development, land use, and some service provision, but also (since 1999) share the tax base. Part of the local tax revenues of each respective *commune* (town) is allocated to a common budget for metropolitan-level initiatives and expenditures. The business tax is governed by Grand Lyon; the property and housing tax by the municipal level.

Map 2.3 Grand Lyon, with Lyon City in the Center, Surrounded by 57 Suburbs

Source: World Bank.

The UC council is made up of representatives from the member cities in proportion to their population. Since 2002, after the creation of conferences of mayors, the member towns have opportunities to discuss in smaller groups their problems and expectations for submission to the UC. (Grand Lyon established an innovative zoning of its territory into nine subzones by means of this consultative power.) Urban transportation services are managed by a separate authority, partly financed by a grant from Grand Lyon, whose main sources of revenues are tariffs and an earmarked tax on enterprises. Since 2000, the area of Grand Lyon has been gradually expanding through annexation of adjacent towns. Although the city of Lyon has only about half a million inhabitants, Grand Lyon contains 58 municipalities with 1.4 million people. The total metropolitan area (Grand Lyon plus three nearby areas) consists of 139 municipalities with a total population of 2 million (more information is available at www.grandlyon.com).

Communauté Urbaine of Marseille, France

Marseille is an example of a transition from voluntary cooperation among local governments to a regional planning and service delivery authority.

The municipalities of Marseille, Marignane, and Saint Victoire created a public corporation in 1992 that focused on a few road and traffic projects. In 2000, 17 cities joined the consortium, and they established the Communauté Urbaine of Marseille (CUM). The area had a total population of 980,000 in 2000. CUM is a metropolitan organization governed by the mayors and councillors of the municipalities. CUM now is responsible for regional economic development, transportation, land use and housing, crime prevention, waste disposal, and environmental policies. It collects a common tax on business and thereby eliminates tax competition among the municipalities. It also achieves more cost-effective tax collection than if each local government collected the tax in its jurisdiction. As this example shows, a local government may be responsible for a service, or in this case, collecting a tax, without necessarily having to execute the task itself. Discussions are ongoing to extend the borders of CUM to neighboring urban communities where there is significant industrial and economic activity and potential (more information is available at www.marseille-provence.com).

Twin Cities Metropolitan Government, Minneapolis–St. Paul, Minnesota, U.S.

The Twin Cities Metropolitan Government is an example of a regional planning and service delivery authority that evolved into a regional government. The Minneapolis–St. Paul metro area had to respond to increasing polarization between two neighboring, decaying inner cities and their rapidly growing suburbs (urban sprawl). The main challenges included a spatial mismatch between affordable housing and available jobs, causing serious traffic congestion; two low-income central cities that provided daytime services to a large working population who did not pay taxes to the core city because they lived in the richer suburbs; and the need for suburban local governments to respond to a continuous need for expensive infrastructure in new residential areas (more information is available at www.metrocouncil.org).

In sum, significant mismatches existed between the social needs and the property tax bases in rich and poor local jurisdictions in different areas. The need to harmonize revenues and expenditures across the region was strong enough to drive the creation of a tax sharing system. This initial voluntary organization of the local governments, in the early 1970s, later grew into a regional planning and service delivery authority to minimize service quality differences among the jurisdictions. It has since evolved into a regional government authorized by the state of Minnesota and subsequently into a public sector corporation.

Metropolitan-Level Government

The responsibilities for regional coordination and sometimes selective service delivery functions may be vested with a separate local government or council (table 2.8). Although they have separate functions, sometimes such local governments

Table 2.8 Metropolitan-Level Government

Model	Characteristics	City examples
Metropolitan local government	A separate, metro-level local government, directly elected or appointed by the partner local governments.	Toronto, Canada (1954–98); London, U.K.; Quito, Ecuador; Cape Town, South Africa (until 2000); Dar es Salaam, Tanzania; Budapest, Hungary; Abidjan, Côte d'Ivoire (until 2001); Shanghai (and other large Chinese cities).
	Responsible for coordination and selective functions, which may or may not include service delivery.	
	Its authority over the partner local governments varies; it can have (a) no substantial authority over them (e.g., in Dar es Salaam); (b) limited authority (e.g., Budapest); or (c) substantial authority over the area's lower-level local governments (London; cities in China).	
	The metropolitan-level local government is in some cases the only local government for the area, with local administrative offices under it (e.g., the metropolitan municipalities in South Africa).	
	Common financial considerations:	
	• A higher-level local government tends to be funded through transfers from a higher government tier and/or through tax sharing among local governments in the area.	
Regional government established by higher-tier government	A higher-level metropolitan (regional) government is established by a provincial or national government for a metropolitan area.	Twin Cities and Portland, U.S.; Abidjan, Côte d'Ivoire (from 2001); Madrid, Spain; mayor of London, U.K. (directly elected); Stuttgart, Germany; Manila, Philippines; Nairobi, Kenya.
	Numerous approaches to structures established by higher-tier governments are possible, including (a) a directly elected institution (Stuttgart, mayor of London); (b) an appointed body (as in the Twin Cities, U.S., and the Ministry of Nairobi Metropolitan Development); and (c) an entity with strong local government representation in which only the chair is indirectly elected or appointed by higher-level government (as in metro Manila).	
	Common financial considerations:	
	• Funding would normally be part of the provincial or national government budget.	

would not be above the other local governments in the metropolitan area in terms of reporting relationships, but rather would be separate entities of equal rank and legal status. Budapest, Hungary, and Dar es Salaam, Tanzania, illustrate such structures.

Metropolitan Local Government
City Government, Budapest, Hungary
Budapest offers a case of a metropolitan local government with broad functions. The city covers an area of 525 km^2 and has a population of 1.7 million (2011), close to 20 percent of the country's population. The local government system of Budapest is unique in Hungary, comprising the municipality of Budapest (called "the city") and its 23 district governments, all equal in rank and legal status (Horváth and Peteri 2003). Both the city and the districts are local governments, not clearly subordinated to one another, and each has specific duties and powers, specified by the Act on Local Governments and the Act on the Capital City.

Although the city was handled as a special case, the district governments received broad mandates. The municipality of Budapest, with an elected mayor and a 33-member general assembly, provides the following public services: maintenance and supervision of hospitals and polyclinics, art and public culture institutions, children's and youth homes, secondary schools and dormitories, social homes providing specialized care, and markets and market halls. The public utilities of the municipality of Budapest now operate as municipal companies.

A legal amendment in 1994, however, gave the general assembly of the city supremacy in important matters of regulation and in revenue sharing and city planning. Regarding the sharing of certain revenues from the national budget and local revenues, the influence of the districts was reduced to voicing their opinions, whereas previously consent of the district mayors was required. In city planning, the city became the primary regulatory authority; previously the districts could

question the general plan. In 1997, the city received additional authority over the development and protection of the built environment. A specific system of urban master plans has since been established, reflecting the strengthened, unified management of the city.

Dar es Salaam, Tanzania–Metropolitan Local Government
Dar es Salaam is Tanzania's largest and most important industrial and commercial center, with a population of about 4 million (approximately 10 percent of the country's population). Its population grows by about 4.3 percent per year. It is one of the fastest-growing cities in the world, expected to reach 5 million by 2030.

Dar es Salaam is legally an administrative region of the country. The regional administration is an arm of the national government, with an appointed regional commissioner coexisting with the three Dar es Salaam municipalities and a Dar es Salaam City Council (DCC), which is another administrative entity for the same area. Box 2.11 provides more information about the governance system of Dar es Salaam.

Two-Level Local Government System with Separate Rank and Legal Status
A two-level system sometimes has a separate, usually elected, level of local government with coordination authority over the lower levels and responsibility for some planning and service delivery functions.[5] We first describe the governance structure in Quito, Ecuador. The following examples also illustrate the influence that a higher-tier (national or state or provincial) government can have and the not uncommon evolutionary nature of institutional arrangements for metropolitan governance. Some cities have used a two-level structure in the past but returned to a one-level local government system (Toronto and Abidjan), and some have returned to a two-level structure after operating in a one-level system for some time (London).

Box 2.11 Metropolitan Governance System in Dar es Salaam

The metropolitan local government system was established in 2000. It is composed of a coordinating Dar es Salaam City Council (DCC) and three municipalities of fairly similar population size, with their respective mayors and councils (shown in different colors on map B2.11.1). As a separate local government, the DCC is made up of six councillors from each of the three municipalities, plus a few representatives of the national government, who elect a mayor from among the members.

The DCC is responsible for coordination among the three municipalities and for a few specific functions, such as management of the city's landfill, its main market, and a main bus terminal. However, it does not have jurisdiction over any land or any authority or direct decision-making power over the other three local governments in the city, which has limited its ability to influence the city's development. Despite strong socioeconomic cohesion and physical integration across the three municipalities, the administrative integration and coordination among them have not yet advanced very far.

The DCC's funding comes from limited transfers from the national government and from facilities that it manages. The three municipalities collect own-source revenues through development levies, agricultural leases, city service levies, land rent, licenses, and fees. Property tax is also part of local governments' revenue in Tanzania, but a national tax authority collects and redistributes the revenues. Revenue collection from property taxes has started to increase substantially after efforts to obtain better identification and valuation of properties, currently being completed by the local governments in the city.

As in many other developing countries, the local governments in Dar es Salaam are highly dependent on intergovernmental transfers, particularly for their capital investments. Transfers in Tanzania include recurrent sector block grants, sector basket funds, and ministerial subsidies, as well as development grants (see table B2.11.1). Recurrent block grants account for about two-thirds of all intergovernmental transfers. Until 2004, Tanzania had a discretionary system of intergovernmental grants. Among its many shortcomings was a tendency toward inequality, allocating a relatively high share to wealthier and urban jurisdictions. Starting in FY 2004/05, a new transfer system was introduced. Both recurrent block grants and development grants are now disbursed to local governments based on formulas.

Map B2.11.1 Dar es Salaam Metro Region

Source: World Bank.

(continued next page)

Box 2.11 *(continued)*

Table B2.11.1 Transfers to Local Governments in Dar es Salaam Metro Region 2009/10 (T Sh millions)

Municipal Council (MC) and City Council (CC)	Ilala MC	Kinondoni MC	Temeke MC	Dar es Salaam CC	Metro region
Education grant	20,852	31,062	19,733	6	71,654
Health grant	10,859	7,106	5,998	273	24,237
Other sector grants	740	618	299	241	1,898
General purpose grants	6,621	2,923	2,483	2,157	14,184
Total recurrent grants	39,073	41,709	28,514	2,677	111,973
Subventions	1,506	2,838	4,196	0	8,540
Recurrent transfers	40,578	44,547	32,710	2,677	120,512
Development grant	6,514	5,368	8,513	10,075	30,471
Total transfers	47,092	49,916	41,223	12,753	150,983

Source: www.logintanzania.net/report4b.asp.

Source: www.logintanzania.net.

The Metropolitan District of Quito

The Metropolitan District of Quito (MDQ) was created by law in 1993 as a second-level local government, covering an area of 4,230 km² with a current population of about 2.5 million. At the lower level are 61 zones and parishes. MDQ has a special status as the national capital, with a directly elected mayor and council (15 members) with strategic responsibilities for economic development, land use, environmental planning, and transportation. It also oversees metropolitan companies for water supply, solid waste management, health, and education services. Financially MDQ depends on transfers from the national government, but it also has its own resource base (taxes and special contributions). Somewhat similar systems exist in Bogotá, Colombia, and Caracas, Venezuela, although they are weaker in practice (Rojas 2007).

Toronto City, Canada

Toronto operated as 13 independent municipalities until 1953, when a two-level system, with an elected metro Toronto government and six additional independent local municipalities, was established. After operating under that two-level system for more than 40 years, during a period of exploding population and economic growth, the seven municipalities were merged in 1995 into one single-level local government, the City of Toronto, an area of 632 km², with a current population of about 2.5 million. With its surrounding urban municipalities, the metropolitan area has about 5 million people. The evolution of Toronto's institutional arrangements is described in box 2.12. It illustrates how institutional arrangements may change as a city's circumstances change.

The transformations in Toronto were driven to a great extent by the desire to increase the effectiveness of urban development and service delivery, including harmonization of service levels across the area. Each time a regional authority was disbanded, something else soon took its place. The provincial government played an important role in the evolution. On metropolitan matters, it is quite common that a higher-tier

Box 2.12 Toronto: Evolution from a One-Level System to Two Levels, and Back to a One-Level System

Stage 1. In the early 1950s, with growing service demands on suburban local governments with limited resources, but with a core City of Toronto that had a solid financial base (a strong property, commercial, and industrial tax base), the political boundaries no longer reflected the socioeconomic realities. At the time, each municipality acted independently with respect to transportation, land use, and housing.

Stage 2. In 1954, Metropolitan Toronto (Metro) was formed by provincial legislation, as a metropolitan-level government for the City of Toronto and 12 suburban local governments. The purpose was to (a) redistribute the wealth of the city to the suburbs, so that they could provide infrastructure; (b) coordinate land use and transportation; and (c) maintain local governments' responsiveness to local needs. The Metro's initial responsibilities were planning, borrowing, property assessment, public transit, roads, and administration of justice. The suburban local governments were responsible for fire protection, garbage collection and disposal, licensing and inspection, local power distribution, policing, public health, general welfare, recreation and community services, and the collection of taxes. Responsibilities were shared for parks, planning, roads and traffic control, water supply, and sewage disposal. Costs were shared based on the property tax base.

Over time, responsibilities changed. Metro took over police, social assistance, traffic control, licensing, conservation, waste disposal, and ambulance services. In 1967, the number of municipalities was reduced from 13 to 6. Property assessment and administration of justice became provincial responsibilities in 1970.

Stage 3. The structure was successful in meeting its objectives of providing infrastructure in the suburbs, maintaining a vibrant core city, and pooling revenues over the whole metropolitan area. However, in the 1970s needs changed as a result of growth outside of the Metro area. Between 1971 and 1975, the provincial government created four regional governments around Metro, and in 1988 it established the Office of the Greater Toronto Area (OGTA) to encourage Metro and the four regions around it to coordinate their waste disposal, regional transport, land use, and infrastructure planning. A forum of the greater Toronto area mayors and the chairs of the regional governments focused on economic development and the marketing of the area.

Stage 4. The current City of Toronto was formed in 1998 through provincial legislation, amalgamating the Metro government and six lower-level local governments to create a single-level government. A Greater Toronto Services Board (GTSB) was created shortly thereafter to oversee regional transit as a separate level of governance for this function. The GTSB was governed by elected representatives from each local government, with limited powers to coordinate decision making among the member local governments. It was abolished in 2001. In 2006, the provincial government created the Greater Toronto Transportation Authority (GTTA) to coordinate transportation, the most critical function in need of coordination.

Source: Slack 2007.

government plays a significant role, not only from a fiscal transfer perspective but to ensure that arrangements exist for reasonable coordination of public services and areawide development.

Greater London Authority, U.K.

London, with a current population of more than 7 million, has since 2000 elected members of the Greater London Authority (GLA), which is a city-wide government with a mayor and assembly. It covers an area of 32 local authorities ("boroughs"), which have independent mayors and councils. Functions assigned to the boroughs include housing, education, social and health services, and responsibility as local planning authorities. The GLA is a higher-level strategic authority to promote sustainable development and define strategy. Its main responsibilities are transport, police, economic development planning, fire and emergency planning, land use planning, culture, and environment and health; it also coordinates London-wide events. However, the GLA has very little fiscal autonomy. More than 80 percent of the revenues of both the GLA and the local governments come from central government grants. Other revenues include a local property tax and user charges. Box 2.13 describes how London arrived at this current structure.

Box 2.13 London: Evolution from a Two-Level System to a Single Level and Back to a Two-Level System

Stage 1. London was governed by a two-level structure from 1964 to 1986, comprising the Greater London Council and 32 local governments, each with its own mayor and council.

Stage 2. In 1986, the Greater London Council was abolished and London's governance instead became a direct responsibility of central government ministers, coordinated by a subcommittee headed by a junior minister for London, using agreements and ad hoc arrangements for regional planning. In 1994, the Government Office for London (GOL) was established to allow the central government to act as a strategic authority, coordinating all entities related to London.

Stage 3. In 1999 the new Greater London Authority (GLA) was created, comprising 32 local governments and the Corporation of London. The lord mayor of London was directly elected in 2002; he can direct a local government to reject (but not to approve) large development applications. Four functions are separate from the GLA Assembly but accountable to it through the lord mayor of London:

- Transport for London is responsible for roads, buses, trains, the subway system, traffic lights, and the regulation of taxis. The mayor appoints a commissioner, chairs the board, and appoints 15 nonexecutive members.
- The London Development Agency (abolished in 2012; its functions are now part of GLA) coordinated economic development and worked in partnership with industry and the public and voluntary sectors.
- The Metropolitan Police Authority has 23 members, of which 12 are assembly members, and six are independent Londoners.
- The London Fire and Emergency Planning Authority is responsible for fire and emergency services. The mayor appoints its chair. There are 17 members, of whom nine are from the GLA and eight are nominated by the association of London local governments.

Source: www.london.gov.uk.

City of Abidjan, Côte d'Ivoire

Abidjan is the former capital and the largest city in Côte d'Ivoire. A polycentric structure, it was originally made up of 10 towns (*communes*), with no large, predominant city center. The current metropolitan area consists of 13 municipalities with a population on the order of 6 million. It is an economic and cultural hub in West Africa and has a high level of industrialization. Abidjan became a municipality in 1956, divided into administrative areas by lagoons (see map B2.14.1 in box 2.14), and has gone through a number of institutional changes since then. The current name of the metropolitan structure is the Abidjan District (in 2001 it replaced the former name, City of Abidjan). Box 2.14 describes the emergence of the current system through three stages.

Regional Government Established by Higher-Tier Government

Metropolitan governance reforms have rarely emerged purely from local government initiatives; rather, a national or provincial government has usually initiated change by either imposing or encouraging it (OECD 2006). For example, sometimes the higher-tier government has proposed that municipalities agree to work together to improve coordination of services such as water, waste management, or public transit. Although many metropolitan governments have been established by a higher-tier government, experience shows that such an institution will often be weak unless it is supported by the local governments with which it must work.

Numerous models or approaches exist to establish regional governments or councils for governing, regional planning, and service delivery, including the following:

- Direct election (e.g., Stuttgart, Germany; London, U.K.; and Portland, Oregon, U.S.)

- Appointment by a higher-tier government (e.g., the Twin Cities, Minnesota, U.S.; and the Ministry of Nairobi Metropolitan Development, Kenya)

- Strong local government representation (the higher-tier government only appoints the chair, as, for example, in Metro Manila, the Philippines).

Three city examples below illustrate different approaches, as well as how higher-tier governments have initiated coordinated governance in metropolitan areas.

Portland Metro Service District, U.S.

Portland has an elected regional authority called the Portland Metropolitan Service District ("Portland Metro"), created by the Oregon state legislature in 1977. It is an authority that gained the support and respect of the local governments in the area based on one function—land use regulation and management. It was originally a consolidation of a regional planning council, a metro service council responsible for solid waste disposal, and the administration of a regional zoo. In 1990 it was given added responsibilities for various facilities (the stadium and the exhibition center) and soon after, several regional parks, cemeteries, and marine facilities. Box 2.15 sheds light on the gradual formation of the Portland metropolitan system by higher government.

The Twin Cities Metro (Minneapolis–St. Paul), U.S.

The Twin Cities Metro is an example of a regional planning and service delivery authority that evolved into a regional government appointed by the U.S. state of Minnesota. Cooperation among the Twin Cities area's many local governments was initially motivated by a need for tax sharing because of significant differences between rich and poor jurisdictions. The initial voluntary organization of local governments evolved into the current Twin Cities Metropolitan Council, whose extensive functions are described in box 2.16.

Box 2.14 Abidjan: Evolution from a Two-Level Local Government to a Regional Government

Stage 1. Reforms in 1978 restored *commune*, or local government, status to the major cities in Côte d'Ivoire. At the time, Abidjan had 10 local governments, differing in size and ability to raise their own funds, each with an elected mayor and set of councillors (see map B2.14.1). At the same time, a higher-level, metropolitan local government, the City of Abidjan, was established, with a council composed of the City mayor and four councillors from each local government. The mayor of the city was indirectly elected by the 10 mayors. The major functions of this metropolitan government were waste disposal; public lighting; sanitation; traffic regulation; maintenance of roads, parks, and cemeteries; and town planning. The local governments in the area were responsible for markets, allocation of plots for public purposes, maintenance of primary schools and clinics (but not school or health policy, or the supervision and payment of staff), and operating social centers; they were to share responsibility with other government levels for pollution and hygiene. Private sector companies managed solid waste removal, electricity, and water. This system functioned for more than 20 years, but the national government interfered in the local governments' carrying out some functions, such as inspection of construction sites and issuance of drivers' licenses. The city had little influence over its finances. National government collected property taxes and remitted them to the local governments, which then paid (often delayed) a fixed portion to the higher-level local government, the City of Abidjan (Stren 2007).

Stage 2. In 2001, the City of Abidjan was replaced by a regional ("district") government of Abidjan. The post of mayor of Abidjan was replaced by that of district governor; this person was appointed by the president of the country and assisted by a district council. This became a higher-tier regional government, above the original 10 local governments, to which three large suburban jurisdictions (local governments) and some rural areas were added. This metropolitan area now has a population of approximately 6 million. Urban planning is a key district-level function. Service delivery is constrained by limited local resources. After an attempted military coup in 2002, security has increasingly become a priority.

Stage 3. In September 2012 (after the presidential election) the District of Abidjan was dissolved by a presidential ordinance and replaced by a governorate (an executive body) under the direct control of the national government. A decision had been taken to separate the finances of the District of Abidjan from the contributions of the municipalities by having local revenues collected in the area shared by the two levels (municipalities and district) according to percentages fixed by law. By early 2013 the reallocation of the previous district revenues was still pending, with several options being contemplated.

Map B2.14.1 The 10 Communes of Abidjan

Source: World Bank.

Box 2.15 Formation of the Portland Metro Government

The Portland Metro is governed by a directly elected Metro Council with seven councillors and an executive officer. It has a strong land use statute, as a tool for regional development, which has included establishing a longer-term urban growth boundary to create a certain degree of predictability for private sector land developers in their business planning. An important feature of the law is that Portland Metro may levy property, sales, and income taxes and issue Metro bonds to finance its investment programs. Complementing the regional Metro authority, the local governments in the area (three counties and 25 cities and townships) have created a coordinating group (called "FOCUS") to develop joint recommendations to the Metro Council. Local governments are also represented on a regional planning advisory committee.

The Metro Council of Portland gets about 15 percent of its revenues from property taxes. More than 50 percent of its revenues come from fees and user charges for facilities that the council operates (a solid waste disposal facility, a zoo, and convention, arts, and expo centers).

In 1973 a state law established an urban growth boundary limiting large-scale development in Portland to prevent excessive sprawl. It limits access to utilities such as sewerage, water, and telecommunications, as well as coverage by the fire and police departments and schools. Originally this law mandated that the city must maintain enough land within its boundary to provide for an estimated 20 years of growth. However, in 2007 the law was altered to require planning for an estimated 50 years of growth within the boundary, as well as protection of nearby farms and rural land. The growth boundary, along with efforts by the city to create economic development zones, has led to the development of a large downtown area, a large number of mid- and high-rise developments, and an overall increase in housing and business density.

Source: www.oregonmetro.gov.

Metro Manila, the Philippines

Metro Manila has about 11 million people and includes 17 municipalities. The extended urban area includes another 4 million people in 18 more local governments. The country has a long history of autonomous local governments resisting control from higher tiers, and people have strong loyalties to their local government units. Nevertheless, most of the various metropolitan-level entities that have existed in Manila were established and appointed by the national government (see box 2.17).

Verband Stuttgart, Germany

The Verband Stuttgart Region (Stuttgart regional association) was created by the Baden-Württemberg state government by law in 1993. The *Verband* is a directly elected, higher-level metropolitan entity composed of 179 local governments including the City of Stuttgart. Its main responsibility is now serving as a public transport authority for the area, but it is also engaged in tourism and regional planning. This governance structure became fairly weak, in large part because it had no authority to tax or levy user charges. Its funding is derived about equally from local governments' contributions and intergovernmental grants from the state of Baden-Württemberg (information from www.region-stuttgart.org; www.region-stuttgart.de/en).

Box 2.16 The Twin Cities Metro (Minneapolis–St. Paul), Minnesota, U.S.

The local governments in the Minneapolis–St. Paul region had particular incentives for institutional change. Over time they had grown closer, but they needed to respond to increasing polarization between decaying inner cities and rapidly growing suburban areas ("urban sprawl"). A spatial mismatch between affordable housing and available jobs caused traffic congestion and a continuous need for expensive infrastructure in new suburban areas. With two low-income core cities and richer suburban communities, the two core city governments had to provide services for a large working population in the city center during the day, who mainly contributed to the tax base of the many suburban areas where they lived.

The Twin Cities case is an example of a regional planning and service delivery authority that evolved into a regional government, and subsequently into a public sector corporation. The current metropolitan area covers seven counties, with about 200 small municipalities, about 100 special service district organizations, and a population of about 3 million. A Twin Cities Metro Council was established by the Minnesota state government in 1974 to adopt development plans and policies and to coordinate the activities of existing regional service delivery agencies. The agency would also appoint their boards and review their annual budgets. The Metro Council was also given the authority to review all projects of "metropolitan significance" proposed by the local governments in the area.

In 1994, the Metro Council was made a public corporation, owned by the state of Minnesota. It received operating responsibilities for metropolitan transport and sewerage service, and its previous functions were strengthened. It also received expanded access to regional property taxes to finance its administration and transport subsidies. This reform changed the council from a regional planning agency with only loose supervisory control over a number of regional agencies into a new regional government with an annual budget allocation from the state government 15 times the size of its previous budget.

A directly elected metro council has been proposed and debated on several occasions but has not yet obtained sufficient support in the state legislature. Currently the council comprises a chairperson and 16 members representing geographic districts, all appointed by the governor of Minnesota and confirmed by the state legislature. The council has the following responsibilities: operation of an extensive bus system; collection and treatment of wastewater; engagement of communities and the public in planning for future growth; forecasting the region's population and household growth; ensuring affordable housing for low- and moderate-income individuals and families; and planning, acquisition, and funding for parks and trails. It also provides a framework for decisions and the implementation of regional systems including aviation, transportation, parks and open space, water quality, and water management.

Source: www.metrocouncil.org.

Box 2.17 Stages of Emerging Metro Manila, the Philippines

Stage 1. In the 1960s, the mayors of Manila and the neighboring municipalities created a league to address pressing growth issues in the region. However, since membership in the league was voluntary, it was unable to coordinate long-term development effectively. In 1975, the Metro Manila Commission (MMC) was formed, following a referendum, to create a single metropolitan area by integrating four cities and 13 municipalities. Under the MMC, all metropolitan legislative and executive authority was vested in a small governing body appointed by the president of the country. The role of the MMC was executive and policy making, and to provide services common to the metropolitan area. The local governments contributed 20 percent of their annual revenues to the MMC.

Stage 2. Popular support for the MMC declined, and in 1990 a new president replaced it with the Metro Manila Authority (MMA). The MMA was responsible for basic urban services, including land use planning, traffic management, public safety, urban renewal, and waste management. It was governed by a metropolitan council composed of the mayors of the 17 local governments in the area and headed by a chair indirectly elected by the members every six months. It continued to collect revenues from the local government units, but the amount was reduced to 15 percent of local governments' annual revenues.

Stage 3. In 1995, the MMA was replaced by the Metropolitan Manila Development Authority (MMDA). The MMDA is a development and administrative unit under the direct supervision of the president of the country. It performs planning, monitoring, and coordination functions but can do so only if it does not diminish the autonomy of local governments on local matters. Its council is still dominated by the 17 mayors of the area local governments, but the chair and a number of the managers are appointed by the president. The MMDA is responsible for almost all traditionally local public services. It derives resources from the central government, a 5 percent contribution from the local governments, and revenues from metro service fees and fines. The MMDA has been criticized for being more of a national corporation than a fully local institution.

Source: www.mmda.gov.ph.

The Ministry of Nairobi Metropolitan Development

Metropolitan Nairobi was established in 2008 by presidential decree to facilitate implementation of a growth and development strategy for the Nairobi metropolitan area of 15 local governments (see map 2.4). Initially it was intended to cover most local government functions, plus promotion and development of a funding framework. To date, the ministry has functioned mostly as an additional channel for national government funding for minor investments in the metro area. This is a case in which the defined "metropolitan area" is much larger than it would be if defined based on socioeconomic cohesion factors, such as the existence of a single economy and labor market. The defined area is 32,000 km². It encompasses four counties with a total of 15 local governments. The population is about 11 million, growing at 3.4 percent per annum. The area is so large because the Kenyan government determined that if a small part of a county was part of the integrated economy and labor market, then the entire county should be included in the area governed by the ministry.

Map 2.4 Metropolitan Nairobi

Source: World Bank.

The Randstad, The Netherlands

The Randstad is a conurbation in the Netherlands that consists of the four largest Dutch cities—Amsterdam, Rotterdam, The Hague, and Utrecht—and the surrounding areas. With a population of 7.1 million, it is one of the largest conurbations in Europe. It covers an area of about 8,287 km². The area figure is the sum of the areas of the four member provinces, although the Randstad is normally not considered to cover the whole of any of them. The Randstad has had a history of strong competition among cities, particularly the two main cities of Rotterdam and Amsterdam. The national government has been instrumental in promoting collaboration, rather than competition, on certain priority subjects for the area through financial incentives and political influence. Recently, local planners have started to refer to the Randstad as the "Deltametropool," consisting of two large metropolitan areas (source: www.randstadregion.eu).

Mexico City Metropolitan Area, Mexico

The Mexico City metropolitan area illustrates a case in which fiscal decentralization policies in the 1990s unintentionally made worse the fiscal disparities of the Metropolitan Zone of the Valley of Mexico (ZMVM) (Raich 2008). Despite state intervention through a system of redistributive transfers, the increased fiscal disparities occurred for three primary reasons: (a) an indirect negative effect of the transfers on local fiscal efforts, including the collection of property taxes; (b) uneven distribution of services and infrastructure in the metropolitan area; and (c) the existence of differing governance structures in the various jurisdictions within the zone. Legal and political complexities made it difficult to mitigate the problems, although the situation has since improved somewhat.

Annexation or Amalgamation of Local Governments

Although the boundaries of an economic region grow incrementally over time, government boundaries tend to change only occasionally, through legal actions. Annexation and amalgamation are sometimes the most effective approach to achieve needed scale, cost sharing, efficiency, and equity in public service delivery (table 2.9). Yet amalgamation tends to be politically controversial, usually requiring the active involvement of a national or a provincial government. Few amalgamations have achieved coverage of an entire metropolitan area, usually because of the local political dynamics. The following are some examples:

- *London, U.K.* The Greater London Authority covers 7.5 million people, but the functional economic area, the greater southeast, has a population of 20 million.

- *Toronto, Canada.* The amalgamation of the City of Toronto (2.5 million people) is sometimes considered both too small and too large. It is too small to cover the metropolitan economic region referred to as "the greater Toronto area" (5 million people) or to address regionwide spillovers related to transport and planning. It is too large to be fully locally

Table 2.9 Annexation of Territory or Amalgamation of Local Governments

Characteristics	Examples
Creates a jurisdiction that covers a larger portion (or all) of the metropolitan area, facilitating equalization within the area (one tax base).	Toronto, Cape Town, Istanbul, Pittsburgh, Madrid, Anchorage
With a larger jurisdiction, residents' access to local government may be affected and local accountability weakened.	
Common financial considerations:	
• Cost savings usually occur through scale economies.	
• Harmonization of service and salary levels across the new local government may be standardized to the local government with highest levels, resulting in higher costs.	
• One-time transition costs need to be taken into consideration.	

responsive and accessible compared with its earlier six separate municipalities.

Some local governments, however, do indeed essentially cover their entire metropolitan economic region (their functional area). Examples are the following:

• *Cape Town, South Africa.* Cape Town's boundaries were drawn by the Municipal Demarcation Board of South Africa[6] in 1998 and now encompass 95 percent of the people who live and work there.

• *Istanbul, Turkey.* Istanbul's administrative boundaries were expanded in 2004 to include areas previously governed by the central government, increasing its area from 1,830 km^2 to 5,340 km^2 (Turan 2011).

Pittsburgh, Pennsylvania, U.S., is a classic example of annexation. In the early 20th century, Pittsburgh successfully undertook the annexation of 12 neighboring municipalities. More recently, new suburban local governments have been incorporated within the jurisdiction of the City of Pittsburgh, in gradual adjustments as the area has changed.

Cape Town, with a population of about 3.5 million, had a two-level metropolitan structure in the 1990s and became one amalgamated municipality in 1998 by consolidating a number of local governments (see box 2.18). It is by area

(2,455 km^2) now the largest city in South Africa. Table 2.10 is a snapshot of the Cape Town budget for the 2011/12 fiscal year with indications of changes of budget lines from previous years.

Anchorage, Alaska, U.S. is another example, a municipality which has grown from 20 km^2 to more than 5,000 km^2 during the last 50 years.

Financial Implications of Amalgamations

Particular financial adjustments are needed when an amalgamation of local governments is considered. For example, how are salaries to be harmonized or duplicate assets to be divested? Amalgamation does not necessarily reduce costs. When Toronto amalgamated six municipalities into one City of Toronto, for example, it unified salaries and services across the six former local government areas, and overall costs went up. Harmonization of service levels often means conforming all to the levels of the local government with the highest expenditure, resulting in higher overall costs for the amalgamated entity. That may outweigh other cost savings that can usually be achieved. One-time transition costs must also be taken into consideration in moving to a new governance structure. For example, Cape Town went through various local governance reforms in a short time and in recent years has seen further structural reforms, territorial changes, new management structures, and new forms of service delivery. Such frequent reorganization may run

Box 2.18 Changing Metropolitan Governance Models in Cape Town, South Africa

The 1996 interim constitution in South Africa allowed for three types of local governments: metropolitan, urban, and rural. The Cape Town Metropolitan Council is a metropolitan government. The constitution also provided for three categories of municipalities. Category A municipalities had exclusive municipal executive and legislative authority in their areas. Category B municipalities shared authority in their areas with a Category C municipality within whose area they fell. Category C had authority in an area with more than one municipality.

A subsequent study recommended a single-level metropolitan government system, with each municipality to cover its metropolitan area, to redress inequalities, promote strategic land use planning, coordinate infrastructure investment, and develop a citywide framework for economic and social development. It was thought that the change would prevent the local governments from competing for investment in an uncoordinated way. In 1998, all Category C municipalities in South Africa, like Cape town (see map),

Source: www.capetown.gov.za.

Map B2.18.1 Population Density in Cape Town, South Africa

Source: World Bank.

became one-level (amalgamated) municipalities like Cape Town shown in the map above.

---

the risk of disrupting local service delivery because of the time and resources that the changes require.

One Large Municipality Covering the Metropolitan Area

Where the geographical area of a municipality essentially coincides with the economy of a metropolitan area, financial management coordination is somewhat less challenging because of less institutional complexity. In other cases allocation of resources across a broad area for service delivery and investments, often with the active involvement of municipal suboffices, presents particular difficulties for a municipal council.

Johannesburg City, South Africa

South Africa has eight large, one-level, metropolitan municipalities, including Cape Town and Johannesburg. The city of Johannesburg is the provincial capital of Gauteng province and the largest city in South Africa, with a population close to 4 million. The municipal city's land area of 1,645 km^2 is large, with a moderate population density of 2,364/km^2. It is the world's largest city not situated on a river, lake, or coastline. Box 2.19 summarizes the way Johannesburg has become a single, amalgamated municipality.

Table 2.10 Budget of City of Cape Town 2011/12

Expenditures	Rand millions	Change %	Revenues	Rand millions	Change %
Employee-related costs	7,091.6	9.1	Property rates	4,582.0	8.9
Remuneration of councillors	108.8	17.9	Penalties and other charges	85.8	6.6
Debt impairment	1,040.0	7.5	Service charges	8,125.7	22.4
			–electricity		
Depreciation	1,392.8	17.0	–water	1,828.1	10.1
Finance charges	766.4	3.6	–sanitation	991.1	10.2
Bulk purchases	5,785.9	22.1	–refuse	820.4	7.6
Contracted services	2,320.2	31.6	–other service charges	625.4	–4.0
Transfers and grants	96.4	10.1	Rental (facilities, equipment)	264.0	8.0
Other expenditure	3,539.8	4.4	Interest from external investments	192.4	–10.0
Total expenditure	22,141.9	100.0	–outstanding debtors	218.3	3.6
Capital Budget			Fines	186.9	3.5

Sources	Rand millions	Change %	Licenses and permits	30.0	4.5
Capital grants and donations	2,715.4	940.2	Agency services	116.0	
Capital replacement reserve	970.9	272.0	–Operational transfers	1,897.8	28.4
External financing fund	1,357.4	85.4	Other revenue	1,912.3	8.6
Revenue	46.3	32.7	Gains on disposal of personal protection equipment	105.0	–66.2
Total	5,089.9	100	Total revenue	21,981.2	100.0

Source: www.capetown.gov.za/en/Budget/Pages/Budget2011-2012.aspx.

Shanghai Municipality, China

Shanghai is another example in which one municipal government covers its entire metropolitan area. Chinese cities have a two-level local government structure, a municipal government with a number of subordinated districts and county governments. All large cities in China operate under the same governance model, in which the municipal jurisdiction includes both urban and large rural areas. District governments tend to be the more urban ones, and counties the more rural ones.

Shanghai Municipality currently has nine districts, defined as its core city, seven semiurban suburban districts, and one rural county (the large island; see map 2.5). Shanghai is one of four municipalities which are treated as provinces and

have corresponding powers. The overall metropolitan area is 6,340.5 km². Despite the fact that a Chinese municipal government covers its entire metropolitan area with a two-level local government system, coordination and financial allocations can still be challenging. Although the core city urban districts tend to have well-coordinated services (transport, water and sewerage networks, etc.), coordination with subordinated suburban local governments, county governments in particular, is often difficult because they are independently governed.

Shanghai is an example in which political economy legacy and culture may influence how an area is practically managed. In this case, the higher-level municipal government tends not to

Box 2.19 The Change of Governance Structure of Johannesburg, South Africa

The population of the greater Johannesburg metropolitan area was about 7.2 million in 2007. An even broader definition of this metropolitan area gave it a population of about 10.3 million at the time. Gauteng province is growing rapidly and experiencing heavy urbanization (more information is available at www.gautengonline.gov.za).

The urban portion of Gauteng is a polycentric region (as depicted in the map below) with a projected population of close to 15 million by 2015 (see map). The city of Johannesburg evolved from a segregated city (with seven white councils and four black councils), through a fragmented stage with one metro council plus four subordinated local councils. The current, integrated stage is a one-level city government, with one tax base that covers the main part of the metropolitan area. In the earlier two-level arrangement, the higher-level local government was responsible for borrowing and debt repayment, and the lower-level government collected most revenues. When finances were tight at the lower level, however, transfers of funds to the higher level tended to be delayed or stopped. Since its

formation, the one-level city government has substantially improved governance and efficiency. It has, for example, issued management contracts for water and sanitation services; corporatized roads department and solid waste functions; sold information technology assets and leased them back; and moved to private management of its properties.

Map B2.19.1 Johannesburg within Gauteng Province

Source: World Bank.

---

interfere with the details of how the subordinated lower governments run their affairs.

Takeaway Messages

Metropolitan areas are becoming "the new normal." With continued urbanization around the world, cities become more economically interdependent with their surrounding settlements and hinterlands, creating metropolitan areas with a single economy and labor market, a community with common interests and joint actions. Such areas need some areawide management for selective

functions. Cooperation among local governments may be encouraged by incentives from a provincial or national government through intergovernmental systems, legal frameworks, or specific financial incentives.

But many governance approaches exist, each with its pros and cons. The main models and approaches are cooperation among local governments; regional authorities or special purpose districts (as bottom-up, voluntary organizations); metropolitan-level governments (either as a second-level local government or as a regional government established by a higher-tier

Map 2.5 Shanghai Core City and Suburban Districts/County

Source: World Bank.

government); and consolidating local government through amalgamation or annexation of territory.

No one size fits all. The most appropriate governance structure depends on the national as well as local context (legal framework, local government responsibilities, issues and opportunities in the area, institutional capacity and tradition, etc.). It may be formed through a bottom-up process by the local governments in the area or as a top-down decision by a provincial or national government. Institutional and financial arrangements may need to evolve over time, as needs and circumstances change. Politics, rather than efficiency and equity, often determines the formation or evolution of metro area governance and finance systems.

Tailored financing arrangements are needed. Examples of financial considerations in regional cooperation include tax sharing agreements to prevent tax and fee competition and to harmonize revenues and expenditures across a metro region; cost sharing or a common budget for metropolitan-level initiatives and services (and entities); coordinated revenue mobilization through user charges, property taxes, earmarked taxes, and so forth; and mobilization of multiple funding sources for large infrastructure with areawide benefits. A municipal development fund at the national level, with multiple funding sources, is sometimes used to support local capital investments in metro areas.

Cooperate, don't compete. This is the essence of a metropolitan approach: to cooperate on certain initiatives or services (while possibly competing on others in terms of service quality and cost-effectiveness). Cooperative agreements may include joint revenue mobilization, funding of investments, and service expenditures.

Choosing a structure. In choosing a governance structure one needs to weigh (a) the potentials for economies of scale and service coordination efficiency and the need to address area spillovers and disparities, versus (b) the impact on residents' access to their government and its responsiveness and accountability.

Division of functions. In any metropolitan governance arrangement, ensure that functions and responsibilities are clear (not overlapping, difficult to misunderstand, etc.) among the involved entities, particularly if specialized authorities or different levels of local government are applied. In addition, be aware of the risk of limited effectiveness with a metropolitan agency with no independent authority (i.e., advisory only).

Clear and reliable sources of funding. For a regional authority or metropolitan-level government to fulfill its functions, it is critical that it be assigned sufficient revenue sources to fulfill its mandates on a sustainable basis.

Local government commitment. To be effective, the metropolitan-level structure must have the support and commitment of all local governments involved, independently if it is formed bottom-up by themselves or top-down by a higher-tier government. Depending on the circumstances, consider allowing individual local governments the flexibility to participate in some or all metro-level functions.

Annex
Cities Used as Examples in This Chapter

Metropolitan Area	Key Metropolitan Features
North America	
Los Angeles County, U.S.	• Providing services for a fee to many smaller local governments in the area under individual contracts; cost-effective for all involved.
Mexico City, Mexico *Zona Metropolitana del Valle de Mexico (ZMVM)*	• Large area as a conglomerate of municipal and state jurisdictions, governed by forming collective bodies (commissions) and bilateral agreements. Characterized by legal, political, and fiscal complexities causing unintended inequalities through the transfer system in the past.
Twin Cities, U.S.	• The initial coordination initiative and authority were motivated by fiscal inequality in the region. • Regional planning and service delivery authority evolved into a regional government of the state; now a state-owned corporation, receiving a portion of property taxes from the region to cover its costs for service provision.
Portland, U.S. *Metro Council*	• An elected metro council formed for land use management, with significant power; now has broader functions and an advisory committee formed by a number of local governments.
Toronto, Canada	• Evolution from a one-level to a two-level system, and back to a one-level system, with amalgamated local governments (and common tax base) after extensive involvement of provincial government.
Vancouver, Canada *Greater Vancouver Regional District (GVRD)*	• Public corporation owned by the member local governments, providing them a number of services (but all local governments do not provide all services through GVRD). • Has access to a variety of funding sources, including user charges; share of property tax; and annual contributions from member local governments.
Washington, D.C., U.S. *Metropolitan Washington Council of Governments*	• Council of 21 local governments with coordination functions but without own decision-making authority (the local government councils must ratify any decisions), except for some transport items.
Africa	
Abidjan, Côte d'Ivoire	• Evolution from a one-level to a two-level regional government system; initiatives by local governments as well as national government.

Cape Town, South Africa	• Many changes in the 1990s, including amalgamation in 2000 into one large municipality, corresponding to the functional economic area and the regional labor market. (Eight such metropolitan municipalities exist across the country.)
Dar es Salaam, Tanzania	• Three local governments plus a Dar city council (at the same level and having no authority over the three local governments) for general coordination and a few specific functions, without any land and with very limited own-source revenues; growing property tax revenues for the local governments but still heavily dependent on transfers from the national government.
Johannesburg, South Africa	• Evolution from seven local governments to a two-level system, to one local government with sector entities.
Nairobi, Kenya *Ministry of Nairobi Metropolitan Development*	• Ministry from 2009 for development of the Nairobi metro area; a new window of national funds for 15 local governments in the area.
Australia	
Melbourne	• State (provincial) government provides (and funds) a number of traditionally local services such as public transportation.
Europe and Cental Asia	
Bologna, Italy	• A flexible approach created by 48 local governments, the metropolitan city council is presided over by the provincial president; local governments may participate in some or all activities of the council.
Budapest, Hungary	• City local government and many district local governments, all equal in rank and legal status; the metropolitan area and the commuter area are being distinguished as two separate planning contexts.
London, U.K.	• Evolution from a two-level to a one-level and back to a two-level system. Greater London Authority (GLA) with little fiscal autonomy; more than 80 percent of both GLA and local government revenues come from central government grants. Authorities for transport, police and fire services, and emergency planning.
Lyon, France	• Planning and service authority with metro tax sharing system; small local governments with cooperative arrangements for service provision.
Marseille, France *Communauté Urbaine de Marseille*	• Common business tax to prevent tax competition among local governments in the area.
Prague, Czech Republic	• One elected local government with subordinated district offices.

Randstad, The Netherland	• One of Europe's largest conurbations with the four largest Dutch cities (Amsterdam, Rotterdam, The Hague, Utrecht) and surrounding areas; joint efforts mainly ad hoc or through national government pressure.
Stuttgart, Germany	• A directly elected, higher-level metropolitan entity, mainly for public transport; also engaged in tourism and regional planning. No authority to levy taxes or user charges (funded by the state and local governments).
Tbilisi, Georgia	• One dominating city (the capital) and a few smaller, less-affluent local governments, with informal, case-by-case coordination efforts to date.

Latin America

Bogotá, Colombia	• The city is divided into 20 localities, each governed by an administrative board of no fewer than seven members, elected by popular vote; the principal mayor designates local mayors from candidates nominated by the respective administrative boards.
Santiago, Chile	• Greater Santiago has 37 local governments but no metropolitan government; functions distributed among various authorities. An "intendant" of the Santiago Metropolitan Region is appointed by the president.
São Paulo, Brazil *Intermunicipal Consortium of Greater ABC Region*	• ABC Council, a political body of the state, local governments, and civil society; active engagement by civil society and private sector, particularly for economic development of the metro area; a flexible, pragmatic approach to regional problem solving but not a government structure.
Quito, Ecuador	• The Metropolitan District of Quito (MDQ) is an elected metropolitan council with broad responsibilities, presided over by an elected metro mayor. MDQ depends on transfers from the national government but also has its own resource base (taxes and special contributions).

East and South Asia

Dhaka, Bangladesh	• A regional planning and development agency for land matters.
Manila, the Philippines	• Strong tradition of local government autonomy, but most metropolitan entities established and controlled by the national government.
New Delhi, India	• The metropolitan area of Delhi is nine districts of the National Capital Territory of Delhi (NCT) and four major satellite cities outside the NCT (in two different states), with various development and service authorities.

| Shanghai, China | • One municipal government for a large area, with a number of subordinated district governments (for the highly urban areas) and subordinated but more independent counties (with large rural areas). |

Middle East

| Istanbul, Turkey | • Annexation of territory earlier governed by the national government. |

Notes

1. Dar es Salaam, Tanzania, is an example where more than 70 percent of the population lives in unplanned settlements. In terms of city area, more than 50 percent of Kampala, Uganda, and more than 70 percent of Kabul, Afghanistan, are informal settlements.

2. This is an example of a two-level system with 179 lower-level municipalities. CAM was created in 1983 and is administered by a directly elected council (which elects a president). CAM took over the previous powers of the province of Madrid. When it was established, the lower-level local governments' powers and responsibilities were significantly reduced.

3. For example, the National Association of Regional Councils and the Association of Metropolitan Planning Organizations. Additional information is available at www .abag.ca.gov/abag/other_gov/rcg.html, including links to all COGs in the United States.

4. The name of ABC region refers to three smaller cities bordering on São Paulo—Santo André, São Bernardo do Campo, and São Caetano do Sul.

5. The source for parts of this section is Enid Slack, "Managing the Coordination of Service Delivery in Metropolitan Cities: The Role of Metropolitan Governance," Policy Research Working Paper, August 2007, World Bank, Washington, DC.

6. Similar consolidations of jurisdictions aimed at covering the "functional area" were done in other parts of the country through the Municipal Demarcation Board, initially creating six (now eight) such large metropolitan municipalities.

References

Abbott, J. 2011. "Regions of Cities: Metropolitan Governance and Planning in Australia." In *Governance and Planning of Mega-City Regions—An International Comparative Perspective*, edited by J. Xu and A. Yeh, 172–90. New York: Routledge.

Bahl, Roy W., Johannes F. Linn, and Deborah L. Wetzel, eds. 2013. *Financing Metropolitan Governments in Developing Countries.* Cambridge, MA: Lincoln Institute of Land Policy.

Brinkhoff, Thomas. 2012. "City Population." The Principal Agglomerations of the World, www .citypopulation.de/world/Agglomerations .html.

Dodge, William R. 1996. "Regional Excellence— Governing Together to Compete Globally and Flourish Locally." Washington, DC: National League of Cities.

Horváth, Tamás M., and Gábor Péteri. 2003. "General Conditions of a Decade's Operation." In *The Budapest Model—A Liberal Urban Policy Experiment*, edited by Katalin Pallai, 359–405. Budapest: Open Society Institute.

OECD (Organization for Economic Co-operation and Development). 2006. "The Governance of Metro-Regions." In *Competitive Cities in the Global Economy.* Paris: OECD Publishing.

Raich, Uri. 2008. *Unequal Development—Decentralization and Metropolitan Finance in Mexico City*. Saarbrucken: VDM Verlag Dr. Muller.

Rojas, Eduardo, Juan R. Cuadrado-Roura, and José Miguel Fernández Güell, eds. 2007. *Governing the Metropolis—Principles and Experiences*. Washington, DC: Inter-American Development Bank.

Slack, Enid. 2007. "Managing the Coordination of Service Delivery in Metropolitan Cities—The Role of Metropolitan Governance." Policy Research Working Paper, World Bank, Washington, DC.

Turan, Neyran. 2011. "Towards an Ecological Urbanism for Istanbul." In *Megacities—Urban Form, Governance and Sustainability*, edited by A. Sorensen and J. Okata, 245–87. Heidelberg: Springer.

World Bank. 2010. *World Development Report 2009: Reshaping Economic Geography*. Washington, DC: World Bank.

Yang, J. 2009. "Spatial Planning in Asia—Planning and Developing Megacities and Megaregions." In *Megaregions: Planning for Global Competitiveness*, edited by C. L. Ross, 35–52. Washington, DC: Island Press.

CHAPTER 3

Municipal Financial Management

Rama Krishnan Venkateswaran

Financial management is a crucial element of municipal management. It enables the local government to plan, mobilize, and use financial resources in an efficient and effective manner, as well as fulfill its obligation to be accountable to its citizens. This chapter covers the basics of the municipal financial management process. It discusses the four fundamental components of public sector financial management: budgeting, accounting, reporting, and auditing, and their applications in local government. Each process is discussed separately, and the chapter also brings out their linkages and synergies.

Figure 3.1 depicts the pillars of public financial management. Let us look at them briefly before we delve into more detailed discussions. *Budgets* provide operational and financial plans for the attainment of the local government's goals. Budgets are developed based on both financial and nonfinancial information. Financial information includes the estimates of

financial resources—both what is available and what is required—to achieve identified priorities. Nonfinancial information includes community priorities, policy, and political considerations.

Accounting involves classification and documentation of various financial transactions of the local government; it provides the basic financial information required for preparation of the budget and financial reports and data to communicate with clients and partners such as lenders or higher-level governments. Accounting information includes specific figures on revenues earned and expenditures incurred within a specific period (usually a financial year) and information on assets and liabilities of the entity. *Financial reports* provide aggregate figures on the government's revenues and expenditures, which help readers to understand the "big picture" of the government's financial position and the efficiency of its financial management. *Auditing* is the process of independent verification of the

Figure 3.1 The Pillars of Financial Management

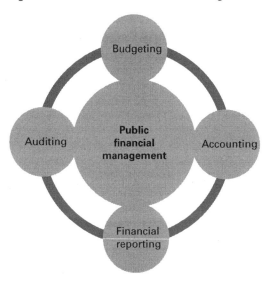

financial information contained in the accounting records and financial reports. It provides assurance to external persons or entities about the credibility of the information.

Budgeting

A budget is the annual financial plan of a local government, which defines its operational and development priorities for the ensuing financial year and describes how the plans will be financed. The budgeting process is vital in laying out the city's choice of expenditure priorities and identifying the resources necessary for the realization of planned expenditures. This section explains the role of budgeting in municipal financial management and helps the reader to understand the objectives of the budget process, the components of a good budget, the steps in the budget process, and the relationship of the budget to other aspects of the financial management process.

Budgeting: Concepts and Practices

Budgeting and budgets are vital in the planning, control, and evaluation of government operations, but budgeting practices are not uniform across countries. "The budgeting process provides the medium for determining what government services will be provided and how they will be financed" (Mikesell 2011). Budgeting is the process of allocating scarce resources across unlimited demands; it is a financial and operating plan for a fiscal year (12 months). The budget contains information about the types and amounts of proposed expenditures, the purposes for which money will be spent, and the proposed means of financing. Although budgets are usually prepared for one financial year at a time, the recent trend has been to plan for three to five years as the basis for the annual budgets. That results in the annual budgeting process becoming part of a medium-term planning and program implementation process, helping the entity to achieve continuity in the planning and execution of its development program.

Budgets as Planning Instruments

The adoption of a budget implies that decisions have been made—on the basis of a planning process—as to how the organization plans to reach its objectives. The planning function in any government is of critical importance for the following reasons:

- *Public goods.* The type, quantity, and quality of goods and services that the public sector produces are not evaluated and adjusted through the market mechanism.

- *Public interest.* The goods and services provided by the public sector are often among the most critical to the public interest.

- *Immense scope.* The immense scope and diversity of modern government activities make comprehensive, thoughtful, and systematic planning a prerequisite to orderly decision making.

- *Participation.* Government planning and decision making generally take place in a joint process involving citizens, their elected representatives, and the executive branch.

Thus, budgets help ensure that governments deliver the services that citizens have demanded, through choices made in a democratic process, and that available resources are used efficiently.

Budgets as Instruments of Fiscal Discipline and Control

Budgets are *instruments of financial control* used by both the executive and the legislative branches of a local government. For example, the mayor, the chief financial officer, or the city manager can use the budget to monitor actual expenses, compare them to plans made at the start of the year, and improve operational efficiency. At the same time, the city council can use the budget to keep track of whether the executive branch is using resources efficiently to address the development priorities that the council has established.

The control function in budgeting involves restraining expenditures to the limits imposed by available financing, ensuring that enacted budgets are executed and financial reports are accurate, and preserving the legality of the government's expenditures. The control function permits development of information for the cost estimates used in the preparation of new budgets and preserves audit trails after budget execution. Box 3.1 presents four principles of a good budget.

Types of Budgets

Budgets have been used for centuries, but the forms, types, and scope of budgets have continued to change. This section discusses the various budget types and their merits and shortcomings, including the challenges of implementing them in practice (adapted from Mikesell 2011).

Administrative

Budgets can be classified according to the administrative entity that is responsible for management of the particular public service or function. Thus, the budget can be organized according to the agency or department that will implement the work for which the funds are provided, such as the health or water department, the education authority, the waste management department, and so forth.

Economic

Budgets can be classified by economic function, that is, by the type of revenues and expenditures, such as taxes, salaries, supplies, and so forth. This kind of classification is also called "line-item" or "object of expenditure" classification.

Box 3.1 Principles of a Good Budget

Those preparing a local government budget should keep the following principles in mind:

Principle 1. Establish broad goals to guide government decision making.

Principle 2. Establish credible approaches for achieving the goals that have been set by developing appropriate policies, programs, and strategies.

Principle 3. Equip the local government with a budget that is consistent with the goals and the approaches that have been decided on.

Principle 4. Enable the local government to monitor and evaluate its performance and to make adjustments to meet contingencies and changing circumstances.

Source: Adapted from NACSLB 1998.

Functional

The functional classification identifies spending according to the intended purpose or objective, for example, education, health, social services, without specifying the (often several) administrative departments that will receive the resources or the expenditure category for which the budgeted funds will be used.

Fixed or Flexible Budgets

Fixed budgets are those specifying appropriations of fixed amounts. The appropriated amounts may not be exceeded, regardless of changes in demand for government services. Earmarked grants from a higher government tier are typical fixed budgets, which can be spent exclusively for the target purposes (e.g., education, health, or roads); unspent amounts may be returned to the grantor. *Flexible budgets* permit the local government to adjust the budget allocations during the course of the year, in accordance with program requirements, and thus enable it to adapt to contingencies and unexpected events.

Line-Item Budgets

Line-item budgets provide for budget allocations in a very detailed manner, by specific allocation for each expenditure item. These budgets are input oriented and describe minute details; as a result the budget documents are voluminous. Although line-item budgets help governments to exercise financial control over each item of expenditure, they do not provide flexibility to adjust spending in accordance with changes in needs and circumstances and do not provide a "big picture" view of what resources are being used for. Table 3.1 is a copy of the budget snapshot of the city of Bangalore, India.

Program Budgets

Program budgets provide budget allocations for a whole program and expect the budget holder to make allocations for the various expenditure categories within it. In this method, local government control is exercised over expenditures for the overall program and not over individual expenditure items. Program budgets are output

Table 3.1 Line-Item Expenditure Budget of Bangalore, India

Source: http://bbmp.gov.in.

oriented. Although program budgets provide the budget holder with flexibility to manage resources efficiently, they also require efficient accounting and control procedures to prevent waste or misuse of resources. Hence governments often start with an efficient line-item budgeting process and then move into preparing program budgets.

Operating Budgets

Local budgets typically consolidate two budgets, an *operating budget* and a *capital budget*. An operating budget (also called a "current budget") is typically larger and more detailed than a capital budget. Operating budgets include revenues from current year transactions (tax collections, rents received) and provide for expenditures that are necessary for day-to-day operations during the year (wages and salaries, office expenses, maintenance expenditures, etc.).

Capital Budgets

Capital budgets include revenues from capital transactions (such as the sale or lease of assets, land, or other property) and provide expenditures for goods and services whose benefits extend beyond one year. That includes allocations for the construction of buildings and acquisition of assets such as plant, machinery, and vehicles. Capital budgets are also called "development budgets" (in some Asian countries). They are nonexistent in many developing countries because they are not legislated by the central government.

Table 3.2 summarizes the main attributes of current and capital expenditures. It is important to distinguish current (also called "operating") and capital (also called "nonrecurrent" or "development") expenditures and to segregate the current and capital budgets. The table supports the view that segregation is possible and very useful for analyzing the financial position of a local

Table 3.2 Attributes of Current and Capital Expenditures

Current expenditures	Capital expenditures
It is an amount spent to acquire goods or services essential for daily operations and is expensed immediately.	It is an amount spent to acquire or improve a long-term asset, such as equipment or buildings.
Its effect is temporary—its benefit is received within the accounting year.	Its effect is long term—its benefit is received for a number of years in the future.
No asset is acquired, nor is the value of an asset increased.	An asset is acquired or the value of an existing asset is increased.
It has no physical existence because it is incurred for items that are used by the organization.	Except for some intangible assets, it generally has physical existence.
It is recurring and regular; it occurs repeatedly.	It does not occur again and again; it is nonrecurring and irregular.
It helps to maintain the business.	It improves the position of the business.
It is normally charged against revenue in the income statement in the year it is expensed.	A portion of the expenditure (depreciation on assets) is shown in the income statement as an expense, and the balance is shown in the balance sheet on the asset side.
It does not appear in the balance sheet.	It appears in the balance sheet until its benefit is fully exhausted.
It reduces the revenue (profit) of the organization.	It does not reduce revenue; the purchase of a fixed asset does not affect revenue.

government, regardless of whether or not national regulation stipulates the two separate budgets.

Budget Preparation

This section describes the steps in the budget process, including the budget cycle, the budget manual or circular, the budget calendar, budget formulation practices, budget estimates, budget approval, and supplementary or revised budgets. It addresses budget processes and how they help local governments maintain financial discipline and accountability.

The Budget Cycle

Public sector budgeting is organized around a cycle within a fiscal year, which allows the system to absorb and respond to new information and thereby allows the government to be held accountable for its actions. The budget cycle consists of four phases: (1) preparation and submission, (2) approval, (3) execution, and (4) audit and evaluation. The first three phases are discussed in detail here, and auditing is discussed in chapter 8.

Figure 3.2 depicts a budget cycle, a continuous process with interlinked phases that do not necessarily occur during the same budget year. Because local governments are required to

approve their budgets prior to the start of the fiscal year, the preparation stage of the cycle takes place prior to the budget year. Similarly, the audit and evaluation stage takes place mostly after the close of the fiscal year. The overall purpose of the budget process is to help decision makers make informed decisions about the provision of services and the development of capital assets, but it also helps promote stakeholder participation in the budgeting process.

Budget formulation. Budget formulation has both policy and procedural aspects. The executive leadership (usually the mayor's office in a city) sets out the detailed policy and program goals that it wants to implement in its jurisdiction. These are usually assembled through a development planning process in which cities prepare medium- and long-term development plans. For example, in India five-year plans are prepared at both the national and provincial levels that lay out the broad development priorities and programs. Based on these five-year plans, provinces and cities prepare annual plans, which in turn form the basis for annual budgets that describe the priorities and programs for a particular fiscal year.

Figure 3.2   The Budget Cycle

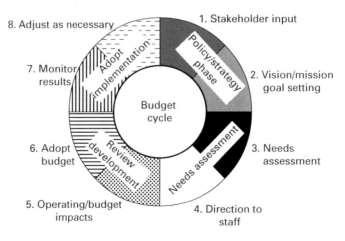

Source: NACSLB 2000.

The National Advisory Council on State and Local Budgeting (NACSLB) in the United States has recommended the following steps to improve the quality of the budget process (Freeman and Shoulders 2000):

- The budget process should consist of activities that encompass the development, implementation, and evaluation of a plan for the provision of services and capital assets.

- A good budget process incorporates a long-term perspective, establishes links to broad organizational goals, focuses budget decisions on results and outcomes, involves and promotes effective communication with stakeholders, and provides incentives to government management and employees.

- The budget process should be strategic in nature, encompassing a multiyear financial and operating plan that allocates resources on the basis of identified goals.

- A good budget process moves beyond the traditional concept of line-item expenditure control, providing incentives and flexibility to managers that can lead to improved program efficiency and effectiveness.

Budget circular and budget calendar. The procedural aspect of budgeting relates to translating policies and plans into budget estimates. Around the first quarter of a fiscal year, the finance department of the local government sends a *budget circular* for the following fiscal year to all local government departments, agencies, or entities. The circular includes (a) the *budget planning calendar*; (b) *instructions* for preparing budget plans; (c) an indication of what *funds* are likely to be available; and (d) overall *priority directions* from the executive leadership. Large municipalities have to create complex budgets that require the harvest of enormous amounts of data and information from every single unit or department. To manage this lengthy process, it is necessary to plan ahead and set up a calendar with specific dates for each unit, specifying the deadline for submission of their financial data to the accounting department. Table 3.3 provides an example of a typical budget calendar that would be issued during the middle of the year before the fiscal year being considered.

Entities in Charge of Budget Preparation or Approval

Local governments usually follow specific guidelines for budget preparation that are provided by higher authorities. Many other players are also involved in the process of preparing the budget. In municipalities in Western countries, the main players are the following:

City council. The city council is responsible for adopting the current and capital budgets for the upcoming fiscal year. Its approval is often issued as a local bylaw or ordinance. The council thus is also responsible for approving modifications to the budget under implementation throughout the fiscal year.

The mayor. The mayor is primarily responsible for the presentation of the city budget to the city council. She or he may delegate the responsibility to a subcommittee of the council, such as a budget committee or standing committee for finance.

Heads of departments. The head of each department, agency, or other independent unit must submit departmental budget plans to the finance officer or the budget committee. The plans should include detailed estimates of the budget needs of the entity for the coming fiscal year (some municipalities require estimates for the next three years as well) and estimates of any revenue anticipated to be collected by the entity.

Chief financial officer. The chief financial officer (CFO) usually leads the day-to-day process of budget preparation and works under the direction of the mayor and the budget committee. The CFO is responsible for reviewing and commenting on the city's budget and its multiyear

Table 3.3 Budget Calendar for Budget Fiscal Year January–December 2010

June 4, 2009	Open budgeting process at division level for budget input.
July 7, 2009	Personnel budget estimates for 2010 to departments for review.
July 2009	Begin citizen survey to help set budget priorities.
July 14, 2009	Close division-level budget plans; open department-level budgeting.
July 20, 2009	Personnel budget for 2010 returned to Finance Department.
July 28, 2009	City council meeting on budget.
August 3, 2009	Finalize fees and service charges.
August 10, 2009	Department budget requests and revenue estimates completed for all funds.
August 20, 2009	Revenue and expenditure summaries due to CFO for review.
September 8–10, 2009	Internal budget review with CFO, department heads, and finance committee.
September 21–25, 2009	Final internal reviews with CFO, department heads, and finance committee.
September 29, 2009	Special meeting with council to present the 2010 Preliminary Budget.
October 7, 2009	Present proposed utility fee adjustments to city council.
October 20, 2009	City clerk publishes notice of public hearing on revenue sources.
November 1, 2009	Preliminary budget filed with city clerk and made available to the public. City clerk publishes notice of filing of preliminary budget and notice of public hearing on budget.
November 2, 2009	Status reports and preliminary budget amendment estimates for 2010 budget to council; public hearing on city's revenue sources and property taxes.
November 14, 2009	Continuation of public hearing on revenue sources and public hearing on proposed budget and levy of property taxes.
December 8, 2009	Second public hearing on budget and council adoption of the budget.
January 1, 2010	Start implementing the new budget.

Source: Adapted by author from a U.S. city government budget calendar.
Note: CFO = chief financial officer.

financial plans. He or she is required to submit periodic reports to the council and mayor on the budget execution progress and the state of the city's economy and finances. The CFO's report should include analysis and evaluation of the city's various operations, fiscal policies, financial transactions, and recommendations.

Legislative Approval of the Budget

Local governments' budgets are prepared by the mayor (or the mayor's designated or delegated representative) and presented before the local government council. After receiving the draft budget document, the council usually turns it over to a committee of the council for scrutiny. The committee will advise the council concerning the budget proposals. In some countries, budgets are prepared by committees of the city council with the help of city executives (such as the standing committee on finance found commonly in local governments in South Asia). As part of its scrutiny, the city council may hold hearings to obtain the advice and opinions of key stakeholders. After completing its examinations, the city council adopts the budget by passing a local appropriations act or council resolution.

The budget thus becomes a local bylaw that cannot be changed by any entity below the council. Should it be deemed necessary, the council may adopt a modified budget, which is called a "supplementary" or "revised" budget. In some countries, regulations require issuing a revised budget if either revenues or expenditures deviate from plans substantially (say, by more than

Municipal Finances

20 percent). Local governments in many developing countries revise the budget just before closing the fiscal year, a practice that undermines the fiscal discipline and control functions of budgeting.

Budget Execution

The *budget execution process* includes the various operations involved in translating the budget statement into decisions and transactions using the budgetary resources. Budget execution commences with the *apportionment* (fund allocation) process, to ensure that the departments or other units receive allotted funds in a systematic manner, so that planned activities are implemented smoothly and without causing cash flow constraints to the city. The apportionment process enables managers to plan and execute spending and projects in accordance with the availability of resources. Once funds are apportioned, departments make *allotments* to their operating units on a monthly or quarterly basis, to control spending during the fiscal year.

During budget execution, multiple subsystems of the city operate in cooperation. Local taxes and other revenues are collected. Cash is managed such that funds temporarily not needed are invested. Supplies, materials, and equipment are procured and paid for. Expenditures incurred are recorded in accounting records and consolidated into financial reports.

Audit

Audits are the final phases in the budget cycle. An audit is an "examination of records, facilities, systems, and other evidences to discover or verify desired information" (Mikesell 2011). The audit seeks to discover deviations from accepted rules and practices and bring out instances of any illegal or irregular transactions or decisions. Audits aim at holding management accountable and preventing repetition of inappropriate actions in the future. The goals of the audit process may vary depending on the purpose of the audit.

Participatory Budgeting—Engaging Stakeholders in Budget Formulation

Participatory budgeting is a democratic process in which citizens or community members are directly involved in decisions about how to spend all or a part of a local budget (www.participatorybudgeting.org). Citizens' involvement varies in form, depth, and breadth. Many local governments have opened up decisions in entire municipal budgets, involving citizen assemblies in setting overall priorities and choosing new investments. States, cities, counties, schools, universities, housing authorities, and coalitions of community groups have used participatory budgeting to open spending decisions to democratic participation. In some cases the local government sets aside a small portion of the budget and entrusts communities to decide priority projects for their neighborhood. Common forms of citizen participation in the budget process are discussed below, along with some challenges to its implementation. Box 3.2 summarizes an example of participatory planning from Kerala, India.

Participatory Budgeting: How Does It Work?

In participatory budgeting, community members make budget decisions through an annual series of local assemblies and meetings. Although there are many models of participatory budgeting, most follow a basic process: diagnosis, discussion, decision making, implementation, and monitoring:

- Residents identify the most important local needs, generate ideas to respond to those needs, and choose budget representatives for each community.

- The representatives discuss the local priorities and together with experts develop concrete projects that address them.

- Residents vote for which of the projects to fund.

- The local government includes them in its budget and allocates funds to implement the chosen projects.

Box 3.2 Participatory Planning in Kerala, India

In 1996 India's Kerala State embarked on a remarkable experiment in local planning and budgeting known as the "People's Plan Campaign for the Ninth Plan" (PPC). The objective of the PPC was to devolve 35 percent of the state development budget from a centralized bureaucracy to local communities, where local people could determine and implement their own priorities. The PPC developed from a series of local-level planning experiments led by the left-of-center parties in the state, led by the Communist Party (Marxist), which experimented with various forms of community mobilization. The PPC unfolded as a sequence of assemblies, seminars, task forces, local council meetings, implementation and monitoring committees, and the like. The meetings were held at the lowest tier of the local government structure, known as the *grama sabha*, in rural localities and the ward committee in urban areas.

These meetings, often facilitated by resource persons from a popular NGO,

discussed and prioritized the various development needs of the community and presented them to the local government council, which consolidated them into a "Development Report." Based on these development priorities, the local government council prepared the annual plan and budget and presented them to the citizens. The plans were then sent to the District Planning Committee, which scrutinized them to iron out inconsistencies, fill in gaps, and thus enable the local plans to be more comprehensive.

The PPC radically improved the delivery of public services, brought about greater caste and ethnic equality, facilitated the increased entry of women into public life, and enhanced democratic practice. The PPC brought about such a radical new model of engaging citizens in community development and decision making that even a change of government in 2001 could not overturn the model.

Source: Franke 2007.

- Residents monitor the implementation of the budget projects.

Where Has It Worked?

The Brazilian city of Porto Allegre started the first full participatory budgeting process in 1989 for its municipal budget. As many as 50,000 people have participated each year in the *orcamento participativo* (the Portuguese term for "participatory budget") that started in Porto Allegre, to decide as much as 20 percent of the city budget. Since 1989, participatory budgeting has spread to more than 1,200 cities in Latin America, North America, Asia, Africa, and Europe (for more details about participation, visit

http://internationalbudget.org). Box 3.3 contains more information on the Porto Allegre experience.

The Pakistan budget law mandates that local governments set aside 25 percent of their local development budgets for "citizens community boards" (CCB). Communities apply to use funds from the CCB budget for small road, drainage, and water improvement projects and commit to pay a portion of project cost (say, 15 percent to 30 percent) as their cash contribution. In Nepal, many water supply projects are initiated, financed, and implemented by water user communities, which receive 50 percent grants from the government, pay 20 percent cash, and borrow about 30 percent of total project cost.

Box 3.3 Participatory Budgeting in Porto Alegre

Participatory planning and management processes in local governance are a precondition to the success of social inclusion strategies where poverty alleviation is a key component. In this perspective, the experience of Brazil's participatory budgeting (OP) is interesting and instructive. The OP has proved to be a more versatile and flexible instrument than originally envisaged. It has offered the poor and the marginalized an unprecedented opportunity to participate in local governance without preempting the statutory powers of elected representatives or the executive authority of municipal officials. Officials and community leaders attest to the OP's impact in promoting a better understanding of the role and functions of local government, a precondition to constructive dialogue, cooperation, and partnership. At the same time there have also been some concerns regarding the outcomes of the OP process, including concerns that funds are allocated to social projects to the detriment of other projects; that investments required for local economic development do not receive as high a priority as they should in a developing country; and that the longer-term perspective is sometimes obscured by the attention to urgent needs.

In addition, the significant commitments of staff time and resources required for effective outreach, organization, and smooth implementation are costs that must be considered.

Despite these concerns, however, there is no doubt that the OP helped trigger a change in the relations between citizens and their municipality, as each side developed a better understanding of the needs, constraints, and roles and responsibilities of the other. The opportunity to participate in decisions regarding the allocation of public funds for projects fostered a shift in the local political culture from confrontational tactics and corrupt political bargaining to constructive debate and civic engagement in governance.

Source: Serageldin et al. 2005.

What Are the Benefits?

Elected officials, community organizations, academics, and international institutions such as the United Nations and the World Bank have declared participatory budgeting a model for democratic government. Why? Their endorsements are based on the following:

- *It gives community members a say.* Ordinary people have more voice, and they get to make real decisions.

- *It produces better and more equitable decisions.* Local residents know best what they need, and budget dollars are redistributed to communities with the greatest needs.

- *It develops active and democratic citizens.* Community members, staff, and officials learn democracy by practicing it. They gain more understanding of complex political issues and community needs.

- *It builds communities and strengthens community organizations.* People get to know their neighbors and feel more connected to their city. Local organizations are able to spend less time lobbying, and more time deciding policies themselves. Budget assemblies connect groups and attract new members.

- *It connects politicians and constituents.* Politicians build closer relationships with their constituents. Community members get to know their elected officials and local governments.

- *It makes government more accountable and efficient.* Local officers are more accountable when community members decide on spending in public assemblies. There are fewer opportunities for corruption, waste, or costly public backlash.

Budget Preparation Techniques

Budget preparation techniques and practices apply the general budget concepts and principles to the formulation of a typical municipal budget. This section identifies and discusses the main components of a municipal budget from both revenue and expenditure sides.

The section will bring together the various concepts through a hands-on exercise in budget formulation. It then turns to the concepts and techniques relating to capital budgeting, including various techniques for appraising investment projects and their applicability in the municipal context. Figure 3.3 is a visual impression of a standard budget; it depicts the form followed throughout this handbook. In contrast to the detailed and lengthy line-item budgets, such short, summary or snapshot budgets are used to

inform management decisions, for reporting, or for communicating with stakeholders, especially citizens.

The Revenue Side of the Municipal Budget

Budget preparation is an iterative process in which draft budget plans and cost or revenue estimates are exchanged vertically between lower-level and higher-level entities, such as departments and their units, or between departments and the city council or its budget committee. Horizontal exchange and coordination across departments, such as service or functional departments and the finance department, are also intensive. Nevertheless, it is the revenue side of the budget that is the logical starting point for three reasons (Lee and Johnson 1998):

- *Preparing entities.* Ascertaining the possible revenues available for appropriation helps the budget preparer to fix the boundaries, in terms of available resources, of the expenditures that the organization can plan.

- *Citizens.* Citizens are usually concerned about taxes and worry at budget time about tax hikes.

- *Politicians.* Political leaders are always conscious that program initiatives leading to higher expenditures, and therefore higher taxes, may have negative effects politically.

Figure 3.3 Standard Budget Structure

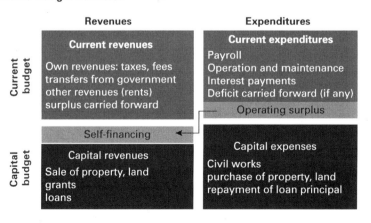

The revenue side of a municipal budget usually has four components: (1) own-source revenues, (2) fiscal transfers from higher governments, (3) shared taxes, and (4) debt or borrowing.

"Own-source revenue" refers to the various tax and nontax sources of revenue that municipalities can collect. They may include property taxes, income taxes, retail sales taxes, and others, depending on national revenue assignment (see chapter 1). Nontax sources include user fees and charges, such as the fee that a vegetable vendor pays to use the municipal market, but also proceeds from the lease or sale of assets. Fiscal transfers are the various grants that higher levels of government provide to municipalities, whether unconditional or conditional. Shared taxes include those that are collected by higher levels of government but whose proceeds are shared with local governments based on a formula. Borrowings are the loans and other forms of debt that municipalities can take on to finance their expenditures (chapter 5 and chapter 7 discuss more details).

At the start of the budget preparation process, the budget office (or the finance or revenue department) surveys the historical trend of revenue collection figures to estimate the resources that can be raised. In addition, the budget office tries to estimate the possibility of increasing tax or other rates or expanding the existing tax base. The budget office will also explore the possibility of new sources of revenue. These efforts are essentially of a technical nature, carried out with a view to presenting options to city management. The city management makes the final call on revenue options, considering their technical, economic, administrative, and political feasibility.

The Expenditure Side of the Municipal Budget

Simultaneously, the budget office informs the departments (or leaders of projects and programs) about the extent of financial support to be expected in the budget and invites their expenditure proposals. The various operating expenditure items, such as salaries and office expenses, are estimated based on historical and current spending trends. The budget office also takes into consideration expected changes in general economic indicators, such as the rate of inflation, in preparing its spending estimates. The plans and information generated and exchanged at this stage also help the units themselves and the budget office to prioritize programs, projects, and expenditures. Usually the budget office gives certain guidelines in advance (through the budget circular) with respect to the various assumptions, trends, and priorities, and that helps the departments and other units prepare their expenditure proposals. The budget office scrutinizes the proposals and finalizes them, often based on bargaining discussions with the respective departments. Those discussions also help the budget office to plan for expenditure management (see also chapter 5).

As mentioned, in the process of preparing the budget, it is essential to collect data on actual revenues and expenses for the last year or two, as well as to propose an estimate of the next year's revenues and expenditures that takes into account changes in policies and events adopted by the governing body. The budget needs to show how much money will be available, where it comes from, and how it will be used.

Capital Budgeting in Municipal Governments

Capital budgeting is a tool for expenditure planning that often includes a multiyear capital improvement plan (CIP) and preparation of an annual capital budget. The capital improvement plan is important because purchasing, development, expansion, or rehabilitation of physical assets requires large money outlays, often beyond the limits of the annual budget. Hence separate, long-term planning is necessary to ensure that projects are evaluated in a systematic manner, from both technical and financial perspectives, to help the city management select a list of projects that are feasible and within the city's operating and financial capabilities. Table 3.4 briefly summarizes the logical flow of a capital planning and

Table 3.4   Logical Flow of the Capital Budgeting Process

Phases	Steps	Results
Planning	Update inventory and assess asset condition.	An inventory of infrastructure with analysis of condition and adequacy of maintenance spending.
	Identify projects.	A project list with rough cost estimates (capital improvement plan).
	Project evaluation	Detailed costing of both construction costs and subsequent operating costs, estimation of any revenue, comparison with strategic plans, and cost-benefit analysis to identify priorities.
	Project ranking	Ranking of projects using capital budgeting techniques.
Budgeting	Financing	Financing arrangements for projects to be included in the budget.
	Budget	Expenditures included in budget proposals of the appropriate departments, their placement in resource envelope available to government, inclusion of project operating costs in the long-term budget forecasts for period when project is completed and running.
Execution	Procurement	Process for selection of contractors for projects.
	Monitoring	Review of physical and financial progress of project; coordination of spending with revenue flow.
Auditing	External audit	Ex-post review of financial records upon project completion.

budgeting process. Capital improvement planning and capital budgeting are different in scope and time frame, but both largely follow the same logic, processes, and techniques.

The capital budget may be a section of the overall budget (as in figure 3.3) or issued as a separate document. The capital budget should have cost estimates for all infrastructure projects that are proposed, including both the investment cost and implications for the operating budget (Mikesell 2011). Capital budget preparation requires ranking project proposals using capital budgeting techniques such as payback period, the net present value method, internal rate of return, or profitability index. They are discussed in detail in chapters 4, 5, and 6.

Issues, Practices, and Challenges in Municipal Budgeting

Though the principles of budgeting are uniform globally, the reality is not. The rules and practices of budget formulation differ from country to country, and even within a country the basic principles, issues, and challenges may vary. Here we put the differences in the rules and procedures aside and

look at a few common issues that affect the budgeting practices of local governments everywhere. This section discusses some practical difficulties that municipal finance officers face, particularly in developing countries, focusing on problems that prevent the preparation of realistic and comprehensive budgets and ways to address them.

Comprehensiveness

As a basic principle, the municipal budget should be comprehensive, covering all areas (each service or function) and aspects (revenue, expenditure, short- and long-term impacts) of functioning. Against this principle, municipal budgets in most developing countries deal only with the revenues and expenditures of core governmental functions and do not include ancillary activities carried out by the city. For example, the municipal budget often does not include the expected revenues and expenditures of municipal enterprises such as a water supply company that is organized and managed as an independent company.

The other concern regarding budget comprehensiveness relates to the extent of decentralization and the transfer of powers and functions to local governments (see chapter 1). Even in decentralized settings, where local governments are expected to take the lead in local development activities, budget allocations from central ministries are often made to line departments and not routed through local governments' plans and budgets. This often creates fragmentation in planning and execution, as well as tensions between local governments and the line departments.

Realism

Budgets are useful to the extent that they are realistic. The four main shortcomings in this regard are political distortions, information shortage, incremental budgeting, and balloon budgeting.

Politicized budgeting. Often in developing countries, budget presentation is an opportunity for political grandstanding by the mayor and city council. As a result, the municipal budget document reads more like a wish list of programs and projects divorced from financial reality. Such a situation arises from weak accountability of city management to its citizens and stakeholders and also from soft budget constraint by the higher-level government. In other words, where there is a strong accountability framework and the national government exerts hard budget constraint, city managements hesitate to announce grand plans and projects without ascertaining that they have adequate financial resources.

Shortage of timely information. Another hurdle to local budgeting arises when local governments do not know beforehand the fiscal transfers that they will receive from the national government. That occurs because of a weak intergovernmental fiscal relationship, or where central governments do not feel obliged to announce in advance the transfers and entitlement payments due. It weakens the ability of local governments to forecast revenues or forces them to make estimates in their budget documents based on guesses.

Incremental budgeting. Local governments sometimes fail to use proper techniques and instruments in preparing budget estimates.

Service or line departments and budget officers often project revenues or expenses by simply increasing the actual results of the current year, adding, say, 5 percent or 10 percent to every line. This is not a bad way to start, since it at least might factor in inflation, but a major trouble is that inflation may have different impacts on revenues and expenses and on different revenue and expenditure items. Realistic estimates should reflect good understanding of future events, along with natural uncertainties. For instance, a 20 percent increase in tax revenues could be realistic if the city council has approved a rate increase or if the tax base is expanding because of the dynamic growth of housing.

Weaknesses in Budget Execution

The most common weakness in budget execution is a disconnect between the budget document and daily expenditure decisions. The signs include (a) huge overspending in some line items without any discussion or higher-level approval; (b) delays in budget execution due to delayed transfers from the central government; (c) unclear distinction between revenue and expenditure items; (d) a revised budget issued at the very end of the fiscal year with huge changes from the initial budget plan; and (e) a huge deficit at year-end, when a balanced or surplus budget was planned. All are results of weak fiscal control and discipline in the municipality.

The central governments in developing countries often approve development grants very early in the fiscal year, rather than the year before. Development projects thus often start at midyear or in the third quarter of the fiscal year. As a result, development funds remain unspent at the end of the fiscal year, causing a large but artificial surplus in the closing budget. It is particularly confusing if there is no clear distinction between current and development expenses. Quite often weak procurement and cash management systems result in overspending or in delayed budget execution, eventually constraining local governments from implementing their budgets efficiently and timely. Councils are often forced to alter their budgets and approve a supplementary budget during the fiscal year, undermining the authority of the budget process, as well as its planning and control functions.

Budget Monitoring

Successful budget execution depends to a large extent on robust budget monitoring by top executives (such as the mayor or city manager) and the city council. Especially in large cities, however, budgets involve hundreds of millions in financial resources and plans and projects in a variety of sectors. The magnitude often reduces the ability of the council and executives to monitor budget execution and exercise control. Management information systems, discussed in this section, are useful tools to track budget execution, identify weaknesses promptly, and take remedial action.

Management Information Systems

A management information system (MIS) involves three primary resources: people, technology, and information. Management information systems are different from other systems, such as an accounting or procurement system, because they are used to analyze activities from the perspective of management decision making. MISs help city governments to realize the maximum benefit from their investments in personnel, equipment, and business processes. All local governments use information systems at all levels of operation to collect, process, and store data; an MIS does those things in a timely, systematic, and comprehensive fashion. MIS data are aggregated and disseminated in the form that city managers need to carry out their functions.

The term "MIS" may conjure up the image of sophisticated computers and highly qualified analysts crunching reams of data and producing complicated spreadsheets and charts. Although management information systems can be very sophisticated, they can also be implemented in very simple ways to support efficient and effective decision making. For example, a city government can use an MIS to track the patterns of its revenues and expenditures. Analysis of revenue collections may show that property tax collections are higher in certain wards of the city, compared to others. That could prompt the city management to investigate the reasons for the variation and redistribute resources to help the areas that are not performing well. There are simple techniques, easy to implement, that can provide useful insights into the efficiency of budget execution. (Chapter 8 includes a detailed discussion of performance measurement.)

Budget-Actual Variances

Budget-actual variance analysis is an old and simple tool for budget monitoring. It is often not possible to create a perfect budget because some future events are unpredictable. But a well-developed and realistic one that is based on the actual financial situation, current and past, can be the best road map to efficient financial management. For example, uncertainties or unexpected financial developments, such as an increase in unemployment because of an economic downturn, or major damage to a water treatment plant due to severe weather, can result in revenue shortages and a parallel increase on the expenses side. Such occurrences will cause differences between the budgeted and actual amounts that need special attention when the budget is revisited and refined. But variances that are not generated by such unforeseen events should be minimized.

Two types of variances occur, favorable or unfavorable:

- Favorable variance occurs when actual results are better than budgeted or planned (F). Costs are lower, or revenue is higher, than expected.

- Unfavorable variance occurs when actual results are worse than budgeted or planned (U). Costs are higher, or revenue is lower, than expected.

Variance analysis is a tool to evaluate variances in revenues and expenses. It reveals whether the government is operating within its authorized resources. A variance, positive or negative, often calls for explanations. Thus, it is important to analyze and understand the causes of variances and take corrective action. Not all variances are worth investigation, however. For example, a variance of only 1 percent of spending is well within the normal range. A variance of 10 percent or more in spending is likely to signal that something is wrong and warrants attention. Proper variance analysis requires some thought to (a) analyze the variances, (b) identify the causes, and (c) take appropriate action.

Variances can occur for many reasons, such as changes in funding levels due to inflation, population change, or government funding decisions and policies. Changes in the cost of services, labor, or material can also cause variances in budgets.

Table 3.5 presents an example of a variance calculation for expense items of a water utility. The table shows a huge total variance of 35 percent that deserves attention and remedies. First, each cost item needs close scrutiny. For example, we might find that the increased cost of water provision is due to an increased energy tariff, which would be beyond the control of management. Meanwhile, the cost of fee collection has jumped by $11,000, which could be acceptable only if fees collected had experienced an even greater increase.

Accounting

This section discusses the basic concepts and principles of accounting, with an overview of its subject matter. The objective of the section is to introduce the reader to the role of accounting as the basis for documenting, classifying, and organizing financial information in a systematic manner. The section also provides a brief overview of the types of accounting and their relationship to auditing and the various accounting standards.

Accounting Concepts and Terms

The role of accounting in managing organizations. Accounting systems are used to provide complete, timely, and accurate information concerning revenues, expenditures, assets, and liabilities. Within a local government, accounting records provide information on billing taxpayers and receiving tax payments, paying employees, and paying vendors and contractors for goods, work, and services. Accounting systems also inform management and external stakeholders about the financial resources, the efficiency of the organization's financial management, and its financial position during and at the end of the financial year (Lee and Johnson 1998).

Difference between accounting and bookkeeping. People often mistakenly use the terms "bookkeeping" and "accounting" to mean the same thing. Accounting is concerned with identifying how transactions and events should be described in financial reports. It is also concerned

Table 3.5 **Example of Variances between Budgeted and Actual Expenses for a Water Utility**

Expense item	Budget ($)	Actual ($)	Variance ($)	Variance (%)
Cost of water provision	140,000	$190,000	50,000 U	36
Cost of fee collection	28,000	39,000	11,000 U	39
Administrative expense	60,000	85,000	25,000 U	42
Other expenses	12,000	10,500	−1,500 F	−13
Total	240,000	$324,500	84,500 U	35

Note: U = unfavorable variance; F = favorable variance.

with designing bookkeeping systems that make it easy to produce useful reports and to control an organization's operations. Thus, accounting is broader than bookkeeping, and accounting requires more professional expertise and judgment. Bookkeeping is the process of recording transactions and other events, either manually or with computers. Bookkeeping is critical to accounting, but it is only the clerical part of the accounting process.

Types of Accounting

Although accounting may seem to be a single term and subject, in fact various types of accounting exist, and each plays a specific role in the financial management of organizations. The most important accounting types include financial accounting, cost accounting, management accounting, and public sector or commercial accounting.

- *Financial accounting* provides information to management and external stakeholders, such as a city council, shareholders, or citizens, on the receipts, expenditures, assets, and liabilities of a municipality. In other words, financial accounting is concerned with the reporting of financial transactions and the financial position of the municipality, monthly, quarterly, and at the close of the financial year.

- *Cost accounting* provides information to management on the cost of operations and helps with measuring and controlling the costs of specific services or functions. Cost accounting is an internal function and generates information relating to historical costs of operations and efficiency. Although cost accounting uses information from the financial records, its methods and processes are different.

- *Management accounting* is a later development of cost accounting in which the data and information from cost accounting are converted into decision reports for management, using various analytical and presentation techniques.

- *Public sector accounting and commercial accounting*, in their basic principles, are the same. Certain specific accounting practices that suit accounting in government organizations create the differences between the two. One of the most visible differences is that local governments in the developing countries use *single-entry cash basis* accounting. In contrast, the vast majority of commercial entities use *double-entry accrual basis* accounting. Furthermore, government accounting is based on the annual budget process, and therefore budget allocations, appropriations, and commitments become very significant.

Key Terms in Public Sector Accounting

Public sector accounting has three building blocks: *allocation, appropriation,* and *commitment*. We briefly introduce these three terms because they keep popping up during discussions on municipal financial management; a detailed discussion is beyond the scope of this chapter. It is important, however, to be familiar with their definitions and implications in the budgeting process. Box 3.4 provides some concrete examples for applying these terms.

Appropriation. An appropriation is the total amount of resources a local government department can spend for the entire fiscal year. Spending authorizations granted by the legislature (e.g., the city council) depend on both the budget system and the nature of the expenditure. Authorizations that permit government departments or units to incur obligations and to make payments out of public funds are usually granted through appropriation, a financing source against which expenses must be matched and reported on the statement of operations. The receipt of an appropriation is recorded at the departmental level only.

Allocation. Allocation is a budget execution process to allocate funds to the program level; it is a percentage of an appropriation that is

Box 3.4 Examples of Appropriation, Allocation, and Commitments

Appropriation example. The federal Environment Protection Agency approved a grant of $200,000 to a city's Division of Debris Removal. This grant is an appropriation or funding for a specific purpose, to enable the division to assist the city in an emergency cleanup of its hazardous yard trash disposal site.

Allocation example. Usually in the educational system, funds may not be provided to schools based solely on academic need, but rather poverty must be considered as the determiner. The purpose of the "allocations" funds is to help disadvantaged children meet high academic standards through food programs, after-school or summer programs, and the like. The district determines the per pupil expenditure (PPE) as a measuring tool, and then schools are sorted by poverty level. For example, if school A has 75 percent poor children, it receives 1.4 times the PPE in allocation funds; school B, with 35 percent of its students in poverty, receives 1.25 times the PPE, and so forth.

Commitment example. In the United States, central government or federal agencies commit funds for large projects. For example, the U.S. Department of Transportation agreed to commit resources to fund a bridge project in the District of Columbia.

earmarked for a specific agency or staff office. The receipt of an allocation is usually recorded at the intermediate and activity levels.

Commitments. Commitments or obligations, also known as "encumbrances," are legal pledges to provide finance. Broadly, a commitment arises when a purchase order is made or a contract is signed, implying that goods will be delivered or services rendered and that a bill will have to be paid later on. The commitment is recorded for the amount of the obligation for one fiscal year.

Budgetary or appropriation accounting. Budgetary or appropriation accounting consists of tracking and registering operations concerning appropriations and their uses. It should cover appropriations, apportionment, any increase or decrease in appropriations, commitments or obligations, expenditures at the verification or delivery stage, and payments. Budgetary accounting is only one element of a government accounting system, but it is the most crucial both for formulating policy and for supervising budget implementation.

Commitments or obligations accounting. This kind of accounting is essential in keeping budget implementation under control. Most developed countries keep registers of their transactions at each stage of the expenditure cycle, or at least at the obligation stage and the payment stage. Commitments or obligations accounting provides the basis for budget revisions. Decisions to increase or decrease appropriations and the preparation of cash plans must take into account commitments already made.

Accounting Standards and Standard Setters

Accounting standards enable accountants to apply a common approach to their treatment of financial transactions, thereby ensuring comparability of financial reports. Although the basic principles of accounting are universal, their application in public and private sector organizations and specific business situations is determined by accounting standards. Accounting standards are usually set by national-level, standard-setting bodies, the ministry of finance, or the office of the auditor general in developing countries. In the United States, the Government Accounting Standards Board (GASB) sets standards for government accounting, and the Financial Accounting Standards Board (FASB) sets standards for the private sector. At the global level, the International Accounting Standards Board (IASB) sets the International Financial Reporting Standards. Similarly, the International Public Sector Accounting Standards (IPSAS) are issued by the IPSAS board, which is a part of the International Federation of Accountants (IFAC) (www.ifac .org). Box 3.5 offers a glimpse of the historical emergence of accounting.

The relationship between accounting and auditing. Auditing is a process of independent verification of financial processes and statements. Thus, auditing commences after the accounts have been prepared and finalized. The audit can be internal or external; the verifier can be an internal person (independent of the entities that complete financial reports) or an external entity, typically a private or central public auditing office. The purpose of an audit is primarily to provide assurance to stakeholders of the credibility of an organization's financial statements. The organization

prepares annual financial statements based on the information in its accounting records. The external audit is an independent verification of them. The auditor expresses an opinion concerning whether the financial statements present a true and fair view of the organization's financial affairs.

Accounting Principles and Practices

This section elaborates the basic principles of accounting and forms the foundation for the remaining discussions on accounting. It strives to help the reader understand the building blocks of accounting for financial transactions. Simple numerical examples illustrate the theory, and exercises help to test one's grasp of the principles discussed.

Accounting is based on a few basic principles:

- *Business entity principle.* This principle requires that every organization be accounted for separately and distinctly from its owners. It also requires a local government to account separately each entity it may control. The reason behind this is that separate information for each entity is relevant to decisions that the entity would make.

Box 3.5 Accounting in Historical Perspective

The first known accountants worked for the religious authorities in ancient Mesopotamia (now Iraq), making sure that people paid their taxes (of sheep and other agricultural produce) to the temples. In trying to keep track of who owed what, they had to issue receipts and IOUs ("I owe you"—a promise to pay) and accidentally invented writing.

Thousands of years later, in late medieval Italy, double-entry bookkeeping emerged.

The man who first wrote down the method, Luca Pacioli, was a Franciscan friar. Double-entry bookkeeping recognizes that all transactions have two aspects—a credit and a debit—and in a properly constituted set of books, the two sets of figures always balance. For those of a particular turn of mind, the balance has a beauty, maybe even divinely inspired.

Source: http://news.bbc.co.uk/go/pr/fr/-/1/hi/magazine/8552220.stm.

- *Objectivity principle.* It requires the information in financial statements to be supported by evidences (invoice, receipt, etc.) other than someone's imagination or personal opinion. The reason for it is to make financial statements useful by ensuring that they present reliable information.

- *Cost principle.* This principle requires the information in financial statements to be based on costs incurred in transactions, consistent with the objectivity principle.

- *Going concern principle.* This principle requires accountants to prepare financial statements under the assumption that the business will continue operating. It is not especially relevant for local governments, as they are expected to exist ad infinitum. However, some of the enterprises that local governments may establish (for example, a local water company) are susceptible to failure and closure.

Accounting Practices

This section introduces the reader to the practice of basic bookkeeping, the chart of accounts and the various books of accounts, computerized accounting, and the preparation of trial balances. It discusses the standard formats or templates for basic accounting records such as the journal, ledger, and cash book and summarizes good principles of maintaining accounting records. This section will help the reader to understand the organization of accounting information through the Chart of Accounts, and consolidation financial records through the Trial Balance and Final Accounts. Finally, a brief discussion sheds light on the role of information technology in the recording and compilation of accounting information, with a reference to standard accounting software packages and integrated financial information systems (IFMIS).

Entries. Regardless of the type of organization or the type of financial transaction, accounts are maintained within sets of books called "journals" and "ledgers." Journals are the *books of original entry,* and ledgers are called *books of final entry*. Transactions are initially recorded in journals when they occur and are later posted to the relevant accounts in the ledgers. Table 3.6 is a snapshot of a journal in which transactions are entered in chronological order from original vouchers.

Accountants using manual systems may still write the same entry several times—first in the journal and then into various ledgers. Computerized systems do this by one keyboard entry that immediately generates all of the required subsequent entries automatically.

T-accounts. In the simplest form, an account looks like the letter *T*. When a T-account is used, increases are placed on one side of the account and the decreases on the other side. That makes it easy to determine the balance of the account. The balance of an asset account is the amount of the asset owned by the entity on the date the balance is calculated. The balance of a liability

Table 3.6 Sample of a Journal (any currency)

#	Date	Voucher no.	Description	Debit amount	Credit amount
1	8/3/2012	1529	Mr. Brown, property tax payment	400	
2	8/5/2012	37245	Mr. Green, water bill payment	125	
3	5/6/2012	525	Electricity (street lighting) bill		1,325
4	8/5/2012	6473	Ms. Watt, rental bill payment	250	
5	8/7/2012	1530	Mr. Moron, property tax payment	820	

account is the amount owed by the entity on the date of the balance.

In the T-account, the left side is called the debit side, abbreviated *Dr,* and the right side is called the credit side, abbreviated *Cr.* When amounts are entered on the left side of an account, they are called *debits,* and the account is said to be *debited.* When amounts are entered on the right side, they are called *credits,* and the account is said to be *credited.* The difference between the total debits and the total credits recorded in an account is the *account balance.* In other words, there is a debit balance when the sum of the debits exceeds the sum of the credits and a credit balance when the sum of the credits exceeds the sum of the debits. Figure 3.4 shows the accounts after Mr. Moron paid half of his annual property tax dues.

Single-Entry versus Double-Entry Accounting

Single-entry accounting systems record transactions line by line, in the order of occurrence, to a simple journal or cash book. Small organizations and some local governments follow single-entry accounting. Rather than use modern accounting systems, they record only one aspect of a transaction in the account books. They may also maintain separate records for some transactions, such as lists of arrears or receivables, or payables, or asset records (discussed in chapter 6). Those records, however, are not integrated into the financial statements and at best are attached as memo items to financial reports. Thus, the single-entry system does not provide a comprehensive picture of the financial affairs of the entity and for that reason

is not a preferred method of accounting. Recall that we have said that any financial transaction essentially has two aspects—the debit aspect and the credit aspect. Modern systems of accounting recognize both the debit and credit aspects, as in the example in table 3.6, and record each transaction as an entry into two (or more) separate ledger accounts. This is called the double-entry accounting system.

Principles and Procedures of Double-Entry Accounting

Double-entry accounting, also known as the double-entry system of bookkeeping, is a system in which each transaction has two fundamental aspects, the receiving of a benefit and the giving of a benefit. Both aspects are recorded in the same set of books. In accounting, the one who receives is a debtor, and the transaction is recorded as a debit on a particular account (dr). The one who gives is a creditor, and the transaction is recorded as a credit on another account (cr). Under the double-entry system, every debit must have a corresponding credit and vice versa, and the total of the debit entries and the credit entries must be equal. In deciding which account has to be debited and which account has to be credited, the accounting equation below should be used:

$$\text{assets} = \text{liabilities} + \text{equity}.$$

The components of the accounting equation can be summarized in the balance sheet. Table 3.7 shows a simple balance sheet of an independent housing management unit of a municipality. In practice, however, local government organizations tend to have more complex balance sheets than that one.

The fundamental principle of the double-entry system lies in analyzing the two changes involved in a business transaction and properly recording both of the changes in the books of accounts. For the accounts to remain in balance, a debit (dr) change in one or several accounts must be matched with a credit (cr) change in

Figure 3.4   Example of a T-Account

Table 3.7 Balance Sheet of a Housing Management Unit of a Municipality

Assets		Liabilities and owners' equity	
Cash	$5,600	Liabilities	
Accounts receivable	$4,200	Notes payable	$10,000
Inventory	$9,000	Accounts payable	$20,000
		Total liabilities	$30,000
Fixed assets		Owners' equity	
Buildings and equipment	$7,000	Capital stock	$7,000
Land	$12,000	Retained earnings	$800
		Total owners' equity	$7,800
Total	$37,800	Total	$37,800

one or several other accounts. Therefore, after a series of transactions, the sum of all the accounts with a debit balance will equal the sum of all the accounts with a credit balance.

The main terms used in double-entry accounting are the following:

Journal. This is the book in which all transactions are recorded at first, using the double-entry format of debit and credit.

Ledger. This is the second process, in which the journal entries are posted to another book known as a ledger. In the ledger, all the accounts are classified and individually maintained. Each ledger (account) has two identical sides—a left side (debit) and a right side (credit), and all the transactions relating to that account are recorded chronologically.

Trial balance. This is the third process, in which the arithmetical accuracy of the books of account, at a point in time, is tested by means of a trial balance. It is an informal accounting schedule or statement that lists the ledger account balances and compares the total debit balance with the total credit balance.

Final accounts. In the final process, the result of the full year's operational activities is determined through final accounts—the "statement of receipts and payments" (called an "income statement" in business accounting) and a balance sheet; these are described in detail in the section on financial reporting.

Examples of Double-Entry Bookkeeping

Let us look at some examples that illustrate the double-entry system of recording business transactions into debit and credit accounts (see tables 3.8 through 3.12).

Example 1: The Municipal Company purchased $7,000 worth of machinery and paid in cash.

Analysis of transaction: Increase in assets (equipment) by $7,000, and decrease in assets (cash) by $7,000.

Example 2: The company borrowed $15,000 from a bank.

Analysis of transaction: Increase in assets (cash) by $15,000, and increase in liabilities (payables, that is, borrowings) by $15,000.

Example 3: The company paid a utility bill of $1,000 by check.

Analysis of transaction: Increase in expenses by $1,000 and decrease in assets (cash) by $1,000.

Example 4: The company generated sales revenue the amount of $12,000; 60 percent of sales was received in cash, and 40 percent on credit.

Analysis of transaction: Increase in revenue (sales) by $12,000, increase in assets (cash) by $7,200 ($12,000*60 percent), and increase in assets (receivables) by $4,800.

Example 5: A partner invested $20,000 in the company.

Analysis of transaction: Increase in assets (cash) of $20,000; increase in owner's equity of $20,000.

Table 3.8 Purchase of Machinery

Ledger entry	Debit	Credit
Equipment	$7,000	
Cash		$7,000

Table 3.9 Borrowing

Ledger entry	Debit	Credit
Cash	$15,000	
Borrowing		$15,000

Table 3.10 Paying a Utility Bill

Ledger entry	Debit	Credit
Expenses (utilities)	$1,000	
Cash		$1,000

Table 3.11 Sales of Goods

Ledger entry	Debit	Credit
Cash	$7,200	
Receivables	$4,800	
Revenues (sales)		$12,000

Table 3.12 Equity Received

Ledger entry	Debit	Credit
Cash	$20,000	
Owner's equity		$20,000

The Chart of Accounts

The *chart of accounts* is basically a structure of identifying numbers assigned to each account to identify various functional areas or segments of the local government. The charts of accounts for local governments are often regulated by higher government entities and issued in laws or ordinances, for example, by the ministry of finance or the office of the auditor general. Because the numbers are assigned in order, local governments are allowed, and even encouraged, to add more detailed subaccount numbers into the regulated chart of accounts.

The chart of accounts in a small municipality may be very simple. The left side of table 3.13 shows a general structure of main accounts; the right side indicates the structure of the numbering of various accounts and subaccounts. A longer number indicates a lower rank of subaccount. Thus, users such as local governments can add more numbers to the end of some account numbers to enable more specific segregation of various transactions, such as the cost of energy use by office buildings (account 1501) or by schools (account 1502).

Bases of Accounting

Accounting systems could be quite different in scope and methodology. Accounting of financial transactions can be different depending on the *basis of accounting*. The "basis" refers to the

Table 3.13 Chart of Accounts

Accounts	Numbers	Sample asset accounts
		101 Cash (cash in hand)
		105 Bank accounts
		150 Buildings
		1501 Office buildings
Assets	100–199	1502 School buildings
		151 Accumulated depreciation
Liabilities	200–299	160 Vehicles and equipment
Revenues	300–399	170 Investments and stocks
Operating expenses	400–499	190 Other assets

timing of recording a financial transaction, that is, whether it is recorded at the time of its occurrence or at the time of the exchange of cash. The former is called *accrual-based accounting,* and the latter is called *cash-based accounting.* These are the two main systems, but there are others that are somewhere in between, which may be called "modified accrual" or "modified cash basis."

Cash-based accounting. In cash-based accounting, record keeping works on a strictly cash-in, cash-out basis. That is, financial transactions are recorded only when money actually changes hands:

- Income is recorded only when money (cash or a check) or revenue is actually received. Therefore, a tax bill issued is not recorded as revenue, only the tax actually paid in and appearing in cash or in the bank account of the municipality.

- Expenses are recorded only when they are actually paid. Thus, an electricity bill received is not recorded as an expense until and unless it is actually paid to the electricity company.

Accrual-based accounting. In the accrual-based accounting system, transactions are accounted as revenues or expenses independent of the movement of cash:

- Income is recorded when it is earned, even if the money has not yet been received.

- Expenses are recorded when they are incurred—not necessarily when they are actually paid.

In accrual-based accounting, total revenues and expenses are shown in the financial statements whether or not cash was received or paid out in a particular accounting period. In other words, income is reported in the period when it is earned, regardless of when it is received,

and expenses are deducted in the period when they are incurred, whether they are paid or not. Using accrual-basis accounting, an organization records both revenues and expenses when the transactions occur. Accrual accounting is the most common method used by businesses and is increasingly used by local governments as well.

For example, if a municipality sells an old truck for $5,000, under the cash method, that amount is not recorded in the books until the buyer pays the money to the municipal cashier or the cashier receives a check from the buyer. In contrast, under the accrual method, the $5,000 is recorded as revenue immediately, when the sale is complete (the contract is signed, and the buyer takes the truck), even if the money is only received a few days or months later. The same applies to expenses. If the water department receives an electric bill for $1,700, under the cash method, the amount is added to the books only after the department has actually paid the bill. Under the accrual method, the $1,700 is recorded as an expense the day the bill is received.

Modified accrual-based accounting. Although most local governments in developing countries use cash-based accounting, several developed countries have been moving toward the use of an accrual basis. However, a strict accrual basis is not feasible for many local governments, and thus most of them have been using modified accrual accounting. That generally means that they account all expenditures, regardless of whether cash is paid out, but recognize revenue only when it becomes both available and measurable, rather than when it is earned. The reason for this choice is their limited ability or capacity to collect billed and due revenues, such as taxes, water or solid waste fees, and so on.

Trial balance. As discussed, in a double-entry accounting system, every transaction is recorded with equal debits and credits. As a result, one knows that an error has been made if the total of the debits in the ledger does not equal the total of the credits. Also, when the balances of the accounts are determined, the sum of the debit balances must equal the sum of the credit balances. This equality is tested by preparing a *trial balance*. When a trial balance does not balance, it indicates an error in the account balances. The error(s) may have been in journalizing the transactions, in posting to the ledgers, in determining the account balances, in copying the balances to the trial balance, or in adding the columns of the trial balance.

However, a trial balance is not by itself a proof of complete accuracy. Some *compensating errors* do not affect the equality of the trial balance because they affect the debit and credit sides equally. Locating errors and rectifying them are

part of the work that accountants do in preparing the final accounts and are not dealt with in detail here.

Manual versus Computerized Accounting Systems

The increasing use of computers in accounting is a significant trend that changed accounting practices beginning in the latter half of the twentieth century. Some Asian countries still rely on manual accounting, often with computer assistance, such that simple Excel tables are created to generate reports, but the legally binding records are manual. Box 3.6 shows the manual ledger of a municipality in Pakistan, with handwritten entries and the fingerprints of illiterate customers. Computerization has changed the

Box 3.6 Manual Bookkeeping in Pakistan

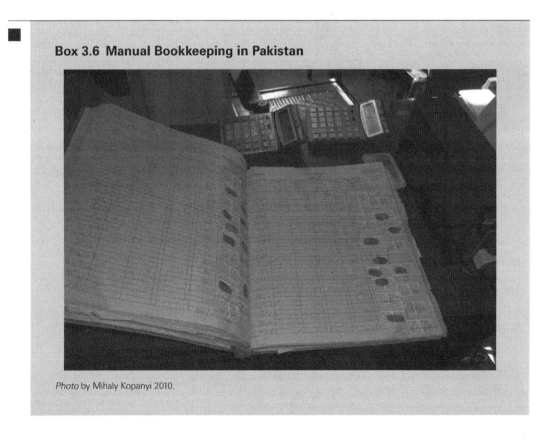

Photo by Mihaly Kopanyi 2010.

defining characteristic of accounting from a focus on recording financial transactions to serving structured information to management and stakeholders.

This interface of accounting with information systems includes people, procedures, equipment, and their interactions. Modern accounting systems are designed to capture data relating to financial transactions and to generate from these data a variety of financial, managerial, and tax accounting reports and visual summaries. These can take different forms, from low-cost accounting software packages in small organizations to very expensive and complicated enterprise resource planning software in big ones. These systems computerize activities such as recording transactions in the journal and ledger, generating the trial balance, and preparing the financial statements. In addition, most accounting software packages come with modules on budgeting, inventory, billing, and the like, increasing their usefulness for municipalities.

Good Practices in Maintaining Books of Accounts

In this section we summarize practical approaches, experiences, and good practices in local government accounting.

- *Basics first.* It is important for municipalities to make sure that they are able to fulfill basic accounting functions such as preparing journals and ledgers, posting transactions on a daily basis, tallying cash balances at the close of a business day, and the like, which will make them better prepared to move into advanced accounting practices such as accrual-based accounting or integrated financial management systems.

- *Double-entry accounting system first.* Local governments should start with cash-based double-entry accounting, recording both

aspects of transactions. Often this is misunderstood as implementing accrual-based accounting, but that is a completely different approach and more difficult to implement. It is better, first, to gain experience working with a cash-based double-entry system and then enhance the municipal accounting system in a stable and systematic manner.

- *Computerize after strengthening business processes.* Although computerization of accounting procedures improves efficiency, if local governments computerize without changing their underlying processes, the effectiveness of the whole system is reduced, since the inefficiencies of the old system persist ("Garbage in garbage out"). Therefore, local governments embarking on computerization should start with a detailed analysis of their financial procedures and systems and identify ways to improve them before computerizing the process.

- *Revenues and expenses are recorded at the time they are earned and due.* This principle is critical in accounting and should be the cornerstone of an organization's accounting for transactions. Often financial officers and city managements are under pressure to paint a rosy picture of their finances. That pressure causes them to recognize revenues much before they are actually collected, or not to pay or record expenses when they are due. If payments due are delayed because of a shortage of cash, or if contractors are paid without delivery of services to prevent budget allocations from being turned back to the ministry of finance at the end of the fiscal year, it is equally problematic. These practices distort the true financial position of the local government and should be avoided.

- *Final accounts should be comprehensive.* The annual financial statements of any entity are intended to provide a comprehensive picture of the entity's financial performance for the stated period. Local governments may have subsidiaries or related enterprises whose finances are not reported in or along with the financial statements. Again, such practices distort the financial picture of the local government. For example, if a municipality owns a water distribution company, even though the company is a separate entity, because it is fully owned and controlled by the municipality, its financials should be included and reported as part of the municipality's off-budget financial reports.

- *Final accounts should be prepared in a timely manner*. Final accounts should be prepared within a reasonable time after the close of the financial year. Although companies are usually required by law to prepare their annual financial statements within a reasonable period (usually three to six months after the close of the financial year), local governments often do not conform to such stringent standards. Timely annual financial statements let stakeholders know the financial performance for the past year. If statements are delayed, their informational value is eroded.

- *Accounts should be audited by independent external auditors*. An annual audit by independent external auditors enhances the credibility of financial statements. The auditors' management letter or opinion also provides valuable feedback that should be acted on. Where no definite arrangement exists for annual external audits, local governments should voluntarily initiate audits of their financial statements, in consultation with the Supreme Audit Institution or with the professional organization of auditors in their country. To enhance transparency and accountability, the municipality should also publish the audit report and opinion in a forum or location where the community and other stakeholders can access them.

- *Invest in capacity building and training*. Staff skills and capacities are very important for the effective and efficient performance of any system. As municipal governments improve their accounting systems and processes, it is important to strengthen the technical and managerial skills and capacities of the staff who manage the systems. Junior staff should be trained in the technical processes of bookkeeping and accounting, and higher-level staff should be trained in financial management concepts and practices to equip them to use accounting data to improve the organization's efficiency and effectiveness.

- *Treat accounts as an information system*. Accounting forms the backbone of the financial record system of any organization. At the same time, the value of accounting is in management's use of accounting information for decision making. In municipal governments, accounting records should not be seen just as historical records of financial transactions. They should be seen as the organization's financial information system, providing valuable information regarding operational and financial efficiencies and conveying the financial performance of the organization to citizens and stakeholders.

Detailed Discussion of Accounting Books and Financial Statements

This section further addresses the details of accounting and bookkeeping practices. In a business, it is normal to encounter a significant volume of transactions of various kinds that have an impact on the entity's financial position. Recording all of the transactions to the general ledger directly may cause mistakes; that is the reason why the process of recording transactions is divided into two steps. First, transactions are recorded in the general journal, which is one of the accounting prime entry books. Second, entries from the general journal are posted to the general ledger, which is composed of the corresponding accounts (or categories) that constitute the balance sheet and income statement. To illustrate, let us assume that a city with double-entry accounting collected property taxes of $20,000 and paid employee benefits of $5,000 on November 20.

Journal

All the business transactions are recorded in the general journal daily and in chronological order. Although the structure and form of a general journal vary depending on business needs, the recording of some data in a journal is mandatory. Table 3.14 shows an example of a general journal template with columns for the mandatory data. They are (a) date of transaction; (b) names or reference numbers of the accounts that are debited and credited; (c) a description of the transaction; and (d) columns for debits and credits to record the exact amounts of each business transaction.

General Ledger

The next step after recording all the business transactions in the general journal and using the T-accounts is to post the transactions to the general ledger accounts.

T-accounts also form part of the year-end posting. During the posting process, one can use the T-accounts to help minimize errors in posting corresponding transactions. The second step thus is to post the journal entries to the general ledger using the T-accounts, as shown in table 3.15. Notice that every transaction is posted both as a debit and as a credit, for example, cash debit $20,000 and property tax credit $20,000.

General ledger accounts classify accounting data into categories, the chief ones being assets, liabilities, equity, revenues, and expenses.

Table 3.16 is a sample of a general ledger template that includes columns for the date and explanation of transaction and debit and credit columns, and shows the balance of the account after the transactions have been posted. The table shows that at the end of the day on November 20, there was a $15,000 cash balance. It is important to notice that "Payroll and employee benefits" is a debit account, and thus the positive balance is a debit, whereas the property tax ledger is a credit account, in which the positive balance is a credit. Finally, the sums of balances are equal: $5,000 + $15,000 = $20,000.

Cash Book

The cash book is a ledger in which all cash transactions (whether cash received or paid) are primarily recorded according to date. It is both

Table 3.14 General Journal

Date	Description	Posting reference	Debit	Credit
Nov. 20	Cash		$20,000	
	Property tax revenue			$20,000
Nov. 20	Cash			$5,000
	Payroll and employee benefits		$5,000	

Table 3.15 Posting Transactions in Three T-Accounts

Cash account			Payroll and employee benefit expenses			Property tax revenue	
Nov. 20	$20,000	$5,000	Nov. 20	$5,000		Nov. 20	$20,000
$15,000		Balance	$5,000		Balance	Balance	$20,000

Table 3.16 Sample Ledger Accounts

Dr			Cash account				Cr
Date	Particulars	J/F	Amount	Date	Particulars	J/F	Amount
Nov. 20	Property tax		$20,000	Nov. 20	Employee benefits		$5,000
	Balance		$15,000				

Dr			Payroll and employee benefits (debit account)				Cr
Date	Particulars	J/F	Amount	Date	Particulars	J/F	Amount
Nov. 20	Cash		$5,000				
	Balance		$5,000				

Dr			Property tax revenue (credit account)				Cr
Date	Particulars	J/F	Amount	Date	Particulars	J/F	Amount
				Nov. 20	Cash		$20,000
					Balance		$20,000

Note: J/F denotes Journal or Folio reference (if any).

Table 3.17 Sample Cash Book

Debit					Credit				
Date	Particulars	V. No.	L. F.	Amount $	Date	Particulars	V. No.	L. F.	Amount $
Nov. 20	Property tax—cash		xx	20,000	Nov. 20	Employment benefits		xx	5,000
	Balance			15,000					

a book of original entry, in which all cash transactions are recorded as soon as they take place (similar to a journal), and a book of final entry, in which the cash aspect of all cash transactions is finally recorded, without posting in the ledger as a cash account. The cash book is one of the most important accounting records for local governments using manual accounting systems.

If we were to take the same transactions given above and record them in a cash book, it would look like table 3.17. The columns of the cash book are as follows:

Date: The date of the transaction.

Particulars: The name of the opposite account against which a cash transaction occurred. A narration of the transaction should be written in this column, below the name.

V. No. (Voucher Number): The voucher number of each item of receipt and payment is also written (cash memo number, payment voucher number, or receipt voucher number).

L.F. (Ledger Folio): This is the page number of the ledger where the opposite account has been opened. This will make it possible to locate the account from the ledger.

Amount: The amount of the transaction. When cash is received, the amount is recorded on the debit side, and when cash is paid, the amount is recorded on the credit side.

Receipts and Payments Account

The receipts and payments account statement shows a summary of inflows and outflows under the various account heads. It includes headings that begin with the cash in hand (opening balance) at the commencement of the year and end with the closing balance at the end of the year.

Local governments prepare a *receipt and payment account* at the end of the year for the purpose of disclosing the results of their financial transactions. Table 3.18 summarizes the consolidated payments and receipts account of a small municipality. This is a very simple, easy-to-follow snapshot, with sufficiently detailed, specific revenue and expenditure items.

Similarly to the cash account, receipts in a receipts and payments account statement are shown on the debit side, and payments are shown on the credit side. Cash receipts and cash payments of both a capital and a revenue nature are also recorded here. However, this statement does not include any unpaid expenditures or any unrealized income related to the period.

The Financial Statements

Local governments with double-entry accounting systems typically prepare four financial statements at the end of the fiscal year: *Trial Balance, Statement of Receipts and Expenditures, Statement of Financial Position* (balance sheet), and *Cash Flow Statement.* Local governments publish or submit to higher government tiers the *Statement of Receipts and Expenditures, Cash Flow Statement,* and the *Statement of Financial Position.*

Table 3.18 Consolidated Receipts and Payments Account for the Year Ended December 31, 2010 (dollars)

Receipts		Amount	Payments		Amount
Opening Balance:			Program Expenses:		
- Cash	500		Salaries: Program staff		18,300
- Bank	25,500	26,000	Salaries: Admin. staff		11,000
Local contribution		10,250	Road develop. works		27,000
Grants from:			Education centers		13,000
- Local agencies		15,500	Health program		9,700
- Foreign agencies		55,700	Other Expenses:		
- Govt. dept.		22,000	Stationery		2,400
Interest from:			Traveling expenses		15,000
- Bank		150	Fuel & maintenance		7,200
- Investment		1,400	Rent		4,200
Loans and Advances:			Loans and Advances:		
Loans taken		45,000	Loans to staff		15,600
Loan refund from staff		10,000	Loans returned		14,800
Advances for administration expenses		5,300	Purchase of land		35,000
Sale of furniture		3,400	Closing Balance:		
			- Cash	1,600	
			- Bank	19,900	21,500
Total		194,700	Total		194,700

Trial Balance

The previous section described how transactions are first entered in journals and the cash book and then posted in the ledger in their respective accounts. At the end of the accounting year, these accounts are balanced. To check the accuracy of postings in the ledger, a statement is prepared containing balances of all ledger accounts on a particular date. A *trial balance* consists of a debit column with all debit balances of accounts and a credit column with all credit balances of accounts.

Table 3.19 is a trial balance of City XYZ, prepared for the 2009 fiscal year by February 28, 2010. The balance of the statement tells little about the financial position of the city, but it indicates that the credit and debit entries are correct because they are balanced. The next section explains how the trial balance is developed, based on the balances of the various ledger accounts, using a sample of T-accounts and the balance of the cash account. This example signifies the importance of checking the accuracy of the posting of transactions and the relationship between the ledgers and the trial balance sheet.

Table 3.19 Trial Balance of City XYZ (dollars)

Account title	Debits	Credits
Cash	42,260	
Accounts receivable	-	
Office supplies	840	
Insurance	2,000	
Payroll & employee benefits	20,500	
Consultant fees	350	
Rent	1,000	
Utilities	250	
Contributions		50,000
Property tax		12,000
Business licenses		5,200
Totals	67,200	67,200

Relation between Ledger Accounts and the Trial Balance

Table 3.20 summarizes the City XYZ example. The T-accounts shown resulted from entering the city's transactions, which were then posted to ledger accounts. From the balances of ledger accounts summarized in table 3.20, the city's trial balance can easily be prepared. Readers should take the time to follow the T-account balances to reconcile how the trial balance is prepared.

Financial Statements

The Statement of Receipts and Expenditures is a key part of a comprehensive annual financial report, which presents the financial statements of the local government. Each year, every governmental organization prepares a Statement of Receipts and Expenditures and supports it by important analysis (such as the management discussion and analysis, or MD&A, in municipal governments in the United States) and in the notes to the financial statements.

The Statement of Receipts and Expenditures reports on total revenues and total expenses. Governmental organizations issue it with a *focus on the entire organization,* including all kinds of activities and all kinds of revenues and expenditures during the fiscal year. In short, the statement shows how much money they have earned (revenue) and how much they have spent (expenses). Table 3.21 is a sample income statement prepared in part from the data presented in table 3.20. Added data show opening balance, transfers, and expenses not shown in table 3.20.

The statement of activities first establishes the change in fund balance as a result of revenue and expenditure balances, then adds the fund balance at the beginning of the reporting period (fiscal year). The sum of these two yields the end-of-period fund balance of $40,500.

Table 3.20 City XYZ—T-Accounts and Cash Account

Contributions revenue		Office supplies expenses			Cash account		
Jan. 10	$50,000	Jan. 20		$240	Jan. 3	$5,200	
		Jan. 31		$600	Jan. 10	$50,000	
Balance	$50,000	Balance		$840	Jan. 15		$350
Payroll and employee benefits expenses		**Insurance expense**			Jan. 20		$240
					Jan. 30		$10,000
Jan. 30	$10,000	Feb. 1		$2,000	Jan. 31		$1,000
Feb. 15	$10,500				Feb. 1		$2,000
Balance	$20,500	Balance		$2,000	Feb. 3	$12,000	
Property tax revenue		**Business licenses revenue**			Feb. 15		$10,500
Feb. 3	$12,000	Jan. 3		$5,200	Feb. 25		$600
					Total	$67,200	$24,940
Balance	$12,000	Balance		$5,200	Balance	$42,260	$24,690
Consultant fees		**Occupancy/rental expenses**					
Jan. 15	$350	Jan. 31		$1,000			
Balance	$350	Balance		$1,000			
Utilities expense		**Accounts payable**					
Feb. 8	$250	Jan. 31		$600			
		Feb. 25		$600			
Balance	$250	Balance		$0			

The Statement of Revenues and Expenditures thus gives a sense of how well the local government entity, as a whole, is operating and reports the following items:

- Revenues such as contributions, program fees, membership dues, grants, investment income, and amounts released from restrictions.

- Expenses such as expenditures, encumbrances, other financing uses, and all expenses of a business type, such as salaries, utilities, and so forth. Expenses can also be reported in categories such as major programs, fundraising, management, and general.

- The bottom line resulting from all the revenue and expenditure items would be the change in the fund balance—the surplus or deficit.

The Statement of Financial Position (Balance Sheet)

The Statement of Financial Position or balance sheet reflects the structure of an organization's assets and the financing sources used to finance those assets, as of a particular date. And as the name indicates, there should be balance between its parts because this financial statement reflects the essence of the accounting equation, which is

$$assets = liabilities + equity.$$

The net assets of a government organization are equivalent to the net worth (equity) of a commercial organization. The Generally Accepted Accounting Principles (GAAP) suggest that net assets be classified as unrestricted (UR),

Table 3.21 Statement of Receipts and Payments (dollars)

Revenues	Unrestricted
Earned revenue	17,200
Contributions	10,250
Program revenues	
Other sources	3,400
Interest and dividend income	1,550
Grants	93,200
Loans and advances	60,300
Released from restricted funds	
Total unrestricted revenue	185,900
Expenses	
Program expense	22,700
Development expense	27,000
Management and general	29,300
Loans and advances	65,400
Other expenses or fund uses	27,000
Total operating expenses	171,400
Change in fund balance	14,500
Fund balance, beginning of period	26,000
Fund balance, end of period (surplus or deficit)	40,500

temporarily restricted (TR), or permanently restricted (PR). Local governments in many countries must classify their assets according to GAAP (as is discussed in more detail in chapter 6). Figure 3.5 illustrates the components of net assets and highlights their meanings.

The term "Statement of Financial Position, or balance sheet" is one used by nonprofit organizations. The statement's purpose is to report assets, liabilities, and net assets as of a specified date. The Statement of Receipts and Payments depicts the overall status of the organization's surplus (or deficit) by looking at revenues and expenses over a period of time (fiscal year). The Statement of Financial Position depicts the overall status of the organization's finances at a fixed point in time (the end of the fiscal year). It totals all the assets and subtracts all the liabilities to compute overall net assets and surplus or deficit.

Table 3.22 shows a sample of a small local government entity's Statement of Financial Position (balance sheet), with restricted and unrestricted, and designated and undesignated assets; it also shows the total assets and the net assets. From the table one can make a number of observations. The table includes current assets (50,000), of which total 40,000 is unrestricted and designated for operations (25,000) and for Board (15,000). There are 10,000 restricted assets, grants from the central government earmarked for specific expenditures.

A Brief Introduction to the Fund Accounting Model in the United States

In the United States, municipalities follow an accounting model called "fund accounting," in which revenues and expenditures are reported under different funds (box 3.7). A fund is a fiscal and accounting entity with a self-balancing set of accounts recording cash and other financial resources. Thus, a local government should have only one *general fund*, but it may have many other types of funds. For example, a city may maintain a separate, special revenue fund for each restricted revenue source, a separate capital projects fund for each major capital project, and a separate debt service fund for each issue of outstanding bonds.

Table 3.23 shows a balance sheet in fund-based accounting of a U.S. city. The general fund in a local government embraces most major government functions, such as police, street maintenance, sanitation, and so on. The balance sheet displays financial assets and liabilities, with memo items on other assets, and it provides decision makers with very specific information on the sources and uses of funds and accrued liabilities.

Municipal Accounting in Developing Countries

This section discusses problems that local governments are facing in developing countries in applying modern accounting principles

Figure 3.5   Logical Frame of Net Assets

Net Assets - Diagram

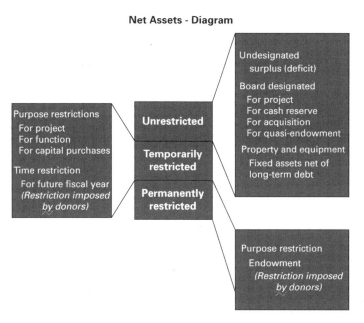

Source: GASB 1999.

and practices. Although the discussion briefly touches upon current debates on these issues, it focuses on how to address them from a municipal management perspective rather than on policy.

Cash or Accrual Basis

Finding a suitable accounting method is a common issue for municipal governments in developing countries. Local governments have traditionally applied single-entry cash-based accounting, as that is the method that central governments follow. As decentralization progressed and local governments started acquiring their own identity, the need to adopt accounting systems and procedures more suited to their business requirements became important. Advisers and consultants often think of local governments as being similar to private enterprises and for that reason have recommended double-entry accrual-based accounting for local governments.

Although it is true that double-entry accrual-based accounting is the state-of-the-art method, whether such accounting is feasible in a local government context also must be considered. Just to name a few main impediments: estimating the value of municipal assets and establishing opening balance sheets are hard to do quickly. Therefore, instead of rushing to implement sophisticated forms of accounting such as full-accrual accounting, it is advisable to build up the capacities of the accounting system and the staff by first transitioning to a *double-entry cash basis* and then perhaps to a *modified accrual basis*. The experience of the local government in preparing accounts using double-entry cash-based accounting will enable it to move comfortably to more sophisticated methods.

Table 3.22 Government Funds Balance Sheet

Municipality date of issue	Total to date	Current year Unrestricted Operations	Current year Unrestricted Board designated	Restricted	Note	Prior year
Assets						
Current assets	50,000	25,000	15,000	10,000	a	42,000
Fixed assets	20,000		20,000			20,750
Long-term assets						
Total assets	70,000	25,000	35,000	10,000		62,750
Liabilities						
Current liabilities	3,000	3,000				3,500
Long-term liabilities						
Total liabilities	3,000	3,000				3,500
Net Assets						
Unrestricted						
Undesignated	22,000	22,000				26,500
Board designated	15,000		15,000		b	
Property, plant equip.	20,000		20,000			20,750
Temporary restricted	10,000			10,000		12,000
Permanently restricted						
Total net assets	67,000	22,000	35,000	10,000		59,250
Total liabilities and net assets	70,000	25,000	35,000	10,000		62,750

a. Restricted for sole use for school health screening program.
b. Amount designated for the School Board discretion on teachers training.

Box 3.7 The Fund Structure of State and Local Governments in the United States

Governmental Funds

Purpose: To account for and report governments' operating and financing activities financed predominantly through taxes and intergovernmental grants.

Basis of accounting/measurement focus: Modified accrual/current financial resources

There are five kinds of governmental funds:

- *General fund*—to account for and report all financial resources not accounted for and reported in another fund

- *Special revenue funds*—to account for and report the proceeds of specific revenue sources that are restricted or committed for specified purposes other than debt service or capital projects (e.g., gas tax revenues required to be used for road repairs)

- *Debt service funds*—to account for and report financial resources that are restricted, committed, or assigned to expenditure for principal and interest

(continued next page)

- *Capital projects funds*—to account for and report financial resources that are restricted, committed, or assigned to expenditure for capital outlays, including the acquisition or construction of capital facilities, such as buildings and highways, and other capital assets
- *Permanent funds*—to account for and report resources restricted in that only the earnings on investments, not the principal, may be used to support the reporting government's programs for the benefit of the government or its citizenry (e.g., maintenance of a public cemetery or park).

Proprietary Funds

Purpose: To account for and report governments' activities that are similar to those carried out in the private sector and financed predominantly through user charges.

Basis of accounting/measurement focus: Full accrual/economic resources

There are two kinds of proprietary funds:

- *Enterprise funds*—to account for and report business-type activities that serve the public at large (e.g., an electric utility)
- *Internal service funds*—to account for and report goods and services provided to departments of the same government (e.g., a centralized purchasing function or motor pool).

Fiduciary Funds

Purpose: To account for and report resources held by governments as trustees or agents for another party or parties.

Basis of accounting/measurement focus: Full accrual/economic resources.

There are two kinds of fiduciary funds:

- *Trust funds*, including
  - Pension (and other employee benefit) trusts—to account for and report resources accumulated to pay pension, health care, and other benefits to the government's retired or disabled employees (e.g., a local government's pension plan for its employees)
  - Investment trusts—to account for and report investment pools in which other governments participate (e.g., a state government pool open to local governments within the state)
  - Private purpose trusts—to account for and report resources held for individuals or external organizations (e.g., a scholarship fund for employees' children, funded by a donation from a citizen)
- *Agency funds*—to account for and report resources held on a short-term basis on behalf of individuals, organizations, or other governments (e.g., taxes collected on behalf of another government). These funds have only assets and liabilities—no revenues or expenses.

Source: http://media.wiley.com/product_data/excerpt/01/EHEP0015/EHEP001501-2.pdf.

Accounting for Operations and Maintenance Costs of Fixed Assets

Most local governments pay a great deal of attention to their capital budgets and to asset creation; often very little attention is paid to asset management. Just as asset creation is critical to building up the local government's capacities for delivering services, asset maintenance and replacement are necessary for sustaining the service delivery capacities created. Therefore,

Table 3.23 Example of a Government Funds Balance Sheet (USD thousands)

	General	Health and urban dev. programs	Community redevelopment	Route 7 construction	Other government funds	Total government funds
Assets						
Cash and cash equivalents	3,418.5	1,236.5			5,606.8	10,261.8
Investments			13,262.7	10,467.0	3,485.3	27,215.0
Receivables (net)	3,644.6	2,953.4	353.3	11.0	10.2	6,972.5
Due from other funds	1,370.8					1,370.8
Receivables from other governments		119.1			1,596.0	1,715.1
Liens receivables	791.9	3,195.7				3,987.6
Inventories	182.8					182.8
Total assets	9,408.6	7,504.7	13,616.0	10,478.0	10,698.3	51,705.6
Liabilities and Fund Balances						
Liabilities:						
Accounts payable	3,408.7	130.0	190.5	1,104.6	1,074.8	5,908.6
Due to other funds		25.4				25.4
Payable to other governments	94.1					94.1
Deferred revenue	4,250.4	6,273.0	250.0	11.0		10,784.4
Total liabilities	7,753.2	6,428.4	440.5	1,115.6	1,074.8	16,812.5
Fund balances:						
Reserved for:						
Inventories	182.8					182.8
Liens receivables	791.9					791.9
Encumbrances	40.3	41.0	119.3	5,792.6	1,814.1	7,807.3
Debt service					3,832.1	3,832.1
Other purposes					1,405.3	1,405.3

Unreserved, reported in:						
General fund	640.3					640.3
Special reserve funds		1,035.3			1,330.7	2,366.0
Capital project funds			13,056.2	3,569.8	1,241.3	17,867.3
Total fund balances	1,655.3	1,076.3	13,175.5	9,362.4	9,623.5	34,893.0
Total liab & fund balance	9,408.5	7,504.7	13,616.0	10,478.0	10,698.3	51,705.5

Amounts reported for government activities are different, because:

Capital assets used in governmental activities are not financial resources and therefore are not reported in the funds.	161,082.7
Other long-term assets are not available to pay for current period expenditures and therefore are deferred in the funds.	9,348.9
Internal service funds are used by management to charge the cost of certain activities such as insurance and telecom to individual funds; the assets and liabilities of the internal service funds are included in governmental activities in the statement of net assets.	2,994.7
Long-term liabilities, including bonds payable, are not due and payable in the current period and therefore are not reported in the funds.	(84,760.5)
Net assets of governmental activities	123,558.8

Source: Authors, adapted from Freeman and Shoulders 2000.

local government financial management should include adequate provision for the operation, maintenance, and replacement of the assets they have created. From an accounting perspective, this would require that the municipality make adequate provision for operating costs (based on the data generated through its cost control systems) and for the depreciation of fixed assets. Chapter 6 discusses asset management in detail.

Weaknesses in Accounting Standards and Practices

While there is no disagreement that reforms are necessary to improve the quality of municipal accounting, a common impediment to such reforms is the absence of well-defined accounting standards and procedures for local governments in most developing countries. Usually accounting standards and procedures are designed for national governments, with local governments expected to follow along. In such cases the utility of the standards for local governments is often reduced because they are not fully responsive to local government requirements, especially in areas such as cost accounting by service and local function, accounting of billing for and collection of fees and charges, local pension funds, and the like. Hence, wherever no specific standards and procedures exist for local government accounting, special efforts should be made to define them by taking into consideration the requirements of local governments. Fixing such weaknesses by reforming the accounting system is full of challenges, in particular when a computerized, automated accounting system is replacing a manual system.

Using Accounting Information for Management Decision Making

This section discusses using accounting information to support management decisions. Some of the material will be revisited in subsequent chapters (including chapters 5, 6, and 8). Here we focus only on cost accounting and on some

analytic tools. The section introduces some of the basic concepts in cost accounting, such as standard costs, cost centers, direct and indirect costs, costing of overhead, and activity-based costing. Some advanced management accounting techniques, such as break-even analysis, are briefly outlined.

Cost Accounting and Cost Management

Cost accounting provides key information for managers, helping them both in operation decisions and in analyzing operational efficiency. In a cost accounting system, the costs of providing services are managed by measuring each service separately, enabling the manager to monitor the cost of delivering particular services such as water, solid waste management, housing, education, or health care. Cost accounting gives the decision maker analytical information that can be used to increase the efficiency of operations.

Role and importance of cost accounting of service delivery. While financial accounting such as this chapter has discussed helps an organization prepare financial statements that give an aggregate view of its revenues and expenses and the resultant surplus or deficit, cost accounting helps an organization obtain a detailed view of the underlying costs that flow into the aggregate financial reports. Such detailed cost information can be used to control costs and to determine appropriate pricing for products and services. In a local government, cost accounting information provides valuable insights to the finance officer, the city management, and the managers of specific service entities on the true costs of providing services. It helps the city government to estimate the extent of cost recovery and sustainability of a service by comparing the cost of operating it with the fees and charges received for it.

Cost accounting information helps the finance officer control costs and make operations more efficient, reducing pressure on the city's budget and avoiding the politically difficult steps of raising user fees and taxes. Cost accounting systems are forward looking and therefore help finance officers model future costs and prices and analyze the financial position of the entity in different scenarios. However, cost accounting systems are still in their infancy in local governments in most developing countries. They need the attention of policy makers. For instance, municipal accounting systems derived from central government accounting do not support accounting of the specific costs of basic services such as water, solid waste management, or public transport. The discussions below give a broad overview of some of the relevant cost concepts.

Basic cost accounting techniques. Cost accounting systems can differ based on the nature of an entity's operations. In an entity that carries out mass production with common work (such as most municipal services, from solid waste disposal to water and sanitation), the system of process costing is adequate. In contrast, if an organization carries out specific services designed for individual customers (such as information technology or construction work), a job order cost accounting method is often used. Although these cost accounting systems are useful by themselves, they have deficiencies, especially when shared costs are involved (i.e., various departments or processes share a service), making it difficult to apportion the costs of jobs and processes accurately. Such deficiencies have led to the introduction of *activity-based costing*.

Activity-based costing. Activity-based costing (ABC) systems refine costing systems by focusing on individual activities as the fundamental cost objects. An activity is an event, task, or unit of work with a specified purpose, for example, removal of wastes from a part of a city, registration of births and deaths, and so forth. ABC systems calculate the costs of individual activities and assign costs to cost objects, such as products and services, on the basis of the activities undertaken to produce each one. For this purpose, the cost accounting systems group activities into *cost pools* and use them as the basis for assigning costs.

For example, a city government may use the same trucks, loaders, labor, and equipment for maintaining parks and sports, health, and school facilities. Hence it may set up a *maintenance pool fund* and allocate the cost of trucks (fuel, labor, repair) by distance in kilometers of transport used. It may allocate the cost of loaders and other equipment based on the time of use for each maintenance project in the areas covered. The logic of ABC systems is that the basis for the allocation of costs is usually the key cost driver, and so the allocation leads to more accurate costing of activities. Though an elaborate discussion about advanced cost accounting is beyond the scope of this chapter, it is useful for local government executives to understand that such sophisticated techniques exist and make accounting of service delivery costs more accurate. In that way they can help improve the quality of municipal financial management.

Cost centers and responsibility accounting. As discussed above, one objective of a cost accounting system is to break down the cost details of a product or service, so that management can identify costs that can be controlled. An uncontrollable cost is one the manager cannot influence. For example, in a municipal government, office expenses are a controllable cost, but insurance premiums on the city's trucks are not controllable because they are not set by the city government. Even then, the manager might save costs by competitive selection of insurance companies.

The concept of controllable costs and expenses provides the basis for a *responsibility accounting system*, in which managers are responsible for the costs and expenses that fall under their control. Prior to each reporting period, the organization develops plans that specify the expected costs or expenses under the control of each manager. Those plans are called *responsibility accounting budgets*. The responsibility accounting system accumulates costs and expenses to include in timely reports to managers about the costs for which they are responsible. The reports are performance reports and compare actual costs and expenses to the budgeted amounts. Managers use performance reports to focus their attention on specific, actual costs that differ from budgeted amounts and decide corrective actions to bring the costs down.

Techniques for Efficient Management Decision Making

Accounting is the language of any business, but increasingly accounting is also assuming greater importance in the management of local governments because they are providing services to their citizens from limited resources. Setting up basic accounting systems allows the efficient recording and compilation of financial data; the data need to be analyzed, structured, and presented to make them useful for management decision making. Several financial analysis techniques help managements to draw meaningful conclusions. The techniques include ratio analysis, trend analysis, financial modeling, and ranking investment projects using capital budgeting techniques, break-even analysis, and other methods. We will discuss break-even analysis, one of the simplest techniques, which can be used in almost any organization. Other techniques will be discussed in chapters 5 through 8.

Break-even analysis. Break-even analysis is a technique widely used in business settings, especially by production management and management accountants. It is a helpful tool in deciding whether or not to purchase equipment, for example, a compactor truck, because it computes how close the operation would be to its break-even level with and without the truck. Break-even analysis simply calculates the level of service

or production at which total variable and fixed costs are equal and the business makes neither a profit nor a loss. That is the *break-even point*. The calculation depends on carefully distinguishing costs that are *variable* (that change when the output changes) and costs that are fixed (that are not directly related to the volume of output). The simplest computation of the break-even point is

break-even point = total fixed costs / (sales – variable costs).

In local governments, financial planning is of major importance. Breakeven analysis reveals how revenue and costs vary with a change in service level, that is, what effect a change in a service or the mix of services will have on revenues. Ideally, the goal is to find a level of output at which the government will reach breakeven—that is, total revenues are equal to or exceed total costs.

Municipal services should approach cost recovery rather than produce extra revenues. However, moving around breakeven may risk generating a deficit, raising a demand for subsidies, or undermining the sustainability of services. Thus, break even analysis is also a useful tool to measure which programs are self-supporting and which are subsidized or need to be. By studying the relationships among costs, service volume, and revenue, municipal management can better approach many planning decisions. Break-even analysis can also be useful when city managers are making lease-or-buy decisions or are dealing with other common issues of day-to-day city management.

Figure 3.6 shows a break-even chart, a graphical representation of costs C at various levels of output, together with the variation of income A from sales or fees. The intersection of the two lines represents the break-even point, at which neither profit nor loss is made. Thus, the entity is facing with losses as long as the volume of output or sale is less than Q_0 and begins to realize net revenues when output or sales exceed Q_0.

Figure 3.6 Break-Even Analysis

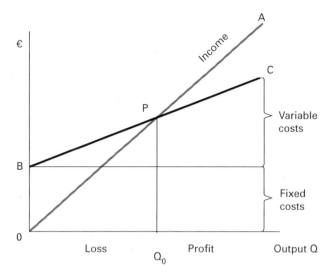

The reason is that services always have an initial investment, which generates a fixed cost even if there is no production.

Financial Reporting

This section builds on previous discussions of accounting to take it to the next level, using accounting information to compile financial reports. Before the content and techniques of preparing financial reports, the importance of financial reporting for transparency and accountability in the public sector is addressed. Also touched on are the roles of participants in the reporting regime, including higher-level governments, line ministries, the parliament and other legislative bodies, oversight institutions such as the auditor general, and the citizens themselves, as well as financial reporting as a tool to communicate with stakeholders.

Financial Reporting: Concepts and Practice

Financial reporting provides a consolidated set of information to a wide range of stakeholders that require information about an entity. Financial reports are means of communicating to the users of financial information material that they use to make choices among alternative uses of scarce resources. The objective stems largely from the needs and interests of those users, who lack the ability to gather the information they need and therefore must rely, at least partly, on the entity's financial reports. Financial reports are also means of performance monitoring (the subject of chapter 8). The potential users of financial reports and their information needs include the following:

- *Investors*. For companies, investors are interested in the entity's ability to generate net cash inflows because their investment decisions relate to the amounts, timing, and uncertainties of those cash flows.

- *Creditors*. Creditors provide financial capital to a local government by lending it cash (or other assets). Like investors, creditors are interested in the amounts, timing, and uncertainty of a municipality's future cash flows. To a creditor, a borrower is a source of cash in the form of interest, repayments of borrowings, and price premium of debt securities.

- *Suppliers.* Suppliers provide goods or services rather than financial capital. They are interested in assessing the likelihood that what a municipality owes them will be paid when due.

- *Employees.* Employees provide services to a municipality, and so they are interested in information to assess its continuing ability to pay salaries and wages and provide incentive payments, retirement, or other benefits.

- *Citizens.* To citizens, a municipality is a source of services. Citizens are interested in assessing the ability of the local government to continue providing those services, as they have a long-term involvement with the municipality and depend on it for services.

- *Governments, their agencies, and regulatory bodies.* Governments and their agencies and regulatory bodies are interested in municipal activities because they are responsible in various ways for ensuring that economic resources are allocated efficiently. They also need information to help in regulating activities, determining and applying taxation policies, and preparing national income and similar statistics.

The above categories of information users and their requirements are applicable in both the private and public sectors, although the kind of information required of a municipal government may be different than what is required from a business enterprise. For example, the national government would be interested in how efficiently the municipality has used intergovernmental transfers to meet development requirements, whereas the citizens may be more interested in knowing about the money spent on local development works.

Financial reporting is but one source of information to permit decision making. Users of

financial reports also need to consider pertinent information from other sources, such as information about general economic conditions or expectations, political events and the political climate, and the industry outlook.

Users of financial reports also need to be aware of the characteristics and limitations of the information in them. To a significant extent, financial reporting is based on estimates, rather than exact measurements, of the financial effects on entities of transactions and other events and circumstances. Hence users of financial reporting have to read the financial statements as a whole, especially the notes and annexes in which the bases and assumptions for the estimates are described.

Characteristics of Good Financial Reporting

According to the Financial Accounting Standards Board (FASB), the following are the qualitative characteristics required in good financial reporting (FASB 2000; Skousen *et al.* 2000):

- *Relevance.* To be useful in making investment, credit, and similar resource allocation decisions, information must be relevant to those decisions. Relevant information can make a difference in the decisions of users by helping them evaluate the potential effects of past, present, or future transactions or other events on future cash flows (*predictive value*) or confirm or correct their previous evaluations (*confirmatory value*). Timeliness—making information available to decision makers before it loses its capacity to influence decisions—is another aspect of relevance.

- *Faithful representation.* To be useful in making investment, credit, and similar resource allocation decisions, information must be a faithful representation of the real-world economic phenomena that it purports to represent. The phenomena represented in financial reports are economic resources and obligations and the transactions and other events and circumstances that change them. To be a faithful representation of those economic phenomena, information must be verifiable, neutral, and complete.

Verifiability implies that different knowledgeable and independent observers would reach general consensus, although not necessarily complete agreement, either

(a) that the information represents the economic phenomena that it purports to represent without material error or bias (by direct verification); or

(b) that the chosen recognition or measurement method has been applied without material error or bias (by indirect verification).

To be verifiable, information need not be a single-point estimate. A range of possible amounts and the related probabilities can also be verified.

Neutrality is the absence of bias intended to attain a predetermined result or to induce a particular behavior. Neutrality is an essential aspect of faithful representation because biased financial reporting information cannot faithfully represent economic phenomena.

Completeness means including in financial reporting all information that is necessary for faithful representation of the economic phenomena that the information purports to represent. Therefore, completeness, within the bounds of what is material and feasible, considering the cost, is an essential component of faithful representation.

- *Comparability*. Comparability, including consistency, enhances the usefulness of financial reporting information in making investment, credit, and similar resource allocation decisions. Comparability is the quality of information that enables users to identify similarities in and differences between two sets of

economic phenomena. Consistency refers to use of the same accounting policies and procedures, either from period to period within an entity or in a single period across entities. Comparability is the goal; consistency is a means to achieving that goal.

- *Understandability*. Understandability is the quality of information that enables users who have a reasonable knowledge of business and economic activities and financial accounting, and who study the information with reasonable diligence, to comprehend its meaning. Relevant information should not be excluded solely because it may be too complex or difficult for some users to understand. Understandability is enhanced when information is classified, characterized, and presented clearly and concisely.

- *Materiality*. Information is material if its omission or misstatement could influence the resource allocation decisions that users make on the basis of an entity's financial report. Materiality depends on the nature and amount of the item, judged in the particular circumstances of its omission or misstatement. A financial report should include all information that is material in relation to a particular entity—information that is not material may, and probably should, be omitted. To clutter a financial report with immaterial information risks obscuring more important information, thus making the report less useful in decisions.

- *Benefits and costs*. The benefits of financial reporting information should justify the costs of providing and using it. The benefits of financial reporting information include better investment, credit, and similar resource allocation decisions, which in turn result in more efficient functioning of the capital markets and lower costs of capital for the economy as a whole. However, financial reporting and financial reporting standards impose direct and indirect costs on both preparers and users of financial reports, as well as on others such as auditors and regulators. Thus, standard setters seek information from preparers, users, and other constituents about what they expect the nature and quantity of the benefits and costs of proposed standards to be, and consider in their deliberations the information that they obtain.

Financial Statements in Action—Policy Perspective

The financial statements of any organization are the income statement, the balance sheet, and the cash flow statement. We have introduced them in the context of accounting, and we now discuss them from a policy perspective.

Local governments prepare various reports for different purposes and target audiences:

Management/internal reporting. In addition to the annual financial statements that are used for reporting to the municipality's external stakeholders are several forms of *internal reporting.* Various departments prepare periodic financial reports and submit them to the financial officer and the mayor for their internal review (weekly, monthly, and quarterly). The local government also prepares and submits reports to higher levels of government reporting on the use of fiscal transfers and other resources received. These reports serve the purposes of monitoring bodies and are not usually shared with other external stakeholders. Box 3.8 summarizes a case in Bangalore, India.

Budgetary reporting. The executive reports to the city council regarding progress in budget execution during the course of a financial year in monthly budgeted/actual reports and variance analyses. These reports are also internal, helping the city council know whether the approved budget is being executed in accordance with

---

Box 3.8 PROOF–A Campaign for Transparency and Accountability in Bangalore

The Public Record of Operations and Finance (PROOF) campaign was launched in Bangalore, India, in July 2002, by four NGOs—Public Affairs Centre, Janaagraha, Centre for Budget and Policy Studies, and Voices. PROOF is a campaign for transparency in municipal governance, conducted in close partnership with the local government to enable government and citizens to work together and ensure that public money is being used for public goods.

PROOF requires that municipal finances related to public services are published and scrutinized by organized groups and the public at large. It focuses on three areas: obtaining quarterly financial statements from the government, developing performance indicators to assess municipal undertakings across the city, and public discussions. These include comparing the city's Revenue and Expenditure Statement to original budget figures and the balance sheet, with detailed information about current and long-term assets and short- and long-term liabilities.

Performance indicators were initially developed for two sectors: education, to assess the performance of Bangalore schools, and health, to assess the performance of the city's government hospitals. The aims of the reviews are to improve public financial accountability and performance, bring government and the public closer together, and provide benchmarks to develop and reshape public expenditure priorities.

Source: http://ww2.unhabitat.org/cdrom/TRANSPARENCY/html/2_6.html.

---

plans and whether revenues and expenditures are being realized in accordance with budget projections. Variants of budget reporting include program reporting and performance reporting. Program reporting describes the execution of a specific program (for example, school rehabilitation). Performance reporting records progress against plans or measured performance targets (such as collection of arrears). These reports are discussed in detail in chapter 8.

Citizen reporting. Citizens are among the most important stakeholder groups and have a key interest in knowing the state of affairs of their local government. For example, how well does the city government deliver services, and how efficiently does it use resources (including the taxes collected) for the development of the community? Quite often, however, citizens find it difficult to understand formal financial statements and audit reports prepared for professionals. To bridge the gap, proponents of social accountability, such as some civic organizations, have started to encourage municipalities to simplify complicated financial statements. Box 3.8 summarizes the example of the PROOF transparency initiative in India. The organization disseminates brochures, briefs, and leaflets that use nontechnical language and easy-to-understand formats such as charts, pictograms, and simple tables with key numbers. Similar initiatives are taking place in such countries as Nepal and Ghana.

Municipal Financial Reporting Formats

This section summarizes financial reporting in the context of municipal government policy. It focuses on content such as the reporting of receipts, payments, assets, and liabilities and the formats and standards used. It discusses good practices in municipal financial reporting, including linking it with performance reporting (discussed more in chapter 8). Some problems that local governments in developing countries face in the preparation of comprehensive financial statements are also addressed.

Formats and Standards in Municipal Financial Reporting—Good Practice Examples

In the United States, the Government Accounting Standards Board (GASB) sets the financial reporting standards for municipal governments. In June 1999, GASB issued Statement 34 "Basic Financial Statements—and Management Discussion and Analysis—for State and Local Governments" (GASB 1999). GASB 34 brought about a significant change in the format and content of local government financial reporting. It was the result of a continuous effort by standard setters in the country to fully meet the needs of financial statement users.

Box 3.9 describes how the government of South Africa has achieved significant progress toward standardized municipal financial reporting.

Each local government prepares two governmentwide financial statements, *statement of net assets* and *statement of activities,* that integrate the revenues and expenses of governmental activities, as explained previously. These statements provide an aggregate picture of the revenues and expenditures of the local government as a whole.

Fund financial statements provide detailed reporting on specific economic activities carried out by a local government, as explained above and shown in table 3.23. These activities are grouped together and reported in eight different fund financial statements. For example, the *enterprise fund* accounts for revenues and expenditures relating to any commercial-type operations (such as water and sewer service or local bus service) run by a city government with user charges or fees. Similarly, there are *fiduciary funds, agency funds, special revenue funds,* and the *pension fund,* which is a trust fund outside the municipal budget.

Management discussion and analysis (usually referred to as "MD&A") is a unique aspect of the reporting requirements introduced by GASB 34. MD&A provides an analytical overview of a government's activities through the year and an

Box 3.9 Municipal Finance Management Act, South Africa

The National Treasury of the Government of South Africa has played a pivotal role in the introduction of financial management reforms across government since 1994 and in local government since 1996. The reform initiative has been implemented through the Municipal Finance Management Act No. 56 of 2003 (MFMA), which is supported by the annual Division of Revenue Act. These pieces of legislation have been aligned with other local government legislation, such as the Structures Act, Systems Act, and Property Rates Act and their regulations, to form a coherent package.

The national treasury's primary objective was to secure sound and sustainable management of the financial affairs of government—national, provincial, and local. That includes regulatory interventions, manuals, guidance, circulars, workshops, seminars, training, internship programs, and hands-on support to municipalities. The national treasury has developed a phased implementation strategy of financial and technical support for local governments, based on the MFMA, including

conditional grants, subsidies, technical guidelines, policy advice, and the placement of international advisers with some municipalities. The strategy takes into account the differing capacities of municipalities to implement the reforms, as well as the need for institutional strengthening, building municipal capacity, and improving municipal consultation, reporting, transparency, and accountability.

The MFMA aims to modernize budget, accounting, and financial management practices, placing local government finances on a sustainable footing to maximize the municipalities' capacity to deliver services. It also aims to put in place a sound financial governance framework by clarifying and separating the roles and responsibilities of the council, mayor, and other officials. The MFMA is required by the country's constitution, which obliges all three tiers of government to be transparent about their financial affairs. It also forms an integral part of the broader reform package for local government outlined in the 1998 *White Paper on Local Government*.

Source: http://mfma.treasury.gov.za/Pages/Default.aspx.

introduction to the figures and results reported in the financial statements. It provides an analysis of the government's financial activities based on currently known facts, decisions, or conditions and helps users assess whether the government's financial position has improved or deteriorated during the year.

Links between Performance Reporting and Financial Reporting

It is important to remember that finance constitutes only one aspect of a local government's responsibilities and performance. Hence reporting of a government's activities should also

include its performance in the achievement of its development goals and programs. The importance of such a results-based approach to government activities is now being recognized all over the world, and several initiatives on performance reporting are being introduced. For example, the Service Efforts and Accomplishments reporting initiative of GASB in the United States attempts to introduce standards for performance reporting along with the standards for financial reporting for local governments. The goal is to assist users of the information (including citizen groups, state legislators, city council members, and other interested persons) to evaluate the efficiency of the services that governments provide and to assess governments' effectiveness in achieving their goals and objectives. Chapter 8 discusses performance measurement in more detail.

Auditing

Auditing helps to ensure that funds are not subject to fraud, waste, and abuse or to error in reporting. Auditing in the public sector also helps to ensure that the entity carries on its business in compliance with the established rules and procedures of public financial management. Without going into the technical details of the auditing process, the discussion in this section focuses on the use of audit reports as tools of accountability, the differences between various types of audits and their relationships, and the audit models in the public sector. It also addresses the meaning and significance of audit opinions, the various types of audit opinions, and audit standards.

Auditing—Basic Concepts and Practices

Auditing is a systematic process of objectively obtaining and evaluating evidence regarding assertions about economic actions and events. It consists of a series of sequential steps, including evaluation of internal controls and testing the substance of transactions and balances. The auditor communicates the results of his or her audit work to interested users through the audit report. The findings of the auditor are expressed in the form of an opinion concerning the fairness with which the financial statements present the organization's financial position, operating results, and cash flows.

Auditing in the private sector is used largely to ensure that the financial statements issued by a firm fairly reflect its financial position. In the public sector, other objectives are equally important, such as compliance with the rules and procedures for public expenditures, and are included in the scope of the audit. Another purpose of auditing in the public sector is ensuring that public funds are not misused or misappropriated.

Types of Audits

A financial audit is a historically oriented, independent evaluation performed for the purpose of certifying the fairness, accuracy, and reliability of the financial data. Financial audits focus on whether financial statements prepared by an entity reflect the financial position of the organization. Auditors examine the accounting treatment of various transactions in the entity's financial statements and whether the information disclosed in the financial statements reflects the underlying transaction. This is the most common form of audit.

A compliance audit focuses on whether the entity complied with certain rules and procedures regarding the spending of money. This kind of audit is usually done in the public sector, so that the auditor verifies the compliance of the entity with the government's established rules and procedures for financial management.

A management audit is a future-oriented, independent, and systematic evaluation of the activities of the organization prepared to help it attain its objectives. A management audit is also called a "performance audit." It evaluates the organization's performance against its stated plans and analyzes the reasons for any variance in performance, with the aim of drawing lessons for the future.

The auditor's findings are communicated through the *audit report*. The audit report is the culminating step in the audit process, and *expressing an audit opinion* is the auditor's overriding goal. The audit report concisely describes the auditor's responsibility, the nature of the examination, and the auditor's findings. The form of the audit report is standardized in many countries.

The introductory paragraph identifies the financial statements covered by the audit report and clearly differentiates management's responsibility for preparing the financial statements from the auditor's responsibility for expressing an opinion on them. The scope paragraph states whether the audit was conducted in accordance with accepted auditing principles. The opinion paragraph conveys the auditor's findings.

For instance, an audit report issued by the company KPMG to the City of Roanoke, Virginia, in the United States, illustrates the structure, details, and depth of an audit report and the messages and issues discussed with management. One interesting finding was the following:

> The City calculates its allowance for uncollectible receivables based on historic data and specific account analysis. We evaluated the key factors and assumptions used to develop the allowance, including possible management bias in developing the estimate, in determining that the allowance for uncollectible receivables as of June 30, 2011 is reasonable in relation to the financial statements of the city. (Roanoke City Department of Finance reports 2011, http://www.roanokeva.gov/85256A8D0062AF37/CurrentBaseLink/N27W8PBL294LGONEN)

We can draw two lessons from this statement: First, the city carries out a careful analysis and makes some assumptions in estimating the uncollectible receivables (arrears). Second, the source data, the analysis procedure, and the assumptions are evaluated by the auditor as adequate.

Types of Audit Opinions and Their Significance

Upon completion of the audit fieldwork, the auditor must decide whether or not an opinion can be rendered. If an opinion cannot be rendered, the auditor must clearly *disclaim an opinion* and give the reasons for the *disclaimer*. If an opinion is rendered, the auditor must decide whether to issue an *unqualified*, a *qualified*, or an *adverse* opinion.

Unqualified opinion. An unqualified audit opinion expresses the auditor's belief that the financial statements present a true and fair view of the entity's financial position.

Qualified opinion. The auditor expresses a qualified opinion if the financial statements contain material differences from accepted accounting standards and practices. Materiality is judged according to whether the differences might affect the conclusions drawn by users of the financial statement.

Adverse opinion. An adverse opinion is expressed when the financial statements contain serious differences from accepted accounting standards. In rendering an adverse opinion, the auditor states that the financial statements do not fairly present the entity's financial position and results of operations, in accordance with accounting standards and principles.

The standards and practices of audit reports and opinions described above are not found in many developing-countries' public sectors. The audits are not risk based, and the auditor's findings do not make any distinctions between material findings and nonmaterial findings. The auditor simply lists his *observations* in the form of *audit paragraphs* or *audit queries* and gives them to the audited entity at the conclusion of the fieldwork. That is considered a *preliminary audit report,* and the audited entity is expected to provide suitable replies to the audit queries raised within a specified time period. If the auditor is satisfied with the replies received, the audit paragraphs or audit queries are dropped, and a final audit report is prepared and submitted to the audited entity. In that system, the auditor does not express an opinion on the financial statements of the entity but instead carries out a "100 percent" check on all financial transactions from both financial and compliance points of view.

Municipal Audit Practices

This section discusses the role of audits in local governments with specific reference to the issues developing countries face. It centers on the weaknesses in public sector audit systems in developing countries, the impediments to regular and timely audits, and the role of the supreme audit institutions (SAIs) in public sector auditing.

External audits play a significant role in enhancing the accountability of municipal governments, in addition to providing valuable feedback to city management on the quality of the city's financial management. However, the experiences in most developing countries indicate that audits do not always play the critical part that they are expected to play for a variety of reasons.

Delayed audits

In most developing countries, government entities such as supreme audit institutions or the office of the auditor general audit municipalities. These agencies often are responsible to audit a large number of ministries, departments, central government agencies, and provincial governments. As a result, municipal audits often have a lower priority than others and are often conducted well after the close of the financial year. In fact, in quite a number of cases, audits have been delayed by years.

Compliance audits

External audits carried out by public sector auditors are often compliance audits in which the auditors verify whether the entity's expenditures are in accordance with the government's rules and procedures. Although verifying that is important, municipal governments also require audits to provide assurances on their financial statements, particularly if they plan borrowing or issuing debt. Local citizens and other stakeholders, such as lenders, are interested in knowing about the quality of the municipality's financial management. They expect the annual external audit to provide the necessary assurances. Hence municipal governments should undergo both financial and compliance audits, done together or separately.

Capacity shortage

Public sector audit agencies often are short on capacity, another factor that causes weak municipal audits. Weak capacities appear in both skills and numbers of auditors. Because public sector audit agencies more often than not carry out compliance audits, undertaking financial audits often poses a challenge to their knowledge and skills. Because the agencies frequently have the responsibility to audit numerous agencies of higher-level governments, they often find it difficult to program municipal audits within a reasonable period after the close of the financial year. A possible solution to this issue is to involve private sector auditors in carrying out the external audits of municipalities, as in the case in Bangladesh summarized in box 3.10. The practice has been successful in several countries but is not widespread. Governments and supreme audit institutions should establish policies and frameworks (including audit standards for municipalities) to facilitate the engagement of private sector auditors.

Audit Follow-Up

Audit follow-up is a critical part of the audit process. In the *management letter,* the auditor points out specific issues that the city management needs to rectify to improve the quality of its financial management and reports. City executives must respond to the audit observations diligently and have them rectified by the time of the subsequent audit. In the public sector, it often does not happen as expeditiously as desired. The reason is that executives often take audits as a criticism of their actions and do not want to admit that they were wrong. Without well-specified public sector audit standards in many developing countries, auditors can make audit observations without understanding the nature and context of an administrative action. That makes it difficult for executives to address the auditor's queries satisfactorily, and some audit queries are left pending for months or years.

Some developing countries have introduced the practice of *audit conferences,* in which the auditor, the audited city, and the supervising line ministry sit together to go over the audit observations and resolve issues through discussions. Such a process expedites, and reinforces the importance of, a prompt response to audit observations

Box 3.10 Use of Private Sector Auditors to Audit Local Governments in Bangladesh

Bangladesh, has approximately 4,500 rural local governments (called "union parishads"). As part of its policy to empower local governments, the government of Bangladesh, with World Bank support, introduced a system of block grants to union parishads in 2006. With increased financial resources flowing to local governments, the central government was keen that financial audits be conducted on a regular and timely basis. However, the comptroller and auditor general (C&AG), who has the constitutional mandate for the external audit of public sector institutions in Bangladesh, lacked the capacity to complete annual external audits of 4,500 union parishads in a regular and timely manner.

An *audit strategy* has helped to address this issue by forming a public-private partnership among the C&AG, the ministry of local governments, and the institute of chartered accountants of Bangladesh, which was contracted to carry out the annual external audits, with the C&AG providing quality assurance for the audit process. The outcome of this innovative approach was that the annual external audits of the union parishads are completed within a reasonable time after the close of the financial year, and the audit reports are made available to the local governments and their stakeholders, enhancing the framework for local accountability.

Source: World Bank 2011.

by city executives. In many local governments, audits are handled by the executives, with little involvement by the municipal council. That needs to change; the council should be fully abreast of the audit observations and make it a priority to ensure that the executives take prompt corrective actions. As a good practice for strengthening social accountability, audit observations and the corrective measures taken could be shared with citizens and other stakeholders, published on the city's website or on public notice boards.

Takeaway Messages

Budgets are developed based on both financial and nonfinancial information and determine how local services will be provided and financed in a fiscal year. The budget is often a local ordinance or bylaw approved by the council or equivalent body of a local government. It is a guiding, financing, executive, monitoring, and evaluation tool that allocates funds and responsibilities and induces actions by local entities and persons to achieve the set goals.

Budgeting weaknesses in developing countries include unrealistic plans and estimates, a shortage of timely information, politicized targets, and balloon revenue targets. Implementation weaknesses include overspending, delayed execution, unclear items, and persistent deficits.

The primary role of the accounting system is to provide and record timely and accurate information on revenues, expenditures, assets, and liabilities to inform stakeholders about the sources and uses of financial resources. The main types of accounting include financial accounting, cost accounting, managerial accounting, and tax accounting. Accounting systems include single-entry and double-entry accounting and cash-based or accrual-based systems, or combinations.

The most advanced system is double-entry accrual-based accounting, but double-entry cash-based accounting is a more realistic option for the local governments in developing countries. Cost accounting and fund accounting are more sophisticated systems that provide more specific information on key activity areas and functions and eventually on local government effectiveness overall.

Computerized accounting (and management information) systems offer convenient solutions in which each transaction is entered only once and automatically posted in various accounts, journals, and ledgers. Computerized systems are generally more accurate than manual systems. Moreover, they shift the focus of accounting from registering transactions to providing timely and structured information to those who need it, such as the mayor and executives, the council, and citizens.

Financial reports are key communication and control tools for local governments. The three main external financial reports are the Statement of Activities, the Statement of Financial Position, and the Cash Flow Statement. Many other reports are used internally, including budget/actual, trial balance, asset register and maintenance, or cost center reports. Accounting and financial reporting are often regulated by national institutions that prescribe standard formats and procedures.

The financial reports are the subjects of auditing, which is a process of systematic collection and evaluation of information on the financial transactions and the financial reports. The three main types of audits include the financial audit, the compliance audit, and the management audit. The results are presented in an audit report, which may include an unqualified, qualified, or adverse opinion by the auditor.

The audit report provides valuable feedback to management and calls for corrective actions. For external stakeholders, an audit report with positive statements is an assurance that the financial reports fairly represent the financial position of the local government. That is a vital message for investors and creditors. Local governments in developing countries are often audited by state auditors who focus on verifying compliance with public sector rules rather than the quality of finances, hence the need for simple self-assessments in order to ensure the accountability of public funds.

References

FASB (Financial Accounting Standards Board). 2000. *Statement of Financial Accounting Concepts*. Norwalk, CT: FASB; www.fasb.org.

Franke, Richard W. 2007. "Local Planning: The Kerala Experiment." In *Real Utopia: Participatory Society for the 21st Century*, edited by Chris Spannos, 130–35. Oakland, CA: AK Press.

Freeman, Robert J., and Craig D. Shoulders. 2000. *Governmental and Non-Profit Accounting*. Saddle River, NJ: Prentice Hall.

GASB (Government Accounting Standards Board). 1999. "Statement #34. Basic Financial Statements and Management Discussion and Analysis for State and Local Governments." www.gasb.org.

Lee, Robert E., and Ronald D. Johnson. 1998. *Public Budgeting Systems*. Gaithersburg, MD: Aspen Publishers.

Mikesell, John. 2011. *Fiscal Administration*. Boston: Wadsworth.

NACSLB (National Advisory Council on State and Local Budgeting). 2000. "Recommended Budget Practices: A Framework for Improved State and Local Government Budgeting, NACSLB." Government Finance Officers Association, www.gfoa.org.

Serageldin, Mona, et al. 2005. *Assessment of Participatory Budgeting in Brazil*. Washington, DC: Inter-American Development Bank.

Skousen, Fred, Earl K. Stice, and James D. Stice. 2000. *Intermediate Accounting*, 14th ed. Cincinnati, OH: South-Western College Publishing.

World Bank. 2011. "Progress Report on Bangladesh Local Government Support Project." World Bank, Washington, DC.

CHAPTER 4

Managing Local Revenues

Maria Emilia Freire and Hernando Garzón

In some important respects, a local government is analogous to a business. It provides services to its customers—residents. In turn, residents must pay for the services they receive (Bird 2011). However, the ways residents pay for services vary substantially. Fees and user charges for water or energy would seem the most obvious ways, but there are many more. For example, if you need a place to sell fruit, you use a stand in a vegetable market; you pay your municipality for the space and for the infrastructure you get. You use the walkway to store construction materials for your house, and you pay a fee for the inconvenience of your neighbors or other pedestrians. Those fees are called "benefit taxation," that is, people pay for the benefits or the utility they receive. They hope that what they pay is in line with the cost of the service that is being provided.[1]

However, most municipal services are not sold and billed like water or energy. Local governments provide services such as police protection, firefighting, street cleaning, street lighting, free parking, and even shelters for the poor and prisons for lawbreakers. These are so-called *public goods* because not only do they benefit the whole community, but individuals cannot reasonably be excluded from their use, and their consumption by one individual would not interfere with consumption by another (e.g., national defense, park services, public lighting). Thus, they need to be paid for by means of taxes that reflect the willingness of the community to finance these services and (in principle) the benefits that individuals extract from them. In this case—of goods whose use cannot be regulated through normal pricing mechanisms—local (benefit) taxes are the most appropriate vehicle of financing.

The sources of revenue for local governments vary across countries but generally include taxes, user fees and charges, and intergovernmental transfers. Other revenues may include investment income, property sales, and licenses and permits. In terms of taxes, property and business taxes are probably the most often levied by local governments around the world. Other local taxes can include income taxes, general sales taxes, and selective sales taxes (for example, taxes on fuel, liquor, tobacco, hotel occupancy, and vehicle registration) and land transfer taxes (or stamp duties). Often, these taxes are collected at the state level and shared with local levels according to predetermined formulas. They are called "shared taxes." To meet capital expenditure requirements, some municipalities charge developers for growth-related capital costs, using so-called development charges or "betterment levies." A land value capture tax is sometimes levied to finance infrastructure.

This chapter discusses the various aspects of managing local government revenues. It relates to the questions addressed in the first chapters, notably how local governments should finance the responsibilities assigned to them and what instruments are best suited to be used at the local level. In a time when demands on local governments are increasing, the capacity to raise local revenues as a complement to other resources is crucial for local governments to ensure adequate provision of services and maintain fiscal balance.

This chapter focuses on local taxes, user charges, and other local revenues, commonly referred as "own-source revenues" (OSRs). Capacity for collecting own revenues is among the most important evidences and factors of local autonomy, accountability, and self-reliance. Transfers, grants, and borrowing play a vital part in financing most municipalities, as discussed in chapter 1. Borrowing and other forms of debt financing are reviewed in chapter 7, in conjunction with the modalities for financing capital improvement plans.

Financing the City and the Quest for the Good Local Tax

Cities collect revenues to provide services and fulfill public functions. But how much revenue should be collected at the local level remains a difficult question. The responsibility of local governments to provide services to their constituencies and their authority to raise revenues are intertwined functions and should be in harmony. As discussed in chapter 1, an important rule of sound fiscal decentralization is that finances should follow functions (Bahl 2002); that is, local governments should be able to access the resources to finance the public services that they are mandated to provide. However, in reality, spending is much easier to decentralize than revenues, and local governments often need financing from upper levels of governments or the private sector to fill the gap.

The Role of Local Revenues—Big Picture

How cities finance their public expenditures is an important issue in urban development. Because every city is different, no single approach will suit all. The appropriate strategy for any city depends on factors such as size, economic conditions, demographic composition, and level of urbanization (Slack 2009).

While there is a consensus that cities' resources should be in line with their responsibilities—for example, larger cities need to spend more and therefore need to mobilize more local revenues—fiscal theory recognizes that local governments have a limited tax base (Bird 2009). Fiscal decentralization has delegated to local governments many functions, from water supply and solid waste management to investment in infrastructure such as streets and roads, flood control, and the like, as well as social services. Regardless of how well these functions are executed, the municipal mandates are clear and can be justified by the fact that local governments are closer to their constituencies and in principle capable of responding more efficiently to their demands. Around the world, local (municipal) expenditures as a share of total public expenditures vary between 45 percent in Denmark and 11 percent in Bolivia.

The rationale for which sort of revenues should be decentralized is much less clear. Local governments have generally lower tax potential than central governments, mainly because some taxes can be collected more efficiently by the central government than local governments. That is the case for customs levies, personal and corporate income taxes, value added taxes, and taxes on royalties.

This largely explains why the local revenue share of all public sector revenues is consistently lower than the share of local spending in total public sector spending (see figure 4.1); it underscores the need for intergovernmental grants to bridge the gap between municipal responsibilities and municipal revenues, as discussed in chapter 1.

It is also true that revenues are often centralized for political rather than merely technical or administrative reasons. Furthermore, local governments often miss the tax potential of their jurisdictions because of lack of information, low institutional capacity, and weak political commitment.

What Is a Good Local Tax?

Fiscal theory suggests that good local taxes have three features: they are easy to administer locally; are imposed on local residents; and do not raise competition with other local governments or the central government (box 4.1). These principles impose serious limits on what can be considered a good local tax. For example, although user charges and property taxes are clearly local

Figure 4.1 Local Share in Public Expenditures and Revenues (2011)

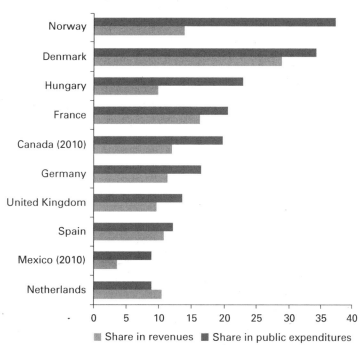

Share in revenues ▪ Share in public expenditures

Source: OECD 2011.

Box 4.1 A Good Local Tax

- Tax base should be immobile, so that local governments can vary the tax rate without the taxable base moving somewhere else.
- The tax yield should be adequate to meet local needs, be stable, and be predictable.
- Tax base should not be easy to export to nonresidents.
- Tax base should be visible to ensure accountability.
- Taxpayers should perceive the tax as fair.
- The tax should be easy to administer.

Source: Bird 2001.

taxes (they are paid by the people who receive the services), other taxes may be collected by the central government and shared with local governments, depending on the governments' fiscal architecture. That is the reason for the existence of so many combinations of local and central government taxes.

To fulfill all mandated and desirable functions, local governments need access to several taxes. Such an arrangement will increase their flexibility to respond to changes in the economy, evolving demographics, changes in the political climate, and other factors. For example, property taxes provide a stable and predictable source of revenues but do not increase with economic growth as fast as income and sales taxes do.

Principles of Local Revenue Management

There are two key principles of local revenue management:

1. The services that municipalities provide should be clearly linked to the revenue sources needed to finance them.

2. Services should be financed by their beneficiaries—"the general benefit principle"—directly or indirectly.

In this context, *private goods* (in the sense that they are excludable, i.e., people who do not pay can be prevented from getting the service,

such as electricity, water, urban transport, waste management, and parking) can be successfully financed by fees or user charges. In contrast, *public goods,* such as parks, street cleaning, and lighting, should be financed by local taxes. Moreover, other factors such as externalities and redistributive spillovers need to be taken into account (see figure 4.2). Redistributive policies and spillovers or externalities exceed the responsibility of the local government and thus should be funded (at least partially) by the central government. Other services, such as education and cultural services, do not fit clearly into any particular category. If seen as a private good (excludable), education should be financed by the beneficiaries, with the possible contribution of local taxes (at least partially and complemented by grants). If seen as a public good and an essential ingredient to improve the country's human capital, central government grants are largely justified (Slack 2009).

The Structure of Revenues in Local Governments

Studying the structure of local government revenues requires distinguishing between sources of revenues and the factors that affect the level of those revenues, such as the size of municipalities, the wealth of the local economy, and who provides public services.

Figure 4.2 The Benefit Principle of Municipal Finance

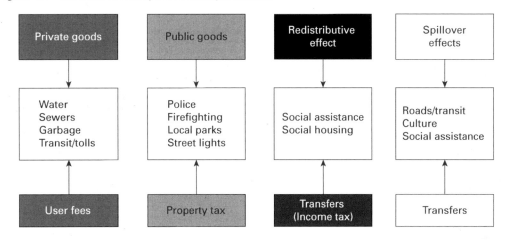

Source: Slack 2009.

Table 4.1 Brazilian Municipalities—Composition of Current Revenues by Size of City, 2003 (percentages)

Population	0 to 5,000	5,000 to 10,000	20,000 to 50,000	50,000 to 1 million	Above 1 million	Brazil
Tax revenues	3.5	5.6	12.1	21.7	36.6	19.6
Intergovernmental transfers	91.1	87.3	73.8	62.3	45.3	66.1
Other revenues	5.3	7.1	13.9	16.1	18.1	14.3
Current revenues	100	100	100	100	100	100

Source: World Bank 2006a.

The structure of local revenues varies among both countries and cities, but some general tendencies are noticeable. For example, as shown in table 4.1 and figure 4.3, the size of the municipality affects the role of local taxes, compared to transfers from the central government, in total revenues. Smaller municipalities have smaller tax bases and therefore are more dependent on the central government. For small cities of 5,000 or fewer, grants are 91 percent of revenues; taxes and other sources account for only 9 percent. In the case of large cities of more than 1 million, grants account for 45 percent and taxes and other revenues for 55 percent. The figures might be somewhat different in other countries, but the Brazilian pattern reflects a general tendency, namely, the *positive correlation between the size of the city and the role of own-source revenues.*

Unlike Brazil, some developing countries must deal with rapid urbanization and megacities with very low own-source revenues, such as large cities in Pakistan that collect only about 7 percent of their spending as own revenues. That is a typical pattern in many Asian and African countries.

Comparing several countries (table 4.2) suggests that the revenue structure of local governments also varies with the development level of the country. Cities in *less-developed countries seem to rely more on grants and transfers.* For example, grants represent 83 percent of local

Figure 4.3 Brazil—Sources of Revenues by Size of Municipality, 2003

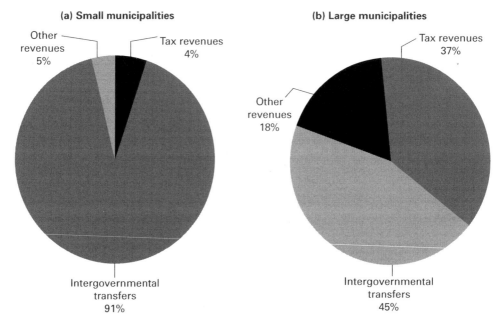

(a) Small municipalities

Other revenues 5%

Tax revenues 4%

Intergovernmental transfers 91%

(b) Large municipalities

Tax revenues 37%

Other revenues 18%

Intergovernmental transfers 45%

Source: Authors based on World Bank 2006a.

revenues in Botswana, 65 percent in Brazil, and 91 percent in Uganda. OECD (Organization for Economic Cooperation and Development) cities rely more on own revenues, either property taxes or income taxes.[2] Property taxes seem to be especially important in Australia, Canada, the United Kingdom, and the United States, reflecting the availability of support in the form of administrative and information processes, as well as traditional and customary factors.

In many other countries, various obstacles make it difficult to use property taxes to finance local governments: weak cadastre systems, confused property rights, no tradition of market valuation, and difficulty in bringing people to recognize a tax on something that they rarely consider selling.

The role of *shared taxes* varies. Many countries prefer to have higher levels of government collect and administer such taxes as property tax,

personal income tax, and business tax and transfer the agreed share to the local level. Shared taxes are particularly important in formerly centralized governments such as the Czech Republic (46 percent of local revenues are in the form of shared income and business tax).

The share of own revenues in total revenues also varies, ranging from 61 percent in Croatia (31 percent if shared personal income tax is excluded) to 9 percent in Uganda. Developed countries generally show a higher share of own revenues and a greater reliance on local taxes. A great variety of local taxes exist, although most countries rely on property taxes, motor vehicle taxes, and sales and income taxes. In addition, a large part of own-source revenue is accrued through surcharges and special revenues. These sources will be discussed in detail in the following sections. Hybrid types of shared taxes are used by many countries, at least in the postcommunist world.

Table 4.2 **Structure of Local Revenues, Selected Countries, 2006 (percentage)**

| | Local taxes | | | | Other revenues | |
	Property tax	Income and business tax	Total local taxes (includes shared taxes)	Grants	(including fees and sale of assets)	Total
Australia	39	0	39	14	47	100
Bolivia	19	8	72	18	10	100
Botswana	8		10	83	7	100
Brazil	4		13	63	24	100
Bulgaria	20	0	20	70	10	100
Canada	38	0	40	42	18	100
Croatia	3	46	61	12	27	100
Czech Republic	6	4	56	28	16	100
Denmark	3	48	51	39	10	100
Finland	2	44	47	29	24	100
France	34	18	45	29	26	100
Germany	5	16	42	34	24	100
Kenya	16	0	21	33	46	100
Mauritius	12		26	67	7	100
Russian Federation	4	23	31	58	11	100
South Africa	17	0	20	25	55	100
Spain	16	10	52	36	12	100
Sweden		58	59	22	19	100
Thailand	8		55	31	14	100
Uganda	3	1	5	91	4	100
Ukraine	2	34	42	38	10	100
Cities:						
Cape Town	25		25	25	50	100
Toronto	42		42	21	37	100
Madrid	12		47	39	14	100
Mumbai	19		65	4	31	100

Sources: DEXIA 2008; Slack 2009; IMF Government Finance Statistics 2007.

Sometimes they are accounted as grants, sometimes as own revenues (see chapter 1). They bring a sense of stability to local revenues because they are defined and collected by the central government.

Revenue Authority

How much tax authority local governments have to respond to increasing urban needs is a key factor of revenue management. Can local governments adjust tax rates, impose new taxes, and adjust user charge schedules? The situation varies across taxes and countries. Tax responsibility can be seen in four ways: authority to establish taxes, to set tax rates, to collect the tax revenue, and to allocate the proceeds (see box 4.2 and chapter 1).

- *Authority to establish local revenue sources.* Local governments' revenues are defined in the constitution or in the law that governs the country's finances. The assignment of tax bases

Box 4.2 Which Revenue Sources Should Be Defined Centrally Rather Than Locally?

User chargers and fees. A general rule in public finance is to charge for services whenever the direct beneficiaries can be identified. When the consumption of a public service benefits both the direct users and the community at large (for example, consuming clean water reduces contagious diseases; that is, it has positive externalities), the central government may intervene to subsidize larger population groups and encourage a greater level of service than if the good were produced and sold by the private market.

Broad-based business levies. Business tax rates are not well suited to be established by subnational governments, but these taxes are increasingly used by local and state authorities. To minimize potential distortions in the flow of factors and goods within a nation, a high degree of national uniformity is desirable for levies such as the corporate income tax and the value added tax (VAT).

Personal income tax. Although the personal income tax is often a national tax, it can also be used locally, even by small units of government, especially in the form of piggybacking on the centrally defined system.

Real property tax. The real property tax is by nature a local tax, given that it has an immobile tax base. It is hard to administer, especially in developing countries where information and valuation are often weak.

Sales tax. Excise and single-state retail taxes are prime candidates for local use, especially if a taxing region is large enough to avoid revenue loss from customers' crossing borders into lower-tax regions. Over time, sales taxes have been replaced by the VAT, a national tax that avoids the cascading effect of the usual sales tax. Although it is a better tax in general, the wide use of the VAT has resulted in a shrinking number of good local taxes.

Business, personal, and corporate income taxes are often shared taxes—they are collected by states or the central government and shared with local governments.

Sources: Bird 2001; 2006.

(local tax sources) is part of countries' fiscal framework. In countries with a unitary system (such as France, Kenya, or Morocco), the tax base is defined by the central government. In federal countries (such as Brazil, Germany, and Mexico), revenue assignment authority is shared between the federal and the state governments. In general, city managers have authority to establish *nontax sources* (e.g., user charges, fees, licenses, permits) and to set to some extent their *local taxes* (e.g., the property tax and, in some cases, the valuation of the tax base).

• *Setting of tax rates.* The authority over tax rates varies among countries. Tax rates are set either by the central government or by the state government, often within a range of values from which local governments can choose (as in Colombia). City governments have gradually gained greater authority (autonomy) to set their own tax rates and user charges, often with the approval of the sector authority (ministry). Tax exemptions or abatements are usually limited by law and are also under city authority.

• *Revenue collection authority.* Local taxes are collected directly by the local government, or collection is outsourced to higher government entities, peer cities (for example, Amman collects property tax on behalf of four cities), or even the private sector (for example, the case of property tax in Kampala). Central governments may collect local taxes on behalf of local governments and transfer the proceeds to each local government (as for Chile's property tax). Federal taxes shared with local governments are collected by the upper level of government and transferred back based on the origin of tax collections. Many of these processes are determined by political, cultural, or historical practices.

- *Revenue allocation authority*. Generally local governments have autonomy to allocate or spend their revenues freely, but sometimes tax proceeds are earmarked for specific purposes. For instance, in Brazil, 25 percent of net local revenues must be allocated to education. In Nepal, 75 percent of general shared tax revenues ought to be spent in development expenditures. Revenues from vehicle taxes are allocated to street and road maintenance in many countries. Revenues from asset sales, fiscal charges on land development, and construction permits are ideally earmarked for specific capital purposes.

- *Valuation*. Particularly in the case of the property tax, valuation is frequently carried out by the higher-level authority to ensure a uniform definition of "market value" (as in Canada). Alternatively, a higher level authority may establish a methodology to determine "market values".

Main Revenue Sources of Local Governments

Estimating how much money will be available to a city can be the most challenging as well as the most important part of preparing a local budget. Estimates that are too high can cause real headaches as the fiscal year progresses. It is better to err on the safe side and underestimate rather than overestimate expected revenues. Local government revenues fall into different groups that are important for both planning and analysis purposes. Finance officers need to be aware of the characteristics of a good local tax: predictability, buoyancy, equity, and local control. Ideally, local revenues are controlled locally and proceeds are stable, predictable, buoyant, equitable, and usable without constraints. However, very few revenues pass this test; property taxes and fees may be the closest ones.

Some local government revenues are very stable and predictable (property taxes); others show wide variations (sales tax). Some are restricted for specific uses (road charges), and others have no restrictions. Depending on the country, some local revenue sources are established by the local council, but many others may be beyond local control. For example, in the United States the constitution of the state of Wyoming (Wyoming 2011) gives local officials very little decision-making authority with respect to taxes and fees. The same is true for Mexico and many developing countries.

Municipal revenues can be classified in different ways, notably own revenues, intergovernmental transfers, and external revenues. Good revenue management also requires distinguishing between current (or recurrent) and capital (or nonrecurrent) revenues, although that is not mandated in many developing countries.

Table 4.3 and figure 4.4 show the classification of local revenues used in this chapter. Revenues are classified into current and capital. Within current revenues are own revenues, transfers, and other revenues. Shared taxes (collected by the central government and shared with subnational entities) sit at the border of own revenues and transfers. Because they often provide a large portion of local revenues (as in Argentina, Serbia, and Turkey), this category has a big influence on own-revenue capacity projections. Shared taxes are commonly considered transfers, even though many argue that they are own revenues if the share is returned to the local government of the jurisdiction where they were collected. The Council of Europe has issued a clarification statement on the matter: "Shared taxes are financial transfers; if they are not in direct relation to the amounts collected locally, they are also considered as grants" (Council of Europe 2006).

Recurrent revenues should be sufficient to finance current (or operational) expenditures; that is, they should be sufficient to finance regular operation and even to generate an operational surplus, which then can be used for financing capital investments directly or by leveraging debt. Failure to generate sufficient current revenues suggests that the municipality is financially unsustainable. Such a municipality will generate arrears (unpaid bills), sell assets and use up its wealth (as some cities in the United States have done temporarily, in response to the fall in tax revenues after 2008), or be bailed out by the central government through discretionary grants (as occurred in Jordan).

Own-Source Revenues

Own-source revenues (OSRs) are funds that local governments raise directly, as opposed to transfers and grants received from higher government tiers. Distinguishing and measuring them is important to assess municipal fiscal creditworthiness, autonomy, and capacity to raise revenues. They are also important with respect to revenue incentives: own-source revenues are the funds that local governments control, can project, and can increase through local decisions, procedures, and actions. Central government transfers and donations could be very significant, but the local government does not control them—there is little or nothing it can do to increase them.

Table 4.3 Structure of Revenue

Categories	Current revenues	Capital revenues
Own-source revenues	Taxes	Asset sale
	Fees/charges	Dividends
	Asset fees	Betterment fees
	Other	Contributions
Revenues from higher government tiers	Shared taxes	General capital grant
	General transfers	
	Earmarked grants	Earmarked grants
External revenues (debt, equity)	Liquidity borrowing	Loans, bonds
		Bond
		Equity

Figure 4.4 Revenues in Budget Context

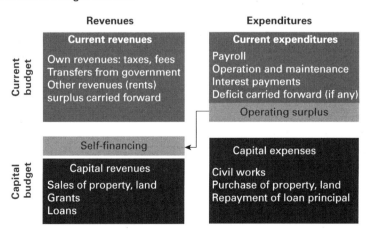

Box 4.3 shows a typical list of OSRs; the 24 OSRs can be grouped into the following categories: *taxes, charges, fees, asset and investment proceeds,* and *other* small revenues. Taxes are levied to finance general expenses; charges finance the costs of services; fees are supposed to cover the direct costs of specific services or functions such as issuing marriage, birth, or death certificates; licenses; or permits. These distinctions are less clear in practice. Some taxes and charges may be called "fees" (as a "water fee"). Some fees are set far above the direct cost of the respective services; for example, business licenses, vocational fees, or building permits, which in fact are taxes, may be called fees to make them politically more acceptable.

Most local governments have a long list of OSRs assigned by law, a handful of which provide the bulk of their revenues. Table 4.4 shows a list of countries in various levels of development. The data suggest that local taxes provide a substantial share of local revenues (37 percent, in this group) and that the property and the income taxes are the most significant (44 percent and 41 percent, respectively). In contrast, Guatemala collects only a sales tax and a small amount of property tax. The table also reflects a great variety of revenue sources across countries. Property tax is the sole local tax source for municipalities in Australia, Canada, and the United Kingdom, whereas local income tax is the main tax revenue in the Nordic countries. One can conclude that

---

Box 4.3 Principal Revenue Sources for Local Governments

1. Property tax (rates) on land and/or buildings
2. Tax on the transfer of immovable property
3. Tax on motor vehicles
4. Local sales tax and/or tax on the sale of local products (or surcharge)
5. Tax on local businesses and services
6. Tax on electricity consumption (surcharge)
7. Tax on nonmotorized vehicles
8. Tax on tourism, hotels, restaurants, and entertainment
9. Tolls on roads, bridges, etc., within the limits of the local government
10. Charges for public works and public utilities such as waste collection, drainage, sewerage, and water supply
11. Charges for markets and rents for market stalls
12. Charges for the use of bus stations and taxi parks
13. Fees for approval of building plans and erection and reerection of buildings
14. Fees for fairs, agricultural shows, cattle fairs, industrial exhibitions, tournaments, and other public events
15. Fees for licensing of businesses, professions, and vocations
16. Fees for other licenses or permits and penalties or fines for violations
17. Fees for advertisement
18. Fees on sales of animals in cattle markets
19. Fees for registration and certification of births, marriages, and deaths
20. Fees for education and health facilities established or maintained by the local government
21. Fees for other specific services rendered by the local government
22. Rent from land, buildings, equipment, machinery, and vehicles
23. Surpluses from local commercial enterprises
24. Interest on bank deposits or other funds

Source: Devas, Munawwar, and Simon 2008.

Table 4.4 Selected Local Government Taxes by Country, 2010

Countries	Local taxes % Local revenue	As percentage of local taxes		
		Income tax	Sales tax	Property tax
Australia	40.1	0.0	0.0	100.0
Austria	66.5	44.3	37.7	8.7
Belgium	33.4	79.8	14.4	0.0
Canada	37.0	0.0	2.0	98.0
Denmark	44.0	93.6	0.1	6.3
Germany	34.9	85.8	0.8	13.4
Ireland	5.7	0.0	0.0	100.0
Japan	57.9	17.2	23.6	13.5
Norway	49.8	90.2	0.5	6.5
Spain	47.0	38.4	50.5	10.9
Switzerland	52.8	87.0	0.0	12.2
United Kingdom	30.9	0.0	0.0	100.0
United States	38.8	5.9	19.8	74.2
Guatemala			26.2	8.6
Average	37.1	41.6	11.5	44.2

Source: IMF Government Finance Statistics.

every country needs to find its own most suitable local tax system.

The next sections will discuss the following sources of local own-source revenues: property tax, sales tax, automobile tax, local personal income tax, local business tax, user charges, utilities surcharges, fees and fines, and other revenues.

The Property Tax

The property tax can be appropriate for financing local services for many reasons:

- Real property is *immovable*: it cannot move away when taxed or when taxes are increased.

- To the extent that there is a clear link between the services funded at the local level and property values, the *accountability* of local governments to local residents can be substantially improved.

- It can be seen as a *benefit tax,* if the services taxpayers receive (roads, garbage collection, or police services) approximate the value that they pay in property tax.[3]

- Being *visible,* the property tax increases accountability, although it may be more difficult for local governments to increase tax rates.

- Residential property taxes are particularly appropriate to fund local governments because they are *borne by local residents*. In addition, local governments have a comparative advantage in identifying and valuing properties because they are familiar with the local base. Land-based taxes have been used for centuries (see box 4.4).

Property tax can fund those local services that cannot be charged directly to the users through user fees and are not covered by grants. The property tax can also be viewed as a form of *benefit tax* or land-based tax that captures part of the value accrued by a piece of land as a result of public investment in that land or in the vicinity. This assumes that adequate valuations are able to measure the impact of the new investment on land prices (Brzeski 2012). In addition, property taxes can be extremely useful

Box 4.4 Land Tax in Old China

One of the oldest land taxes was used in China for more than 2,000 years. It was established at one-tenth of the product of land and was used to finance infrastructure and security. The taxes were paid in produce. The farther the land was from the capital, the bulkier was the produce used to pay the land tax.

Source: Wikipedia.

for land management, as they discourage land speculation and promote the productive use of urban land.

Property taxes have also some drawbacks, the most important being:

- The high cost of accurate valuation of property values

- The political difficulty of enforcement

- The apparent inelasticity of property values with respect to GDP or national income (property values respond less quickly to changes in GDP than incomes or sales)

- The fact that few jurisdictions update property values on an annual basis. That means that to maintain property tax revenues in real terms local jurisdictions would have to increase the tax rate regularly and this leads to taxpayer resistance and discontent.

These shortcomings explain the relatively smaller role that property taxation plays in developing countries and the small share of revenues that property tax yields in most developing cities. In OECD member countries, the property tax represents 2 percent of GDP; in developing countries it is between 0.3 percent and 0.7 percent of GDP (Slack 2009; Bahl, Martinez-Vasquez, and Youngman 2008). In Australia, Canada, Ireland, South Africa, and the United Kingdom, property taxes provide most of the local revenues (DEXIA 2008). In summary, property tax is not

for everyone. In countries where property rights are not clear, where property boundaries are subject to litigation, where there are multiple claims on land, where land registration is not functioning well, and where the judicial system is absent, then the property work does not work. It is fair to say that in those contexts, fiscal cadastres should not be promoted and that street addressing and the connection between the street addressing data base and the local fiscal registers, focusing on occupancy and street level instead of property rights and plot boundaries should be favored.

Despite the theoretical arguments in favor of the property tax as the best local tax, the difficulties that most countries encounter in trying to use it well have led some tax experts to believe that "governments in developing countries are not able to administer a well-functioning property tax" (Bahl, Martinez-Vazquez, and Youngman 2008) because of the drawbacks listed above. More recently, however, programs have been introduced, as in Colombia, that may indicate how property taxes can be better managed. In Colombia, property tax now accounts for 40 percent of city revenue (see box 4.5). In addition, some developing countries have started to use computer-aided, mass valuation systems (CAMA), which enable annual updating of the tax base (see box 4.6). This modeling process is being introduced in six large cities of Tanzania under a joint World Bank–GIZ project (TSCP). A well-functioning CAMA system, established in Moldova under a World Bank

Box 4.5 Updating the Cadastre to Increase Tax Revenues—The Case of Colombia

Despite general skepticism, the case of Bogotá has proved that political will, technical expertise, and investment can significantly increase property tax proceeds. To raise finances for a planned first subway line, in 2008 the mayor of Bogotá initiated a major updating of the physical records and taxation values of 2.1 million properties. As a result, property tax revenues increased by US$171 million and reached 40 percent of own revenues by 2010. The cost of improvement was less than US$15 million.

Colombia has four cadastre agencies under the National Geographic Institute Agustin Codazzi, that are in charge of establishing the property tax base for its large cities, which are responsible for setting their own rates and collecting the property taxes.

For quite a while, the property tax base of Bogotá had not been updated, and the city was forgoing important revenues during a boom in the real estate market. To capture those gains, the city refurbished tax administration and revaluated the properties. The cadastral value increased by 47 percent, from US$ 66.5 billion in 2008, to US$98 billion in 2010. The key elements behind this success included improved human resource management, introduction of information technology, engagement of stakeholders and career civil servants, openness to review the project's results, massive improvement in assessment techniques with econometric modeling, and mitigation of the project's impact on the property tax through a ceiling on the tax increase. The accompanying chart, figure B4.5.1, shows the gradual increase of tax dues (white) and the revenue forgone through the ceiling on tax increases.

The reassessment exercise led to dramatic increases in cadastral values and property tax bills. To minimize the resistance of taxpayers, Bogotá's city council adopted an increased ceiling, to change the property tax proportionally to the logarithm of the property's value. This had two benefits: (a) it separated the technical updating of the cadastre from the political implications of increasing the property tax; and (b) property owners no longer observe jumps in their property tax, which creates predictability and certainty over the medium term and lessens resistance. The ceiling cut about 20 percent of the additional revenues for 2009 and 2010. These results are in line with the idea of Bahl, Martinez-Vazquez, and Youngman (2010) that "revaluation is not inexpensive, but the consequences of failure to revalue, at least periodically, can be even more costly" (4).

The reassessment work included three components: the *physical* revision of changes in parcels' physical configuration; *legal changes*, through the verification of ownership; and *economic changes* through assessment of property values by researching the real estate market. All these components required human and technical resources proportional to the number of plots and inversely so to the time available for the process. The cadastre update of 1,212,000 urban plots costs the city about US$7.8 million, or US$6.50 per property. Hundreds of temporary workers carried out the physical updating, representing about 35 percent of the total cost. The economic and market analysis represented about 23 percent of the total cost. The rest was spent for technology and administration.

Next steps. Bogotá is trying to implement two strategies: annual updating of the cadastral database and improving the structure of the property tax rate. The city is looking for methods that would allow updating the physical and economic information on

(continued next page)

Box 4.5 *(continued)*

Figure B4.5.1   Property Tax Potential Revenue 2004–10

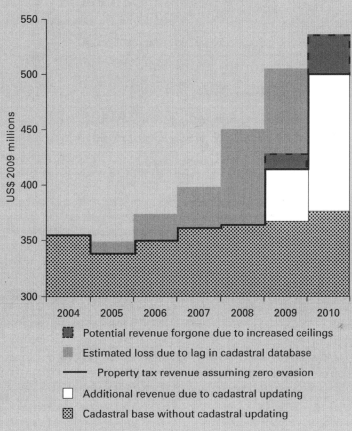

Legend:
- **▨** Potential revenue forgone due to increased ceilings
- **▨** Estimated loss due to lag in cadastral database
- **——** Property tax revenue assuming zero evasion
- **☐** Additional revenue due to cadastral updating
- **▨** Cadastral base without cadastral updating

properties without the massive amount of fieldwork and number of assessors. The physical information will be updated by focusing on new construction activities, using information from the urban curators who issue construction permits, the registry office about changes in ownership, the department of urban planning to monitor changes in land use regulations, and aerial photographs to guide the cadastre staff. The economic information will be obtained by using market samples, with individual assessments of a sample of properties sold in a neighborhood. The rate policy will be changed by introducing rates differentiated by land use and higher rates for vacant land.

The secrets of success. Among the factors leading to the effort's success were strong political support; the technical capacity of the cadastre agencies to revalue properties; and a clear policy to avoid sudden increases in tax bills.

Source: Ruiz and Valejos 2010.

Box 4.6 Computing the Tax Base of a Building in Village X

A house is included in the national cadastre as item # 407 in the ward 080604 (Mt. Michael) with the following elements: the use is for single-family residence; has one floor; total area = 434 m², of which 358.4 m² are constructed; the building is 60 years old. The following table shows the value assessed for purposes of land assessment. The tax base is assessed as follows:

$Vt^* =$	*	Vcx	*	Ax	*	$C_a x$	*	$C_i x$	*	$C_q x$	*	C_v
109,122		609		358.4		1.00		0.9		1.01		0.55
Assessed value		Unit value of buildings		Area of construction		Coefficient of use		Coefficient of location		Coefficient of quality and comfort		Coefficient of age

project with the support of SIDA (Swedish Development Association), has been in use for over a decade.

Performance of the property tax depends on the city's administrative capacity and efforts, which can make or break the system. The operating costs can be upstream (identifying the property and the payer) and downstream (billing and collecting). To make it worthwhile, the property tax administration and operating costs should range from 2 percent to 5 percent of mobilized revenues. A recent survey found that in Turkey, large municipalities collect substantial property tax revenues, whereas hundreds of small municipalities collect less property tax than their costs of administration and collection (Peteri and Sevinc 2011). The potential of property tax is, however, very important, and cities should invest in the capacity required to make it the good instrument that it is meant to be (Brzeski 2012). Ultimately, if the property tax is really going to be made operational, the central government has to make significant efforts to increase capacity and improve cadastres and take on a good deal of at least the initial political costs.

To tax real property, local governments need to follow at least three steps:

1. Identify the properties that are being taxed.

2. Assess the property value and tax base.

3. Set the tax rate.

Property Identification and Fiscal Cadastre

The first step in levying a property tax in one city is to identify the existing real estate properties, their size, use, location, and owners. This is best done with the preparation of a fiscal cadastre, which includes information on each property, including physical description, a notation of ownership, and the assessed value of land and improvements. A complete inventory of all parcels and assigning a unique tax identification number to each property allows a quick tracking of the parcels.

Some countries have a well-developed land cadastre that has been maintained for decades. It identifies the plot boundaries, improvements, ownership, deeds, and other legal requisites. The land cadastre is the basis of ownership transactions and focuses on the legality, the precise boundaries, and zoning regulations. If

Figure 4.5 Cadastre Information (personal files)

it exists, the land cadastre is the best source in establishing a fiscal cadastre. Figure 4.5 shows the land cadastre of a rural property within a set of plots identified in South Portugal in 2006. The identification reference—for example, 0084-R-L10—means that the plot is located in the city of Porches (0084), is a rural parcel (R), and is located in grid L10.

Establishing and updating land cadastres is a time- and money-consuming exercise usually carried out by central government entities under the supervision of the national geographic department to ensure consistency and lower unit costs. Municipalities can use information available in the land cadastre as a basis to design and establish an integrated system for managing the property tax. When land cadastres are not available, local governments

can use simplified procedures in establishing fiscal cadastres (discussed below).

Fiscal cadastres can be prepared without such precise, legally binding identification of the boundaries, deeds, subdivisions, and so forth. They require only good identification, some technical details on land and improvements, ownership or user information, the tax value assessment, and billing records. Property identification may be difficult in developing countries and transition economies. Land cadastres or maps may not exist or may be outdated, ownership information may be incomplete, and data on land records may be kept in separate departments. Figure 4.6 depicts the relationship and sequence among the cadastre, the identification of plots, the assessment of the areas and value, and the billing of the taxes.

Figure 4.6   Information Flow to Assess the Property Tax Base

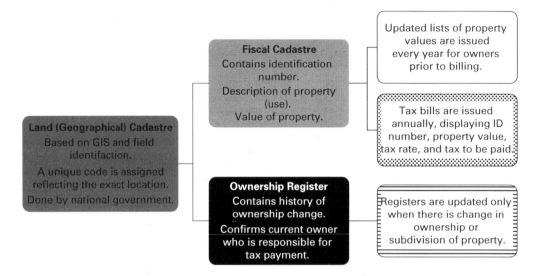

Assessment of the Tax Base

Authorities always emphasize that property is assessed for taxation purposes. In theory, that would mean that the property value is a good estimate of the market value. In reality, property tax is often levied without reference to estimated market value. The general principles of assessing the property tax base and how it can be estimated and updated by applying various models are discussed below.

Tax base models have different typologies, depending on how the property is assessed or valued (Brzeski 2012). Although multiple methods exist, *area-based* and *value-based* assessments are the two main method categories:

- *Area-based assessment* uses the area (or usable area) of the real property assets (for example, square meters of land and improvements) and the characteristics of the plot—urban, rural, close to main centers—to compute its taxation value. This method is used in the Czech Republic and Poland.

- *Value-based assessment* estimates the property value through its market value or the land

register value. This method is used in France and the United States. The market value of the property can be based on the capital land value, the capital value of land and buildings, or annual rental value.

Fiscal experts such as Enid Slack (2009) favor the market value approach, as it is closer to the right cash flow value, captures any improvement in the area, and is more transparent. Developed countries tend to use the market value assessment. Developing countries use a mixture of the two, beginning with area assessment and capturing some market value elements in the unit tax for buildings and land. Area-based models have the advantage of being simple and incurring lower costs. Once the cadastre is prepared, the design is registered, and basic values are given to land and buildings using a unit price system, annual updating requires much less data. It typically requires the area's measurements and type of use (urban, rural). No market data or valuation work is required, which leaves little room for disputes and appeals. Furthermore, area-based models do not require frequent reassessments, which plague value-based systems. However, its revenues are not buoyant and do not increase with market booms. It is, however, recession-proof in that it is independent of market recessions.

Area-Based Assessment

Under an area-based assessment system, the tax jurisdiction estimates the value of a unit (in general, a square meter) of land area, a square meter of building, or some combination of the two. Where both measures of area are included, the assessment of the property is the sum of an assessment rate per square meter multiplied by the size, for example, L_s, t_i, b_i,

L_s = land size (m²)

B_s = building size (m²)

$p_{li,}$ = assessed price of m² land (function of use, and characteristics)

$p_{bi,}$ = assessed price of m² building (function of conservation, quality, and use).

The value assessed will be

$$V = L_s p_l + B_s p_b.$$

The unit value of land and buildings reflects (a) the location—in general, properties in the center of town command higher prices than those in the periphery; (b) the level of conservation of the building; (c) the profitability of rural land; and (d) the use of structures. The example depicted in box 4.6 suggests that area-based models rarely use area solely; they estimate a value that captures the factors that substantially influence market value, such as location, quality, comfort, and age. In short, most area-based models are interconnected with market values, but the relationship is more distant and perhaps less systematic than in the value-based models discussed below.

One of the problems with area-based models is that they are slower in including increments in land value associated with public investments, although some calibration is possible by using coefficients of additional value-influencing factors (Brzeski 2012). Capturing some market

factors in an area-based assessment is important to ensure the fairness of the assessment. That is especially true because citizens see visible differences among properties, and they do so mostly by looking at factors that the market would recognize, such as proximity of infrastructure, access to energy, and the like.

Value-Based Assessments

Value-based assessments follow two main approaches: *market value* or *rental value*. Market value is defined as the price that a willing seller and a willing buyer would agree to on a given property. It can apply to capital land value, or capital land value plus buildings, or buildings separately, or annual rental value. Under the rental value (or annual value) approach, property is assessed according to an estimate of its rental value or net rent. Table 4.5 summarizes the various value-based assessment approaches and indicates the countries applying them.

Value-based assessments are supposed to be close to the market value, but market value can be observed only when a property is sold. Because only a minority of properties are sold in a year, taxable values are just good estimates. Assessing or reassessing market values needs strong support in the form of reliable and up-to-date property data, with building details, and equally reliable and market-based evidence of unbiased sales transactions. These methods require regular reassessment and revaluation, which pose not only technical but also political challenges even in the highly developed countries.

Annual rental value. The annual rental value models use the rental value of the property as the tax base. A net value or a gross value can be used depending on whether the maintenance expenses are borne by the owner or the tenant. The annual rental value models capture a number of market factors in estimating fair rental value. However, policy considerations are also involved, such as preferential rates for owner-occupied properties (as are customary in Pakistan; see table 4.6).

Table 4.5 Assessing the Property Tax Base—Alternative Approaches

Tax base	Definition	Measure used	Where used	Tax rates established by local governments (LG) and the range of tax rates
Assessed unit value, or area based	Size of property adjusted to account for quality and structures	M² of land and building area, adjusted	Armenia, Belgium, Bulgaria, Denmark, Germany, Israel, Italy, Poland, Portugal, Spain	Portugal: LGs set the tax rate, within 0.7 percent and 1.3 percent. Denmark: LGs within 1.6 percent and 3.4 percent. Spain, Poland, and Italy: LGs within a cap set up by central government. Germany: set up by local governments. Bulgaria: 0.15 percent of value of property.
Market value	Price of potential sale or purchase	Comparable sales	Australia, Canada, Hungary, Japan, Netherlands, South Africa, United States	In Hungary, set by local government.
Rental value	Value in current use	Net rental Income	France, India, Ireland, Morocco, Pakistan, United Kingdom	In United Kingdom, as function of a cap. In France, local governments with a cap.
Self-assessment	Sales price	Determined by owner of property	Peru, Turkey	

Sources: Slack 2009; DEXIA 2008.

Table 4.6 Annual Rental Value Tables—Punjab, Pakistan

Residential Property—ARV Valuation Table

		Self-occupied				Rented			
		Land rental value (Rs/sq yd)		Building rental value (Rs/sq ft)		Land rental value (Rs/sq yd)		Building rental value (Rs/sq ft)	
Class	Property situated Main/Off roads	Up to 500 sq yds	Over 500 sq yds	Up to 3,000 sq ft	Over 3,000 sq ft	Up to 500 sq yds	Over 500 sq yds	Up to 3,000 sq ft	Over 3,000 sq ft
A	Main roads	0.4	0.3	0.4	0.3	4	3	4	3
	Off roads	0.3	0.25	0.3	0.25	3	2.5	3	2.5
B	Main roads	0.3	0.25	0.3	0.25	3	2.5	3	2.5
	Off roads	0.25	0.2	0.25	0.2	2.5	2	2.5	2
C	Main roads	0.25	0.2	0.25	0.2	2.5	2	2.5	2
	Off roads	0.2	0.15	0.2	0.15	2	1.5	2	1.5

Source: Ellis, Kopanyi, and Lee 2007.

Annual rental value systems may not yield good revenue if areas have rent controls. The Pakistan annual rental value table may look like an area-based system, but the unit taxes (e.g., 0.4 rupee per square yard) were estimated from market samples of actual rental transactions.

Other simplified tax base variants. Table 4.7 shows the prevalence of property taxation around the world. Other tax base variants include (a) a unitary flat tax, for cities that need cash and decide to use the same tax for all properties (Ireland); (b) and initial acquisition value, by which cities use historical acquisition values as

an expression of the premium for long-term residence (because the initial value does not change over time, the tax base is highly inequitable); and (c) banding of values; that is, properties are classified as belonging to a certain established "band" of values.

Updating the property tax base and improving tax administration represented a significant investment for Bogotá city; the total cost was nearly US$17 million (over 2009 and 2010), which was repaid by the additional tax proceeds well within one year. Table 4.8 summarizes the direct cost of updating the database.

Table 4.7   Methods Used to Assess the Property Tax Base

Region	Countries	Capital land value	Capital value land and buildings	Capital value land and buildings separate	Capital value buildings only	Annual rental value	Area based	Unitary flat tax
Africa	25	1	8	3	4	7	11	6
Asia	24	2	6	2	0	11	11	0
W. Europe	13	0	9	0	0	6	0	0
E. Europe	20	1	6	0	0	0	15	0
Latin America	16	2	14	1	0	1	0	0
Total	98	6	43	6	4	25	37	6

Source: Muccluskey, Bell, and Lim 2010.

Table 4.8   Updating the Property Tax Database in Bogotá

Item	Cost US$ thousands 2009	Percent	Observations
Administrative support	557.8	7.1	Management and administrative staff including selection of personnel to be hired.
Support staff and material	954.8	12.2	Project headquarters, vehicles, attire, secretaries, and assistants.
Mapping	392.2	5.0	Digitizing staff, carrier officers to supervise.
Communications	79.1	1.0	Staff and contractors, managing relations with communities and media.
Economic component	958.1	12.2	Assessors, carrier civil servants, econometric modeling team.
IT support	560.5	7.2	Hardware and program assistants, IT support staff.
Temporary employees	4,330.3	55.3	Over 460 technicians and professionals.
Total	7,832.8	100.0	

Source: Ruiz and Valejos 2010.

CAMA. Computer-aided mass appraisal has become widely used in the United States, Canada, and Western Europe in the last two decades. It has been introduced to developing countries with great success, as it enables the assessment of a property tax base with much less data and cost (Eckert 2008).

CAMA is a process to estimate a *hedonic price* index for a class of real estate, such as residential properties, from a representative sample of sold properties from the entire population (Eckert 2008). The index relates sales prices to the physical and location features of the sold properties. The weights (or the coefficients of the estimated regressions) are then used to value unsold properties. In this way, local governments can have a valuation of the universe of unsold properties. CAMA brings an easier way to assess the property tax base, and in a way, it

has revolutionized the administration of property taxes (see box 4.7). The traditional valuation methods require a great deal of data on sales and rents and are therefore expensive to use in transitional and developing countries. Recent improvements in spatial analyses of location, using GIS and low-level technology, have reduced the amount and type of data needed for CAMA.

In countries in transition where there is an existing property tax, CAMA can be very useful in recalibrating models to achieve more market-oriented results. In countries without a tax, CAMA, with some low-level technology and external ground data, can establish a working property tax at a reasonable cost in a relatively short time. In Kosovo, a property tax was established in 30 cities in 18 months. In Cape Town, a general revaluation was done in two years using CAMA. Further updates can be done in months

---

Box 4.7 Developing a Computer-Assisted Mass Appraisal Model

The development of a CAMA method follows several steps:

Data collection. Data are gathered concerning both sold and unsold properties, including and inventory of property characteristics, location, and other factors that may affect value. Data can be qualitative or quantitative and categorical (good, fair, poor) or continuous (e.g., number of beds). Data are then analyzed in terms of distribution and to identify outliers. Data are fitted into multiple regression analysis to identify the strongest predictors of the value of the property in analysis.

CAMA modeling. The appraiser developing the model uses various techniques to develop an appraisal model that replicates the market in assigning value to the various features of a property. Such techniques may include linear or multiple regression statistical analysis, or

modification of existing or accepted models. A linear model is the easiest and can be estimated as follows:

$$P = A_0 + A_1 X_1 + A_s X_2 + \cdots + A_n X_n,$$

where P is the sale price of the property; X_i is the attribute of the property—location, quality, size, and use.

A_i is the estimated weight that will be used later to assess the value of the unsold property.

A key part of the modeling process involves continual testing of the model to determine if it is accurately predicting the value of properties. Once a CAMA model is developed by the appraiser for a class or subclass of property, it is then applied to all properties, sold and unsold, in that class or subclass. This ensures that all properties in the class or subclass are treated equitably.

Source: Eckert 2008.

(Eckert 2008). The problem is that collection rates and valuation efforts often do not keep up with the speed of the new systems. In Kosovo, collections are less than half the amount billed annually, and local governments are not valuing properties, so the base is eroding almost as fast as it was created.

Establishing Tax Rates

Once the tax base is chosen, the next element is to set the tax rate, which usually is a local government function. Local governments set property tax rates in different ways:

- They can choose one rate for all assessed properties (the simplest way) or use different rates according to whether the government is taxing land or buildings or urban or rural land; according to location and type of infrastructure available; or according to use (residential, commercial, industrial).

- The central government may put a cap on the local tax rate, as well as a limit on abatements and exemptions.

- Property tax rates may be updated annually using an inflation index that maintains the real value of the tax proceeds and minimizes political controversies.

- In some cases, as in Australia, Canada, and the United States, local governments determine their expenditure requirements, subtract the amount they expect to receive from other revenues such as grants and other taxes, and divide the residual amount by the assessed property value to get the property tax rate. This process undergoes several iterations before the increase in tax is announced, for a sudden increase in tax rate would have to be justified and supported by similar market value increases rather than merely by the wish of the local government to spend more.

Changing rates or adjusting the base is subject to policy decisions. In Bogotá, property tax rates vary from 3 percent in the rural areas to 30 percent for vacant urban land taxed on a rental value basis. The last reform in 2007 focused on updating the basic cadastre and keeping it current on an annual basis. The results have been impressive, although the city has established tax increase ceilings to avoid upsetting the taxpayers with sudden hikes in their property tax bills (described above in box 4.5). Assessed tax values have increased several times, and collection results have also improved.

By contrast, in many transition and developing economies, the national government may set the rates for property taxes, in the form of either a cap or a range of rates. Local governments may vary rates by class of property, for example, residential, commercial, and industrial (India, Pakistan). This is justified because needs and consumption of public goods vary, and when local governments want to attract businesses, these taxes may come into play. Often local governments can establish their own tax rate, within a range of values agreed with the central government.

Billing, Delivery, Collection, and Enforcement

Billing, delivery, collection, and enforcement ("downstream activities") have a substantial impact on the performance of the property tax. Many local governments understand their importance and have a keen interest in maximizing the results. Some of these activities can be outsourced to the private sector, provided there are good incentives for effective collection and enforcement (Brzeski 2012). Billing and delivery may be a challenge in countries without good property addressing systems (box 4.8).

Although voluntary compliance is always preferred, enforcement is unavoidable and requires procedures for dealing with tax arrears and noncompliance. Public awareness of simple, swift, and effective procedures, including judicial sale or arrest, usually induces voluntary compliance. Additional encouragement to compliance can be achieved when payment is easy to make

Box 4.8 Property Tax in the West Bank

Local taxation in the West Bank is fairly difficult considering the particular circumstances. However, despite the constraints, the property tax is collected in 29 towns, and property tax revenue represents about one-fifth (19.16 percent) of the total current budget.

Source: World Bank 2010.

(electronic payment via the Internet, or payment at the local post office) and tax bills provide information about how the money is spent, rather than about the penalties for noncompliance. Tax arrears are relatively small in developed countries (4 percent or 5 percent in Canada and the United States), but they can reach 40 percent to 50 percent, as they have in the Balkans, Kenya, and the Philippines.[4]

Disputes and complaints are dealt by the compliance office of the property tax authority, as they may be based on incorrect information. When the taxpayer is not satisfied, the issue may follow the administrative process of arbitrage and tax tribunals.

In sum, the property tax is a good tax for local governments—the tax base is fixed, and when the proceeds are used to pay for local services they approximate a user fee (Ingram 2008). In addition, property tax revenue is predictable and stable, a clear advantage for local governments that do not have much diversity in revenues. In developing countries, however, the property tax may be difficult to implement. First, administration may be costly, especially the initial investment in property identification and staff training. New techniques, such as computer-assisted mass appraisal, can significantly reduce the cost of valuation. Second, local governments may tax more nonresidential property because it is easier to obtain revenue from a deeper pocket. However, that might be counterproductive, since businesses are mobile and may leave town. Third, local governments cannot rely on property tax for purposes other

than the provision of public goods. For expenditures such as education and health, transfers from the central government are the best direct source of revenue. Ironically, it is in those countries where the property tax is used to fund teacher wages that the yields and systems are the most significant (e.g., Montgomery County, Maryland, and Fairfax County, Virginia, in the Washington, D.C., metropolitan area). Simplified procedures, such as area-based assessments (as are used in Bangalore) and self-assessments (introduced in such cities as Bogotá), have led to significant increases.

In many countries, the property tax is under attack (Ingram 2008). Its unpopularity comes from its visibility—taxpayers are faced with large tax bills once or twice a year. Many taxpayer revolts can be traced to rapid increases in property tax bills, and many recent reforms involve limiting increases in property tax bills from year to year. The visibility of the tax is also a virtue in that it provides an incentive for citizens to scrutinize the expenditures of the local government, promoting fiscal discipline and citizen involvement. For many local governments with limited technical capacity, the biggest difficulty in implementing a property tax is obtaining accurate information on the properties to be taxed and their value. Without this basic information, local authorities will have a hard time designing and implementing an efficient and fair real estate tax.

The debate over whether the property tax is the best local tax is still very much alive and, as indicated earlier, property tax is not for everybody. But a larger number of experiences around the world provide information on how local governments have dealt with their particular circumstances and have succeeded in using property taxation to finance their functions (Bahl, Martinez-Vazquez, and Youngman 2008; 2010).

General Consumption or Sales Taxes

Local sales taxes are general consumption taxes charged at the point of purchase for certain goods and services. The tax is set as a percentage of the price of the purchased product. A sales tax is a regressive tax, meaning that its impact decreases as a payer's income increases. Ideally, a sales tax is fair, has a high compliance rate, is difficult to avoid, and is simple to calculate and collect. A conventional or retail sales tax attempts to achieve that ideal by charging only the final or end user. It is unlike a gross receipts tax, which is levied on the intermediate business that purchases materials for production or ordinary operating expenses prior to delivering a service or product to the marketplace. The sales tax prevents so-called tax cascading, or pyramiding, in which an item is taxed more than once as it makes its way from production to final retail sale.

General consumption taxes include retail sales taxes and value added taxes (VATs). Local retail sales tax rates are in general about 2 percent to 5 percent and are collected by the cash counters of stores and from other final sales transactions. They are very important for local governments. In Spain, they account for half of local revenues; in Austria, 30 percent; and in the United States, 25 percent.

Local sales taxes have two main benefits: (a) they provide an elastic source of revenue—that is, when the economy grows, so do retail sales, providing more revenue for the local government; and (b) they are transparent and easy to collect. They also have shortcomings: evasion problems can sometimes be serious, and large rate differentials between neighboring local governments lead to people crossing the border to make purchases in the lower-rate city. Local sales tax can be a small surtax attached to the central or provincial or state tax system. Sometimes cities introduce an additional, "piggyback" tax or surcharge of 1 percent or 2 percent. That could be a good way to go, since it is easy both technically and politically and would avoid high compliance costs.

Value added tax (VAT). In most countries, the general sales tax (or gross receipts tax) is levied as a value added tax at the central government level, although there is some experience with state or provincial VATs as well, as in Brazil. Many analysts believe that the sales tax is not a good tax and suggest that it should be abolished and incorporated into a comprehensive value added tax (Werneck 2008). Turnover sales taxes have been gradually replaced by national VATs in many countries, leaving local governments without an important local tax. In such cases, tax revenue sharing arrangements have been devised to distribute part of the tax proceeds among local governments. Such sharing ought to be in the nature of a grant and not based on origin. However, the infrastructure needed for an effective VAT is fairly big, including proper accounting practices, which may be lacking in developing economies, where sales without receipts or electronic registers are common and so is the informal sector.

Local governments outside the United States seldom levy general sales taxes. The exception is Brazil, where they are a major form of municipal taxation (the *imposto sobre servicos,* or ISS), imposed on all services except communications and interstate and intercity public transportation, which are taxed by the states. The ISS is imposed on retail sales at the minimum rate of 2 percent; maximum rates differ by the type of service, with the maximum being 5 percent of gross revenue. The main problem with gross receipts taxes is that they tax business inputs and cause tax cascading effects, with consequent distortions to the organization of production, as businesses attempt to reduce tax liabilities.

Selective sales taxes on automobiles (such as fuel taxes and vehicle registration) are another type of sales taxes. They have a double benefit in that they discourage road use and at the same time produce revenues that are often earmarked for road maintenance.

Local Personal Income Tax

Income taxes are used at the local level but to a much lesser degree than property or retail sales taxes. Local personal income taxes can be of two types: a surtax on the central or state income tax (a piggyback tax) or a separate, locally administered tax. The second type is less common because it is more difficult to implement and very expensive to administer.

Local income taxes are not common in developing countries. Rather, local governments in less developed countries (e.g., in Pakistan, Serbia, Turkey) receive a substantial share of income tax revenues through tax sharing systems such as those outlined in chapter 1 (Bird 2001). Nevertheless, income taxes can be justified at the local level on the grounds that local governments are increasingly being called upon to address issues of poverty, crime, regional transportation, and other regionwide needs. To the extent that local governments are required to provide social services, a small tax on incomes is probably more appropriate than a property tax because the local income tax is more closely related to ability to pay.

The local income tax is a big revenue raiser in Nordic countries, yielding revenues of up to 15 percent of GDP. Municipalities in Denmark, Finland, and Sweden impose local income taxes on their own, parallel to the national income tax, because they are directly responsible for social services and health. They use the tax base assessed for national income tax purposes (a similar system is used by the state governments of the United States). In these countries, the local personal income tax constitutes the main source of local revenues (85 percent in Finland and Denmark; almost 100 percent in Sweden; 16 percent in Belgium). To prevent the local government from overtaxing, the public tax ceiling has become a formal agreement in Denmark, Norway, and Sweden (Slack 2009).

Local Business Tax

Local business taxes, or taxes on economic activity, take various forms. The tax can be a corporate income tax, a tax on capital or labor; a nonresidential property tax; or it can be a license fee or other charge to commerce or industry. In the European Union, 10 countries use a business tax, which contributes between 15 percent and 30 percent of local governments' revenue. The local business tax is more important than any other local tax in Germany, Hungary, Italy, and Luxembourg (see table 4.9 and box 4.9).

The local business tax is calculated on different bases, depending on the country. The two main approaches are stock base or flow base.

Table 4.9 Main Local Business Taxes in the European Union

Country	Name of tax	Base	Percentage of tax revenues	Percentage of total revenues
Austria	Municipal business	Value of salaries	20	10
France	Professional tax	Rental value of capital assets	43	19
Germany	Local business tax	Company profit	43	19
Hungary	Local business tax	Net turnover tax: difference between revenues and cost of production	38	12
Italy	Regional tax	Net value added	54	24
Spain	Economic activity tax	Profit on economic activity	9	3

Source: DEXIA 2008.

Box 4.9 Local Business Taxes around the World

In Côte d'Ivoire, the main local tax is a local business tax (*patente*). It is a set of fixed taxes that vary according to the type, size, and location of a business. This tax produces one-third of total revenues in Abidjan. A similar tax exists in Morocco, where six tax rates are applied to several hundred categories of businesses, classified by rental value and type of business. In Tunisia, the business tax is levied at a rate of one-fifth of 1 percent of gross business income.

Hungarian local governments collected 86 percent of their own-source revenues from local businesses, with a maximum rate of only 0.3 percent but on a base of gross sales. In addition, a small communal tax, at a fixed amount per employee, is levied based on businesses' average number of employees. In Ukraine, a simplified system was introduced consisting of fixed rates on gross sales by sole owners, plus a 10 percent sales tax on gross sales by enterprises.

In Latin America, local business taxes are quite common. Argentina has a local tax on gross receipts at rates between 1 percent and 12 percent. Colombia's business tax ranges from 0.2 percent to 1 percent of gross receipts. Sometimes a tax is levied on the firm's wealth. Chile imposes a tax of 2.5 percent to 5 percent on firms' net wealth; Ecuador imposes a similar tax at 3 percent. In Kenya, the business tax is in the form of a license fee, a flat contribution that is not related to the income or assets of the business.

Source: Bird 2001.

Using stocks (e.g., payroll, the number of employees, value of property assets, capital goods) to determine the tax base enables local governments to have relatively stable tax revenue from one year to the next. Many view it as unfair, since it ignores businesses' ability to pay and discriminates among stocks or specific assets. That is not the case when the tax assessment is based on flows (e.g., profit, added value, or net turnover); that is more equitable for businesses but is sensitive to change in the economic environment and provides less-predictable tax revenue. Box 4.9 provides a summary of how business taxes are used in different countries.

Local business taxes are often popular with residents and elected officials because (a) they are more responsive to economic growth than property taxes; (b) cities have more discretion over the level of the business tax than any other tax rate; and (c) no one is sure about the incidence of the tax, so it is easy to claim that it is partly exported to nonresidents. One good economic argument in favor of local business taxation is that it can be seen as a proxy for a *benefit tax*. However, public services benefiting specific businesses would be better paid by appropriate user charges, as well as a property tax. When these charges are not feasible, some form of broadly based business tax is justified.

Local business taxes have several shortcomings. First, local business taxes are generally not equitable and may accentuate disparities among cities; they lend themselves to being exploited. Second, from a policy viewpoint, a high business tax can hurt employment and investment, especially in economic downturns. That is the reason that the local business tax in the European Union has been revised in many countries to exempt small firms. Third, corporate income taxes are difficult to administer because the payers have to determine how much income is attributable to the local jurisdiction imposing the tax; especially when firms have businesses in several jurisdictions, that process is technically complex. For instance, in Turkey, the large cities gain exceptionally high local taxes from corporate income because they host the headquarters of large firms that operate around the country. For transitional economies, a local business tax is one of the easiest taxes to levy, whereas their limited administrative capacity often makes the use of other taxes, such as the property tax, more difficult.

It is odd to notice that although economists agree that local business taxes are inefficient and distort economic decisions, most governments at all levels ignore such advice and impose them anyway (Bird 2006). They do so on the basis that if the proceeds are used to provide services to local businesses, the use of a business tax at the local level is totally compatible with the benefit principle. In addition, local governments often have very few tax alternatives. Being able to tax local businesses, without arousing the opposition of their entire constituency, can be a powerful argument in its favor. Countries with long experience of using local business taxes include Brazil, Canada, Germany, Hungary, Japan, Kenya, Ukraine, the United States, and most West African countries.

Motor Vehicle Taxes

The motor vehicle tax is becoming more common in urban areas in both developed and developing economies. Vehicle taxes are consistent with the criteria of equity, ability to pay, and the benefit principle. Generally there is a positive correlation between the market price of vehicles and the level of income of their owners. Vehicle taxes are easier to manage in comparison to other local revenue sources. The characteristics of vehicles are well known, and so are the average market prices, based on mileage and physical condition. Tax enforcement is relatively easy and effective, considering that for this particular tax, enforcement is usually done directly by the police.

For instance, not having an up-to-date vehicle registration (i.e., proof of tax compliance) may result in a fine, removal of plates, or vehicle impoundment. Just as with all other local taxes, effective and efficient management of the vehicle tax requires a complete database on vehicle owners and a credible enforcement system. In many countries, this is typically a shared tax with local governments receiving 50 to 100 percent of the yield. National governments are usually reluctant to give taxing power over cars to local jurisdictions. Doing so can create tax competition between jurisdictions if the registry rules are leaky.

Vehicle registration fees are also better for reducing local pollution and congestion because these negative externalities are largely localized by owners' registration and vary by engine size, vehicle age, axle, and weight. These factors affect the amount of pollution, congestion, and road damage more than would fuel consumption.

Fuel taxes are typically national and aim at financing intercity roads and externalities. Fuel purchase is also less localized, so that a fuel tax is less efficient in reducing local externalities than congestion charges or tolls, which can vary by time of day and location (Slack 2009). Cities that levy a fuel tax often piggyback on state fuel taxes because the administrative costs of levying their own tax would be too high. The earnings from this tax are generally earmarked for local roads and transit services or environmental remediation.

Administration remains the core and main challenge for an effective vehicle taxation system. Adequate updating of a motor vehicle database should be automatic. That means that the vehicles database is updated as part of the transfer of ownership when the sale of a vehicle is completed. For instance, the plate of a sold car remains with the seller, and the new owner must obtain a new plate. This provides strong support to timely ownership records, since driving without a plate or registration is a criminal charge. Tax rates for the purpose of tax assessment need to be transparent, and tax payment obligations and deadlines need to be communicated to all owners on a yearly basis. A stamp on the plate or windshield is a simple, cheap, and transparent instrument. Enforcement needs to be credible, and impounding vehicles should be considered an enforcement option.

Congestion taxes are a recent type of tax designed and implemented in large cities with the objective of discouraging the use of private cars and reducing congestion and pollution in the city center. The tax has been successfully implemented in London, Milan, Singapore, and Stockholm. Congestion and pollution have been substantially reduced, and the proceeds of the congestion tax have been used to finance the renovation of major public transit systems, notably the subway in London. The methods to compute and levy the tax vary; for example, an average tax charged during particular hours (London, between 7 a.m. and 6 p.m.) or as a function of the congestion in the city and the hour of the day (Singapore). The congestion tax is an example of a win-win situation in which a fiscal tool generates revenues for the local government and also leads to less carbon emission. It promotes the use of the mass transport system, contributes to improving air quality, and generates time savings in commuting, hence increasing urban productivity.

User Charges

User charges are paid by consumers to the local government for private goods and services, such as water, electricity, waste collection, or public transport. A user charge is a charge per unit of output, for example, the water tariff per cubic meter of consumed water, the electricity bill for a given consumption of kilowatt hours, and the fee per trash bin or per kilogram to collect solid waste. User charges or user fees have an interesting economic rationale. Well-designed user fees allow residents and businesses to know how much they are paying for services. When proper prices are charged, governments can make efficient decisions about how much to provide, and citizens can make efficient decisions about how much to consume. In theory, user charges affect behavior and promote an optimal level of consumption that is reached when the price equals the cost of providing an additional unit of the service (see box 4.10).

User charges are subject to local politics and often are set below costs, particularly in developing countries, with multiple negative consequences, such as the following: (a) The service provider owned by the municipality may reduce the quality, time of availability, or coverage of services (for instance, water is provided only three or four hours per day in most Pakistani cities). (b) The provider requires subsidies from the municipal budget, so that the costs are eventually paid by the same customers or taxpayers. (c) Underpricing a service (by not charging enough for it) can result in overconsumption. In contrast, user fees for water that are based on marginal cost encourage water conservation, discourage water consumption for low-value uses (e.g., watering the lawn or washing the car), and postpone the time when new investment is needed (Devas 2001).

User charges are also an important way to provide economic signals, both to consumers, concerning the scarcity of services, and to providers, about the demand for services that needs to be met. User fees also ration the use of existing facilities and give appropriate capital investment signals. In other words, they can reduce the demand for infrastructure: "Whenever possible, local public services should be charged for rather than given away" (Bird 2001). Cost recovery is a basic economic principle but may be in conflict with social justice in that some low-income groups may not be able to afford cost-recovery-level tariffs. Thus, appropriate tariffs may require targeted subsidies to ensure access to public services for the poor.

Designing User Charges

Determining the proper domain and design of user charges is quite challenging. In theory, municipalities should charge for private good services the same price as would be charged in a competitive market.

Box 4.10 Water Tariffs—An Example of User Charges

A water tariff is a price charged for water supplied by a service provider. It is supposed to recover the costs of water treatment, storage, transportation, and delivery. Water tariffs vary widely among cities. Tariffs (often average cost pricing) can be set below costs (which leads to overconsumption), at the level of cost recovery, or above the level of cost recovery to include a predetermined return on capital.

Water tariffs are set based on (a) financial criteria (cost recovery); (b) economic criteria (efficiency pricing based on marginal cost); and sometimes (c) environmental criteria (incentives for water conservation). In addition, social considerations play a role, such as a desire to avoid too great a burden on poor users. Water tariffs include at least one of the following components: a volumetric tariff, in which metering is applied, or a flat rate, with no metering. The tariff for a first block on an increasing block tariff (IBT) is usually set very low to protect poor households. The size of a first block can vary from five to 50 cubic meters per household per month. In South Africa, the first block of six cubic meters per household per month is provided free (free basic water).

International comparisons. Linear volumetric tariffs are the most common form of water tariff in OECD countries. Tariffs whose unit costs go up with the level of consumption—increasing-block tariff systems—are used by about half of the water utilities in OECD countries, such as Spain. Flat rates are still reported in Canada, Mexico, New Zealand, Norway, and the United Kingdom. As for developing countries, a recent sampling of 94 utilities indicated that one-third used increasing-block tariffs and the remainder used flat fees. The highest water tariff in the world is found in Scotland, equivalent to US$9.45 per cubic meter ($m^3$) in 2007. The lowest is in Ireland, where residential water is provided free. The lowest residential water and wastewater tariffs were found in Ljubljana, Slovenia (equivalent to US$0.01 per m^3); Saudi Arabia (equivalent to US$0.03 per m^3); Havana, Cuba; and Karachi, Pakistan (equivalent to US$0.04 per m^3). The highest water and wastewater tariffs were found in Copenhagen (US$8.00 per m^3), Honolulu (US$7.61 per m^3), and Glasgow (US$5.89 per m^3). An even higher combined water and wastewater tariff can be found in Essen, Germany, a city that was not included in the OECD survey. The tariff in Essen is equivalent to US$8.41 (€5.61) per m^3, according to a survey carried out for the weekly magazine *Der Spiegel*. Many utilities charge higher tariffs for commercial and industrial customers than for residential users as a way to subsidize residential customers.

Source: Easter and Liu 2005.

Four Methods of Computing User Charges

- *Marginal cost pricing* is the ideal way to compute a user charge, as it approximates the market price in perfect competitive market, that is, the cost of producing an additional unit of the good. This principle is difficult to apply because it requires complete information on the cost of the product, as well as the opportunity cost, that is, the value of the alternative use of resources if they were not used for the good or service being offered. Other concepts are important, including the long-term marginal cost; that is, the cost of expanding the facility, including infrastructure and capital costs.

- *Average cost pricing* is a more practical method that guarantees that all costs will be recovered. The prices are easier to calculate: all the financial costs required for providing a certain service are divided by the number of consumers or the volume sold, which produces the appropriate user charge.

- *Average incremental pricing* uses the average cost price but asks how much it would cost to serve an additional consumer.

- *Multipart tariffs* unbundle the service and charge for each component according to its price elasticity. Multipart tariffs make it possible to set a fixed charge for basic consumption, with progressively higher charges for greater consumption, to help low-income customers through built-in subsidies in the tariff structure. Some of these pricing techniques may also consider higher unit-prices during peak hours of consumption (e.g., electricity supply), as well as separate fees for new connections to the existing network. These one-time fees usually cover part of the capital cost of the investments in the services' main infrastructure.

Difficulties with User Charges

The biggest difficulty with user charges is the suggestion that they harm low-income families, who cannot afford to pay them. Many studies have shown that this is not true, as the poor tend to pay higher prices for privately sold water. A consensus exists that relatively simple pricing systems, such as a low initial charge for the first block of service use, can deal with most inequity concerns.

A second problem is the cost of metering or implementing the price system. Charging the marginal cost of water requires metering, and the installation of meters has a cost. Costs are also associated with obtaining the information that municipalities need to price services correctly. For example, they need to know long-term capital costs, infrastructure investments that will be needed, and so forth. Many municipalities lack the necessary expertise to price correctly.

Some practical issues regarding the implementation of user charges include the lack of technical knowledge on how to set an adequate user charge structure; the lack of a cost accounting system to determine the actual cost of service provision that would need to be recovered to ensure service sustainability; and a fairly weak enforcement system due, in some cases, to shortsighted interest in short-term political gains at the expense of the financial sustainability and quality of municipal services. However, even if average cost is the adopted method, local entities and their public facilities would do well to employ user charges. They discourage overconsumption and provide a steady stream of revenue to local governments.

Surcharges on Utilities

Utility surcharges are levied on household services, such as water, electricity, telephones (landlines and mobile phones), and cable television (box 4.11 is a summary of the surcharges in Fairfax County, Virginia). They are widely used because recovery tariffs are well accepted and the surcharge is typically a small addition to the generally acceptable bills. Surcharges[5] constitute an emerging form of taxation for developing countries. They act as increases in utility tariffs, and they may discourage the consumption of services. In general, however, people believe that they meet the criteria of a broad tax base and fairly low tax rate, making these taxes more affordable and politically acceptable.

In practice, these surcharges should be used for specific purposes, notably to increase the efficiency of the services being taxed. An example is the energy fund in Alameda County, in California, established in 1995 to finance energy-saving projects to make electricity cheaper for consumers in the longer run (see box 4.12).

Municipalities in the West Bank offer another unique case, where surcharges are the largest

Box 4.11 Charging Willing Buyers

There are 11 various taxes and surcharges imposed on cable TV, Internet, and phone services in Fairfax County, Virginia, in the United States. The charges increase the direct service fee by 11.9 percent. The largest items include a communications sales tax of 6.43 percent and a federal subscriber lines charge of 6.07 percent. The smallest are nearly invisible: a federal regulatory recovery fee of 0.08 percent, a cost recovery surcharge of 0.06 percent, and a federal excise tax of 0.18 percent.

Box 4.12 Surcharge for Energy Saving

Alameda County, California, in the United States, collects utility surcharges to finance energy saving investments. All proceeds are deposited in a Designated Energy Fund. The money is used to increase the efficiency of planned projects, help pay for projects with long payback periods, and cover gaps in project financing.

Source: http://californiaseec.org/documents/best-practices/best-practices-alameda-county-ac-fund.

local revenue source. Municipalities impose surcharges on both electricity and water, which provide substantial general local revenues. These two surcharges generated half of all local revenues—36.0 percent and 14.3 percent, respectively—in 2008 (World Bank 2010).

Fees, Permits, and Licenses

User fees include license fees, such as those for registering marriages and births, fees for providing a copy of a marriage or birth certificate, or pet registration. These fees aim to reimburse the cost the local administration incurred to provide that service or document. However, a number of license fees are in fact taxes, set high above actual costs. These typically include business or professional license fees, building permits, and others.

Taxing by charging high fees. Charging excessive fees has become a popular practice in developing countries. These seem to be cheap and easy

revenues, but they have substantial implications that policy makers need to be aware of. In some countries *business licenses* constitute an important revenue source. Businesses are relatively easy to identify, and enforcement is based on the need for a license to operate legally. Business licenses also serve other purposes, such as compliance with public safety ordinances and regulations on hygiene, for example, in restaurants, schools, and sport facilities. However, excessive license fees may discourage business development and eventually be transferred to customers.

Construction permits or building licenses in rapidly growing cities may generate significant revenues. (Teheran offers an extreme case, in which building permits provide two-thirds of the city's revenues.) They offer easy identification, ability to pay, and practically automatic enforcement—no payment, no license. Construction permits serve other purposes, such as public safety and compliance with zoning rules and regulations and minimum construction specifications. However, high building permit fees may have negative effects on willingness to pay user charges over time; some developers argue that they have paid the fee for water, road, and waste removal by paying a high license fee in advance.

Land development fees and construction permits are by far the most important local government revenues in many developing countries, including most of the post-Yugoslav countries. In some of the Balkan countries, land development fees constitute a large share of local governments revenues (50%). This has a number of implications on the level of vulnerability of the municipal revenues structure as well as the way municipal land is dispensed of and the way cities of the region urbanize. The 2008 financial cricis has shown the need to diversify the sources of revenues. Abolishing these fees would curtail new investments, but allowing local governments to set them at any level hurts business and encourages illegal construction. One alternative is for the central government to impose rate ceilings, as in Albania. The tax base could be set per square meter, by zones, or on estimated construction costs.

Professional licenses are sometimes used in developing countries, typically for specific high-revenue professions such as lawyers, doctors, and real estate agents. In some countries, however, the costs of collection and enforcement may be greater than the revenue they generate. The use of electronic forms has reduced the cost of administering these taxes.

Development impact fees are one-time charges applied to offset the additional public service costs associated with new development. Development impact fees are usually applied at the time a building permit is issued and are dedicated to provision of the additional services—such as water and sewer systems, roads, schools, libraries, and parks and recreation facilities—made necessary by the presence of new residents in the area. The funds collected cannot be used for operation, maintenance, repair, alteration, or replacement of existing capital facilities and cannot just be added to general revenue. They are essentially user fees levied in anticipation of use, expanding the capacity of existing services to handle additional demand. The amount of the fee may not be arbitrary but must be clearly linked to the added service cost.

Fines and Penalties

The category of fines and penalties primarily includes motor vehicle traffic violations and penalties for late payment of taxes and user charges. Their use varies from one city to another. Fines and penalties can be a significant revenue source for urban traffic management in medium-size and large cities. Amman City, Jordan, has introduced a computerized system for recording and penalizing traffic violations. Because half of the country's population lives in, and the other half often travels into, Amman, it has improved traffic rule compliance and generated substantial revenue for the city.

Current Revenue from Assets

Current revenue from assets is mainly rent from leases of municipal land and buildings. Table 4.10 summarizes the main capital revenue categories.

This category of revenues applies to municipal real estate used in retail and wholesale activities; for example, municipal food markets and municipal urban land and buildings. Asset revenues often have great potential. Potential revenue

Table 4.10 Main Capital Revenue Categories

Categories	Capital revenues
Own-source revenues	Asset sales
	Betterment fees
	Contributions
	Current surplus
Revenues from higher government levels	General capital grant
	Earmarked grants
External revenues	Loans, bonds, and equity

from assets is sometimes underutilized because inventories of municipal fixed assets are generally incomplete and outdated, or they may never have been developed. To improve revenues from land assets, cities can benefit from (a) more transparent management of fixed assets; (b) a legal requirement that city governments submit yearly balance sheets to the overseeing authorities explicitly reporting on fixed assets; (c) a competitive system to set rents and award leases; and (d) good contract management and enforcement, supported by a transparent, reliable, and up-to-date asset revenue database. Further details and discussion on the management of local government assets are included in chapter 6.

Other Recurrent Revenues

"Other recurrent revenues" is a residual category that indicates possible misclassification if it is too large. A figure greater than 5 percent may mean that the revenue manager does not have an accurate account of the items included as revenue. It also signals a lack of transparency that hurts accountability. A large "other revenues" segment also could be a result of balloon budgeting, as when the local finance department puts a large sum in the category to ensure a formally balanced budget. This is a highly inappropriate budgeting practice that violates basic disciplines and distorts budget execution.

Capital Revenues and Main Sources of Capital Investment Financing

In many countries revenue accounting requires segregating current (also called "recurrent" or "nondevelopment") revenues and capital (also called "nonrecurrent" or "development") revenues. The reasons behind this distinction are (a) the basic principle that a municipality should finance its regular operations from recurrent revenue flows; (b) that nonrecurrent revenues are better accounted in, and used for, capital or

development expenditures; and (c) that the sale or long-term lease of assets (either land or property) reduces the wealth of the municipality, and thus the proceeds should be accounted for in the capital budget and reinvested to finance local public infrastructure to ensure that the wealth of the community remains the same or grows. Many developing countries do not require the preparation of separate current and capital budgets. However, this distinction is essential for local governments to secure proper revenue management and to pursue development. Some important capital revenues are discussed in detail in chapters 6 and 7, but they are briefly summarized here for the sake of a comprehensive description of the capital budget.

- *Own-source capital revenues.* This category includes (a) proceeds from the sale or lease of assets (land or building); (b) betterment fees or other development levies, including quasi-tax construction permits and land development fees; (c) contributions from beneficiaries of local public goods; and (d) sometimes operation surpluses from the previous fiscal year, which may be allocated to the capital budget or set aside as reserves. Municipalities should put great or major emphasis on their own capital revenues because they are under the most direct control of the municipality. Using asset sales, betterment levies, and contributions requires a clear strategy interlinked with the urban planning, zoning, and development plans (discussed in chapter 6).

- *Capital transfers and grants.* Transfers and grants are allocated by many central governments not only as general block grants or current grants, but also as separate transfers for general capital investments. They may also be earmarked grants for specific investments, such as water and sanitation, roads, health, culture, or education. Earmarked or target grants may require copayment by the municipality and perhaps also by the beneficiaries.

Some of these grants may be competitive, and accessing them may require application and local policy decisions. Some capital transfers aim to fund delegated services and develop infrastructure in services for which the local governments are not responsible. Proceeds from earmarked grants are best spent precisely for the set purpose and in the exact amount.

- *External revenues.* Borrowing by local governments is justified, especially to finance long-term investment plans, provided that debt service is ensured and does not jeopardize the fiscal stability of either the local or the higher levels of government. Operational surpluses and own-capital revenues can be used for cofinancing or repaying debt; they play an important role in estimating and ensuring municipal borrowing capacity and creditworthiness (discussed in more detail in chapter 7).

- *Donations and public contributions.* Local or foreign donors or philanthropists may donate a capital item or money to be used for the purchase of a capital item in their homeland or in a disadvantaged area. They may want publicity for their donation, which the municipality can arrange to acknowledge their sponsorship (such as naming the library).

- *Public-private partnerships.* Capital costs can be paid by means of partnerships between the private sector and the municipality. In most cases the private sector partner will have a profit motive, so the terms and conditions must be carefully defined to protect the community's interests.

Land-Based Revenues to Finance Local Investment

Land is a good instrument to finance local investment. Investment in infrastructure increases the market value of land, and it is a good practice to have the public sector recover some of that additional value so that more infrastructure can be financed. As mentioned in chapter 5, there are several ways in which local governments can tap their land assets to mobilize revenue. The most important include betterment levies (or land value capture), sale or lease of public land, public-private partnerships, and impact fees (Peterson 2009).

Land value capture taxes are levied to capture the increment in land value attributable to public investment. These taxes are also known as "land value increment taxes," "betterment levies," or "valorization taxes" (Slack 2009). Betterment levies are directly levied on the owners of property whose value has improved because of the government's investment in nearby public infrastructure, such as street paving; water, sewer, and drainage systems; bridges; public lighting; or rail or bus rapid transit. To contribute to the financing of these types of projects, part of the project cost is typically distributed across the beneficiaries. In Jordan, beneficiaries pay 50 percent of the cost of road development and pavement, in cash advance or installments.

For example, a subway increases demand for housing and offices on properties located nearby, which in turn will result in higher prices being charged for those properties. In addition, zoning changes that accompany investments in infrastructure—for example, increased densities along the subway line—will boost land values. A land value capture tax is a way for the public sector to tax some or all of the private windfall gain created by the infrastructure. Box 4.13 summarizes the main steps in valorization.

Some Latin American cities finance street improvements, water supply, and other local public services through a system of taxation known as *valorization* whereby the cost of public works is allocated to property owners in proportion to the benefits conferred by the works (Bird 2001). The benefits are estimated on the basis of the market value of the benefited plot. The valorization charge is a lump-sum levy, although it can be paid in installments (box 4.14 provides examples of land-based revenues that reduce speculation).

Box 4.13 Computing Land Value Valuation

1. Calculate the cost of the project.
2. Divide by the number of the beneficiaries.
3. Determine the zone of the influence of the project. That is, where will property values increase as a result of the project? Rail stations will have larger zones of influence than a school or a theater.
4. Distribute the tax within the zone. Closer properties will pay a higher portion. The distribution of valorization charges involves a considerable amount of administrative discretion.
5. Collect the tax before construction. Often the tax will not cover the total costs of the project, and project costs are often underestimated.

Source: Slack 2009.

In addition to valorization contributions, Colombia has been levying a *plus valia* or land value increment tax (also called a betterment tax) since 1980. This tax is designed to recoup the benefits that are a consequence of "urban actions," including changes in the classification of land from rural to urban and specific public works typically related to the expansion of the urban road network. Valorization revenues can be substantial, depending on the actual construction of such projects. In Cali, they accounted for 31 percent of city revenues in 1980. Betterment levies are more common in developed than in developing economies. Usually they operate as a surcharge (i.e., additional levy) on the property tax bill.

Land sales have been used by cities such as Cairo, Cape Town, Istanbul, and Mumbai (Peterson 2009). These sales have generated revenues of US$1 billion to more than US$3 billion, dedicated primarily to infrastructure investment. The value of these transactions is large in relation to the investment they will be financing. In addition, some countries may have become too reliant on land sales (e.g., China and the Balkans). Local governments have become dependent on land sales to finance capital expenditures, which have contributed to sprawling and land sales on the periphery of cities.

Improvements in land-based instruments and the use of public land assets to promote local development have also become more common, including the revival of downtown Washington, D.C., and the private-public partnerships now common in the financing of large urban projects, including subways (Shanghai), waterfronts (Baltimore and Washington, D.C.), and Olympiad Villages (Barcelona).

Other issues concerning land-based financing relate to the volatility of land markets. Although using one-time land sales to finance one-time infrastructure projects is adequate, including expected revenues from the sale of land assets in a multiyear budget may pose some financial risk, as the revenues may not materialize at the expected values.

Land sales often lack transparency and accountability. The majority of land sales are conducted off-budget, and the large sums involved may invite corruption and institutional capture by the selling agency. Special legislation that earmarks the revenues from land for capital investment can protect receipts from being diverted to operating budgets. Table 4.11

Box 4.14 Land-Based Revenues, Speculation, and Leapfrog Development

Public transportation investments often increase nearby land values. All too often, however, land near public transportation (such as bus, tramway, and rail stations) remains vacant because landowners, speculating on future land price increases, tend to hold out for prices in excess of what buyers and renters will pay today. This drives developers to seek cheaper sites farther away from public transportation and other urban infrastructure amenities. Once this cheaper land is partially developed and inhabited, its occupants create political pressure to extend transport services to their area. Once the infrastructure is extended, land prices in the remote area begin to rise, choking off new development there (even though land is available within the existing urbanized area) and driving developers and users even farther away. This cycle is partially responsible for "leapfrog" development, also known as "sprawl." Transportation infrastructure, intended to facilitate development, thus chases it away. The resulting sprawl strains the transportation, fiscal, and environmental systems on which communities rely.

Several local governments in the United States use a *value-capture technique* that is embedded in their property tax. This *split-rate property tax* creates an incentive for landholders to develop high-value sites or sell to those who will. It reduces the tax rate on assessed building values and increases the tax rate on assessed land values. It thus motivates affordable compact development by making more land available for development close to public transportation and reducing building costs. The split-rate property tax can also help local governments raise revenues to finance infrastructure. This technique's ability to foster affordable compact development might help bridge the gap between those who advocate making city development compact by setting growth boundaries, and those who fear the impact of growth boundaries on affordable housing. An econometric study, published in the *National Tax Journal*, found that transforming the traditional property tax into a value-capture, split-rate tax would shrink an urbanized area. In reality, an urban area would not shrink, but new development would tend to occur within the existing urbanized area, rather than outside it.

Source: Rybeck 2004.

---

summarizes the potential and issues concerning land-based taxes.

Revenue Administration Issues and Challenges

In any local government, the department of revenue has the main responsibility for determining and collecting taxes due, at the least cost to taxpayers, and fostering the highest degree of public confidence in the integrity, efficiency, and fairness of the process. Revenue administration departments are also expected to assist the units in charge of budgeting, financing, and appraisal of real estate and any other local tax bases. Revenue administration capacity is a function of four key elements:

- Identification and registration of local residents liable for payments (tax, fees, charges)

- Assessment of payment obligations (for both taxes and other charges)

- Billing and collection

- Enforcement of payments.

Table 4.11 Land Financing Instruments

Instrument	Description	Requirements	Problems
Sale of public land	Public land assets are sold, with proceeds used to finance infrastructure investment.	Inventory of land assets, market valuation, and strategic decisions about best use, open auctions for disposing of land that is sold.	Needs competency for inventory and sale. It may result in sprawl (China). Difficult to implement if the agency does not benefit directly from the sale.
Betterment levies	Public sector taxes away a portion of land value gain coming from infrastructure projects.	Difficult to implement on a parcel-by-parcel basis; simplified approach adopted by Bogotá is better.	Needs experience with the instrument, as in South America.
Impact fees	Developers pay the cost of systemwide infrastructure expansion needed to accommodate growth.	Strong analytical capacity to estimate the infrastructure cost implications of development at different locations.	Need to develop simplified approaches that capture the concept of recovering the off-site cost of growth without overwhelming technical demands.
Acquisition and sale of excess land	Public sector acquires land surrounding the infrastructure project and sells land at a profit when project is completed and land value has increased.	Social contract is needed on who should benefit from land value gains resulting from public infrastructure, the original landowner, public sector, displaced occupants, etc.	It is difficult to reach agreement on the proper exercise of eminent domain.

Source: Peterson 2009.

Identification and Registration Functions

In principle, taxpayers and beneficiaries of municipal services must register with the local revenue administration. However, they do not always do so. The degree of compliance varies with the particular tax or user charge. To identify the missing taxpayers, local governments can use different methods. One method used for property taxations is aerial photography or satellite images, to obtain accurate information on property size and location and check consistency with identification of taxpayers. Another method is to cross-check consistency between the number of beneficiaries of household services (for example, solid waste collection and water) and the number of households actually served. Finally, Street Addressing is often a very important tool to increase the accuracy of taxpayer lists. Many street addressing programs have had great impact on capturing the local tax base by reconciling the street addressing data base with the fiscal registers of the tax department.

Assessment Functions

Assessing the tax base is the first step in determining the tax obligations, particularly in the case of property and business taxes. In practice, however, information on both taxpayers (the tax roll) and the value of the tax base is sometimes incomplete and outdated. For instance, new subdivisions or transfers of property are not recorded on time, and the people who bought or inherited the property do not show up in the tax records. The same problem may occur with the establishment of a new industry or business, which may not be recorded or registered in a timely manner. These are particularly acute problems if the data are maintained only in paper records and updated manually. Comprehensive, computerized tax records are important to ensure that changes in ownership cannot take place without being recorded in all relevant fiscal systems.

Similarly, for user charges, the consumption of water or electricity by individual users needs to be established, but sometimes the databases of beneficiaries may be outdated. The probability of underregistering is smaller than for property taxes, as users have the incentive to register so as to receive the service. Illegal connections for water, sewers, and electricity are common in some developing countries. Detecting and registering, or disconnecting, illegal connections is difficult for both technical and sometimes political reasons. The effect is free riding, since the volume of water provided is much higher than the consumption of those who pay (see box 4.15). Bulk metering and comparing metered and unaccounted volumes of services help the identification of areas, and eventually customers, with illegal connections.

Billing and Collection Functions

Once the tax bases are assessed, the next step is to bill and collect payment. Unfortunately, in many situations the names and addresses are unknown. Street addressing[6] and resident identification have become important programs to improve tax collection in both formal and informal urban areas. The main point is that under most legal enforcement systems, a taxpayer or subscriber is not legally responsible for payments of which he or she has not been formally notified. Therefore, a basic condition for an

---

Box 4.15 The Free Rider Paradigm and the Need for Local Taxes

The free rider paradigm describes the situation in which everyone benefits from a good program (for example, firefighting or green spaces), but some people do not pay because they know other people will. In sum, a free rider is a person who receives the benefit of a so-called public good without paying for it. In the case of firefighting or defense, free riders will have their lives and property protected without contributing to the cost. Economists hate free riders because they fear that free riding will prevent necessary services from being provided. If paying for defense or firefighting is voluntary, many people might free ride, making the service uneconomic. The popular solutions to free riding are coercion and taxation. To prevent the free rider problem, payments for public goods are made compulsory, usually in the form of a tax or compulsory levy.

Source: http://www.kingwatch.co.nz/Christian_Political_Economy/free_riders.htm.

effective collection system is a working billing (and mailing) system.

Unfortunately, although 100 percent of taxpayers are obliged to comply with tax obligations, only a portion of them are actually registered (in some countries as few as 50 percent or 60 percent). In addition, not all registered taxpayers pay their taxes. Collection efficiency in normal circumstances reaches 95 percent in developed countries but is just 70 percent, or even less under poor practices, in developing countries.[7] In this context, it does not make sense to increase tax rates as a means to increase tax revenues. That would only penalize the taxpayers already registered and paying taxes but do nothing about those who are unregistered. The challenge to revenue managers is to broaden the base; that is, to get more taxpayers registered and interested in paying. Actually, one could argue that broadening the tax base could make it possible to reduce tax rates, which in turn would improve tax compliance.

Revenue Collection Enforcement

Another critical step in revenue administration is the enforcement of payments. Weak enforcement can be caused by lack of penalties for noncompliance. Furthermore, clear and unbiased records and timely reminders about unpaid bills and accumulated arrears are vital parts of the enforcement system. If taxpayers know that the tax records are weak, they are less willing to pay. In the course of implementing tax reforms, governments sometimes grant partial amnesties on tax debts that have accumulated over many years. Tax amnesties (that is, a one-time discount, forgiveness of penalties, or deduction of tax arrears) are usually granted to encourage improved compliance on current payments. Conversely, denial of service, such as car registration, could be used to encourage payment of other taxes.

Easy and convenient payments are vital elements of effective collection. People are less willing to pay if they must walk to a faraway office, or wait in line for hours, or payment is restricted to cash or check. Internet and electronic banking payments reduce transaction costs for taxpayers and collection hurdles for the administration staff.

Poor revenue enforcement may be due to a combination of various factors: (a) lack of accountability of the local government; (b) lack of political will; (c) weak institutional and administrative capacity; (d) lack of incentives for both revenue collection and enforcement; (e) lack of a policy of publicizing good use of tax proceeds; and (f) payment informality and corruption. Indeed, surveys in many developing countries have shown very clearly that taxpayers (even poorer people) would be ready to pay more taxes if services improved and if government was more transparent. Sometimes corruption is so common that taxpayers refuse to pay because they believe that resources will never be used to improve the living conditions of the population. A study of six African countries found that 30 percent to 70 percent more revenue could be collected at the local level if people paid what they were supposed to (Action Aid 2011). Improvement in this regard would make more money available to be invested in services for the poor and marginalized.

What can local governments do?

Ask people why they refuse to pay taxes, and the answers might surprise you. You may think that people prefer to keep their money, but it may be that people think that the tax collectors keep the collected money for themselves. People refuse to pay because they do not think the local government will spend the tax money properly. When you know the reasons, you will be able to address the most pressing problems facing tax collection and at the same time make tax collection more just.

One way to find out why people refuse to pay tax is to do a survey in your local area. Ask people how they experience the tax collection system and what it would take for people to pay their taxes. Interviews with as few as five people can give you a good idea of where there might be problems (see box 4.16). Using personal stories, for example, about the abuse of power by tax collectors, can be a very effective way of informing people about the problems in your local tax system.

Failure to comply is a less severe problem among beneficiaries of municipal services because it may be easier to cut their water or electricity if they do not pay their bills. A big challenge for municipal revenue administrators is creating an up-to-date database on taxpayers and subscribers to municipal services and implementing an enforcement system.

Revenue collection often remains poor because the local government does not know how much it could collect under good conditions. For example, although revenues may be increasing 4 percent to 5 percent a year, the potential could well be a doubling of the annual collection amount. Box 4.17 illustrates simple methods to estimate potential revenues.

Good practices in enforcement can be as easy as following up with a phone call to taxpayers when there is a delay in payment. An incentive is offered to waive the penalty if payment is made immediately or no later than a specific date. If needed, a reminder notice is sent to the taxpayer's street address or e-mail address. A visit is made to the taxpayer to obtain a signed notification. Alternatively, the bill is given to a collection agency. As a last resort, the case is sent to a municipal tax court if the taxpayer

---

Box 4.16 Reasons Why People Do Not Pay Taxes—Survey in Tanzania

Opinions on tax in Tanzania
In Tanzania a survey among taxpayers showed interesting results on why the local government was not able to collect much tax:

- 58% answered that tax collection was low because people did not feel that their tax money would be spent well by the local government.
- 48% answered that they thought tax collection was low because the tax rates were too high.
- 46% answered that the problem was that tax collectors were dishonest.
- 38% answered that the problem was that tax collectors harassed the local population.

A big surprise was that 73% of the people interviewed said that they would be willing to pay more tax if public services improved. This shows that the biggest problem in low tax collection is not necessarily that people prefer to keep their own money. If the budget is fair and just, more people will also be willing to pay taxes.

It also shows that how taxes are collected can be very important. If tax collection involves corruption, intimidation, or even violence, tax collection will also be low. Civil society can play a key role in addressing these problems by uncovering them and demanding that they be changed.

Source: http://www.actionaid.org/sites/files/actionaid/budgets._-._elbag_handbook_series.pdf.

Box 4.17 How to Estimate Potential Revenues

There are several ways to estimate local government potential revenues. The three most commonly used are described below.

1. **Average per capita revenue: national vs. city.** The method compares the per capita revenue of a given tax (e.g., sales tax) at the national level (NA_{pc}) with per capita revenue obtained at the city level (CA_{pc}). If the city average is below the national average, and there is no apparent justification—for example, the city is small or less affluent—then the difference between the two is the potential revenue (PR_s) for that particular tax multiplied by the number of inhabitants (P_i).

$$PR_s = (NA_{pcs} - CA_{pcs}) * P_i,$$

where PR_s is potential revenues by source, NA_{pcs} is national average per capita by source, CA_{pcs} is the national average per capita by source, and P_i is the population of city i.

2. **Estimated vs. actual revenue from taxpayers.** This method compares the total revenue that would be obtained if all taxpayers pay the average obligations and the actual income received on that particular tax. This is especially useful in the case of the property tax.

$$PNR_{pt} = (ENP * AR_{pt}) - CC_{pt},$$

where PNR_{pt} is potential additional *net* revenue from the property tax, ENP is estimated number of taxable properties, AR_{pt} is average yearly revenue per property, and CC is current yearly collection from property taxes.

3. **Estimated vs. actual revenue per subscribers.** Given the *actual* number of subscribers (e.g., water consumers) and given the average annual payment per subscriber, one can estimate the potential income and the difference between that potential and the actual tax collection.

$$PNR_{si} = (ENP * AP_{si}) - TP_{si},$$

where PNR_{si} is potential net revenue from service i, ENP is estimated number of properties (beneficiaries) in the city, AP_{si} is average yearly payment per subscriber to service i, and TP_{si} is total yearly payments from current subscribers to service i.

---

refuses to pay. Taxpayers are informed of all these legal actions, as well as future steps to expect if they fail to make payment. The challenge to the city's tax administration is to implement and enforce these procedures legally through a tax court. Typically, just a few cases need to be enforced; if they are broadly publicized, it usually generates an immediate rise in tax compliance.

Developing Local Institutional Capacity

Lack of institutional capacity hampers local revenue managers in estimating how many taxpayers are missing from their tax rolls, how many of those who are registered are inactive, and how much is actually being evaded in tax payments. In addition, even when taxpayers are registered and active, sometimes there is no complete and reliable information on their tax liabilities, tax

Box 4.18 Success in Increasing Own-Source Revenues in Maputo

The city of Maputo, in Mozambique, has increased its own-source revenues by almost 30 percent since 1998 through revenue management reforms supported by World Bank projects. These have enabled Maputo to increase its tax base, taxing more properties and initiating adjustments in user fees for certain services (notably a new, incremental solid waste fee). Legislative reform, tariff studies to inform policy and management decisions, and prioritization of both revenue and expenditure management have created institutional shifts for revenue enhancement. The use of rigorous analysis, initiated through tariff studies, has identified the ratio of expenditures that can be financed with own-source revenue, the relative proportions of fiscal and nonfiscal revenues, and measures to increase revenue collection efficiency. It has provided an empirical basis for decisions to expand the property tax base and improve tariff setting and collection of user fees.

Source: World Bank 2007.

payments made, and their balances (taxes in arrears are practically unknown). Furthermore, for many taxpayers that are actually registered, their addresses and information on their current economic activities are incomplete or outdated, making billing and tax enforcement fairly difficult. Introduction of modern computerized management information systems helps resolve many of these everyday matters (box 4.18 describes measures undertaken in Maputo, Mozambique).

The challenge to tax administrators, and revenue managers in general, is therefore to gradually overcome current weaknesses by using management information systems to upgrade their institutional capacities to identify taxpayers (and subscribers to services), assess their payment obligations, ensure accurate and timely billing, and enforce collection.

Incentives to Improve Revenue Collection

Many local governments lack the appropriate incentives to encourage tax compliance. Typical problems with incentives include the following:

- Tax payment is not comfortable. Taxpayers may have to stand in line for long periods to find out what they owe and make payments. There are no online payments, nor are there contracts with banks to receive tax payments.

- A substantial part of taxpayers' records are still kept manually, and electronic records between the treasury and accounting are not integrated.

- Mail payments are unreliable because of poor service and can also be costly.

Various solutions for these problems exist:

- Implementation of a taxpayer address system for billing tax liabilities, to reduce transaction costs in tax compliance

- Integrated electronic systems to manage taxpayers' current tax accounts

- Unified billing systems

- Provision for taxpayers to pay by mail, through banks, or through e-mail

- Setting up "tax help desks" to help taxpayers comply with their obligations

- Separate systems for large and small taxpayers.

Street Addressing and Tax Systems

A major source of improvement in revenue collection and management is adoption of a modern street addressing system that can provide the tax authorities with reliable information on the location of taxpayers and taxable businesses. Examples around the world confirm the utility of street addressing projects in improving the performance of tax systems.

Improving the performance of the existing tax system

One of the main benefits of the address directory is the ability to obtain information on economic activities and the population not listed on the tax rolls. It improves the efficiency of the property tax by supplementing incomplete property records. Box 4.19 explains a project implemented in Senegal. The process, managed by the tax department, involved reconciling the address directory with the taxpayer rolls to create a tax register that includes both.

Street addressing and property tax reform

A number of urban development projects in francophone Africa that include a street addressing component provide an opportunity to reexamine the municipal taxation system, and in particular the property tax system, so that it can be adapted to the local context in a cost-efficient way.

Rather than struggle under a cumbersome and complex taxation system based on antiquated, largely unenforceable tax laws, municipalities are moving toward simplification of tax laws and adopting a property taxation approach more closely aligned with existing capacities and resources. For example, in Burkina Faso, Mali, and Togo, property taxation reform has been coupled with street addressing projects conducted under the auspices of World Bank–financed urban development projects. The cities of Ouagadougou, Bobo-Dioulasso, and Lomé carried out street addressing initiatives in conjunction with the implementation of a local tax on all types of residences, using a simplified basis more in accordance with household capacity to pay. This type of residence tax was inspired in part by the urban tax in Morocco and the old Tunisian rent tax. On the whole, the assessment of taxes on a simplified basis and the use of an address directory have reduced procedural

---

Box 4.19 Development of Tax Registers in Senegal

The Senegal program aimed at determining the number of people not listed on the tax rolls by comparing the rolls with address directories and incorporating address information on the tax rolls. The project included several steps:

1. Assess the performance of tax enrollment and collection operations for business taxes and license fees and for the property tax (names of taxpayers surveyed, amounts assessed, and so forth).

2. Close the information gap between the address directory and the existing tax rolls.
3. Include address information on tax rolls and assessment notices.
4. Locate addresses not surveyed (businesses, dwellings, mixed-use properties).
5. Conduct additional field surveys.
6. Create a register of all potential taxpayers.
7. Determine tax amounts and create rolls or registers for collection of advance payment.

Source: Farvacque-Vitkovic 2005.

Box 4.20 Tax Department Involvement in Street Addressing Surveys in Niger

The city of Niamey spearheaded a street addressing initiative using funding from the International Association of Francophone Mayors (AIMF). It established several mixed teams consisting of municipal agents, a representative of the water company (SEEN), a representative of the electric company (NIGELEC), and a cadastral agent. Each street and door number was penciled onto the cadastral map on paper. The team leaders filled in each door number on survey forms, according to the cadastral reference for the plot. In this way, the two directories were reconciled with one another in real time. When an area being assigned addresses has not yet been surveyed and entered in the cadastre, the subdivision plan also held by the cadastral and municipal agents is often used. This type of dual codification system, for street addressing and cadastral purposes, makes it possible to reconcile the address directory with the other directories kept by the government and utility concessionaires.

Source: Farvacque-Vitkovic 2005.

complications (box 4.20 summarizes experiences in Niger).

Supplement the cadastre with street address data

In the event that such a cadastral reform proves to be overambitious, a less sweeping program can be adopted by using street addressing data to supplement the information in the cadastral unit. If fieldworkers experienced with maps have no problem identifying individual properties, the same will hold true for tax or treasury agents responsible for tax auditing and collection, as mentioned above in regard to the tax registers. This type of intervention would take a two-pronged approach: (a) incorporate the addresses into the cadastral data and (b) establish a correspondence between addresses and cadastral references for plots that are so identified.

The fact that a cadastral documentation is inadequate or nearly nonexistent and often out of date does not preclude the implementation of innovative property taxation systems, in which street addressing initiatives can play a fundamental role. The innovation lies partly in requiring citizens to participate in the costs of the city (rather than taxing property that is often unregistered) and partly in seeking simple solutions.

Revenue Enhancement Programs

Developed countries initiate gradual, annual, incremental changes in their well-established revenue systems. In contrast, developing countries require comprehensive reforms for improving their local revenue administration, establishing databases, and substantially enhancing institutional capacity on most fronts, from assessment, billing, and collection to enforcement and remedies (see box 4.21 and box 4.23). Donor agencies, such as the World Bank, or bilateral donors, such as the French, German, U.S., or Swiss agencies, often provide substantial financial and technical support for these reforms, which can be seen as lifetime investments for the participating cities, often with good and short recovery of invested costs.

Box 4.21 What to Do When in Financial Stress

The financial crisis of 2008 led many local authorities into financial stress, mainly because expected revenues did not materialize and expenditures could not be cut to accommodate the fall in revenues. Without the ability to borrow to finance short-term deficits, many local governments faced tough decisions. The road map followed by many local governments includes common-sense steps. (a) Figure out what is going on: if the source of the problem is a decline in sales tax, is it a short-term or a structural problem? (b) Communicate what is going on: the public should be told the origin of the problems and why services are being reduced or taxes increased. (c) Rethink priorities and reallocate resources to the most important programs. (d) Avoid short-term remedies such as using one-time revenues or carryovers from previous years or deferring infrastructure maintenance. (e) Use new revenues after doing the homework of cutting costs; that is the only way the public will accept new taxes. Strengthen long-term financing planning. (f) Keep morale of personnel high.

Fremont, California, used a four-point plan to survive recession. In July 2003 the mayor explained the situation: Sales tax revenues had dropped by 25 percent, business tax by 30 percent. No growth was projected. In addition, hotel and motel tax receipts had declined by more than 50 percent during the preceding two years. Property taxes had slowed down. In view of this situation, the council decided on a plan to raise revenues and consolidate long-term revenues. It included (a) cutting spending and reducing services; (b) increasing local activity and promoting consumption from local sellers; and (c) thinking creatively about sources of new growth (for example, Sterling, Illinois, invested in brownfields redevelopment to spur economic growth).

Source: International City Management Association 2003.

Box 4.22 Financial Recovery Action Plan in Kampala, Uganda

The city of Kampala became bankrupt in the mid-2000s, with enormous overdue liabilities (about 30 percent of annual budget) and poor revenue collection. The council adopted a detailed Financial Recovery Action Plan (FRAP) and implemented it in the following years under a World Bank project (KIIDP).

The plan was based on a 31-page FRAP action matrix, with specific assumptions, forecasts, actions, responsibilities, and budgets assigned. The city managed to stabilize its budget, increased property tax collection threefold, and worked out its overdue liabilities over five years. Property tax collection was improved by a computerized database, timely billing, reminders, and good communication, including a leaflet attached to each bill that explained the use of property tax revenues, noting that two-thirds of property tax revenue is used for improving services in the same collection zone.

Source: World Bank 2006b.

Box 4.23 Main Steps in Revenue Enhancement Programs

1. Develop baseline indicators on both *current* subscribers and *current* taxpayers. Estimate the *actual* number of beneficiaries and the potential number of taxpayers to compare performance before and after the implementation of any proposed revenue management plan of action.
2. Update databases (registers) of service subscribers and taxpayers, through third-party information, direct field surveys, and self-reporting requirements.
3. Expand street nomenclature to update addresses, which are needed for billing, collection, and enforcement of user charges, local taxes, and other revenue sources.
4. Upgrade the current billing and collection system for both user charges and local taxes (including hardware, software, office equipment, and staff training).
5. Update the property tax information on property owners, physical characteristics of the properties, valuations, and their corresponding tax assessments (i.e., the municipal cadastres), and make the updating automatic and electronic.
6. Implement a transparent system of incentives to reward early compliance with tax payments and user charges.
7. Implement a transparent system of disincentives (penalties) for late payment of user fees and local taxes.
8. Develop baseline indicators for *actual* and *potential* user charge collection by service, and *actual* and *potential* tax collections by tax source, to measure performance in local revenue collection efficiency.
9. Establish minimum standards in the provision of the different municipal services, determine *actual* standards, and evaluate performance in adherence to standards.
10. Determine the number of units of services supplied and establish the unit cost per service.
11. Compute expected cost based on minimum standards; determine *actual* cost, and measure expenditure efficiency performance.
12. Compute the user fees (user charges) that reflect the actual cost of providing each service. This information constitutes basic input for monitoring and assessing performance in expenditure efficiency by municipal service.
13. Develop benchmarks, indicators regarding unit cost for main municipal services. The unit cost indicators should differentiate between construction costs (i.e., capital outlays per unit of public works) and associated operations and maintenance (O&M) costs.
14. Develop a system for the legal enforcement of user fees and local taxes, together with a system of appeals.

These reforms are often parts of, or to some extent conditions of, large infrastructure investment programs aiming to ensure financial sustainability of the built assets and long-term sustainability of the improved services.

The World Bank supports dozens of such programs or program components annually in all continents. The case study in box 4.5 summarizes the case of Bogotá; boxes 4.18 and 4.20 show West African cases. Box 4.22 summarizes the Kampala Financial Recovery Action Plan (FRAP), showing the complexity and demanding nature of a revenue enhancement program (see also chapter 5). The impact of infrastructure investments on land and real estate prices and the expected revenue from betterment taxes need careful projection and realistic timing. Street addressing programs take time, and their revenue impact will be strong and visible after two or three years, rather than just a few months. Guiding, monitoring, and managing revenue enhancement programs and projecting revenues require an expert team and a good combination of qualitative and quantitative analysis.

Serbia has gone through a comprehensive reform of local taxation. An important reform included the transfer of the property tax revenue policy and administration from the central to the local governments. After legislative changes in 2006, the cities started reforming their own systems and achieved remarkable results—40 percent to 90 percent increases in tax revenues by 2009.

The typical difficulties experienced before and during the reforms included the following:

- Small human capacity and inadequately trained staff

- Lack of technical equipment and software

- Outdated, vague databases inadequate for billing and enforcement

- Unwillingness of other government agencies to hand over basic data.

The case of Serbia provides a good example of the importance of incentives and points to the fact that cities collect more taxes when the tax authority is devolved to the local level (table 4.12 shows the remarkable results achieved in Serbia

in three years). Despite Serbia's progress, tax bills are still very low, the tax base is poorly registered, and total collection averages less than 1 percent of GDP.

Internal Accountability in Revenue Collection

In many developing countries, the system of local accountability in revenue collection by municipal internal controllers and the city council is fairly weak. The little time that is generally allocated in the budget process to debate the revenue budget (in contrast to the much longer time devoted to reviewing and disputing the expenditure budget) is a good indicator of the fairly weak internal accountability in revenue collection. Similarly, municipal external and internal audits focus more on the expenditure side than on revenue performance. Thus, revenues forgiven, missed, or lost often remain hidden from the council or policy makers.

The Revenue Budget Cycle

Typically a local government budget process consists of at least seven steps: revenue forecast, setting expenditure limits, budget preparation, budget negotiation, budget approval, budget execution, and budget evaluation. The circular nature of the budget is known as the *budget cycle*, as each step uses the output of the previous one and helps the step ahead. Figure 4.7 depicts the revenue budget cycle (see chapter 3 for more

Table 4.12 Collection Improvement Results of Property Tax Reform in Serbia

Cities	2006	2007	2008	2009	2006/2009
	SRD millions				Percent
Belgrade	2,439	2,625	3,694	4,792	196
Kragujevac	110	138	184	180	164
Vranje	37	37	44	54	146
Vrnjacka Banja	20	18	23	28	139

Source: City to City Dialogue Program, WBI, 2012.

Figure 4.7 The Revenue Budget Cycle

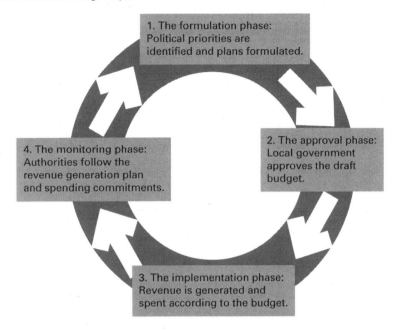

1. The formulation phase: Political priorities are identified and plans formulated.

2. The approval phase: Local government approves the draft budget.

3. The implementation phase: Revenue is generated and spent according to the budget.

4. The monitoring phase: Authorities follow the revenue generation plan and spending commitments.

details on budgeting). The cycle spans one year and is repeated every fiscal year. In countries where the budget year starts with the calendar year (i.e., from January to December), budget preparation starts as early as April of the preceding year to give the technical team enough time to assemble facts, past realization rates, and trends to be used in the projections, and to prepare the basic revenue projections around which the overall budget unfolds. Budget preparation requires the projection of the locality's revenues (all the categories discussed previously), plus projections of the intergovernmental transfers and special taxes or revenues collected for special purposes (e.g., land-based revenues).

The second step in the budget cycle is the setting of expenditure limits or budget ceilings. The local government tentatively sets budget ceilings across all its administrative units. Such ceilings generally are the maximum a local government can spend in a fiscal year. The sum of all these departmental ceilings is the budget ceiling for the whole local government. These expenditure ceilings are determined based on the revenue forecast and the municipal development plan. The municipal budget director receives and reviews with each department or administrative unit that unit's expenditure proposals. He or she reaches agreement within the local government and prepares a budget proposal. Then, as the third step, the mayor submits the budget proposal to the municipal council for its discussion and approval. The following sections review five phases of the revenue budget process: revenue planning, revenue forecasting, discussion and approval, implementation, and monitoring and auditing.

Revenue Planning

Revenue planning is crucial for local governments, as it provide the means to assess whether they will be able to meet expenses; that is, the operating budget and the provision of services. Capital expenditure planning (included in the capital budget) is carried out in response to the needs for expansion and rehabilitation of infrastructure and service coverage. The planning of other capital revenue for the financing of multiyear development plans depends on (a) any balance surplus in the operating budget, (b) capital grants, and (c) long-term credit for local public investment (chapter 7 further develops the concepts of capital improvement planning and its financing).

Revenue Forecasting and Trend Analysis

Local governments need to forecast the revenues they will be collecting in order to plan expenditures.[8] As discussed before, the local government revenues come from taxes, fees, licenses, user charges, and intergovernmental transfers. To forecast the revenues accruing from each source, local governments can use simple projections (looking at past trends) or can try to understand what factors influenced the past behavior of tax revenues to enhance the quality of the forecasts (figure 4.8 depicts New York revenues from 1993 to 2009).

For example, most taxes will fluctuate with changes in income and economic activity, as well as tax rates. If forecasters know how different taxes are linked with economic variables (e.g., GDP and employment), they can use macroeconomic projections prepared at the national level and their knowledge of their city to make accurate projections for the city's own revenues. That is, the analyst tries to find the link between the

Figure 4.8 Local Revenues and Price Indexes in New York City, 1993–2009 (percent)

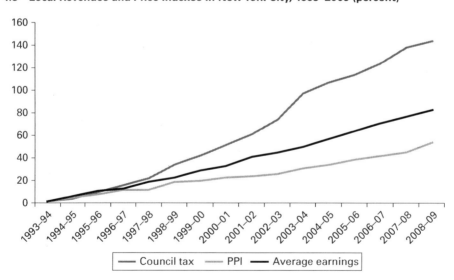

Source: www.osc.state.ny.us/localgov/training/chapters/myfp/two/rev_aid.htm.

factors that drive revenues (income, production, tax rates, building permits issued, retail sales, etc.) and the revenues that government collects (property taxes, user fees, sales taxes). The ability to project future resources is critical to avoid budgetary shortfalls.

Revenue forecasts can be made for aggregate total revenue or for individual revenue sources, such as sales tax revenues or property tax revenues. There is no single method for projecting revenues. Different methods tend to work better for different types of revenue. Similarly, there is no standard time frame over which to attempt a forecast. The local government might look ahead to the next year's budget, while managers of a city water system may be concerned about a 20-year time horizon. Finally, revenue forecasting is intimately tied to the public policy process and is thus subject to considerable scrutiny and even political pressure.

Guajardo and Miranda (2000) suggest a seven-step process to include economic and political factors in projecting local revenues:

1. Select a time period over which revenue data are examined. The length of time depends on the availability and quality of data, the type of revenue, and the degree of accuracy sought.

2. Examine the data to determine any patterns, rates of change, or trends that may be evident. Patterns may suggest that the rates of change are relatively stable or changing exponentially. Table 4.13 shows the behavior of key taxes in the last five years in both nominal and real terms; that is, taking into account changes in prices.

3. Consider to what degree economic conditions, changing citizen demand, and changes in government policies affect the revenue. These assumptions determine which forecasting method is most appropriate.

4. Project revenue collection in future years. The method selected depends on the nature and type of revenue. Revenue sources with a high degree of uncertainty, such as new revenues and grants or asset sales, may require some sort of *qualitative* forecasting method, such as consensus or expert forecasting. Revenues that are generally predictable will typically be forecast using a quantitative method, such as a trend analysis or regression analysis (see box 4.24).

5. After the projections have been made, the estimates are checked for reliability and

Table 4.13 Revenue Data and Growth Factors for Forecasting

| | Historical series (revenue collected in US$ millions) | | | | Growth in percent | | Projection alternatives |
Local taxes	2008	2009	2010	2011	Nominal	Real	Function of
Sales tax	45	48	50	52	4.9	2.4	GDP
Property tax	15	16	18	17	4.2	1.7	Price index
Business tax	7	7	9	10	12.6	8.9	GDP
User charges	9	9	10	12	10.1	6.6	GDP
Surcharges	0.9	0.9	1	1.2	10.1	6.6	GDP
Total	76.9	80.9	88	92.2	6.2	2.5	
Price increase	3 percent	4 percent	2 percent	5 percent	3.66		

validity. Conducting a sensitivity analysis assesses reliability. The key parameters used to create the estimates are varied, and if this leads to large changes in the results, the projection is assumed to have a low degree of reliability.

6. Monitor and compare revenue collection with the estimates. Monitoring serves both to assess the accuracy of the projections and to determine whether there is likely to be any budget shortfall or surplus.

Box 4.24 Methods for Calculating Growth Rates and Projecting Revenues Years Forward

Percent Change: The first option compares consecutive time periods using the following formula:

Percent change = [(CR − PR)/PR]* 100, (Eq.1)

where CR = Current Revenue and PR = Past Revenue.

Average Growth Rate: For a longer period, the same change formula can be used, but the total percent would be divided by the number of years (N):

Average growth rate = {[(CR−PR)/PR] /N}* 100 (Eq. 2); for $(t_n - t_o)$.

However, for such longer periods, the use of the first and last year may be suitable only when the revenue changes are rather uniform. A more accurate growth rate would be obtained using compound growth rates.

Compound Annual Growth Rate (CAGR): CAGR takes into account the first and the last value of the particular time period but includes the effect of the annual compounding periods in the final growth rate. The results are fairly reliable if the changes from one year to the next are rather smooth. The CAGR can be computed as CAGR $(t_n - t_o)$ = {[(Vt$_n$/Vt$_o$)* 1/ $(t_n - t_o)$] − 1}* 100 (Eq. 3), Vt_o = initial value,

Vt_n = last value, and $1/(t_n - t_o)$ = number of years or using the basic formula of

$$VT_n = VT_o (1 + r)^{n-1}$$

and solving for r:

$$r = \{exp[ln(VT_n/VT_o)/N] - 1\}* 100.$$

Arithmetic Mean Growth Rate: Alternatively, if the time series is characterized by volatility in yearly revenues, the first and the last year might not be representative; in such cases, it may be better to use the arithmetic mean growth rate (also known as the Arithmetic Mean Return—AMR). The formula of the AMR is as follows:

$$AMR = 1/n(X_1 + \dots + X_n), (Eq. 4)$$

where n = number of time periods of one year, and X_i = percent revenue change for period i; computed as [(CR − PR)/PR]* 100 (Eq. 1) $i = 1 \dots to \dots n$.

Linear Trend Growth Rate: Another option is to compute the CAGR of the trend line, calculated by the least squares method. This would provide the growth rate of the trend in revenues for the particular time period. For example, Excel automatically draws the trend line, calculates the trend equation, and R^2, which indicates the quality of the forecasting trend.

7. Update and adjust the revenue forecast as conditions affecting revenue generation change. Fluctuations in collections may be caused by unexpected changes in economic conditions, policy and administrative adjustments, or changing patterns of consumer demand.

Projecting Individual Sources of Local Revenues

The first step in projecting local government revenues is to classify the revenues according to a given methodology and identify the economic and other factors that affect each of them. Some revenues are very sensitive to economic changes (e.g., sales and business taxes), while others depend far more on policy decisions or long-term development trends (property tax). Some are fairly predictable (automobile tax), whereas others are erratic (fines). Some are controllable, and others are completely out of the control of municipal executives. Some represent large sources of revenue, whereas others do not make a discernible difference to the bottom line (parking violations).

In projecting local revenues, it is useful to ask four questions: How sensitive is the tax to economic change? How predictable is it? How much control can local governments exert over the proceeds? How important is the impact of the tax on the local government budget?

Property taxes and other property-related tax items (transfer tax):

- Sensitive to economic change?   Not significantly
- Predictable?   Yes
- Controllable?   Yes
- Large source of revenue?   Yes

Real property taxes usually represent the largest portion of local government revenues in developed countries. The tax base is normally fairly stable, at least in the short term, and local policy makers determine both assessment and tax rates. There are two methods to project real property taxes:

- Assume it is kept constant at the current price level.
- Assume a conservative adjustment for projected changes in total assessed value.

In the United States and other countries where property tax is the main fiscal instrument of municipalities, local authorities try to establish property taxes so as to cover the local government expenses. This often leads to big increases in tax rates and opposition from the taxpayers. The charts in figure 4.9 show two possible policy scenarios used in New York City. In the first, a dynamic increase of property tax eliminates the deficit; in the second scenario, a constant property tax rate would yield an increasing deficit.

Sales tax and other non-property taxes:

- Sensitive to economic change?   Yes
- Predictable?   No
- Controllable?   No
- Large source of revenues?   Yes

Sales tax and other non-property taxes such as utility, restaurant, or hotel occupancy taxes are major revenue sources for counties, cities, or towns. It is useful to track the sales tax separately from other non-property taxes because it is affected by different factors.

In some U.S. cities, local sales taxes are collected by the state and distributed to counties and certain cities that preempt the county tax. Many counties share sales tax revenues with other local governments according to formulas based on factors such as population and property values.

Figure 4.9   Property Tax and Revenue Forecasting Scenarios

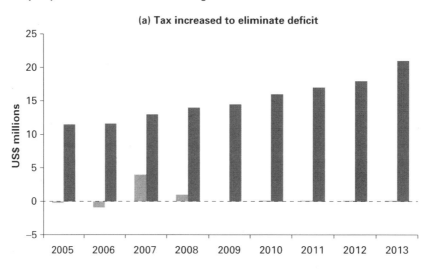

(a) Tax increased to eliminate deficit

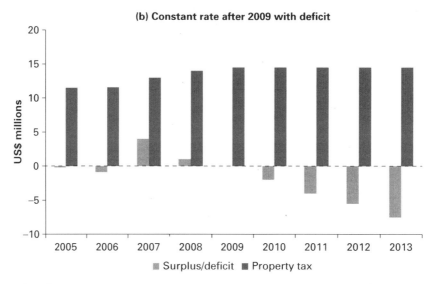

(b) Constant rate after 2009 with deficit

■ Surplus/deficit   ■ Property tax

Source: Office of State Controller 2010, http//www.osc.state.ny.us/localgov/training/chapters/myfp/two/rev.

Sales and most other non-property taxes are more volatile than the property tax because they are affected by changes in the economy with very little lag. They are also subject to policy changes at the state, county, and sometimes municipal level, including changes to the rate (if the revenue is shared with the government doing the projection), changes to the base (such as sales tax free weeks), or even municipal preemption of a portion of the rate by a city.

Recent history will help local governments determine the starting point for their sales tax

Figure 4.10   Sales Tax Collections, Year-over-year, 1991–2009

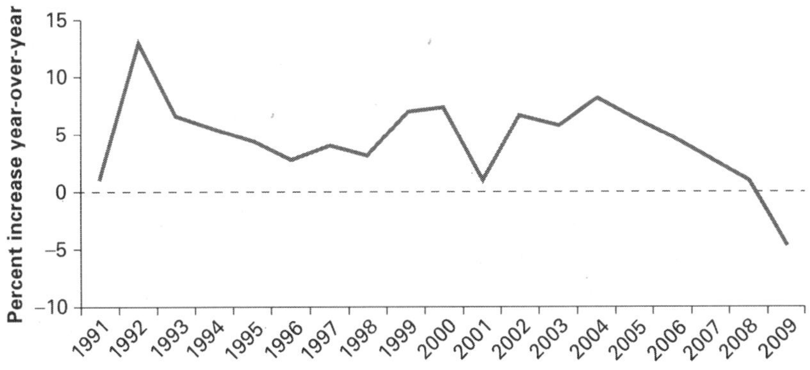

Source: Office of State Controller 2010. http//www.osc.state.ny.us/localgov/training/chapters/myfp/two/rev.http//www.osc.state.ny.us/localgov/training/chapters/myfp/two/rev.http://www.osc.state.ny.us/localgov/pnbs/research/snapshot/080919snapshot.pdf

projections, and information about the local economy (up or down) will provide important factors to take into account. Many central government departments (e.g., ministry of economy, central bank, or department of planning) publish forecasts for the factors that influence non-property tax revenues, including national gross domestic product (GDP), employment trends, retail trade, and wage growth. Figure 4.10 shows that sales tax revenues are sensitive to economic cycles and dropped from 2008 onward.

In the United States, local data (but not projections) can be obtained from the Bureau of Labor Statistics and the U.S. Census Bureau. Local governments should be particularly conservative in projecting this revenue source because it is large and can be volatile. Several questions should be considered:

- Has there been a change to the sales tax rate?

- Has there been substantial economic change, such as in unemployment or retail growth?

- Has there been a change in interest rates that may affect spending and therefore the sales tax collected?

Other local revenues:

- Sensitive to economic change?   No

- Predictable?   Depends

- Controllable?   Depends

- Large source of revenues?   No

Other local revenues include fines, licenses, sale of property, interest earnings, and other small sources of revenue. If a locality aggregates some or all of these into a single category, it is best to project based on steady recent trends or by holding them constant, adjusting if necessary for major known changes to large revenue sources. If a locality is doing a line-item projection, these should be projected according to the most reasonable trend, such as inflation or known fee increases, or held constant.

State and federal transfers and grants are generally beyond a locality's control. Timing and the relative health of the state budget affect most of its aid categories. It is a generally accepted practice to hold state aid revenues constant, unless there is a reasonable possibility of a decrease or the solid expectation of a specific increase. Table 4.14 summarizes the

Table 4.14 Predictability of Main Local Revenues

	Property tax	Sales tax	Other local taxes	Transfers
Sensitive to economic change	Not significantly	Yes	Yes	No
Predictable	Yes	No	Mixed	Mixed
Controllable	Yes	No	Yes	
Large source of revenue	Yes	Yes	No	Yes
Forecast methods				
1.	Remain constant	Function of GDP, employment	Indexed to inflation	Remain constant
2.	Cover deficit			

Source: Prepared by authors using information from New York Office of State Controller, http://www.osc.state.ny.us/localgov /training/chapters/myfp/two/rev_aid.htm.

characteristics of the main revenue sources for forecasting purposes.

There are some exceptions, however. Certain state aid programs are reimbursed based on local costs or participation (many school aid grants fall into this category). Localities may contact the state agency administering the program for assistance with these types of aid projections. Federal grants are generally specific to certain programs, some of which can be start-up grants, meaning that the local government must continue to fund the program after the federal aid ends. Generally, therefore, federal aid is a small but variable revenue source.

Forecasting methods range from relatively informal qualitative techniques to highly sophisticated quantitative techniques. In revenue forecasting, more sophisticated does not necessarily mean more accurate. In fact, an experienced finance officer can often guess what is likely to happen with a great deal of accuracy. In general, forecasters use a variety of techniques, recognizing that some perform better than others depending on the nature of the revenue source. Box 4.25 summarizes the nature of two main forecasting methods.

Forecasting in revenue enhancement programs is quite different from regular forecasting. Forecasting with qualitative techniques is particularly important when a substantial revenue reform is planned and taking place. These reforms can be seen as long-term investments (computerization of the various databases, expansion of databases by identifying new customers, legalizing illegal connections, etc.). They require not only substantial amounts of money and time, but often firm political support. Forecasting revenues under these circumstances requires a team of experts, who must set specific actions and calculate the expected one to five years ahead, using a combination of qualitative and quantitative techniques.

The Revenue Budget Debate

Budget debates at the local government level focus more on how to use the resources available than on how to obtain them. Exceptionally, local administrations are required by city councils or the ministry on local governments to explain the assumptions made in forecasting the revenues. In this context, the main task of the revenue manager is to present to the city council proposals for how to (a) encourage tax payments through facilities and incentives; (b) upgrade revenue billing and collection through expanding the city's street address system; (c) upgrade and integrate taxpayers' current accounts through electronic management information systems; and (d) mobilize

Box 4.25 Revenue Forecasting Techniques

Revenue forecasting projects future revenue streams, including business sales projections or estimations of revenue collected in taxes for a government entity. The ability to estimate revenue accurately is vital to successfully building an annual budget.

Judgmental forecasting relies less on data and more on judgment, using the assessment of a person or committee based on past experience or perhaps past trends. Such forecasting does best when the conditions are unpredictable or rapidly changing. Sometimes it uses the experience of a small group of experts familiar with the nature of government activity. For example, a small municipality may gather together a group of local real estate professionals experienced in

potential revenue, either with currently available revenue sources or with new revenue sources such as betterment levies.

As we have said, analysis of the local budget focuses more on expenditure levels and composition than on the revenue side. Often revenues are overestimated, leading to higher spending than is justified. For instance, the revenue forecast may assume an unrealistic collection of tax arrears or may include revenue from the expected sale of municipal land at a much higher price than is realistic. These odd practices usually result in municipal fiscal deficits or unfinished local infrastructure projects.

Revenue Budget Approval

Once proposed expenditures and revenue are agreed upon, the annual municipal budgets is approved. Budget approval requires voting on the budget bill in the municipal council and issuance

the market to judge the growth of real estate. Their opinions and knowledge will help project how much tax revenue the municipality might expect in taxes on new housing sales, for example.

Time-series forecasting uses trends based on historical data compiled over the course of several years or instances. Forecasters relying on this basic method look at data evolving over time. Such issues as cyclicality and seasonality might influence the forecast results.

Four methods are usually mentioned: (a) naïve–constant increase, (b) using time series such as moving average models, (c) causal models, and (d) judgmental forecasting.

Source: Garrett and Leatherman 2010.

of a budget resolution. Sometimes the local budgets require the approval of the state or central ministry in charge of local governments. More common is the need to have state governments approve the municipal budget, as in Mexico. In general, budgets need to be balanced for approval, but the meaning of "balanced" varies. In many cases it includes the use of external resources to finance planned and approved investment expenditures (see also chapter 7).

Given the usual bias in favor of revenue overestimation, prudent fiscal policies would require a rigorous analysis of the methods and assumptions used to project the components of municipal revenue. This function is usually the responsibility of an internal control unit in the municipal administration. The economic commission of the city council, the city councilors in general, and in some countries the ministry of local governments or its equivalent may be involved. The challenge to a city council (including the economic commission) and to a municipal internal controller is to ensure that the revenue forecast is realistic, in order to prevent fiscal deficits or unfinished public works, among other possible outcomes.

Revenue Budget Execution

The challenge in revenue execution is to ensure the collection of an amount equal to or greater than the forecast. In practice, the actual collection of a given tax often turns out to be less than predicted. For some taxes the actual collection may be higher, eventually canceling the collection that was less than predicted. This is the normal situation in most budget executions that occur within fiscal discipline, avoiding excessive and repeated overprojections (and underprojections) of revenues. In contrast, in the absence of rigorous discipline local governments are characterized by low revenue collection efficiency and significant budget deficits. Therefore, the challenge in revenue execution, particularly in those municipalities with soft budget constraints, is to take advantage of and learn to use their own resources (i.e., their revenue base) and live within their means, rather than rely on distorting cross-subsidies from the central government. Table 4.15 describes relevant indicators to monitor revenue performance.

Typically, monitoring of revenue collection is done on a monthly basis by revenue source, as well as for the aggregate of all sources. If substantial differences are observed, remedial action is taken for the cases that depend on factors under the control of the revenue administration department, such as weak billing or limited enforcement. Several objective indicators may be used to monitor performance in each of the main functions in revenue administration. These issues are further discussed in chapter 8 in the context of municipal financial performance monitoring.

An example of the use of cost-efficiency performance indicators is the case of the Borough of Sutton in London. The borough has implemented a program on cost savings or cost efficiency in service provision (called "value for money," or VfM), as illustrated in box 4.26.

Revenue Mobilization Strategies

An overall strategy in revenue management, and in municipal financial management in general, consists of linking key municipal functions, such as (a) revenue collection to service provision, (b) cost of service provision to beneficiaries, and (c) user charges to expenditures by service. Each of these strategies is explained below.

Table 4.15 Revenue Performance: Monitoring and Evaluation Indicators

Main functions	Effectiveness (%)	Accuracy (%)	Cost efficiency	Retrieval time
1. Taxpayer identification and registration	Registered tax payers/total residents	Registries with errors/total registries	TCR/RT Average cost per registry	Electronic H, hours D, days
2. Tax billing	Number of taxpayers/ taxpayers billed	Bills with errors/ total bills	Total cost of billing/TT	E, H, D
3. Tax collection	Revenues collected/ total accounts	Total value of accounts received/ total accounts	Total collection costs/ total accounts Average cost per account	E, H, D
4. Tax enforcement	Arrears recovered/ total arrears	Delinquent accounts/total accounts	Total cost of recovery/ total delinquent accounts	E, H, H

Box 4.26 Value for Money Strategy—London Borough of Sutton

The London Borough of Sutton has established a "value for money" strategy and used benchmarking to drive the council's efficiency program. A key objective of the strategy was to balance flexibility with a systematic and objective assessment. The process also required the support of service managers and appropriate member involvement.

A benchmarking system provides a guide to comparative performance across all service areas, taking into account particular local pressures. Potential areas of efficiency savings are identified using an assessment tool known as a "VfM quotient," which uses data from the Audit Commission and the Chartered Institute of Public Finance to provide automatic assessments of each service's value for money. Automated production of these reports frees officers' time for more intensive research into performance and results. Service areas are then charged with selecting one or two significant areas of potential efficiency savings to be subjected to particular focus through efficiency challenge workshops. This ensures

that service managers are involved at an early stage. The workshops involve councilors, relevant service managers, other council staff, and external consultants. Ideas that the workshops identify are then consolidated into an efficiency program that informs the financial and corporate planning process.

Efficiency projects are categorized into four areas:

- Customer services—transferring process from back-office to front-facing customer service staff
- Invest-to-save projects
- Procurement projects
- Transitional services—combining similar functions of the council or with other partner organizations.

These areas are supported with specialist staff and funds. Members play an active role by taking personal responsibility for providing ideas and oversight of selected projects. Regular reports are produced to ensure that senior officers and members can monitor progress.

Source: Audit Commission U.K. 2009.

Linking Tax Revenue Collection to Service Provision

Local taxpayers are often reluctant to pay taxes because they do not know whether those revenues are well and in accord with their preferences and priorities. The primary concern is that local taxes may be used mainly to pay for municipal workers and municipal bureaucracy, or even worse to benefit the local administration. One of the strategies to regain trust in the local government is to open the accounts and display the direct link between local taxes and the provision (or expansion, rehabilitation,

and maintenance) of basic economic and social infrastructure, such as streets, public lighting, sidewalks, or roads. (Box 4.27 shows the leaflet used in Kenya to inform taxpayers about the sources and uses of the taxes they pay.) This is similar to the idea that fuel taxes are used to fund road maintenance or that water tariffs pay for the maintenance of the water infrastructure. This type of revenue allocation and use (which accords with the principle of benefit taxation) should be transparent, be made known to all local residents, and be supported by social audits to encourage tax compliance

Box 4.27 Citizens' Information Leaflet, Kenya

Kenya's citizen's budget

In 2011 the Kenyan Ministry of Finance published a six-page citizen's guide to the national budget. The document presents some of the key figures from the budget in diagrams and bullet points. For example, this pie chart is from the document. The citizen's budget provides information about how much money each sector will receive and how much has been earmarked for the poor, as well as a lot of other information. The citizen's budget also explains briefly what the government intends to do about important areas, such as creating youth employment and cushioning the poor from rising food prices.

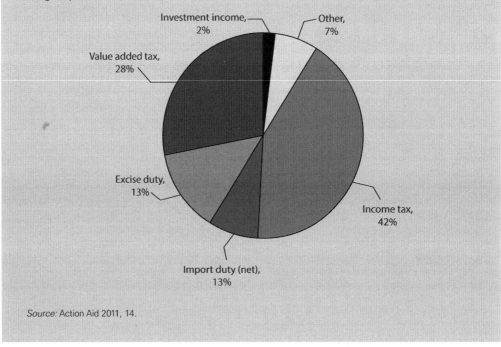

Investment income, 2%
Other, 7%
Value added tax, 28%
Excise duty, 13%
Income tax, 42%
Import duty (net), 13%

Source: Action Aid 2011, 14.

and local revenue mobilization efforts in general.[9] Two ways of doing that are linking costs to beneficiaries and linking expenditures to user charges.

Linking the cost of service provision to beneficiaries. Linking the cost of service provision to its beneficiaries improves transparency and the efficiency of resource allocation (discussed further in chapter 5). For instance, using property taxes to upgrade a water distribution system and subsequently using water user charges to maintain the quality of service are consistent and make sense in the eyes of the taxpayer.

Linking user charges to expenditures by service. User charges should be set at a level that will enable financing of the actual cost (O&M) of providing the service, as mentioned before, making service provision financially sustainable. In practice, the local government needs to have good knowledge of the cost of providing each service;

that requires good accounting and budgeting systems by service. Therefore, one of the main hurdles to setting adequate service fees is the establishment of accounting and budgeting by service, accounting by *cost centers,* or *fund accounting.* User charges can then be set at a level that recovers the actual cost of service provision and is consistent with the best consumption. Benchmarking can also enhance expenditure efficiency and user charge collection performance.

Improving Revenue Collection Efficiency

Electronic databases. All information on taxpayers and subscribers to services should be managed in electronic databases. Centralized databases keep track of outstanding financial obligations to the local government, payments, and arrears. Identification of taxpayers can benefit from crossing different databases. For instance, the names of water subscribers could be electronically crossed with the addresses and names of property taxpayers to broaden the tax base (box 4.28 summarizes the case of Ghana).

One-stop shops. To improve revenue collection efficiency, one-stop shops have been established in many cities in developing countries. They are meant to have up-to-date information on the clients' (i.e., taxpayers' and service subscribers') current accounts. All information is accessible in one office, so that clients do not have to visit several different, perhaps remote, offices for their complaints or inquiries to receive attention.

Box 4.28 Improving the Property Tax in Ghana

In Ghana, the World Bank has supported property tax reform through both urban and land administration projects, such as the Local Government Development Project; Second Urban Project (SEC Cities); Fifth Urban Project; and Second Land Administration Project. Project support has built capacity for district assemblies to overcome the constraints to property tax collection, most notably the dual system of land delivery (traditional and public) that has created a complicated system of property rights. Revenue mobilization from property taxes has also been constrained by failed attempts to create accurate official land registries and the limited base of landowners with official titles.

The Second Urban Project, for instance, has improved registration systems by linking an updated street addressing system with land cadastres and by harmonizing the legislative framework on land administration with customary law on land ownership. The reform increased revenue generation capacity in five cities. The percentage increase in property tax revenue collected by the five assemblies from 1988 to 1997 ranged in nominal terms from 2,713 percent in Accra to 62 percent in Tamale. The street addressing initiatives made it possible to locate and compile a register of taxable individuals and businesses. Still being rolled out in secondary cities, the street registration system in Accra and Tamale has enabled district assemblies to accurately determine their tax base, and it presents opportunities for augmenting revenue performance in both primary and secondary municipalities in Ghana. The new legal framework has made taxation a viable land management instrument by standardizing land ownership criteria and creating a basis for land valuation.

Source: Farvacque-Vitkovic et al. 2008.

Box 4.29 Benin Increases Its Revenue Capacity

Benin's two-phase Decentralized City Management Program (DCM I and DCM II) has enhanced revenue mobilization capacity in three primary cities (Cotonou, Porto-Novo, and Parakou) and three secondary cities (Abomey-Calavi, Lokossa, and Kandi). During DCM I, the three primary municipalities increased their total revenues by 82 percent, 148 percent, and 131 percent, respectively. The second phase of the program established municipal structures for improving tax billing and collection. Tax collection efficiency has also improved through a significant decrease in administrative expenses.

The program introduced computerized budget management systems. The integrated taxpayer and user database has enabled municipalities to track compliance by taxpayers and identify potential taxpayers. The automation and computerization of tax collection have reduced recovery costs for locally and centrally administered urban taxes. On the policy side, the program supported development of clear tax recovery procedures and implementation guidelines for finance department staff.

The alignment of central and local government revenue management systems has reduced tax administration costs and improved coordinated management of revenues and expenditures. The *Ministère des Finances et de l'Economie* established a central unit for each municipality to control revenues and expenses, in line with central government accounting procedures. Capacity building for the *Circonscription Urbaine* and line ministry staff has improved their efficiency in property and professional urban tax collection, budgeting, and accounting.

Source: Farvacque-Vitkovic et al. 2008.

A decentralized city management program to enhance revenue mobilization is illustrated by the experience of Benin in revenue collection efficiency (box 4.29).

Municipal Revenue Policy

Municipal revenue policy starts with identification of the issues affecting municipal revenue performance. Some of those issues may require actions at the national policy level, such as the size of and formula for intergovernmental transfers, the assignment of local taxes, and the establishment of tax rates (and ceilings for user charges). Others may be solvable at the local level. The system of intergovernmental fiscal transfers discussed in chapter 1 is out of local control, and thus it is better to focus on local actions.

At the local level, revenue issues deal with deficiencies in the coverage of those liable for taxes and nontax payments. Examples include the adequacy of identification and registration of taxpayers; the currency of the tax assessments, such as valuations of property; and the accuracy and currency of cadastral records. What are the deficiencies in the billing and collection of taxes and fees? The enforcement and remedy systems are also important to making sure that taxes are paid equitably.

Policy Tools

What are the tools that local governments can use to make sure revenues are enhanced, identified, and collected in the most efficient and equitable fashion and that problems identified can be promptly addressed? In general, sound revenue policy needs to look for means to enhance revenues, broadening the efficiency of the coverage of local tax bases, so that tax rates can be the lowest possible. Similarly, covering all the subscribers of services allows for the lowest user charges, which in turn enhances affordability and access to services.

Most local governments need the following for successful revenue management:

- *A credible enforcement system.* Political resistance may be attenuated if resources are allocated to improving the quality and quantity of public goods and services.

- *User charge set at a level to recover the operation and maintenance costs of service provision.* Local revenue policy needs to ensure the financial sustainability of municipal services.

- *Cost accounting systems by service.* To be able to set user charges at a level that ensures cost recovery for each service, the municipality must track the cost of each. It is practically impossible to set adequate charges without knowing the operation and maintenance costs of municipal services.

- *Affordable user charges.* Local governments need to adopt a policy regarding user charges that addresses issues of ability to pay. Two approaches are generally applied: (a) price regulation, which often implies a general subsidy, or (b) targeted subsidies to households. Price regulation usually distorts the true cost of service provision, leading to excess demand requiring overproduction and to unsustainability. Failing to solve the problem of cost recovery is not the best way to approach inability to pay.

- *Outsourcing revenue collection.* Outsourcing may be viable for user charges, including the administration of services. Ultimately the objective is sustainable service provision according to set standards.

- *Public-private partnerships.* Services financed by user charges, such as water and solid waste collection, in principle have the potential to be provided in partnership with the private sector; that typically ensures revenue collection efficiency, sustainability, and good standards in service provision.

Revenue Policy Impact Analysis

Any tax revenue policy will affect people's income and savings. The following are some items that need to be considered when setting prices or tariff rates:

Efficiency. Any municipal revenue policy should aim to finance local public goods and municipal services efficiently and equitably. Efficiency considerations are important to avoid unnecessary over- or underconsumption of services. In the case of water tariffs, if tariffs are too low, people will overconsume, and revenue will be insufficient to cover operation and maintenance. If the tariff is too high, people will not be able to afford a social optimum of the service being supplied.

Impact on the distribution of income. Taxes and user charges affect local income distribution. Local inequities produced by fiscal policy may worsen poverty levels, or they may reduce the concentration of wealth. In this respect, revenue policies may be neutral, regressive, or progressive with respect to their effects on local income redistribution. Progressive revenue sources (e.g., income taxes) generally streamlines aggregate local demand for public goods and services, which ultimately improves local economic growth.

Impact on the absorption capacity of new taxpayers. Improvement in the management of local revenue often results in increases in the taxes that residents should pay. This is particularly true when new land valuations are made for purposes of the property tax. In this case, local revenue administrators ought to offer a plan for a gradual increase in tax obligations to facilitate

Box 4.30 Criteria for Tax Choice

Local governments need to make choices on where to put emphasis across available instruments. In many cases, the options are limited and described in the constitution or regulatory framework, and the degrees of freedom left to the local government may be limited. However, it is useful to share a framework for cases where such potential exists.

There are several criteria to evaluate the best local taxes to be used by the local government. Bahl (1996) suggests five criteria: administrative ease, yield, equity or incidence, neutrality, and political feasibility. Taxes can be easily classified according to these criteria.

Let's take four major taxes: property tax, sales tax, income tax, and vehicle taxes. One can model how much each tax would need to be increased for a given amount of revenue needed and simulate how the municipal council would vote. Would administrative ease and political feasibility be the most important criteria? Or would yield and buoyancy be more important (maybe in a situation of financial stress)? What about equity (or progressivity)? Would the municipal council consider that property taxes are more progressive than sales tax, although the latter is much easier to implement or increase?

tax compliance. For instance, if revaluations are made every five years, then the corresponding increases in the tax could be divided into proportional increases over the next five years. An alternative is to use an annual price index to adjust the value of the tax base gradually, without big jumps, as has been done in Colombia.

Box 4.30 summarizes the criteria local governments can use to help in choosing the best taxes that are adapted to their particular circumstances.

The Role of Target Subsidies

Regardless of how well the revenue structure is planned and administered, some residents will be unable to pay user charges. Typically they are the poor, the unemployed, and the disabled. In theory, such groups should be protected by the safety net of regional or central governments, which should provide target subsidies to those who need them, perhaps using the local government as a conduit. The subsidy can be targeted to a specific use, as is the transportation voucher in Brazil, which is available to all

workers in the formal market. The federal government and employers finance it. It is a great policy to help poor workers commute to the labor market.

In the absence of direct subsidies, cross-subsidies can help the poor access a service by having the richer pay a higher tariff and allowing the poor to pay less. These cross-subsidies are often implicit in the user fee structure; for example, charging a smaller unit price for low consumption. Cross-subsidies are particularly used in water and energy services. Another way that the poor are helped through tax policies is exemptions from taxes. For example, in some countries owner-occupied property of widows and senior citizens without the ability to pay is exempt from the property tax. Additionally, specific programs to subsidize only basic, minimum consumption of some household services, such as electricity and water, may assist people unable to afford their monthly payments.

Many developing countries fail to follow these simple practices; instead, they often keep tariffs generally low under the argument of protecting the poor. As said, that is the least efficient way to protect the poor and has multiple adverse effects, such as overconsumption by the rich, loss of revenue that must eventually be covered by the general budget, and low quantity and poor quality of services (e.g., unclear water available one hour per day).

The main question, however, is who should pay for the subsidies? In practice, the local government pays in revenue forgone. Subsidies on basic consumption of services, such as water and electricity, should be financed from at least three sources: (a) *other consumers,* or those who pay the higher fees because of the cross-subsidies implicit in the fee structure; (b) *local taxes*; and (c) *state transfers* from the central government to deal with poverty and social issues (safety net).

However, local governments are not expected to take care of inequality concerns, which are the responsibility of the central government. If local governments were to increase taxes to improve the living conditions of their poor, local residents might resent the policy and decide to leave the community for another jurisdiction, where tax revenues are reinvested in the physical infrastructure of the city. Unfortunately, taxpayers are often selfish, and they prefer that the central government be the one to address poverty.

Takeaway Messages

A solid financial structure is essential to the success of cities in meeting the challenges of urbanization. The financial structure affects the quantity and quality of services, the efficiency with which those services are provided, whether the costs are shared across the city in a fair and efficient way, and both citizen access to government and local government accountability to citizens.

The choice of revenue tools is also important. The benefit model of local government finance starts with the premise that the main role of the local government is to deliver goods and services to local residents. Wherever possible, local government services should be paid for on the basis of the benefits received. Where the beneficiaries can be identified and where the services are not primarily redistributive in nature (e.g., social security), user fees are recommended. This is the case of water, sewers, recreation, and transit.

Revenue sources are combined in different ways by local governments, in line with the culture and the legislative framework. There are, however, some common features:

- Most local own-source revenue comes from the property tax and from sales and business taxes. Income taxes are used mostly in Northern Europe countries.

- Property tax is a good local tax because the base is immobile and the tax is visible. However, it requires technical capacity and political commitment. Often politicians avoid the property tax because it is too visible. If taxes and valuations are kept updated and transparent, taxpayers are likely to accept the advantages of the property tax. Much progress is still needed in developing countries, where the property tax represents a very small proportion of tax revenue and where the infrastructure for setting up a property tax is often not in place.

- Land-based revenues have been used recently to finance infrastructure in developing countries, and they are likely to be important revenue for the future. Land sales and leases (Cairo, Mumbai), betterment levies, and improvement fees are ways to capture the value of public land. They can also be used as the contribution of the public sector in private-public partnerships, notably in large projects. Examples are the Shanghai Metro project and the São Paulo Metro 4 Station.

- Another recently used source of local revenues is the congestion pricing or congestion tax used in London, Singapore, Milan, and Stockholm with the aim of reducing traffic, congestion, and pollution. The benefits of these taxes have been visible: carbon emissions have dropped and the revenues raised were used to expand and improve the public transport infrastructure.

In time of financial stress, many local governments are living in the moment. Cities need to reflect about the factors that have led them into fiscal distress and take the actions that will improve their situation in the medium and long term. Quick fixes (such as selling a physical asset) will not work. Reconsidering the allocation of resources and identifying potential increases in existing tax rates (even if temporary) are the best ways to deal with any financial crisis in an open and transparent way.

Notes

1. The difficulty of measuring the individual utility that a given person extracts from using a public service justifies the use of proxies in financing the service, notably progressive income taxes or proportional property taxes (Musgrave and Musgrave 1976).

2. Particularly in the Nordic countries; for more information, see OECD Fiscal Decentralization Database, http://www.oecd .org/tax/federalism/oecdfiscaldecentralisation database.htm#C_4.

3. This principle is often at odds with the principle that the rate of the property tax should be set so that when applied to a given base it yields the amount of money the local government needs to provide basic services. This means that everybody is paying a different amount for the consumption of the same public services on the assumption that the "utility" of these services is proportionate to one's wealth.

4. In many countries, collection rates look much better than they are because local property tax systems do distinguish collection of old unpaid

liabilities (arrears, fines, and penalties) from collection of current annual tax dues.

5. Some consider that utility surcharges are essentially benefit taxes illegitimately charged on excludable goods because it is easier to collect these than general taxes on pure, nonrival, public goods. However, surcharges could be good instruments to finance new development, for example, supporting green development, when imposed on energy.

6. Street addressing is the system that generally assigns a specific nomenclature (or address) to each location (i.e., plot of land, dwelling, building, etc.), making identification possible. Under the most modern system, this information is supported by GIS maps.

7. This difference could be exaggerated, given the difficulty in separating the potential number of taxpayers (whether registered or not), the registered taxpayers, and those actually receiving a tax bill.

8. Derived from Garrett and Leatherman 2010.

9. The term "social audits" refers to the role of civil society organizations in formally overseeing the operations of the local government, particularly the implementation of local development projects.

References

Action Aid, International Governance Team. 2011. "Budgets, Revenues and Financing in Public Service Provision." http://www.actionaidusa .org/sites/files/actionaid/budgets_revenues _and_financing_public_service_provision _hrba_governance_resources.pdf.

Audit Commission U.K. 2009. London Borough of Sutton. http://www.auditcommission. cov.uk/SiteCollectionDocuments /AuditCommissionReports/National Studies/23042009summingupREP.pdf.

Bahl, Roy. 1996. "Fiscal Decentralization: Lessons for South Africa." In Restructuring the State and Intergovernmental Fiscal Relations, edited by Bert Helmsing, Thomas Mogale, and Roland Hunter. Freidrich-Ebert-Stiftung.

———. 2002. "Implementable Rules of Fiscal Decentralization." In *Development, Poverty and Fiscal Policy*, edited by M. G. Rao, 253–77. New Delhi: Oxford University Press.

Bahl, Roy, J. Martinez-Vazquez, and J. Youngman. 2008. *Making the Property Tax Work: Experiences in Developing and Transitional Countries*. Boston: Lincoln Institute of Land Policy.

———. 2010. *Challenging the Conventional Wisdom of the Property Tax*. Boston: Lincoln Institute of Land Policy.

Bird, Richard. 2001. "Setting the Stage—Municipal and Intergovernmental Finance." In *Challenges of Urban Governments*, edited by M. Freire and R. Stren. Washington, DC: World Bank Institute.

———. 2006. "Local Business Taxes. In *Perspectives in Fiscal Federalism*, edited by Richard Bird and François Vaillancourt. Washington DC: World Bank Institute.

———. 2009. "Tax Assignment Revisited." In *Tax Reform in the 21st Century*, edited by J. Head and R. Krever, 441–70. New York: Wolters Kluwer.

———.2011 "Subnational Taxation in Developing Countries: A Review of the Literature." Policy Research Working Paper 5450, World Bank, Washington, DC.

Brzeski, W. Jan. 2012. "Global Position Paper on Property Tax Reforms." International Property Tax Institute, Toronto, Canada.

Devas, Nick. 2001. "Financing Cities," Insights #38, November, http://www.id21.org/insights /insights38/ insights-iss38-art01.html.

Devas, Nick, A. Munawwar, and D. Simon. 2008. *Financing Local Government*. Commonwealth Secretariat Local Government Reform Series, London.

DEXIA. 2008. *Sub-National Governments in the European Union*. Organization, Responsibilities and Finance, Paris.

Easter, K. W., and Y. Liu. 2005. "Cost Recovery and Water Pricing for Irrigation and Drainage Projects." Agriculture and Rural Development Discussion Paper 26, World Bank, Washington, DC.

Ellis, P., M. Kopanyi, and G. Lee. 2007. "Property Taxation in the Large Cities of Punjab Province, Pakistan." *Journal of Property Tax Assessment and Administration* 4 (2): 31–52.

Eckert, Joseph. 2008. "Computer-Assisted Mass Appraisal Options for Transitional and Developing Countries." In *Making the Property Tax Work*, edited by R. Bahl, J. Martinez-Vasquez, and J. Youngman. Cambridge, MA: Lincoln Institute of Land Policy.

Farvacque-Vitkovic, C. 2005. *Street Addressing and the Management of Cities*. Washington DC: World Bank.

Farvacque-Vitkovic, C., M. Raghunath, C. Eghoff, and C. Boakye. 2008. "Development of Cities of Ghana—Challenges, Priorities and Tools." Africa Region Working Paper 110, World Bank, Washington, DC.

Garrett, T. A., and John C. Leatherman. 2010. *An Introduction to State and Local Public Finance*. http://www.rri.wvu.edu/WebBook/Garrett /chapterfour.htm.

Guajardo, S. A., and R. Miranda. 2000. *An Elected Official's Guide to Revenue Forecasting*. Chicago: Government Finance Officers Association.

Ingram, Gregory. 2008. "Foreword." In *Making the Property Tax Work: Experiences in Developing and Transitional Countries*, edited by Roy Bahl, Jorge Martinez-Vazquez, and Joan Youngman. Boston: Lincoln Institute of Land Policy.

International City Management Association. 2003. IQ Report, vol. 35, no. 8, August.

Muccluskey, W. J., Michael E. Bell, and Lay C. Lim. 2010. "Rental Value versus Capital Value. Alternative Bases for the Property Tax." In *Challenging the Conventional Wisdom on the Property Tax*, edited by Roy Bahl, Jorge Martinez-Vasquez, and Joan Youngman, 119–57. Cambridge MA: Lincoln Institute of Land Policy.

Musgrave, Richard A., and Peggy B. Musgrave. 1976. *Public Finance in Theory and Practice*, 2nd ed. Tokyo: McGraw-Hill Kogakusha Ltd.

Peteri, G., and F. Sevinc. 2011. "Municipal Revenues and Expenditures in Turkey." UNDP–LAR Project, UNDP, Ankara, Turkey.

Peterson, George E. 2009: Unlocking Land Values to Finance Urban Infrastructure; World Bank PPIAF, Washington DC.

Ruiz, Francisco, and Gabriel Valejos. 2010. "Using Land Registration as a Tool to Generate Municipal Revenue: Lessons from Bogota." World Bank, Washington, DC.

Rybeck, Rick. 2004. "Using Value Capture to Finance Infrastructure and Encourage Compact Development." Washington, DC: District of Columbia Department of Transportation.

Slack, Enid. 2009. *Guide to Municipal Finance*. The Human Settlements Financing Tools and Best Practices Series, UN HABITAT, Nairobi, Kenya.

Werneck, R. 2008. "Tax Reform in Brazil: An Evaluation at the Crossroads." PUC Texto par Discussao, N 558. Rio de Janeiro: Pontificia Universidade Catolica.

World Bank. 2006a. "Brazil: Inputs for a Strategy for Cities. A Contribution with a Focus on Cities and Municipalities." Report No. 35749-BR. World Bank, Washington, DC.

——. 2006b. "Uganda at a Glance." World Bank, Washington DC.

——. 2007. "Implementation Completion Reports for Maputo Municipal Development Program (MMDP) I." World Bank, Washington, DC.

——. 2010. "West Bank and Gaza, Municipal Finance and Service Provision." Sustainable Development Department, Middle East and North Africa Region Report. World Bank, Washington, DC.

Wyoming. 2011. *"Guidelines for Preparing the Municipal Budget—A Handbook for Municipal Elected Officials.* Available at http://www.wyomuni.org/vertical/Sites /percent7BAA188EFF-AB49-49A3-ACFE -6BC586C039AD percent7D/uploads /percent7BD4C29F11-6798-4AE1-AD5C -0E67ABFAF498 percent7D.PDF.

CHAPTER 5

Managing Local Expenditures

Lance Morrell and Mihaly Kopanyi

Local governments throughout the world are under increasing financial pressure to do more with less. Although not all local governments have the same level of responsibility for providing services, most of them face a rapidly growing demand for urban services as a result of the continuing fast growth of the urban population. However, the capacity of those local governments to supply urban services and to undertake the necessary infrastructure development is severely constrained by a shortage of fiscal resources. Although the situation is the result of many factors, the problem has become more extreme following the financial crisis of 2008, which intensified the general need to increase efficiency and to manage financial resources more effectively.

Although the demand on local governments for more services at a lower total cost will continue, the ideas and tools that this chapter presents will provide local government officials, and in particular finance officers, with the means to increase the efficiency and cost-effectiveness of municipal services and functions. Even though the nature of the services that municipalities provide varies by size and local situation, the concepts presented in this chapter, together with those in chapters 3 and 4, apply to most local governments.

The objectives of this chapter are to introduce concepts designed to strengthen the abilities of local government administrators, members of local councils, department heads, and finance staff to manage and control the level of expenditures, so that local services can be provided efficiently and effectively and the tax burden on citizens minimized.

Expenditure Management Concept and Principles

Throughout the world, legislatures and specialists are discussing the importance of fiscal discipline and operational efficiency. The concept of expenditure management is to ensure that the funds available to local governments are spent on improving service delivery and achieving government objectives efficiently and effectively. Shortcomings in expenditure management result in the arbitrary allocation of resources and inefficient operations, which are common in many developing countries. Expenditure management systems are the tools that enable local governments to ensure that revenue budgets are realistic and expenditures are consistent with the revenue forecasts. These systems also help to ensure that strategic priorities receive the needed budgets and that the various public services are provided at reasonable cost.

What Is Expenditure Management?

Expenditure management focuses on ensuring that funds are allocated and used to achieve agreed priorities and that information is available to enable governments to plan and monitor the performance of their programs and the impact of their expenditures. Its tools include planning resources and expenditures; allocating or appropriating resources and transferring funds to entities and functions; controlling and executing expenditures and the release of funds; and monitoring expenditure performance. They will be discussed in more detail in the following sections.

Expenditure Management Entities

Several entities are involved in expenditure management, each fulfilling specific aspects and functions of the overall expenditure management of a local government; and the allocation of functions depends on (local) legal and political circumstances:

- *Council and mayor.* Members of the local government council focus on ensuring that the services demanded by the taxpayers are provided efficiently, that the funds collected are used appropriately, and that the government's policies and internal control procedures

are being followed. The council sets rules, provides guidance, discusses expenditure performance analysis and decides on corrective actions, and communicates expenditure performance to external entities, such as the central government and the citizens.

- *Finance department.* The treasurer or the head of the finance department focuses on ensuring that each line department receives a budget sufficient to provide the agreed services; the funds allocated to the various departments are used for their intended purposes; and systems and procedures are in place to monitor and evaluate recurrent and capital expenditures.

- *Line departments.* The heads of the line or functional departments focus largely on managing and controlling their specific costs, for example, in a solid waste services department, investing in and maintaining machinery and the costs of fuel and wages.

Expenditure Management—Big Picture Issues and Challenges

The scheme in figure 5.1, introduced in chapter 3, illustrates the perspective and roles of the mayor, the council, and the finance department in expenditure management. Among other functions, they need to focus on the big picture of municipal finances, as they are responsible for ensuring that total revenues are sufficient to cover the total expenditures of the municipality or, in other words, that the budget is balanced (see also chapter 8).

The balanced budget. The local situation and challenges to a large extent depend on a country's fiscal architecture and specifically the level and depth of decentralization (explained in more detail in chapter 1; see also Ebel and Vaillancourt 2007). As a result, comparing structures and revenue and expenditure balances requires careful understanding of the country's situation. Nevertheless, some general principles and basic

Figure 5.1 Revenues in Budget Context

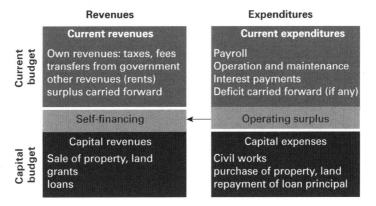

Revenues

Expenditures

Current budget	**Current revenues** Own revenues: taxes, fees transfers from government other revenues (rents) surplus carried forward	**Current expenditures** Payroll Operation and maintenance Interest payments Deficit carried forward (if any)
	Self-financing ←	Operating surplus
Capital budget	**Capital revenues** Sale of property, land grants loans	**Capital expenses** Civil works purchase of property, land repayment of loan principal

Table 5.1 Jhelum City Budget (PRs millions)

	2004–05	2005–06	2007–08
Current revenues	91.9	130.9	115.5
Current expenditures	30.0	42.8	47.5
Current balance	61.8	130.1	117.8
Development revenues	14.8	25.1	15.5
Development expenses	36.1	144.1	188.3
Development balance	(21.3)	(119.0)	(172.9)
Closing balance	40.6	11.2	(55.0)

structures provide a useful basis for analysis and comparisons, including the balanced budget principle and the division of functions among government tiers, for example.

Municipalities should plan for and maintain balanced budgets for both legal and pragmatic reasons. Figure 5.1 depicts an ideal situation that is realistic in developed countries, namely, current revenues exceed current expenditures and provide a substantial operating surplus that is available for self-financing a portion of capital expenditures. Thus, a balanced budget includes three balances: current balance (with surplus), capital balance, and balance total. Well-managed municipalities, even in developing countries, plan and execute their budgets with these

triple balances, as does Jhelum city (population 200,000), in Pakistan, as shown in table 5.1. The 2007/08 budget suggests that although municipal borrowing is prohibited in Pakistan, delayed payment to developers (forced credit) is apparently an option.

Hundreds of municipalities in developing and transition economies face persistent current deficits—in part because of the global financial crisis. That means that they fail to finance regular operations from current revenues, and either accumulate deficits over years or finance operations from capital receipts; that is, they are using up the wealth of the community. Table 5.2 shows the budgets of a big (over 3 million) Pakistani city and a medium-size city in Croatia.

Although the two budgets look similar, the current deficit is more persistent in Pakistan, while it is temporary in Croatia and due largely to the global economic downturn. Despite their current deficits, both of these cities finance development, largely with state grants, and in Croatia, with loans. Needless to say, a current deficit is an unhealthy situation that should be fixed. A persistent current deficit may indicate either soft budget constraints, meaning weak expenditure control, or a vertical imbalance, meaning a mismatch between expenditure and revenue assignments, which should be corrected by the central government.

Table 5.2 Budgets of a Big City in Pakistan and a Medium-Size City in Croatia

Multan budget (PRs thousands)	2008–09	2009–10	2010–11	Rijeka budget (€ thousands)	2008	2009	2010
Current revenues	5,318.7	4,719.5	5,850.5	Total current revenues w balances forward	128.4	120.7	119.5
Current expenditures	4,054.0	4,761.8	6,138.7				
Current balance	1,264.7	−42.3	−288.2	Current expenditure	124.2	122.4	127.6
Capital or dev. receipts	1,018.0	1,403.0	0.0	Net operating balance	4.2	−1.6	−8.1
Capital expenditures	1,420.0	868.0	965.0	Capital revenues/financing	32.2	17.2	33.6
Capital balance	−402.0	535.0	−965.0	Capital expenditures	36.4	15.5	25.5
Total balance	862.7	492.7	−1,253.2	Capital balance (surplus/ deficit)	−0.2	8.6	8.5
				Overall closing balance	4.0	7.0	0.4

Expenditures by functions or sectors. The level of fiscal decentralization largely determines the structure of expenditures by function or service sector. The Nordic countries of Europe are deeply decentralized, with a broad scope of functions devolved to the local governments. Other European countries remain more centralized, with few functions assigned to the local level. Like them, most of the municipalities in the developing world have limited functions. For example, municipalities in Jordan are largely responsible for local roads, street lighting, and solid waste management; other functions are performed by central government entities.

Figure 5.2 shows a very clear relationship between decentralization and the size and structure of expenditures by function. Municipalities in decentralized countries cover a large share of public expenditures (in Denmark, 35 percent of GDP); spend the bulk of their budgets on social services; pay in part for some urban services, most of which are provided by private entities; and spend only a small portion of their budgets on administration. The opposite side of the picture shows cities in centralized countries paying a small share of municipal expenses (in Turkey, 5 percent of GDP), with minor responsibilities for social services; substantial spending on urban services; and a large portion of their small budgets covering administrative expenditures.

Municipalities in the developing countries tend to be similar to the more centralized European countries, with small shares of total public expenditures, minor functions in the provision of social and urban services, and a large share of their budgets going for administrative expenditures. Some even argue that local employment is their prime function. The citizens, however, may not feel that the local government serves them and thus may not be willing to pay higher taxes if the bulk of the budget is spent for administration rather than services. Lessons can be drawn from the assignment of functions, as well as national traditions, to determine the structure of expenditures, and expenditure control should be assessed against those characteristics.

Table 5.3 shows the emerging situation of the Russian Federation following the political transition. Russian municipalities are substantially responsible for the provision of social services (low-income housing, health, and education). The table suggests that over time they have rationalized expenditures by, among other things, privatizing part of the housing stock. They increased expenditures on urban services, education, and health. They are also specifying expenses more precisely, reducing the

Figure 5.2 Expenditures by Function and Decentralization

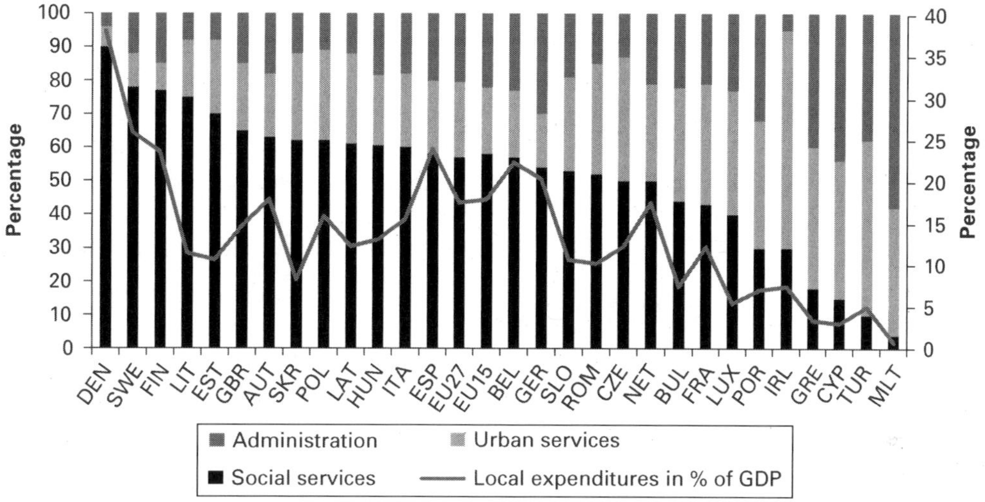

Source: http://epp.eurostat.ec.europa.eu/portal/page/portal/statistics/search_database.

Table 5.3 Municipal Expenditures by Function in the Russian Federation (%)

Function	1996	2002
Local administration	3.3	6.7
Infrastructure and economic services	8.3	9.9
Housing and communal services	26.6	19.5
Culture	2.1	3.0
Education	25.6	33.2
Public health	14.5	15.5
Social policy	7.2	7.6
Other	12.4	4.6
Total	100.0	100.0

Source: Chernyavsky and Vartapetov 2004.

undefined "other expenditures" line item from 12.4 percent to 4.6 percent.

Expenditure Management—A Battlefield between the Finance and Line Departments

Budget planning is an iterative process driven and controlled by the treasury or finance department and usually by a finance committee of the council (explained in more detail in chapter 3). The finance department sets the budget calendar and communicates policy decisions and guidelines. Against these the line departments draft their budgets and submit proposals to the finance department for review and negotiation (see figure 5.3). The finance department is responsible to enforce key policy targets (including the balanced budget), to consolidate the departmental budgets into the municipal budget, and to submit it for approval by the mayor and council. It is a lengthy process, with competitions, battles, and sometimes harsh discussions between the finance and other departments.

The functional or line departments are primarily responsible for fulfilling their tasks from the budget allotted to them, thus controlling their expenditures. Therefore, during the planning process they have a vested interest in increasing their budgets over the previous year's amount. Sometimes battles occur between the finance department and other entities in discussions of expenditure plans. Table 5.4 shows how a school

Figure 5.3 The Iterative Budgeting Process

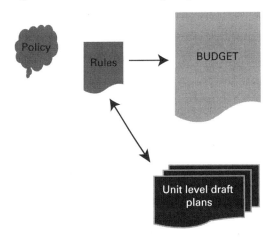

Table 5.4 Expenditure Plan Submitted by a School to the Finance Department

	Revised Estimates 2011 (Rs)	Plan 2012 (Rs)
Gross expenditure[a]	32,500,000	36,125,000
Revenues from tuition[b]	8,000,000	10,120,000
Net financing need	24,500,000	26,005,000

a. The costs of energy and utilities will increase total expenses by 5 percent, and four part-time professors will be hired, based on approval by the school board.
b. Applications suggest that the number of students will increase by 10 percent, and tuition will be increased by 15 percent.

supports its expenditure plan with specific information about changes from the previous (base) year.

The negotiations between the finance and line departments are particularly difficult when the departments are requested to cut expenditures, a challenge that municipalities have been facing all over the world, including in the United States, because of the economic downturn after 2008. In such cases detailed and specific measures are required to achieve revenue increases and, more important, expenditure cuts, including reducing the number of police and spending on park maintenance. Finance departments should identify, and offer to decision makers, alternative solutions to achieve needed budget restructuring.

An Effective Expenditure Management System

An effective expenditure management system must include three elements:

1. *Milestones.* It is necessary to plan for future expenditures with clear and measurable milestones to monitor actual performance.

2. *Spending control.* It is necessary to control expenditures so that actual spending is consistent with the budget and plan.

3. *Evaluation.* Expenditures must be monitored and evaluated to ensure that they are in fact conforming to agreed-on plans.

The overarching objective of expenditure management, as said, is to improve the use of resources. To fulfill that objective, local governments must promote achievement of three interrelated outcomes:

1. *Aggregate fiscal discipline*—ensuring that actual expenditures are consistent with actual total revenues, to keep government spending within sustainable limits

2. *Allocative efficiency*—consistency between budgets allocated to programs and activities that promote the strategic priorities of the communities

3. *Operational efficiency*—the provision of public services at a reasonable quality and cost.

Although those three outcomes are reasonable, they must be achieved by local governments that are by their nature complex organizations, with numerous and often conflicting political agendas and competing special interests. One group within the local government may want a tax increase to improve a specific local service; another group may lobby to increase pension payments to employees; the interests of community groups may differ from those of developers or local businesses, and so on.

The Expenditure Management Cycle

Expenditure management should be seen as a continuous cycle that includes reviewing and setting policies, developing and approving plans, mobilizing and allocating resources, implementing plans and controlling expenditures, monitoring accounting expenditures, and evaluating and auditing expenditure performance. Figure 5.4 depicts the expenditure cycle, and box 5.1 illustrates some actions that can be taken to improve expenditure management. We begin by briefly explaining the elements of the expenditure management cycle; more details will be discussed in the subsequent sections. Box 5.1 summarizes

the key requirements for improving expenditure management.

Policy Setting

The cycle begins with, and is driven by, the policies that the local government is trying to achieve. To begin the process, government officials must review current policies to determine if they are still valid and, together with the various stakeholders, identify new or modified policies that are important to the communities. An example might be introducing a development fee that requires local property developers to finance upgrades of trunk infrastructure when developing adjacent properties. Another example could be requiring that housing developers ensure that 15 percent of all new housing units are affordable for low-income groups.

Planning

After a transparent review of, and agreement on, the local government's policies and strategies, plans need to be finalized for each department

Figure 5.4 The Expenditure Management Cycle

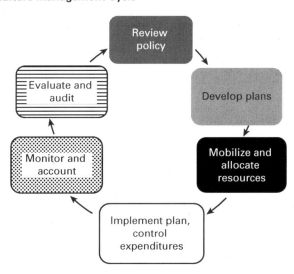

Source: World Bank 1998, 32.

and unit. In developing effective plans, it is essential that measurable milestones are identified to enable performance to be monitored. The implementation plans should enable government officials to make midcourse corrections or to expand or contract some programs if actual levels of revenues or expenditures alter the initial plans.

Resource Allocation

The next step of the cycle is to mobilize and allocate the resources needed to achieve the policies and then implement the planned activities. At this point, the sources of revenue (discussed in chapter 4) must be reviewed, and realistic revenue budgets must be developed and compared with the estimated expenditures (procedure discussed in chapter 3). This budgeting or planning process is iterative, as estimated expenditures may be greater than realistic revenue projections. Thus, the process will need to continue to the point where the *estimated expenditures* for the agreed plans and programs are adjusted to be consistent with the *revenues* that realistically can be generated. Some weaknesses that

frequently affect resource allocation are listed in box 5.2.

Expenditure Control

Once plans have been developed and fully funded to address the agreed-on strategic policies, the local government will proceed to implement the plans and to properly account for and control both revenues and expenditures. Various tools and procedures can be used to perform adequate expenditure control at every level of the local government and in each department and unit authorized to spend funds.

Accounting and Monitoring

The next step in the expenditure management cycle is to account for each expenditure, adequately ensuring that costs are applied to the specific activities (cost centers), and then to monitor the results through financial and technical means.

Evaluation and Audit

The final step in the expenditure management cycle is to review and audit the results of the

Box 5.2 Weaknesses in Resource Allocation and Use

Weaknesses that undermine expenditure management, and public financial management in general at the local government level, include the following:

- Poor planning
- Lack of links among policy making, planning, and budgeting
- Poor expenditure control
- Inadequate funding of operations and maintenance

- Little relationship between budget as formulated and budget as executed
- Inadequate accounting systems
- Unreliability in the flow of budgeted funds to agencies and to lower levels of government
- Poor cash management
- Inadequate reporting of financial performance
- Poorly motivated staff

Source: World Bank 1998, 5.

---

programs to evaluate objectively whether or not the agreed-on outputs and outcomes are being achieved. The results of these evaluations will provide critical information to all stakeholders during the review of government policies that will be part of the next annual policy review program.

Each of these items is discussed in more detail in the following sections, but the question may be raised as to where the cycle should begin. The objective of a local government is to deliver those services that the population demands and is willing to pay for in the form of taxes and fees. Thus, the policy framework should be the place where the planning and expenditure management cycle begins and ends.

Example: The economic and demographic changes in many East European cities require consolidating schools by closing some and moving students from unsustainable schools to growing areas nearby. Closing a school is among the hardest of decisions, charged with both interests and politics. Ideally the decision on which of five schools would be closed should be made based on detailed analysis, since the answer to this simple question is not straightforward. Thus, the local government contracts a consultant to analyze the situation based on clear and hard numbers, to

recommend solutions, and to conduct or facilitate stakeholder consultations. Once the proposed plan has been fully developed and its cost determined, it is presented to the communities for discussion. After a number of stakeholder meetings and revisions to the plan, stakeholders agree that the local government should organize a referendum for the citizens of the zones affected and decide which school to close based on popular vote With this strategic policy decision in place, the finance and education departments will prepare revenue and expenditure plans to support eventual implementation. Those plans would contain measurable outputs and outcomes, as well as intermediate targets to enable officials to monitor and evaluate the results.

Review and Develop Policies and Plans

What is an expenditure management policy? In a broad sense, it is a way of making choices about planned expenditures in the years ahead (next year, or the next three to five years). Many players are involved in the policy-setting process. The elected officials (mayor, council, etc.) and their respective constituents are critical in defining the new policy agenda (e.g., spending more on education, and maybe less on roads, because education is a high priority). Policy options and plans are also frequently developed internally by service and line departments. As with the example above on a school rationalizing program, once policy options have been agreed on, the service and line departments are essential in developing cost estimates and implementation plans, and the finance department must identify ways to finance the costs.

Arguably the most difficult part of the expenditure management cycle is to review policy options and decide on those policies that are most appropriate for a specific local government. A major reason why this step is so difficult is that it is not merely technical but largely depends on the political process and is thus subject to the involvement of special interests. It is crucial that the elected officials in the government provide legitimacy to policy decisions and the resource implications over the life of the policy by being at the center of the process of reconciling what is affordable, given the level of revenues that can reasonably be expected, and what is being demanded of the various sectors.

What is the right package of policies depends on (a) the priorities of the society, (b) the costs of programs and activities needed to meet those priorities, and (c) the objectives of special interest groups. A program may be relatively inexpensive but not fall in a priority area. Or a program may be in a priority area but be much more expensive than another program in some other priority area. In either case, the program is not right. To establish priorities, one needs to know the preferences of the citizens and have a participatory process in place. Functional and service departments and municipal agencies or enterprises are responsible for and active in estimating and articulating customers' needs and priorities in their competency area. Often they have a vested interest too. Therefore, the policy formulation process induces competition among departments, agencies, politicians, and interest groups, as well as among project proposals.

Example: Local elected officials may use their influence with a department to gain its support for certain projects which would benefit the officials and their constituents. The projects may be high priorities for the local communities but may not have the impact of others are supported by the department or government because of the influence of a few elected officials (the "bridge to nowhere" in Alaska is an example; see box 5.3).

Incorporating Financial Constraints and Examining Alternatives

The policies and projects that elected officials and their staff support must recognize the hard budget constraints imposed by realistic revenue forecasts and the recurrent costs of proper operation and maintenance of assets. Analyses must be based on realistic revenue and expenditure assumptions and include, as much as possible, alternatives for decision makers to consider, as well as clear and verifiable indicators that can be used to monitor and evaluate progress in developing and implementing each alternative.

For good functioning, government officials must coordinate the drafting and analyses of options by the departments, and the data and underlying assumptions used must be made available to all to ensure transparency and encourage a high degree of realism in the process. Neither the analyses nor the conclusions will satisfy all constituents, and that is why transparency is essential.

In some cases, for example, a department may withhold information regarding its best estimate of the full cost of a program to get the program approved. Once a budget has been provided and work started, perhaps based on half of the actual estimate of its cost, future budget allocations will normally be easier to obtain.

Neither transparency nor large-scale policy dialogue is common in many developing countries. Rather, proposals are drafted by department experts behind closed doors, or by consultants, and not communicated to stakeholders because consultations are a time-consuming and sometimes painful political process. Indeed, sector departments have the professional expertise to draft proposals or discuss alternatives, but they may have vested interests, too. In addition, in some cases mismatches occur between government policy and the actual expenditures, as shown in box 5.4, either for political reasons or because of resource constraints issues.

Well-organized analyses and participatory budgeting (explained in chapters 3 and 8) are increasingly used to support informed decisions that reflect citizens' priorities. Chapter 8 discusses an effective data collection, analysis, and decision process that is used increasingly, including in developing countries. Municipal and financial audits start with developing structured databases and proceed to completing analyses, comparing results with benchmarks, and eventually preparing a specific action plan for improving local services and financial performance, including time frames.

Higher bodies such as the council or central government (financier of operations and development) use municipal audits to control and measure the performance of municipal entities. Performance management can also be supported by specific performance contracts between a municipality and service entities, whether public, private, or mixed ownership. The central government may also set performance targets, condition grants on the municipality's meeting them, and enforce such an arrangement by a municipal contract (see chapter 8 for more details).

Example: Fairfax County, Virginia, U.S., decided that it wanted to extend the mass rapid transit system out to the international airport. Elected officials from a number of jurisdictions and many of their constituents supported the extension, and the relevant staff and consultants began developing various technical alternatives and cost estimates. Among the options under consideration was whether to locate the station at the airport on ground level or underground. The technical analysis indicated that the above-ground option was substantially less expensive. But the underground option would not change the landscape, and thus it was more appealing

Box 5.4 Mismatch between Policy Goals and Expenditure Allocations in Guinea

A 1996 public expenditure review (PER) in Guinea revealed a complete mismatch between the government's stated policy priorities and its actual priorities, based on expenditure allocation. Although the government designated primary education, public health, and road maintenance as priorities, funds often were allocated to other areas instead. No system existed for costing out policy proposals or subjecting them to rigorous scrutiny. An exercise to cost out the policy mix that would be needed to meet the government's stated priorities revealed that the share of priority programs in total spending would need to triple over the succeeding four years, implying drastic cuts in other expenditures to remain within the budget. The report also showed that actual allocations to meet the recurrent costs of investment projects fell far short of what would be required for adequate operation and maintenance.

Based on the findings and recommendations of the PER, the government of Guinea launched an initiative to define affordable policies. Four line ministries began revising their medium-term policies and costing out their implementation. The government also began preparing a medium-term expenditure framework for the four ministries (initially), in the context of its economic reform program, and central ministries began preparing a macroeconomic policy document to help the cabinet make intersectoral allocation decisions. The ministry of planning took steps to improve the predictability of the macroeconomic framework.

Source: World Bank 1997.

to many. After numerous public hearings, revisions, and reviews of the cost and financing assumptions, the decision was made in favor of the lower-cost, ground-level option because it was more consistent with the estimated revenue stream.

Budget Plans

No good expenditure control system can operate without adequate budget plans. The expenditure budget is the result of the planning process discussed above. Expenditure budgets are often very detailed. For example, the expenditure budget of Lahore, a city of 7 million, is about 400 pages long, with detailed line items for each and every unit, function, and action. The council discusses these very detailed budget plans, but the expenditure managers in finance departments use, and submit to the council, short budget summaries for easy communication (see chapters 3 and 8). Strategic discussions and decisions on the budget require such short budget snapshots.

Box 5.5 shows a general budget template and a real budget snapshot from a Nepali city. The two templates, albeit in different order, follow the same logic, namely, they separate (a) own expenditures, (b) delegated expenditures that are financed by earmarked grants from higher government tiers, and (c) capital expenditures. Own expenditures are those activities that have been devolved to the local level; what activities are delegated depends on the local circumstances.

The Mechinagar budget shown in box 5.5 offers further information, including (a) that "current expenditures" are fully assigned, which means that there is no "other" category that is not attached to specific functions, and (b) that unassigned "miscellaneous" expenditures are the

Box 5.5 Snapshots of Expenditure Budgets

Sample expenditure plan	2008	2009	2010	2011
Total expenditures	**Actual**	**Actual**	**Actual**	**Plan**

EXPENSES ON DELEGATED FUNCTIONS

1. Preschool education
   - Wages
   - Operating
   - Repair and maintenance
   - Capital investment
2. Primary and secondary school
3. Health care
4. Social assistance and poverty alleviation
5. Public order and civil protection
6. Other

OWN EXPENDITURES

1. Infrastructure and public services
   - -Current expenditures
     - Direct expenditures
   - -Capital expenditures
     - Direct expenditures
     - Subcontracts
2. Environment protection
   - Wastewater
   - Solid waste
3. Social, cultural, recreational expenditures
4. Local economic development
5. Social housing
6. Urban development
7. Civil security
8. Transfer to sublocal government entities
   Support to public utility companies
9. (subsidies, grants, equity, in-kind)
   - Utility 1
10. Loan repayment
11. Interest charges
12. Guarantees called (paid by the municipality)

(continued next page)

Box 5.5 *(continued)*

Expenditure Budgeted vs. Actual Mechinagar City, Nepal				
	Actual 2007/08	**2007/08 % share**	**Budget 2007/08**	**Variance 100-A/B%**
52 Salaries	10,661	14.96	11,035	3.39
53 Allowances	252	0.35	385	34.45
54 Travel and per diem	692	0.97	705	1.83
55 Services	384	0.54	480	19.98
56 Rent	178	0.25	180	1.21
57 Repair and maintenance	544	0.76	550	1.09
58 Office supplies	905	1.27	915	1.07
59 Newspapers	49	0.07	50	1.94
60 Fuel	567	0.80	600	5.53
61 Clothes/food allowance	351	0.49	355	1.18
64 Food (prisoners/animals)	295	0.41	310	4.8
65 Financial asst./donations	41	0.06	50	17.29
66 Contingencies	4,772	6.70	5,282	9.66
68 **CURRENT EXPENDITURES**	19,692	27.64	20,897	5.77
69 **DEBT PAYMENT**	4,000	5.61	4,000	0.00
71 Health	668	0.94	700	4.58
75 Fin. assistance	1,144	1.61	1,159	1.25
76 Miscellaneous	3,140	4.41	3,850	18.44
77 **DELEGATED PROGRAMS**	4,952	6.95	5,709	13.25
78 Furnitures	22	0.03	50	56.47
79 Vehicle	99	0.14	150	34.17
80 Machinery equipment	305	0.43	11,210	97.28
81 **ORDINARY CAPITAL**	425	0.60	11,410	96.27
82 Land/building purchase	365	0.51	365	0.14
83 Building construction	250	0.00	1,300	80.80
85 Other dev./construction	41,815	58.69	58,136	28.07
86 **CAPITAL INVESTMENT**	42,180	59.20	59,801	29.47
87 **TOTAL EXPENDITURE**	71,249	100.00	101,817	30.02

Note: Template from Municipal Finances Self-Assessment (MFSA-see chapter 8) and budget of Mechinagar, Nepal.

largest item in the delegated programs, which signals improper budgeting and uncertainty of control. As for development expenditures, one can also notice (c) that the city singles out expenditures on land and buildings but reports all other urban construction (e.g., roads, drainage) in one line that represents over half the total budget; it would be better to separate that line into the main investment categories. The Actual/Budget (A/B) column shows (d) that by end of the fiscal year, large differences appear between planned and actual investments, a common situation in developing countries because of delays in allocation of grant funds, delays in construction, or both.

Donor-Funded Projects

Many developing countries receive support from development partners, bilateral or multilateral donors. Receiving a project free makes local governments happy but often makes them myopic too, in that they tend to ignore or hide the longer-term implications of operating and maintaining the assets received. For proper expenditure management, it is important that local governments ensure that the recurrent costs that these donor-funded projects entail are properly captured in future budgets. This is not always easy or even possible since many projects are implemented outside of the normal budget process. However, local governments must actively analyze all government and donor-funded projects to understand the implications of operating and maintaining them and should account them on-budget instead of off-budget.

Many projects are structured by, paid for, and implemented by external agencies, with no money transferred to the local budget. There is nothing wrong with that; from an accounting perspective these are in-kind contributions. However, two challenges must be considered: First, these projects need to be integrated in the longer-term plans of the municipality, be included in a medium-term budget, and be part of the category of highest-priority projects. Second, the financial implications need to be planned for and budgeted. Even if it is not possible to incorporate the projects into the normal budgeting process, notations about them must be shown in the budget to ensure that provision for the recurrent costs they entail will be in place when they have been completed. Unless provisions are made in the budgets for the outer years, the risk increases that the staff, equipment, and supplies needed to make use of the assets (for example, a school, a health clinic,

or a road) will not be in place after construction is complete.

Example: Some donor projects are managed externally by a project unit hired by the donor. Thus, the local government may not be properly informed about the details concerning costs, implementation schedules, and, more important, about the timing and amount of recurrent costs. In such cases direct budgeting of these projects in advance or detailed and timely accounting of actual costs is not possible. Possibly some agreed-on amount of total support can be made note of as an off-budget memo item. In the case of an in-kind donation, such as a school building, the local government must operate it by hiring teachers, paying electricity and water bills, and making repairs. It must budget for and perform those operation and maintenance functions immediately upon taking over the building from the donor.

Multiyear Budgets and Capital Investment Plans

Policies generally take more than one year to implement, and when a government is preparing only a single-year budget, implementation becomes more difficult. To ensure that the true cost of a program is recognized and the desired outputs and outcomes are realized, it is best to budget over a longer term, such as three to five years. This section discusses the use of multiyear budgets or investment plans.

Table 5.5 presents the three-year, rolling, medium-term budget for the city of Johannesburg, South Africa. It compares the adjusted actual results for the current year with the budgets for the next three fiscal years. The budget, along with a great deal of other financial information, is posted on the city's website.

What Is a Capital Investment Plan?

A capital investment plan (CIP) is a multiyear (usually three to six years) program of capital investment projects, prioritized by year,

Table 5.5 Multiyear Budget for the City of Johannesburg

	Actual 2010/11 (R millions)	Budget 2011/12 (R millions)	Change (%)	Estimate 2012/13 (R millions)	Estimate 2013/14 (R millions)
Revenue	26,430	29,371	11.1	32,843	36,875
Expenditure	25,960	28,266	8.9	31,348	34,217
Surplus (deficit) before tax	469	1,104	135.4	1,495	2,657
Tax paid	59	295		286	303
Surplus for the year after tax	410	809	97.3	1,208	2,354
Capital gains and contributions	1,976	2,701	36.7	3,315	3,427
Surplus with capital gains and contributions	2,386	3,510	47.1	4,524	5,782

Source: http://www.joburg.org.za.

with anticipated start and completion dates, annual estimated costs, and proposed financing methods. The plan is usually approved by an elected body, such as a city council, and after approval, it can be used to secure financing from donor institutions or banks. The approved CIP connects midrange plans with the annual budgetary process. The plan is reviewed and revised annually, and an additional year is added. When the process is fully established, the CIP becomes a rolling plan linked to the annual budgeting process. Each year, the previous year is removed from the CIP period, a new year is added, and current-year capital budget expenditures become part of the approved annual budget.

Capital investment planning by local governments often includes investments (assets) by the local government itself and by its entities, including enterprises established and owned by the government for the provision of municipal services (such as utility companies). The plan may also include investments by the private sector through public-private partnerships (PPPs). *The Guidebook on Capital Investment Planning for Local Governments* (World Bank 2011) contains more details (chapters 4 and 7 of this book also discuss specifics of the CIP).

In many developing countries, projects funded by central or regional governments often represent the majority of local public investments. The imposition of centrally planned projects reduces the incentives of local policy makers to engage in the time-consuming CIP process. Such projects create a number of complications for local governments:

- The projects are often selected without adequate consultation or coordination with local governments or their stakeholders and as a result may not reflect local priorities.

- Project schedules may conflict with capital projects of the local governments themselves.

- Once completed, such projects often have a major impact on local budgets because the local government is expected to pay their operations and maintenance costs, frequently creating a substantial budgetary liability.

Financial Capacity of Local Governments

A critical input in the capital investment planning process is knowledge of the local government's capacity to fund capital investments. Its capacity includes the feasibility of incurring debt and attitude toward borrowing (chapter 7 discusses external sources of financing). Knowledge of financial capacity should include the government's recurrent obligations and the annual revenue stream that will be available to ensure effective operations and maintenance or finance debt. Unless the local government has the ability to fund and implement a capital investment program, the list of projects prioritized through the CIP process is nothing more than a "wish list" of local needs and preferences. Considering that most local governments can finance only a few priority projects in any one year and only a small percentage of their total capital needs, the realistic assessment of financial capacity is essential.

Few would argue with the idea that bad planning leads to unsatisfactory results. With capital projects, bad planning and weak expenditure management generally lead to too many projects being started (too wide an investment) but not completed on time, or at all, because of a lack of financial resources (too shallow a pool of financing). The impacts of bad capital planning are also evident in extended construction schedules and poor quality of construction due to lack of money. Such wide but shallow investments result in poorly constructed capital projects and also deny citizens the improved services that would have resulted from the government's actually completing critical, high-priority capital projects.

When municipalities have infrastructure systems that provide fee-based services (for example, water, sewerage, etc.), some part of the user fees should be dedicated for capital investment, including maintenance and repair (M&R) costs,

restoration, and recapitalization. Establishing the levels of such tariffs or fees is of critical importance (box 5.6 provides an example of the steps involved). It is good practice to base such tariffs on full cost recovery, a rare case in developing countries. It usually would imply that the tariffs would cover M&R costs, operations costs, debt service (that is, payment of loan interest), and depreciation.

Problems common in the CIP process include the following:

- Capital investment plans do not include realistic assumptions about funding and financing, resulting in a series of wish lists.

- Capital investment decisions are made without reference to life cycle costs and management.

- Capital investments require that the local government assume an unrealistic and unsustainable level of debt.

- Local governments plan for or establish public-private partnerships without clear justification and without the capacity to manage them effectively.

- Capital investment priorities are distorted by the availability of funding, or the lack of it, for specific activities. For example, funding or grants may be available to local governments for specific types of investments (such

---

Box 5.6 Main Steps in Setting New Tariffs

1. Calculate the existing cost of service.
2. Develop alternative scenarios.
3. Calculate the cost of each.
4. Calculate tariffs by scenario.
5. Compare tariffs to willingness to pay.
6. Recalculate tariffs.
7. Discuss results with stakeholders.
8. Select the preferred scenario.
9. Build public support.
10. Present to the tariff-setting body and secure a tariff change.

Source: USAID 2006, 46.

---

as roads or health clinics), regardless of locally identified priorities. Funds may be provided by the central government to support line ministry programs or by donor agencies that are committed to supporting specific types of investments.

- The capital investment program may include too many projects (too wide) with too little funding (too shallow). It may overemphasize roads, versus everything else, because roads are politically popular and their planning and financing are the easiest to control.

The process of capital investment planning and budgeting is a dynamic and iterative one that generally involves four stages:

1. Financial planning

2. Project identification and prioritization

3. Program and project management

4. Monitoring and evaluation.

Expenditure Management — Budgetary Controls

To this point, the chapter has defined the concept of expenditure management and reviewed the steps in the expenditure management cycle. The previous two sections discussed reviewing and developing policies and plans for recurrent and capital expenditures. The next element in the expenditure management process concerns the procedures to control actual expenditures to ensure that services are being provided in a cost-effective manner.

As stated earlier, an effective expenditure management system must include three elements:

- Plan for future expenditures, with clear and measurable milestones to monitor actual performance.

- Control expenditures so that actual spending is consistent with the budget and plan.

- Monitor and evaluate expenditures to ensure that they are in fact conforming to agreed-on plans.

Local governments in developing countries face numerous entrenched obstacles in controlling expenditures, some of which are inherent in the budget process:

- A disconnect between the budget and government policies

- Lack of clarity of objectives in budget preparation

- Emphasis on fighting for resources rather than results

- Difficulties in planning in the single-year framework, complicated by the unpredictability of budgetary resources

- Accountability undermined by a lack of clear objectives and anticipated results

- Fragmentation of the budget, with lack of coherence among the parts.

When reviewing ways to improve their budgeting and expenditure controls, it is important to keep in mind that local governments are in the business of delivering services. When budget processes are plagued by challenges such as those listed above, it is difficult for local authorities to prioritize spending strategically because they may be unable to learn what the spending is actually accomplishing.

One very effective means to control expenditures is to ensure that the budget and other critical documents are readily available for all to see. It has been well documented that such increased transparency can increase the efficiency of governments, and it also makes the misuse of public funds less likely. With the increased use of the Internet, local governments are able to provide their stakeholders and potential investors with easy access to relevant information about their finances, the services they are providing, and much more. Two examples of local governments' making effective use of the Internet to make their operations more open and transparent are the websites of the city of Johannesburg, South Africa (http://www.joburg.org.za), and Fairfax County, Virginia, U.S. (http://www.fairfaxcounty.gov).

Budgetary Control Is Essential

After a budget has been approved, it is normal to issue a warrant (or similar document) to those authorized to incur expenditures, specifying the items of expenditure under their control and the approved provision for each. To provide effective control, it must be clear who is responsible for authorizing each expenditure item (accounting officer). The same applies to each revenue item, in that one person needs to be responsible for its collection (also discussed in chapter 3).

The degree of delegation of authority to incur expenditures varies among local government systems and individual authorities. No one system is necessarily better or worse than another, but adequate systems depend on the size of the authority and the ability and capacity of the staff. Generally speaking, it is better to delegate authority to incur expenditures to the operating departments to which the budgets have been provided. Centralized control can lead to operating departments' feeling without power and thus perhaps not as responsible. Regardless of which unit has authorization to incur expenditures, a system of monitoring and oversight is essential. Areas where monitoring and oversight are critical include the hiring of staff and the level of wages paid them (although that is often compromised by the highest council or mayor level) and contracting with private firms for services that should have been done in-house.

Weak control over administrative costs is typical in local governments, particularly in developing countries. It is a critical shortcoming because administrative expenditures, particularly wages, salaries, and benefits, are among the costliest line items. But also, reckless hiring of staff, hiring of close relatives of the top personnel, and paying generous compensation frequently signal weak expenditure management. They make citizens unhappy and reluctant to pay taxes that appear to be mainly used for the benefit of the local administration. Getting away from these kinds of practices requires clear policy and strong political support for expenditure control procedures.

Budget adjustments are inevitable during the year for a number of reasons. An absolute increase in a department's budget (supplementary estimate) would normally require approval by the authority's chief financial officer, and often by the council, since it affects the overall budget. Reallocations within a department's budget (*virements*, or the transfer of items from one financial account to another) are normally within the power of that particular department to authorize.

Control of expenditures requires active management of each item and regular, up-to-date information. That means that transactions must be entered promptly in the authority's accounting system (chapter 3 discusses accounting, as well as the importance of good record-keeping systems). Progress on each item must be monitored continuously, and variations from budgeted amounts identified and understood. Depending on the reasons for the variation, appropriate action must be taken either to correct the problem or, if the current situation is different from what was expected during budget preparation, to adjust the overall and departmental budgets.

Controlling Payments Is Essential

Payment systems should incorporate internal control procedures, such as requiring multiple signatures for payment authorizations and checks, preparation of all checks from the accounting system, and so on. However, care must be taken to not include so many checks and balances that payments are unnecessarily delayed. In some governments, authorization procedures can require as many as 25 steps before a payment can be released.

While the logic behind such complex and time-consuming procedures is to strengthen internal control, in reality the reverse is normally the case.

Payment systems must be related to budgets to ensure that no payment is processed unless a prior commitment was approved and tied to a specific budget line item. Before payments are made, they should be reviewed to ensure that no errors were made and that all necessary approvals and supporting documentation have been received. Payments for goods need to be compared to contractual prices and conditions, and payments for salaries and wages should be verified by the physical presence of the labor force. Cases have been known of municipalities having deceased staff still on their payroll. The picture in figure 5.5 is a nice example of a manual cashbook with fingerprints of illiterate people who received cash support in Pakistan.

Managing Tariffs and Subsidies

Expenditure management officers and units are crucial in managing tariffs, or fee schedules, which require particular attention to controlling and/or reducing associated formal or hidden subsidies. These tasks are important both in planning and in implementing the budget. This section summarizes the critical areas to manage, the basic principles, and common practices. The guide *Managing Municipal Services* summarizes basic principles and practices (USAID 2006). As this publication makes clear, cost analysis is the first step, and among the most important, in tariff setting or approving tariff changes (see also box 5.6).

These issues are particularly important in developing countries, where most tariffs for services are below the level required to recover their cost and thus induce budget expenditures. Another argument to mention is that politicians, especially before elections, are often enthusiastic and very generous in "protecting the customers" by fighting against tariff increases, while also promising to expand basic urban services. These unfunded promises often create headaches for financial departments because it is a hard fact that the budget—and eventually the same citizens—will cover the subsidies. Furthermore, uncontrolled subsidies raise fairness issues because they support all customers, including those who could afford to pay full costs. In some cases they are regressive, conferring greater benefit on the rich because they consume more of the subsidized services (e.g., water, gas, electricity). Finally, subsidies create particular difficulties when the local government gives them to private providers under service contracts. Subsidies can be a rather substantial share of the budget. Box 5.7 shows the case of a Croatian city that spends more than 12 percent of its annual budget on subsidies to the operations of local public utility companies.

Expenditure Control in Tariff Setting

Tariff setting may seem to be the domain of the revenue managers. The fact is that revenue and expenditure managers should work on it hand in hand. Expenditure control is a real challenge because tariffs are generally sluggish and often determined by tradition, constrained by customers' willingness and ability to pay or by tariff agreements. A tariff based on *cost-plus pricing* is

Figure 5.5　Manual Cashbook

Source: Photo Mihaly Kopanyi.

Box 5.7 Supporting Public Utility Companies in a Croatian City

	Euro	%
Public transport	4,640.0	4.1
Waste management	2,077.8	1.8
Maintenance of roads and public spaces	1,087.4	1.6
Producing and distributing heating energy	501.2	0.4
Water supply and wastewater treatment	2,904.0	2.6
Others	2,506.8	1.6
Total	13,717.2	12.1

not advisable without good understanding of the costs, nor is it politically feasible.

There might seem to be a big difference between setting tariffs for and subsidizing services being directly provided by local government–owned entities, on the one hand, and working with private providers, on the other. From the expenditure control perspective, however, the real difference is that private provision requires making the tariffs, costs, and subsidies more explicit. A municipal department can get financial support by simply changing its budget appropriation or can hide a subsidy in various ways. However, when a municipality works with a private company, the private partner wants to ensure that all terms and conditions are in the contract, including the agreed tariff, rules for changing tariffs, subsidies from the municipality, if any, and so forth. In short, most tariff-setting and subsidy issues are very much the same, regardless of who owns the service entity, since eventually the customers and the municipality will pay the costs. Tariff setting in public-private partnerships is discussed in the Public-Private Infrastructure Advisory Facility (PPIAF) guidelines (Shugart and Alexander 2009). Regulated tariff setting in PPP arrangements has been very successful in the Chilean water sector (Chavez 2002).

The finance department plays a critical role in tariff analysis, negotiation, and approval; the department should scrutinize tariff proposals and the underlying expenditures, efficiencies, and subsidies. A very simplified form of a tariff, measured in unit costs, is the following:

Tariff = capital expenditures + operation expenditures + allowed revenue,

or in a more popular form:

Tariff = CAPEX + OPEX + allowed revenue.

What constitutes capital expenditures (CAPEX) is a difficult question. In general, it is the cost of amortization of service-related assets and debt service. However, the finance department should carefully assess what relevant assets should be included in the capital base. Should obsolete assets be included? Is it better to compare the city's utility to a well-organized entity (benchmark company) or to the national average? The utility might own excess capital in the form of vacant land, unused or abandoned assets, or a luxury leisure compound in the mountains. Are all of these included in the asset base for tariff setting, or only the assets directly related to the specific service? The cost of certain capital expenditures should be recovered separately and not included in the overall tariff rate, for example, connections for water supply and sewage services. Because these costs directly benefit a specific user or facility, the cost of that connection should be recovered directly from the beneficiary in the form of a fee and not included in the overall tariff rate, which applies to all the users of the entire system.

Similarly, in the case of operations expenditures, excess labor, inefficient operation (such as huge water losses), oversized marketing, training expenditures, or donations for sports or charities should not be part of the calculation of the fair and true operation expenses of the service-providing entity. The operation of large utilities might be so complex that answering those questions requires an analysis in depth of CAPEX and OPEX, and that might justify hiring an external specialist to support informed decisions about tariff levels.

The basic tariff-setting principles are well recognized and obeyed in developed countries but are often overlooked, compromised, or unknown in developing countries. Good tariffs should pass three tests. They should

- Ensure cost recovery, financial feasibility, and a good price signal for providers;

- Ensure affordability and a good price signal for customers; and

- Avoid cross-subsidies, or preferably, any subsidies at all.

Current practices in transition and developing countries tend not to meet these criteria. One of the reasons why municipalities fail to meet these principles is pressure from the elected officials to provide services to their constituents at rates that are below cost. One of the direct impacts of such political pressure is that municipalities have insufficient revenues to properly operate and maintain their systems, resulting in poor levels of service and premature deterioration of the assets. Interesting examples include the water sectors in India (TERI 2010) and Chile (Chavez 2002) and district heating in Russia (Adrianov et al. 2003). As shown in table 5.6, many water companies in India are heavily subsidized, including two of the three in New Delhi. The companies cover some operation and maintenance costs themselves, but rather than collect tariffs from customers, they receive subsidized payments from the local governments—disconnecting service provision costs from revenues.

The typical challenges in developing countries include the following (see also box 5.8):

- Initial investments or network expansions are often financed by central government grants and not accounted for in tariffs; historical tariff levels often fail to cover the costs of operation and fair maintenance. As a result, services are often intermittent, with low quality and low coverage. The providers have no incentives for either cost savings or service improvement. The situation often is unsatisfactory to both providers and users.

Table 5.6 Managing and Financing the Water Supply in New Delhi

Geographic areas	Water supply functions of service companies		
	Capital works	Operation and maintenance	Revenue function
Municipal Corporation Delhi (MDC)	Yes	Yes	Yes
New Delhi Municipal Corporation (NDMC)	Yes	Bulk supply only	Bulk payment from NDMC
Delhi Cantonment Board	Yes	Bulk supply only	Bulk payment from Cantonment

Source: TERI 2010, 38.

- Price signals are distorted by low tariffs for all customers, which may create perverse incentives to overuse resources, ignore losses, and accept excessive tariffs to cope. For example, the poor may purchase water from tankers, which costs 10 times more than piped water would cost.

- Cross-subsidies are frequent. Commercial and industrial customers often pay excessive tariffs ("because they can afford to pay"). A cross-subsidy also occurs between those who pay fees and charges and those who do not.

The billing and collection systems are often defunct, in part because of a lack of reliable property data. Developing a computerized land and real estate cadastre offers a solution but is both time-consuming and expensive. Cities in developing countries that fail to obtain resources for a cadastre project could benefit from alternative instruments such as street addressing. They may establish a fiscal database by attaching a code to each property for tax and fee collection purposes. The code does not provide full legal reference to the property but is used for revenue collection purposes (discussed in more detail in chapter 4).

Once the provider has a robust set of house and business addresses, preparing bills for services provided becomes much easier. Box 5.9 describes an application of street addressing in waste collection for the city of Conakry, Guinea. Through a World Bank–financed urban project, the city designed a street addressing system to enable it to address poor collection of solid waste.

Low tariffs and lack of cost controls may result in blanket subsidies of various kinds to municipal enterprises, including agreed annual block grants, discretionary grants at the end of the fiscal year (often justified as a need to pay salaries), or payment of their unpaid utility bills. For example, the Water Company of Lahore has paid about half of its electricity bills in recent years; the remainder was paid by the finance department when the electricity company complained. *Blanket balance sheet subsidies* are among the worst in supporting services because they discourage enterprises from improving services and reducing costs. In addition, balance sheet subsidies are often ad hoc and based on political connections rather than measured needs; they work like entitlements when neither the company nor its customers account them as subsidies.

Managing Subsidies

Sustainable services require stable cost recovery, which in turn often results in tariffs' being

Box 5.9 Street Addressing to Support Household Waste Management in Conakry, Guinea

Household waste management in Conakry in the late 1990s was initially the sole responsibility of municipal authorities. Unsanitary conditions in that city led to efforts to clarify and assign the tasks of solid waste collection, transfer, and treatment. The responsibility for waste collection was turned over to small and medium-scale enterprises (SMEs), which could bill the users directly. This system called for a precise delineation of each entity's coverage area and the establishment of waste transfer points.

The task of transferring waste to the existing landfill was handled by the city's Public Solid Waste Transfer Department (SPTD). The Second Urban Project (UDP 2), financed by the

World Bank, had just completed its first street addressing project and published a street map, which at the time was one of the few such documents that were up-to-date. The street map, data dase, and street index developed as part of the street addressing program served as a guide to delineate collection zones for the various SMEs. The installation of street signs simplified this process and made it easier to fix collection zone boundaries and routes and to set up transfer points. The street addressing system thus played a highly positive role in launching an operation that indisputably owed its success to the concentrated efforts of several authorities, operators, and donors focused on a radical transformation of the city's image.

Source: World Bank 2005, 26.

unaffordable for some in the society. Although, as a matter of principle, subsidies should be avoided or reduced to a minimum, fair and broad provision of services often requires some form of subsidy, particularly in developing countries. A simple cost recovery tariff would exclude poor citizens entirely or partially. However, it is equally important to limit the use of subsidies and avoid unnecessary use of public resources. The section below discusses options for accommodating the poor, various forms of subsidies, and finally the allocation and targeting of subsidies.

Targeting the Poor

Various means and instruments are available to support access by the poor to a fair share of public urban services, whether water, electricity, public transport, social housing, district heating, education, or health. Table 5.7 summarizes them and their implications. Expenditure managers need to be aware of these options and their specific

implications to advise the council in reaching informed decisions. The table also shows that well-targeted subsidies can produce substantial savings, along with fairer provision of services to the poor. In Nyiregyhaza city, Hungary, the private providers together with the municipality established a support fund (RÉS, or gap foundation) to subsidize the poorest of the poor, paying two-thirds of a household's bills if the household paid one-third (Tausz 2004).

Forms of Subsidies and Implications

From the expenditure management perspective, it is important to distinguish the forms of subsidies—capital versus operation. It is important for management to understand the differences between the two, what types of subsidies are being provided, and who are the primary beneficiaries.

Operation subsidies support the costs of operation and regular maintenance of the various

Table 5.7 Options for Poor Customers

Targeting option	Description	Application examples
Service-level targeting	Provision of lower quality or reduced scope of services (applicable for segregated zones; self-selection of this service is advisable if possible).	• A public tap instead of house connection to water. • Community containers for waste collection instead of door-to-door collection of waste bins. • Building smaller housing units with simpler amenities. These services might still require a subsidy but much less than the full services.
Income-based subsidies	Household income or proxy indicators, such as salary or electricity consumption, determine subsidy.	• The target group pays a portion of the tariff, and the municipality pays the rest to the provider based on actual fee collection. • Volume-based tariffs: a low tariff for basic volume and a high tariff above basic level. • Electricity consumption is the basis of "communal charges" for solid waste or a basket of basic services. • Elderly people pay half-fare for public transport.
Other measures of poverty	Property value as proxy of poverty—an official poverty list (sensitive politically and socially).	• Property value is the basis of a "communal tax" that covers a basket of basic services. • Households on the poverty list pay a third of their bills.
Geographic targeting	Households in a specific geographic area pay lower tariffs, fees, charges.	• Slums or other areas defined as poor may pay smaller tariffs for selected services.

Sources: Prepared by authors using DANCED 2002; Chavez 2002; and Kopanyi, El Daher, and Wetzel 2004.

services. Operation subsidies appear in various forms, including explicit and implicit; and demand-side and supply-side. It is important to stress that the central and/or the local government will eventually pay for the subsidies, whether the service entity is public or private. Table 5.8 summarizes the various forms and means of providing operation subsidies and sheds some light on their possible impact.

Capital subsidies are common throughout the world but are more prevalent in developing countries. The central or the local government may provide a grant to cover a portion of a service entity's investment, or all of it. The central or local government, or international donors, may provide assets as in-kind donations. These practices have a number of major implications: (a) the cost of the donated capital is often not accounted fairly in the entity's balance sheet; (b) capital subsidies distort tariff setting because capital costs (i.e., amortization) are not built into the tariff; (c) the investments may not be sustainable, so that another grant or subsidy may be required for major refurbishment, replacement, or expansion of an asset in time; (d) the donor of an asset may not provide a subsidy for its operation and maintenance, and the municipality may fail to budget the expense; and (e) old capital subsidies create difficulties in forming public-private partnerships because their value is often unknown.

Finally, and most important, capital subsidies are not targeted. Because they benefit all users,

Table 5.8 Forms and Means of Operation Subsidies

Form of subsidy	Means of subsidies	Effects
Supply-side subsidies		
Explicit	Performance grant to provider.	Guaranteed revenue amount paid based on fulfilled agreed minimum performance (e.g., volume of service).
	Target grant to provider to pass through to target groups.	The municipality pays or subsidizes a portion of the tariff or fee.
Implicit	Annual block grant to provider.	Entitlement; no incentive for improvements.
	Discretionary, ad hoc grant also called balance sheet subsidy.	Filling the income gap, the subsidy bails out the entity, often end of the year.
	Forced subsidy, payment of providers' arrears to suppliers.	The entity elicits the subsidy by failing to pay its bills.
Demand-side subsidies		
Explicit	Cross-subsidy.	Differentiated tariffs for various groups, such as commercial and industrial versus residential; could be adverse.
		Volume-based banded tariffs provide incentives to saving scarce resources (water, electricity); fair; good price signal.
		Tariff based on capacity (diameter of water connection pipe, electricity meter capacity).
		Subsidy forced by nonpayers. When fee collection is poor, those who pay in fact subsidize those who avoid payment. A tariff increase to cover the missing income would further charge those who are already paying.
	Credit to the poor.	Creates incentives with respect to both demand and supply.
Implicit subsidy	Low tariff forced by the council.	Subsidy to the demand-side, but not accounted for as a subsidy; distorts price signals to customers. Undermines financial sustainability and induces supply-side subsidy or deterioration of assets and services.

they waste public resources as those who can afford to pay the full costs enjoy the subsidies. Thus, the finance department should calculate and communicate to stakeholders (such as the council) the true costs of services, including capital expenditures, and may aim for the gradual inclusion of capital expenditures in tariffs, fees, and charges.

As we have said, urban services in developing countries are often operated with low tariffs that cover neither the capital investment nor operation and regular maintenance. The first step toward addressing that situation could be achieving the recovery of operation and maintenance

costs, gradually reducing operation subsidies, which require clear measurement, effective allocation, and targeting (box 5.10 illustrates water subsidies in India).

Subsidy Allocation and Targeting

The overarching objective is to use subsidies fairly to maximize revenues for covering the cost of operating and maintaining services. That can be achieved by the careful allocation and targeting of the subsidies. The following steps and considerations are useful in meeting those objectives:

- Scrutinize the operation and maintenance expenditures of the service provider to ensure

Box 5.10 Water Subsidies in Delhi, India

Huge subsidies are being given to customers through subsidized tariffs. According to the chief minister, who is the chairman of the board of the National Commission of Tariffs (NCT), as much as 60 percent subsidies are being factored in the domestic tariffs in Delhi. These subsidies are meant for the poor, but the poor are hardly connected to the system because connection charges are so high. Thus, the middle-to-high-income customers enjoy the low tariffs. Further, the poor have to incur coping costs to meet their water needs from tankers. Hence benefits are not reaching the target users.

Source: TERI 2010, 35.

that it is allocating the minimum required subsidy.

- Ensure explicit, transparent, measurable, and accounted-for subsidies.

- Identify the target groups, their needs, and their ability and willingness to pay.

- Select the appropriate subsidy options.

- Select the appropriate method of transfers attached to performance.

- Set rules for subsidy implementation and enter into a contract with the provider, if possible.

- Monitor, enforce rules, and evaluate the implementation and impact of the subsidies.

- Estimate, decide or plan, and budget the volume of subsidies the government is able and willing to cover (an average per customer, per service, or per provider).

- Communicate the use of subsidies to key stakeholders.

Table 5.9 illustrates the various tariff options. It is based on a real water supply project in a small town in Nepal. The project is running a huge deficit of NPR 450,000, or 33 percent. A willingness-to-pay survey indicates that most households could easily pay higher tariffs and still pay less than 5 percent of household income. The table summarizes the situations of three groups of customers grouped by household (HH) income, with 5 percent of income serving as a proxy for ability to pay for water. The detailed tariff analysis was carried out because the town initially agreed on a flat rate of NPR 100 "because the people can pay only that." However, the town soon discovered that the combined costs of operation, maintenance, and debt service $(O + M + DS)$ were well above the total revenues that such a flat rate would produce.

The analysis suggests that local policy makers have a number of options. A flat rate of NPR 300 would result in financial feasibility but would create an unbearable burden for poor households. The target service would drop the subsidy if in-house connections paid NPR 300 per month and poor families paid NPR 60 per month for community taps installed for five-family groups. This variation seems attractive but not feasible because connections to the houses have already been installed. Better-off families could afford to pay NPR 360 per month, which would allow household connections for the poor families for NPR 60 per month. Poor families would then receive a large cross-subsidy paid for by the better-off families. Many more options could be considered. The last two lines of table 5.9 compare two possible options, including one with differentiated

Table 5.9   Tariff Options for a Small Water Supply Project in Nepal

	Household income over NPR 10,000	Household income NPR 3,000 to 10,000	Household income below NPR 3,000	Total number of connections	Total revenue NPR per month	Total cost (O + M + DS) NPR per month	Subsidy per month (NPR)
Number of households	900	2,700	900	4,500		1,350,000	
5 percent of HH income (NPR)	750	375	100				
Current situation: flat tariff NPR 100	100	100	100	4,500	450,000	1,350,000	900,000
Option 1	300	300	60	3,780	1,134,000	1,350,000	216,000
Option 2	360	360	60	3,780	1,350,000	1,350,000	0.0
Option 3	300	300	300	4,500	1,350,000	1,350,000	0.0

Note: O + M + DS = operations, plus maintenance, plus debt service; HH = household.
Option 1: In-house connection for rich and medium-income families for Rs 300 per month and community taps each for five poor families for Rs 60 per month per family fee.
Option 2: Target service Rs 360 per HH in house and Rs 60 per HH for community taps.
Option 3: Household connections for all and flat rate Rs 300 for each HH regardless of income level.

services and differentiated tariffs, each affordable for the particular household groups.

What lessons can one take away on tariff setting and subsidies? There are many, but let us summarize a few of the main ones: (a) finance departments have a critical part in analyzing, monitoring, and controlling expenditures incurred under the various tariffs and associated subsidies for basic urban services; (b) expenditure control requires solid information and deep understanding of the underlying costs to estimate realistic and justified subsidies; (c) subsidies should be targeted, explicit, and well accounted; and (d) the total volume of annual subsidies should be estimated and communicated to key stakeholders, including decision makers such as the council, line departments, and the budget committee, as well as the citizens at large and the customers of the specific services.

Principles of Procurement and Expenditure Tracking

Procurement takes many forms and encompasses the acquisition of goods (bulk products such as energy and fuel), real property, capital equipment (trucks), built assets (hospitals, schools, roads), and services (including office accommodation, cleaning, and security, and even banking services). Procurement is at the heart of delivering public services. It involves large amounts of public money, and it is the largest single source of allegations of corruption and government inefficiency. Because procurement is central to so much of what local governments do, effective procurement is critical for expenditure management.

Generally, all well-designed procurement systems require high levels of transparency, fair and open competition, and selection of the best-qualified supplier. The implementation of those systems is often difficult and time-consuming. As a result, many local governments tend to ignore procurement rules and instruments. They purchase goods and services arbitrarily and pay more than they should for inferior goods and services.

Because of the importance of procurement, its close supervision is essential. Most procurement systems, if implemented as designed, will deliver similar results. Frequently, however, as we have said, the systems are not implemented for the following reasons:

- Lack of well-qualified procurement specialists

- Lack of policy and practice in saving money through good, competitive procurement

- A culture of limited transparency

- Poor definition of specifications

- Pressure on key officials from special interests.

The Procurement Cycle

Although the steps in procuring an item will vary somewhat based on the cost of the item being procured (less expensive items usually use less complicated procedures), in general the steps in the procurement cycle are the same (figure 5.6 depicts the competitive bidding process):

- Define the requirements.

- Understand the allocation and sharing of risk (especially for activities involving public-private partnerships).

Figure 5.6 Competitive Tendering Process

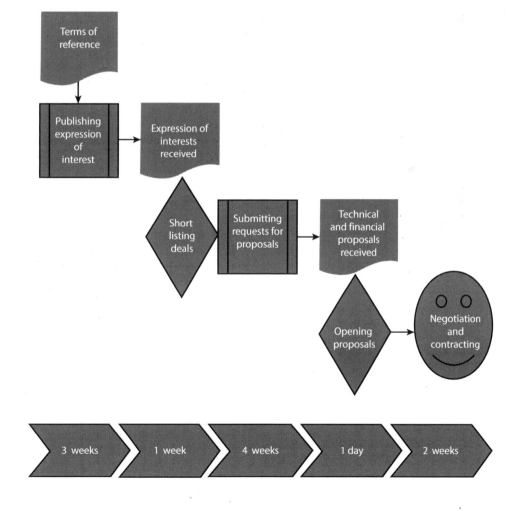

- Prepare terms of reference (ToRs) and detailed specifications, whether for goods or civil works, so that it is clear what is expected to be provided and by what date.

- Advertise the proposed procurement to attract the widest possible interest.

- Request that companies submit expressions of interest (EOIs) based on a brief description of the activity to be procured.

- Evaluate the submissions and select a small number of firms, contractors, or suppliers to participate in the final competition.

- Send the TORs or detailed specifications and the applicable commercial terms in a letter of invitation to the short-listed firms or the pre-qualified contractors. requesting submission of technical and financial proposals no later than a clearly specified date.

- Evaluate the proposals and select the *lowest evaluated bidder,* that is, the best price for the specifications required; invite that firm for contract negotiations.

- Negotiate and sign the contract.

- Begin work.

Procurement Plans

To ensure that only approved items are procured, it is essential to have well-developed and transparent procurement plans that specify the goods, services, and civil works that the government has decided to procure (table 5.10 is a snapshot from a city's procurement plan). The plan should indicate the expected time to complete each phase of the procurement process; it should estimate when implementation is to start and when it is to be completed.

Such a plan will enable management to monitor the process for delays and inefficiencies and track the expenditures. It will indicate to all stakeholders what is being planned; any changes to the plan must be explained and supported by a sound project rationale. To ensure that the plan reflects the most current thinking, it should be updated regularly, perhaps annually, and made available to all stakeholders.

Competitive Procurement

Local governments often lose money because of inadequate procurement. The fact that fair and transparent competition is the foundation of procurement sounds simple and obvious, but it is often ignored. The major reason is that it can take up to six months, or more than one year for large infrastructure projects. Municipal officers might feel that it is a waste of time if they fail to understand the enormous losses that they risk in a rush for sole-source procurement. Competitive procurement may also be avoided if the project has not been properly planned and approved by the council. Sometimes the procurement must be completed quickly so that funds can be spent before the end of the fiscal year. Other reasons are vested interests by some officers, council members, and politicians, or simply corruption. Figure 5.6 depicts the competitive tendering process for a medium-size project.

Competitive procurement has various forms and options; what is adequate depends largely on the size and nature of the procured good or service. Very large projects may require international tendering, if sufficient capacities are not available at the national level, as is often the case in small or medium-size developing countries. Medium-size projects might be better tendered nationally. In the modern world, competitive tenders are not limited to goods but extend to services, including security, office space, event management, and banking, which is especially important. Municipalities can gain financially by selecting partner banks competitively. Finally, simple shopping or single-source selection is still adequate for procuring a small quantity of goods or hiring specialists (table 5.10 shows various procurement forms in the local procurement plan).

Table 5.10 Project Procurement Plan

Ref. no.	Contract description	Est. cost ($ millions)	Procurement method	Pre-qualification	Domestic preference	Prior review	Expected bid opening	Comments
Works								
CW-1	Drainage system	6.770	International competition	No	Yes	Yes	April 16, 2012	
CW-2	Traffic management	8.94	International competition	No	Yes	Yes	May 25, 2012	
Goods								
EQ-1	Computers	0.45	International competition	No	No	Yes	January 16, 2012	
EQ-2	Stationery	0.05	Shopping	No	No	No	June 5, 2012	
EQ-3	Advertising	0.045	Direct	No	No	No	July 5, 2012	
Consultancies								
TA-1	Management information system	0.750	International competition	N/A	N/A	Yes	August 7, 2012	

Critical Steps in the Procurement Process

Many local governments follow the procurement process depicted in figure 5.6, some only because it is required by a donor. Most local governments in the developing world, however, are inexperienced in critical elements of the procurement process; as a result, they often feel the burdens but miss the benefits of good procurement. Box 5.11 summarizes a procurement reform in Uzbekistan.

The most critical steps, which make a procurement effective or failed, are the following:

- *Terms of Reference* (ToR). It is necessary to spend sufficient time, and perhaps money, to prepare an adequate ToR document. The ToR should be very specific in defining objectives, scope of works, and tasks to be completed; include very specific, measurable, time-bound outputs; and provide a payment schedule corresponding to the tasks. A brief and vague ToR will neither guide the contracting partner nor encourage a clear and strong commitment. Moreover, it will not provide solid ground for the local government to enforce the agreed actions and demand value for money.

- *Selection of the short-listed companies and the final bidder.* Many local governments appear weak in setting up selection committees with competent and committed members. They often take the selection as a formality rather than a critical step, fail to find the best candidate, and then obtain substandard results (such as poor products, delays, or weak

---

Box 5.11 Introducing Competitively Tendered Franchises in Uzbekistan

Urban public transport services were traditionally supplied in Uzbekistan by state-owned enterprises that enjoyed areawide or citywide monopolies. Beginning in late 1997, however, as part of the transformation of this former socialist economy into one that functions on market principles, the Uzbek government implemented radical changes in the organization and regulation of urban public bus transport services.

Through a gradual and carefully planned process, which included experiments in a few cities, a study tour to London, and progressive scaling-up to all secondary cities, responsibility was given to the city administrations to organize all bus services on the basis of exclusive route franchises. These franchises were allocated through a competitive tendering process that was open to private companies and associations of small owner-operators, as well as state-owned enterprises. Tendering was the responsibility of a special commission in each city, chaired by a deputy mayor and operating under precise rules set by a transport regulatory agency in the central government. The main selection criteria included bidders' discounts, if any, from the passenger fare ceiling, proposed service frequency, and bus fleet characteristics. Franchise duration, initially set at six months and renewable once for another six months, is progressively being extended (it now lasts for one year).

These reforms, completed in two years, have resulted in impressive changes. Numerous private operators have entered the public transport market, many new jobs have been created in the emerging bus service sector, and a healthy competition has developed, particularly for the rapidly growing minibus services. Private operators now supply more than 50 percent of all urban transport services. A bus route franchising system is now also being implemented in Tashkent.

Source: World Bank 2002, 10.

---

consultant reports). They may fill selection committees with personnel ex officio, who lack expertise and sometimes have a vested interest in supporting one specific candidate.

- *Contracting.* Even the best ToR and selection would fail if the contract signed is weak and does not protect the local government's interests. Sometimes the selected partner provides what is alleged to be a standard contract and insists that it is the best, used by many municipalities, and has no room for improvement or change. Accepting such a contract is a dangerous practice. Often just the opposite is true: the "standard contract" is neither standard nor best. In short, a municipality must prepare its own contract (hiring a good lawyer, if needed), must ensure the best conditions, protect its own interest, and negotiate hard.

Procurement Principles

Sound principles of public sector procurement will contribute to strengthening local governments' administration by controlling expenditures and improving the delivery of public services. Some basic principles of public sector procurement include the following:

- *Lowest evaluated bidder.* Procuring entities are under pressure to select the bidder offering the lowest cost. But most procurement systems specify selecting the contractor offering the best price for the specifications required— or the *lowest evaluated bidder*. Governments need to be wary about selecting a contractor offering an unrealistically low price: experience suggests that such a contractor will attempt to increase the bid price through a series of change orders or will provide goods or services below specified quality.

- *Value for money.* Value for money is a measure of the efficiency with which the financial resources of the government are used. Value for money is represented by a number of factors, not only price; for example:

  — The suitability of the goods, equipment, or services purchased

  — The useful life and durability of the goods or equipment

  — Operation, maintenance, and servicing costs

  — The administrative costs of the selected purchasing method

  — The delivery period

  — Future transportation costs

  — Storage costs

  — The time it takes to procure the goods.

- *Transparency.* The people have a right to assurance that correct procedures have been applied, and the primary tool to deliver that assurance is transparency. Not only does transparency in procurement assure the public that the correct procedures are being employed, but it also encourages suppliers to compete for the contracts that the government and its agencies award. Transparency in procurement procedures also helps to reduce the risk of fraud and corrupt practices.

- *Accountability.* Accountability is a keystone of any procurement system. It is used to ensure that officials undertaking tasks carry out their responsibilities with the due diligence that is owed to both the government and the people.

- *Equity.* All eligible suppliers should receive notice of all procurement opportunities. The principle behind this is to ensure that all national and international bidders, suppliers, contractors, and consultants have a fair basis on which to compete for contracts funded by the government. It eventually helps save money too.

- *Effectiveness.* The ultimate role of a specific procurement exercise should always be remembered: Procurement is only a means to achieve a specific objective. Any procurement that fails to facilitate the objective of the procurement is ineffective.

- *Efficiency.* Government should never overlook the need for speed and efficiency in the procurement process. The more that nonessential administration encumbers the procurement process, the more funds are diverted from meeting the government's primary objective. The longer the procurement process takes, the higher the real cost to the government.

- *Ethical standards.* Everyone involved in procurement activities must comply with the government's code of ethics. Although the particular provisions of the code will vary, they should include a stipulation that no individual shall use his authority or office for personal gain. That includes accepting or requesting anything of material value from bidders, prospective bidders, or suppliers, for the individual, his or her spouse, parents, children, other close relatives, or any other persons through whom the individual might gain direct or indirect benefit from the gift. The code should also address issues such as conflicts of interest, disclosure of personal relationships, and confidentiality and accuracy of information.

E-procurement

"E-procurement" is a nickname for electronically managed procurement processes, in which all phases of a procurement are completed on the Internet or by electronic means. The municipality announces the project by calling for expressions of interest, then issues a request for proposals through the Internet. Likewise, the bidders are supposed to submit their bids electronically and receive confirmation and results digitally. More and more governments are experimenting with e-governance systems in efforts to reduce corruption in government procurement. In the case of Thailand, progress toward such a system has been limited because Internet access is limited in

much of the country and is comparatively expensive. However, e-auctions and e-procurement for public projects have recently begun to emerge.

Other e-governance initiatives include some in the realm of commerce. To reduce person-to-person interactions between businesses and government officials, it is becoming increasingly common for countries to offer business license applications and submissions online. In the developing world, where governance processes are many times dysfunctional, many countries are simply digitizing dysfunctionality.

Contract Management

Too often, the management of contracts made with customers, vendors, partners, or employees is delegated to engineering or procurement units, with little or no involvement by the financial and legal staff. This is a critical error. Contract management includes three critical areas: (a) contract structuring, negotiation, and signing; (b) contract monitoring during implementation; and (c) releasing payments (or collecting dues). Local governments in developing countries often fall short in all three areas. Box 5.12 presents points to remember for successful contract management and some reasons why some entities fail to manage contracts successfully.

Contracting. The contract is critical in procurement. Contracts are vital in ensuring compliance with terms and conditions, as well as documenting and agreeing on any changes that may arise during project implementation. Many local governments often go into contracts with a limited understanding of the financial and legal implications. Doing that is particularly dangerous in public-private partnerships, many of which have failed because of disproportionate allocation of risks, responsibilities, and financing between the private and public partners. A famous case was the Dar es Salaam water public-private partnership, which failed in three years. Eventually, the private partner walked away, leaving the

Box 5.12 Key Elements for Successful Contract Management

- A documented plan for managing the contract to ensure a focus across the organization on delivering value for money
- Key performance indicators to measure and drive the performance of suppliers
- Detailed agreement on the required outputs and the expected performance and quality of service to be delivered
- Monitoring whether the service is being delivered according to specifications and to make sure that the costs of the service are no higher than expected
- Continual assessment and management of risks to service delivery and ensuring that business continuity plans are in place, so that critical services continue to be delivered through a range of contingencies
- Regular testing and price benchmarking to ensure achievement of value for money
- Clear legal procedures to implement financial penalties in the event of poor supplier performance
- Administration and change management activities focusing on cost monitoring and forecasting, ordering, payment and budget monitoring procedures, resource management, forward planning, management reporting systems, and asset management

Why Do Organizations Fail to Manage Contracts Successfully?

- Poorly drafted contracts
- Inadequate resources assigned or available to the contract management team
- The government or customer team does not match the supplier's team in skills or experience, or both
- Appointment of the wrong people, leading to personality clashes
- Poor understanding of the context, complexities, and dependencies of the contract
- Failure to check supplier assumptions presented in their proposal
- Lack of clarity in the authorities and responsibilities related to commercial decisions
- Lack of performance measurement or benchmarking by the customer
- Failure to monitor and manage retained risks (statutory, political, and commercial)

Source: Authors, based on World Bank 2005.

---

city with huge costs and a water supply system without an operator.

Contract monitoring. Contract monitoring is particularly important in implementing large infrastructure projects. It includes monitoring expenses and the stages of physical completion to ensure that the two are moving at the same relative pace. Municipalities with limited capacity often contract out construction monitoring, in which case the one doing the monitoring must be monitored too. In critical phases, progress reports must be scrutinized thoroughly and progress verified on-site by a municipal engineer to ensure that payments are released based on verified progress and the completion of work invoiced. Not only do developing countries fall short of good municipal capacities, but the capacities of construction companies and construction monitoring firms are weak too. An infrastructure investment capacity assessment in Pakistan found that the shortage of construction capacities (engineers, skilled workers, machinery) was a greater impediment to infrastructure development than lack of funds (World Bank 2007).

Cost control and release of payments. From the expenditure management perspective, the most critical area of contract management is controlling contract implementation and releasing payments on a timely basis consistent with the contract. More important, payments should be based on verified progress. The World Bank has introduced technical audits to complement financial audits to monitor where and how money is used in Bank-funded infrastructure projects.

Variation orders. Some contractors may offer a low initial price for services, goods, or work (perhaps by a narrow margin) and later propose changes or variation orders because of unforeseen expenses. Some expenses might be truly unforeseen, such as a drastic change in fuel prices or special situations underground that cannot be detected during planning. But too often, change orders are a means for the contractor to increase the price of the contract (and the profits) to compensate for an unrealistic initial proposal.

Change or variation orders are also a common form of corruption. Thus, requests for technical variations are not matters only of engineering but need close scrutiny by the financial staff, who have the power to reject invoices and delay or deny payments if unjustified expenses or fraud is suspected. Change orders are usually associated with the physical work, but financial management also needs to be involved to determine the impact of cost increases on the budget and financing. Finally, if change orders are due to slow payments, that is an administrative issue that needs to be examined with an eye to efficiency, as well as for any indication of kickbacks.

Expenditure Management Systems

Local government entities manage expenditures through various systems and instruments, including those for accounting, internal control, cash management, procurement, and contract management. These systems play multiple roles in the life of local governments. This section focuses on their role in expenditure management.

Accounting Systems

Budgets are not the product of accounting systems. After the budget has been approved, the accounting system will record and report on the actual results, so that comparisons to the budgeted amounts can be presented and the activities of the authority controlled (discussed in chapter 3). Accounting systems must be designed to provide management with timely information that can be used to control the activities agreed to in the budget and which are within the capacity of the institution and its staff to operate.

Figure 5.7 shows a copy of a daily report from the automated financial management information system (FMIS) of Chiniot City, Pakistan. The mayor and the chief financial officer receive a snapshot every morning; they can also access the reporting system remotely (from home or while traveling) through the Internet.

Internal Control Environment

Among the most important reasons to have a strong internal control environment is to reduce exposure to corruption risks. Corruption is technically defined as the abuse of entrusted power for personal gain. Notice that this definition is not limited to the abuse of public office: corruption can occur in transactions between private parties as well.

A problem encountered by nearly all anticorruption efforts is that corruption is very difficult to measure accurately and comprehensively. That makes it difficult to track progress toward combating it. So the goal of anticorruption efforts should be to reduce the prevalence of corruption by making it more difficult and costly to engage in such practices. To do that, one must recognize that corruption is not a transactional problem but rather an institutional problem. In places where corruption is rampant, selectively punishing

Figure 5.7   Daily Financial Snapshot: Financial Management Information System of Chiniot City, Pakistan

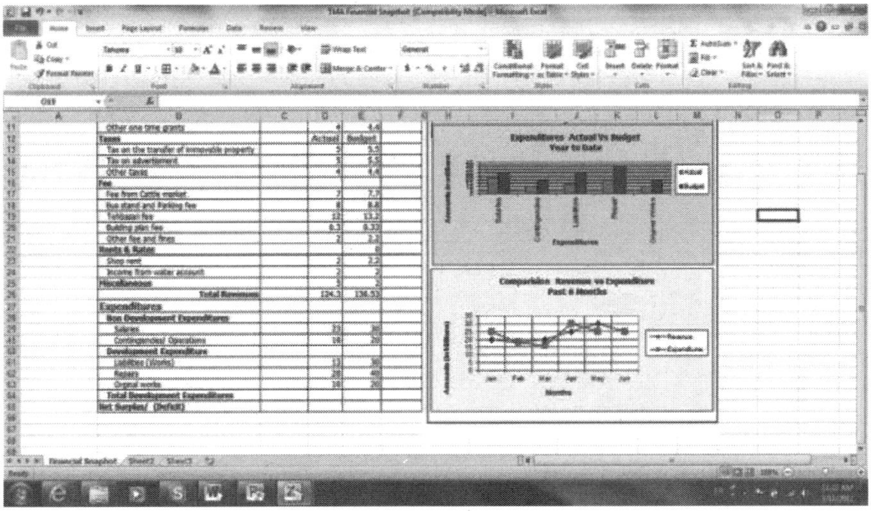

Source: World Bank 2008.

people for individual acts will not change the underlying environment that makes corruption prevalent in the first place.

But whereas corruption is intrinsically difficult to fix, local governments can reduce their exposure to corruption risks and make it more difficult for such transactions to take place. An effective expenditure management system, with robust internal controls and monitoring and evaluation systems, is critical in a local government (see box 5.13). Moreover, management must constantly be aware of "red flags" indicating that weaknesses in the internal control environment have resulted in increased vulnerability to corruption. Actions that management can implement include the following:

- Analysis of variances between planned and actual financial and operational performance

- Trend analysis and comparative trend analysis of the movement and variation of transactions between cities or sections of the same city that cannot be explained

- Increasing transparency of all financial and operational information

- Use of hotlines for the public to report service delivery or other concerns

- Increased use of technology to increase automated transactions.

The situation described in box 5.13 illustrates the dynamic nature of corruption and the importance of vigilance by all government officials for signs of weakness in the control environment, which if not addressed could lead to corrupt behavior.

Cash Management

The cash management function is generally found in the finance or treasury office under the management of the finance director.[1] The objectives of cash management are to bring funds into the local government's finance office or treasury as quickly as possible, pay the funds out as efficiently as possible, and

Box 5.13 Bypassing an Integrated Financial Management Information System to Embezzle Public Funds

The government of an African country that we have worked with implemented an integrated financial management information system (IFMIS) for the central government and the major local governments. Among the local governments to implement the new system was the capital city. The early evaluations of the implementation were positive. A feature of the system strongly supported by the city treasurer was that no disbursements could be made unless the item had been budgeted for and all required documentation had been received and approved by the responsible official. As the system had been designed by a major international software company and the evaluations from the first round of implementations had been positive, confidence was high that the internal control environment in the capital city had been improved. However, it was later learned that the city treasurer had never destroyed the manual checks that were used extensively with the previous accounting system. In addition, the Office of the Auditor General had not required that its representative permanently working in the capital city offices rotate after the specified number of years, in contravention of its normal procedures.

After several years it was discovered that the city treasurer was, on a regular basis, writing manual checks on the pension fund account to a fictitious company. In collaboration with the town clerk, checks were deposited with a colleague working for a commercial bank, in an account controlled by the town clerk. Because the auditor who had not been required to rotate from his position was also involved with this scam, these people were able to steal a substantial amount of money from the city before they were eventually caught and sentenced to jail.

make effective use of the funds until they are needed for operating expenses. This office may have one employee responsible for the entire function. Depending on the size of the local government, the functions may be organized so that one employee is assigned to collections and bank deposits, other staff process disbursements, and still others are concerned with short-term investments.

Whether the system is centralized—which means that one department is responsible for all collections—or decentralized, prudent internal control suggests that the finance official responsible should limit the number of offices that collect revenue and should implement procedures to protect the government's funds and enforce efficient cash management practices. Box 5.14 lists some of the benefits of efficient local government cash management.

Local governments collect money owed in a variety of forms and from a large number of locations. It is one of their main functions. Revenues come from fines, fees, taxes, licenses, permits, and special assessments. It is important that internal control procedures be developed and regularly updated to ensure that all funds owed are properly collected and reported. All receipts (revenues) should be received in a timely manner, credited to the proper accounts, and deposited in the correct bank account as quickly as possible. As discussed in chapter 3, modern, computerized accounting systems and integrated financial management information systems can greatly facilitate bank reconciliations.

Box 5.14 The Benefits of Efficient Cash Management

- Efficient cash handling and control systems increase certainty that payments are made properly by the due date and that receipts are passed without delay to the responsible bodies. They also reduce operational risk and the scope for mismanagement or fraud.
- By minimizing the volumes of idle cash held by government bodies, most of which is unlikely to be fully remunerated, and reducing the payment authorities (and checks) in transit or awaiting clearance, the government gains direct savings in the form of borrowing that is no longer needed.
- The linkage of government accounts (so that balances are netted through a single account at a bank) not only reduces gross balances, but improves visibility of flows—opening up opportunities for active management—and reduces risk, whether through exposure to the banking system or to financial market movements.

- A wide range of financing instruments—Treasury bills and other short-term borrowing and lending—gives a government greater flexibility in how best to manage its financing needs; it is able to avoid the risk of high borrowing costs associated with less flexible arrangements.
- Active cash management policies, by offsetting flows in and out of the ministry of finance account at the central bank, remove one of the major influences on short-term changes in money market liquidity. This in turn reduces one of the elements of uncertainty in the central bank's liquidity forecast and therefore makes monetary policy interventions less problematic. More generally, it can reduce the volatility of short-term interest rates and uncertainty in money markets.
- Efficient cash management contributes to the development of an efficient short-term securities market, as well as being facilitated by it.

Source: World Bank 1998.

As stated earlier, expenditure management systems are intended to increase the efficiency of local governments and reduce the overall cost of providing services. Collecting revenue is one of the major areas where efficient systems can have a big impact on the cost of doing business. If collection rates are allowed to decline, the result is a "tax on the local government." The uncollected portion of rightfully owed revenues will reduce the amount of funds available for providing services. An example of a cash forecast is presented in table 5.11; the cash balances can be reconciled with the bank deposit balances of the municipality.

Cash flow fluctuation. Accurately predicting the peaks and valleys of cash flows is one of the most difficult aspects of cash management. A cash flow forecast is a schedule of expected receipts and disbursements for a given period. The types of forecasts prepared and their frequency will depend on several factors. Governments with predictable cash flows and sufficient cash reserves can usually get by with an annual forecast. An annual forecast provides an overview of the expected cash position by month. Most governments prepare an annual forecast and use it to make longer-term investment decisions.

Table 5.11 **Simple Annual Cash Forecast (thousands of dollars)**

Cash category	Opening balance	Jan.	Feb.	Mar.	Apr.	May	....	Dec.	Total
	1,000								1,000
Property tax		250	250	300				100	900
Land tax		50	25						75
Other revenue			10		15	10		100	135
Payroll expense		−25	−25	−25	−25	−25		−25	−150
Other current expenditures		−10	−10	−10	−10	−10		−10	−60
Capital expenditure				−150	−100	−575			−825
									0
Net change		265	250	115	−120	−600		165	75
End balance		1,265	1,515	1,630	1,510	910	.	1,075	1,150

Local governments with volatile cash positions, erratic cash flows, or changing demographics may need more frequent and detailed forecasts. A *monthly cash forecast* estimates weekly cash positions and helps monitor the accuracy of the annual forecast. It is more operational than an annual forecast. This type of forecast is common because most local governments experience fluctuating cash flows and liquidity problems. A *weekly forecast* estimates daily cash positions and can help in monitoring the accuracy of the monthly forecast. It can be useful for governments that need to monitor their cash positions closely. As presented in chapter 3, modern computerized accounting systems and integrated financial management information systems can greatly facilitate the preparation and monitoring of cash forecasts.

Measuring and Improving Expenditure Management Performance

One problem for local government officials is the lack of opportunities to learn from the experiences of other governments. That problem is being addressed through Public Expenditure and Financial Accountability Assessment (PEFA), a program that provides a diagnostic tool to measure the quality of administrative systems in public finances and compare them at an international level.

Public Expenditure and Financial Accountability Assessments

Public Expenditure and Financial Accountability assessments aim to support reforms in expenditure management, as well as other aspects of public financial management. The results of each assessment are reported in concrete and standard terms. PEFA lays down three main requirements for sound financial management:

- *Discipline:* Public finances must be dealt with in a disciplined manner.

- *Strategy:* Resources must be allocated in accordance with strategic objectives.

- *Efficiency:* Tasks must be performed efficiently.

In an attempt to reduce the overlap that existed in measuring countries' financial management performance, the Public Financial Management Performance Measurement Framework was developed through extensive consultations between donors and governments. It was designed to be an integrated framework to measure and monitor countries' public financial management systems, processes, and institutions over time. It has recently been adapted and used in a small sample of municipalities. The individual items in the framework are scored on a basis of A (good) to D (not so good), and aggregate scores are developed from the scores on the subitems. Since its creation, a large number of assessments have been conducted, and many more are in various stages of preparation and planning (see http://www.worldbank.org/WBSITE /EXTERNAL/PEFA).

The municipal assessments prepared by PEFA include ones for the canton of Lucerne and the city government of Addis Ababa. The reports contain rich reviews and discussion of expenditure management by the two local governments and also findings developed by the assessors using the PEFA methodology that has been developed for municipalities. The assessments are useful for finance officers in other local governments both to learn more about the methodology at the local government level and also to learn how other governments are addressing, or not, issues that are generally common to all local governments. The scores achieved by the city of Addis Ababa

for one of the indicators in the PEFA municipal assessment[2] are shown in table 5.12.

Municipal Audits (Municipal Financial Self-Assessment and Urban Audits) and Municipal Contracts

Municipal audits are another monitoring tool for enhancing transparency, accountability, and performance in local finances. The World Bank has introduced municipal audits in a number of Bank projects and the MFSA template and methodology are increasingly being used by local governments in various regions of the world. The Municipal Finances Self-Assessment (MFSA), which uses some PEFA indicators, goes into municipal finances in greater details, including (a) assessment of the financial situation of a municipality; (b) review of revenues and expenditures on an annual basis; and (c) identification of specific, monitorable measures for improvement (details are discussed in chapter 8). Municipal audits can be completed as self-assessments or using third-party experts.

Along with the MFSA or independently of it, the Urban Audit (methodology developed by the World bank and customized to local contexts by

Table 5.12 Cash Flow Assessment from Addis Ababa Public Expenditure and Financial Accountability (PEFA) Assessment

Indicator	Score	Explanation
Predictability of availability of funds for commitment of expenditure.	C+	Single dimensional scoring method
1. Degree to which cash flow forecasting and monitoring are carried out.	B	A cash flow forecast is prepared for the fiscal year and updated quarterly.
2. Reliability and time horizon of the periodic information during the year providing the ministries, departments, or agencies (MDAs) with information about maximum limits and payment commitments.	B	Entities of the city government of Addis Ababa are provided with a reliable indication of actual resource availability for expenditure commitment a quarter in advance.
3. Frequency and transparency of the adjustments made to the budgetary allocations available at a level higher than MDA administrations.	C	Budget adjustments of various amounts are frequent during the fiscal year (for last two fiscal years), and they are made transparently.

Source: Authors, based on World Bank 2005.

Box 5.15 Summary of Results of Municipal Contracts in Senegal and Mali

A World Bank-financed project in Senegal (The Urban Development and Decentralization Program UDDP/Programme d' Appui aux Communes - PAC) has reached a large number of municipalities (and citizens) through the signing of municipal contracts and has succeeded in funding and supporting a large number of urban development projects. More important, the project has contributed positively to long-term capacity building and institutional reform in local governments in urban finance and organizational management. Financial capacities of the municipalities have increased considerably, and positive results were achieved in broadening the tax base and increasing local tax collection.

The project changed the behavior of many municipalities in these areas, with a positive impact on the sustainability of the results. Ownership by the Senegalese central government and the municipalities was strong,

illustrated by the fact that nearly 25 percent of project costs came through cofunding. Municipal contracts have served as a platform for donor harmonization in the country and for channeling bilateral and multilateral interventions. Greatly contributing to the positive results has been the fact that the project was implemented in a time when the political environment was supportive of decentralization. New legislation on decentralization had recently been introduced, and municipalities were willing to cooperate.

In comparison, the municipal contract approach was less successful in Mali. Despite the satisfactory implementation of the physical component of the project, in provision of urban services and investments in infrastructure, the institutional reform and capacity-building component did not achieve the expected results in large part due to lack of supervision and monitoring.

Source: VNG International 2010, 42.

local users themselves) can be a powerful investment programming tool. It aims to help local governments (1) assess their level of services and infrastructure, (2) locate and quantify the gaps and (3) prioritize and select municipal investments programs. Both audits/self-assessments contribute to enhance transparency, participation and accountability in the decision-making process over what and how priorities should be financed, shedding light on the use of public funds in the municipal space.

Municipal audits can form the basis of *municipal contracts*. Municipalities may sign contracts with their central governments containing performance indicators defined by the municipal audits and supported by performance grants. Box 5.15 presents a summary of municipal contracts in Senegal and Mali. The audits enable

cities to improve their expenditure management through a municipal contract that manages and regulates relations between the state and the local government. A municipal contract has as its foundation a comprehensive analysis of the municipality's characteristics, its urban features. and its organizational and financial capacities (MFSA + Urban Audit). The analysis enables management to establish priorities for investments, programming, and the funding needed to support the operation of municipal services and any needed adjustments to the municipal staffing and organizational structure.

Managing Capital Expenditures

Managing capital expenditures is somewhat different from managing current expenditures.

All the rules discussed in the context of current expenditures are valid in managing capital expenditures, plus two more: *evaluation of capital investment projects* and *procurement and contract management*. Because of the bulky nature of capital projects, procurement of development and construction services and contract management are vital in managing capital expenditures. The opposite is also true—procurement and contract management is important in managing some current expenditures, such as purchasing fuel, energy, water, or office stationery in bulk.

Managing capital expenditures is again an area in which local governments in developing countries are lagging and thus often experience substantial losses. For example, at the advent of computerization (and perhaps also today) it was common for each school in a city to receive a small budget, go to the next-door shop, or maybe a friend's shop, and buy information technology equipment. Some clever cities moved in a different direction: they combined all the computer needs for schools, offices, and other entities and issued a tender to buy, say, 200 computers and 50 other pieces of equipment (printers, servers, etc.). With competitive tendering, they may have saved 30 percent or more of the costs, or they could have bought 30 percent more equipment from the same budget. The same thing could happen if a water main needed to be replaced and the next-door entrepreneur is selected, behind closed doors, for the construction work.

Evaluation of Capital Investment Projects

Procurement of capital investment projects is intertwined with the evaluation of the projects, before and often during the tendering process, as the companies bidding are often requested to add their knowledge and assist in selecting the final form of the project. These decisions require comparing project alternatives in both technical and financial terms. The process is iterative; it may start with drafting two to three main technical options and discussing them with stakeholders, but financial feasibility and expenditure control must be the driving forces. Often, after financial feasibility is scrutinized, the engineers need to go back to work out details of the preferred modality.

Capital projects can be evaluated using a variety of methods—and in fact should be done that way—with varying levels of sophistication. We introduce the three most common methodologies. They are *net present value, internal rate of return,* and *cost-benefit analysis* (each relies on discounting the cost of the benefits of proposed investments to present value). The *payback rule* and *average accounting return* are other methods that can be used, but they are not described in detail in this material. These methods will be revisited in chapter 7, which discusses external sources of financing in assessing viable capital investment projects. Other useful methods also exist that are not discussed here.

The need to use these methods in evaluating capital projects applies not just to those that generate revenue directly, such as water and sanitation, slaughterhouses, and markets, but also to those that are expected to generate increased economic activity, such as roads. In each case, the expected financial or fiscal benefits and the increased operating and maintenance costs must be compared to the initial capital investment to determine the relative financial or economic merits of a project and evaluate competing investments. These issues are discussed in more detail in chapter 6, on asset management.

Net Present Value

In evaluating any capital project, it is important to determine how much value is added or created by undertaking it. The difference between the value added (usually increases in cash flow) and the cost of the investment is the net present value (NPV) of the investment. Since the cost of the investment usually occurs in year one (or at least the first several years), and the increases in value to a government (in the form of increased cash flows) generally occur in the future, it is essential to bring this stream of benefits back to their present value so that they can be accurately compared to the cost of the investment. The future value is brought back to present value by applying a discount rate to those future streams of cash flow. The discount rate (it is also called the "reference" or "hurdle" rate) that is used in making this calculation, in the case of a local government, could be the cost of borrowing long-term funds. An investment should be accepted if the net present value is positive and rejected if it is negative.

The concept of present values is discussed in detail in chapter 7. Briefly, however, the purpose of present values is to compare the future of cash flows of alternative investments (positive or negative) by applying a discount rate to bring them back to present value. Once the future cash flows are discounted back to the present, management can compare alternatives more accurately and decide which would be better. The discount rate (or hurdle rate) is generally the entity's cost of capital. For a government, the discount rate would be the rate at which the government can borrow. To further complicate an already difficult concept, the discount rate used to calculate the present value of future cash flows should, if possible, correspond to the life of the asset. For example, in evaluating investments with a 10-year life, the discount rate should correspond to the rate at which government could borrow funds for 10 years.

Example: The department of public works is comparing two models of road grading equipment for its maintenance unit. The *heavy duty model* that costs $30,000 will result in estimated net cash flows of $9,000 per year for the next five years; the *economy model* costs $20,000 and would raise net estimated cash flows by $5,800 per year for the next five years. The hurdle rate is 10 percent. Table 5.13 summarizes the results and calculations. The calculation shows that the heavy duty model is superior because the NPV is $4,117, versus $1,977 for the economy model. Furthermore, since the NPV exceeds zero, the heavy duty model should be purchased.

Internal Rate of Return

The internal rate of return (IRR) is the most important alternative to net present value. As with the NPV, one must compare investments, usually in year one, to benefits in the form of increases in cash flow in future years. However, whereas the discount rate in the NPV is a known value (the cost of capital), with the IRR, the discount rate is what makes the NPV of the net cash flows from an investment equal to zero. Based on the internal rate of return method, an investment is acceptable if the IRR exceeds the required return (hurdle rate) and should be rejected if it does not.

Example: Let us again take the example of the two pieces of road grading equipment and calculate the internal rate of return for each. The IRRs confirm the results from the NPV analysis, namely, that the heavy duty machine is the best option. It has a 15.2 percent internal rate of return, whereas the economy machine has only a 13.8 percent IRR. Both IRRs are higher than the hurdle rate (the cost of long-term borrowing for the city), but the better machine is financially better too. Table 5.14 summarizes the results and calculations.

Whereas the net present value is the more reliable of the two methods and always indicates the correct alternative investment, in practice, the IRR is frequently preferred because it provides a single rate that can be more easily compared to the cost of borrowing, rates of inflation, and so forth.

Cost-benefit Analysis

Cost-benefit analysis is a policy analysis tool that uses both NPV and IRR methodology. The objective of a cost-benefit analysis is to quantify the total costs of a project over its lifetime and compare them with the value of the total benefits that are expected from it. This is done by discounting to present value the estimated stream of benefits and the stream of costs, and then comparing the present value of the costs with the present value of the benefits. As can be imagined, it is extremely difficult to calculate accurately the lifetime cost of an investment or its corresponding benefits.

Table 5.13　Net Present Value Analysis of Two Equipment Models (dollars)

Hurdle rate 10%	Year 0	Year 1	Year 2	Year 3	Year 4	Year 5	$NPV = \sum Y_i - Y_0$
Initial investment, heavy duty model	30,000						
Revenues (net cash flow)		9,000	9,000	9,000	9,000	9,000	
Discount factor $d = (1 + 0.1)^n$		1.10	1.21	1.33	1.46	1.61	
Net present value CF/d	−30,000	8,182	7,438	6,762	6,147	5,588	4,117
Initial investment, economy model	20,000						
Revenues (CF = net cash flow)		5,800	5,800	5,800	5,800	5,800	
Net present value CF/d	−20,000	5,273	4,793	4,358	3,961	3,601	1,987

Note: NPV = net present value; CF = cash flow; d = discount factor; i = years from 1 to 5.

Table 5.14　Internal Rate of Return Calculation

Hurdle rate 10%	Year 0	Year 1	Year 2	Year 3	Year 4	Year 5	$NPV = \sum Y_i - Y_0$
IRR calculation HD		1.152	1.327	1.529	1.761	2.029	
PV (IRR HD = 15.2%)	−30,000	7,813	6,782	5,887	5,110	4,436	27
IRR calculation economy		1.138	1.295	1.474	1.677	1.909	
PV (IRR Economy = 13.8%)	−20,000	5,097	4,479	3,936	3,458	3,039	8

Note: IRR = internal rate of return; HD = heavy duty; PV = present value; i = years from 1 to 5.

Table 5.15　Sensitivity Analysis (dollars)

Sensitivity analysis using data from table 5.14	Year 0	Year 1	Year 2	Year 3	Year 4	Year 5	$NPV = \sum Y_i - Y_0$
12% less net cash flow		7,920	7,920	7,920	7,920	7,920	
NPV of the heavy duty model	−30,000	7,200	6,545	5,950	5,409	4,918	23
12% cost overrun	−33,600	8,182	7,438	6,762	6,147	5,588	517

Therefore, it is essential to apply some judgment in the form of a sensitivity analysis.

Sensitivity Analysis

While each of these methods, and the others mentioned earlier, will provide a clear indication of the best investment alternative for a particular project, capital expenditure analysis is only as good as the assumptions used in making the calculations. What is the probability of correctly estimating the exact stream of benefits from any capital project? Or what is the probability of correctly estimating the additional operating costs and the timing of those costs? For that reason, it is essential to accompany any evaluation with a rigorous sensitivity analysis, regardless of the type or number of other methodologies used in making those calculations.

The objective of a sensitivity analysis is to select those assumptions that are the most critical to the evaluation, such as a sales price, labor rate, or collection rate, and assume different values for them, higher and lower than the base case scenario (see table 5.15).

Example: Using the results of the road equipment investment analysis from table 5.13, one can test, first, the impact of a possible risk, that the net cash flow gained using the heavy duty machinery would be 12 percent less than the base case scenario. Table 5.15 shows net present value of $23. Thus, this investment would remain feasible as long as the net cash flow does not drop below $7,900 per year. Second, one can test the impact if the machinery eventually costs about 12 percent more than planned, say, because of a change in foreign currency exchange rates. The results in table 5.15 show that the investment would remain feasible, or even a bit better. One can say, though, that the difference between the two sensitivity results is not significant.

Medium-Term Expenditure Framework—Multiyear Budgets

In many cities, budget preparation has become highly informal—ad hoc measures are used to deal with financing and implementation difficulties; expenditures outside the budget are common; and multiple budgets are produced with no single comprehensive budget. Cost estimates that the various city departments submit do not attempt to reflect any policy objectives or strategic benchmarks; they simply represent uniform increases over the previous year. And because most of these cities operate with a single-year budget framework, every year the budgeting process starts from scratch. Chapter 3 offers a more comprehensive discussion on budgeting.

Medium-Term Expenditure Framework

What is done by the central government's medium-term expenditure framework (MTEF) needs to be clearly differentiated from what is done by local governments. Central governments typically rely on a medium-term expenditure framework that is a rolling, three- to five-year budget, which links policies to expenditures. An MTEF has the potential to link the often-competing short-term imperatives of governments with the medium- and longer-term demands of the budget. In technical terms, an MTEF is a framework for integrating fiscal policy and budget procedures over the medium term by linking a system of aggregate fiscal forecasting to a disciplined process of maintaining medium-term

budget estimates that reflect existing government policies. Local governments do not normally make use of an MTEF; their use of multiyear budgets generally accomplishes the same objective of linking policies to expenditures over a three- to five-year time frame.

The PEFA assessment report for the city of Addis Ababa stated that a three-year medium-term expenditure framework was introduced at the city level for the first time for the budget of 2007/08. The assessment indicated that the MTEF includes revenues and expenditures and is rolled out every year. The section on capital expenditures[3] is classified by sector and covers road, education, health, water and sewerage, land development, and other categories.

Multiyear Budgets to Support a Policy Environment

As indicated in the discussion of the expenditure management cycle, policies should lead the budget process. However, it is difficult to budget for new programs, whatever they may be, within a one-year budget. A multiyear budget enables local governments to continue with their normal budget preparation processes and present in the outer years the introduction of new policy initiatives. The multiyear format enables governments to present new revenue policies to support new services (expenditures) that are needed to support new policies and programs demanded by the population.

A multiyear budget is prepared in the form of a rolling budget, in which the first year has the same level of revenue and expenditure detail found in a normal budget and the outer years have more tentative numbers designed to demonstrate commitment toward a particular set of policies and levels of expenditures. Moving outward from year one to year three, the revenue and expenditure estimates become "softer." As year one is nearing completion, the budget estimates for year two (now the next year) become firmer, and an additional year, year four, is added

Table 5.16 A Multiyear Budget

Category	Year 1	Year 2	Year 3	Year 4
Revenue				
Property tax	100	105		
Land tax	10	12		
Other	5			
Total	115	117	120	
Expenditures				
Salaries	45	47	48	
Material	10	11		
Maintenance	3	3		
Total current expenditures	58	61	62	
Capital expenditures	25	26	27	

to the planning horizon. A simple example of a multiyear budget is presented in table 5.16.

The chief characteristics of a multiyear budget are the following:

- It is a medium-term fiscal framework that provides revenue forecasts for a three- to five-year period and also forecasts the economic environment in which it is anticipated that the budget will be operating.

- It contains spending projections that are consistent with revenue projections.

- It links budget allocations to program impact.

- It includes a robust monitoring and evaluation program to develop an impact analysis and provide feedback for the review of policy objectives.

Key mechanisms that promote strategic decision making by core decision-making bodies are the following:

- Consultation and debate on policy issues

- Transparency and accountability

- Decision making that is underpinned by resource availability

- Proper management and sequencing of the process for assessing policy considerations by the municipal cabinet.

Capacities Necessary to Implement a Multiyear Budget

A multiyear budget requires program managers and department heads to design and plan their activities around established government policies and priorities. It forces managers to demonstrate how proposed activities relate to government and sector objectives. Because it is a plan to support prioritized programs over multiple years, the budget becomes the main vehicle through which the local government implements agreed-upon policies and fulfills its mission.

To implement a multiyear budget process, a local government must be able to do the following:

- Establish clearly defined policy objectives, along with the desired outputs and impacts.

- Design public programs and targeted services to bring about the desired outputs.

- Calculate a realistic estimate of the resources needed to properly implement the programs.

- Develop an effective mechanism to coordinate with various departments and special interest groups (including harmonization of donor activities).

- Have budget discipline.

- Have procedures for estimating the forward costs of programs.

- Implement an effective monitoring and evaluation system that provides policy makers with critical information regarding the effectiveness of the programs.

- Generate political leadership committed to improving expenditure management systems and procedures and increasing the level of transparency in government.

A multiyear (program) budget differs from the traditional line-item budget by focusing on the expected results of services and activities, rather than on inputs such as salaries and supplies. In a program budget, revenues and expenditures are linked to multiyear programs that meet the municipality's goals, objectives, and strategies. Significantly, a program budget identifies the anticipated results and outputs of investments. Ideally, a program such as a neighborhood street and sidewalk improvement program should be clearly delineated, have minimum overlap with other programs, be results oriented, and lend itself to quantifiable measurement. Planning, budgeting, administrative control, and reporting will be carried out within the framework of this program structure. Some of the problems that have been encountered with multiyear program budgeting relate to having good baseline data, methods to gather the data, and specific, well-defined targets (see chapter 3 for a more thorough discussion of program budgeting).

The Shift toward Performance-Based Budgets

The output of a private sector company is the product that it sells, and the aim of that company is to maximize profits through the sale of its product. The company has an incentive to improve the quality of its output, as higher-quality products lead to higher sales revenue. The company also has an incentive to minimize the cost of producing its output, as cost efficiency and high-quality expenditure management lead to lower costs and higher profits. The objective of the company is to make money, and it accomplishes that by producing and selling its output (Coca Cola sells soda; Toyota sells cars, etc.).

What about the public sector? What is the objective of a government, and how does it achieve it? In democratic societies, governments exist to provide services that neither the market nor individual citizens can adequately provide. So the outputs of a government are the services that it provides.

Chapter 3 reviewed the various types of budgets. Traditional or line-item budgets are the most common, but performance-based budgeting is receiving more attention because it focuses on outputs rather than inputs. As discussed in chapter 3, budgets can be of several kinds: line-item, performance, and program (summarized in tables 5.17 and 5.18).

Traditional to Performance-Based Budgeting

Budgeting is a way of estimating and allocating resources to achieve an objective of a local government in delivering services. Performance-based budgeting establishes accountability by linking the commitments of the executive branch, which agrees to achieve stated results in return for continued funding or other incentives. It also makes governments more accountable to citizens. Performance information helps policy makers put a monetary value on programs. Performance-based budgeting forges a link between planned activities and outcomes.

In summary, performance budgets use statements of missions, goals, and objectives to explain why money is being spent. It is a way to allocate resources to achieve specific objectives based on program goals and measured results. Performance budgeting differs from traditional budgeting because it focuses on results rather than the money spent and on what the money

Table 5.17 Types of Budget Formats

Format	Character	Organization	Purpose
Line item	Commodity/service inputs	Items purchased	Control
Performance	Activity/workload	Tasks/outputs	Management
Program	Public goals across agencies	Outcomes/customer response	Planning

buys (results) rather than the amount that is made available.

The major elements of performance-based budgeting are defining goals and objectives, developing measures of performance aligned with those goals and objectives, linking spending decisions to results (outcomes), and accountability for results. In recent years, the emphasis on outcomes and the importance of delivering the benefits of agreed-upon programs to their recipients and participants has made performance-based budgeting a hot topic. Table 5.19 illustrates the logic behind the hierarchy of inputs, outputs, and outcomes or performance.

In many ways, the need for and attraction of performance-based budgeting come from the shortcomings of the traditional budgeting process, which results in a negotiation between managers and funding authorities over relatively small percentage changes from the previous year's budget.

Those negotiations rarely reach issues of efficiency and effectiveness. Performance-based budgeting is not just about performance. It is instead a process by which a particular type of budget is prepared. Performance-based budgeting should be viewed as having the following six steps:

- Identify desired outcome.

- Define the data necessary to measure performance and the systems needed to collect the data on a regular basis.

- Select an outcome performance measure.

- Set a goal.

- Report results.

- Implement consequences.

It is hard to refute the theory of performance-based budgeting. Unfortunately, the process is complex and frequently difficult to implement. Some of the issues that need to be overcome include the following:

- Identifying and developing the right performance measures and indicators

- Developing accounting systems to support performance-based budgeting

- Creating incentives for decision making based on performance

- Getting the needed "buy-in" from all branches of government

Table 5.18   Flow of Service Provision

Nature of service provision	Street repair
Inputs:	Line items:
Labor, materials, and equipment	Tons of gravel; contractor payments
Activity:	Performance:
Street repair	Lanes paved
Program result:	Program outcome:
Increased speed and safety of travel	Reduced commuting time

Table 5.19   Performance Budgeting Logic Model

		Outcomes		
Inputs	Outputs	Short term	Medium term	Long term
Staff costs	Workshops	Awareness	Behavior	Conditions
Materials	Outreach	Knowledge	Decisions	Environment
Equipment	Inspections	Attitudes	Policies	Social
Technology		Skills		Economic
				Civic

- Overcoming the concern of agencies that too much attention is focused on a small number of indicators

- The difficulty of measuring outcomes, especially intermediate ones

- Incomplete understanding of the relationship between expenditures and outcomes.

Because of its complexity, it is uncommon to see performance-based budgeting used for an entire entity, such as a local government. However, many local governments use performance-based budgeting for certain activities or departments because it is important to link expenditures to agreed-upon policies and programs. The U.S. state of North Carolina implemented performance-based budgeting in its local governments.

Example: The city of Sunnyvale, California, U.S., has adopted a performance-based budget for improving child-care services. Box 5.16

Box 5.16 Performance-Based Budget for Child Care Improvement in Sunnyvale, California

Service Delivery Plan 52404 — Facilitate Child Care Services

Facilitate the Child Care Program by:—Staffing the Child Care Advisory Board;—Monitoring child care legislation;—Conducting advocacy/leadership activities; and—Coordinating and monitoring existing child care support services, so that:

Service Delivery Plan Measures	FY2001/2002 Adopted	FY2002/2003 Adopted	FY2003/2004 Adopted
• Served Child Care Advisory Board Members rate staff support as "good" 85% of the time	0.00%	85.00%	85.00%
• 90% of the Child Care Advisory Board work items are completed according to Council's approved work schedule	0.00%	90.00%	90.00%
• Served collaborative agencies rate staff support as "good"85% of the time	0.00%	85.00%	85.00%

	Costs	Products	Work hours	Product costs
Activity 524009 — Staff the Child Care Advisory Board				
Product: A Work Plan Completed				
FY 2002/2003 Adopted	$18,494.14	1.00	338.23	$18,494.14
FY 2003/2004 Adopted	$19,181.38	1.00	338.23	$19,181.38

(continued next page)

Box 5.16 *(continued)*

	Costs	Products	Work hours	Product costs
Activity 524010—Monitor Child Care Legislation				
Product: A Bill Tracked				
FY 2002/2003 Adopted	$10,461.35	6.00	180.39	$1,743.56
FY 2003/2004 Adopted	$10,838.66	6.00	180.39	$1,806.44
Activity 524011—Conduct Advocacy/Leadership Activities				
Product: An Activity Completed				
FY 2002/2003 Adopted	$15,408.38	1.00	270.58	$15,408.38
FY 2003/2004 Adopted	$15,935.43	1.00	270.58	$15,935.43
Activity 524012—Coordinate and Monitor Existing Child Care Support Services				
Product: An Organization Monitored				
FY 2002/2003 Adopted	$10,789.93	4.00	202.94	$2,697.48
FY 2003/2004 Adopted	$11,213.66	4.00	202.94	$2,803.42

Totals for service delivery plan 52404:	**Costs**	**Work hours**
FY 2002/2003 Adopted	$55,153.80	992.14
FY 2003/2004 Adopted	$57,169.13	992.14

Source: www.sunnyvalecity.com.

summarizes a portion of that budget. The program includes situation analysis, performance targets with outputs and outcomes, and specific actions with specific budget allocations.

Monitoring and Evaluation

Monitoring and evaluation are the next stage of the expenditure management cycle, although they could be important both during (midterm) and after implementation of the annual budget or specific projects. A number of instruments and methodologies are used for monitoring and evaluation. This section briefly discusses three, namely, variance analysis, comparative cost analysis, and benchmarking.

Variance Analysis

Revenue and expenditure levels need to be reviewed regularly—monthly or quarterly—to ensure that they conform to the budget and to determine if they are on track to achieve the stated policy objectives. An activity can be analyzed in a number of ways, in terms of both financial and operational performance, but an analysis of the variances between planned and budgeted amounts and actual results is arguably one of the best methods.

Given that budgeted levels will generally be different from actual levels, explanations of the resulting variances should be restricted to those that exceed a certain percentage, such as plus or minus 10 percent of budget. Table 5.20 shows a

Table 5.20 Variance Analysis

Category	Budget	Actual	Variance	Variance (%)	Explanation
Revenues					
Taxes	10,000	10,500	500	5.0	
Grants	15,000	10,500	−4,500	−30.0	Delayed or canceled?
Total	25,000	21,000	−4,000	−16.0	
Expenditures					
Labor	4,500	4,600	−100	−2.2	
Material	3,000	2,800	+200	6.7	Unpaid bills?
Total	7,500	7,400	+100	1.3	

case in which four items vary by less than the 10 percent threshold but the category grants differs significantly because of delays; the cost of materials indicates substantial savings that might be a result of unaccounted bills.

When the planned level of activity—developed after extensive review during the budget process—is compared with the actual results, the variance provides useful information to decision makers. However, variances, small or large, do not by themselves explain the underlying reasons, such as whether the budget preparation process was flawed or the environment for the activity has changed. Thus, the variance analysis is just a signal that must be followed by specific inquiries and corrective measures; those may include changing the budget plan by issuing a supplementary budget or warning the respective departments to exercise more stringent expenditure control.

Comparative Service Delivery Costs

It is difficult to compare two objects and draw firm conclusions, but if the two objects are generally similar, such comparisons are possible. That would be the case for comparisons of basic urban services, such as the costs of solid waste removal, street lighting, and education, provided in different cities or in different parts of the same city. Service comparison can provide useful information, but the contextual differences among locations must be understood.

Example: It is possible to compare costs per ton of waste removed, costs per child educated from kindergarten through ninth grade, costs per kilometer of road maintained, and so on. The comparisons in absolute terms will not mean much because each city or part of a city has different characteristics, such as being farther from the landfill, for example. But they can indicate areas of expenditure that need more examination. Comparisons can also provide interesting lessons regarding procedures to control costs or improve services that might be transferred to other areas. For example, fuel consumption by solid waste trucks (or any other truck) should be monitored on a daily basis and irregularities investigated. If one or two trucks of a 20-truck fleet consume much more fuel than the others, say, 30 percent to 50 percent above average, an inquiry would establish whether the use of those trucks has changed, whether they need urgent engine maintenance, or even the possible theft of fuel.

Benchmarking Service Delivery Standards

The task of expenditure management is to ensure that the funds available to local governments are spent on improving service delivery and achieving objectives efficiently and effectively (Helgason 1997). However, what is the level of service that was agreed to? How much solid waste removal or street cleaning constitutes an acceptable level of service? Benchmarking is an instrument that can be used to improve the performance of the public sector and the services that are provided.

Benchmarking is becoming a central instrument for improving the performance of the public sector. Under the right conditions, comparisons can be an important driver of performance. The basic idea behind benchmarking is simple:

- Find an organization that is best at what your own organization does.

- Study how it achieves those results.

- Make plans for improving your own performance.

- Implement the plans.

- Monitor and evaluate the results.

In other words, benchmarking is an attempt to identify and implement best practice. Although the idea is simple, putting it into practice may be more complex and challenging. Knowledge of differences in performance can be an important incentive for improvement, but achieving improvements will still require significant effort and leadership. Moreover, it is not sufficient to copy practices from other organizations. Best practices have to be evaluated and adjusted to the needs of an organization.

Benchmarking has been introduced into the public sector through two main strategies:

- *A top-down approach,* in which benchmarking is imposed externally, usually by central government agencies, such as the finance department or another agency. Externally imposed benchmarking can be used by a department to set targets for one of its subsidiary agencies. In this case, benchmarking can be used instead of more direct control by introducing competitive pressures.

- *A bottom-up approach,* in which local government departments or service entities (such as a water utility) develop their own benchmarking projects and try to find appropriate

benchmarking partners. Finance departments can support such initiatives by helping agencies to find benchmarking partners and to achieve relevant expertise.

Experience has shown that both approaches have value; governments should develop procedures to apply both. For example, externally imposed benchmarking may give incentives for organizations to initiate more detailed process benchmarking. Benchmarking projects driven internally may increase the level of commitment and ownership of the management and staff in the particular department.

In designing departmental benchmarking efforts, consideration needs to be given to the following questions:

What is benchmarked?

- Processes

- Results

Against what is an organization benchmarked?

- Other organizations

- Standards

How is benchmarking used?

- For continuous improvement

- For evaluation

A close relationship exists between results benchmarking and process benchmarking. Results benchmarking identifies the processes that need improvement. Process benchmarking improves the processes, contributing to better results.

Organizations can be benchmarked against other organizations or against a standard. Benchmarking against other organizations is an important source of learning, as organizations are constantly challenged by developments in other organizations. However, benchmarking is not copying. The interaction between the organizations involved can be an important source of improvement.

Box 5.17 explains the growing importance of International Organization for Standardization (ISO) standards and certificates, also a kind of benchmark, in the local government sector. Benchmarks that are identified by an organization can become a form of "best practice" standard. Benchmarking against standards can be important, as standards or quality models are in many cases based on the best practices of many organizations. Benchmarking against a standard can be an interim step toward benchmarking against other organizations, particularly if many organizations benchmark themselves against the same standard. The organizations can then compare their scores against those of other organizations, identify their weak and strong sides (or processes), and seek to reduce the weaknesses by benchmarking their processes against those of better-scoring organizations.

Box 5.17 International Organization for Standardization Certificates — Improving Municipal Performance and Cost Control

ISO is the well-known acronym of the International Organization for Standardization, a nonprofit organization headquartered in Geneva, Switzerland, that develops and publishes a wide range of standards and issues *ISO certificates*, often via partner domestic entities. The ISO 9000 family of standards is related to quality management systems and designed to help organizations ensure that they meet the needs of customers and other stakeholders while meeting statutory and regulatory requirements related to the product.

ISO 9001 deals with the requirements that an organization wishing to meet the standard has to fulfill. An ISO 9001 certificate is issued by an independent registrar after it has been verified that a company or supplier has implemented the ISO 9001 quality management system and follows all its requirements in daily operations. Over a million organizations worldwide are independently certified. The ISO 9001 certification is recognized and appreciated globally because it provides a means for customers to improve the delivery of quality services by contracting with companies that meet a set of rigorous standards.

The vast majority of ISO 9001 certificates are issued for private firms as part of their quality compliance; they are particularly useful in international trade and services. However, municipalities and their utility companies are increasingly obtaining ISO certificates in the United States, Europe, and the developing world. For instance, many municipalities in Eastern Europe have obtained ISO certification, including ones in transition countries such as the Czech Republic and Hungary. Municipalities in the United States typically certify their key service entities, such as those for fire protection, water and sanitation, education, and health, and those overseeing building codes or public housing. The ISO helps streamline services, reducing the cost of operation, and also lowers the costs of insurance and financing. Municipalities in Eastern Europe start with ISO 9001 certification of the entire municipal administration. Some argue that it may help them obtain cheaper insurance or even bank borrowing if a credit rating has not yet been obtained.

Source: http://www.iso.org/iso/home/about.htm.

By combining the results of the variance analysis of expenditures with analysis of the actual service delivery against the benchmarks, management is able to determine its level of efficiency and effectiveness in providing services. The example in table 5.21, which concerns costs of road maintenance activities, provides some useful information. The national averages obtained from the road authority can be used as benchmarks:

- The cost of resealing was significantly above the benchmark, probably because of deferred maintenance and bad road conditions (but that needs verification).

- The cost of resurfacing gravel was below the benchmark, perhaps because of incorrect costing (some costs may be accounted for as resealing).

- Asphalting was high above the benchmark; this has no logical reason and thus needs inquiry.

Feedback for Budget Planning

The expenditure management process is driven by evaluations of results, and that is why it is so important that outputs are specific and measurable. They are a critical source of data to begin developing the next year's budget. The information developed from the monitoring and evaluation process, combined with changes and adjustments to the policy framework, enables departments to determine more accurately the level of resources that will be needed to deliver the desired level of services and new policy outcomes.

Audit and Oversight

Financial and specialized audits are discussed in detail in chapters 3 and 8. Because of the importance of oversight in expenditure management, however, it deserves some reference in this chapter. As stated earlier, expenditure management is shared among different positions in the local government organization. The concept of oversight applies primarily to the members of the local government council and to the central government.

Role of Oversight in Expenditure Management

Oversight is a means of holding the executive accountable for its actions and ensuring that agreed-on policies and plans are implemented in an effective and efficient manner. One of the pillars of a strong internal control framework is a robust system of oversight to monitor the performance of the executive. Normally, the most common form of oversight is that provided by the elected officials (the local council, parliament, etc.), but realization is growing that communities can also be significant in monitoring the performance of both contractors and government officials. The role of communities is more prominent in developed countries that have histories of transparency, freedom of speech, and representation.

In both long-established and new democracies, parliaments have the power to oversee the government through tools and mechanisms that typically are outlined in the constitution and laws. Legal frameworks vary from one country to the next, but the oversight functions assigned

Table 5.21 Benchmarking Road Maintenance

Activity	Kilometers			Shillings (millions)			Shillings (million per kilometer)	
	Plan	Actual	Variance	Plan	Actual	Variance	Actual	National average
Resealing	25	20	−5	100	105	−5	5.3	4.0
Resurfacing gravel	15	17	2	125	120	5	7.1	8.0
Resurfacing asphalt	5	5	0	150	160	10	32.0	30.0

to a parliament should also be given to the local government council. It is the responsibility of local elected officials to ensure that their constituencies are receiving value for money. In addition, the principle of subsidiarity applies to the oversight provided by the local councils, who are supported by the community, which has a strong vested interest in ensuring that the agreed upon quantity and quality of services are provided.

In performing their oversight functions, local councils can implement the following practices:

- *Establish an audit committee* to work with independent auditors and review their reports.

- *Meet independently with the auditors* to review their findings regarding the internal control system and other compliance matters.

- *Establish committees to oversee the activities* of individuals or a small number of departments.

- *Establish a finance and budget committee* to work closely with the finance department to ensure that the local government is managing its resources and expenditures effectively.

- *Meet regularly with constituents* to listen to their concerns, observations, and possible complaints regarding the performance of contractors and the quality of services provided.

To ensure that oversight can be implemented effectively, information about the workings of government must be available to stakeholders on a timely basis and in a format that is understandable. For instance, the financial transparency home page for Fairfax County, Virginia, stipulates that the county "is moving forward on providing residents with more financial transparency. The term *financial transparency* describes efforts to make comprehensive, unfiltered information available to everyone, enabling a clear view of the government's operations and how tax dollars are spent."

On its financial transparency home page, the county has provided financial reports, budgets, annual audits, procurement contracts, and staff compensation plans. The site also indicates that further work is under way to provide even more financial information to the transaction level (for additional information, see http://www.fairfaxcounty.gov/finance/transparency). Although most local governments may not be able to provide the level of financial information made available by Fairfax County, they can begin to make more information available to increase the level of transparency as a means to strengthen oversight.

Expenditure Management and Political Economy

Local governments operate in a complex environment influenced by local culture, politics, and special interests. Heads of finance departments and their staff must be mindful of political pressures while developing and implementing budgets, accounting for activities, and monitoring and evaluating results. One of the best means to mitigate the risks posed by such special interests is to ensure that policies, plans, budgets, and results are openly provided to all concerned stakeholders and community groups.

This expenditure management chapter closes with a brief discussion of the links between expenditure management and the political environment. Political influence is intertwined with most local government activities, in part because local governments always need political support and reconfirmation for programs (decision makers need political approval). But political influence also appears without demand for it, and it is particularly strong where spending is at stake.

Political Pressure from Local Special Interest Groups

Expenditure management focuses on ensuring that funds are allocated and used to achieve agreed-upon priorities and that information is available to enable governments to plan for and monitor the performance of their programs and the impact of their expenditures.

An effective expenditure management system must include three elements.

- It is necessary to plan for future expenditures with clear and measurable milestones to monitor actual performance.

- It is necessary to control expenditures so that the actual spending is consistent with the budget and plan.

- Expenditures need to be monitored and evaluated to ensure that they are in fact conforming to the agreed-on plans.

The problem of specials interests is frequently not given proper attention in designing development projects or other investments at the local government level. An example of the potential impact of special interests is described in box 5.18.

Political Pressure from the Central Government

In many countries, local governments are hindered by political and administrative interference from above. The central government can disturb local expenditure management by giving or withholding money, projects, or staff.

Political projects. The most typical problem is undertaking projects on purely political bases, without consultation with the local stakeholders. One project proposal sent to a donor for funding literally argued that the "market street should be asphalted, because the Governor's house is located at the end of that street." Politically granted projects may create contingent liabilities for the local government, which must fit their operation and maintenance costs into the local budget.

Unfunded mandates. Another typical intervention by the central government is to assign formerly central functions to the local

---

Box 5.18 Potential Impact of Special Interests

The U.S. state of New Jersey identified the need to construct a new tunnel linking the state with New York City. After the required environmental studies and technical engineering designs were completed, agreement was reached that the Trans-Hudson Express Tunnel would be jointly financed by the state of New Jersey, the Port Authority of New York and New Jersey, and the federal government.

The objective of the tunnel was to increase access for the thousands of people who commute daily from New Jersey into New York City. The effectiveness of the tunnel was questioned by many, however, because it did not connect to train stations but ended under the basement of a major department store,

Macy's. Thus, the nickname of the project was "the tunnel to Macy's basement." A new governor of New Jersey stopped work on the tunnel, saying that the risk of cost overruns was placed unfairly on his state. Work was subsequently restarted because of pressure from numerous sources.

Virtually no one questioned the need to expand rail capacity between the two jurisdictions. However, even though the project would potentially benefit one company tremendously by requiring that thousands of commuters pass through or near its store twice a day, little has been written about that impact of this potential special interest in the design and implementation of the project.

Source: Based on information from Wikipedia.

governments. This seems to be consistent with the devolution principle, but the center often fails to allocate also the corresponding resources or taxing power. The result is called an "unfunded mandate." Similar effects emerge, for example, when a national ordinance increases the salaries of teachers or other public servants but provides no corresponding transfer of funds. The local governments then must cut expenses elsewhere. They often do so by deferring maintenance of assets or reducing services.

For example, in Uganda, the Kampala city council required privately owned motorcycle taxis (called "boda-boda") to register their vehicles and pay a small registration fee. However, shortly after this local tax was imposed, the president abolished it to boost his popularity as he sought reelection in 2006. Kampala and other local governments were denied a source of locally generated revenue because of political pressure from a politician at center.

Political interference is not restricted to developing nations. For example, in the United States, in 2003, the governor of the state of Virginia extended the time that a person must spend in jail after three drunken driving arrests from five days to 15 days. But the local jails are not administered by the state government; they are administered by county governments Thus the directive from the state imposed additional costs on localities that were required to house people in jail for longer periods.

Takeaway Messages

Key messages from this chapter include the following:

- Expenditure management should be seen and performed in a cycle of policy setting, planning, execution analysis, and audit, which feeds into the next cycle and policy setting.

- Effective expenditure management requires close and timely monitoring and analysis of both operating and capital expenditures, comparing clear and measurable targets to solid baseline data, and initiating corrective actions as required.

- Monitoring and evaluation not only measure and control results but also facilitate cost control and decision making, for example, about whether or not to contract out specific services.

- A number of well-tested, effective instruments are useful for expenditure analysis, including plan/actual variance analysis, forecasting, and benchmarking results to local, national, or international indicators. Net present value, internal rate of return, and cost-benefit analysis are among the most important techniques applied along with a rigorous sensitivity analysis.

- Setting, monitoring, and controlling tariffs are vital elements of effective expenditure management. They are useful tools to control providers, regardless of the institutional form of service provision, such as department, legally independent municipal entity, public utility, public-private partnership, or fully private provider.

- Cost recovery is a basic principle but may require subsidizing certain local services, particularly in developing countries. Municipalities in developing countries tend to rely on untargeted supply-side subsidies (grants to service entities). In contrast are more explicit, demand-side subsidies that target the poor or other communities, while requiring full cost coverage by households and businesses that can afford to pay.

- Modern computerized accounting, budgeting, and cash and financial management systems are key instruments for effective expenditure control. To make these effective, a proper internal control environment and performance-based systems are needed.

- Managing capital expenditures requires long-term planning of both capital investment projects and financing; transparent and competitive procurement; and strong capacities for contract management.

- A medium-term expenditure framework is a robust instrument for supporting effective expenditure management and for performance monitoring. It should be combined with disciplined audits and financial and regulatory oversight.

- Expenditure management is not merely a technical process but also a very political one. Thus, effective expenditure management requires good understanding and management of the political economy implications of the plans and decisions.

Notes

1. This section was prepared based on World Bank 1998, chapter 2.
2. More details are available at http://ec.europa .eu/europeaid/what/economic-support /public-finance/documents/ethiopia _addisababa_pefa_report_2010_en.pdf.
3. The entire assessment can be found at http://ec.europa.eu/europeaid/what /economic-support/public-finance /documents/ethiopia_ _addisababa_pefa _report_2010_en.pdf.

References

Adrianov, Valentin, Sergei Sivaev, Raymond Struyk, and Emin Askerov. 2003. *Russia's Winter Woes: Tariff Setting for Local Utilities in a Transition Economy.* Moscow: Institute for Urban Economics.

Chavez, Carlos. 2002. "Public-Private Partnership and Tariff Setting: The Case of Chile." Paper for the OECD Global Forum on Sustainable Development, Paris, April.

Chernyavsky, Andrei, and Karen Vartapetov. 2004. "Municipal Finance Reform and Local Self Governance in Russia." *Post-communist Economies* 16 (3), September.

DANCED (Danish Co-operation for Environment and Development). 2002. "Solid Waste Tariff Setting—Guidelines for Local Authorities." Proposal for the Department of Environmental Affairs and Tourism, Tanzania, April.

Ebel, R., and F. Vaillancourt. 2007. "Intergovernmental Assignment of Expenditure Responsibility." In *The Kosovo Decentralization Briefing Book.* Prishtina: Kosovo Foundation for an Open Society.

Helgason, Sigurdur. 1997. *International Benchmarking Experiences from OECD Countries.* Paper presented in Paris, February.

Kopanyi, M., S. El Daher, and D. Wetzel, eds. 2004. *Intergovernmental Finances in Hungary, A Decade of Experience.* Washington, DC: World Bank Institute.

Shugart, Chris, and Ian Alexander. 2009. "Tariff Setting Guidelines." Public-Private Infrastructure Advisory Facility (PPIAF), Working Paper No. 8, World Bank, Washington, DC.

Tausz, Katalin. 2004. "Managing Household Arrears in Utility Services—Social Policy Challenges and Responses." In *Intergovernmental Finances in Hungary, A Decade of Experience,* edited by M. Kopanyi, S. El Daher, and D. Wetzel. Washington, DC: World Bank Institute.

TERI (The Energy and Resource Institute [India]). 2010. *Review of Current Practices in Determining User Charges and Incorporation of Economic Principles of Pricing of Urban Water Supply. New Delhi, India.* New Delhi: TERI.

USAID (U.S. Agency for International Development). 2006. *Managing Municipal*

Services, Assessment and Implementation Toolkit. Washington, DC: USAID.

VNG International. 2010. "Effective Aid through Municipal Contracts." The Hague, Netherlands: VNG International.

World Bank. 1997. *The State in a Changing World. World Development Report 1997*. Washington, DC: World Bank.

———. 1998. *Public Expenditure Management Handbook*. Washington, DC: World Bank.

———. 2002. *Cities on the Move, a World Bank Urban Transport Strategy Review*. Washington, DC: World Bank.

———. 2005. *Public Expenditure and Financial Accountability (PEFA), Performance Measurement Framework*. PEFA Secretariat, World Bank, Washington, DC.

———. 2007. "Pakistan Infrastructure Implementation Capacity Assessment." South Asia Region, Report 41630-PK, World Bank, Washington, DC.

———. 2008. "Punjab Municipal Service Improvement Project." Staff Progress Report, World Bank, Washington, DC.

———. 2011. *Guidebook on Capital Investment Planning for Local Governments*. Urban Development Series. Washington, DC: World Bank.

Select Bibliography

Farvacque-Vitkovic, Catherine, Lucien Godin, Roberto Chavez, and Lorence Verdet. 2005. *Street Addressing and the Management of Cities*. Directions in Development. Washington, DC: World Bank.

Institute of Public Finance. 2008. "Communities and Local Government Delivering." Institute of Public Finance North West e-Government Group, March 2008, Munich.

Obidegwu, Chukwuma. 2005. *The Medium-Term Expenditure Framework: The Challenge of Budget Integration*. East Asia Decentralizes Making Local Governments Work, World Bank paper, Washington, DC.

PEFA (Public Expenditure and Financial Accountability). 2010. Addis Ababa PEFA report, http://ec.europa.eu/europeaid /what/economic-support/public-finance /documents/ethiopia_addisababa_pefa _report_2010_en.pdf.

Shah, Anwar, ed. 2006. *Local Public Financial Management*. Public Sector Governance and Accountability Series. Washington, DC: World Bank.

World Bank. 1991. *Urban Financial Management A Training Manual*. By James McMaster, Economic Development Institute. Washington, DC: World Bank.

CHAPTER 6

Managing Local Assets

Olga Kaganova and Mihaly Kopanyi

Local governments own or control large asset portfolios, including physical assets such as land, buildings, infrastructure, vehicles, and equipment and financial assets such as investments, ownership in enterprises, bonds, or bank deposits. Good management of the physical assets is important for local well-being for multiple reasons. For example, these assets represent the local public wealth; they are the material base for local public services. Maintaining and operating assets are the bulk of local expenses. The assets are important resources for local economic development. The financial assets both supplement and support the development and use of the physical assets; the two main asset clusters can be seen as transient forms of each other. For example, we can finance a new bus stop from financial savings or sell a piece of land to obtain the money; these are typical decisions in asset management. Despite its importance, systematic asset management is often neglected, with no focal managing entity in many municipalities, particularly in the developing world.

This chapter summarizes for practitioners the main economic attributes of assets; the concept of asset management strategy; and forms, ways, and means of asset management. It underscores that asset management should be a defined activity in a local government and provides a framework and practical tools for good asset management, for improving existing practices, and for interlinking asset management with financial management. The chapter introduces some simple tools for financial analysis, indispensable for good asset management. It also discusses some critical technical issues, such as how to improve the attractiveness of municipal land to investors or induce competition in land auctions to maximize proceeds. Some more advanced instruments and institutions, such as land-based financing, land and asset strategy, special purpose corporations, and development agencies, are also introduced.

Municipal Asset Management

Municipal asset management is a process of making decisions and implementing them regarding operating, maintaining, refurbishing, acquiring, or developing physical assets cost-effectively, with the ultimate objective of providing the best possible service to local citizens. In this sense, asset management is among the municipal functions that have the most direct effect on the lives of local citizens. Thus, shortcomings in asset management often have visible and painful consequences. For instance, a new water supply system is great, but it is painful if, in a few years, service drops from 24 hours a day to 16, then eight, or even less than two hours a day, as a result of poor maintenance; that is not an uncommon case in Asia. The "asset management framework" denotes a system with rules, procedures, and entities to manage the assets of a local government.

Classifying Assets

Municipal assets exist in many different forms, each of which may require different understanding and perhaps a different approach. Thus, classifying assets is the first important step toward good asset management. Several useful ways of classifying municipal assets are summarized below.

By Material Form

One can distinguish physical (or tangible) and nonphysical (financial, intangible) assets. The most important physical assets are also known as "fixed" or "capital" assets. They include real estate (land, buildings), infrastructure, equipment, and vehicles. For the sake of simplicity, this chapter refers to physical assets simply as "assets," unless reasons exist to use another name or to refer to a specific form of asset. Nonphysical assets include investments, shares of companies, bonds, bills, or cash.

Physical assets are understood as all kinds of resources that the local government can own, control, use to produce economic value, or exchange for money. Large and even midsize urban governments own or control quite large and diverse asset portfolios, which typically can include the following:

- Administration buildings and premises (parts of buildings)
- Public housing
- Schools and kindergartens
- Medical clinics
- Cultural facilities (libraries, museums, theaters)
- Sport facilities (stadiums, football fields, tennis courts, swimming pools)
- Parking garages
- Water, rainwater, and sewerage facilities and networks
- Street lighting
- Streets, roads, plazas, parks, and forests
- Agricultural land
- Parking lots
- Vacant land
- Cemeteries
- Farmers markets
- Commercial real estate
- Production facilities and repair shops
- Storage
- Landfills
- Cars and specialized vehicle fleets, such as ambulances, garbage trucks, and tractors.

By Ownership

Classification by ownership reveals who owns the public assets in a municipal jurisdiction. Some assets are owned by local governments themselves; some are owned by the central, state, or provincial government but used by the local government; and some assets have mixed ownership (such as state-municipal ownership or public-private partnerships). The local government may lease some assets from the private sector.

By Function

This term stresses what each asset group is used for. Common categories here may include property for administration; for social services (health, education, culture); for urban infrastructure (water and sanitation, solid waste management, transport, communication); vacant land; and income-generating assets.

By Service Responsibility

One can distinguish *core assets* or *mandatory assets* important to fulfill local functions prescribed by law. Assets that are not necessary for performing assigned functions are called "non-core assets" and can be considered as reserved wealth or surplus property ("private domain" property). For example, vacant land can be used for future urban development or sold to obtain money for funding expansion or renovation of core services, such as sanitation networks or building a policlinic. Non-core assets can be used for services or functions not mandated by

law but which reflect the priorities of the local citizens (e.g., subsidized housing for low-income families, a sport or cultural center). Service responsibilities are often reinforced by legal limitations.

By Legal Limitations

Classifying assets by legal limitations reveals what local government can do with the asset. In countries that have adopted Roman law principles (e.g., France, Hungary), government-owned properties are divided into two major groups. "Public domain" implies that the property cannot be alienated (sold or mortgaged) and might also carry limitations on its use and management arrangements (box 6.1 describes a case in Hungary). "Private domain" implies that the property can be disposed of and regulated similarly to a privately owned asset. Although the legal rules are particular to a country or region, many of them aim to distinguish between inherently public domain property and property that is inherently private domain, which happens to be owned by a public entity but can be sold, exchanged, or altered without a direct impact on services.

Asset Management Approaches

Asset management appears in two main contexts and forms in the life of a municipality. Assets can be seen as a group or portfolio or as

---

Box 6.1 Example of Changing the Status of Municipal Property in Hungary

An elementary school building is nearly abandoned because of an aging population and competition from nearby schools. But it cannot be sold or converted to commercial use because it is a *public domain property*.

For its status to be changed requires the following: (1) the municipal council votes to

close the school and changes the school zones to ensure school access for all families affected; (2) it votes to change the legal status of the building to "private domain"; and (3) it then can sell or lease the building for other purposes.

Source: Kasso and Pergerne-Szabo 2004.

individual service objects maintained for their useful life, or "life cycle." For example, a road that is maintained and improved can serve people for centuries (or even thousands of years). Both portfolio and life-cycle approaches are equally important, as they represent different contexts, times, or situations in the local government's life. It is also true that various asset management activities typically belong to different local government units. The service or technical units (departments of roads, transport, housing, etc.) focus on managing assets over their useful life cycle (some might be short; some quite long). The finance department, the budget committee, and the council need to approach the entire asset portfolio and making decisions across users, services, and asset forms.

Portfolio Management

In portfolio management, assets are elements of the total wealth of the municipality. In portfolio management, assets are compared with one another and decisions are made to serve the local community as the material base of the local services and functions. Within this portfolio concept, asset management is a process of decisions on acquisition, holding, use, refurbishment, or disposition of assets for attaining the goals of a local government either in financial terms or by expanding or improving local services. Each group of assets can be seen as a portfolio within the total portfolio, and decisions often compare alternatives across these portfolios. Physical and financial assets are two main portfolios to compare in decisions, such as whether to build water infrastructure or to make a financial investment in a water company that will build the network and provide water.

As said, the elements of the portfolio are exchangeable; they can replace or supplement each other and thus can be seen as transient forms of money and physical assets. For example, a local government that does not have sufficient resources to repair three schools may decide to sells some land to generate the money to repair the schools. The composition of the asset portfolio will then have slightly changed, but the total wealth of the community, especially from the social value viewpoint, increased via the reinvestment of the money from the land sale in socially significant property.

Life-Cycle Asset Management

The second common understanding of asset management implies the strategic management of physical assets during their life cycle. A life cycle could be short for a truck, say, 10 years, or could span centuries. For example, the GT road, a 2,500-kilometer (km) major road between Kabul and Kolkata, has existed since the third century. The term "life cycle" refers to planning, creating or acquiring, using, managing, and maintaining a facility and disposing of it when it is no longer required. Managing assets through their entire useful life cycle is particularly important for local governments.

The cycle suggests perpetual movement. Referring to the diagram in figure 6.1, logically the cycle starts at the northwest, with clear identification of needs, objectives, functions to fulfill, and the costs and risks associated with the selected options (e.g., buying simple, multifunction trucks or special compactor trucks for transporting waste). The next section of the cycle includes setting service performance, estimating demand, analyzing financial and technical options, designing, and procuring. The next parts of the life cycle include construction; commissioning; operation; maintenance; refurbishment (a road every 15 years), with continuing performance monitoring; and divestiture (as an old truck) or decommissioning and redevelopment (as the demolition of an old school built in the 1920s and its replacement with a new school).

Figure 6.1 Asset Life Cycle

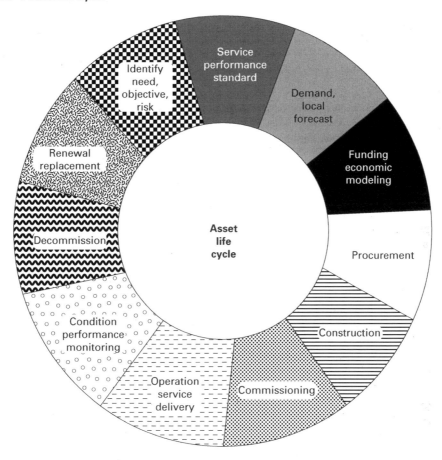

Asset Management Functions and Interlinks

No municipality would exist or survive without a sufficient portfolio of assets, which it needs to fulfill its various vital functions.

Asset Functions

The main reasons why managing assets should be central to local governments are listed below:

- *Material base*. Assets constitute a material base for municipal service delivery. Indeed,

referring to the list of typical assets shown above, many of them are used for core services that government is responsible for, whether they be local public records held in the city hall, water service, or schools. The quality of life in a particular jurisdiction and its attractiveness for people and businesses depend, to a substantial degree, on the quality of public infrastructure and related services.

- *Wealth*. Physical (capital) assets normally constitute the biggest share of local public wealth, as the example in table 6.1 illustrates. We can see that physical assets are the bulk of the wealth in both of these local governments, Los Angeles County and Warsaw, Poland. We can also notice big differences in local circumstances. Warsaw is loaded with land, which is a big reserve, whereas the value of its improvements and infrastructure is relatively low. In contrast, Los Angeles owns a much larger share of capital assets in buildings and infrastructure, and a third of the total is in financial assets (including equity investments); both play major roles in service delivery.

- *Liabilities*. Assets also can be associated with direct or contingent liabilities. For example, leakage of a main water or sewer line or eruption of an old water main is a liability of the owner municipality or its water company. Land that turns out to be contaminated may require costly remediation before the government can use or sell it. Real estate used as collateral for municipal borrowing has a direct liability risk of being lost if the local government fails to repay its loan on time.

- *Operating expenditures*. Holding a property incurs costs (electricity, water, cleaning, repair). Even holding vacant land has some costs, such as protecting it from squatters or from illegal dumping. Physical assets owned and controlled by local governments may

constitute a major expense, especially if they are properly maintained and repaired. For example, the cost of operation is the second largest after salaries in municipal expenses in Germany.

- *Source of revenue*. Government property can be a major source of revenues, whether one-time, as a sale of surplus property, or recurrent, including leasing land and commercial properties or granting concessions for operating municipal parking lots.

- *Economic development*. Local property holdings are often so large, especially in urban areas or in countries where land is owned by government, that they have a major impact on spatial and economic development, including by the private sector. The government can, in fact, have more control over physical assets than over local taxes and fees.

- *Values beyond the economic value*. Government property can have important value other than its "formal" (book or market) value, a factor that needs to be considered in decisions regarding some properties. For example, an old movie theater in a small town that is not functioning and not sustainable financially still may have substantial sentimental value for the generation of citizens for whom it was the center of entertainment in their youth.

Table 6.1 Assets in the Balance Sheets of Local Governments

Asset type	Los Angeles County, U.S. (%)	Warsaw. Poland (%)
Total assets (financial and capital)	100	100
Capital assets, total of which	67	94
Land and easements	28	80
Building, improvements	15	8
Infrastructure	20	8
Equipment	2	NA

- *Corruption.* Government real estate is historically prone to corruption and conflict of interest in many countries. For that reason managing it requires transparency and good governance.

Asset Management Interlinked with Other Areas of Local Governance

The idea that local government asset portfolios require special management is just emerging in most developing countries. Good asset management requires a multidisciplinary approach. It overlaps with real estate and public financial management and often also involves enterprise management (see figure 6.2). Given its nontraditional nature, asset management often does not fit well into more traditional areas of local government activities, such as budgeting.

Further, as figure 6.2 indicates, good asset management, especially in medium-size and large jurisdictions, requires specific expertise in both real estate markets and management. Local governments need such experts, either on staff or under contract for specific tasks. The *Guidebook on Packaging and Marketing Municipal Land to Investors*, from the Urban Institute, shows an example of how a real estate company marketed municipal land (for more information, see Urban Institute 2012a).

Figure 6.2   Interlinks between Asset and Other Management Areas

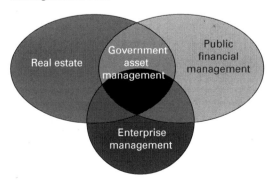

Asset and Financial Management

Asset management and financial management are linked in numerous ways. In particular, as figure 6.3 illustrates, each asset management activity has multiple implications for financial management. For example, if it is decided to acquire a new property (e.g., to build a school), the project has to be included in the municipality's capital investment plan; the municipality must identify and secure sources of financing and process the project through the capital budget.

Framework for Strategic Asset Management

Why do governments need property and infrastructure at all? The simple and traditional answer is, to be able to provide services to their citizens according to legal requirements or local traditions. For example, if primary education or fire protection is the responsibility of the local government, school buildings and fire stations (along with fire trucks) are needed. In practice, local governments often own properties for many reasons. Some property has accumulated historically by default; some are symbols of power and prestige. Some is confiscated because of unpaid taxes or was abandoned by the owner. Among nontraditional reasons for owning property, two stand out: (a) to support local economic development and (b) to generate additional, nontax revenues. Another important consideration is that the government is a guardian of public property that should be preserved for future generations, such as forests, parks, grazing lands, and wetlands.

Strategic asset management of real estate and land has four components: inventorying, analytical accounting, portfolio management, and asset strategy and implementation (summarized in table 6.2). If it does not cover these components in a satisfactory way, a local government may face substantial losses either in wealth or in service scope and quality.

Figure 6.3   Management of Physical Assets and Implications for Local Finance

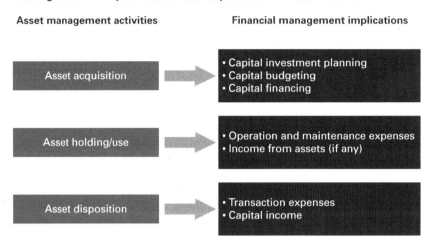

Asset management activities

Financial management implications

Asset acquisition → • Capital investment planning
• Capital budgeting
• Capital financing

Asset holding/use → • Operation and maintenance expenses
• Income from assets (if any)

Asset disposition → • Transaction expenses
• Capital income

For strategic management of municipal engineering infrastructure (e.g., water, wastewater, roads), the framework that is conceptually similar but adjusted to infrastructure specifics is presented in box 6.2. Notice that this framework emphasizes that financial planning and life-cycle management are at the core of good asset management.

Inventorying

Maintaining clear and up-to-date asset records and inventories is vital, since we cannot manage something if we do not know it exists. Poor land records encourage corruption, encroachment, crime, and health hazards. For instance, hundreds of millions of people live on municipal land without permits (slums discussed in chapter 2), and abandoned land is often used for illegal waste disposal, inducing environmental and health hazards. Protecting municipal property may be costly, but removing people, businesses, or waste from land is often far more expensive. In the developing world, many municipalities are unaware of the extent of their assets or, at the very least, the property and infrastructure over which they have domain if not possession. An

asset inventory can be established in various ways, but it is easiest if there is a reliable land cadastre in the country. Without a cadastre, an initial asset inventory can be prepared during a street addressing survey (Farvacque-Vitkovic et al. 2006). The survey identifies the general layout of municipal streets, records street length, attaches a metric numbering system to the buildings, and notes the type of use of each plot (residential, business, utilities, empty lot, or other use). If the addressing survey is supplemented with identification of urban fixtures (public standpipes, bus shelters, telephone booths, and the like) or specific surveys of street systems or utilities, simple use of the address directory will provide the basis for an asset inventory. Other information can be gradually added to the inventory, such as the ownership status of the facility or land, property appraisals, and estimated cost of upkeep.

Analytical Accounting

The analytical accounts on properties are like personal identity cards for the properties (they used to be handwritten on cards). They should note key legal and technical information such

Table 6.2 Framework for Strategic Asset Management

Inventorying

- Develop and maintain comprehensive records of properties owned by the local government (including properties managed and used by various municipal departments and enterprises).

Analytical Accounting

- Develop and maintain a property management and accounting system on a property-by-property basis (including all revenues, costs, and occupancy/tenant records), specifically for the purpose of asset management (should not be confused with the bookkeeping records).
- Include the value of each property in the accounting database and include financial liens against each property.
- Formalize in writing the contractual relationships regarding property with all tenants and users of municipal property.
- Use private sector property management approaches for improving government property management.

Portfolio Management

- Formulate a strategic role for real estate in attaining municipal goals.
- Develop classification of real estate by its role in performing governmental functions and apply this classification while conducting an inventory.
- Develop and use class-specific financial tools and performance standards.
- Monitor property and portfolio financial performance.
- Implement a portfolio management approach, including proactive management of social use and surplus portfolios.
- Make transparent rules on how municipal property (including land) is allocated to third-party (private, nongovernmental) users.
- Develop and implement policies aimed at rationing property demands and consumption by governmental departments and social users.
- Introduce a transparent process of multiyear capital investment planning.
- Make asset managers accountable through regular reporting.

Strategy and Implementation

- Develop and implement an asset management strategy as a guiding document.
- Establish a centralized real estate authority for overseeing or direct control over asset management.
- Devise written policies and decision-making roles for the acquisition, holding, and disposition of assets.
- Develop in-house real estate expertise and use outside real estate professionals as needed.
- Set up incentives for more efficient use and management of municipal property assets.

Source: Kaganova 2008.

as size, location, ownership, and use, but also any rent contract and revenues; the date, nature, and cost of main refurbishments and replacements; and even scheduled future renovations four to five years ahead. Municipalities in the developing world often lack analytic records and correspondingly lack strategic management. They can only react to negative events, for example, having to repair a water main after it has exploded. Without scheduled cleaning of sewer mains, in many Asian cities from Karachi to Dhaka clogged mains cause a mix of storm

Box 6.2 Essential Elements of the Framework for Infrastructure Asset Management Planning

1. What do you have and where is it (inventory)?
2. What is it worth (costs, replacement rates)?
3. What is its condition and expected remaining service life (condition and capability analysis)?
4. What is the level of service expectation, and what needs to be done (capital and operating plans)?
5. When do you need to do it (capital and operating plans)?
6. How much will it cost, and what is the acceptable level of risk(s) (short- and long-term financial plan)?
7. How do you ensure long-term affordability (short- and long-term financial plan)?

Source: Managing Infrastructure Assets, 2005.

water and wastewater to back up onto the streets, and people must walk in it for days. Poor analytic accounts often mean lack of money set aside for proper maintenance.

Portfolio Management

As a basic principle, local governments must aim to expand services, and to do that they have to increase public wealth. The principal rule of portfolio management is that proceeds from asset divestitures should be reinvested into another form of capital assets. Thus, divestitures should be part of a plan to invest for better services or wealth. Sometimes cities sell properties without good marketing and at prices below market because they are in desperate need of cash for operating expenses. In doing so, they are consuming public wealth, wealth of the current and future generations.

Asset Strategy

Asset strategy has multiple interrelationships with other areas of municipal management. It is linked to urban planning, for example, through a long-term master plan that indicates

the direction and nature of development and expansion of the city, as agricultural land is transformed into urban, defining where new public facilities will be needed. Long-term plans also help the city develop based on citizens' priorities. A medium-term capital improvement plan, with specific proposals, signals what to sell for generating money (if needed) and what to build in the next three to five years. Operating with this approach, the local government needs to look at all local assets as portfolios in which elements are changed, developed, or replaced to implement the city's strategy.

The frameworks for strategic asset management presented in table 6.2 and box 6.2 are quite ambitious and require time and effort to understand and implement. However, a local government can consider the table and the box menus and begin with those items that have the highest priority in local circumstances and are politically and administratively feasible. Such an approach, tailored to local realities, has worked well in a number of transitional countries such as Croatia, Kyrgyzstan, and Serbia. A subset of activities from the list were implemented, to various degrees,

Box 6.3 Croatian Cities: Initial Asset Management Model

1. Introduction of an information system on the property-by-property level
2. Transitional issues
3. Property classification
4. Real estate and business appraisal
5. Operating statements for income-generating properties or portfolios
6. Intensive financial analysis of portfolios, properties, and projects
7. Deregulation of business rentals and improvement of rental practices
8. Quantification and monitoring of direct and indirect property-related subsidies obtained by tenants and users of local government's real estate
9. Reporting on property
10. Management consolidation
11. Comprehensive asset management plan

Source: Kaganova 2008.

by several cities in Croatia (Varazdin, Split, Rijeka, Karlovac). Box 6.3 summarizes the Initial Asset Management Model, which addressed 11 priority actions from the list in table 6.2.

Entities in Charge of Asset Management

Asset management is complex and is usually a joint activity of units and entities in a local government. Even units dedicated to asset management, such as a property department or a municipal company, usually cover just one particular form or segment of assets, such as a municipal land corporation that manages vacant land. The next section summarizes the work of the main local entities in charge of asset management.

The Council

The council or local assembly plays two roles in asset management—it is the highest representative of the local public ownership and chief decision maker but is also the highest regulator of asset management in the broad sense.

- *Chief decision maker.* The council is the highest body to approve large-scale, high-value asset transactions, especially those related to asset alienation (sales, use as collateral for borrowing) or acquisition. For example, the

council should approve asset strategy for a list of assets above a value threshold that are subject to disposition during a coming year, along with a capital investment program. The council may appoint an asset committee of council and external members to draft strategy, policy, and regulations; analyze large, difficult cases; and advise the council on options (see Urban Institute 2012b).

- *Regulator.* The council issues local regulations that define the rules; for example, a local ordinance on procedures for leasing and selling municipal assets or environmental and safety regulations that affect the use and management of assets.

The Mayor's Office

The office of the mayor prepares documents that go to the council for approval and signs major real estate contracts on behalf of the local government. The council may also delegate asset transactions below a certain value threshold to the mayor.

Departments

Most municipal departments are engaged in asset management. A number of them are focused more on portfolio management, such as the departments of finance and legal affairs. Others deal with individual properties, for example, the departments overseeing works, services, and infrastructure.

- *The finance department* (sometimes along with the treasury) defines fiscal targets related to asset management for the next budget year, for example, expected revenues from land and property sales or leases or gains from planned reductions in property-related operating expenses. The finance department or the treasury unit deals specifically with the financial assets, including cash, bonds, shareholdings, or other securities, for several related reasons. On the one hand, financial and intangible assets are part of the city's wealth and assets; on the other hand, they are intertwined with the physical assets. Financial assets represent reserves that can be used to finance real asset investments. Money gained from sale of assets can and should be treated as financial assets, as long as it is not used to fund physical assets again. Investing financial assets is a risky business, and clear prudential rules are required to ensure that the invested money is not lost. In this sense physical, financial, and intangible assets are transient forms of one another in the asset portfolio. The management of financial assets is discussed further in chapter 7.

- *The legal department* often deals with matters related to asset acquisition and disposition; for example, it will prepare and often sign lease and sales contracts and keeps all legal documents related to local government asset ownership.

- *Specialized departments,* such as the department of works and services, often are responsible for implementing capital investment projects.

- *Line departments* usually monitor, guide, and represent the users of municipal properties, with shared responsibility for operation, maintenance, and repair of the physical assets used. For example, the department of education is a user of some municipal buildings or premises and also may share some work with schools that report to it (such as assembling annually the schools' requests for capital repair funding).

- *Budgetary units* and semibudgetary service units (schools, health centers) are users of properties and often are responsible for their day-to-day operation and maintenance.

Municipal Companies

Municipal companies exist in most countries and often hold, use, and manage large portfolios of municipal land, other real estate, infrastructure facilities and networks, and movable property such as equipment, cars, and specialized vehicles. Municipal companies vary widely in purpose and legal (corporate) form. They can be utilities or specialized companies, such as municipal land development corporations (discussed also in chapter 2).

- Municipal companies as independent legal entities are considered municipal investments. Ideally assets donated at the establishment of these companies are accounted as divestitures or invested assets; however, in developing countries the ownership status of many assets, such as land parcels or water pipe networks, is blurred. Thus, most of the physical assets these companies use are recorded on the balance sheet of the companies, not in local government folios. Two problems are common in such cases: (a) local governments do not have data on land and buildings held by the companies, whereas the companies may hold more land than they need; and (b) the property is exposed to business risks if the companies are engaged in commercial activities.

- Municipal service companies may create contingent liabilities for the municipality.

First, the service responsibility remains on the shoulders of the municipality if the company defaults; as a result, municipalities often heavily subsidize their service companies to maintain vital services. Second, the municipality, as the sole owner, has full responsibility for the debts and guarantees of its companies and may default itself as a result of a default by its company. Local governments often have partial ownership (some percentage of shares) of various corporate entities, with shared gains and risks.

- Local governments may establish specialized government agencies that are hybrids of a sort: they combine a regulatory power of the government with elements of the corporate structure and powers of a company. Examples include the Urban Renewal Authority of Hong Kong, or the Water Service Authorities in India and Pakistan. Such agencies, with mixed authority and investor functions, can entail intrinsic conflicts of interest and thus are not recommended for general practice.

Public-Private Partnerships

Specific facilities or properties and sometimes whole portfolios can be managed, during various stages of the property life cycles, by public-private partnerships (PPPs). Under common good practices, the private partner manages the entity under a contract between a local government and the private partner. Assets either remain in full public ownership (management contract) or become part of a joint venture if a separate legal entity is created (more details in chapter 7).

Improving Asset Management in Local Government

Asset management is complex and requires both professional skill and consistent effort. Improving asset management from scratch requires a concerted initial effort and must be continued as a routine activity over the years.

This section addresses the challenges of initiating asset management improvement. Four specific steps or groups of tasks are vital in the effort.

Challenges

There are four main challenges to improvement of asset management: The first is the *political cycle*. Good asset management requires long-term commitment and leadership, which often conflicts with the election cycle mentality of politicians. A visionary mayor or treasurer is needed to initiate and continue improvement of asset management. The city council also needs to be educated on its importance.

The second challenge concerns the *sequencing of actions*. There is no obvious or universal sequence, and so it has to be defined locally. Intentions should also be tailored to the *human capacity* of the local government and its ability to adopt new techniques. Last, better asset management needs strong *ownership of the process;* it cannot be introduced by consultants. The local government needs to internalize the process; consultants or providers of technical assistance can only facilitate or supply approaches, techniques, and training. Box 6.4 summarizes the case of Kathmandu, which exemplifies the difficulty of correcting previous poor asset management.

Initial Steps to Improving Asset Management

Practical experience shows that initial steps to improving asset management include the following:

- *Identification of problems and areas needing improvement.* Such an assessment, coupled with recommendations on means to achieve improvement, often requires outside experts working jointly with knowledgeable people in the local government. For example, energy efficiency audits are effective new instruments for asset management improvement.

- *Focal person.* Someone in the local government should become responsible for the process.

Box 6.4 Campaign Asset Management—Road Widening in Kathmandu

The recent case of Kathmandu, Nepal, shows that abandoned assets and inconsistent asset management induce costly corrective actions and severe tensions. The local government of Kathmandu has not maintained its road assets or protected its ownership of public roads for decades. The city owns 15- to 20-meter strips of land along main roads. The roads, however, were built decades ago and were narrow, covering typically only eight to 10 meters with asphalt road and walkways. The rest remained abandoned "no-man's land," with no ownership rights enforced by the city. Encroachment on these belts along city roads has grown over time in Nepal.

The Kathmandu Valley Town Development Enforcement Committee launched a campaign early in 2011 to widen 400 kilometers of city artery roads, based on a notice published in *Nepal Gazette* on July 4, 1977. The enforcement followed the ruling 33 years later and resulted in the need for demolishing an

enormous volume and value of assets. Road widening is now vital for developing the city, but it means demolition of structures including all or part of shops, homes, and commercial buildings built over decades.

The government will provide compensation for only those structures that were built before the 1977 public notice. As a result, many owners will lose their shops or living space without compensation. Huge tensions and demonstrations erupted when the government started bulldozing the illegal structures, as shown in the accompanying photo (figure B6.4.1). Although as a basic principle nobody should build structures on public land, it would have been better to enforce the ownership rights of the city in a timely manner and avoid demolishing properties. Because of the desperate need for better roads, the street widening gradually won strong citizen support. About half the new roads had been built by the end of 2012.

Figure B6.4.1 Demolished Buildings to Enforce Right of Way

Source: Himalayan Times, February 4, 2012.

- *Task force.* If an asset management unit or department does not already exist, it is not advisable to start by creating one. Instead, it is better to establish an asset committee in the council or a temporary, cross-department task force on asset management, under the auspices of the mayor or treasurer.

- *Action plan.* It is imperative to identify priorities and adopt an action plan. The task force should work according to the specific set of priorities established based on the assessment recommendations. Moreover, the task force should act strictly according to its action plan (refer to box 6.3 above, on Croatia's experience).

Inventorying Capital Assets—Step 1

If inventory records do not exist, inventorying capital assets will be the highest priority for a local government and its task force on improving asset management. Usually various records exist that can be used as initial sources of data for an inventory, such as accounting, land, and technical records, though they may be uncoordinated, inconsistent, and incomplete. The legal department or line departments typically have some records of existing capital assets that will be useful to feed into the inventory. Often asset ledgers are maintained by accountants of local governments. Department managers and technical experts can also provide valuable information on the current condition of capital assets. The goal is to identify all capital assets, arrange them into clusters and logical order, and then assemble data for their management. If a street addressing program has been implemented, it will be extremely helpful for identifying and locating municipal assets. The Urban Audit (discussed in Chapter 5) can be another important tool to help (1) identify/inventory, (2) locate and (3) map existing municipal assets. See box 6.5.

Grouping Assets

Assets are often grouped in the records by asset type, by service sector, or by holder or manager (i.e., municipal department). Typical groupings might be as follows:

- Utility and sanitation assets, including sewer and water systems, solid waste facilities, and municipal electric and lighting systems

- Highways, roads, and bridges

- Public buildings (in large cities, this portfolio can be further specialized: government use, education, sport, culture, public housing, etc.)

- Land or rights to land

- Certain improvements to land other than buildings

- Certain equipment, vehicles, and furnishings.

Table 6.3 shows an example of a basic inventory of buildings. The task force should decide what data need to be collected. It is important to make sure that the data collected and maintained satisfy practical asset management needs, and not only formal bookkeeping requirements regulated by the central government. For example, readers will notice that table 6.3 records such characteristics as building condition and occupancy but lacks an important column on estimated market value of properties.

Geographic information systems (GIS) are becoming increasingly affordable for local governments. They help tremendously in the precise identification of assets, as well as provide interactive maps for strategic planning and daily asset management. However, as summarized in box 6.5, it is better to start simply. Inventorying should be driven by practical asset management needs and local realities. In places where useful inventory records do not exist, it is wise to start the inventory from a simple Excel spreadsheet, which later can be imported into a more advanced database that can be linked to GIS.

Table 6.3 Example of a Basic Building Inventory

NN	Property current function	Address	Cadastre number	Total floor area, sq. m	Land area, sq. m	Year of construction	Building condition	Building book value, thousands, local currency	Current occupancy, %	Notes
1	2	3	4	5	6	7	8	9	10	11
1	Administrative building	Chapichi St, 4	170,477	7,500	2,600	1985	good	80,670	80	
2	Kindergarten local government 1	Sevani St, 2	NA	580	350	1980	satisfactory	3,500	100	
3	Kindergarten local government 2	River St, 57	NA	990	690	1964	bad	NA	33	Repair planned
4	Culture Center	Karmin St, 39	NA	6,500	4,500	1984	bad	61,732	50	

Land and Infrastructure Inventorying

Land inventorying and inventorying of infrastructure assets (networks) are usually more complex than inventorying buildings and premises. The basic elements of a land asset inventory are as follows:

- Location of parcel, in address form, and cadastral coordinates with map, if possible

- Size of parcel in square feet, square meters, acres, or hectares

- Ownership or entity having legal control rights, plus any leasing, right-of-way, deed, mortgage, or other legal obligations to third parties

- Current use, that is, actual use(s), with the most important distinction being vacant or built-up, with further typology for built-up. The land use description can be expanded to include qualifiers about construction on the parcel (legal or illegal; size of building, structure, condition, and dates of main installation and refurbishments).

- Legal restrictions on development or use, including zoning or other limitations on development, use, or sale

- Classification for management, including distinguishing whether properties are core assets used for mandatory functions of the government, are used for noncore activities, or are surplus property available for future public uses (see Step 2 below).

The land inventory can be compiled as a separate exercise by the local government, as part of a national cadastre agency's systematic registration that aims to identify and register all private and public land, or as part of a street addressing program. A combination of all could happen; a local government effort to inventory its land, coordinated with systematic national registration, can be the most effective approach. However, experiences show that preparation of a full land cadastre in urban areas can require a decade or more. Where a national land cadastre for public properties does not yet exist, a separate inventorying initiated by a local government should be pursued as part of a street addressing program, regardless of whether some precise cadastre data might be missing. In either case, how to organize a realistic and inexpensive process will depend on a number of factors, one of which is what kind of maps are available for the process. The best case is a digital parcel map from the cadastre superimposed on a recent aerial photo or satellite image.

Developing an asset inventory might be a long and incremental process, and it is important to conduct it by stages and according to priorities: (1) list assets, starting from the most important, then (2) gradually add legal, technical, and value data. To continue to be useful, land and building inventory records need to be regularly updated to capture changes in property ownership, land uses, and legal restrictions. An important issue to address at some moment is to decide in which local department the land inventory database should be housed and maintained.

Infrastructure inventorying should start from defining key components of the systems to be inventoried. Typical municipal infrastructure systems may include the following:

- Water systems: wells, river diversions, dams, transmission lines, water treatment plants, treated water storage facilities, distribution pipelines, fire hydrants, pumping stations, and water meters

- Wastewater systems: collection pipelines, manholes, pumping stations, wastewater treatment plants, sewage lagoons, sludge disposal areas

- Storm drainage systems: canals, ditches, pipelines, manholes, storm water inlets, flood control reservoirs, erosion protection, dikes

- Solid waste collection and disposal facilities: collection containers, collection vehicles, recycling facilities, landfills

- Streets and roads: roadway surfacing, adjoining sidewalks, adjoining lighting, signage, bridges, traffic control devices, drainage systems.

Specific basic data will vary for each category of infrastructure elements but in general would include the length (or quantity) of the elements; size (according to some classification); age (according to 5-to-10-year intervals), if known; material; and condition. For example, inventorying of roads by local governments in Ethiopia included the following categories:

- Importance: arterial road, subarterial, collector, and local

- Surface: asphalt, gravel, all-weather (unclassified), and earth roads

- Size (width): >30-meter reserve; 25–30-meter reserve; 20–25-meter reserve; 15–20-meter reserve; 5–10-meter reserve.

Location of elements can be identified with the help of handheld devices that have become increasingly available and inexpensive. As with inventorying land and buildings, it makes sense to prioritize and stage the inventorying of infrastructure, and it is important to periodically update the records as a part of asset management.

Classify Capital Assets—Step 2

What to do with a particular physical asset depends on why a city has that asset at all. For example, it may have a school building with a roof that needs replacement, but by law the local government is responsible for primary education. The asset might also be a nonfunctional, decrepit old movie theater that is in the municipal portfolio for historical reasons, whereas the city has no legal obligations to run movies. These examples illustrate a fundamental principle of good asset management, namely, that the asset portfolio should be aligned with the functions and responsibilities of the government. Properties can be usefully sorted into groups according to municipal function:

- *Mandatory* properties needed for performing the local government's functions as stipulated by law

- *Discretionary* properties needed for performing voluntary functions supported and performed for social, political, or other reasons

- *Surplus or income-generating* properties not needed for either of the first two but in the portfolio for historical or business reasons.

Legislation usually defines some functions as exclusive or shared responsibilities of local governments. Often, the functions include provision of water and sewers, local roads and parks, cemeteries, preschool and primary education, and local culture and sport. However, very often the law is silent regarding the quantity or composition of facilities that the government needs to fulfill the functions. For example, exactly which cultural facilities should a government provide? How many sport fields, parks, and social (subsidized) apartments? Because the law is silent, those become matters for local government budget and policy to decide. For example, should a local government operate and maintain all sports facilities in its territory? How much of the cost should be shifted to users through fees?

Wise asset management is not just building and maintenance, but also implies adjustment and remodeling of assets to suit current needs and priorities. For example, during recent renovation of a school built in the 1970s, the city of Katowice, Poland, redesigned the internal floor plans, so that usable floor area substantially increased, and new classroom and workshop spaces were carved from previously unused, empty halls and corridors.

Financing Principles and Goals

For rational responses to uneasy questions regarding financing assets, it is useful to formulate financial principles and goals for each group of properties and follow them in asset management.

A. Use of properties for mandatory functions should be optimized by the following practices:

1. Increasing the efficient use of public facilities by requiring budget organizations to justify and reasonably minimize their demand for space

2. Minimizing operating costs, without jeopardizing property condition and value

3. Locating government offices and services in functional, not prime, areas and in modest, adequate buildings and facilities

4. Understanding the best use of an asset and undertaking cost-benefit analyses to justify governmental use of particular properties

5. Investment in the repair and replacement of mandatory properties, as an absolute priority over investment in discretionary and surplus properties.

B. Assets for discretionary functions should be optimized by the following:

1. Analyzing actual costs and sharing them with stakeholders, to facilitate the best decisions

2. Generating program alternatives to reduce direct and indirect, property-related subsidies as much as possible, particularly by means of the following:

   — Requesting users or their sponsors to maintain the property themselves

   — Encouraging users or sponsors to lease unused portions of premises or territory to other commercial or nonprofit entities and accurately account to the owner for resulting net revenues, and making appropriate adjustments to subsidies

   — Establishing clear contractual relations with the users, which stipulate mutual responsibilities for property maintenance and allocation of the costs and revenues

   — Monitoring use and occupancy to ensure that unused space is reassigned to more important users

— Arranging the sharing of facilities by multiple groups.

C. Use of surplus property should also be optimized:

1. Leasing property for the most profitable use to maximize revenues

2. Periodically evaluating the income-generating performance of these properties using alternative investment benchmarks

3. Making selective capital improvements to enhance income generation

4. Selling underperforming properties to generate one-time revenues that can be put to better use (Such sales need to be timed carefully, to avoid quick sales in depressed markets.)

5. Reducing maintenance costs and liability on properties that cannot be leased or sold

6. Ruling out investment in acquisition or construction of new surplus properties on principle (It is not good policy for local government to engage in speculative real estate.) and especially if capital investment needs of the mandatory properties and facilities are not yet provided for (A local government should not invest in building a shopping mall, especially if the local schools or roads are not in perfect repaired condition.).

Usually, neither the classification nor the financial policy principles are required by law. However, because this issue is strategically important and will have both short- and long-term effects on the local citizens, it is recommended to have the classification approved by the local elected body.

Establish Policy for Good Asset Management—Step 3
Adopting explicit written policies on key asset management issues is a good practice. Many local governments in the developing world have no such policies, in part because of the limited discretion of officials and politicians. Lack of written policies does not imply that there is no policy, however, because existing practices, whatever they are, always shape some informal, perhaps vague, policy. Table 6.4 suggests key issues to address and key principles to take into account in formulating written asset management policies (for a detailed discussion, see Peterson and Kaganova 2010).

Ensure Transparency and Inform the Public—Step 4
Transparency is a simple, inexpensive, and effective way to support good asset management and curb corruption and conflict of interest. In asset management, many violations of public interests take place at specific moments in the property life cycle. The areas prone to violations include (a) property acquisition or reconstruction; (b) property disposition (sales); and (c) allocation of rights in property to third parties, including rights of use or lease to the private sector or transfer to municipal enterprises. These are the areas where anticorruption mechanisms should be built into the asset management process (Péteri and Schaeffer 2007).

Transparency of Information
The simplest form of transparency is transparency of information. Pure facts about municipal property, if properly disclosed, constitute a powerful instrument to make local governments and decision makers accountable (box 6.6 summarizes the case of Kyrgyzstan). Hence it is good to introduce at least annual asset reports, presented to the local elected body (council, assembly), published, and made available to the public. The report should be factual and specific and should summarize information on property holdings, transactions, and investments. Good practice reports would contain information and data on the following key areas:

Table 6.4 Asset Management Policies

Policy issue	Key principles to include
Valuing and pricing assets for allocation or disposition	• Market valuation should be required before any transaction, even among government entities (for example, when municipal land or property is contributed to municipal enterprises or public-private partnerships).
	• Allocation of surplus property, including vacant land, for private use should take place in exchange for the property's market value, whether in money or in-kind; any deviation from this rule (giving the property free or for less than its market value) should be preapproved by the elected body.
Allocation: Procedures of land and property allocation	• Procedures should be transparent, according to written rules.
	• Allocation should be mainly in the form of competitive procurement, with cases permitting noncompetitive allocation carefully limited by the rules.
	• Allocations should mainly be for the highest price offered, with other options (such as multiple criteria for choice of winner) limited to special cases only.
Rights: Which rights are allocated	• Ownership or limited, temporary rights such as leases.
	• Permitted land uses and mandatory land use parameters (e.g., a flow-to-area ratio) defined clearly before land is allocated.
Proceeds: Use of sale proceeds	• Revenues from sales of capital assets should be used for capital investment or repayment of long-term debt only, to maintain the wealth of the municipality and share it with next generations.
Acquisition: How to acquire land from the private sector	• Acquisitions only according to priorities for capital investment preapproved by the local elected body as a part of capital investment planning.
	• Based on voluntary purchases as much as possible (i.e., minimizing expropriation).
	• Voluntary purchases should be based on open solicitation of proposals from private sector sellers.
Transparency	• Issues of transparency of information on capital assets (see text under Step 4).

Source: Peterson and Kaganova 2010.

Box 6.6 Power of Information Transparency

An inventory of municipal land in one of Kyrgyzstan's cities revealed that 86 hectares of municipal land had been allocated to 178 various private land tenants (legal entities and physical persons) free of charge, which was against the law and also represented a very large portion of municipal land, given that land leases made up only 11.5 hectares. When this information was presented to the mayor, he paled, literally, because he immediately recognized negative legal and public relations implications, in addition to forgone revenues for the city budget.

Inventory and tenants: Inventory of municipal property assets (buildings, land) directly controlled by the local government, its budgetary organizations, and municipal enterprises.

A *directory of public properties* (land, buildings, premises) used or leased by private and nongovernment tenants, with key characteristics of tenancy (for how long, at what price or payment).[1]

Transactions with public property: A directory of all acquisition and disposition transactions: from whom acquired, for what price, and through what procedure (e.g., public auction, unsolicited bid, debt-equity swap, donation, compensation of owners on lost property, confiscation), and file copies of contracts.

Capital investments: Quantitative, project-by-project information on municipal capital investments.

Transparency of Procedures

Another important part of transparency is transparency of procedures and decisions. All rules regarding allocating public property to nongovernmental users should be in writing and made available to the public (in an asset policy statement). The public should have access to key events related to public property, such as meetings of city government and auctions or opening of sealed bids.

Mass Media

It is impossible to overestimate the importance of mass media and watchdog groups in building public demand and expectations regarding transparency. At the same time, ensuring that public disclosure of information and asset management proceedings are open to the public should not be left to journalists but should be codified in law, or at least local regulations.

Finally, broad awareness and education campaigns are needed. Even formulating requests for information or asset management reports requires some technical knowledge, and that

is lacking in most countries in general. Hence there is a need to educate governments, the public, watchdog groups, and mass media.

Financial Implications of Asset Management

Good asset management has multiple ties with financial management and benefits from using the tools of financial analysis. Financial management benefits from information generated in asset management, which can identify forgone revenues as well as financial gains for the municipal budget, support service cost reduction, and help quantify service efficiency, as well as identify areas for financial policy intervention.

Identifying Potential Gains for the Municipal Budget

Let us think for a minute of property-related opportunities for budgetary gains in a city or town. Table 6.5 addresses such opportunities.

Financial Analysis of Property or Portfolio

Good asset management is not possible without financial analysis of properties and portfolios. Some basic analysis tools for improving asset performance are mentioned below (more details in Urban Institute 2012b). This section offers a brief summary of areas, activities, and tools of financial analysis, including valuation of individual properties or portfolios, income statements on assets, analysis of subsidies, financial analysis instruments and methods, financial planning, and life-cycle costing of assets. This chapter focuses on how to use these rather than on the underlying mathematics and financial or statistical theory.

Valuation

Knowing an asset's value is important in many situations: when property is considered for allocation for a specific use; when its performance is evaluated; when it should be priced for selling or

Table 6.5 Main Asset-Related Revenue and Saving Opportunities from a Budgetary Viewpoint

Sources of forgone revenues	Potential savings on expenses
Operating revenues	*Operating expenses*
• Hidden price subsidies to private lessees, users of municipal property (land tenants, retail tenants, NGOs). • Low rent collection rate, below the private sector benchmarks. • Self-inflicted limitations on rental revenues from municipal land and property, from excessive limitations on property use.	• Operation and maintenance of municipal properties and infrastructure is one of cities' biggest operating expenses (in Germany, it is second only to salaries; in Warsaw, it is about 12 percent to 20 percent of the city's total operating expenses). Optimization of management and operation can save 10 percent to 15 percent of this cost without reducing property holdings or outsourcing maintenance and operations. • Rationalizing property portfolios against need, costs, and benefits (e.g., less floor space per employee, moving two departments or services into a single building, and the like). • Own or lease? Moving to owned buildings instead of leasing space in private ones can be justified in the long term in some cases.
Capital revenues	*Capital expenses*
• Selling land or property at the bottom of the real estate market. • Undisposed surplus properties that could be sold. • Self-imposed limitations on revenues from municipal land and property sales because of excessive limitations on property use.	• More efficient capital investment project implementation and replacement of public expenses by private through PPPs. For example, public land can be provided to a private developer to build a public parking garage in exchange for the right to use a portion of the site for mixed-use development. • Selling a government property that is difficult and costly to maintain (office building, plant) and leasing back sufficient parts of it from the private buyer.

Note: NGO = nongovernmental organization; PPP = public-private partnership.

leasing out; or when the city needs to estimate its wealth, to name a few. Which values do asset managers need to know and why? In this regard, there are two groups of government properties. For properties that can be alienated (sold), the market value (the price a willing buyer would offer in fair competition)[2] is the key to monitoring and controlling performance. As part of the real estate management process, the financial performance of each property is evaluated against its market value, often estimated by collecting real transaction prices of comparable property.

The Book Value

The book value of properties functions like a birth certificate that reflects a one-time, real value attached to the property; the record remains in the accounting ledgers forever. Traditionally, accounting values should by law reflect the historical cost of acquisition or development, reduced by depreciation calculated by the formula defined by central government regulations. More advanced accrual accounting systems account the depreciation as costs and set funds aside for future replacement of the given asset. They may also incorporate periodic adjustment of initial construction costs for inflation or major refurbishment. An important conceptual issue to recognize is that the book value of a property has limited meaning for decision making in asset management. The book value of a property does not indicate the price a willing buyer would offer, and so it has limited connection to the current market value unless it was incurred very recently.

For local public assets that are not alienable under any reasonable assumptions (such as bridges, roads), the contemporary approach is to estimate the so-called replacement cost, that is, how much it would cost to rebuild a property or structure of similar quality. One can also estimate the life-cycle cost, which consists of the acquisition cost and the cost of operating, maintaining, and repairing the property during its lifetime.

Estimating Market Value

Contemporary property valuation practices rely on three main appraisal methods or approaches to estimating market value, each used to the extent that recent valid and relevant data are available:

- *Replacement cost.* This approach sums the estimated construction cost to replace the building, including architectural and other "soft" costs, and the market value of the land.

- *Sales comparison.* Before putting it on the market, the potential price of a property can be estimated by collecting price data on similar properties recently sold in fair market transactions. If this is the only relevant information obtainable, there remains the question of how similar those sold properties are to the property being priced.

- *Income capitalization.* This approach estimates the value of the property based on its revenue stream under its current use. In its simplest form, this approach uses the formula

Market value = annual net *cash flow* divided by a *rate of return.*

The result depends on two main factors: the present use and the "hurdle interest rate," meaning the rate the municipality could realistically obtain for a comparable investment. Thus, the estimated market value is adequate to the extent that the present use reflects the real potential of the building.

Box 6.7 summarizes the main valuation methods used for different kinds of property.

It is important to remember that the appraisal of a property is only an estimate of its value,

---

Box 6.7 Which Valuation Method to Use?

The type of property may influence the selection of an appraisal approach. The following are examples:

- *Apartments and houses not rented.* The sales comparison approach is probably best. The cost approach may be helpful, but for older properties it may require a large adjustment for depreciation to obtain a helpful result.

- *Business rental property.* Income capitalization and sales comparison are the most useful. The cost approach may be useful for newer properties.
- *Vacant land.* Sales comparison is the main practical approach because there is no income to capitalize, and there is no construction. The approach called "residual land value" can be used as well.

Source: Urban Institute 2012b.

which ultimately is determined in the market-place. An appraisal based on multiple approaches to value is more credible than one based only on a single approach. The projected value strongly depends on the appraiser's perspective. For example, if a building generates net revenue of 20,000 rupees per year, and the hurdle rate of return is 9 percent, then it signals a value of about 222,000 rupees for the municipality. However, a willing buyer who feels that the building can produce 40,000 rupees per year might easily offer 300,000 rupees or more for the property in competitive bidding. This example illustrates that these valuations are just opinions, and results depend on the reality of the assumptions behind the valuation. Another lesson is that the municipal asset managers should be aware of the ways of thinking of willing buyers.

The most important methodological issue related to valuing local government properties is to introduce into local government practice the notion of market value, as it is understood in international practice and in the private sector. The problem is that some local governments use nonstandard definitions that underestimate the wealth concentrated in real estate and distort the city's ability to judge its equity position.

Municipalities often sell a building at a price that is too low because they do not account for the fact that their present revenue stream is low compared to the market. They also have to determine the hurdle rate to consider—the bank short-term deposit rate, the borrowing rate, the yield of bonds? In short, it is wise to compare not only the market value of a building but also the yield rates and revenue streams of comparable assets. For example, what is the revenue base for the planned sale of a 5,000-square-meter covered market that generates 200,000 rupees per month, when a comparable market in another part of the city earns 400,000 rupees per month? The discrepancy might result from poor lease contracts or corruption, in which case basing the price on revenue of 200,000 rupees per month might be a

mistake. The reference revenue could well be in the range of 400,000 rupees per month.

Operating Statements for Properties or Portfolios

Rational evaluation of the financial performance of properties requires information on all revenues and all expenses associated with each. A standard format is an *operating statement,* which consists of a summary of income and expenses (also called an "income statement"). It is important to be flexible in formatting the statement, adding or deleting classes of income and expenses as appropriate. Box 6.8 presents a template income statement for a housing unit, with guiding notes.

It is useful to establish the report so that the actual results can be compared item by item with the budget and with the results from the previous year. For portfolios of homogeneous properties (such as rental apartments), a portfolio-level income statement also should be produced.

A common problem in many local governments is that financial performance data are seldom collected on a property-by-property basis. Very often, data are not collected (especially about expenses) or are presented only at an aggregated level (such as costs of fuel, electricity, or labor). Therefore, it is essential for the local government to introduce and continuously use formats for property income statements. Furthermore, *all* relevant revenues and expenses for each property, and in particular management and administrative costs, should be included. Sometimes it is difficult to attach administrative costs (called "overhead") to properties. An easy way to overcome the difficulty is to use one of the measured costs, such as electricity, or the total measured costs, to distribute the overhead costs proportionately. Box 6.9 sheds light on an interesting case of a Nepali shopping mall.

Note that income statements are useful for all government real estate properties, not only for income-generating ones. For properties that are not income generating, such as a city hall or

Box 6.8 Asset Operating Statement for a Housing Management Unit

Operating or income statement for a housing management unit.

Revenues	Thousand dollar
Gross Potential Income (1)	1,000
Less Vacancy Loss (2)	50
Effective Gross Income	950
Operating Expenses (3)	
Repairs	100
Heat	60
Electricity	50
Water	20
Trash Removal	20
Insurance	30
Taxes	50
Communal Fee	30
Property Management Fee	50
Miscellaneous (4)	10
Total Operating Expenses	420
Net Operating Income	530
Financing Costs	
Mortgage Interest	90
Overhead Costs	
Appraisal	10
Other (5)	5
Total Overhead	15
Net Income	425
Less Mortgage Principal Payments (6)	100
Net Cash Flow (7)	325

Notes

1. *Gross potential income* includes actual rents and other income plus amounts that would have been collected if vacant spaces were leased. This income can be further broken down into types of income such as rents, late payment fees, vending machine revenues, copying charges, etc. If rents are artificially low to provide a subsidy to the tenant, that subsidy may also be included as an addition to the amount actually collected.

2. The amount of rent lost due to vacancy and collection losses, as well as subsidies in the form of rent reductions. Deducting this from *gross potential income* results in *effective gross income*.

3. The categories under *operating expenses* should be modified to include other types of expenses. Some of those listed may be unnecessary and can be deleted.

4. *Miscellaneous* expenses are those that do not fall into any of the other expense descriptions but are too small to justify their own line item description.

5. The category *Other* may include certain accounting, legal, and other charges that are incurred as a result of the requirements of the owner but that are not necessary for the successful operation of the property.

6. *Mortgage principal payments* require cash but add to the wealth of the owner by reducing the outstanding debt on the property. Conversely, interest payments, while requiring cash, do not reduce the debt and therefore do not enhance the wealth of the owner. Debt is a result of the circumstances of the owner. The property itself can operate equally with or without the debt.

7. *Cash flow* is the amount of cash, positive or negative, received by the owner as a result of holding the investment.

For the purpose of simplicity, depreciation is not considered as an expense in this sample statement, but it should be added as such if a depreciation fund exists in which the depreciation is accumulated for future replacement of the property.

schools, cash flow will always be negative, but it is still important to know the information for comparisons with other properties, especially of the same type. Comparing detailed operating costs may make it possible to identify costs that can be reduced.

Financial Analysis

A variety of indicators can be used to measure the effectiveness of the management of a portfolio of properties and the individual properties in the portfolio. These financial indicators, calculated by the asset manager or under his or her direction, provide insights about the performance of the assets and can suggest opportunities for improvement (for more detail, see Urban Institute 2012b).

Asset management requires experience, judgment, and the ability to analyze and interpret data. Data are useful only if they are properly understood; otherwise, inappropriate decisions might be made. The asset manager must use judgment in interpreting the results of calculations.

Indicators for Investment Comparison

Surplus or income-generating property should be treated as invested property and analyzed against other feasible investments. The underlying logic is very simple and straightforward: the local government does not need this property for its core functions. Property that it retains should produce returns that are competitive with those of other available investments, such as bank deposits or state securities, taking into account the degree of risk. If the property is not generating sufficient returns, its performance should be scrutinized to see if and how the performance could be improved. Should the effort fail to produce higher returns, the owner should consider selling the property and reinvesting the proceeds in other assets (either financial or infrastructure) or using them to repay long-term debt. Before these decisions are made, it is useful to consider the real estate market cycle. When putting properties up for sale, it is useful to launch a good marketing campaign.

Income capitalization triangle. The income capitalization triangle is the simplest formula for analyzing investments:

$$R = I / V,$$

where R = capitalization rate, I = income, and V = (book) value.

The concept is that each of these three characteristics can be calculated if the other two are known. In particular, the capitalization rate (rate of return) R can be calculated if annual income and property value are known (estimated). The capitalization rate can be used as a rough estimate of investment performance for one year. A key for the correct use of this rough estimate is to understand that I (income) should be the *net operating income*, that is, the income left after all expenses are paid out from the revenues gained.

It must be noted that in the above equation R is dependent on V as well as I. If the estimated value is too high, then R may appear too low. It will seem that the cash flow is too low relative to value, but it could be perfectly acceptable if a lower, more accurate value were to be used. Likewise, if the value is shown to be too low,

R appears more attractive than is justified. Thus, it is important to use realistic value data.

Net operating income. Net operating income or net cash flow is an absolutely necessary basic characteristic for any income-generating property, because it shows whether the property really generates net income or in fact generates a net loss. What can be done when an asset manager sees that the income-generating property does not produce satisfactory returns? First, they should scrutinize the entire chain of property management to find any overlooked opportunities to improve financial results (see table 6.6). Either income needs to increase or expenses need to decrease, or both.

Return on investment. Return on investment can be calculated for each property, or for property types, or for the entire property portfolio. This analysis is useful because it offers the opportunity to compare an individual property with the entire portfolio. If a property is producing a return below the average of comparable properties in the portfolio, it should be examined to determine if operational aspects of the property could be changed to improve its performance. If no improvements are likely, perhaps the property should be sold and the proceeds invested in other assets.

Likewise, a property performing above the average may be retained as an important component of the portfolio. However, it may be performing in an unsustainable manner and, in its excellent position, may be a candidate for sale.

Table 6.6 How to Increase Net Operating Income

Increase income:	Decrease expenses:
• Increase rent to true market level by auctioning the lease, upon contract expiration, or renegotiating the current contract.	• Save on maintenance and repair without compromising property value.
• Decrease vacancy time.	• Reduce utility expenses.
• Increase collection rate.	• Minimize management expenses.
	• Revise norms for contributions in reserve or replacement funds.

If the property is subject to debt, such as a mortgage, then it is important to be careful in calculating the return on investment. It can be calculated in two ways. First, we can calculate the *return on asset* (RoA), meaning the income before deducting the interest paid, compared to the value of the asset, as the performance of the asset is not changed by financing. The rents and operating costs will be the same with or without debt. Second, we can calculate the *return on equity* (RoE), meaning the net income after deducting the interest paid, divided by the value of the equity (that is, the value of the asset minus the amount of the debt). RoA and RoE show the performance of the investment differently, and it is good to see and analyze both.

For example, a one million dollar property with a $400,000 debt has equity of $600,000. If it produces $100,000 income before interest expense, the return on assets is 10 percent (100,000/1,000,000). If the interest expense is 8 percent of the $400,000 debt, or $32,000, then the income after interest is $68,000, and thus the return on equity is 68,000/600,000, or 11.33 percent.

Other ratios. The operation statements for each property allow asset managers to use simple ratios to compare one property to another within the same category and identify properties that perform worse or better than others. Frequently used ratios are the following:

Operating expense ratio = total operating expense/effective gross income,

or, complementary to that formula,

net income ratio = net operating income/ effective gross income.

Comparisons of line items of income and expense on a per-square-meter basis are also very useful in comparing rental apartments, offices, or shops. These ratios may be within different ranges for different types of properties; for example, residential rental income is usually lower than income from commercial rentals.

Discounted Cash Flow Analysis

The discounted cash flow analysis is a more comprehensive technique for analyzing income from property or investments. It provides an estimate of the market value of a property or project based on estimated future revenues and expenses, which are diverse and incurred over time. It is especially useful when a need exists to make a financially sound choice among two or more alternative uses of the same property or among alternative investment projects.

Figure 6.4 shows a schematic representing benefits, or revenue inflow, and expenditures, or money outflow, of a Tanzania landfill over 20 years and the results of the discounted cash flow. The initial investment t_0 is negative (blue column). The white field depicts the growing flow of operating expenses, and the other white columns illustrate the periodic refurbishments. The revenue from tipping fees and waste recycling starts with zero, during construction of the landfill, and increases gradually as collections cover a larger part of the city and the number of households increases (black field).

The dark gray column shows the discounted flow of revenues; the light gray shows the discounted flow of expenditures. The investment of 1.1 billion shillings is projected to generate 1.2 billion shillings net present value, the difference between the discounted revenues and the discounted expenditures. This investment is projected to have a 21 percent internal rate of return, against the reference discount rate of 12 percent. Figure 6.4 may help in understanding the two important terms used in discounted cash flow analysis, namely, "present value" and "internal rate of return."

Present value. Present value is the sum of the discounted flow of revenue or expenses using a reference discount rate (such as inflation, but

Figure 6.4   Present Value of Costs and Revenues of a Landfill in Tanzania

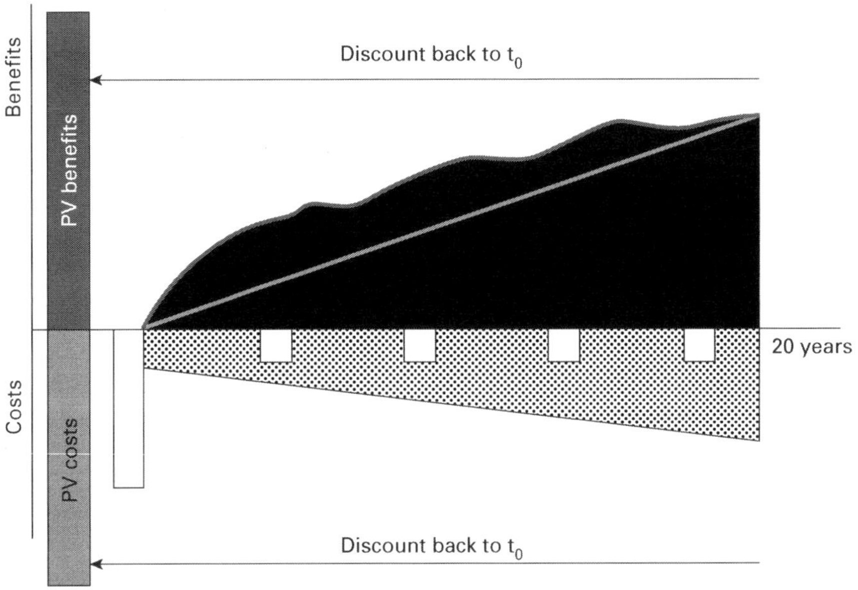

Note: PV = present value; t_0 = initial investment.

usually higher); the net present value of an investment is the difference between the present values of the revenue and the expenditure flows. A simple formula shows how to calculate the net present value of an asset or investment with a diverse flow of revenues and expenditures, as is typical in assets:

$$NPV = \frac{(R-E)_1}{(1+r)^1} + \frac{(R-E)_2}{(1+r)^2} + \ldots + \frac{(R-E)_n}{(1+r)^n},$$

Where NPV = net present value of the asset

R = revenue flow (all kinds of revenues in each year 1, 2, ... i, ..., n)

E = expenditure flow (all kinds of revenues in each year 1, 2, ...i, ..., n, including cost of operation, maintenance, and replacements or refurbishment)

r = reference interest rate (such as the rate of return of similar investments, the borrowing rate, or yield on state bonds).

Internal rate of return. The net present value leads to calculation of the internal rate of return, which is an interest rate that would make the discounted flow of revenues equal to the discounted flow of expenditures. In other words, this is the highest possible market interest rate that would enable the investment to repay all the expenses without losses, but would not generate net revenue.

Discounted cash flow analysis is based on the premise that money is worth more today than if one must wait until a later date to receive it. Simply stated, would you rather be given one million dinars today or one year from today? Clearly, it is better to receive it today and invest it for a return during the year. So future revenue is worth less than present revenue. The purchase of an asset today (or the decision to keep it and receive its value today) entitles its owner to receive the cash flow it produces and eventually the proceeds of its sale. The discounted cash flow is today's value of the future flow of revenues from the operation and the eventual sale of the asset. The amount of the discount is a percentage that should reflect returns in the investment market. A higher discount rate means that future revenues are worth less today, while a lower discount rate results in a higher value today. Likewise, revenues further in the future are worth less today than revenues received sooner.

Occupancy Rate

Occupancy is an indicator of the use of premises (usually rental) during a year. It does not measure what the tenant does in using the space but only that a tenant has the right to use the space under a lease. It does not measure whether the tenant pays the agreed rate and on time. A variation is vacancy, in which *vacancy % = 100 % of time – occupancy % of time.* Occupancy can be measured for each property, a group of properties, or for the entire portfolio.

Indicators for All Types of Property

The above indicators are not relevant for properties that do not produce income, such as administrative buildings. It is assumed that these properties perform a necessary governmental or social function rather than generating revenue. With respect to these properties, the asset manager must ensure that they are truly needed by the local government and that they are fully in use (vacancy can be measured). If not, there may be opportunities to lease portions of them to generate additional income and reduce the burden on the city budget. Likewise, social housing is intended to meet a social need and not to produce a large cash return, but the income statement is relevant for social housing. For social housing and administrative properties, other indicators are useful, as shown below.

Operating analysis. Many indicators can be created to better understand the operations of a building, usually based on costs (or revenues) per square meter:

- Heating costs per square meter
- Water costs per square meter
- Repair costs per square meter
- Electricity costs per square meter
- Rent per square meter.

The unit cost ratios are useful in comparing properties, provided the properties themselves are comparable. Although administrative and other properties may have no measurable return on investment, their operating costs are subject to analysis and improvement. This is particularly true if the property is comparable to income-producing assets in the portfolio. Administrative offices may be comparable to leased surplus offices, for example, and operating costs can be compared. Likewise, social housing may not produce market rates of rent, but expenses should not exceed those of similar properties that are not subsidized.

The above ratios are useful in energy audits, which are detailed assessments of energy use by schools, offices, health and sports facilities, and so on. They analyze energy use, leaks, and potential savings such as insulation of walls, recycling, and so on. As mentioned in chapter 5, International Organization for Standardization (ISO) analysis and certification also support energy savings and cost reduction, including reduction of building insurance fees.

Deferred maintenance. Underinvestment in property and infrastructure maintenance often results in their deterioration and devaluation. Local governments around the world, but particularly in developing countries, defer maintenance to balance budgets and spend the saved money for other purposes. Postponing maintenance temporarily may be a natural part of life; but it has long and deep negative consequences when it becomes a general practice. It is further aggravated when no records are kept on postponed or deferred items of maintenance. Monitoring deferred maintenance is important. Some rough estimates at least may be obtained by comparing annual planned and actual expenses on building and infrastructure repair. Deferred maintenance remains hidden unless an engineering assessment and plan spell out maintenance protocols, that is, the timing and nature of due maintenance, such as road resurfacing every seven years, truck engine refurbishment after 200,000 kilometers, or refurbishment of a vegetable market every five years. The analytical accounts of each property should indicate both the due and the effective maintenance time and estimated or actual costs.

Quantifying and Managing Property-Related Subsidies

Subsidies are common in both central and local governments. Ideally a subsidy should be direct and targeted, meaning that the government may support a target social group (extremely poor families, those with disabilities, the aged), a culture or religion, or a sports event, with a transparent, well-defined amount of cash or in-kind benefits (such as food or the free use of a hall for an event). Subsidies are matters of policy decision, and they are among the special functions of local governments. However, subsidies can also be hidden, and they can be counterproductive, for example, if everyone benefits from below-cost public transportation instead of only elders or students. Subsidies are often not quantified or accounted as a separate budget line, remaining hidden among the costs of a service provider such as the water company or housing department. That provider then requires budget support to cover its annual losses.

Rent subsidies are also common, as when local governments give land or built-up premises to various private sector or NGO (nongovernmental organization) tenants at below market rents. Under this practice, the local government forgoes potential income (that it could earn by leasing premises at market prices). Such preferential rental rates are also, in practical terms, indirect subsidies to the tenants:

$$Indirect\ rental\ subsidy = (market\ rent) - (actual\ rent).$$

Nevertheless, decisions on such indirect rental subsidies are completely political. Decision makers should be well informed about the size and costs of the subsidies, and the asset managers should provide them with that information. In particular, for each property, asset managers should know at least the estimated market rent. That allows the size of the subsidy to be calculated by estimating the unit subsidy (market minus actual rent per square meter) multiplied by the rental area. The template in table 6.7 is a useful tool to summarize, analyze, and communicate to decision makers the hidden subsidy

Table 6.7 Estimating Indirect Subsidies to Rental Tenants (in shillings)

Tenant	Address	Area (m²)	Actual rent per m²	Market rent per m²	Subsidy per m²	Total indirect subsidy to tenants
Mr. Smith	Main Street	45	50 Shs	90 Shs	40 Shs	1,800 Shs
Ms. Brown	Post Street	38	50 Shs	70 Shs	20 Shs	760 Shs
Clear air NGO	Broad Street	120	60 Shs	120 Shs	60 Shs	7,200 Shs
Total forgone revenue						9,760 Shs

provided to organizations in the form of discounted rent.

It is important to be aware that not only are such subsidies forgone revenues, but they also create distortions to the local economy because they provide unfair competitive advantage to tenants who pay below-market rent. Why, for example, should a private art gallery be at a serious disadvantage because it must pay higher rent than the gallery registered as a public institution, which is eligible for subsidized space? If reduction of these subsidies is established as a goal, the way to achieve it is obvious: premises with subsidized rent should be those whose market rents are the lowest, in other words, the most modest premises in both quality and location. In particular, subsidized premises should not be in prestigious areas.

In sum, policy makers (such as the council) should be well informed about forgone revenues because revising existing policy and practice can lead to fairer economic conditions for tenants of municipal rentals, more revenues for municipal budgets, and greater transparency about who receives public subsidies (direct or indirect) and how much. The most complicated cases are those in which land is given to investors at discounted prices for the sake of local economic development and new employment.[3]

Incentives for Local Government Employees

Examples from around the world indicate that properly structured incentives for government employees and government units can result in positive outcomes that would be practically impossible to obtain otherwise. For example, in the wake of the municipal financial crisis, Montgomery County, Maryland, in the United States, introduced an innovative incentives program for its employees. All employees are encouraged to identify and suggest possible savings related to municipal assets. If a suggestion is implemented and the savings materialize, the employee who made the suggestion receives a direct monetary bonus.

Financial Planning

Asset-associated financial planning has two major elements. One is related to the fact that capital assets have a long, useful life. For example, buildings and infrastructure facilities and networks are useful for 25 to 75 years, or even longer. Therefore, expenses related to these assets need to be planned and executed for their useful lifetime; that is called "life-cycle costing." The second element is that local governments always have many capital investment needs, such as repairing and renovating existing buildings and networks, acquiring new equipment, building new roads, and so forth. That implies that those capital expenses need to be planned ahead for about three to five years. A useful tool for that is called "capital investment planning" (also discussed in chapters 5 and 7).

Life-Cycle Costing

The costs associated with the useful life of a property include its acquisition costs (that is, land acquisition and construction), annual costs, and disposition costs. The annual costs, in turn, comprise such items as maintenance and repair, operation costs, and expenses for restoration and modernization (or accumulation of funds for replacement at the end of the asset's useful life). The annual costs depend on the type of facility, materials and equipment used, climate, the cost of labor, and so forth. In practice, they also depend on the current condition of the facility—if preventive maintenance and repairs have been deferred for the past several years, the current operating expenses could be higher than they would otherwise be. Further, annual costs can differ dramatically within one system. For example, in water systems, the most expensive operations usually are water pumping and water treatment. As a result, a water supply service may spend most of its annual costs on electricity for pumping the water and labor for operating and maintaining the facilities and network. A social rental department pays only repairs and maintenance labor and materials, as tenants pay most of the operating expenses, such as electricity, telecommunication, or water.

Maintenance and repair (M&R) costs are distributed unevenly during a life cycle and depend on the kind of asset. Figure 6.5 depicts the life-cycle costs of various assets over a 50-year life cycle. The small columns signal regular, small maintenance instances; the tall columns indicate larger costs or major refurbishments and substantial expenditures.

Similarly, annual operation costs, compared with the initial construction cost, vary substantially by type of asset and constitute a substantial amount. The total M&R and operation costs over an asset's life are often much larger than the initial construction cost (table 6.8).

Sometimes the total life-cycle cost can be lowered by redistributing the costs along the cycle. For example, spending more to build a facility might result in overall savings on M&R and operations costs. The same can be true for the costs of certain types of repairs, replacement, or renovation. For example, replacing an old air conditioning system with a modern, energy-efficient one can lead to substantial savings in annual energy costs, so that in a few years the investment is recaptured and life-cycle saving begins.

Three methods are commonly used to plan for operating and maintenance costs of both existing and planned municipal assets:

1. For approximate or preliminary planning, it is common practice to base estimates of annual operating and maintenance costs on a percentage of the estimated or original construction cost. However, this method is the least accurate and cannot be recommended as good practice.

2. Another method uses historical costs. For additions to or modification of existing facilities, identifying historical costs and adjusting those values, based on required or desired changes to the previous operating and maintenance program, is an effective approach for estimating future operating and maintenance costs.

3. The most accurate method requires the preparation of a detailed operating and maintenance work plan for the facility or system, including a description of all anticipated operating and maintenance activities, a description of each work activity, a detailed staffing plan, power costs, materials costs, replacement costs of equipment having a short life expectancy, etc.

Notice that having and implementing operating and maintenance work plans for infrastructure and buildings is a core element of good practice in life-cycle management.

Another component of the annual cost is restoration and modernization (R&M) expenses, which are also called "recapitalization" or "depreciation." Municipalities that use accrual accounting compute cost and account asset depreciation (see also chapter 3). However, for those that use cash accounting, as is typical in the developing world, it is also allowed and is good practice to budget depreciation costs annually. They are then accumulated in a special depreciation fund, earmarked exclusively for restoration and modernization of assets or their replacement at the end of their useful life. Depreciation funds cover the whole portfolio (for example, all schools in a city or the water and sewer infrastructure).

Funding for R&M may be seen as sacrificed money when a local budget is constrained. In particular, local politicians might feel that establishing a reserve fund dedicated to future investment or refurbishment is a poor use of resources, when there are always immediate needs for other expenditures. However, failing to fund M&R or R&M costs properly results in deferred repairs and maintenance, which reduce the useful life of the assets.

Capital Investment Planning

A capital investment plan is a rolling, three- to five-year plan that summarizes the strategic development program for the upcoming period, including a detailed list and information on

Figure 6.5 Annual Maintenance, Management, and Repair Costs of Facilities, Washington, D.C.

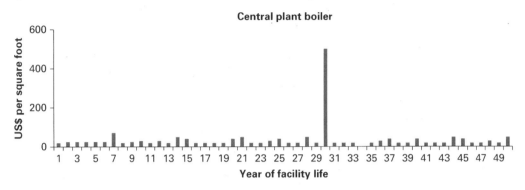

Central plant boiler

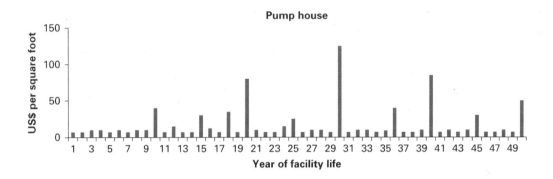

Pump house

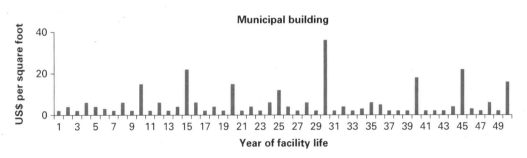

Municipal building

Source: Authors, based on data from Whitestone Research 2010.

planned priority investment projects, the timing of their implementation, funding sources identified and approved, and main technical characteristics. Capital investment plans build a bridge between the longer-term visions, the master or development plans, and the annual capital expenditure budgets (World Bank 2011). The rolling capital investment plan is a systematic, simultaneous evaluation of potential projects; it should be revised annually by transferring the current year to the capital budget and including one additional year. The capital investment

Table 6.8 Examples of the Life-Cycle Costs for Different Facilities, Washington, D.C.

Facility	Initial or replacement cost		Annual M&R (average) and operations costs		M&R and operations costs, in 50-year life cycle
	$ per sq. foot	%	M&R, % of replacement cost	Operations, % of replacement cost	% of replacement cost
Central plant, boiler	640	100	6.4	4.9	561
Pump house	640	100	3.0	19.4	1,117
Municipal building	264	100	1.7	5.1	340
Public library	230	100	1.7	5.1	338

Source: Whitestone Research 2010.
Note: M&R = maintenance and repairs.

planning process facilitates coordination among the local government entities that are responsible for project implementation (discussed in more detail in chapter 7).

Taking a Strategic View of Municipal Assets

A strategic view of municipal assets considers the entire portfolio and draws policy conclusions to support decisions to prevent deterioration and maximize value. The asset strategy is part of the broad strategy of the municipality, which uses assets to fulfill its functions and goals. From this perspective, analyzing the asset portfolio aims at identifying how to improve the performance of the assets in fulfilling municipal goals and short- and medium-term targets. For instance, in times of financial distress, financial stability might be the prime objective. That might require selling assets that induce losses or are too expensive to maintain. When financial conditions are good, the question is more how to acquire assets for priority services, to enhance their quality, or to support local economic development.

Analyzing assets' performance is an important part of capital improvement planning, in which main asset acquisitions, renovations, or divestitures are taken into consideration and accounted for in the rolling plan. Figure 6.5 illustrates that as

part of an asset's life cycle, additional investments are required a few years after installation. Analysis of asset portfolios focuses on effectiveness, and investments in securities or commercial properties might show the highest financial return. However, it should be kept in mind that unless such financial investments are made for the creation of a strategic reserve, they do not support the main function of the municipality, which is to provide the citizens with good services. Investments in commercial properties bring multiple risks that the government is not suited to manage, and they are not recommended.

What Can Be Learned from the Balance Sheet?

A balance sheet can provide a useful perspective on the asset portfolio by revealing assets and liabilities (details on the balance sheet are discussed in chapter 3). Table 6.9 shows the key categories of assets and liabilities that can commonly be found on a local government asset-liability balance sheet. One of the questions to ask is whether it would be beneficial to rebalance and restructure the physical assets, or assets and liabilities. For example, does it make sense to sell some surplus commercial properties that the government happens to have and invest the proceeds in needed infrastructure? Should surplus land and property be sold to repay debt?

Table 6.9   Asset-Liabilities Balance Sheet

Assets	Liabilities
Fixed assets • Land • Infrastructure • Buildings • Equipment *Financial assets* • Investments in enterprises • Securities, bonds, etc.	• Debt, including that secured by municipal property or by a property-generated income stream • Third-party guarantees • Pension obligations • Long-term, property-related paying obligations (leases, public-private partnership repayment) • Other contingent liabilities (e.g., remediation of land contamination)

Obviously, to obtain an undistorted picture of assets requires knowing the market value of land, especially that part of it that could be sold. Similarly, built-up properties that can be classified as surplus should be appraised, at least roughly.

The financial analysis tools discussed above, such as the capitalization rate, discounted cash flow, and net present value analysis, are practical methods for comparing the value of surplus land and property with the total annual capital investment budget. Comparison of alternatives is necessary in making decisions regarding asset divestiture or investment, that is, whether it is wise to sell assets that provide little or no cash revenue and invest proceeds in shares, bonds, or joint equity ventures that seem to offer higher gains.

Municipal Enterprises

Municipal enterprises are established because independent and focused management can perform better than municipal line departments, which often are not suited for daily management of most local service delivery. Municipal enterprises are independent legal entities, often under direct municipal ownership. They work under an appointed director. Sometimes they are corporatized companies governed by a board. Municipalities in the developing world do not perform well in controlling their enterprises, despite the fact that the enterprises may represent the bulk of municipal wealth (Kopanyi

and Hertelendy 2004). Assets transferred to enterprises are no longer part of the municipal balance sheet, but from a strategic and operational perspective it is wise to improve municipal control over them.

How to Control Municipal Enterprises

Very often municipal enterprises hold or own large portfolios of property that originally was municipal. Those holdings can be lucrative assets (vacant land, revenue-generating rentals). Usually, enterprises obtain these assets free from local governments as in-kind equity donations, and their value is not accounted for on the municipal balance sheet or known to the local government. Revenues from these assets are usually retained by the companies and not shared with the municipal budget. The municipality can and should strengthen its control over the enterprises substantially by using governance instruments such as are applied in the private sector:

- ***Establish contractual relations*** with the enterprises regarding their use of assets given to them (e.g., a performance-based service contract with a water, transport, or solid waste company).

- ***Improve the governance*** of the enterprises to protect assets (e.g., hire professionals to represent the municipality on the enterprise board or as executives of enterprises solely owned or majority-owned by the municipality; exercise strong oversight over management, and so forth).

- **_Take back assets_** to the direct control of the local government; transfer back land or property that is surplus to the enterprises' operations. That is possible if the municipality is the sole or majority owner of the enterprise. Even so, retransferring assets requires legal action, as it is a divestiture by, and reduction of the equity capital of, the enterprise.

- **_Improve reporting_** by rigorous scrutiny of the financial reports and audits of the enterprises. Some municipalities also prepare a consolidated annual report that includes reports on the investments and enterprise portfolio, annexed to the closing financial report (budget and balance sheet).

After establishing good control and governance of municipal enterprises, local governments may consider the option of creating a financial holding that owns all the municipal enterprises and shareholdings on behalf of the municipality. This is a German model (_stadtwerke_) followed in some European countries and is also similar to development authorities established in India and Pakistan. Benefits from such a holding, if it is governed well, include robust capital; good security for borrowing; possible pooling of demand for debt to obtain a better interest rate; and opportunity to rebalance assets to support a strategy for the entire portfolio. However, this option may discourage direct involvement of the local government in outsourcing delivery of services to the private sector through concessions and similar instruments.

This model also contains a risk that the holding, which may have a balance sheet larger than the municipality's, might grow out of control of the municipality and become self-serving rather than responsive to the municipal needs. Moreover, because of its size ("too large to fail"),

the holding might be dangerous for the municipal budget, as in the case of the Debrecen Holding in Hungary. It started in 2000 with great promise: big investments, big development projects, independent borrowing. By 2010, however, its debt became unmanageable, unpaid bills amounted to about 5 million euros, and eventually the municipality was forced to bail it out. Lessons suggest that the financial holding is not a suitable tool of municipal asset management for developing countries.

The governance and control of municipal enterprises in developing countries often suffer from ineffective boards filled with appointed municipal administrators and politicians. Such board members lack expertise or motivation (or both) to work effectively to guide and control the executives and the operation. The boards may look similar to those used in the developed countries but be ineffective because of different corporate cultures and local circumstances.

Instruments of Land-Based Financing

Land-based financing is a set of instruments that local governments across the world use to convert their land or land-related regulatory powers into funding for infrastructure or delivery of infrastructure services (Peterson 2009). There are three distinctive types of instruments, including sale of land or buildings or transferring land to public-private partnership ventures; using regulatory instruments for generating revenue; and taxing or charging developments. Cases of these instruments are discussed briefly below.

Converting Government-Owned Land and Property into Money or Infrastructure

Public property can be transformed into money or infrastructure by disposition or equity participation. The simplest way is to dispose of surplus land or built-up property and use the revenues for capital investment in other locations. The term "dispose" may imply sale, that is, conveyance of full ownership to a buyer, or conveying temporary rights, such as a long-term lease. Obviously, for this instrument to work the land or property should be in a desirable location within an active real estate market, and the sale should take place at a time when private demand is strong. For example, impressive sales in Istanbul and Cairo took place at the top of the market, before the market crash in 2008–2009:

- In Istanbul in 2007, the auction of an old bus station and former administrative site produced $1.5 billion, which is equivalent to one-and-a-half times the city's municipal capital spending in 2005.

- In Cairo in 2007, an auction of desert land for new towns generated $3.14 billion—equivalent to about 10 percent of total national government revenues and 117 times greater than the (very low) total urban property tax collection in the country.

However, systematic dependence on revenues from government land, especially land sales, is very risky for several reasons. First, land is a limited resource, and its sale cannot be a sustainable revenue source. Moreover, dependence on land sales provides pervasive incentives for spatial expansion and urban sprawl, which fuel future unsustainability. Land markets are also volatile and cyclical, making land sales not a stable revenue source. To mitigate the risks, land sale revenues should be placed in a special, multiyear budgetary fund that would buffer fluctuations of the land market.

Another instrument from the same group is contribution of a government site into a PPP, in exchange for obtaining a needed public facility without spending public money. The private partners in such PPPs recoup their spending in profits from a commercial part of the land development. Such a land-for-infrastructure scheme is tied to a site, but no public funding is needed. For example, in Kuwait City most of the public infrastructure (public garages, highway rest stations, markets) has been built through such arrangements. Private developers sandwiched public garages for the central city into their mixed-use skyscrapers built on government land, with retail below a garage and office floors above. Similarly, in Bethesda, Maryland, a public parking garage was built by a private developer underneath its mixed-use building in exchange for the 99-year lease of the site.

Converting Municipal Power into Money or Infrastructure

Another tool from this group converts municipal power to define land uses and land use parameters (land use planning and land use control) into money or infrastructure through the sale of development rights. That is, the local government sells to developers the right to exceed the planned parameters of land use (e.g., floor-to-area ratio, maximum number of floors, maximum land coverage) in exchange for money or building public infrastructure. This kind of arrangement has been broadly employed (e.g., São Paulo, Brazil; Lima, Peru; Stuttgart, Germany; Bethesda, Maryland, U.S.). It is also used in some Indian states as a form of compensation to private owners of land when parts of their parcels are expropriated for public infrastructure.

Similarly, it is possible to capture for the municipal budget a part of the gain in value of land (military, railroads) that occurs when it is rezoned. For example, in the United States and Serbia, surplus military properties have been sold to the private sector, and local governments have thus shared in the gain created by rezoning of the land from "special use" (military) to "commercial use."

Using Government's Power to Extract a Public Share from Private Gains

Finally, the local government can use legislative or regulatory power to extract a public share from private property gains by taxes, fees, or in-kind contribution. This tool is used in several forms in various countries.

A betterment fee can be charged property owners whose property value increased as a result of public infrastructure built or improved in the vicinity. However, experiments with betterment fees in Australia, Poland, and the United Kingdom were unsuccessful and were abolished, formally or de facto. The lone country with a steady record of success in some cities is Colombia.

Developers' exactions and *land dedication* (Russia, Serbia, United States) and *impact fees* (Serbia, United States) all require private developers to contribute infrastructure or land for public uses in connection with their real estate development projects. Developers' exactions in the United States are related to on-site infrastructure, and impact fees are related to off-site infrastructure. In the Balkans, this kind of fee is called a "land development fee" and is supposed to cover off-site infrastructure, while on-site is paid by developers directly. A good system of impact fees requires a strong analytical base and a long-term investment plan to differentiate accurately the impact of new development on infrastructure cost by location, land use, lot, and building size. In many countries, such as in the Balkans, such fees are set up arbitrarily, without any relation to the cost of infrastructure, and used practically as a general tax on new development, especially nonresidential uses.

Such cases illustrate that the use of land financing instruments provides one or both of two main benefits: direct, immediate revenues for funding infrastructure or reducing debt *or* public infrastructure facilities' being obtained without spending public money. In addition, many of these instruments transfer some risks to the private sector.

Specifics of Strategic Land Management and Administration: "The Devil Is in the Details"

Land is often the most valuable asset of local governments if it is valued at its market price (see the example of Warsaw in table 6.1). That implies that the quality of land management is especially important, and as has been said, inventorying land is the very first step. The next actions in strategic land management have some specifics that are useful to know.

Strategic Land Classification

The basic elements of land classification have been outlined above. It requires identifying parcels needed for mandatory and discretionary functions, and surplus land. Figure 6.6 summarizes the logical frame and specific actions.

One of the questions that will unavoidably emerge is how much vacant land will be needed for future use for public purposes. That depends on what kind of urban development is planned. For predominantly residential areas, a general rule is that about 28 percent to 35 percent of the territory should be publicly owned for use as roads and for social infrastructure (schools, hospitals, etc.). Nonresidential areas may need a smaller share of public land. If there is insufficient land for public uses in areas planned for new development, the land should be acquired. If, however, the municipality owns land, but development is not planned in the immediate future, a course of action must be determined: Is it better to sell the land now, spend the proceeds for current needs, and buy land when development goes ahead? Or is it better to hold the land? Although there is no universal answer, it is useful to remember that in many growing urban areas, land values generally increase faster than inflation or returns on other investments. Therefore, the land, if it is already owned, can be a good investment.

A spatial development plan, at least a basic one, is necessary to know exactly where the

Figure 6.6 Classification of All Municipally Controlled Land

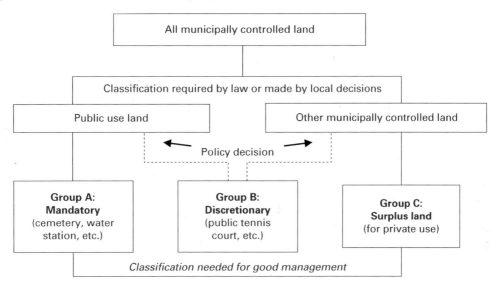

streets, roads, and public facilities of the future are supposed to be. Such a plan allows the separation of future public use land from other vacant land, which would be classified as surplus. The latter type of land can be very valuable and also needs strategic management. A possible approach to such a land decision is depicted in figure 6.7, which sorts all vacant sites into four groups (see Urban Institute 2012b for more details).

Ways to Enhance the Value of Municipal Land

Local governments, as landowners, have unique power over the value of land that they offer to investors and the prices that investors are willing to pay. Revenues from land sales, PPPs, and sales of development rights can increase by two to five times if the most profitable uses of land ("highest and best uses") are permitted by land use plans and regulations. Moreover, changing land use parameters may switch land value from negative (meaning that the private sector will not be interested without subsidies) to positive.

If these powers are used wisely, municipalities can increase revenues from allocating land and become more attractive than other municipalities to investors. A number of tools exist for enhancing land values and prices:

- *Offer a prepared site, not "raw" land, but a prepared subdivision site with basic infrastructure.* Providing internal and external roads and off-site hookups to water and sewerage makes the land ready to use when construction is completed and removes a major uncertainty for investors. However, in preparing land for investors, the municipality must take into account environmental and social implications. For example, it should have a resettlement action plan that summarizes negative social impacts, such as loss of houses and cropland, and spells out specific actions to compensate affected citizens or entities (for more details, see English and Brusberg 2002). Fair treatment of people—even if they are encroachers—is fundamental to any good land project.

Figure 6.7 Classification of Surplus Municipal Land

- Golden reserve. "Golden reserve" is the nickname of sites in prime locations, placed under a moratorium from being sold or leased to investors for at least 10 to 15 years. The land can be released from the moratorium when the government needs funding for major infrastructure projects. The local council should approve the list of sites under the moratorium and issue a binding document. Meanwhile, the sites can be used as public spaces or leased for short-term uses like parking lots.

- Large construction sites. Sites suitable for capital construction should be released to investors via auctions or other forms of competitive procurement. The release should be planned and preapproved by the local elected body (annual program) and timed to the real estate market (no sales at the bottom of the market).

- Small plots. Small holdings that cannot be built up as independent real estate can be offered to owners of neighboring sites.

- Other sites. Sites not suitable for capital construction for various reasons (shape, location, slopes) can be leased for temporary light construction uses.

Table 6.10 Example of How Permitted Land Uses Influence Land Value

Scenario 1 (according to the detailed development plan):	Scenario 2 (according to a market study conducted by real estate experts):
Greenfield site, 10 hectares; permitted land uses are an "industrial zone," defined as production asset management warehouses; auxiliary offices up to 14% of total floor space.	Greenfield site, 10 hectares; permitted land uses are production asset management warehouses; offices; retail asset management–related warehouses (such as a showroom, discount retail store, furniture store, or home improvement center).
Floor area:	Floor area:
Production management warehouse: 60,000 m^2	Production management warehouse: 40,000 m^2
Office: 10,000 m^2	Office: 10,000 m^2
Total: 70,000 m^2	Retail management warehouse: 20,000 m^2
	Total: 70,000 m^2
Prices expected at auction:	Prices expected at auction:
Euro 14.5/m^2, on average	Euro 15/m^2 (office/warehouse), on average
(or 1,448,272 euros for the entire site).	Euro 37/m^2 (retail/warehouse), on average
	(or 2,164,077 euros for the entire site).

Source: Urban Institute 2012a.

- *Broaden permitted land uses and land use parameters.* The example in table 6.10 illustrates how permitted uses influence the value and attractiveness of land for potential buyers. In particular, it shows a common case in which a detailed development plan for a greenfield industrial zone stipulates that only production and warehousing can be developed on the site. Under this condition, an expected price at auction could be, at best,

14.5 euros per square meter, on average. If, however, permissible land uses were expanded to allow some retail and retail-related warehousing, the average expected price could go up to 21.6 euros per square meter. That would translate to about 715,805 euros of additional revenues for the municipal budget.

- *Reduce government-related risks and costs for investors.* Three main types of risks can be removed:

  Legal risk—make sure that the city has "clean" rights to sites offered to investors.

  Financial risks—make all costs related to site acquisition and development known to investors in advance.

  Timing risk—make the time for obtaining permits and infrastructure hookups predictable.

  If these risks are not eliminated, investors will hedge against them by reducing the price they are willing to pay.

Good Disposition Procedures and Contracts: Why Do They Matter?

Good disposition procedures matter because they indicate how interested the local government is in being a good business partner for private investors and how qualified it is to do so. Any uncertainty in the land procurement process or in land lease or sale contract increases investors' risks and reduces their trust that the process is not corrupt. In some countries, local residents and businesses still do not have a choice and would accept even shaky land rights and unclear contracts. However, relying on that undercuts the municipality's long-term competitiveness both domestically and internationally. Listed below are some basic features of a good land procurement and marketing process (for more information, see Urban Institute 2012a).

- *Local ordinance.* The procurement process should be defined in a formal document, preferably a *local ordinance on land allocation and disposition* approved by a local elected body.

- *Competition.* The process should be open and competitive, with minimal limitations (if any) on participation.

- *Auctions or sealed bids.* For the majority of sites, the process should be an open auction or sealed-bid competition, with the winner in either case selected based on the highest price or rent offered. Selecting winners based on other or multiple criteria should be permitted in special cases only, predefined in the ordinance on land allocation and disposition.

- *Public announcement.* A public announcement of the auction or competition should have sufficient information for potential bidders.

- *Time.* A sufficiently long marketing period should be provided after the public announcement. For simple and relatively small sites, the time between the announcement and auction should normally be at least 45 days. For larger or strategic sites, or when demand is weak, the period should be at least 90–120 days.

- *Inform the public.* The public should be provided with information on the results of the procurement, including the identity of the winner, the purchase price or rent, and any conditions or limitations on the site and transaction. Information should be provided by written notice posted in public places and on websites, and the information should be entered in the local public property inventory.

- *Delegate the task.* The local governments should have the right to delegate, by written agreement, responsibility for organizing and conducting land procurement under the established procedures.

Using Real Estate Brokers for Disposing of Surplus Land

Large real estate sales call for a high-quality and properly targeted marketing campaign to attract good investors. The best solution is to hire a professional real estate company or agent with a good brokerage record. They can distribute the information on your sites through their databases of clients and organize the marketing to potential buyers. The marketing agent should be selected through procurement.

If a local government decides to conduct its marketing without the involvement of a private real estate broker, it should at least consult informally with local real estate agents. In any event, publishing an advertisement in a local newspaper is absolutely not enough. The marketing campaign must have other elements, such as a billboard directing people to websites with asset management auction information; brochures; and online postings. Information should be provided to all local real estate companies, the chamber of commerce, and so forth.

Leasing or Privatizing Municipal Land

Which rights should be given to private economic actors (citizens, companies) when government land is allocated to them for private investment? There are two major cases in which that question is acutely important. The first is the case in which moving land from public to private ownership is not allowed in the country. Investors may only obtain term rights, such as leases, but the central government may be interested in investigating its options. The second is the case in which private ownership exists, but local governments may decide what rights they want to convey to investors in a specific case.

Experience in former socialist countries indicates that when they have a choice, investors in most cases strongly prefer land ownership, not land lease (see below). This signals, at the very least, two things: First, countries without private land ownership, but which are surrounded by countries with ownership, will lose some investors, who will go to places they find more secure. Second, in countries where both options exist, cities granting ownership will have an advantage in competition with their neighbors for investment.

Nevertheless, both options have proponents and opponents, often based on ideology. On the one hand, practically all prosperous societies in the contemporary world have grown on fundamental respect for private ownership of land and property.[4] On the other hand, some believe that land was created by God for everybody's use and cannot be in private ownership. At a more pragmatic level, there are costs and benefits associated with each option.

Arguments for and Benefits of a Long-Term Lease

- Under a long-term lease, local government can exercise a level of control over the speed of development, as deadlines for building on the land should be included in the lease contract. The contract may also have a provision for termination if the investor does not build on time. These provisions create a certain protection against land speculators who are buying the land for resale at a profit, not for immediate development. (Conditions requiring that construction be completed in a set time can be attached to sale contracts as well.)

- Local government will get land and improvements back after the expiration of a lease. It must be said that that can be more a curse than a blessing, as Chicago, Kuwait City, and Johannesburg have learned. In those places investors stopped maintaining buildings 10 to 15 years before expiration of their lease, as they lacked incentives. At the end of long-term leases, the cities have found themselves owners of deteriorating commercial properties that have nothing to do with governmental functions.

Costs and Risks of a Long-Term Land Lease

- Investors prefer ownership to land lease. The first reason is that owned land can be used as collateral for borrowing to supply construction finance. Second, in many countries, investors trust law and state for protecting their ownership rights more than they trust local governments and lease contracts. The quality of land lease contracts in most such countries has been inadequate to protect either private or governmental interests. To investors, this implies that they are exposed to high risks, among which are the risks of extortion, pressure by corrupt officials using loopholes, and uncertainties in lease contracts.

- The land-leasing model is also more expensive and complicated to administer. First, it implies the need to maintain parallel systems for registering leasehold rights of land tenants and their ownership rights in improvements. Second, local governments become holders of large portfolios of lease contracts, and those must be monitored and managed, adding to the cost of land management. Third, a single property tax is not applicable because taxation of buildings and payments for land must be administrated separately.

- The land-leasing model requires sophisticated legal knowledge on the part of participants and can unintentionally give advantage to foreign investors over small domestic lessees. The lease agreement is a binding contract, and parties entering into it must be fully aware of their legal obligations under the terms of the lease. That is not something that small landholders in most developing countries, who cannot afford to hire qualified lawyers, will understand. The quality of the lease itself is crucial. Omission of key provisions—for example, who owns what at the date of termination, or provisions for renewal—can lead to multiple cases of litigation, as happened in Kuwait, or mass protests, as happened in Hong Kong

SAR, China. One can surely assume that small local lessees are at highest risk under the lease model, as they often do not have good lawyers and shrewd negotiators at their disposal. As a result, the land lease system often unintentionally discriminates against them and favors experienced foreign interests. This should be recognized as a policy issue.

- The land-leasing model is associated with higher transaction costs. Trading of land leases incurs higher transaction costs than does trading of owned land because an investor must sell the building and separately transfer the lease through the local government, which costs additional time and money, compared to a single sale of a fully owned property. For the same reason, properties located on leased land usually have lower liquidity than ones on owned land. Altogether these complexities make investment in leased land less attractive to investors.

If investors sense that municipal leases are too risky or too expensive, given all the time and money required to obtain them, they will just go to private sellers or to other cities or countries.

Policy Implications

What, then, are the key policy implications for local governments of decisions whether to sell or lease?

- Local governments that would be the first in their country to start selling land into private ownership most probably will have an advantage in attracting investors over governments that prefer land leases.

- It is impossible to predict whether an investor will buy land for immediate development or for speculative investment to resell. However, a government can consider whether a person or company has a timebound, quality development plan in its selection of a buyer.

- If doubt exists, a wise local policy could be to try both options simultaneously, monitor outcomes, and correct the policy based on evidence. In practical terms, that means putting some parcels up for auction sale and some into long-term leases. In monitoring outcomes, some core indicators would be the answers to such basic questions as the following:
  1. Are higher prices paid for ownership (everything else being equal)?
  2. Do the intervals between contract signing and a request for a building permit differ between the two options?
  3. Do the construction completion times differ?
  4. Does the amount of investment depend on the land rights?

Who should decide, and how? Given that the decision may have a serious influence on the competitiveness and prosperity of the municipality, *local policy makers*—the elected body and the mayor—should have joint responsibility for lease or sale decisions.

Advanced Asset Management: Public-Private Partnerships and Land Development Corporations

Asset management is a highly technical area, and as is shown in figure 6.2, it requires professional real estate expertise. When such expertise is not involved, many costly mistakes are made, often without even being recognized.[5] Attracting experts qualified to manage large property portfolios and enabling them to act efficiently are often impossible within rigid government administrative structures (i.e., pay levels, decision-making processes). Moreover, rational management of capital assets requires actions and operations—such as selling surplus land to the private sector—that governments sometimes are not allowed to do. Finally, as already discussed, the private sector can bring not only expertise and efficiency but direct funding for public capital investment as well. These are the main reasons why two advanced asset management instruments—public-private partnerships (PPPs) and land development corporations—have emerged and become noticeable in asset management.

Public-Private Partnerships

The prevailing form of PPPs is based on a contractual relationship between the government and the private partner (which can be a consortium of private entities). A less common form (and generally not recommended for local governments) is a joint legal entity, established by the government and the private partner, usually with shares held by the initial partners or publically traded. PPPs vary broadly. On one end of the spectrum are simple management contracts of three to five years, under which a private partner operates and maintains some government facility (such as a public garage) or provides a service that traditionally would be provided by a municipality (such as street cleaning). It is important to mention that PPP arrangements are very sector specific and require a good combination of technical, financial, and institutional governance expertise. A contract that suits a water supply PPP is not appropriate for one that operates a bus service or a shopping mall.[6]

At the other end are complex, long-term PPP arrangements, such as Design-Finance-Build-Operate-Transfer (often referred as DFBOT). For example, a private partner in a PPP can design, build, and operate several public schools for a local government (a very common arrangement in the U.K.). The partner will also provide financing for the capital investment, and the local government will repay the costs (and a profit) to the private partner over the next 30 years through an agreed annual fee. Private partners in well-structured, long-term PPPs can do various things, including providing financing and expertise and taking on specific risks.

Long-term PPPs associated with capital investment are the most complex instruments among all that local governments might use, and for that reason, only a minority of local governments are likely to use them. Moreover, as with borrowing, PPPs are usually possible only if the local government has a certain level of financial autonomy.

It is certainly recommended that any local government engage only gradually in PPPs, starting with simpler, short-term forms, such as outsourcing operations and management of selected municipal services or facilities. The government can enter into long-term PPPs after gaining experience with simple contracts (see also chapter 7).

Land Development Corporations

Local governments sometimes establish land development corporations as special purpose entities. They are quite common in South Asia, for example, the Delhi Development Authority in India and the Lahore Development Authority in Pakistan. International experiences with these entities vary widely. Land corporations usually operate under the commercial code, as private companies do, and they have more independence than departments or small units of the local government. A central idea of this corporate model is that it allows combining private sector efficiency with public value goals. On the efficiency side, the corporate model establishes incentives for the company to make its operations cost-efficient and self-sufficient. It makes it possible to accelerate all processes, to promote flexibility and entrepreneurship, and to attract and retain private sector experts in real estate and finance.

The scope and functions of land development corporations vary widely. For example, they may include land acquisition, equipping with infrastructure, and releasing improved land onto the market; building housing for low-income families; or managing properties used by government functions. The corporate model can also provide some protection for strategic land management and long-term planning from the whims of politicians, who may be keen to interfere in land transactions when they are managed by government directly.

On the social values side, land corporations can harmonize relationships with local communities concerning what is being developed, as well as secure the environmental sustainability of buildings and neighborhoods developed. Land corporations can also stimulate local economic development and the regeneration of declining areas in cities through targeted development projects.

At the same time, experiences with government land development companies raise a number of concerns regarding governmental involvement in land and housing development and associated risks. Thus, a risk exists that government companies might take monopolistic positions in land supply and housing supply. That is potent with market distortions, including price hikes (Singapore), or the opposite, oversupply (the Republic of Korea), and may create a direct governmental liability and burden for public finance (Dubai).

The true costs of such government land corporations to taxpayers are often underestimated, even in full-fledged market economies like Canada. In particular, land is often contributed by various governments into their land corporations (or purchased from other governmental agencies) at historical cost instead of market value, and this hidden public subsidy to corporation projects is not accounted anywhere.

A very high risk (and a common practice, at least in many former socialist countries) is that such corporations, like most municipal companies historically, may operate without proper governance, accountability, and transparency. They also tend to become involved in speculative real estate development, which should not be a part of government operations either directly or indirectly. It is often unclear whether these corporations exist primarily to generate revenues for the government or to serve other purposes. A common case is that such companies consume all their revenues, despite the said hidden subsidies from central or local government. For instance, the Lahore Development Authority has a larger budget than the city district government. It has engaged in huge land transactions and has big financial reserves, but it has not paid money into the budget of the city district government in the last decade.

These experiences suggest that it is vital to avoid empowering land corporations with regulatory authority in tandem with the right to operate as a business in the same jurisdiction. That many land authorities in South Asia operate that way raises conflicts of interest and makes the land transactions even less measurable and less transparent and more prone to corruption. Such arrangements also may create unfair competitive advantage over private investors.

Finally, in considering establishing a municipal company to manage municipal land or other capital assets, such a company's activities should be seen as part of a bigger picture of strategic and well-thought-out management of capital assets. Before a local government establishes such a company, time, effort, and expertise must be invested in the critical stage of *conceptual design*. In particular, the key policy, governance, business, and organizational contents have to be formulated and agreed upon in specific terms, before they are codified in legal documents and translated into company actions.[7]

Asset Management Strategy— Putting the Puzzle Together

How can city managers ensure that the instruments discussed in this chapter become parts of a complete and coherent program and have a lasting effect on the municipality's government— especially if the mayor and council may change in the next election? The *asset management strategy* is a special, important document and a tool that helps. The purpose of this document is to summarize both the general principles and the specific tasks of the strategy, including an *action plan* to improve asset management. It is recommended that this document be developed during the 6-to-18-month period after asset management improvements have started. This implies that the strategy should be a real working document, based on practical achievements and realistic intentions related to asset management.

Who Should Develop the Strategy?

In the best case, the temporary asset management task force should be empowered to draft the asset management strategy as one of its outputs. A mayor or treasurer should lead in drafting it and in presenting it to the council.

An asset management strategy includes several key sections:

1. Formulation of the mission, goals, and principles of asset management

2. Commitment to full inventorying and accounting of all properties for asset management purposes

3. Summaries and reviews of portfolios

4. Classification of all real property items among the three functional groups—mandatory, discretionary, and surplus (income generating)— and formulation of financial goals and a management strategy for each group

5. Formulation of asset policy principles, to the extent that the local government is ready to commit to them, to maximize revenues and ensure proper maintenance

6. Identification of local regulations that require some changes to improve asset management, and recommendations for specific changes (for example, liberalization of the ordinance on business rentals; modification of the ordinance on land allocation)

7. A list of specific actions for each group of properties and for separate properties, when necessary (for example, when there is a

change of tenants or managers; to improve use; or to recommend disposal)

8. Suggestions for organizational changes in asset management to ensure effective interdepartmental coordination

9. Identification of the person in charge of implementing the strategy (for example, the members of the task force)

10. A realistic mechanism and time schedule for implementing the strategy that reflect the local government's priorities.

Who Should Adopt the Strategy?

The best-case scenario is if the local council or assembly adopts the strategy as a guiding and binding document, like a local ordinance. But even if it is not a binding document, the strategy will be useful, as long as it is used as guidelines in practice. The strategy should be periodically (annually) revisited to measure progress, ensure its continued relevance, and update as necessary.

Takeaway Messages

For policy makers: Municipal governments across the world control large portfolios of physical assets (land, buildings, infrastructure, and vehicles and equipment), which usually contain the lion's share of local public wealth and which these governments manage on behalf of local taxpayers and citizens. Good management of these assets is critical for public financial well-being and the quality and sustainability of local services. It contributes to local economic development and the quality of life.

Better asset management produces multiple benefits: very real savings and additional revenues for the local budget; better-quality assets and services to citizens; and more trust between people and government.

For municipal staff and technical experts: Any government, be it a beginner or a sophisticate in asset management, can find in this chapter useful ideas, a framework, and practical tools for managing its assets better. They include inventorying assets; using transparent procedures for allocating assets for private use; aligning or classifying assets according to their role in delivering services that the government has to provide; using the market value of assets for decision making; establishing a depreciation fund for funding asset replacement; monitoring key indicators (e.g., asset-related costs and revenues); introducing life-cycle management for infrastructure and buildings, starting from planning operating and maintenance expenses for existing and new capital assets; using advanced instruments such as strategic asset management plans; and so forth.

A critical message is that asset management is a technical area, and so municipal staff members must build expertise and pay attention to regulatory, procedural, real estate, and infrastructure operating details. They should also be creative and inventive and have incentives to adopt those attitudes. Hiring experts from outside government who have specialized knowledge in real estate appraisal, property management, and the like, to assist governments on specific issues also can be justified.

Notes

1. Corruption, favoritism, or conflict of interest often happens through allocating public property to various users under preferential conditions—free of charge or for a below-market price. Disclosure of information on conditions substantially reduces corruption.

2. The market value of land, by definition, is the probable price the land should bring in a fair transaction, after being put on a competitive and open market for a reasonable time, with the buyer and seller each acting prudently and knowledgeably, and assuming the price is not affected by undue stimulus.

3. No universal formula exists, but see the further discussions in Urban Institute 2012a; 2012b.

4. Some rare exceptions exist. In New Zealand, the crown owns the land, and private parties hold fully and freely tradable, perpetual land rights called "fee simple." Those rights are not different in any respect from private ownership.

5. Fascinating examples of the complexity of "ordinary" real estate decisions that cities can face are explained in Hentschel and Utter 2006.

6. The Public-Private Infrastructure Advisory Facility (PPIAF) is a multidonor trust fund managed by the World Bank that provides technical assistance on PPP structuring to governments in developing countries. For more details, visit http://www.ppiaf.org.

7. For more on land corporations, see http://www.urban.org/UploadedPDF/412299-Government-Land-Development-Companies.pdf.

References

English, Richard, and. Frederick E. Brusberg. 2002. *Handbook for Preparing a Resettlement Action Plan.* Washington, DC: International Finance Corporation, World Bank.

Farvacque-Vitkovic, Catherine, Lucien Godin, Hugues Leroux, Florence Verdet, and Roberto Chavez. 2006. *Street Addressing and the Management of Cities.* Washington, DC: World Bank.

Hentschel, John, and Marilee Utter. 2006. "U.S. Cities—An Entrepreneurial Approach to Municipal Real Estate Asset Management." In *Managing Government Property Assets: International Experiences,* edited by Olga Kaganova and James McKellar. Washington, DC: UI Press.

Kaganova, Olga. 2008. "Integrating Public Property in the Realm of Fiscal Transparency and Anti-Corruption Efforts." In *Finding the Money: Public Accountability and Service Efficiency through Fiscal Transparency*, edited by Gábor Péteri, 209–22. Budapest: Local Government and Public Service Reform Initiative/Open Society Institute. http://cps.ceu.hu/publications/joint-publications/finding-the-money.

Kasso, Zsuzsa, and Piroska Pergerne-Szabo. 2004. "Asset Management in Secondary Cities." In *Intergovernmental Finance in Hungary—A Decade of Experience,* edited by M. Kopanyi, S. El Daher, and D. Wetzel, 381–403. Washington, DC: World Bank Institute.

Kopanyi, Mihaly, and Zsofia Hertelendy. 2004. "Municipal Enterprises in Hungary." In *Intergovernmental Finance in Hungary—A Decade of Experience,* edited by M. Kopanyi, S. El Daher, and D. Wetzel, 337–61. Washington, DC: World Bank Institute.

Managing Infrastructure Assets. 2005. National Guide to Sustainable Municipal Infrastructure, Canada, http://www.fcm.ca/Documents/reports/Infraguide/Managing_Infrastructure_Assets_EN.pdf.

Péteri, Gábor, and Michael Schaeffer. 2007. "Property Devolution and Local Government Asset Management." In *The Kosovo Decentralization Briefing Book,* edited by Robert D. Ebel and Gábor Péteri. Budapest: OSI.

Peterson, George E. 2009. *Unlocking Land Values to Finance Urban Infrastructure.* Washington, DC: World Bank and PPIAF.

Peterson, George E., and Olga Kaganova. 2010. "Integrating Land Financing in Subnational Fiscal Management." Policy Research Working Paper 5409, World Bank, Washington, DC.

Urban Institute. 2012a. *Guidebook on Packaging and Marketing Municipal Land to Investors.* Washington, DC: Urban Institute. http://www.urban.org/publications/412532.html.

———. 2012b. *Guidebook on Real Property Asset Management for Local Governments.* Washington, DC: Urban Institute. http://www.urban.org/publications/412531.html.

Whitestone Research. 2010. "Whitestone Facility Operations Cost Reference, 2010–2011." 15th annual ed. www.whitestoneresearch.com.

World Bank. 2011. *Guidebook on Capital Investment Planning for Local Governments.* Washington, DC: World Bank. http://web.worldbank.org.

CHAPTER 7

Managing External Resources

Maria Emilia Freire

In response to rapid urbanization, local governments all over the world are facing the challenge of providing new and improved infrastructure and basic services to increasingly demanding constituencies. The problem is compounded by the irreversible trend toward decentralization, which has delegated to local governments the execution and financing of large portions of the city investment program. Within an appropriate institutional framework and financial controls, many countries have allowed local governments to mobilize external finance for infrastructure through access to debt markets and private sector participation, resulting in better leveraging of own resources and savings. Fortunately, the financial sector of most emerging economies has developed rapidly, and local authorities now have access to a number of financing alternatives and to information on what has worked well in the past and what is needed to enter the financing markets. Experiences with local governments' access to external debt have informed local and

central governments about potential overborrowing and reinforced the need for prudent policies and close supervision.

This chapter analyzes how local governments can leverage and manage external resources to meet the demand for infrastructure development. We define external resources as the resources that accrue to the local government other than from its own revenue (taxes, fees, and fines), intergovernmental transfers, and capital revenues (discussed in chapters 1 and 4). Thus, *external resources* include market-based borrowing and private sector participation, private grants and philanthropic aid, and international aid and development assistance.

The chapter starts with a discussion of the importance of municipalities' having a multiyear capital improvement plan (CIP) to guide the use of external financing. It highlights the difficulties of collaborating across departments and standardizing feasibility studies. Project selection techniques such as cost-benefit analysis and net present value are mentioned as tools for prioritizing investments.

The chapter continues with a description of the characteristics of municipal borrowing and bond issue and discusses instruments that help municipalities access credit markets. Discussion of subsovereign debt regulations points out that national governments are often concerned that local jurisdictions may borrow above their payment capacity and default on their debt service, forcing the national government to finance these unfunded debts.

After exploring the potential of public-private partnerships in financing local investments, the chapter presents the types of external assistance available to municipalities, the emergence of new areas for local investment (including energy efficiency loans), and a review of philanthropic aid for municipalities.

Why Do Local Governments Need to Mobilize External Resources?

During the next 20 years, the need for infrastructure to promote growth and service delivery is projected at hundreds of billions of dollars a year worldwide. A large part of the responsibility for raising the necessary funds falls to the cities in developing countries, where much of the expected urban growth will take place. The Asian Development Bank estimates that in Asia alone nearly US$100 billion worth of new urban infrastructure will be needed annually to fill gaps and keep pace with this unprecedented urban growth. Financing requirements for water supply, sanitation, solid waste management, and slum upgrading in urban areas are estimated at US$25 billion per year—US$50 billion if urban roads are included (Sood 2004)—and an extra US$32 billion will be needed for maintenance (ADB 2011). The figures for other regions are similar. In China, subnational governments are responsible for 80 percent of government spending; in France, Indonesia, and Turkey, more than half of public investment takes place at the subnational level (Canuto and Liu 2010). Recent estimates indicate that the available resources from local governments are at most 10 percent of the total requirements. Thus, leveraging and managing external resources are both inevitable and strategic.

How can local governments finance capital investment? Local governments have several options. First, they can use current surpluses and grants from higher government tiers. They can also tap into local credit and capital markets and public-private partnerships or even attract donations from philanthropic or charitable organizations or international donors. The next section sheds light on these options before detailed discussions in the following sections.

Investments from Net Operating Surplus

Local governments can use their net operating surpluses to finance investment on a *pay-as-you-go* basis, which means that the expenditures will be financed in line with the generated annual surplus. The net operating surplus is the amount of operating revenues that can be used to finance capital expenditures, left over after paying salaries, operational and maintenance expenses, and debt service (discussed in chapters 3, 4, and 8). It implies that investment projects will be built from and at the pace of the available operating surplus. This is different from the *pay-as-you-use* method (common in project financing), in which borrowed funds are disbursed and then repaid from the proceeds generated by the project.

Paying as you go, or relying exclusively on an annual operating surplus, limits the capacity of local governments, given that in most cases the operating surplus is small. Because many infrastructure projects are large, limiting capital spending to the annual revenue stream would make it very difficult to finance such projects as a landfill or a major road. Pay-as-you-go financing often results in a large number of small, short-lived projects rather than large strategic investments. Since large investments play a vital role in creating local activity and eventually expanding local government revenues, depending on pay-as-you-go to finance infrastructure leads to missed opportunities. Moreover, a growing city with good services attracts businesses and housing development that help generate new own-source revenues.

Capital Grants

Local governments often rely on intergovernmental capital grants in developing countries. Grants are the principal source of long-term finance for developing basic infrastructure in many small and poor municipalities. For growing municipalities with adequate wealth and self-supporting projects (for example, urban transport), grants can help leverage and mobilize additional finances. Grants can also be used as a guarantee for borrowed money, resulting in lower risk and better terms.

Local Credit and Capital Markets

Local governments can access local credit and capital markets. The economic concept behind such access is that the long-term nature of infrastructure projects justifies long-term funding. Let us take the example of a solid waste plant. It is likely to cost much more than what a medium-size municipality could finance in a single year out of its current surplus. Moreover, even if the

municipality could finance the plant out of its own revenues over, say, three years, it may not be fair to do so since the plant will be used by future generations over 20-some years. Financing long-lived infrastructure investments with long-term debt spreads out the payment of the plant over time, so that those who benefit from it in the later years contribute to the financing as well. The debt financing alternatives depicted in figure 7.1 include a wide range of options, from borrowing from public banks to issuing debt in international capital markets, depending on the circumstances of a given local government.

Using debt financing has other benefits as well. It disciplines local governments by forcing them to determine major investment priorities and lock in the required financing, so that the decision does not have to be revisited every year. In addition, the ability to finance the construction of an entire facility in a timely fashion saves considerable money, in some cases more than the cost of interest on the loan.

Public-Private Partnerships

When local governments partner with the private sector in financing and building new infrastructure, they create a public-private partnership (PPP). PPPs have expanded fast in the past 30 years, and there are many lessons that can help local governments select the best type of PPP

Figure 7.1 Sources of External Financing for Local Governments

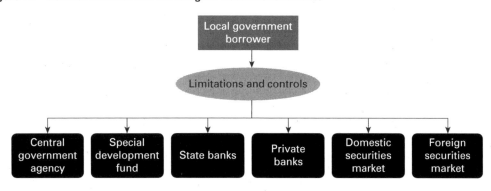

for delivering public services in alignment with their own technical capacity and responsibilities. Experience has shown that the contribution of PPPs in the municipal realm has been particularly important in improving the efficiency of service delivery, notably in such sectors as water supply and solid waste management.

Donations

Local governments may also benefit from private donations and funding from charitable organizations or international donors. Local patriots (or expatriates), for example, may donate an educational, cultural, or health facility in exchange for posting their name on the building. International organizations like the U.S. Agency for International Development (USAID) may donate various infrastructure. In some cases these funds are free and do not require repayment; however, many may require cofinancing from the local budget or fulfilling other policy conditions.

Guarantees

Guarantees have a role to play in using external resources. There are two types: (1) A higher government tier may provide guarantees as a financial support to the local government, making borrowing cheaper. In some cases borrowing can be concluded only with a guarantee by a third party (government or private bank). (2) Local governments may also request that independent entities such as utility companies borrow and may issue a municipal guarantee to support the transaction. In this way, the municipality saves cash from the budget, although it is assuming a contingent liability, that is, the risk that the borrowing entity will fail to pay its debt service and force the local government to step in and pay.

Conditions for Obtaining External Resources

The preconditions for obtaining external resources will be discussed in detail below, but it is worth highlighting a few general conditions for effectively acquiring and using external funds. A solid *capital investment program* with well-defined and appraised development projects is an important instrument for attracting funding consistent with the objectives of the municipality. It is also important to demonstrate that the external funds are used to finance target projects that are sustainable over a longer term and that have sufficient budget for operation and maintenance. Finally, timely and good financial reporting, a clear and balanced budget, and an operational surplus are vital to making the case with potential financiers or donors for the reliability and consistency of the municipal plans.

For prudent borrowing, the local government must have a strong financial position and the capacity to pay the principal and the future interest on the loan on time. It is useful to distinguish between (a) debt or borrowing by the local government to finance its own projects, to be paid off out of the operating surplus, and (b) debt incurred by the municipality on behalf of particular utilities or investments that will generate revenues and pay their own debt service. In the first case, one needs good financial reporting with clear projections showing an operational surplus of municipal revenues (that is, creditworthiness) or a credit rating issued by a rating agency such as Standard & Poor's. Debt in project finance (such as a water plant) needs a solid financial analysis of the project and its projected revenues. If the new project benefits from an implicit or explicit municipal guarantee, the creditworthiness of both the municipality and the new project should be evaluated. Financial feasibility is vital to borrowing funds for projects that are expected to generate enough cash flow to service the new debt. Overlooking these aspects and making overoptimistic projections have caused severe financial problems in many municipalities. The case of Harrisburg, Pennsylvania (see box 7.1), illustrates the importance of making realistic assumptions when deciding whether to borrow or to guarantee the borrowing of a public entity.

Box 7.1 Harrisburg, Pennsylvania: A Bankrupt City

Harrisburg, the capital city of Pennsylvania, filed for bankruptcy protection from creditors in mid-October 2011. Harrisburg is the largest municipality to file for bankruptcy since Vallejo, California, in 2008. The decision was triggered by two factors that heightened the financial difficulties the city was experiencing in debt service to its bond holders: debt service arrears had reached US$60 million.

The main factor was the US$320 million guarantee the city had provided for a waste incinerator. The project was supposed to be self-financing, but its failure left the city on the hook for the debt. In many cases, cities are too optimistic about the capacity of the project to generate enough revenues; and

when the incinerator failed to pay for its own debt, Harrisburg was called to honor the debt.

The second factor was the disagreement between the city and the State of Pennsylvania, which prohibited Harrisburg from imposing a tax on commuters into the city to address its financial problems. The state held that, instead of imposing the commuter tax, the city would have to sell off revenue-generating assets and eventually raise taxes on its citizens. The city argued that the poverty rate was about 29 percent and that taxing citizens would turn Harrisburg into a "ghost town." Claiming bankruptcy protection provided the city with a better set of tools.

Source: Tavernise 2011.

Feasibility Studies

Feasibility studies are vital instruments and preconditions for prudent borrowing. Local governments in developing countries often pay insufficient attention to their importance. They may order a feasibility study that includes a few hundred pages on the technical design of the project, which is a critical part of a feasibility study, but retain only a few pages for discussing the financial issues. In reality, these documents are not feasibility studies: feasibility studies should have detailed and thorough financial analysis, including realistic assumptions about future revenue flows and risks, sensitivity analysis, and instruments and commitments for effective collection of the projected revenues, which are all essential for assessing the financial feasibility of the project. Furthermore, it is vital to involve the customers in a timely way and to reach agreement on feasible and affordable tariffs at this stage.

A solid capital investment program with well-defined and appraised development projects

helps ensure that the borrowing is consistent with the objectives of the municipality (see chapters 5 and 6). To maintain alignment of the local government's borrowing with these objectives, most countries have specific regulations on how much and for what reasons local authorities can borrow. Whenever the local government has borrowing capacity and the projects are justified, using debt to finance investment is economically sound.

Planning Infrastructure: The Capital Investment Plan

While long-term municipal investments require long-term financing instruments, such investments should also be selected and designed in the context of a longer (3-, 5-, or 10-year) development plan. *Capital investment planning* is both a procedure and an instrument for selecting, developing, and implementing an investment program under a rolling multiyear framework

Figure 7.2 Framework for Drafting Capital Investment Plans

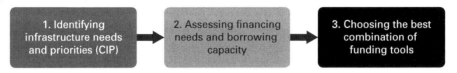

that guides, corresponds to, and is transformed into the annual development plan. The preparation of a local capital improvement plan usually includes three phases: (a) identification and prioritization of the infrastructure needs and required capital expenditures; (b) assessment of the external resources needed, local priorities, and what is feasible (within current legal and financial constraints); and (c) determination of the best combination of resources and funding, as depicted in figure 7.2. An approved CIP is often a published document that informs both the potential financiers and the stakeholders (citizens, firms, potential investors, and municipal entities). Figure 7.3 shows the front page of the CIP and annual strategic investment plan published together for the city of Charlotte, in the United States.

Identifying Infrastructure Needs and Selecting Priorities

Local governments decide—in multiple interactions within their own administration and in dialogue with their constituency—which investments have priority and how to finance them. During budget preparation (see chapters 3, 5, and 6), line departments or other entities and stakeholders assess the city's need for new investments, expansion, or repair of existing infrastructure. This initial list of priority projects is often long and includes many competing proposals. The department of planning or a development committee of the municipal council is assigned to evaluate, rank, and shortlist the proposals based on socioeconomic and policy priorities as well as on funds available.

Assessing Financial Need and Borrowing Capacity

The finance department explores main financing options and proposes financing alternatives for each priority project, ensuring that the whole package fits into the overall funding capacity of the city, including borrowing. The capacity of a local government to borrow depends on two factors: the *projected local revenues* that can be used to pay for or cover future debt service and the size and structure of the *existing debt* (that is, the average maturity and interest rates, which together determine the debt service for the upcoming years).

Future revenues and expenditures are projected as a function of internal variables (such as the fiscal effort of the municipality and its wage policies) and external variables (such as economic growth). Other risks need to be considered, such as the political risk to external variables (for example, changes in grants or tax-sharing rates or failure of higher-level government to cofinance the project as initially promised). Changes in intergovernmental finance arrangements can also undermine the capacity of local governments to adequately project their stream of revenues and investment capacity. Ongoing projects that have received financing or grants from other levels of government need to be taken into account, as they may require some budget allocation for counterpart funding. Box 7.2 shows the complexity of issues to be addressed in defining financing options and limits in a 10-year development plan in San Francisco.

Assessing borrowing capacity is a key action for local governments. It provides a concrete value for how much a local government can borrow while

Figure 7.3 Capital Investment Plan for Charlotte City

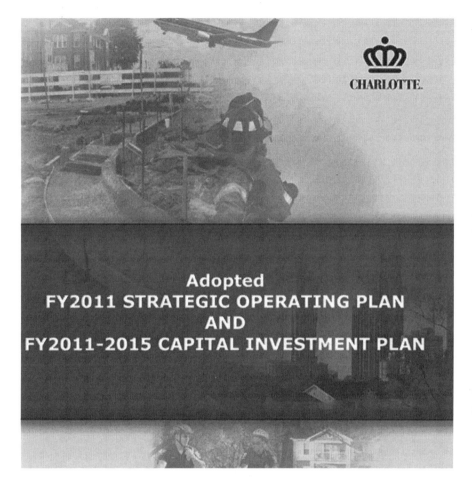

maintaining fiscal balance over the course of full repayment of the debt. It prevents overborrowing and reduces the possibility that local governments will default on their debt. National governments or local rules aiming to reduce the risk of defaults often limit local borrowing by using simple parameters such as *debt stock* or *debt service flow* (debt as a percentage of net revenues). For example, in Brazil, municipalities can borrow if their debt stock remains below 60 percent of their operating revenues or if their debt service (the interest payments on outstanding debt and amortization)

remains below 15 percent of operating revenues. In this way, local governments are able to estimate how much they can borrow in a given year and how many projects can be included in the final, multiyear capital plan.

Choosing the Best Combination of External Financing

Once the local government estimates how much it can raise in the credit market (and how much concessionary finance it is likely to receive), it will be able to choose the best combination of

Box 7.2 San Francisco: The 10-Year Capital Plan, FY 2012–21

In 2006, after decades of underfunded infrastructure, the mayor and board of supervisors approved San Francisco's first citywide, 10-year capital plan. It was the first time San Francisco had thought comprehensively about its infrastructure and developed a plan to address the most pressing deficits. Since then, the city has received voter approval for major seismic improvements and for increased funding of its streets program; for a wide range of new libraries, parks, hospitals, pipelines, transit lines, and museums; and for increased support for the "state of good repair" renewal needs.

The projects were selected based on the availability of funding and the priority of each project. Departments with their own revenues—for example, the San Francisco International Airport and the Public Utilities Commission—finance most of their capital needs out of user fees. Programs that serve the general public (such as fire stations) rely primarily on funding from the city's general fund and debt financing.

The FY 2012–21 capital plan expects US$24.8 billion in funding. This plan includes capital expenditures to be funded by the local government (called the general fund): US$4.8 billion-plus for projects in sectors that finance their expenditures out of cost recovery (transport and utilities) and special large projects that have financing guaranteed and are on a project finance basis. The US$4.8 billion financed by the local government general fund is actually half the proposed US$9.8 billion budget that the city had to cut because of lack of revenues. The overall package includes US$1.18 billion in current revenues (pay as you go), US$2.4 billion in new debt (in the form of general obligation bonds), and US$1.3 billion in previously authorized but not issued general obligation bonds. The city's borrowing capacity is determined by two approved restrictions: (a) property taxes will not be raised to cover the new debt and (b) the debt service of San Francisco's local government will not be above 3.5 percent of the city's own (discretionary) revenues. This restriction implies that new debt can be raised only after the old debt is repaid.

Source: San Francisco Capital Plan 2012–21, http://www.sfgov2.org/ftp/uploadedfiles/cpp/Final_FY09-18_Capital _Plan_All_Sections(1).pdf.

external resources that matches the duration of the projects and that will result in lower overall debt service.

The mayor and the municipal council review the shortlist before deciding on the priority of the projects. The resulting document is a multiyear CIP that includes the priority projects, explains how they fit with the vision of the city, and maps out how they will be financed. Both the five-year capital plan of Charlotte city (figure 7.3) and the San Francisco 10-year plan (table 7.1 and box 7.2) illustrate how the investment plan is organized

and financed, as well as how the city tries to fit the investment plan into its existing resources and debt capacity.

From Capital Investment Plan to Financing Plan

Preparing Capital Investment Plans

Many local governments prepare rolling, multiyear capital investment plans every year, which name the priority capital projects for which financing is guaranteed (see also chapters 5 and 6).

Table 7.1   San Francisco's 10-Year Capital Plan by Department

US$ millions

Sectors	General fund	External and self-financing	Total
Public safety	1,777	0	1,777
Health and human services	1,129	565	1,694
Infrastructure and streets	1,033	6,550	7,582
Education and culture	678	778	1,456
Neighborhood renovation	92	4,179	4,271
Transportation	0	7,842	7,842
General government	165	0	165
Total	4,873	19,914	24,787
Pay as it goes	1,183	0	0
Debt	3,690	0	0

Source: San Francisco Capital Plan 2012–21, http://www.sfgov2.org/ftp/uploadedfiles/cpp/Final_FY09-18_Capital_Plan_All_Sections(1).pdf.

CIP preparation starts with the identification of the infrastructure needs of the city, including deficiencies in coverage and the need for expansion or renovation of existing infrastructure.

If the city has developed a city development strategy—that is, a medium-term economic vision of what the city wants to be in the future—then most certainly the strategy includes a capital investment plan identifying the investments needed to attain that vision (World Bank 2002).

However, even if a city has a development strategy, it needs more detailed information for the particular projects included in the annual development plan. The proposals come from individual departments in the municipality. For example, the education department may propose the construction of two new schools and repairs on 13 classrooms, and the transportation department may propose the pavement of six streets totaling 10 miles of road.

The information provided typically includes the following elements:

- *Municipal information* includes a city vision and strategy and how the project fits into the city's vision of itself, its demography, and its business or social needs.

- *Title and description of the proposed project* include, for example, the size, location, and cost of a school and how long it will take to be completed.

- *Financing* includes the proposed financing over the next five-year period, as well as the cost of completing each phase of the construction and its estimated operating and maintenance costs after completion.

- *Environmental impact* includes how the project will affect the environment, both positively (by reducing greenhouse gas emissions) and negatively (by generating pollution or traffic).

- *Past performance* includes municipal spending on infrastructure and in the particular sectors (education, roads) in the previous five years.[1]

Once the municipal authority defines its investment priorities and selects the individual projects (possibly in conjunction with key business and civil representatives), the next step is to decide how to finance the plan. This is basically an iterative process, since financing options—project-based financing, budget financing, general obligation bonds, or public-private partnerships—influence not only the total funds available but also the list of priority projects. Thus, after looking into financing options, the municipal authority might revise the priority list to avoid unfunded high-priority projects and also to ensure that funding opportunities are put to best use.

Some cities have developed municipal contracts that outline a priority investment plan (based on an urban audit) and a municipal improvement plan (based on a financial audit or on a financial self-assessment of the municipality). Those cities with municipal contracts in place carry out the selection of priority investments on a very participatory basis, typically involving citizens and interest groups (see box 7.3), and the final selection is based on the financial capacity of the local government. Such a model has been very effective in Africa, among other places, where over 200 municipalities have implemented several generations of municipal contracts, thereby introducing accountability in public spending. The financial self-assessment of the municipality will be further discussed in chapter 8.

Besides funding options and CIP structuring, local governments also need to discuss how to include the legally independent utilities—for example, the water utility and the solid waste management company—into the broad CIP with independent financing (possibly using project-based financing and user fees) with the approval of the

Table 7.2 Financing the City Investment Plan of the City of Charlotte, 2011–15

Financing sources	US$
Financed by general fund	256.7
Bonds (participation bonds)	203.6
Independent utilities	2,131.2
Total	2,591.5

Source: Charlotte 2011–15 Capital Investment Plan, http://charmeck.org/city/charlotte/Budget/Documents/FY2011 Strategic Operating Plan.pdf.

council. Most likely, the city budget will include its own revenue, transfers from the central and state government, local taxes and borrowing, and external resources. The revenue-producing utilities are normally included in the CIP, and their revenues and expenditures reported explicitly but outside the municipal budget.

Let us take the case of the Charlotte city investment plan summarized in table 7.2. The city spent two years preparing the full plan, based on dialogue with the business community. The objectives were to promote economic development and better living conditions for its citizens. The total cost for 2011–15 is US$2.5 billion, financed by general revenues (10 percent) and by borrowing and special bonds issued to the general public (8 percent), with the rest financed by large municipal enterprises operating in self-financing sectors such as water and sewer, aviation, and storm water, whose capital plans can be funded by service charges.

Project Selection Tools

To choose among capital investment projects, local governments should have a clear sense of priorities and criteria to help them value and compare projects. Once the list of potential projects is put together, staff of the local government evaluate them according to criteria established in advance and rank them in line with those criteria (such as costs and benefits) and according to their merits or relative profitability as well as feasibility and preparedness. The analysis is often carried out by the technical staff of the planning department, sometimes in parallel with the project department of the development bank or with a central government entity. This is often a time-consuming task because departments in government have different ways of appraising or preparing projects, and often project benefits and costs are hard to quantify.

Many times, however, projects are selected on political grounds (for example, a project for which the mayor has received a special allocation) or because they are financed by the central government and may not be subjected to the prioritization exercise. Ideally, the central government's projects should be accounted for and listed in the CIP plan to the extent that reasonable information is available. The lack of coordination across government tiers not only is inconvenient to citizens but also creates extra costs (see box 7.4).

Although it is widely accepted that political preferences, preparedness, and feasibility are important in the choice of priority projects,

useful analytical tools and indicators are available that should be used when possible for selecting or prioritizing capital projects:

- Cost-benefit analysis (CBA)

- Internal rate of return (IRR)

- Net present value (NPV).

These instruments are critical indicators of feasibility. They indicate how much a project is worth and help rank technically different projects. Chapters 5 and 6 also discuss these instruments. A short summary of them from the financing perspective is included below. However, most local governments do not have internal capacity to apply these instruments and hire consultants, especially for conducting a cost-benefit analysis for projects that may need donor or lender financing. For projects funded from governments' own resources, simpler evaluation criteria are used.

Cost-Benefit Analysis

Cost-benefit analysis is an economic decision-making approach used to assess whether a proposed project, program, or policy is worth doing or to choose between several options. Such an analysis compares the total expected costs of a project with the total expected benefits and establishes whether the benefits outweigh the costs and by how much. In a CBA, all kinds of direct and indirect benefits and costs are expressed in money terms and are adjusted for the time value of money. This process is often very complex and

---

Box 7.4 Lack of Coordinated Plans

A city in Pakistan resurfaced its main street under a donor project, but a few weeks later the department of public health commenced replacement of the sewer main on the same street, carved up the new road, and failed to fix the surface properly. A multiyear plan approved and shared with government would have saved both time and money.

Table 7.3 Cost-Benefit Analysis of a Bus Terminal Project over 10 Years

US$ thousands

Costs and benefits		Present value
Costs		
Direct project costs		
	Cost of design	100
	Civil works	2,000
	Financing costs	300
	Operation and maintenance	5,000
Other costs	Noise	200
	Pollution	800
Total		8,400
Benefits		
Direct revenues for the investor municipality	Fees from buses	4,500
	Parking fees (cars, motorcycles)	1,500
	Lease fees from cafe, restaurant	500
	Taxes	1,000
Indirect revenues	Travel time saving	300
	Jobs, wages, profit	1,200
Total		9,000

time-consuming, especially as one tries to monetize special benefits and costs. In this way, all flows of benefits and all flows of costs over time (which tend to occur in different magnitudes and at different points in time) are quantified and expressed in *present value terms*. Future streams of costs and benefits are converted into a present value amount using a discount rate. Table 7.3 summarizes the costs and benefits of a bus terminal project, translated into present values, after nonfinancial costs (such as noise, pollution) and benefits (time saving) are also estimated in financial terms. For instance, estimating the time savings needs special surveys, such as traffic counts, to quantify the number of passengers on various days, to measure the commuting time before the

project and after, and to attach value to the time based on income estimates.

Discount Rate

The first challenge in the cost-benefit analysis is to compare various costs and benefits independently of the year in which they happen; this calculation requires translating the nominal values into present values. For calculating the present value of future revenues, we use a discount factor d, which is the inverse of a discount interest rate r; thus, $d_i = 1/(1+r)^i$ in any future year (i). The d discounts the value of money over time rather than compounding it. For instance, a nominal or future value of 2 million (in any currency) in revenue over three years would be $2 + 2 + 2 = 6$ million. However, if the discount rate is 5 percent, the earnings of the first year would be the nominal 2 million, but in year 2, the present value of the earnings would be only $2/(1.05) =$ or 1.82 million; and in the third year would be only $2/(1.05)^2 =$ 1.65 million. Using the $R*d_i$ formula, $2*1 + 2*0.952 + 2*0.907 = 5.719$ million total present value of this revenue stream.[2]

The choice of the discount rate reflects the value we give to time, based on local circumstances and opportunities. How do we choose a discount rate? We may use the long-term borrowing rate, inflation rate, or capital market yield, since typically these are real opportunities. We may use a rate reflecting the yield typical in similar projects, similar services, or similar investments. But we need to be pragmatic in choosing the adequate rate, and it is always better to compare the various discount rate options:

- A low discount rate implies that we value the future generations on the same basis as ourselves.

- A high discount rate means that we value the present generation more than the future ones and that the costs inflicted on future generations are less important than those we bear today. The rate chosen makes a large difference in the assessment of investments with long-term effects such as climate change, and thus discount rates are a source of controversy.

The *net present value* is the difference between the initial investment plus discounted revenues and the discounted costs during the active life of the project evaluated at a given discount rate. The NPV should be greater than zero for economically justified projects. A negative NPV suggests that we would lose rather than generate real-term money with the planned investment.

The *internal rate of return* is the discount rate at which total costs, including the initial investment, equal the total benefits of the project. If the IRR is greater than the ongoing comparable long-term interest rate (for example, the bank deposit rate), the project is considered economically justified (meaning that we would gain more than by simply depositing the money in a bank).

To apply the above, consider C_i the cost of a project in year i and R_i the benefits in year i. The total cost of the project will be $\sum C_i$, the total return will be $\sum R_i$, and the total net value = $\sum R_i - \sum C_i$.

Adjusting for time, we would derive the net present value as

$$NPV = \sum R_i/(1+r)^i - \sum C_i/(1+r)^i,$$

where r *is* the interest rate and i would be the years 0, 1, 2, ..., n.

When the net present value is greater than zero, the discounted revenues are greater than the discounted costs, indicating an economic or business justification for the project.

The internal rate of return is the discount rate that makes the net present value equal to zero, that is, the largest discount rate at which the total benefits are equal to the total costs. If the IRR is greater than the current market interest rates (or the price of the capital for the government), the project is certainly worthwhile implementing. If the IRR is less than the price of money, the project should not go ahead. The more profitable the project is, the higher the IRR will be.

Often, we use cost-benefit analysis to measure the benefits of alternative interventions or to calculate an outcome with and without an intervention, as in the example of the proposed covered market in Newville in box 7.5.

Box 7.5 Cost-Benefit Analysis, Internal Rate of Return, and Net Present Value: An Example

To introduce the concepts of cost-benefit analysis, internal rate of return, and net present value, let us start with a simple example. The local government in Newville received the following proposal. A group of retail businesses would like to develop a covered market. They propose that the municipality invest US$10 million in infrastructure. In return, the business community will pay a US$2 million annual lease fee for the first six years. The mayor has to decide whether this proposed business makes sense.

What do you think?

The cost of the project for the municipality is US$10 million. The returns are US$12 million total. At first sight, the project will pay for itself and yield a net value of US$2 million. It seems that the mayor could approve the project.

(continued next page)

Box 7.5 *(continued)*

Is that so? What about the value of time?

Taking the time into account, we see that the US$2 million in year 2 or year 3 is not the same as the US$10 million spent in the first year. It has less value as time passes; and what if a bank offers 8 percent annual interest for the six-year time deposit?

To help the mayor make a decision, we display the annual costs and annual earnings in a single worksheet and use a discount rate to make the values comparable over time (see table B7.5.1).

Let us take these values to our mayor. The cost would be US$10 million; the return would be US$2 million a year and US$12 million in total. Thus, we would have US$2 million net at the end of the period; it looks nice.

Let us now choose a discount rate to convert the nominal values into present value. Let us choose the 8 percent rate that the bank has offered to the municipality for a time deposit. What would be the result? By using the formula $NPV = \sum R_i / (1+r)^i - \sum C_i / (1+r)^i$, the r would be 8 percent, and we would need to compute the present values of revenues and costs for the six years. Table B7.5.2 shows the results.

Lessons

The present value of the total cost does not change, because there was only one cost item; but the present value of the revenue stream has changed. The present value (PV) of benefits with the 8 percent discount rate would be only US$9.246 million, which is actually lower than the cost of the project. The net present value is US$–0.754 million. Therefore, it is not a good idea for the city to finance the project under these conditions, since the city could gain more from depositing that money in a bank. But also, based on the calculations, the local government should request the business community to commit or contract to pay a higher annual fee, say, US$2.3 million, which would ensure a higher rate of return and a positive net present value.

Table B7.5.1 Current Values

US$ millions

Year	0	1	2	3	4	5	6	Total
Cost = C	10							10
Benefits = B		2	2	2	2	2	2	12
Net value ($\sum B_i - C$)	–10	2	2	2	2	2	2	2

Table B7.5.2 Calculation of Net Present Value with an 8 Percent Discount Rate

Year	0	1	2	3	4	5	6	Present value
(1) Compounded discount rate		1.08	1.166	1.26	1.36	1.469	1.587	
(2) Cost = C	10							10
(3) Benefit = B	0	2	2	2	2	2	2	
(4) Discount factor $d_i = 1/(1+r)^i$		0.926	0.858	0.794	0.735	0.681	0.630	
(5) Net benefit NB = $R_i/(1+r)^i = d_i * B_i$		1.852	1.715	1.588	1.47	1.361	1.26	9.246
(6) Net present value ($\sum NB_i - C$)	–10	1.852	1.715	1.588	1.47	1.361	1.26	–0.754

Financing Alternatives: Loans or Bonds

Local governments in developing countries rely mainly on grants to finance infrastructure; however, many have tried to expand and diversify their financing by mobilizing market-based options as an alternative. Typically, these options include the following external resources:

- Borrowing from financial institutions or specialized development banks

- Accessing capital markets or issuing bonds

- Engaging private sector participation through contracts, leases, and concessions.

The success of local governments in leveraging market-based funds for local investment varies a great deal, depending on the depth of the local credit markets, the quality of local governance, and how the private investors perceive the risk of the individual local authority. Some countries have had long-standing experience in raising private debt for urban infrastructure (see box 7.6). Local authorities in North America rely mainly on municipal bonds, while in Western Europe municipal banks have been created to help local authorities. Bond financing is not necessarily an incremental supplement to other instruments; it could be quite significant, if the capital market is robust. For example, the market for municipal bonds in Canada and the United States is larger than the market for corporate bonds.

In developing or emerging economies, local governments' access to credit markets is hindered by various factors:

- Local services such as water supply and solid waste plants are not attractive to private investors, who fear that the projects have limited cost recovery and long gestation.

Box 7.6 Local Government Borrowing in North America and Western Europe

The U.S. municipal bond market was originated in response to the country's urban expansion in the 1850s. Municipal investment in North America was largely financed by *specific purpose revenue bonds* (issued to finance a particular project), also called project financing; others preferred using *general obligation bonds* (see below for the description of types of bonds). The central government endorsed decentralized financing by conferring tax-free status on municipal bonds and contributing to state revolving funds and bond banks so that smaller municipalities could benefit from bond resources without being penalized for their small size.

Western Europe leveraged the historical preferential access to long-term saving deposits and government contributions to establish municipal banks and financial institutions. Examples of municipal banks include Dexia Credit Local of France, BNG of the Netherlands, Banco de Credito of Spain, and Credit Communal of Belgium. The 2008–10 financial crisis affected these large banks as they launched some nontypical products to compete with other financial institutions. As a result, some entities were nationalized and were totally overhauled, as was the case of Dexia Credit Local, which was rescued by massive public capital and the administration totally changed. But all have continued their role of working with municipalities, although now restricted to domestic local authorities.

- Local governments often have a weak fiscal position with a small current surplus and unpredictable transfers from higher government tiers.

- Local capital and financial markets are emerging and do not offer good products for local governments.

Capital Markets: Issuing Municipal Bonds

Municipal bonds have been widely used in North America to finance local government investment but are much less popular in Europe, especially in France and Germany, where local governments largely borrow from specialized banks like Dexia.

What Is a Municipal Bond?

A municipal bond is a debt obligation issued by a local authority with the promise to pay the bond interest (coupon) on a specified payment schedule and the principal at maturity. Thus a bond works like a loan: The issuer is the borrower (debtor), the holder is the lender (creditor), and the coupon is the interest. The purpose is similar to a bank credit. The issuer (the local government) sells bonds to the general public (often through an investment bank) and uses the proceeds from the sale to finance capital projects such as schools, sewer systems, and the like. (Box 7.7 explains underwriting, a process for issuing bonds.) A bond may be printed and traded like a bank note,

although bonds are increasingly issued only electronically, without a printed paper form, creating considerable savings for the issuers.

Bonds bear interest at either a fixed or a variable rate. The date on which the issuer repays the principal—that is, the bond's maturity date—may be years in the future. Short-term bonds mature in one to three years, while long-term bonds generally will not mature for more than a decade.

Individual investors hold about two-thirds of the roughly US$2.8 trillion of U.S. municipal bonds outstanding, either directly or indirectly through mutual funds and other investments. Bond investors are typically seeking a steady stream of income payments, and compared to stock investors, they may be more risk averse and more focused on preserving than on accumulating wealth with more secure but lower yields.

Municipal bonds have been extraordinarily successful in raising capital for infrastructure investments in U.S. cities, in part because the federal government grants tax-free status to municipal bonds. The U.S. municipal bond market grew from US$66 billion in 1960, to US$361 billion in 1981, to US$2.8 trillion in 2010 (Shapiro 2010). In 2010, more than 50,000 entities issued a record US$327 billion in municipal bonds (Platz 2009).

Outside the United States, the market for subnational debt has grown in the past 10 years from US$270 billion to US$396 billion, with the average maturity increasing from 7.14 to 9.45 years.

Box 7.7 Underwriting

The most common process for issuing bonds is through *underwriting*. In underwriting, one or more banks buy an entire issue of bonds from an issuer and resell them to investors. The security firm thus takes on the risk of being unable to sell the issue to end-investors.

Central and local governments usually issue bonds by auctions, where both the public and banks may bid on them. However, the costs can be too high for a smaller loan, in which case the bond is issued as a private placement bond, which is held by the lender and does not enter the large bond market; this process represents a special form of bank lending.

Municipal bond financing has already been undertaken in many countries; box 7.8 gives examples of cases in Africa, Latin America, South and East Asia, and Europe. For Latin America, cities in Argentina, Brazil, Colombia, and Mexico have issued both general revenue and specific purpose bonds. The city of Aguascalientes was the first Mexican city to issue a municipal bond in 2001 for the sum of Mex\$90 million. Currently, three other Mexican cities have outstanding bond issuances totaling US\$1.86 billion (Fitch Ratings 2009).

Types of Bonds

There are several types of municipal bonds, including general obligation bonds, revenue bonds, and structured bonds.

Box 7.8 Municipal Bonds in Developing or Middle-Income Countries

- *Rio de Janeiro* was the first city in Latin America to successfully issue a bond in the international capital markets. The city issued a bond in July 1996 to refinance its existing debt (with an interest rate of 10.3 percent for US\$125 million over three years). The bond was unsecured, despite the fact that this was the first time the city had issued international debt. Since then, tight fiscal regulations have prevented municipal bond issuances in Brazil (Platz and Schroeder 2007).

- *Bogotá* followed Rio's example and issued international bonds in 2001; US\$100 million were sold at a 9.5 percent interest rate and a five-year term to raise funds to finance infrastructure projects. The bonds received global ratings by Fitch Ratings of BB+ and Standard & Poor's of BB. The 2001 Bogotá bonds had no sovereign guarantee.

- *Zimbabwe* issued municipal bonds with sovereign guarantees, as have *Sofia* in Bulgaria and *Moscow* and *St. Petersburg* in the Russian Federation.

- Issuers in *Asia* include Japan, the Republic of Korea, Malaysia, and the Philippines (Peterson, G. and P. Annez 2008). Since 1991, at least 13 local Asian governments have issued bonds totaling US\$34.5 million (Platz 2009). The issues have ranged between US\$148,000 and US\$500,000 with maturities of two to three years. China is revising legislation to allow municipalities to access the bond market, given the increasing pressure of Chinese cities on bank credit. China has used bonds in an indirect way.

- *Indian* municipalities such as Ahmedabad Municipal Corporation have raised about US\$290 million, mainly to finance water supply and sewerage systems. To reduce the risk and increase the marketability of these bonds, the India Securities Exchange Board is issuing guidelines to increase the transparency of issuances and protect investors' interests.

- The city of *Johannesburg* is the only city in South Africa to have issued municipal bonds in recent years, although *Kigali*, Rwanda, is also contemplating this possibility. Johannesburg has launched four institutional bonds totaling US\$506 million. South Africa is the only African country that issues municipal bonds. In 2004, the city of Johannesburg purchased a partial bond guarantee from the Development Bank of Southern Africa (DBSA) and the International Finance Corporation (IFC), guaranteeing 40 percent of the bond's proceeds.

Source: Ngobeni 2008.

General Obligation Bonds

General obligation bonds are serviced from the general revenues of the local government, such as Rio de Janeiro, Buenos Aires, or Johannesburg (see boxes 7.9 and 7.10). The municipality uses its full set of revenue sources, including its taxes and fees, intergovernmental transfers, and unconditional grants, to service the outstanding debt and interest. If the local governments have outstanding debt and the market doubts that they will generate enough general revenues to pay the debt service, a portion of those revenues is deposited into an escrow account to ensure the timely servicing of the bonds.

Revenue Bonds

Revenue or special purpose bonds are secured by the anticipated revenues from the project being financed. For example, in a freeway project, the tolls will be used to pay the bonds; in a water project, the tariffs will do the same. In the case of the Madurai Municipal Corporation, India, the local government issued a revenue bond to finance 27 kilometers of the Madurai inner-ring road. The bond issue generated US$23 million, with a 10-year maturity at a 12 percent interest rate. A special enhancement scheme and guarantee fund enabled the issue to be rated AA+. The bonds were to be repaid by the tolls charged for use of that road.

Box 7.9 General Obligation Bond Issue by Novi Sad

The city of Novi Sad, Serbia, issued the first municipal bonds in Serbia in 2011, for a total of €35 million. The bonds were issued at an annual rate of 6.25 percent for a 12-year maturity, with a grace period of 2 years. The resources will finance the completion of the Boulevard of Europe and the construction of 100 kilometers of sewerage networks. UniCredit Bank in Serbia was the underwriter. Some economists believe that the desire to put the city on the capital market map was the primary reason for issuing the bond, not economic or financial considerations.

Source: Novi Sad 2011.

Box 7.10 Long-Term Bond Issue in the City of Johannesburg

In 2004, the city of Johannesburg tried to access the bond market with a general obligation bond to lower the general cost of the debt. The bond issue had several objectives: (a) to extend the maturity of existing debt; (b) to finance long-term infrastructure projects; (c) to refinance existing high-cost bank debt; and (d) to diversify funding sources beyond bank lending. The city looked for funding beyond 10 years, but to do so at a reasonable price required credit enhancement. IFC assisted in structuring the operation and provided a partial credit guarantee (for 40 percent of the total) shared with the Development Bank of South Africa. As a result, in June 2004 Johannesburg managed to issue a US$53 million 11.9 percent bond to mature in 12 years. Fitch Ratings gave the city an A−rating. The bond issue was oversubscribed 2.3 times.

Sources: IFC 2004; Platz 2009; Amim 2010.

Structured Bonds

Structured bonds are secured by revenue sources that differ from the revenues generated by the project itself. For example, the province of Mendoza, Argentina, issued international bonds to restructure its domestic debt. The provincial government used the province's expected oil royalties to secure the payment of the bonds, both to service the bonds and to redeem them at maturity.

In developing countries, investors concerned about the creditworthiness of local governments tend to prefer structured bonds, since the local government ensures that the bonds will be paid regardless of any internal or external development. That is done through the intercept of intergovernmental transfers, as well as oil revenues; that is, before transfers or royalties are deposited in the local government account, a sum is taken out (intercepted) to pay the debt service.

Risk and Credit Ratings

Credit ratings are assessments of the creditworthiness of a given local government or bond issue made by recognized rating agencies. Basically, the rating indicates the risk that a particular government will not pay the bond's interest and principal on time. Box 7.11 summarizes the evolving ratings in emerging economies (for more details, see Peterson 1998).

The assessment of risk is based on the economic and financial conditions of local government, past fiscal indicators, the structure of debt and pending payments, and the future factors that may affect the creditworthiness of the local governments. A high (investment-grade) rating by a reliable credit agency is particularly beneficial. In general, insurance companies and provident funds (funds financed by contributions from members) are the main purchasers of municipal bonds, and they need to be sure that the assets are secure. However, credit ratings are expensive, and municipalities may need to assess whether the advantages associated with the rating are less than the expected gain from having their bond rated.

Rating Agencies

Rating agencies play a key role in providing the market with information on the capacity of a given local authority to issue debt and pay it on time. The rated municipalities must share their key financial data with the public and enforce their own fiscal discipline.

Three major rating agencies for municipal bonds account for 95 percent of all international ratings around the world:

- Moody's Investors Service

- Standard & Poor's

- Fitch Ratings.

Ratings combine quantitative analyses and judgment about the capacity of the municipality to repay the debt on time; results are published with specific scores (rating grades). In assigning

---

Box 7.11 Ratings in Emerging Economies

Ratings are mandatory for local governments in India, when the issue maturity is more than 18 months. Emerging economies that have local government ratings include Argentina, Brazil, Bulgaria, India, Kazakhstan, Malaysia, Mexico, Morocco, Poland, Romania, the Russian Federation, South Africa, Turkey, and Ukraine. Mexico has been particularly active in promoting the preparation of credit ratings for local governments as a base for both bank credit and bond issue.

---

a rating for general obligation bonds, the rating agencies assess the following factors:

- The local and national economy

- Debt structure

- Financial condition

- Demographic factors

- Management practices of the local government and the legal framework.

Rating agencies use mathematical ratios to compare an issuer to others. But a rating is not a scientific evaluation, and subjective judgment plays a fundamental role in the rating assigned. In the case of Moody's rating, for example, the notation ranges from Aaa (strongest creditworthiness) to Baa (average creditworthiness). Table 7.4 summarizes the different notations of the three rating agencies. There are grades C and D, too, but clients are better off avoiding having their performance rated if they are likely to receive such a low grade.

A bond rating performs the function of a credit risk evaluation. It does not constitute a recommendation to invest in a bond and does not take into consideration the risk preference of the investor. However, the market follows credit risk ratings quite closely, and in the case of bonds, the rating is often the single most important factor affecting the interest cost. Although municipalities are rated on their merits, the country rating is considered a ceiling for subnational entities; thus, the rating of a city cannot be better than that of the host country.

Comparing Bonds and Bank Credit

Are all local governments able to issue bonds? No. Only local governments with considerable investment programs, good ratings, and long-term financial needs will be able to do so. Borrowing from commercial banks or bond banks or syndicating a loan might be better options for smaller local governments, given the advantages of issuing bonds. How can one compare the loan or bond alternatives? Advantages and disadvantages of bonds and loans are explained below and summarized in table 7.5 and box 7.12.

Bonds Have Advantages

Among the benefit of bonds are that local governments receive all the money they need up-front, rather than gradually, as with the typical disbursement process in banks, and that the funds are usually obtained more cheaply than through bank credit, often by two or three percentage points. The terms of the funds are also fixed for the whole period of the issue and cannot be changed or recalled.

Bonds Have Shortcomings

Among the shortcomings of bonds are the following:

- *Preparing a bond issue is complex.* It requires good data, understanding and disclosure of financial and economic information on the local government, and knowledge of the market to ensure that the issue is placed at favorable terms.

Table 7.4 Investment-Grade Ratings of Three Rating Agencies

Rating	Moody's	Standard & Poor's	Fitch Ratings
Best quality	Aaa	AAA	AAA
High quality	Aa1, Aa2, Aa3	AA+, AA, AA−	AA+, AA, AA−
Upper-medium grade	A1, A2	A+. A	A+, A
	A3	A−	A−
Medium grade	Baa1, Baa2, Baa3	BBB+, BBB, BBB−	BBB+, BBB, BBB−

Table 7.5 Comparison of Bonds and Bank Lending

	Bonds	Bank lending
Cost	High transaction costs with expensive preparation	Simple and fast transaction without costs, except for syndicated loans
Maturity	Relatively longer term	Short term
Interest rates	Fixed rates	Floating rates
Repayment	Redemption at maturity	In installments
Merits and demerits	Fund raising from extensive investors; high credit rating is required for the issuance.	The credit rating is not required; banks may offer "relationship lending" based on the trust built on previous interactions with the bank rather than on specific clear risk indicators (but pros and cons remain).

Box 7.12 A Comparison of Bonds and Bank Lending

- *Long term or short term.* Bonds can be used for short-term and long-term investments and cover a variety of needs, including infrastructure development. Generally speaking, a bond is meant to finance a long-term investment, whereas a bank loan is more suitable for short-term needs.
- *Accessibility to the market.* The bank loan is open for most municipalities (provided they have a regular stream of income), while the bond market implies costly and cumbersome hurdles for the aspiring local authority. Only those that have gone through the process can operate in the bond market, but once the local government is accepted in the market, the administrative and search costs of borrowing capital drop significantly.
- *Flexibility and information.* Most local governments use bank credit. Local banks satisfy liquidity needs and provide a set of banking services on a daily basis. Eventually, banks engage in a long relationship with municipalities that benefits the latter whenever the need for capital arises. The relation between the bank and the local government provides flexibility in loan conditions. Borrowers can pay off the loan partly or totally, at any time, with little or no warning. A downside, however, is that lenders can also change the terms of the deal, although borrowers can (in theory) move their accounts elsewhere, assuming another lender is available. In any case, banks are entitled to manipulate lending terms almost at will.
- *Reputation on the bond market.* Local governments need to build up a reputation. Local government is better protected from unilateral change in conditions, since the issue of bonds involves standardized terms and conditions, depending on the terms on which the capital is borrowed. Although *standardization* strengthens the ability to reach a wider range of investors, helps lower search costs, and acknowledges liquidity—bond proceeds are immediately available to the borrower without any conditions and regardless the timeline of project implementation— it makes renegotiation in the case of difficulties virtually impossible.

Source: Platz 2009.

- *Bond issuing is expensive.* Local governments (issuers) need to pay fees to the rating agency, fees to the bank that sells the bonds to the public (underwriter), fees for the operations in the capital market, and the cost of marketing and publicity. For instance, Fitch Rating's fee for rating municipal bonds can reach up to US$750,000 per issue (see www.fitchratings .com). The cost depends on the time and effort it takes to evaluate the bond issuer. Given the lack of data on small municipalities, rating can be really expensive for them. Small or medium municipalities can rarely issue bonds because of the high cost of such issues and because potential investors are not very interested in small issues.

Several countries have made an effort to develop local rating capacity to help municipalities improve their data and increase their capacity to borrow from the market. Box 7.13 summarizes the case of Mexico and the efforts put forward by the central government to establish a culture of local government rating that can be used by the entire banking system when lending to the local governments.

Conditions for a Successful Bond Issue

The success of municipal bond markets depends on the size and debt of the domestic financial market and the legislation regulating local government borrowing. Domestic capital markets develop with the growth of domestic pension

---

Box 7.13 National Rating in Mexico

Mexico stimulated local government credit ratings with the regulations introduced in 2004 by the national banks and securities commission. The regulations mandate that banks make provisions (that is, earmark reserve funds for potential defaults) that increase with the maturity of the outstanding debt and in proportion to the risk level determined by the credit rating assigned by one external rating agency. If the local government entity is not rated, banks assign the highest risk level, and their motivation to lend to such an entity is obviously diminished.

Source: Annez and Peterson 2008.

Box 7.14 Modernization of Local Investment Finance in Mexico

Local Mexican authorities did not have direct access to capital markets. Most of their financing was obtained through the official bank (Banobras) in the form of short-to-medium term bank credit. The adoption of the national rating obligation that was used first for banks had powerful implications for the development of the local debt markets. Local Mexican governments can now access funds from insurance companies and investment banks. The debt issues are expanding, with reserve funds that require the issuer to deposit three years of debt payment as a guarantee to investors.

Source: Annez and Peterson 2008.

funds (as in Chile and Mexico; see box 7.14), the decentralization of services and revenues to local governments, and the strengthening of local institutions, including improved capacity to produce financial reports according to standard practice. In countries where pension funds and the insurance companies are authorized to invest in local government debt, the capacity of local government to issue paper is substantially enhanced.

Legislation is also necessary to explicitly authorize the local governments to issue bonds, including publication of the information that needs to be made available and how the issue is compatible with the institutional framework in place. The debt of the local authorities is always regulated by a law on public debt, followed by a special regulation on local debt. This law regulates at least three issues: (a) debt authorization for each type of local government; (b) types of authorized debts (short term, long term, loans, and bonds); and (c) establishment of a debt limit.

Throughout the history of the United States, the print media have actively provided critical information to investors. Rating agencies appeared in 1909 and ever since have played an important role in emerging and established markets. In the past 60 years, ratings have become a "sine qua non" for most corporate or public issuers seeking to mobilize large sums of capital. Ratings can be especially important for lesser-known issuers that seek to gain footholds in the domestic market or access to international markets (Platz 2009). Unfortunately, the financial crisis of 2008–09 and the role played by some rating agencies have seriously affected confidence in these agencies.

Subsovereign Debt Regulations

While many local governments have accessed long-term financing, some have failed to pay their debts on time, leading to increasing costs, embarrassment for the central government, and eventually bankruptcy. Several such cases—mainly in the 1990s—have discredited local governments in the financial markets and explain why commercial banks are reluctant to lend to local authorities without adequate guarantees from higher government tiers. In the United States, famous local bankruptcies, including Orange County, California; New York City; and Washington, DC, occurred in the 1990s. At present, a new surge of local governments is filing for bankruptcy, as the debt issued to finance investments (such as sewers and incinerators) has mushroomed and local governments find themselves in arrears and close to default. Box 7.1 summarizes the situation in Harrisburg, Pennsylvania, a city that defaulted because it had issued a guarantee to the builder of an incinerator.

Reasons and Rules for Debt Regulation

To restore the confidence of the private sector in the municipal sector and keep local governments' debt within their paying capacity, most countries have passed legislation establishing the limits and conditions for local government borrowing. Some countries prohibit municipal borrowing (Chile, China, and Pakistan, for example). But in the majority of cases, the controls apply to the maximum amount local governments can borrow (or the debt ceiling), the type of borrowing allowed (generally, local governments are not allowed to borrow abroad), or what types of expenditures can be financed with borrowed funds (in general, capital expenditure).

Brazil has introduced tight debt limits to avoid repetition of the debt crisis in the 1990s, when large municipalities such as Rio de Janeiro and São Paulo had to be bailed out repeatedly and the national government absorbed their subnational debt. When national governments allow the local or state governments to borrow in foreign currency, they implicitly assume a responsibility to bail out those governments in case they do not pay on time. Indeed, the reputation of a nation in the international markets can be seriously affected when a large local government defaults.

Brazil's law of fiscal responsibility mandated fiscal discipline from local governments, an important step that indicated a clean break with the overborrowing of the past (see box 7.15). Since most of the 5,560 Brazilian municipalities had approached their debt limits, the national government prohibited new municipal debt issuance in 2000. At the same time, Mexico promoted the development of domestic markets for local government debt and encouraged the use of local government credit ratings (Platz 2009).

The regulations on local government borrowing are typically focused on four rules:

- *The use of the loan proceeds.* The loan should finance long-term investment projects, not current expenditures.

- *The debt limit.* The debt stock (total debt outstanding) or debt service (payment of interest and amortization on the debt stock) should be limited to a certain percentage of revenues.

- *Sources of financing.* In general, no foreign loans are allowed.

- *In case of default.* Who pays if default occurs, or what revenues can be intercepted to pay the debt, must be specified.

Most OECD and European Union (EU) member states allow local borrowing for capital investment purposes as well as liquidity (short-term) loans but require them to be paid back within the budget year. Some of the controls used in the OECD member states apply to debt stock, guarantees, revenue to secure debt, purposes, and intermediaries (see box 7.16 for a detailed list of rules in selected countries):

- *Controls on the debt stock or on debt service* (that is, amortization plus interest) place limits on the amount of debt, generally defined as a percentage of annual revenues. In Brazil, debt stock cannot be greater than 60 percent of current revenues; debt service should be lower than 25 percent of current revenues.

- *Controls on guarantees* apply to the issuance of guarantees and types of collateral a local government may offer to a lender. Municipal guarantees are justifiable in support of essential service projects but should not be used for supporting commercial or revenue-generating investments.

- *Controls on revenue to secure debt* apply to the type of revenue that may or may not be used for debt servicing.

Box 7.15 Brazil's Fiscal Responsibility Law

The Fiscal Responsibility Law of May 2000 governs the expenditures and debt of municipalities. The law includes explicit hard budget constraints: caps on how much a municipality can borrow and caps on particular expenditures. For example, debt service cannot be higher than 25 percent of current revenues, personnel expenditures cannot be less than 60 percent of net current revenues, and total debt stock to net revenue can be no more than 100 percent. If a municipality does not respect the spending limits, it is not allowed to make contracts or conduct credit operations. In addition, municipalities produce quarterly reports to the central government. Mayors are not allowed to incur any new expenditures six months before the end of their term.

Sources: Platz 2009; Melo 2005; World Bank 2002.

Box 7.16 Municipal Debt Controls in Selected Countries

- *Austria.* Individual criteria; no general rule for local governments and differing absolute or relative limits.
- *Brazil.* No foreign debt is allowed; debt service should be at most 15 percent of net revenues; debt stock should be at most 100 percent of net revenues. Borrowing from the central bank and upper levels of government is forbidden.
- *Czech Republic and Poland.* Debt service must be less than 15 percent of revenues. Five-year debt service projections are required.
- *Denmark.* No municipal borrowing is allowed with a few exceptions. Automatic permission is granted for fee-based borrowing for public utilities.
- *France.* Operational surpluses from prior years must exceed debt service payments. No other restrictions apply.

- *Germany.* Each local government has borrowing limits, and explicit approval is needed from the state.
- *Ireland.* Each municipal borrowing must be approved by the Ministry of Finance.
- *Italy.* Municipalities must have balanced accounts. Debt service payments may not exceed 25 percent of current revenues. Loans must have terms of at least 10 years. The State Treasury sets the maximum legal interest rate.
- *Norway.* Borrowing is allowed for investment only.
- *Spain.* Total municipal debt may not exceed 110 percent of annual revenues.
- *United Kingdom.* Credit approval ceilings are given each year by the government to each local government.

- *Controls on the purposes* apply to the types of projects for which a municipality may borrow. Most countries allow municipal borrowing for long-term infrastructure projects only.

- *Controls on intermediaries* are restrictions on the types of lending institutions, including currency, interest rates, fees, and other loan terms.

Informal or Exceptional Borrowing Practices

Despite clear legislation on how much to borrow, local governments often circumvent borrowing limits. This is especially the case when management systems are not rigorous and local governments may assume that they will not be caught for a while. During the 1980s and 1990s, this was the usual practice in most municipalities in Argentina, Bolivia, and Brazil. How could these governments get away with bypassing the limits?

- First, local governments may decide to ignore or *hide limits.* They may accept loans from local banks and fail to register them in the official budget documents. When the loans are due, local governments have to produce the payment or ask the state or central government to bail them out.

- Second, local governments may take a vendor's loan in the form of a *deferred payment,* often with a much higher interest rate than the market, or just delay paying bills to suppliers. This practice is often harmful to the private sector, as vendors may find it difficult to survive without being paid. In Greece and

Portugal, the recent financial difficulties have forced some vendors out of business, as they have been unable to collect local governments' payments.

Borrowing through Special Entities

Municipalities like to borrow through their enterprises, some of which are called special purpose vehicles (SPVs), or through the public utility companies, which are 100 percent owned by the municipality. This is the typical case in China. Local Chinese governments are prohibited by law from borrowing from domestic or foreign banks or issuing debt. To circumvent this restriction, local governments use their special vehicles (or enterprises financed 100 percent by municipal capital) that have authority to borrow. Large metropolitan areas such as Beijing and Shanghai have used SPVs extensively for borrowing to finance huge development projects. This is a big transparency and budget control issue. The size of local government debt is unknown, as local authorities are not obliged to report the debt of their SPVs. As a result, Chinese authorities are considering whether to relax the previous restrictions and allow local governments to access capital markets under clear and transparent rules.

Checklist for Debt Managers

To comply with the constraints and legal frameworks imposed by the central government, local officers find it useful to apply some metrics or rules of thumb to ensure that their debt remains manageable; that way, the debt can be paid without much disruption to the other service provisions. Table 7.6 provides a simple checklist for debt managers.

Given the uneven size of debt service, the debt officer will need to carefully analyze the fluctuation of interest payments and debt amortization (principal repayment). For that reason, it is important to avoid using simple trends to project the debt service, as it might be surprisingly large in some years ahead, particularly if a portion of debt stock is in bonds that require repayment of the principal in bulk at the end of the bond period. To avoid trouble in debt service and severe liquidity crises, local governments might need to build a debt service reserve fund to ensure their ability to repay debts in a timely way. Figure 7.4 illustrates volatile debt service fluctuations. In this illustration, the municipality needs to budget properly to avoid problems in 2014, when the annual debt service will jump from the range of 90 million (in any currency) to 190 million; another challenge will come in 2017.

Table 7.6 A Checklist for Debt Managers

Indicator	What to do?
Debt structure: long vs. short term, domestic vs. foreign, flexible interest rates vs. fixed	Check if it is sustainable and look for unevenness and bunching of payments (balloon payments).
Debt service: % of net revenues	Should be at most 15% over the planning horizon.
Total debt: stock as % of net revenues	Should be at most 60%; higher than that will lead to high debt service and problems in the future.
Total debt per capita	Check with cities at the same level of development.
Deciding among debt programs	• Using net present value of alternative debt profiles to choose the best approach for the intended debt structure. • Modeling and simulating revenue and expenditure flows. • Defining the baseline and alternative scenarios. • Choosing the discount value.

Figure 7.4 Example of a Municipality's Debt Service Fluctuations, 2012–17
millions in any currency

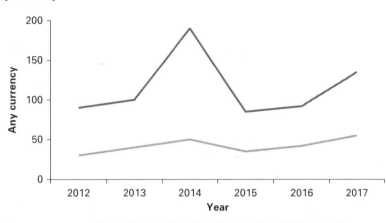

The financial market turbulence of 2009 seems to have contaminated local governments. Bond issues became too complicated and embellished with opaque clauses that eventually backfired on the local governments, leaving them little alternative to refinance. Overoptimistic projections for revenue-producing projects, together with ongoing discussion between cities and states on what taxes to raise and what assets to sell, have led to a difficult situation. Eventually both Harrisburg city (see box 7.1) and Jefferson County (box 7.17) filed for bankruptcy protection.[3]

Borrowing not only expands the financing capacity of local governments but also entails the risk of insolvency. The reasons include overoptimistic revenue projections, economic cycles that reduce own revenue collection, volatility of transfers, collection inefficiency, and underperformance of revenue-generating projects. Thus, local financial officers and political leaders alike should be aware of the insolvency risk and the potential consequences of failure in debt servicing. Some countries, such as Hungary, South Africa, and the United States, follow legislated procedures in which a court-appointed trustee (United States)

or an administrator appointed by higher government (South Africa) takes over financial control of the troubled municipality. The trustee restricts expenditures and manages satisfying creditors from the sale of marketable assets and revenue savings, with fair sharing of the losses among stakeholders. The overarching objective is to maintain minimum services and functionality of the local government, to satisfy creditors to a fair extent, and to implement actions to restore financial sustainability (Canuto and Liu 2013).

Most of the developing countries implement ad hoc interventions, with no rules for managing the insolvency situation. Actions include selling some assets, intercepting revenues from higher government, and often bailouts by higher government. These actions serve the same main purpose—maintaining services—but are often ineffective, reduce the accountability of local officers, soften budget constraints, and raise the issue of fairness. The revenue intercept is widely used but often ineffective, as only a portion of revenues can be intercepted, and thus it cannot eliminate huge debts. The bailout is often unfair because well-managed municipalities get

Box 7.17 Jefferson County Files for Bankruptcy Protection

Jefferson County, Alabama, followed in the footsteps of Orange County, California, whose bankruptcy was triggered by the county's investment in risky interest rate derivatives through the encouragement of an investment bank. In 1994, Orange County filed for bankruptcy protection, citing US$1.7 billion in liabilities. It was the largest municipal bankruptcy in U.S. history until November 2011, when Jefferson County listed US$4.23 billion in liabilities, including US$3.14 billion in sewer debt, US$800 million in school construction, and US$305 million in general warrants.

The problems of Jefferson County are linked to two issues: (a) the investment in an expensive sewer system for the county and (b) the financial structure of the bond that financed that investment. Like Orange County, Jefferson County allegedly owes part of the debacle to the financial adviser who structured and sold most of the US$3.1 billion sewer bonds that led to the bankruptcy, along with risky financial swaps that did just the opposite of protecting the county from changing interest rates. Bonds sold to investors to finance the work contained clauses that accelerated payments and interest rates if certain bond market conditions came to pass. Those conditions were deemed unlikely at the time, and the clauses were described as money savers for the county in the long run. But the clauses were triggered by the extraordinary bond market conditions in 2008, leading to accelerated payment schedules and penalty interest rates. An initial debt of US$1 billion more than tripled.

The final straw in Jefferson County's financial problems came when its occupational tax was ruled unconstitutional in 2011, slicing US$66 million from its annual income. The decision to file for bankruptcy was based on the belief that it would be easier to have a debt reduction ordered by the courts than to negotiate with individual bondholders.

Source: Church, Selway, and McCarty 2011.

nothing, whereas reckless spenders may receive a huge ad hoc grant from the central government based on their need to pay for salaries, water, or energy. In sum, rule-based insolvency procedures are more effective, are in harmony with the market, and better support market-based external financing.

Credit Enhancement and Loan Guarantees

Credit enhancements are devices that mitigate or reduce the risks in debt transactions. The main risk in lending money to local governments is the risk of default, that is, the risk that the local government does not have enough money to pay the debt interest and amortization when they come due. That failure may happen because of the local government's limited resources, because of poor revenue collection, because of some extraordinary and unforeseen event like a natural disaster, or even because of changes in central government regulations.

In countries where municipal borrowing is undeveloped, banks insist on a variety of security arrangements, such as mortgages, claims on municipal real estate, or revenue intercepts. Debt may be influenced by what properties the municipalities may legally offer as security. If only a few properties are available for security, then banks and municipalities will need to develop other loan structures that rely on cash flow from general or

Figure 7.5 Log Frame for Credit Guarantees

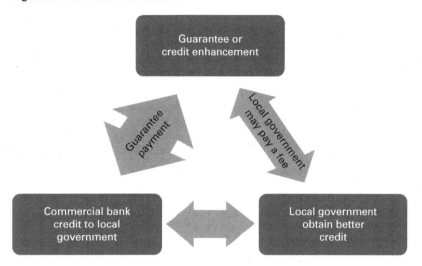

dedicated revenues. To reduce the perceived risk of municipal borrowing, local governments can access several types of credit enhancement or loan guarantee instruments. Figure 7.5 summarizes the logical frame and the positive impact of guarantee instruments. For example, the local government may buy a guarantee for a fee and obtain better debt conditions. Or the guarantor may step in and continue debt service on behalf of the local government in case of its inability to service the debt. The guarantor may pay just a portion (for example, half) of the interest due, and the debtor may absorb the loss (called a "credit guarantee") or pay the entire debt service until the local government restores its financial position (called a "full financial guarantee").

Revenue Intercepts

The revenue intercept provision means that payments from higher levels of government (transfers) can be pledged to the repayment of debt. The intercept provision is widely used as a good guarantee mechanism, especially when local governments borrow from the private sector. It is worth mentioning, however, that revenue intercepts

have several potentially negative impacts: the lenders may neglect due diligence, the intercept may transfer all business risk to the borrower municipality or central government, and the intercept may raise equity issues because some municipalities benefit from intercepts while others meet their fiscal responsibilities. Revenue intercepts became unmanageable in Argentina and Brazil in the 1990s, leading to severe legal restrictions.

Guarantees and Credit Enhancement

Guarantees and credit enhancement offer comfort to lenders who may be reluctant to lend to local governments when there is not enough information and financial transparency. A good example is the Unit Guarantee Corporation in the Philippines, which provides credit guarantees for municipalities that seek to finance infrastructure projects through debt issuances (see box 7.18). However, local governments need to take into account that when they provide a guarantee to a project or public enterprise, they should be sure that the project can generate enough revenue to pay its own debt. The cases of Harrisburg,

Box 7.18 Loans to a Local Government without Sovereign Guarantee

The Local Government Unit Guarantee Corporation, Philippines (UGC), was created in 1998 as a private financial credit guarantee institution. It is owned by the Bankers Association of the Philippines (38 percent), the Development Bank of Philippines (37 percent), and the Asian Development Bank (25 percent). The UGC has a co-guarantee agreement with USAID to cover infrastructure projects for local government units. UGC aims to make private financial resources available to creditworthy local governments; these resources will improve the capacity of local authorities to submit infrastructure projects to the capital markets and to receive commercial banking loans. UGC guarantees cover up to 85 percent of principal and interest; bonds are guaranteed 100 percent of principal and interest subject to an interest rate cap. The guarantee fee ranges from 1 percent to 2 percent a year. For borrowers who do not have an identified stream of revenues, there is a reserve fund created from the monthly gross revenues of the borrower.

Source: Alam 2010.

Pennsylvania (box 7.1), and Johnsville, Jefferson County, Alabama (box 7.17), have shown the negative impact of guaranteeing projects of uncertain profitability.

The Infrastructure Guarantee Fund in Korea, and FINDETER in Colombia have the same function of protecting the municipal lenders and ensuring that local governments pay their debts. At the multinational level, USAID has established a facility—the Development Credit Authority (DCA)—to encourage the development of credit markets in emerging economies. Today, the DCA has a presence in most developing countries.

Since the DCA was established in late 1999, more than 267 partial credit guarantees have facilitated more than US$2.3 billion of private capital debt financing in more than 64 countries. Through the DCA guarantee mechanism, USAID is able to leverage an average of 28 dollars in private sector funds for every dollar spent by the U.S. government. Claims on the DCA portfolio are approximately 1 percent, demonstrating that the targeted borrowers are both a creditworthy and a profitable source of business (for more information, see http://www.usaid .gov/our_work/economic_growth_and_trade /development_credit).

Special Purpose Vehicles and Pooled Finance Arrangements

Although large municipalities can access either bank or capital market resources, small local governments may not have the expertise or resources to finance the transaction costs involved in issuing bonds. Pooling municipalities' debt and their projects can reduce the costs and risks of the operation. Special arrangements can work for emerging markets that have large needs for infrastructure finance. Municipal bond banks and special purpose vehicles are well developed in North America, notably in Canada and the United States. Special purpose vehicles have been used in Asia too. Box 7.19 describes the case of the Tamil Nadu Water Fund.

Special Purpose Vehicles

A special purpose vehicle is a legal entity created to fulfill narrow, specific, or temporary objectives. SPVs are used by the private sector when a

Box 7.19 The Water and Sanitation Fund in Tamil Nadu

The Water and Sanitation Pooled Fund (WSPF) in the state of Tamil Nadu, in India, was the first pooled-financing bond in South Asia. It was installed in August 2002 as a special purpose vehicle. It pooled the water and sanitation requirements of 13 municipalities and towns and raised Re 301 million by issuing an unsecured municipal bond in December 2002. With a 15-year tenor, it is the only true long-term financing instrument in India. The bond relied on multiple credit enhancements, including a guarantee for 50 percent of the principal amount from the USAID Credit Authority. The bond issuances by WSPF are contingent on the prior approval of the state government. The state has mobilized nearly Re 3,000 million within five years through India's first bond by a joint public-private investment with the Tamil Nadu Urban Development Fund.

Source: OECD 2010.

firm wants to make an investment but does not want to risk its unrelated assets. Similarly, a local government transfers assets to an SPV (such as a "Housing Development Ltd.") for management or may use an SPV to finance a large project, risking only the invested assets, achieving a narrow set of goals without putting its entire wealth at risk. SPVs established as joint ventures of local government and private partners to finance projects are an integral part of the public-private partnerships common throughout Europe.

SPVs are also used in the public sector to separate the public nature of the municipality from profitable endeavors. A special purpose vehicle is like a specific firm with a very clear mandate to perform a certain function. It can be owned by a private company, by a municipality, or by a public-private partnership. The characteristic of an SPV is that it does not put in danger the capital of its main shareholders. In this sense, the Chinese municipalities have created and used SPVs to borrow to finance infrastructure and bypassed the prohibition on borrowing directly. In such cases, the expenditures and revenues of the SPV are not included in the local governments' budget and are not an object of public scrutiny. Chinese municipalities have widely used SPVs and local government–owned companies to issue municipal bonds, as they are banned from doing so themselves. There is little market scrutiny of the underlying financial conditions and little information available about the size of outstanding debt of this kind. The Shanghai Urban Development Investment Corporation has issued bonds to help finance transport investment, and many other localities in China have issued bonds through SPVs and their companies, using the corporate bond model.

Hybrid Forms of Loans

In poor countries, the hybrid loan, a combination of a market loan and grants, is an important tool for accessing resources. The hybrid reduces the debt service of the loan and makes it affordable to the local authority. A good example of this is the hybrid financing of Ouagadougou (box 7.20).

Debt Management and Institutional Framework

Managing the debts of a local government is a challenging task. It requires perpetual attention and the use of sophisticated tools to measure borrowing capacity in light of projected future

Box 7.20 The Hybrid Financing of Ouagadougou

The capital of Burkina Faso has more than 1.2 million inhabitants. The local government wanted to invest in upgrading the local market, which accommodates 2,900 traders. Its objective was to strengthen and improve the central covered market, as well as market-places in secondary towns. Economic and financial analysis determined the amount of revenue to be expected from the shoppers, as well as the amount of municipal savings that could be allocated to debt service. Because many communities would not be able to afford the debt payment, the available grant was allocated by priority to the poorest communities. On average, the loan was €2 million and a grant was €3.15 million. The variable rate loan is at a very concessionary rate (euribor less 1.86 percent), with a maturity of 20 years plus 5 years of grace.

Source: Paulais 2013.

revenues and liabilities and must also comply with national regulation. Because municipalities seem to have difficulty controlling their indebtedness, many national governments impose rules and limits aiming to restrict municipal debt. Furthermore, lenders often fail to do their own due diligence because they assume that municipalities cannot go bankrupt, or that there is an implicit sovereign guarantee, or because they do not understand the difference between public finance and market operations.

How Much Can a Local Government Borrow?

Borrowing capacity is the maximum amount of new debt that a local government can issue without hurting its capacity to deliver services and serve existing and new debt. It depends on how much money it has to repay and service the new debt today, reduced by its commitments payable in the future, but increased by its likely future revenues.

Often, legal constraints and debt caps impose additional limits, but the most important is whether the local government will have the capacity to pay the outstanding and new debt on time. Having a good sense of how much a local government can borrow or how much debt it can issue is fundamental to ensuring that a planned investment will be implemented without hurting the long-term fiscal stability of the local government.

Local government borrowing capacity depends on four factors:

- *The municipality's economic and financial prospects.* When the municipality's prospects for economic activity and tax receipts are good, borrowing capacity is greater than in a time of economic crisis and scarce revenues. In a system of intergovernmental transfers, the risk associated with the central government's transfer policy should also be taken into account.

- *The characteristics of the new loans or bonds, interest rates, and maturities.* If the city can issue debt with long maturities and low or concessionary interest rates, the borrowing capacity will be greater than if the municipality has no alternative but to borrow on commercial terms.

- *The structure and size of debt stock.* If a local government has an outstanding debt with low maturities and high interest rates, and if various debts coincide and induce a cluster of payments at the same time, it is likely that debt service absorbs an important portion of the local government's current revenues. Sometimes, a local government obtains new debt to restructure the stock of debt, stretch the average terms, and lower the annual burden of debt service.

- *The institutional framework and the limits imposed by the national or higher-level government or by the local constituency itself.*

Balloon Payment Risk

Borrowing capacity is a serious matter that can be tested by simplified mandatory indicators such as debt stock or new debt as a percentage of net operating revenues. But for larger borrowing, a more detailed cash-flow analysis is required that covers the entire repayment period of the new debt. Local governments in the developing world often calculate the historical trend of their debt service and net revenues and the said mandatory indicators to justify debt capacity. These projections may ignore or hide potential balloon payments, which may occur because the grace periods of the various loans or the final payment of bond principals coincide and cause an extraordinary expenditure a few years ahead. These are often honest mistakes, but many local governments hide the balloon payments intentionally because they want a particular project. Good feasibility studies with thorough financial analysis and cash-flow analysis for the entire loan period are vital to avoiding or mitigating balloon payments. Creditors can also mitigate these risks by requiring the borrower to set aside a debt service reserve fund that gradually deposits funds for 6 to 12 months of debt service. In the case of revenue-generating projects as well, creditors may request that the borrower set up an escrow account and deposit in it all revenue collected from the project, disbursing the debt service first before other payments are due.

Debt Management Strategies

A debt management strategy is a plan that the local government intends to implement over the medium term to achieve a desired composition of the debt portfolio (World Bank 2009). It ensures that the government's financing needs and payment obligations are met at the lowest possible cost consistent with a prudent degree of risk. Debt management strategies help local governments decide how much to borrow, what the best combination of debt instruments is, and what actions to take to ensure that debt stock and debt service do not become too large to be properly paid. When we speak of debt management strategy, we often refer to the following objectives and processes:

- Choosing debt instruments and terms for new debt, taking into account the existing stock.

- Ensuring that the local government debt is in line with the repayment capacity estimated by a detailed cash-flow analysis.

- Creating debt service reserve funds to ensure that the borrower can meet several months of debt service payments, as creditors often require.

- Selecting debt alternatives using net present value approaches to compare various medium- and long-term debts.

Choosing debt instruments may look simple for most local governments, but for large cities, the treasurer or finance chief faces difficult trade-offs between alternative instruments. For instance, if foreign interest rates are lower than domestic interest rates, foreign currency debt may seem attractive. However, the trade-off becomes less clear once we take into account the exchange rate risk, which will determine the eventual cost of foreign currency debt after possible devaluations of the local currency. Since local governments do not have revenues in foreign currency, their exposure to exchange rate risk is very high. For that reason, most countries do not authorize local governments to borrow in foreign currency. Box 7.21 describes the crisis that triggered regulatory change in Argentina.

Aligning Local Debt with Capacity

Ensuring that local debt is in line with repayment capacity is part of the analysis of borrowing capacity discussed above. However, managing the risk exposure embedded in the debt portfolio and making sure that the city is paying the least possible for a given debt stock are important parts of debt management strategy. For example, short-term loans and flexible interest rate loans are more risky, more volatile, and usually more expensive than longer-term loans. Restructuring debt portfolios of cities in fiscal distress often begins with refinancing the short-term debt and obtaining federal government guarantees to allow longer maturities and lower rates, if possible. The choice between debt instruments (bonds and bank credits) is also fundamental. The interest rates of bonds are lower in general, but costs are associated with them, including the cost of financial transparency and disclosure. Loans could also be renegotiated, however, whereas renegotiating bonds is virtually impossible, in part because of the large number of bondholders.

St. Petersburg is a good example of a city that, after passing through some rough times during the transition to a market economy, managed to reduce the average maturity of its loans, its outstanding debt, and its debt service (box 7.22).

Box 7.21 Challenge in Foreign Currency Borrowing

In the late 1990s, the Argentine cities of Mendoza, Rio de Janeiro, and São Paulo borrowed in foreign currency to refinance their domestic debt because the foreign interest rates were substantially lower than the domestic interest rates. While the cities benefited at first from substantial reductions in debt service, the exposure to currency devaluation became too risky. The central governments learned lessons, and both Argentina and Brazil have forbidden subnational governments to borrow in foreign currency.

History tends to repeat itself: Hungarian municipalities enthusiastically borrowed in Swiss francs with low interest in the early 2000s; then many became bankrupt after 2010. The crisis fueled a debate over whether the lenders shared responsibility.

Box 7.22 St. Petersburg's Experience with Debt Management

To deal with its debt problems, St. Petersburg has centralized the management of its debt and adopted a strategy focused on four goals:

- Minimizing the cost of borrowing by improving the city's credit rating

- Reducing exposure to foreign currency risk
- Lessening the burden of domestic borrowing by extending maturities
- Ensuring the effective use of guarantees to promote capital investments.

Source: Platz 2009.

Municipal Finances

St. Petersburg has grown faster than the national average, accounting for more than 15 percent of the foreign direct investment into the country. The city has borrowed extensively in both domestic and external markets and then suffered several setbacks. After some serious restructuring, it centralized management of its debt, which is now in the hands of the Committee on Finance. The debt unit issues periodic reports and monitors and actively manages risk.

Comparing Debt Alternatives

Net present value is a useful instrument for assessing how loans with different maturities and conditions compare, taking into account current market rates or other relevant discount rates. Banks are often better informed and more sophisticated than municipalities and offer complex alternative proposals with various interest rates, repayment schedules, and conditions. Net present value analysis helps in comparing competing offers by showing their true cost. (Maturity profiles are also important factors in identifying the cost of debt.) Comparing loans and bonds is particularly interesting, as loans often disburse gradually and are also paid back over time, whereas bonds can be disbursed all at once and payment can be delayed to the end of the bond period (bullet-type bond). Bonds can also be issued in tranches and paid back at regular intervals, without a bullet final repayment. Organizing data so that the debt servicing and debt maturity profile can be readily determined is an important function of the debt management officer.[4]

Creating Institutions That Reduce Market Failures in Municipal Borrowing
Financial Intermediaries

To ease impediments in local borrowing, central governments, often helped by international organizations, have created financial intermediaries to enhance the capacity of local governments to access debt markets. To help identify the best option for different local governments,

Figure 7.6   Log Frame for Debt Instruments

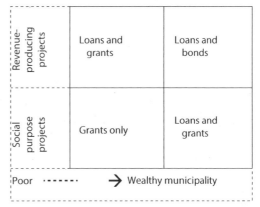

the Philippines government uses the log frame presented in figure 7.6. For local governments that are poor and finance social purpose projects, the best financing is a grant from government or donors. If the investment generates revenues, loans can be used, regardless of the wealth of the community. Bond issuance, however, should be reserved for wealthy local governments that are financing revenue-generating projects.

Institutions that help local governments access the credit market include the following:

- Investment development banks

- Specialized institutions, such as municipal development funds (MDFs), that channel borrowed and grant funds to local governments (for example, the Municipal Development Fund Office, the Philippines; the Town Development Fund, Nepal; the Tamil Nadu Urban Development Fund, India; and the Municipal Development Fund, Georgia)

- Credit enhancement mechanisms such as the Local Government Units Guarantee Corporation in the Philippines and the Infrastructure Credit Guarantee Fund in Korea

- Special purpose vehicles, such as the Water and Sanitation Pooled Funds in Tamil Nadu and Karnataka, in India, that raise finance for small municipalities; the Investment Fund for Urban Development in Vietnam; and the Urban Development Investment Corporations in China.

Resuming Bank Lending to Local Governments

The initial reluctance of the banks to lend to municipal governments has been reduced over time as banks have had some successes. For example, in South Africa, some commercial banks are ready to contribute to the investment programs in large cities. In Morocco, commercial banks have provided substantial refinancing of the public investment programs in some years. In Cape Verde (as in many other countries), an international donor uses the commercial banks to allocate its resources to local authorities, using clear guidelines on risk and repayment conditions. A similar example is FINDETER—a two-tier financial institution in Colombia—which was established to coach the market and encourage market-based finance in municipalities.

New Instruments

New instruments have been developed according to the needs and characteristics of the local authorities. For example, the United States has very successfully used state revolving funds, which are funded partially by the federal government, to leverage state funds in financing priority sectors such as water and sanitation. In addition, the so-called green financing instruments were developed to encourage emerging economies to invest in activities that will diminish greenhouse gas and carbon dioxide emissions.

Borrowing from Development Banks and Financial Institutions

In developing economies, municipalities often work first with commercial banks to manage their cash flows, and they occasionally borrow to manage their responsibilities for recurrent expenditures. However, borrowing large sums of money to finance long-gestation, long-lived capital investment projects is not as frequent. There are several reasons for this. First, bank regulations in general limit their capacity to lend for long-term projects because their deposit liabilities are mostly short term and volatile. Second, commercial banks in general do not have the expertise to assess municipal projects or their risks. In this context, commercial banks either refuse to finance municipal investment or charge high interest rates or require significant collateral to secure themselves against the perceived local government risk.

To take into account these constraints, many countries have established specialized financial institutions to provide long-term credit for municipal infrastructure projects:

- The Infrastructure Development Finance Company, in India, was established in 1997 to offer long-term private finance for infrastructure projects as well as to provide technical assistance. The institution was initially sponsored by the government of India but over time has been purchased by the private sector.

- The Development Bank of Southern Africa established a development fund in 2001 to provide grants and technical assistance to municipalities for implementing infrastructure projects. The bank raises funds from domestic and international capital markets, institutional investors, and bilateral and multilateral development finance institutions. It provides loans for municipal infrastructure, urban renewal, water, sanitation, health care, transportation, and education, for example.

- The Caixa Economic Federal Brazil manages several programs and extends technical assistance to the municipalities eligible for financing at subsidized rates.

Bond Banks

Because many local government loans are small, pooling individual credits or bonds is beneficial, especially for large lenders. Bond banks, established by the federal governments, collect all the borrowing needs of municipalities and issue a single class of bond backed by a diversified portfolio of borrowers. This arrangement reduces investor risk and lowers the borrowing costs of the local governments; an example is the Water and Sanitation Pooled Fund, in India, described in box 7.23.

Bond banks have been used extensively in Canada and the United States since the 1970s. Special-sector bond banks established by the Federal Clean Water Act 1984 helped municipalities issue bonds backed by federal grants and by matching contributions from the states. Outside the North American continent, examples of bond banks include the Kommunalbanken in Denmark, the Kommunivest in the Netherlands,

and the Infrastructure Finance Corporation in South Africa.

Specialized Institutions: Municipal Development Funds

Municipal development funds (MDFs) have been instrumental in building domestic municipal credit markets, while strengthening local governments' capacity to prepare and appraise projects and channeling finance to subnational entities on behalf of donors (Clark et al. 2008). This makes it feasible to reach and fund small subprojects suited to the needs of smaller cities. Central governments have created MDFs as a way to offer municipalities longer-term credit at interest rates lower than those offered in the domestic market. At the same time, they often provide technical assistance in project design and structuring and training to municipal staff on project finance and implementation.

Municipal development funds are pooled financial arrangements combining capital grants from state and central governments and loans from donors. Subsidized credit is then made

---

Box 7.23 Syndication and Access to Market: The Water and Sanitation Pooled Fund

The Water and Sanitation Pooled Fund is a fund common to small cities in the state of Tamil Nadu set up to finance water and sanitation projects. In 2003, this common fund issued a bond for US$6 million to be repaid from the water tariffs of a group of municipalities.

To be successful, the issue required three levels of guarantees:

- *Escrow account:* The municipalities deposit their payments in an escrow account.

Source: USAID 2003.

- *Reserve fund:* This fund carries 1.5 times the annual debt service.
- *Partial credit guarantee:* A guarantee (provided by USAID DCA) covers 50 percent of the loan.

The final rate was 3 percent below the market rate charged by the Tamil Nadu Urban Development Fund. In addition to funding, the pooled fund also provides advice to member municipalities.

available to local governments to finance infrastructure projects. Local authorities are evaluated on their capacity to repay the loans. MDFs have worked as revolving funds most of the time. More recently, some MDFs have accessed debt markets and issued bonds to increase their financial base for helping local governments.

MDFs can act as a first-tier bank and lend directly to local governments, or they can serve as a second-tier bank by lending to commercial banks and encouraging them to on-lend to local governments. Lending to local governments is often accompanied by technical assistance and support in project design and selection. Beyond lending, MDFs provide municipalities with technical capacity, project appraisal, and oversight of local project preparation and construction (World Bank-IEG 2009).

More than 60 countries have established MDFs, generally with the backing of international agencies. Examples of MDFs include the following:

- *Bolivia,* Servicio Nacional de Desarollo Urbano

- *Colombia,* Findeter

- *Czech Republic,* Municipal Finance Co.

- *Georgia,* Municipal Development Fund

- *Jordan,* Cities Villages Development Bank

- *Latvia,* Municipal Development Fund Latvia

- *Morocco,* Fonds d'Équipement Communal

- *Nepal,* Town Development Fund

- *Panama,* Fondo de Desarollo Municipal

- *Parana State (Brazil),* Paranacidade

- *Philippines,* Municipal Development Fund Office

- *Senegal,* Fund of Local Communities

- *Sri Lanka,* Local Government Loans Fund

- *Tamil Nadu (India),* Tamil Nadu Urban Development Authority

- *Tunisia,* Caisse des Prets et de Soutien des Collectivités Local

- *Vietnam,* Local Development Investment Funds

Experience with MDFs has been mixed, with good and some not-so-good results. It is critical to ask whether (a) the MDFs are supposed to be temporary intermediaries that help municipalities gain experience in debt financing, including preconditions, selection of instruments, and the design and implementation of large projects, or (b) they are supposed to help municipalities move gradually toward the local financial and capital markets to eventually gain direct access to funds. MDFs seem to be quite successful in fulfilling the first function but less so in leading municipalities to the markets. Some successful MDFs are briefly discussed in box 7.24.

The World Bank and the Inter-American Development Bank have been particularly committed to the establishment of municipal development funds. Between 1998 and 2008, the World Bank Group financed 190 municipal development projects. One-fourth of the projects helped create municipal development funds. The projects focused on four main priorities: (a) financial management improvement, such as integration of municipal accounts and training of financial staff; (b) improvement of tax records; (c) access to credit markets; and (d) support to the development of credit ratings and supervision capacities.

Not all experiences have been successful. In Africa, five MDPs were unsuccessful, as municipal revenues were overestimated and the loans were not repaid (e.g., Zimbabwe and Nigeria), or the commercial banks that were supposed to participate declined, fearing the lack of financial capacity of the municipal sector. In Asia, MDFs had a good start with Tamil Nadu, but later on, the financial market had developed in India, interest

Box 7.24 Successful Municipal Development Funds

Bangladesh. The Bangladesh Municipal Development Fund started operations in 2002 as a government-owned company to provide financial support to local governments for financing urban infrastructure. It was supported by a line of credit from the World Bank for US$78 million. All types of urban projects are eligible; the interest rate was established at 9 percent. The project has been very successful: 113 municipalities have used credit from the fund. Because all of them have to deposit 10 percent of their loans into an escrow account (to guarantee adequate and timely repayment), the secondary impact of the fund has been a generalized increase in own-source revenues. Local governments have also improved their asset management systems and accounting procedures.

Brazil. The Parana State Urban Development Fund (FDU) was created in the state of Parana, Brazil, in 1998. It was financed by the state budget and a loan from the World Bank and later on by the Inter-American Development Bank and retained earnings. FDU's assets are projected to grow from US$311 million in 2001 to US$1 billion by 2015. FDU lends to municipalities in Parana as well as to urban utilities. Interest rates vary according to the program, but they have been highly subsidized. Loans are 100 percent guaranteed by state transfers to municipalities or by the revenues accruing to public utilities. FDU was the first of many urban development funds in Brazil. Their major role was educating Brazilian municipalities to enter the credit market and to improve project selection and supervision.

India. The Tamil Nadu Urban Development Fund (TNUDF) was established within the World Bank–financed Tamil Nadu Urban Development Project and initially named the Municipal Urban Development Fund (MUDF). By 1996, the government-owned MUDF had financed over 500 subprojects in 90 out of 110 municipalities in Tamil Nadu. Building on that success, the MUDF has been converted into an autonomous financial intermediary, with participation of private capital and management and renamed TNUDF. An asset management company—a joint venture between the Tamil Nadu government and private investment companies—now manages the TNUDF. The new arrangement has brought private sector management expertise to the selection and financing of subprojects sponsored by either public or private agencies and has facilitated the access of creditworthy municipalities to the private capital market. A separate grant window has been created for poverty-oriented investments, such as slum upgrading and the cost of resettlement. This grant window is managed by an asset management company that also provides technical assistance to municipalities in preparing investments and improving their financial management.

Senegal. Senegal's Fund of Local Communities, created under the Urban Development and Decentralization Program, played a major role in strengthening the capacity of the local authorities to manage investment resources, raise revenues, abide by borrowing constraints, and prioritize expenditures. With the help of municipal contracts (introduced at the same time), the fund was a key piece in consolidating the decentralization process in Senegal.

South Africa. The Infrastructure Finance Corporation has a structure similar to that of the Parana urban development fund. It lends to municipalities—especially large metropolitan areas—to finance infrastructure and water supply. The sources of funds include domestic and international markets, raised through bond issues and long-term loans extended by international financial institutions. The loans granted to municipalities are in general at a fixed rate with up to 20-year maturities.

Source: Sood 2009; Alam 2010; Freire and Petersen 2004.

rates went down, and the attractiveness of these funds was substantially eroded. In Pakistan, the MDF focused mostly on grant financing.

MDFs continue to operate and help municipal governments improve their capacity to borrow directly from the market. When municipalities or the credit markets are ready to work directly with each other, MDFs may become suddenly uninteresting. They may lack the tools to compete with aggressive commercial banks, which by now have understood the characteristics of local governments, know the legal framework, and are ready to lend at competitive rates. In these conditions, MDFs may have sufficient funds to lend but lack potential clients (Tunisia and Morocco). Then the need is for sufficient flexibility to allow those funds to be used to strengthen smaller or less-competitive projects or local governments.

External Assistance Available to Local Authorities

Multilateral and bilateral institutions have long been involved in financing local governments and improving their capacity to go to the market to raise funds for their projects. As noted above, the World Bank and USAID have encouraged MDFs and municipal bonds. In India, for example, the promotion of the municipal bond market was part of USAID's Financial Institutions Reform and Expansion Project.

To gain official external support, local governments either contact the representatives of those institutions directly (for example, the Inter-American Development Bank, the World Bank Group, the Asian Development Bank, the African Development Bank, and the European Bank for Reconstruction and Development, or EBRD) or use the information issued regularly by the ministry of planning or ministry of development when so-called wholesale projects are being prepared to help local governments. In general, the international financial institutions and the national governments use some entry criteria in selecting the local governments that will benefit from the loan. The criteria include fiscal indicators (as a proxy for the capacity of the local government to pay the debt and finance the counterpart funding), past performance in project implementation, and budgetary and accounting practices. In addition, local governments may need to show that their strategies are consistent with the main objective of the wholesale program, such as poverty alleviation, competitiveness, or extension of basic services.

The World Bank: IBRD and IDA Assistance for Municipal Development

Multilateral support can be grants or loans. The large part of the multilateral assistance is in the form of subsidized loans, especially for poor countries eligible for credit from the International Development Association (IDA) with highly concessionary assistance. Box 7.25 shows the loan terms from the International Bank for Reconstruction and Development (IBRD), or the World Bank, and IDA credits. In either case, local governments face substantial transaction costs associated with these grants or subsidized loans. Before a city or central government receives the

---

Box 7.25 IDA and IBRD Lending Terms

- IBRD terms include 20 years maturity and a six-month Libor, plus a 0.5 percent spread.
- IDA terms include 40 years maturity, 10 years grace, and 0.75 percent commission.

---

assistance, substantial improvements have to take place at the institutional, operational, and reporting levels.

Rarely do local governments receive direct loans from international organizations. In the most common case, a project is prepared and negotiated with the local government, but the central or the state government assumes the role of borrower and on-lends the funds to the local government, with or without an add-on disbursement fee. The funding is disbursed through a central facility or MDF or second-tier facility and then allocated to specific local governments according to prior agreement or some allocation formula. The exception is loans to large cities, such as Cairo, Mexico City, Mumbai, Rio de Janeiro, São Paulo, and Shanghai, where the World Bank has financed projects directly, although often with a sovereign guarantee.

EU-EBRD Municipal Finance Facility

The Municipal Finance Facility was an initiative of EBRD and the European Commission, to develop and stimulate commercial bank lending to small and medium municipalities and their public utility companies in countries that joined the EU in 2004. They included the Czech Republic, Estonia, Hungary, Latvia, Lithuania, Poland, the Slovak Republic, and Slovenia, followed by Bulgaria and Romania. The facility combines EBRD financing, in the form of long-term loans or risk sharing, with EU Phare grant support in the form of a maturity enhancement fee and technical cooperation for partner banks or public utilities.

Objectives

The facility aims at encouraging the commercial banks to lend to small and medium municipalities, to enhance the banks' ability to assess risks of municipalities and to manage their loans in the sector, to provide local governments access to medium- and long-term financing, and to help them prepare and implement feasible and financially sound infrastructure investments suitable for credit financing.

EBRD provided up to €75 million in long-term lines of credit from 10 and 15 years to partner banks for on-lending to local governments in euros or local currency. Partner banks make loans of up to €5 million, each with a maturity of 5–15 years, available to local governments for investment in infrastructure. EBRD provides for risk sharing for up to 35 percent of the partner bank's risk on a portfolio of loans to local governments. EBRD's support acts like a guarantee, and the bank will step in with risk funding only in the event that a municipal loan defaults. For municipalities, EU funds provide support for project preparation, loan application, and project implementation.

Criteria

Participating municipalities should serve a population of less than 100,000 people. They should have sound financial management and a good cash flow. Investments can be in infrastructure such as local transport, district heating, water supply, sewerage, solid waste management, public roads, and parking.

The Inter-American Development Bank and the World Bank have developed their own subsovereign municipal financing facilities that provide infrastructure finance to creditworthy municipalities without the central government guarantee.

Environmental and Energy-Efficiency Loans and Credits

Energy efficiency and climate change have gained special prominence in the past 10 years, leading to the development of specific programs to help local governments and national entities. International financial institutions, bilateral donors, and private institutions have developed specific products to educate the local authorities and prepare projects that are self-financing. A typical project is retrofitting a public building to make it more energy efficient. For example, Los Angeles was able to finance the retrofitting of the city's central offices, with the cost financed by three years of savings on energy bills. Russia is moving fast on this front as well. In November 2009, Federal Law 261-FZ ("On Energy Efficiency Improvement and Energy Saving") was adopted to help the country reduce its energy intensity by 40 percent by 2020. These regulatory changes have important implications for local governments and cities, including the development of new energy-efficiency competencies and responsibilities, including sustaining achieved results in local public buildings and utilities; supervising installation of metering devices; maintaining local information systems on energy efficiency in buildings (such as energy audit results, energy passports, energy-efficiency measures, and savings reports).

The World Bank and IFC have put together a wide range of programs that lead to sustainable financing for Russian cities.

Climate change is leading to global warming and consequent serious economic disruption and dislocation of millions of people. Policies devised to control emissions and pollution include regulations and standards, as well as economic instruments such as taxes and charges, tradable permits, voluntary agreements, subsidies, and financial incentives.

A growing number of cities have obtained substantial financing of vital local services through the Clean Development Mechanism. The mechanism provides a link between reducing a city's carbon footprint and the changes in behavior needed to effect that reduction (see box 7.26 for the example of Lahore City, Pakistan). Those changes come about through

---

Box 7.26 The Lahore Composting Carbon Finance Project

The Saif Group, through Lahore Compost (Pvt.) Ltd., has set up its first composting plant at Mahmood Booti, Pakistan, under an agreement with the city district government of Lahore. The project was set up on a build-operate- transfer basis, whereby the project will be transferred to the city after 25 years. This is the first public- private partnership in Pakistan on such a large scale in the area of municipal solid waste recycling.

The project was validated and registered as a Clean Development Mechanism project with the United Nations Framework Convention on Climate Change in April 2010. It produces up to 150 tons of compost daily from 1,000 tons of municipal solid waste supplied by the city. Lahore Compost uses an aerobic process with open windrow technology to achieve the maximum level of mature product and a safe environment and to reduce waste disposal by half. The composting process normally takes around 60 days to complete with regular processing (see figures B7.26.1 and B7.26.2).

The project was verified in 2011 by the United Nations Carbon Authority, and since then the volume of carbon reduction is validated every year. Thus, the project has been benefiting from the carbon credits that are expected to generate about US$6 million in total revenues over five years and that support the financial viability of the project. Besides its financial and environmental benefits, the project generated about 50 jobs,

(continued next page)

Box 7.26 *(continued)*

including more than 20 for unskilled workers, most of whom are former scavengers.

The carbon credit is free money, but the transaction cost is paramount. Verification of the project requires plan management to provide laboratory-quality evidence and checks and balances to prove emission reduction, which will eventually be good for the public too.

Figure B7.26.1   Turning the Windrows

Figure B7.26.2   Validation

incentives in the form of carbon credits provided to cities for reducing their greenhouse gas emissions. In 2007, the Municipal Corporation of Mumbai financed a landfill closure and gas capture project at the Gorai landfill, drawing on carbon credit financing. The Asian Development Bank financed the project through the certified emissions reduction (CER) carbon credits fund. One CER amounts to a saving of one ton of carbon dioxide.

Jordan

The greater Amman municipality handles half the solid waste generated in Jordan. With US$25 million in World Bank financing, the city of Amman has expanded existing transfer sites and its existing landfill site (World Bank 2010). The design of the landfill site includes provisions for recycling recoverable materials and landfill gas recovery. The latter is captured to generate "green" electricity and will amount to 160,000 megawatt hours that will be channeled to the national electricity grid. In addition, the certified emissions reductions resulting from the project are estimated at 950,000 tons of CO_2, which will generate a further US$15 million in CER revenue by 2014, while the electricity sale will generate revenues estimated to reach US$25 million by 2019.

Morocco

In 2006, Morocco enacted its first law on solid waste management. In 2007, it launched a 15-year municipal solid waste program in urban areas. The goals included 90 percent coverage by 2021, sanitary landfills in all urban areas, the closure and rehabilitation of 300 existing open dumps, and the promotion of solid waste reduction and recovery. The program aims to improve solid waste management practices in Morocco, which were among the worst in North African countries at 0.05 percent of gross domestic product spending per year, compared to 0.2 percent in the Arab Republic of Egypt and 0.1 percent in Lebanon, Syria, and Tunisia. Gas capture projects will capture and flare methane from landfill sites, reducing emissions by 0.7 to 1.0 million tons of CO_2 equivalent per year and earning Morocco revenue from carbon emission reductions sold under the Clean Development Mechanism. Generating revenues to the sector through carbon trading is an added incentive for municipalities to tackle solid waste problems while also mitigating climate change (World Bank 2010).

Bolivia

Santa Cruz, Bolivia, has about 1.3 million people and is growing 6 percent each year. Sanitation services are well provided by 10 cooperatives, but coverage is limited to 32 percent of the population. Among the projects for improving the situation are four wastewater treatment plants whose methane gas is being transported to a flare by a system of tubes. This project is funded by an emission reduction purchase of US$2.09 million by the Community Development Carbon Fund and the Bio Carbon Fund. The local cooperative SAGUAPAC receives the proceeds from this purchase and is responsible for implementing the project, which is estimated to cost US$1.48 million to install and US$24,000 a year to operate and maintain (Jaguari 2007).

India

The 18 million urban dwellers in Karataka, India, have water coverage for less than four hours a day. To improve the efficiency of water provision, the government has launched a program to improve energy efficiency and reduce greenhouse gas emissions. The program has been implemented in six cities, with energy savings of 16 million kilowatt hours and reduction in total emissions of 13,620 tons of CO_2. The resulting emissions reductions—about 60,000 emissions reduction units—will be purchased by the Community Development Carbon Fund. The gross revenue will amount to between US$600,000 and US$900,000, which will be shared among the participating municipalities.

Private Sector Participation

Public-private partnerships have gained importance as an alternative way for local governments to finance infrastructure and deliver efficient public services. The private sector brings not only capital and knowledge but also access to technology and management practices that result in greater efficiency. PPPs are characterized by the sharing of investment, risk, responsibility, and reward among partners. That shared responsibility also makes the project more responsive to consumer needs. In the context of this chapter, the main issue is that many PPP arrangements offer financing alternatives to municipalities. Cities can save public funds by engaging in a PPP with a private investor and may use their public money instead for additional public projects that would not attract private investors. By handing over public assets to private operators, the municipalities can save on costs of operations, provided that the private firm is more efficient and runs the service with same quality at less cost.

Private or Public Delivery of Services

In principle, it should be normal for the private sector to deliver the local services, such as water, energy, and so forth, that are considered private goods. Competition among private firms would ensure that the services are provided at the lowest possible cost. In some cases, however, competition does not work. One example is public goods such as city street lighting, police, and security, for which cities cannot charge the user because people cannot be excluded from receiving the service. A second example is those instances in which large investments are at stake, leading to a de facto natural monopoly, for example, the local water service. In this case, private sector operation by itself (in a monopolist situation) may not aim at the lowest possible price. Table 7.7 summarizes how the public and the private sectors can operate in several urban services.

Forms of Public-Private Partnerships

The contractual form of a PPP varies depending on the type of service, who owns the assets (the local government or the private partner), who bears the risk, and the duration of the contract.

Table 7.7 A Typology for Delivery of Urban Services

Urban service	Type of good	Role of public sector	Role of private sector
Urban transport	Private (with positive externalities), merit good.	Ensure efficient solutions and serving low-income people.	Operate and construct systems.
Piped sewerage systems	Public good; monopolistic; positive externalities.	Direct public provision.	Can be contracted for specific works.
Water supply	Quasi-public good; has positive externalities.	Regulation required to ensure public health.	Can deliver but is regulated.
Land service, infrastructure, and household connections	All goods are private and can be delivered by the private sector.	Regulations to address environment and safety considerations; zoning.	Deliver infrastructure, finance development, charge consumer.
Slum upgrading	Large component of public good.	Finances public good: water and sanitation.	Community can deliver and build large part of the services.
Solid waste collection	Private good (positive externalities).	Public sector ensures provision and coverage.	Private sector delivers the service.
Waste disposal	Quasi-public good.	Public direct provision.	Deliver under contract.

Source: Batley 2001.

Table 7.8 Types of Public-Private Partnerships

Type of PPP	What they do	Characteristics
Management contracts and BOT	Transfer responsibility for operation and maintenance of a local government–owned business to the private sector for generally up to five years.	Local government retains ownership and funding of the project. It offers some performance objectives by which to judge the effectiveness of the firm in charge of the maintenance and operation.
		Examples: Lahore composting plant BOT; the bus transport service in Hanoi.
Leases	Local authority owns the assets, but the private sector leases the asset and takes care of the maintenance and operation.	Risks are shared; leases can go 5–20 years.
Concessions	Private sector takes responsibility for the maintenance and operation and for the investment in the facility.	Concessions are for 25–30 years. Contracts are very detailed, outlining performance standards, required investment, and mechanisms for adjusting prices and tariffs.
		The Transmillenio bus system; the Senegal urban water concession.
Joint ventures	Private sector holds shares in this structure. Over time, the local government may sell the other shares to the private sector.	The local authority may give daily management to the private partner.
Full or partial ownership	Private sector owns full or part of the service or structure.	With complete divestiture, the private sector takes full responsibility for operations, maintenance, and investments. All assets become private as well.

Source: Delmond 2009.
Note: BOT = build, operate, transfer.

Table 7.8 illustrates the main types of PPPs. In their simplest form, we have management contracts for service delivery that last for one to three years, with assets belonging to the public sector. In the case of build-operate-transfer arrangements, leases, and concessions, the assets are public, but the risk is now private or shared and so is the investment to be made. Concessions can go for up to 25 years. Divestiture is the most extreme case of privatization. It happens when all assets are bought by the private sector and there is no intervention of the public sector any longer (the rail system in the United Kingdom in the 1980s, for example).

PPPs Have Significant and Measurable Benefits

The main benefits of PPPs include the following:

- *Cost savings.* Local governments will realize cost savings in both the construction of capital projects and the operation and maintenance of service.

- *Risk sharing.* Local government can share the risks with the private partner. Such risks include cost overruns, difficulty complying with environmental regulations, and the risk that revenues may not be sufficient to pay operating and capital costs.

- *Improved service.* PPPs can introduce innovation in the company that organizes and carries out the service delivery. They can also introduce new technologies and economies of scale that often reduce costs.

Several decades of PPPs have provided empirical evidence that confirms the positive impacts of engaging private partners in service delivery. Private sector involvement in most infrastructure sectors brings greater efficiency and satisfaction to the consumer. Prices go down significantly, the quality of service improves, and service is extended to the target community. This result is especially evident in the case of telephones, energy, and water service. Labor productivity increases substantially, sometimes by 50 percent. In the electricity sector, the number of connections per worker has jumped from less than 500 per employee before privatization to 750 after privatization. Distributional losses have also fallen substantially, in some cases from 20 percent and 40 percent in electricity and water, respectively, to 10 percent and 20 percent, after privatization (Andres et al. 2008).

PPPs Also Have Risks

Privatization tends to be associated with some negative images. The first contracts were based on unjustified optimism and show some carelessness in design and performance criteria. The local government did not have enough information on the sector in question or enough leverage over the private partner, which made it difficult to monitor the performance of the partnership and take corrective measures. One effect of poor contracts is the high rate of renegotiation and cancellation of PPPs. In Latin America in the 1990s, PPP contracts in the water sector were renegotiated in 74 percent of cases in the first 18 months (Batley 2001).

Nevertheless, the rate of cancellations is now particularly low, suggesting that once the technical details are solved, the local government and the private sector partner are comfortable with the agreement. The most contentious features of the renegotiated contracts seem to be the level of lowest tariff, the investment requirements, and weak regulatory bodies. Sometimes the initial contracts suffer from lack of communication with the public at large, the absence of social programs, contract violations, and ineffective and unpredictable conflict resolution mechanisms.

The main risks in PPPs include the following:

- The main risk is the loss of control. PPPs that entail significant investments by the private partner often allow the partner to become very involved in making decisions on how services are to be delivered and priced, against the best interests of customers.

- Political risks are also common. An incomplete regulatory environment and corruption can transform the public-private partnerships into an opportunity for abuses and political turmoil.

Despite some concerns about the lack of local technical expertise, PPPs are being used throughout the developing countries. For example, in Uganda, local governments can contract out the provision of services and are encouraged to do so. Contracts are in place for solid waste management, road maintenance, retail markets, car parks, and even property tax collection. For land development, property is leased to private contractors for 15 years.

Successful PPP Cases

The number of successful PPPs in municipalities continues to go up. Four are especially interesting: the Bogotá Transmillenio bus system concession contract, the bus transport service in Hanoi, Lahore's composting plant BOT, and the Senegal urban water sector concession. In all cases, the contracts were very clear, the clauses that deal with problems were well defined, and the private sector contributions of investment, tariffs, and rate of return were wisely negotiated. Moreover, the preparation process was rigorous and took into account the demand for the services being provided, the earnings streams, the costs of the investment, the likelihood of private sector interest, and an adequate PPP format for the project. As a basic principle, a prefeasibility study should be prepared before submitting the project for private sector bidding. Good PPPs follow that rule, and failed partnerships may have bypassed the prefeasibility study. Boxes 7.27 and 7.28 shed light on these issues.

Although the advantages of PPPs for cities are well established, local governments should carefully examine the need for technical and financial expertise, so that they can negotiate the contracts

---

Box 7.27 Feasibility Analysis for a Sanitary Landfill

Increasingly, Asian cities are looking to the private sector for capital investment in the solid waste sector. In the assessment phase, a number of different types of analysis and data would be needed for a potential PPP project in this sector. Because of significant economies of scale for sanitary landfills (costs per ton decrease as the size of the facility increases), the private sector will be looking to ensure a certain flow of waste into the facility to guarantee revenues for recycling and disposal operations. Thus, part of the feasibility stage will entail collecting data on existing and projected waste quantities and waste densities from different sources.

To determine which service options could be viable, cost analyses would be performed on different disposal options. This would include a review of capital requirements and projections of the operations and maintenance costs and full amortization of each. The land to be allocated to new facilities would also need to be appraised and valued.

The demand analysis would require a study of the willingness and capacity of residents to pay for improved services. The potential recipients of services would be asked about their opinions on service options, costs, and methods of payment.

The feasibility of undertaking waste recycling as a source of revenue should also be explored, together with on-site recycling and composting activities, which minimize waste generation, as a voluntary alternative to payment of the full service charge.

Source: CIDA 2011.

Box 7.28 Water PPP in Argentina

In the case of Aguas de Tucuman, Argentina, when water tariffs went up overnight and the quality did not improve as expected, the public sector tried to activate some of the contract clauses with little impact. The international water company ended up suing the state government for breaching the contract.

Source: Andres et al. 2008.

with full control. Renegotiations of PPPs, as mentioned above, have been the norm in the water sector in Latin America. Troubled PPPs also occur in Africa; box 7.29 describes a situation in Dar es Salaam, Tanzania. These experiences do not invalidate the benefits of PPPs but show the need for good preparation and improved technical skills. Fortunately, international financial institutions and bilateral aid agencies provide a great assortment of technical assistance to ensure that the partnerships are designed with rigor, reflect the uncertainties of the sector, and provide measures to bring the contract back in line when necessary.

PPPs and the Poor

A good opportunity for the private sector to engage profitably in city projects, while also benefiting the poor, is through innovative products specifically designed to meet the needs of the poor at prices they can afford and delivered in ways that fit their lifestyles (box 7.30 illustrates

---

Box 7.29 Dar es Salaam: A Failed Water PPP

Many cities have struggled through first PPPs but learned from them. That was the case with water and sanitation in Dar es Salaam. The sector was constrained for 30 years by lack of investment. In 2002, a British-German-Tanzanian joint venture—City Water Services—was awarded the tender for a 10-year lease to manage the technical and commercial operations of the water and sanitation system of the city. Three years later, in May 2005, the government accused the operator of failure and terminated its contractual arrangement. The apparent reasons were failure to extend the agreed coverage, to follow the procurement rules, and to pay the agreed return to the city.

Ten years later, the city is revisiting its strategy and is welcoming PPPs; it plans to invite private investors to participate in public transportation projects and in real estate development. A decade of learning by doing has provided excellent guidelines on how to engage in a public-private partnership that respects and abides by the principles of the local government.

Source: Sway 2011.

Box 7.30 "Urban Concessions" PPP in Brazil

In São Paulo, Brazil, new public-private partnerships—called "urban concessions"—are being developed in which impoverished parts of the city will be converted to private operation in exchange for the execution of an infrastructure plan. The concessionaires will recoup their investment and obtain profit from the redevelopment of expropriated properties during the concession period. It is envisioned that the property owners will receive compensation according to predefined criteria, while sitting tenants may either be relocated to low-income housing or obtain a rental grant.

the challenges of meeting those requirements). Potential areas include financial services, such as the Kuyasa Fund in Cape Town. Another example is the SKS Microfinance in India, in the area of housing. In the area of solid waste management and recycling are the Quezon City Materials Recovery Facilities, in the Philippines, and the New Delhi Municipal Council in India. The latter officially subsidized waste pickers—usually the poor—who pick up waste from residents' doorsteps and contribute to the 33 percent waste recovery rate by private, independent recyclers.

Increasingly, output-based aid (OBA) has been used to structure subsidies to the private sector to ensure that performance targets—particularly those related to service provision to the poor—are adequately met. OBA basically links the payment of subsidies to the demonstration of specific service delivery or outputs: for example, the connection of a specified number of customers to the electrical grid or to the water distribution network. Private providers must therefore carry their own risks of nonperformance and provide their own finance up-front (in most cases) to meet the performance targets and obtain the OBA grant. OBA has been found to be especially effective in extending water connections to slum areas through one-time fee subsidies for network extension and connections, as in cities in Ethiopia, Indonesia, Mozambique, and the Philippines (GPOBA 2008; World Bank 2005).

Some Lessons Learned

Public-private partnerships have great potential for enabling local governments to expand services at reduced cost and with greater efficiency. But for the best use of PPPs, local governments need to know more about the specific sectors in which they are working and the legal covenants that they may need in case of disagreements with their private partners. Success depends on a locality's long-term vision, its capacity to regulate service providers and service quality, and its ability to enforce regulatory controls. In moving forward, local governments need to pay attention to the design of contracts, methods for resolving disputes, and the technical details both before and after signing a PPP contract.

Clear norms for supervising the delivery of the service need to be included in the contract and be subject to good supervision. If local governments do not possess the requisite knowledge and skills to pursue a PPP on their own, they should not hesitate to seek outside assistance, as long as they understand the overall vision and guiding principles of the PPP arrangement. Local decision makers must also have a firm understanding of the risks they will assume under a PPP, as well as their contingent liabilities should things not go as expected.

Philanthropic and Individual Contributions

In addition to other financing options, municipalities should seek philanthropic aid. Since the end of the 1990s, philanthropic aid has increased dramatically. The total amount comes to about US$5 billion a year worldwide, of which 75 percent comes from U.S. foundations. These foundations have more than tripled their contributions over the past 10 years, with contributions over the period totaling US$44 billion in 2007 (Paulais 2013; Foundation Center 2009). The Bill and Melinda Gates Foundation is the most important world foundation Most of the funds are channeled through nongovernmental organizations, often European ones (for example, Switzerland is the headquarters of many foundations, such as the World Global Fund to Fight AIDS, Tuberculosis, and Malaria; the Red Cross; and others).

Local authorities rarely have direct access to philanthropic aid, unless through state or national government. In 1995, the Soros foundation (the Open Society Institute) helped establish the National Urban Reconstruction and Housing Agency, in South Africa, and has extended further help to subsidize low-income mortgages. In 2007, a Gates Foundation contribution reinforced the capacity of local governments in the water and sanitation sector.

Local governments do, however, engage the general public in making specific contributions to fund development projects. For example, in the city of Uzgen in the Kyrgyz Republic, the local government engaged the population in raising funds for improving the water system. The city has grown very fast, and the water system had not kept pace. The city could not afford a World Bank loan because it did not have the necessary counterpart funds (3 percent of the total cost). The city administration designed and implemented a successful public relations campaign to convince residents to make a one-time contribution to raise the funds. To solicit funds for the first stage, the local administration mobilized students to raise awareness of the importance of potable water and to convince their parents to contribute. Later, a similar process took place in which the city was able to expand its water coverage from 35 percent to 65 percent of the residents (Kaganova 2011).

Community funds are growing in importance, especially to help low-income families address shelter needs. These funds establish and strengthen local savings groups that provide collective finance for shelter improvement, leverage resources from the national government and foreign donors, and can be important in promoting community development.

They can also contribute to infrastructure at significant savings (Mitlin and Muller 2004). One example is the Slum Dwellers International, a network that incorporates savings and lending activities for shelter improvement. Over the past 15 years, the organization has evolved into an international movement with affiliates in more than 12 countries. It has helped millions of households access land and improved housing with small grants. Other examples include the Cambodia Urban Poor Development Fund, the Bann Mankong (secure housing) in Thailand, the Community Mortgage Program in the Philippines, PRODEL in Nicaragua, and the Jamii Bora Trust Low-Cost Housing Scheme in Kenya.

The Jamii Bora has created a successful low-cost housing program of about US$12.5 million (commercial and residential). The organization purchased 293 acres of privately owned land and has constructed houses with a combination of members' savings, market finance, and donations from well-wishers. Members finance the housing units (about US$3,000 each) with loans from the trust, about $45 per month per household. Maintenance costs are covered through monthly fees of approximately US$7 charged to households (UN-HABITAT 2005). Community funds in India and Thailand have grown substantially with the help of the central government and foreign donors.

Capitalized by donors, Community-Led Infrastructure Financing is a fund for the urban poor that supports community-initiated housing and infrastructure projects with the potential for scaling up. It works with the National Dwellers Federation and other large community organizations to provide consistent approaches and maximum leverage. The goal is to increase the access of poor urban communities to commercial and public sector finance for medium- to- large-scale infrastructure and housing initiatives. The organization provides bridging loans, guarantees, and technical assistance; undertakes rehabilitation projects; and attracts commercial, local, and public sector finance for further schemes (http://www.homeless-international.org).

Takeaway Messages

Many local governments have substantial needs to expand infrastructure and provide basic services. Given the long-term nature of municipal infrastructure, it is possible and efficient to use long-term funds to finance these projects. This ensures that the generations that will enjoy the benefits of the project are also those who pay for them.

However, it takes time and experience for local governments and financial institutions each to know and understand how the other operates. Until they do, central governments step in to regulate how much local governments can borrow, what they can borrow for, and which revenues they can pledge as guarantees. In many countries (such as Chile), local governments are not authorized to borrow. In others, the central government borrows on their behalf.

Local governments that are interested in and can access external financing should follow some key steps:

- Select projects that are worthwhile to finance with market (expensive) resources.

- Make sure they have a good financial position (measured by a net operating surplus).

- Project their balance sheets and find out whether new borrowing is in line with the constraints imposed by the national legislation.

- Compare alternative forms of borrowing, including banks and capital markets.

- Understand when public-private partnerships are efficient ways to finance expensive infrastructure and what enforcement provisions are needed to be sure that the public sector gets its fair share.

- For municipalities that are not used to borrowing in the market, institutions such as public investment banks and municipal development funds can assist in introducing them to the rigor of market-based finance.

Enhancement instruments such as guarantees are also used to make municipal projects less risky for creditors and to attract potential investors.

Sometimes a local government will face financial stress and eventually bankruptcy. It is always useful to understand what can go wrong when you borrow to finance a project and how the local government can remedy or take action in case revenues are less than expected, the costs are higher than planned, or some other factor has turned for the worse (as when the borrowing is in a foreign currency and a devaluation of the national currency occurs).

Notes

1. Most capital improvement plan processes require that submitters of proposals identify not just benefits and cost (broken down by phases of execution) but also a list of all necessary permits, licenses, and ownership or right-of-way documents required for approval of a project, to obtain finances, and to start construction.

2. Computing Present Value—An Illustration

Discount interest rate $r = 5\%$	Base year	Y1	Y2	Y3
Compounded interest rate $(1 + r)^i$	1.000	1.050	1.103	1.158
Discount factor in year i $d_i = 1 / (1 + r)^i$	1.000	0.952	0.907	0.864
Present value of cash flow $PV = CF_i {}^* d_i$	2.000	1.905	1.814	5.719

3. Municipalities can file for bankruptcy in a few countries, for example, in Hungary and the United States. Unlike the corporate bankruptcy that may end up with liquidation, municipal bankruptcy is a protective procedure in which the basic services are aimed to be maintained, while noncore assets and commercial investments are sold and services and staff perhaps reduced, to satisfy the creditors, who also share the risk of being compensated only partially.

4. For more details and guidance on municipal borrowing structure, see Petersen and Crihfield 2000.

References

ADB (Asian Development Bank). 2011. *Urban Infrastructure Financing.* http://www.adb.org /documents/periodicals/intersections/2011 /Urban_Infrastructure_Financing.asp.

Amim, Munawwar. 2010. "Municipal Infrastructure Financing: Innovative Practices from Developing Countries." Commonwealth Secretariat Local Government Reform Series, No. 2, Marlborough House, London.

Andres, Luis A., L. Guasch, T. Haven, and Vivian Foster. 2008. *The Impact of Private Sector Participation in Infrastructure: Lights, Shadows and the Road Ahead*. Washington, DC: World Bank.

Annez, P., and G. Peterson. 2008. *Lessons for the Urban Century: Decentralized Infrastructure Finance in the World Bank*. Directions in Development Series. Washington, DC: World Bank Institute.

Batley, Richard. 2001. "Public-Private Partnerships for Urban Services." In *The Challenge of Urban Government*, edited by Mila Freire and Richard Stren. Washington, DC: World Bank.

Canuto, Otaviano, and Lili Liu. 2013. *Until Debt Do Us Part: Subnational Debt, Insolvency, and Markets*. Washington DC: The World Bank.

Church, Steven, William Selway, and Dawn McCarty. 2011. "Jefferson County Files for Bankruptcy." *Bloomberg News*, November 9. http://www.bloomberg.com/news/2011-11-10/alabama-s-jefferson-county-declares-biggest-municipal-bankruptcy.html.

CIDA (Canadian International Development Agency). 2011. "PPP Guide for Municipalities: Cities Development Initiative for Asia." CIDA. http://www.cdia.asia/wp-content/uploads/PPP-Guide-for-Municipalities2.pdf.

Delmond, Jeff. 2009. *Private Sector Investment in Infrastructure–Project Finance, PPP Projects and Risks*. 2nd ed. Alphen aan den Rijn, Netherlands: Wolters Kluwer.

Foundation Center. 2009. *Philanthropy Annual: 2009 Review*. http://foundationcenter.org/philanthropyannual.

Freire, Mila, and John Petersen. 2004. *Access to Sub-National Credit*. Oxford: Oxford Press; Washington, DC: World Bank.

GPOBA (Global Partnership on Output-Based Aid). 2008. "GPOBA Activities." Global Partnership on Output-Based Aid. www.gpoba.org.

IFC (International Finance Corporation). 2004. *Structured Finance: The City of Johannesburg*. Washington, DC: IFC.

Jaguari, Sergio. 2007. *Contribution of CDM Projects to Sustainable Development Case Study: Bolivia*. Washington, DC: World Bank.

Kaganova, Olga. 2011. *Guidebook on Capital Investment Planning for Local Governments*. Washington, DC: World Bank.

Melo, Luis. 2005. "Financial Decentralization and the Law of Fiscal Responsibility in Brazil." In *City Finance*, edited by George Peterson and Patricia Clarke Annez. Washington, DC: World Bank.

Mitlin, Diana, and Anna Muller. 2004. "Windhoek, Namibia: Towards Progressive Urban Land Policies in Southern Africa." *International Development Planning Review* 26 (2):167–86.

Ngobeni, Jason. 2008. "Asking the Right Questions: Johannesburg Completes a Groundbreaking Municipal Bond Issue." PPIAF Gridlines 22 (Public-Private Infrastructure Advisory Facility). World Bank, Washington, DC.

Novi Sad. 2011. "Information Memorandum for the Issue of the City of Novi Sad Long-Term Debt Securities." Novi Sad, Serbia.

OECD (Organisation for Economic Co-operation and Development). 2010. *Innovative Financing Mechanisms for the Water Sector*. Paris: OECD.

Paulais, Thierry. 2013. "Financing African Cities—The Imperative of Local Investments." AfD and World Bank, Washington, DC.

Petersen, John, with John Crihfield. 2000. "Linkages between Local Governments and Financial Markets: A Tool Kit to Developing Sub-Sovereign Credit Markets in Emerging Economies." Working paper, World Bank, Washington, DC.

Peterson, George. 1998. "Measuring Local Government Credit Risk and Improving Creditworthiness." World Bank Working Paper 37855, World Bank, Washington, DC.

Peterson George and Annez P. 2007. Financing Cities. Fiscal Responsibility and Urban Infrastructure in Brazil, China, India, Poland

and South Africa. World Bank and Sage Publications, Delhi.

Platz, Daniel. 2009. "Infrastructure Finance in Developing Countries: The Potential of Sub-Sovereign Bonds." United Nations Department of Economic and Social Affairs, Working Paper 76, New York. http://www.un.org/esa/desa /papers/2009/wp76_2009.

Platz, Daniel, and Frank Schroeder. 2007. *Moving beyond the Privatization Debate: Different Approaches to Financing Water and Electricity in Developing Countries: Dialogue on Globalization.* New York: Friedrich-Ebert Stiftung. http://library.fes.de/pdf-files /iez/04877.pdf.

Shapiro, Mary. 2010. Speech of Mary L. Schapiro, Chairman of the Securities and Exchange Commission, at the SEC Open Meeting on Municipal Securities Disclosure. Washington, DC. May 26. http://www.sec.gov/news /speech/2011/spch012011mls.htm.

Sood, Pryanka. 2004. "India: Experiments in Local Governments Accessing the Private Capital Markets Provide Promising Results." In *Subnational Capital Markets in Developing Countries: From Theory to Practice,* edited by Mila Freire and John Petersen, 413–42. Washington, DC: Oxford University Press and the World Bank.

Sway, Idda L. 2011. *The Failure of Public Private Partnerships in Water Delivery Services: A Case of Dar-es Salaam City, Tanzania.* Saarbrücken, Germany: LAP Lambert Academic Publishing. http://www.cdia .asia/wp-content/uploads/PPP-Guide-for -Municipalities2.pdf.

Tavernise, Sabrina. 2011. "City Council in Harrisburg Files Petition on Bankruptcy." *New York Times.* October 21.

UN-HABITAT. 2005. *Financing Urban Shelter: Global Report on Human Settlements.* London: Earthscan and UN-HABITAT.

USAID (U.S. Agency for International Development). 2003. "Pooled Finance Model for Water and Sanitation Projects: The Tamil Nadu Water and Sanitation Pooled Fund (WSPF)." USAID Note, USAID, Washington, DC.

World Bank. 2002. *Cali: A City Development Strategy.* Washington, DC: World Bank.

——. 2005. "Output-Based Aid: Supporting Infrastructure Delivery through Explicit and Performance-Based Subsidies." OBA Approaches Note 5, World Bank, Washington, DC.

——. 2009. *Improving Municipal Management for Cities to Succeed.* Washington, DC: World Bank.

——. 2010. *The Cost of Environmental Degradation: Case Studies from the Middle East and North Africa.* Washington, DC: World Bank.

World Bank–IEG. 2009. "Improving Municipal Management for Cities to Succeed." Internal Evaluation Group Special Study, World Bank, Washington, DC.

World Bank and IMF (International Monetary Fund). 2009. *Developing a Medium-Term Debt Management Strategy: Guidance Note for Country Authorities.* Washington, DC: World Bank and IMF. http://www.idfc .com/.

CHAPTER 8

Achieving Greater Transparency and Accountability: Measuring Municipal Finances Performance and Paving a Path for Reforms

Catherine Farvacque-Vitkovic and Anne Sinet

Given the rapid urbanization occurring in countries all over the world, local governments everywhere face the challenge of providing infrastructure and basic services to increasingly demanding constituencies. This situation is compounded by the irreversible trend toward decentralization in which central governments have delegated to local governments the execution and financing of large portions of local investment programs. Most municipalities face heightened fiscal stress and often have to do more with less to meet residents' needs; how well local governments meet those constituent needs is often measured by using methods initially developed by national or state administrations for exertion of control over local entities or by banks for analysis of financial risk.

Performance measurement should be designed to assess not only the efficiency and effectiveness of the municipal services specifically but also the productivity of the municipal departments. Performance can be measured along several dimensions: *efficiency,* which is the relationship between services or products and the resources required to produce them; *effectiveness,* which indicates the quality of municipal performance or the extent to which a department's objectives are achieved; and *productivity,* which combines the components of efficiency and effectiveness in a single indicator that refers generally to the municipal staff and internal performance of the organization.

In summary, performance measurement is a broad concept which tries to get better answers to two major questions:

1. Are we doing the right things?

2. Are we doing things right?

Why Is Municipal Finances Self-Assessment Imperative?

Municipal Finances performance measurement is important because it provides an opportunity to obtain a clear picture of the financial situation of the municipality and support dialogue with key stakeholders (Central government, financial partners, citizens). It also provides an opportunity for benchmarking (ratios) and helps evaluate how effectively and efficiently public funds are being used.

The Anglo-Saxon world has been pushing the envelop on developing methodologies for dealing with these questions. Municipalities have used performance measurement for sometime in Canada, the United Kingdom, and the United States. In these countries, the culture of performance measurement has been widespread for several decades. However, the effectiveness of those methods is regularly subject to debate, and the picture is mixed: in most countries, public administrations are not accustomed to thinking in terms of results but more in terms of volume. Moreover, the performance measurement also needs to evaluate how local governments' efforts are perceived and to help determine a course of action. This is a complex, demanding, and costly process.

Despite the obstacles mentioned above, the culture of financial performance measurement is spreading beyond the English-speaking countries. Moreover, the concept takes on a new meaning in developing countries, where local revenues are often insufficient to meet basic needs and where the effectiveness of public expenditures is even more crucial.

Finally, the world economic crisis and its impact on public finances have greatly contributed to promoting the measurement of municipal financial performance (Paulais 2009). The overarching objective is to increase accountability and transparency in a context of skewed financial resources.

From Analysis of Municipal Finances to Performance Assessment

The analysis of a municipality's financial situation is the first step in performance measurement. The calculation of the financial situation depends on country-specific accounting data and procedures and on the generic systems of revenues and expenditures customized at the local government level (including municipal agencies dedicated to water, solid waste etc.) The key ratios and indicators are directly inspired by methods developed by external entities such as the central or state administrations for control and supervision and also by the banking system and rating agencies for risk analysis and do not contain any home-grown inputs from local governments.

The assessment of the effectiveness, efficiency, and quality of budget planning and implementation (performance measurement) is more challenging. These assessments focus on the effectiveness of the expenditures or resources used, specifically, what the municipality did with its budget that was visible or useful for the population and whether services performed gave the optimum value for money. Does the population's perception of value for money coincide with the municipality's effort?

The central governments have had to scale back their benchmarking initiatives in view of the highly complex decentralized systems now in place, local investment financing (public-private partnerships and cross-financing arrangements), and the distribution of responsibility among the municipality and its departments and agencies. In addition, the diversity of local governments' situations (size of the municipalities, economic potential, existing intercommunal arrangements, and the like) has made it more and more difficult to establish comparable financial benchmarks for municipalities, even for local governments in the same country.

All these reasons have contributed to developing the Municipal Finances Self-Assessment (MFSA) as a reliable way to monitor internal investment planning and budget processes and to convince external partners of the sustainability of a city's finances and financial management.

Toward Municipal Finances Self-Assessment

The MFSA templates are presented at the end of this chapter. It focuses on five main topics: (a) how to calculate a municipality's financial position; (b) which financial ratios to select; (c) how to make financial projections; (d) how to appraise financial management; and (e) how to summarize lessons learned from the previous steps and incorporate them into a municipal finance improvement plan.

Subsequently, the chapter is structured around three main sections:

- First, the chapter focuses on lessons learned from performance measurement practices and experiences in developed countries and assesses how to adapt performance measurement in the context of developing cities.

- Second, it reviews the four key reporting mechanisms commonly used for measuring municipal finances performance: (a) State supervision, (b) risk analysis by financial partners, (c) internal financial follow-up by municipal staff and (d) reporting to citizens.

- Third, it presents the Municipal Finances Self-Assessment (MFSA) and guides the reader through its use and application.

Section 1: Measurement of Municipal Finances Performance: Lessons Learned

Three main systems can be considered as representative of a typology of generic situations:

- *The system for measuring municipal performance in Canada and the United States.* This system has introduced the culture of performance measurement in local governments and in the broader public sector. However, even if performance measurement is widespread in the United States and a few other countries, most municipalities have only a limited ability to measure their performance because of workload issues, and it is often not clear whether the quality and efficiency of services correspond to the resources required to achieve them.

- *The European approach to measuring municipal financial performance.* The European approach is illustrated through the French model, which focuses on a sound analysis of the financial condition of the municipality and on whether the amount of revenue allows a sufficient degree of flexibility in decision making. The culture of performance evaluation as applied to finance began with the debate on how well basic municipal responsibilities like water supply and environmental services were being managed, as well as what municipalities' "social responsibilities" are.

- *Performance measurement in nonmarket economies.* Countries that do not have market economies have also developed integrated municipal finances evaluation, but their systems are oriented toward the achievement of strategic national goals to which all local governments have to contribute. The financial resources of the municipalities are allocated through complex equalization mechanisms in line with the quantitative objectives assigned. This system generates specific audits and supervision to verify whether the quantitative performance targets are reached and, if necessary, to adjust the financial resources provided to the local governments by the central administration. Most of these countries have embarked on a transition, but because changes in intergovernmental systems are slightly less rapid than in other components of the national economy, cumbersome procedures are still visible.

The above classification is, by no means, exhaustive: it is a general overview of the main systems and is helpful in determining the key lessons and best practices that could help foster better financial management processes and improve the financial position of municipalities.

Lessons from Canada and the United States: The Need for Advanced Performance Measures

In the United States, municipalities have used regular financial self-assessments for a long time. One could say that municipal performance measurement was born in the United States at the beginning of the 1930s. This early development is linked to the substantial responsibility historically assumed by local officials for fiscal decisions and services to their population and to the earlier appropriation of results-oriented management by the public sector (box 8.1 sheds light on this evolutionary process).

The law traditionally required local officials to periodically provide upper levels of government with statistics on service delivery performance and cost accounting. This obligation was justified by the number of state grants in local budgets[1] and by the need for the state administration to have control over the disbursement of those grants.

Since the 1980s, there has been a renewed interest in measuring municipal performance, in particular with the generalization of municipal bonds as the main mechanism for local governments to finance investment projects (also discussed in chapter 7). In addition to the traditional ratios for calculating the capacity of the municipality to repay its debts, the municipality has to prove that it is well managed. The ratios and indicators focus on investment and operating costs and on the quality and quantity of services provided.

By most counts, more than half of all U.S. cities were applying performance measures of some type in the late 1990s (GASB 1997; Poister and Streib 1999). Local performance measures were instigated by the Governmental Accounting Standards Board established in 1984 with the agreement of the Financial Accounting Foundation and the ten national associations of state and local government officials; the purpose was to establish and improve standards of accounting and financial reporting for U.S. state and local governments.

Financial conditions and management practices of local governments have become key components of the rating analysis conducted by specific agencies and, consequently, of the capacity of the municipality to get its bonds subscribed at the lowest cost.

Therefore, most U.S. municipalities now show a strong commitment to the effective use of performance measures, at least to get ready to reply specifically to the state auditor and to the rating agencies involved in the process of bond issuance. But they also want to improve their internal management (results-oriented systems), budgeting practices, and strategic planning processes over the medium and long terms.

The entire scheme is supported by population surveys and communication policies targeted to citizen communities and customers.

Box 8.1 U.S. Experience in Municipal Performance Measurement

Public performance measurement can be traced back at least to the 1930s, when Herbert Simon elaborated the concept of efficiency and studied performance measures in U.S. municipalities (Simon 1947/1997) (see Ridley and Simon 1938).

A significant milestone in the early days of performance measurement was the rise of government research at the New York Bureau of Municipal Research. It was focused mainly on performance budgeting or cost accounting, based on the question, How can the executive act with broad discretion and still be subject to legislative oversight?

In more modern times, concern for measuring the performance of public entities arose with the interest in program budgeting in the 1960s and program evaluation in the 1970s. Studies have promoted the use of performance measures and provided instruction on how to develop and use them (Hatry and Fisk 1971; Hatry et al. 1988), while other authors focused on how to incorporate them into larger management processes (Epstein 1984).

Even though many assume that public management relies mainly on importing ideas and models from the private sector, there are a long tradition and extensive experiences in the public sector with performance measurement, mainly in the United States and other Anglo-Saxon countries.

Performance measurement in the public sector means the measurement of performance indicators for efficiency (minimizing input for given output), effectiveness, and equity, which are intended to be used in administrative and political processes to improve rational decision making.

However, results of a survey of municipal governments in Canada and the United States show that there is limited use of the balanced scorecard. Most municipal governments, however, have developed measures to assess their organizations' financial performance, customer satisfaction, operating efficiency, innovation and change, and employee performance. Respondent administrators, in general, have confidence in the quality of the performance measures, and about half reported that these measures were used to support various management functions. The respondent administrators also have a good understanding of the balanced scorecard, and the implementers are positive about their experience.

Source: Williams 2004.

Box 8.2 illustrates the role of performance measurement in communicating with citizens. Early on, these policies became part of the municipal performance self-assessment implementation, contributing to the development of a real culture of performance measurement in local public administration.[2]

The format for performance measurement requires a combination of budgetary and physical aspects, related mostly to development of infrastructure and services and their implementation costs. Each municipality develops its own presentation with no compulsory format, and today there are many examples and applications that illustrate the efforts made by Canadian and U.S. municipalities on performance measurement.[3]

The reports, generated locally, are complemented by regular independent audits regulated by law and focused mainly on the

Box 8.2 Vancouver: Communicating Municipal Priorities and Performance

The images are examples of communication tools created by the city of Vancouver, to illustrate budgeting and spending. Every two years, the city conducts a two-step community survey to gauge citizens' opinions on public services and their priorities. Results help city officials determine what issues are most important to residents and how the city is performing and provide information for the budget planning process.

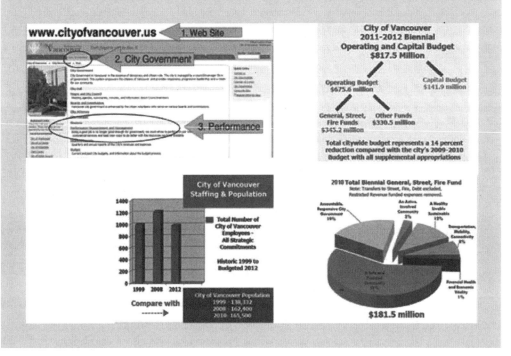

generally accepted accounting principles. For several decades, municipal performance measurement has been integrated tightly into the broader municipal management system and procedures.

But performance compared to what? A performance measure is virtually valueless without comparison with relevant baseline data. The first step developed by U.S. municipalities has been putting in place an internal gauge and to compare results from one year to the next or from one service or department to another and to point out main trends.

External comparisons (that is, comparisons among municipalities), however, are still poorly developed for various technical and political reasons. Two examples of performance measurement are provided in box 8.3: the Ontario, Canada, Municipal Performance Measurement Program and the New York City Citywide Performance Reporting.

Figure 8.1 illustrates specific performance measurement indicators by main municipal services and assessment of the operating costs of roads. The figure shows that the indicators are simple, practical, and sector specific.

Table 8.1 Perspectives on Performance

Service delivery	Financial management	Human resource management
Core performance indicators related to government goals focus on issues such as infrastructure capacity, literacy and numeracy levels, crime rates, and water quality. The aim is to develop outcome-based indicators to provide information on progress toward long-term targets. The needs and the progress are published in community status reports. They are presented as percentages of achievement.	*Level indicators relating to resource management.* These are aimed at tracking the effective and efficient use of financial resources in such areas as local taxation and invoice payment. Indicators are spending per capita (population) for the main services provided to the population: police, environmental services, fire, transportation, etc. The change over 1, 5, or 10 years is given. Operating and investment expenditures can be distinguished from each other.	*Indicators that provide information on strategic human resource issues, such as reductions in staff, the extent of diversity in the workplace, and staff turnover.* Some municipalities introduce extensive surveys of employees to measure their satisfaction and identify emerging issues. The objective is to develop business planning processes and create results-oriented job descriptions to enable all employees to understand how their work contributes to citywide goals.

Source: Boyle 2004.

Box 8.3 Municipal Performance Measurement in Ontario and New York

Service efficiency measures in Ontario, Canada, municipalities. The Ontario government's Municipal Performance Measurement Program requires municipalities to submit financial and related service performance data to the province and public on a range of services provided by municipalities (including general government, fire, police, roadways, transit, wastewater, storm water, drinking water, solid waste, parks and recreation, library services, and land use planning). The program has several objectives:

- To promote better local services and continuous improvement in service delivery and government accountability
- To improve taxpayer awareness of municipal service delivery
- To compare costs and level of performance of municipal services both internally (year to year) and externally among municipalities.

The list of indicators includes:

- General government operating costs and total costs for governance and corporate management as a percentage of total municipal operating costs.
- Operating costs and total costs for police services per capita.
- Operating costs and total costs for paved roads per lane kilometer storm water and operating costs and total costs for collection and conveyance of wastewater per kilometer.

New York City performance reporting. The New York City website http://www.nyc.gov offers a good and innovative example of the performance measurement policy implemented by U.S. municipalities and of the communication policy as a component of its interactive system (flexible, easy to use). Oriented mainly toward citizens and users, the performance scheme provides regular information on spending and funds allocated to the primary expenditures items: critical performance indicators are provided for all city agencies, with monthly updates and automatic evaluation of trends within specified program areas.

It relies on a formal internal framework of data collection and treatment (citywide performance reporting), with integrated operational data residing in disparate databases developed and maintained by separate agencies.

Figure 8.1 Performance-Based Measurement Examples from Two Jurisdictions in Canada

(a) Measuring road performance, in Durham, Ontario

OPERATING COSTS/TOTAL COSTS FOR PAVED (HARD TOP) ROADS PER LANE KILOMETER		
	Durham 2009 result	**Durham 2010 result**
Operating costs for paved (hard top) roads per lane kilometer	$6,053.91 per paved lane kilometer	$7,034.05 per paved lane kilometer
Total costs* for paved (hard top) roads per lane kilometer	$19,019.01 per paved lane kilometer	$23,876.73 per paved lane kilometer

The following narrative is an integral component of the above noted performance measurement results. These results should not be used to compare data from one municipality to another unless the influencing factors discussed in the narrative are also taken into consideration.

* **Total costs** means operating costs as defined by MPMP plus interest on long term debt and amortization on tangible capital assets as reported in the Financial Information Return.

General comments	The costs for paved roads can be influenced by: • Frequency of freezes and thaws • Frequency and severity of rainfall events • Age and condition of the network • The proportion of heavy trucks in the traffic stream • The municipality's pavement standards • The volume and type of traffic using the roads
Detailed comments	The Region of Durham road system is composed entirely of arterial roads. Compared to local roads or residential streets, arterial roads face enhanced impacts of higher volumes of traffic (particularly truck traffic) and consequently experience a more rapid rate of deterioration and, in addition, demand a higher level of service than non-arterial roads.

(b) Performance-measuring indicators for municipalities in Ontario

Service area	Measure
General Government	Operating costs for governance and corporate management as a percentage of total municipal operating costs
Fire protection	Operating costs for fire services per $1,000 of assessment
Police protection	Operating costs for police services per person
	Violent crime rate per 1,000 persons
	Property crime rate per 1,000 persons
	Total crime rate per 1,000 persons
	Youth crime rate per 1,000 youths
Roads	Operating costs for paved (hard top) roads per lane kilometer
	Operating costs for unpaved (loose top) roads per lane kilometer
	Operating costs for winter maintenance of roadways per lane kilometer maintained in winter
	Percentage of paved lane kilometers where the condition is rated as good to very good
	Percentage of winter events where the response met or exceeded locally determined municipal service levels for road maintenance
Transit	Operating costs for conventional transit per regular service passenger trip
	Number of conventional transit passenger trips per person in the service area in a year
Wastewater	Operating costs for the collection of wastewater per kilometer of wastewater main
	Operating costs for the treatment and disposal of wastewater per megaliter
	Operating costs for the collection, treatment and disposal of wastewater per megaliter (Integrated System)
	Number of wastewater main backups per 100 kilometers of wastewater main in a year
	Percentage of wastewater estimated to have by-passed treatment
Storm water	Operating costs for urban strom water management (collection, treatment, disposal) per kilometer of drainage system
	Operating costs for rural storm water management (collection, treatment, disposal) per kilometer of drainage system

Main Lessons Learned from Canada and the United States

The municipal finance assessment applied in Canada and the United States focuses on the level of service provided to the population through workload or outcome ratios and service indicators. The main objective of the measure is to help determine expenditures through a results-based budgeting approach that connects resource allocation to specific, measurable results that reflect agreed priorities.

One impressive lesson learned from U.S. municipal performance measurement is the importance given to communication of performance indicators to communities and citizens, with the clear objective of increasing public confidence in government. Confidence begins with the ability to spend money wisely. Yet, budgets are often full of administrative details seemingly disconnected from the vision and the strategic direction of the municipality. The objective is to connect resources with results so that budgeting is a strategic management and communication tool for legislators and city managers.

However, in actuality, the performance measurement applied in most U.S. municipalities is limited to workload or output measures and does not inform the public about the efficiency, effectiveness, or productivity of the municipality (see Ammons 2001). Despite the general expansion of the performance measurement systems among local U.S. governments, it is difficult to get comparable data, even today. The administrations are very cautious about publishing benchmarks and performance scores, because of the many external factors that influence the results (see above) or the inconsistent accounting practices across municipalities for overhead costs, employee benefits, capital acquisition, depreciation, and the like. This situation is common to numerous other countries and illustrates the limits of a too-ambitious performance measurement system.

Consequently, it is important to design a system for measuring financial performance in harmony with the objective and capacity of the municipality itself.

The European Experience

Except in the United Kingdom, Europe has no tradition of internal performance measurement. To measure the performance of municipal finances through the service delivery effort and cost efficiency is not part of the culture. However, financial ratios and the general financial position of municipalities are usually under tight control of the mayor and his staff, the central government administration, and now even the European Commission:[4] the volume of finance, its year-over-year increase, the balance between the current and the capital investment budget and debt ratios are common concepts shared by most local officials. Municipal finance assessment is widespread but focuses mainly on balancing ratios and trends.

Financial ratios are published annually by state agencies (the ministry of finance or ministry of the interior) or even by national associations of local governments (figure 8.2). A fair amount of information on local finances is available in most European countries but, again, primarily on financial position and revenues. Only partners involved in the local development sector and experts or consulting firms make use of this information.

Service budgeting is not commonly assessed, as it is the prerogative of municipal councils to decide on priorities, generally on the basis of the program or agenda on which they were elected.[5] Consequently, performance measures focus more on financial sustainability than on efficiency and budgeting policy.

Figure 8.2 Municipal Debt per Citizen and Total Debt in 10 French Cities

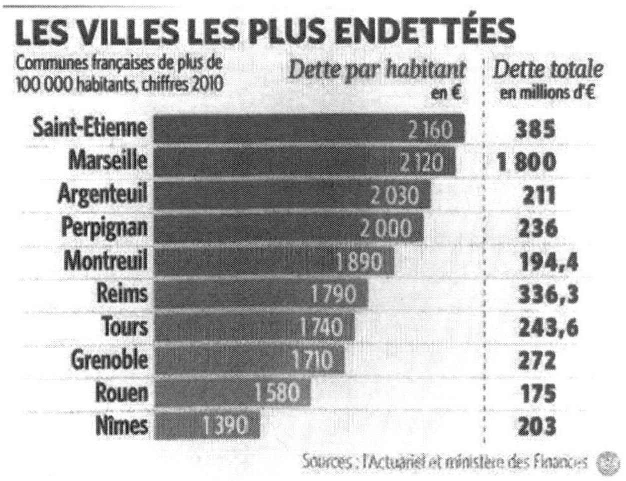

LES VILLES LES PLUS ENDETTÉES

Communes françaises de plus de 100 000 habitants, chiffres 2010	*Dette par habitant* en €	*Dette totale* en millions d'€
Saint-Etienne	2 160	385
Marseille	2 120	1 800
Argenteuil	2 030	211
Perpignan	2 000	236
Montreuil	1 890	194,4
Reims	1 790	336,3
Tours	1 740	243,6
Grenoble	1 710	272
Rouen	1 580	175
Nîmes	1 390	203

Sources : l'Actuariel et ministère des Finances

Source: Agence Française de Notation 2010.

However, under the constraints of the financial crisis, more aggressive attempts to renew the assessment of the municipalities and, in particular, of their financial situation have been initiated. The objective is generally to reclaim budgetary leeway while maintaining a high commitment to social welfare. People are increasingly aware that the best way to achieve this objective is to modernize the state administration and make it more effective. As with the decentralization process, most of the services are now provided by local governments, so that municipalities are directly concerned with the need for modernization and professionalization.

Citizens and taxpayers are also very keenly involved in how state and local government decisions affect the environment, the overall quality of services, and, ultimately, the quality of life.

This trend is confirmed through various rankings that force local authorities to enlarge the scope of their financial assessment and include evaluation of the quantity and quality of services provided by the municipal budget or in partnership with the private sector (figure 8.3). These rankings have had a visible influence on improving city management, at least for the largest cities (those with more than 100,000 inhabitants). Figure 8.3 shows the population's degree of satisfaction with municipal budget expenditures on sectors such as urban services, economic development, police and security, schools, culture, and sports.

City satisfaction indexes provide comparative benchmarks on living conditions, local taxation, level of services, business incentives, and private investment attractiveness; they gradually become targets toward which the local elected officials and their staff work. Even if their mandate does not encompass all the functions of public service delivery, municipal governments have included population

Figure 8.3 Municipal Expenditures on Selected Sectors and Citizen Satisfaction

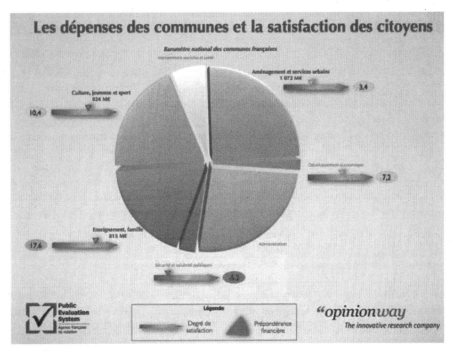

Source: Agence Française de Notation 2010.

mobility and globalization in their policies and know they have to compete with other cities to ensure their development. Among the top priorities for most large and medium-size cities in Europe are the quality of services provided to the population, social welfare, housing, environmental protection, and the investment climate.

This evolution in municipal financial assessment, however, has to overcome various technical issues: (a) the accounting classification is often an ineffective way to estimate the cost of a service or an investment project; (b) service delivery involves a lot of partners or providers only partially under the control of the municipality; and (c) the performance results can vary significantly from one year to another, making it difficult to appraise a situation fairly, particularly for small and medium-size municipalities that do not have the same amount of investments each year.

Traditional financial analysis does not address those issues properly. The citizen satisfaction surveys are among the most powerful instruments for filling these gaps. Since all basic services are well provided in these countries, the surveys give more importance to tariffs and policies and to environmental and sustainability aspects.

Adapting Performance Measurement in the Context of Developing Cities: Key Conditions for Success

In most developing countries, measurement of municipal financial performance is new and part of the change management process. Experiences with performance measurement and practices are few in these countries, and the challenge is to promote its development as an integrated component of good governance and skilled city management.

Municipalities can adapt existing methods and prove they are able to both assess their own situation by themselves and act on key findings. Self-assessment will not preclude the institutionalized auditing process carried out by state auditors and will not substitute for financial assessments carried out by financial partners like banks, which will also intervene for their own purposes in their own way. However, it is very clear that the municipalities that are able to carry out self-assessment will be far better positioned to report to their central government and to their citizens and prepare bankable projects, thereby gaining confidence and trust from both their internal and external partners.

Some conditions might help in the dissemination and scaling up of performance measurement. Among them are: (a) the level of decentralization or the importance given to the decentralization reform process even if all the issues are not solved; (b) the pressure to increase local investment and to mobilize resources for it; and (c) the transparency of communicating financial data and the effort to support municipal capacity building.

Condition 1: The Extent of Decentralization

Increased decentralization and emphasis on reform are expected to exert pressure on national and local governments to disseminate information on their financial situation and financial management efficiency.

The extent of decentralization can be roughly estimated by how much leeway local governments have in making financial decisions and how much municipalities contribute to national public finance. On this basis, the contributions of municipalities to the national public capital investment effort through taxes and other revenue streams and to the living conditions of their population often appear as prerequisites to instituting measures of municipal financial performance. In most developing countries, local governments' contribution to the national public investment effort is weak (less than 10 percent of total public investment), or it falls under the direct control of the central government with little connection to considerations of municipal financial performance.

Condition 2: The Involvement of Financial Partners

The involvement of financial partners (banks, specialized financing institutions, or the financial market) in the financing of local government investment programs generally provides an effective incentive for improving municipal finances: to gain access to credit and become creditworthy for medium- and long-term commitments, municipalities need to present satisfactory financial ratios to secure the confidence of their financial partners.

In most developing countries, the contribution of the banking sector to the financing of the local government sector is limited (at least in the absence of state guarantees). Measurement of financial performance will help stimulate local investment financing from the banks, the specialized institutions, or the financial markets and thereby contribute to a virtuous circle of improved performance.

A substantial source of external funding comes from donors and development agencies.

However, either local governments are ill equipped to prepare financially sound investments programs, or donors lack the tools that would give them the confidence to go ahead with project or program funding. This is a recurrent problem everywhere. In the Balkan countries, for example, the need for investments is great, but the EU complains that it cannot disburse in the absence of good project proposals from municipalities. The World Bank has been implementing municipal development projects for the past 30 years, and yet it seems to reinvent the wheel and the rules of the game every time a new project comes along and, in many cases, the performance-based grants, which are often recommended or implemented, fall short of major transformational reforms in municipal finances and practices. The financing of municipal infrastructure subprojects is the opportunity to stimulate a common understanding of municipal finances assessment and its path to reforms.

Condition 3: Data Collection and Dissemination

Anyone who has ever worked in developing cities will confirm that, in most cases, the availability of data is an issue, and yet every time a donor-funded project is prepared, a huge data collection effort gets under way. There are several problems with data collection: What data and for what purpose? Are the data reliable and pertinent? Who should be using and maintaining the data? Why do the data get lost and go unused after external project funding expires? How do we make data open and available to the public and other stakeholders? In the case of municipal financial data, the key starting point is the definition of terms. In many cases, poor accounting classification can be a constraint. The abuse of the data and misinterpretation that could send wrong policy signals are other reasons for the difficulties

faced in instituting performance measurement in developing countries.

Even if those conditions are challenging, evolution is already visible in some developing countries, especially when cities are ranked according to living conditions and competiveness that clearly reflect the policies implemented by the municipalities on basic services, housing and social policies, quality of urban space, employment, and the like.

All such policies refer to municipal finance and management in various degrees: even if central agencies or concessions to the private sector are mostly responsible for providing these facilities, municipalities have their role and contribute more or less to the image of the cities. Their capacity to program the priorities, to implement and coordinate the projects, and to pay for maintenance are crucial to improving urban living conditions. Municipal finance is thus located at a strategic crossroad.

Figure 8.4 summarizes Morocco's effort to link improvements in municipal finance to the urban development process. Both examples give greater responsibility to local governments for increasing the performance of public services, under tight control from the state government. In both cases, the municipal financial situation is considered essential to improving the effectiveness, efficiency, and productivity of the contribution of the municipality to urban development.

The city rankings in Morocco include selected dimensions for assessing the quality of life and the competitiveness of those services which are directly under the responsibility of the municipalities and Wilayas such as health, education, housing and basic services, infrastructure, real estate, and civil services. The borrowing eligibility guide of the Morocco Municipal Credit Institution (Fonds d'Equipement Communal) prescribes eligibility criteria for the municipalities: (a) an indebtedness rate that is less than 40 percent (of total annual repayment to global resources); (b) a net operating surplus that enables

Figure 8.4 Example of Performance Measurement and City-Ranking Criteria in Morocco

Attractivité	
Qualité de vie	**Compétitivité**
▸ Santé ▸ Education ▸ Climat et environnement ▸ Culture ▸ Logements et services de base ▸ Développement social	▸ Poids économique ▸ Infrastructures et accessibilité ▸ Ressources humaines ▸ Attractivité foncière ▸ Présence administrative

La qualité de vie évaluée selon 6 sous thèmes (Coef.1)	❶ Santé (Coef.2)	• Nombre de lits pour 10 000 habitants (coef.1) • Nombre de CHU (coef.2) • Nombre de médecins pour 10 000 habitants (coef.3) • Nombre de personnel paramédical pour 10 000 habitants (coef.1)
	❷ Education (Coef.2)	• Scolarisation primaire et secondaire (coef.3) • Etudiants du supérieur (coef.2) • Réussite au baccalauréat (coef.2) • Infrastructures scolaires (coef.3)
	❸ Climat et environnement (Coef.2)	• Climat (coef.3) • Proximité de la mer (coef.1) • Proximité de la montagne (coef.1) • Environnement (coef.1)
	❹ Culture (Coef.2)	• Patrimoine culturel (coef.1) • Nombre d'écrans de cinéma (coef.1) • Nombre de bibliothèques (coef.1) • Nombre de festivals nationaux (coef.1) • Nombre de festivals d'envergure internationale (coef.3)
	❺ Logements et services de base (Coef.2)	• Disponibilité du logement (coef.1) • Prix de l'habitat (coef.2) • Équipements (eau et d'électricité) (coef.3)
	❻ Développement social (Coef.2)	• Indice de Développement humain (coef.2) • Emploi : évolution de l'emploi (coef.2) • Sécurité (coef.3) • Pauvreté (coef.3)
La compétitivité évaluée selon 5 sous thèmes (Coef.2)	❶ Poids économique (Coef.2)	• Marché de consommation local (coef.1) • Marché de consommation étranger (coef.1) • Développement industriel et commercial (coef.1)
	❷ Infrastructures et accessibilité (Coef.2)	• Accessibilité aérienne (coef.2) • Accessibilité ferroviaire (coef.2) • Accessibilité routière (coef.3) • Accessibilité portuaire (coef.1) • Capacité hôtelière (coef.2) • Capacité de restauration (coef.1)
	❸ Ressources humaines (Coef.2)	• Taux d'analphabétisme (coef.1) • Taux de réussite au baccalauréat (coef.1) • Taux de diplômés des études supérieures (coef.1) • Coût de la main-d'œuvre (coef.1)
	❹ Attractivité foncière (Coef.2)	• Prix du foncier (coef.3) • Présence de services de conservation et de cadastre (coef.1) • Existence de P2I (coef.2)
	❺ Présence administrative (Coef.2)	• Présence d'un CRI (coef.2) • Présence d'un consulaire (coef.1) • Présence d'une Cour d'appel (coef.2) • Présence d'un tribunal de commerce (coef.1) • Présence d'une wilaya (coef.1) • Présence d'un chef-lieu de province (coef.2)

Source: La Vie Eco 2011 (Moroccan newspaper).

the municipality to pay its total debt (loans contracted previously plus new loans); (c) a cash contribution to the project of at least 20 percent of project cost; and (d) adequate human, material, and organizational means to complete the project.

Performance measurement is included in several World Bank projects in Africa. The Senegal Urban Development and Decentralization Program (UDDP) developed in 1990's opened the path to many other similar projects in Africa where the model was cloned and implemented. The Senegal UDDP introduced for the first time the concept of municipal audits and municipal contracts in Africa. The Municipal Development Agency (ADM) supported 67 municipalities in implementing a sustainable priority investment program and provided them with a financing plan that combined soft loans, grants, and savings. The plan included: (a) physical investment and financial performance improvement plans as part of the municipal contracts signed by the municipalities and the ADM; (b) physical investment financing, an incentive to improve municipal financial performance, in which loan reimbursement is a driving force for increasing revenue; and (c) strictly monitored trends in line with the *Financial Ratios Guide* (figure 8.5) published by the ADM.

Figure 8.5   Ratios Guide Senegal

Source: Agence de Développement Municipal (ADM).

Section 2: Measurement of Municipal Financial Performance: Key Traditional Reporting Mechanisms

Four different methodologies for measuring municipal financial performance are illustrated below: (a) state supervision; (b) risk analysis by financial partners; (c) internal financial follow-up by municipal staff and officials; and (d) democratic dissemination. The first two methodologies are driven by municipalities' external partners. Their objective is to exercise judgment on the financial condition of the municipality. The two others are generally implemented and used internally to improve the management of the financial condition and to communicate with the outside world (citizens and partners). The objective of this section is to present these different methodologies and to show how they can guide municipal performance measurement.

From State Supervision to Democratic Dissemination: Overview

The tools and procedures used by central governments to carry out their supervisory role are numerous but quite similar all around the world. State government administration applies a matrix of monitoring indicators that aim to determine whether the municipal budget or accounts conform to public accounting rules and to the objectives set by national policies governing volume and allocation.

The *risk analysis* of municipal finance carried out by the financial partners (bankers and rating agencies, for example) follows international standards, allowing for the specific requirements of the country. These requirements can be more or less detailed, depending on the nature and magnitude of the project or program to be funded.

Internal financial monitoring focuses on municipal financial management and complements financial analysis and assessment. In the case of municipalities, the methodology does not follow international standards but is generally influenced by methodologies used by the corporate sector.

Democratic dissemination covers various initiatives that help municipalities better communicate their financial performance to their constituents. The key objective is to show to citizens how the municipality is keeping its promises and how it is striving to do its best to improve service delivery and its citizens' quality of life.

Reporting and Accountability to the Central Government and State Oversight and Monitoring

Around the globe, central governments supervise and monitor local government finances. In most cases, local government finances account for less than 5–10 percent of total public finances, and the performance measurement focuses mainly on administrative supervision or control of local budgets and decision making (see the section on budgetary control below).

When the percentage of local government finances is higher than the usual 5–10 percent, state oversight and monitoring become an economic issue. The measurement changes and focuses more on enhancing the transparency of local government finances to stimulate economic growth, to develop municipal credit, and to enhance regional competitiveness. Tools and methods are necessarily more sophisticated and directly involve local governments in tandem with the central government through vertical subnational performance monitoring systems.

Budgetary Control

There are as many budgetary indicator grids as countries. They are usually completed by the ministry of finance or the ministry of interior. The state auditor or treasurer prepares statements of position based largely on accounts and cash balance. The objective is to confirm whether the budget of the municipality conforms to public accounting rules and to national policy objectives as they apply to volume and allocation, for example.

With the progress of decentralization, central government administrations have developed a set of ratios to introduce targets and benchmarking in local government financial management and to anticipate possible overspending or overborrowing that would likely destabilize public finances. Typically, ratios focus on the following items and objectives (see also table 8.2):

- Is the budget well balanced?

- Is the appropriation of mandatory expenditures such as salaries and debt service sufficient?

- Are capital investments (the development budget) greater than 40 percent of the total budget?

- Is the fiscal autonomy of the local government enough? Are the intergovernmental transfers less than a certain percentage of the current revenue?

- Are budget preparation and approval on schedule?

Key indicators used in west and central Africa provide a useful example of targets and benchmarking:

- Date of budget approval.

- Is the budget well balanced and sincere?

- Are mandatory expenditures listed?

- Is the Y-1 budget deficit less than 5 percent of operating revenue?

Table 8.2 Key Mandatory Municipal Finances Ratios

Information on local taxation				
	Tax potential	Tax pressure	Per capita	Average (strata)
Three taxes (Property tax, Land tax, Housing tax or local residence tax)				
Business tax				
All four taxes				

Compulsory key ratios	Amount	Average (strata)
1 Actual operating expenditure per capita		
2 Local Tax receipts per capita		
3 Actual current revenue per capita		
4 Total capital investment expenditure per capita		
5 Debt outstanding per capita		
6 Intergovernmental operating transfer per capita (DGF)		
7 Salaries/total operating expenditure		
8 Tax pressure (actual or potential)		
9 Operating expenditure + debt repayment/actual current revenue		
10 Capital investment expenditure/actual operating revenue		
11 Debt outstanding/actual operating revenue		

- Are salaries and wages less than 20 percent of current revenue?

- Is the capital investment budget greater than 40 percent of total expenditures?

- Is debt service less than 12 percent of current revenue?

The effectiveness of monitoring depends on several factors:

- The availability of data and the quality of the accounting management, often limited to cash management.

- Capacity of the central government to manage the information and react appropriately in case of difficulties.

- Capacity of the local government to handle the technical challenges of providing data and to act on implementing recommendations. This ability is particularly relevant in countries where local governments are implementing part of the national budget through delegated functions with revenue coming mainly from intergovernmental transfers.

In France, Finance Law 1999 stipulates that even if there is no longer prior control over municipal budgets, municipalities have to calculate 11 key ratios every year and communicate them to the central government. These ratios are published by the Ministry of Interior and provide a clear vision of the trends in local finances. Table 8.2 lists the typical compulsory ratios based on French and international practices.

Local Government Collection and Dissemination of Financial Data

When local government finances contribute a higher share of gross domestic product (GDP) and public finances, central governments want to have better knowledge of what is happening in the municipalities and to be able to share that information with other local governments to increase their contributions to the improvement of national public finance goals.

Central administrations publish more and more sophisticated statistical yearbooks or ratio handbooks that profile the financial performance of local governments and include local budget data in state accounting.

This type of monitoring of subnational financial performance requires accuracy and is often produced by specialized departments in the central government. For example, in France, at least two ministries (the Ministry of Finance and the Ministry of Interior) and the National Institute of Statistics publish detailed statistics every year on subnational finance and budgetary issues. In parallel, the National Associations of Local Governments publish its own statistics.

Figure 8.6 shows two pages from a white paper, which is published every year by Japan's Ministry of Internal Affairs and Communications. It assesses the status of revenues, expenditures, flexibility of the financial structure (ordinary balance ratio, real debt service ratio. and debt service payment ratio), outstanding local government borrowing, data on local public enterprises, and information on efforts to promote of the soundness of local public finance.

Reporting and Accountability to Financial Partners

In addition to state supervision and monitoring, guidance provided by the financial partners of the local governments is crucial to improving the measurement of municipal financial performance.

It is generally acknowledged that public funds will not be enough to bridge the financing gap

Figure 8.6   Illustrations from Japan's White Paper on Local Public Finance, 2011

 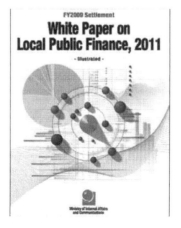

Source: MIAC (Japan).

for much-needed investments and that external funding from national banks or capital markets will be required. The financial partners need a higher degree of information on financial performance measures:

- *Conditions for getting intergovernmental transfers from the central state.* These conditions depend on allocation criteria (operating or current transfers, subsidies to specific investment projects, and the like) and rules. Central administrations are demanding that local governments meet increasingly challenging standards of financial performance, including those for receiving the automatic allocations of grants.

- *Conditions for obtaining bank credit (commercial or donor).* These conditions will highlight mainly those ratios that demonstrate the creditworthiness of the local government through what is generally named risk analysis. If a guarantee from the state is required by the bank or donor, the state government will follow its own procedures to assess the creditworthiness of the local government.

- *Conditions for launching municipal bonds.* These conditions require rating and benchmarking the client (local government) and analysis of the project's financial sustainability.

Financial partners have a crucial responsibility to promote the measurement of municipal financial performance in addition to the monitoring by the state and to the requests for accountability from the citizens.

Intergovernmental Transfers as Incentives for Increasing Measurement of Municipal Financial Performance

Transfers are the primary means by which central governments direct and affect the volume of resources channeled to municipal budgets.

Many cities around the globe are very dependent on such transfers, which remain a large share of their revenues.

The *fiscal equalization grant* is frequently used in developed as well as in developing countries. However, it may have negative effects on the financial performance of the municipalities and has to be carefully implemented. In general, the perverse effects of this very common category of intergovernmental transfers are, first, that the costs of serving numerous small and medium-size local governments are very high; second, that these grants can discourage municipalities from making their own efforts to mobilize local resources better; and, third, that they serve the disadvantaged cities at the expense of the richest.

Performance grants encourage efficient local financial management practices through specific criteria such as "fiscal effort," that is, the amount of revenue collected by the local government as a percentage of its fiscal potential, for example, or the percentage of revenue allocated in the budget to social and priority investments.

However, incentive-based intergovernmental transfers and performance grants are generally demanding and not easy to set up: they require a complete and detailed national database and reliable information on the financial performance of local governments to allow national comparisons, city classifications, and indexing. Local authorities are often critical of the way calculations are made by central governments and of the lack of transparency in the process.

In the case of the French experience on intergovernmental transfers, the calculation of the *dotation globale de fonctionnement* (annual allocations) requires 65 numbers and data on each municipality, including different categories of population data, and also many data on taxation policy implemented by the local government (gross and net fiscal basis, exemptions, fiscal rates, and so forth).

Criteria for transfer allocations often emphasize optimal distribution of funds and correction of structural or long-term fiscal imbalances among a large number of local governments (sometimes several levels of subnational governments), and devote little attention to municipal financial performance. There is a huge literature on these issues with positive examples such as Brazil, Mexico, and South Africa but also with more questionable experiences in places such as Tunisia or Vietnam (see chapter 1).

Measurement of Municipal Financial Performance and Bank Risk Analysis

The development of subsovereign credit without the guarantee of the state government has put pressure on local governments to improve financial information and implement measurements of internal financial performance.

Bank risk analysis focuses on the financial sustainability of the borrower and on its capacity to pay back the loan, with the key ratios below recognized as valid in most situations:

- Existing and future debt as a percentage of current revenue

- Operating surplus as a percentage of current revenue

- Cash balance at the beginning and end of the year

- Resource projections (growth potential)

The criteria vary in accordance with the amount of the loan, the category of the financing (project financing or budget financing), and the institutional and economic context of the country and city.

The main characteristic of risk analysis compared to previous approaches is that it includes financial projections based on the duration of the loan amortization (the financial and physical depreciation of the assets being financed), an unusual exercise in most municipalities in developing countries. It can include broader risk analysis such as country risk analysis, features of the local government system, degree of decentralization, fiduciary environment, and rules: Who is responsible? Who sets the tariffs? Who sets the tax policy? Is annual repayment a compulsory expenditure in the accounting procedure? Table 8.3 provides guidance for financial risk analysis issued by the Network of Associations of Local Authorities of South-East Europe (NALAS) to partner municipalities.

The international donor organizations are strong financial and professional supporters of helping municipalities build creditworthiness and risk analysis capacity.

Measurement of Municipal Financial Performance and Access to Capital Markets and Public-Private Partnerships

Rating procedures focus on financial and nonfinancial performance criteria of local governments and can include assessment of the feasibility and sustainability of specific projects to be financed (that is, project risk). The three main international rating agencies—Moody's, Standard & Poor's, and Fitch Ratings (see chapter 7) publish their main assessment areas but do not disclose detailed procedures and internal scores. National rating agencies (often partners of the big three) are becoming increasingly instrumental in supporting municipal ratings and financial assessments. More and more municipal self-assessments are also completed and generally use the same or similar international standards as the big international rating agencies.

Table 8.3 Guidance on Risk Analysis and Ratios

Financial risk analysis			
Surplus Generation and debt servicing ability	**Cash flow adequacy**	**Capital structure**	**Liquidity and financial flexibility**
• Analytical distinctions with profitability	• Focus on debt service capability	• Leverage	• Sources of liquidity
• Type and structure of debt	• Analytical distinctions with profitability	• Type and structure of debt	• Potential calls on liquidity
• Analysis of cash flow coverage and cash generation ability	• Type and structure of debt	• Hedging arrangements	• Short-term debt maturity
	• Analysis of cash flow coverage and cash generation ability	• Off-balance sheet obligations	• Bank credit facilities
		• Asset values	• Unencumbered assets and debt capacity

Ratios	**Definitions**	**Interpretation**
Ratio of recurrent revenues to total revenues	Measures the degree to which a local government relies on recurrent revenues.	A ratio of 100% or close to 100% may be inappropriate for a local government that is funding the acquisition of significant nonfinancial assets.
Recurrent revenues per capita	Measures the relative burden of taxes and user charges on local taxpayers and service users.	A higher level of operating revenues per capita indicates a relatively high burden of taxes and charges.
Ratio of own-source revenues to total revenues	Measures a local government's own-source revenues compared to its total revenues.	A relatively high percentage of own-source revenues (maximum indicator 100%) indicate that the local government is more reliant on recurrent, predictable revenues to fund its activities.

Source: Josifov, Pamfil, and Comsa 2008.

The six most significant analytical areas are listed below; each of them refers to several criteria:

- Legal and economic framework

- Economic base of the services area

- Municipal finances

- The municipality's existing operations

- Managerial assessment

- Project-specific issues

The rating agencies often carry out baseline credit assessments; box 8.4 explains the four main factors.

Many central governments do not allow their subnational governments to tap into the capital market through municipal bonds. In

Box 8.4 Baseline Credit Assessment

As of late 2006, Moody's had rated 249 local and regional governments in 30 countries around the world, outside the United States. The number of local government ratings had more than doubled since 1998.

Moody's uses two explicit factors to establish the rate: (a) the local government's intrinsic credit strength; and (b) the likelihood of extraordinary support from another entity to prevent a default. The four analytical inputs are:

- The baseline credit assessment of the local government
- The supporting government's rating
- An estimate of the default dependence between the two entities
- An estimate of the likelihood that the other entity would provide extraordinary support to prevent the local government's default

Source: Rubinoff, Bellefleur, and Crisafelli 2008.

Africa, only Johannesburg and Lagos have launched municipal bonds. In Morocco, the Municipal Credit Institution has a long experience with pooling municipal bonds through the Caisse des Dépôts et de Gestion.

Reporting and Accountability to Citizens (Social Accountability)

What is Social Accountability? In practice, Social Accountability is an evolving umbrella covering several components and a menu of options such as: (1) Citizen monitoring/oversight/feedback on public sector performance; (2) User-centered public information access/dissemination; (3) Public complaint and grievance redress mechanisms; (4) Citizen participation in resource allocation decisions such as participatory budgeting. How do we define open government? The Transparency and Accountability Initiative (which includes a number of partners such as the Ford Foundation, the Open Society Foundation, and the U.K. Department for International Development) proposes the following definition: Three key principles form the basis of an open government:

(a) transparency, that is, providing the public with essential information about what the government is doing; (b) civic engagement that allows members of the public to contribute ideas and expertise so that their government can make policies with the benefit of information from widely dispersed constituents of the society; and (c) accountability that ensures that governments are responsible to the public for their decisions and actions.

Communicating and Sharing Information: Open Data, Open Government

A vast menu of tools and methods has been developed to address the open government agenda in the recent past. Most of these have targeted central governments, but few have attempted to work with local governments. Those efforts that have focused on local governments include expenditure tracking, third-party monitoring, beneficiary feedback, and participatory budgeting.

Expenditure tracking (BOOST). Boost is a tool that helps monitor public spending using disaggregated data from the financial management information/treasury systems, including information on spending at the sub-national level. Boost has been introduced in Kenya, Moldova, and Togo, where central governments have been willing to put their treasury data online. BOOST platforms are under development in a number of countries. In some instances, geo-mapping techniques can be used within BOOST to track the use of public funds. Another tool is Public Expenditure and Financial Accountability (PEFA), a program supported by the World Bank. The PEFA program is a multi-donor partnership between seven donor agencies and international financial institutions—including the World Bank—to assess the condition of a country's public expenditure, procurement and financial accountability systems and develop a practical sequence for reform and capacity building actions (http://www.pefa.org/en/content/resources). It can be applied at both the national and the municipal level; yet very few cities have applied it—only Dakar in 2009 and Ouagadougou in 2010, as well as some experimental work carried out in Kosovo.

Third-party monitoring. Increasing attention is being placed on equipping civil society organizations (CSOs) with the proper tools to provide a third-party perspective on public affairs. One key issue is that, often, these organizations are not independent entities and may not provide the best unbiased perspective.

Beneficiaries' feedback. Citizen report cards and scorecards, E-petitions, and reporting based on information and communication technology are tools designed to enable citizens to speak up and report their discontent with the quality and coverage of municipal services. Many cities around the world are conducting beneficiary surveys and providing a space either on an E-platform or through more structured face-to-face community meetings for citizens to raise their concerns and be part of the decision-making process.

Participatory budgeting. Perhaps, the best example of citizen participation comes from the participatory budgeting experience. Participatory budgeting started in 1989 in the municipality of Porto Alegre, the capital of Brazil's southernmost state, Rio Grande do Sul, and was intended to help poorer citizens and neighborhoods receive a larger share of public spending (see box 8.5). Throughout the 1990s, participatory budgeting spread to other municipalities in Brazil and to other countries in South America, including Bolivia, Guatemala, Nicaragua, and Peru, and various forms of participatory budgeting have taken root in other parts of the world. Such programs offer citizens from poor and historically excluded groups access to the decision-making process. However, most of the time only a small share of the total budget focusing on small neighborhood investments is actually open for citizen 's participation. The lion's share of the budget with the key capital investments is not, drawing criticism that, in many cases, real participation is only given lip service.

Social Accountability: Magic Bullet or Just Hype?

What does the evidence of Social Accountability impact tell us? There has been a number of excellent literature reviews and the evidence for many, so far, seems inconclusive. The "What Next" question is key to successfully address the next generation challenges. There is both a need to (a) bring rigor to the process and to the tools; (b) to move away from confrontation and (c) to better understand the fine line between demand and supply. Social accountability mechanisms, in many ways, raise a lot of expectations on the demand side but fail to provide the answers on the supply side. Local governments are not necessarily the bad guys, drenched in corruption and faulted with poor governance. The reality is that many local governments would like to provide better services but are faced with many competing demands in a context of very limited financial resources and low capacity. It is very important to understand the constraints of the supply side. This is why audits/self-assessments are so important and combining complementary audits is so crucial because they help provide a full picture and create a coallition among key stakeholders. Interestingly enough, Social Accountability tools seem to have predominantly been applied in social development/community driven projects (CDD) on essentially small scale projects. Their application in cities on larger scale projects has been limited. There is great opportunity for merging social audits with urban and financial audits, giving more in-depth meaning to the accountability and transparency agenda.

Section 3: Toward a Generic Framework for Measuring Municipal Finances Performance: The Municipal Finances Self-Assessment

The World Bank has developed over the years a framework for local government assessments (municipal audits) that has been tested, implemented, and customized in a growing number of municipalities. The Municipal Finances Self-Assessment (MFSA, also called financial audits) is part of it. It has proved to be a powerful instrument for improving governance and accountability, modernizing management practices, and paving the path toward change and reforms (box 8.6).

The objective of the MFSA is to assess a city's financial health and to identify specific actions

Box 8.6 Improving Local Governments Capacity: The Experience of Municipal Finances Self-Assessment (MFSA) in South East Europe

The MFSA methodology was developed by the World Bank and has been customized for South-East Europe by the World Bank with the support of international and local experts. This adaptation required a common understanding of terminology and a clear definition of budget items (categories) on both the revenue and the expenditure sides. The template or framework of analysis was validated by all stakeholders.

1. One important lesson from the MFSA process is the recognition by participating municipalities of the need for municipal departments and staff to share information and data among the Technical Departments, the Public Utility Companies (PUCs) in charge of service delivery, Tax Services, State Treasury, and so forth. This has typically not been the case. Creditworthiness assessments, municipal finance projections, and financing strategies require data inputs from various sources that are not reported in any of the typical mandatory accounting reports. The MFSA provides a platform for consolidating and reconciling these information sources.

2. The C2C dialogues and the embedded MFSA process helped make a vital connection between financing, urban planning, land management, and ultimately investment programming and service delivery. The series of seven City to City Dialogues was structured in a way that helped close that loop. Several factors have a fundamental impact on the way cities urbanize and on the future of urban investments: the fact that a large share of local revenues come from land development, that

these revenues are highly volatile and subject to global financial stress, that there is a pressure to sell and develop land, and that urban planning functions and issuance of building permits have been quickly devolved to largely unprepared local governments. It is essential that the region start a conversation on these important issues—a conversation that should include all levels of government, the citizens, the service providers, the private sector, and the donor community. The C2C series has helped launch this conversation in a forum where these issues could be discussed safely, problems could be unbundled, and solutions could be identified. The MFSA process clarified the need for a more global and integrated approach that combines MFSA with Urban Audits (Land, Infrastructure and Services Self-Assessment), which a number of municipalities have begun to pursue.

3. The debates launched as part of the MFSA-Urban Audit, as well as the findings of the NALAS Fiscal Decentralization Study and the World Bank Municipal Finances Review underlined the need to assess the progress of fiscal decentralization in the region.

4. The municipal staff from some 25 cities and municipalities in the region (including capital cities) took part in this experience and more municipalities have expressed a desire to join in. Scaling up and institutionalizing these tools are the next steps to be taken in collaboration with regional, national, and local stakeholders.

Source: C. Farvacque-Vitkovic, S. Palmreuther, T. Nikolic, A. Sinet.

to improve mobilization of local resources, public spending, public assets management and maintenance, investment programming, and access to external financing (borrowing plus donor funding).

The MFSA performs several functions: (a) it reviews municipal budgets (revenues and expenditures), financial management practices, savings capacity, investment efforts, and financial projections for the next five years; (b) it provides some benchmarking through a set of simple and comparable key indicators and ratios; and (c) it defines key actions to be included in a municipal finance improvement plan with a clear definition of what concrete actions will be included, how these actions will be implemented and by whom, the timeline for implementation, and the implementation cost (if applicable).

The MFSA is sometimes carried out in parallel with an urban audit that provides a snapshot of the city's quantity and quality of services and infrastructure and identifies a municipal investment program (box 8.7). The World Bank has also developed a framework for the urban audit that, like the financial audit, has been tested, implemented, and customized in a growing number of municipalities. The urban audit has for its main objective the gathering of baseline information on the existing condition of infrastructure and services, the identification of patterns of urbanization and pockets of poverty, and the spatial location and quantification of the gaps, leading to the identification of a priority investments program and a priority maintenance program.

MFSA Innovations

The MFSA has introduced some innovative features. First, it relies on municipal staff themselves, using an integrated approach, to assess the financial situation in their municipalities. Second, it puts city officials in the driver's seat in determining the best and most realistic actions to include in their improvement plans.

Third, it encourages city officials to share their findings with other municipalities from the region. Fourth, it helps assess the extent to which such a monitoring tool or dashboard can be integrated into city management operations. This task is typically outsourced to external auditors so that local governments are not direct owners of the process. In addition, assessments are typically carried out on an ad hoc basis rather than being used as a regular monitoring tool. The MFSA is therefore a radical departure from normal practice; and it promotes the following mutually reinforcing objectives:

- To promote financial self-assessment at the municipal level as part of the management change process in local public administrations: **Accountability**.

- To encourage local governments to share information with other municipalities, and to inform central government, local government associations, and citizens about their current situation: **Visibility in the use of public funds**.

- To encourage financial and other relevant municipal departments—asset management, urban and strategic planning, and the mayor's cabinet—to work together on capital investment plans and municipal programs securely anchored in financial feasibility: **Prioritization**.

- To monitor the financial situation and act on a set of key initiatives to improve the mobilization of local resources, rationalize public expenditures, and improve financial management practices: **Efficiency and transparency**.

- To agree on a common set of concepts, methodologies, and internationally accepted indicators, and to improve communications and negotiations with banking institutions and donors: **Access to external funding**.

Box 8.7 Urban and Financial Audits: A Potentially Powerful Combination

Integrated urban and financial audits in Senegal. In the middle of the 90's. the World Bank initiated in Senegal an interesting and innovative municipal development program (Urban Development and Decentralization Program-UDDP/PAC). This program is based on the concept of municipal audits and municpal contracts and aims to encourage local governments to take greater responsibility in investment planning and financing and to provide them with the tools needed to better assess their needs and manage their day-to- day functions. Municipal audits, including a Financial Audit and an Urban Audit, led to the identificaton of a Municipal Program/Municipal Contract. All municipalities in Senegal have, by now, signed and implemented several generations of municipal contracts. Since its inception in Senegal, the model has been cloned in many countries in Africa and today over 200 municipalities distributed in 10 countries have signed one or several municipal/city contracts (Burkina Faso, Cameroon, Cote d' Ivoire, Guinea, Madagascar, Mali, Mauritania, Niger, Senegal, Rwanda). Figure B8.7.1 illustrates the critical steps in implementing financial and urban audits/self-assessments.

Risk analysis and innovative financial analysis solution in Tunisia. Tunisia has also been a precursor in municipal audits and municipal contracts. The Third Tunisian Municipal Development Project, supported by the World Bank, began in 2002. Out of 260 municipalities, about 132, including the city of Tunis, were facing financial problems serious enough to delay repayments of the loans to the National Municipal Development Fund. The situation was critical for the 71 municipalities with no savings capacity and for the 61 municipalities that had insufficient savings to service debt or to mobilize Municipal Investment Program funds.

The principal objective of the project, which was financed by the World Bank and the Agence Francaise de Developpement (AFD), was to restructure the 132 most financially strapped municipalities. The means set up to achieve this objective were:

- *Adjustment plans* specific to each municipality to enable them to return to normal financial status.
- *"City contracts"* with objectives, terms, and methods for implementing and monitoring the Municipal Investment Plan, as well as the respective obligations of the local and central governments.

The adjustment plans were designed on the basis of audits of the financial and organizational circumstances and of the management practices (objectives, adjustment activities, resources and timetables, performance indicators, and monitoring procedures). "Structural adjustment program contracts" were signed by the Ministry of Interior, city authorities, and the National Municipal Development Fund. This started several generations of municipal improvement plans for Tunisian municipalities.

(continued next page)

Box 8.7 *(continued)*

Figure B8.7.1   Critical Steps in Implementing an Integrated Urban and Financial Audit

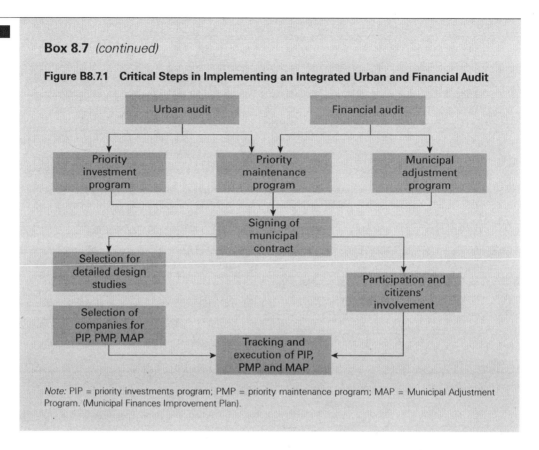

Note: PIP = priority investments program; PMP = priority maintenance program; MAP = Municipal Adjustment Program. (Municipal Finances Improvement Plan).

The Municipal Finances Self-Assessment (MFSA): Template Description

The template of the Municipal Finances Self-Assessment is detailed in the following pages. It provides a framework for analysis and decision-making which local governments can use and adapt to their specific situation. An Excel format of the template is provided at http://siteresources.worldbank.org/EXTURBANDEVELOPMENT/Resources/MFSA-Template.xlsx which potential users can download and use directly.

The main modules of the MFSA are the following (see figure 8.7):

- *Module 1.* Collect and organize relevant information on city finances and urban

management issues (city profile) (steps 1 and 2).

- *Module 2.* Perform a historical analysis and create summary tables (revenue, expenditures, and financial situation) (steps 3–5).

- *Module 3.* Perform financial projections (step 6).

- *Module 4.* Evaluate financial management tools and processes and prepare a Municipal Finances Improvement Action Plan (steps 7 and 8).

Key findings from the MFSA will shed a light on several aspects of municipal finances:

- Financial sustainability of the local government, based on operating surplus, capacity

Figure 8.7 Modules of the Municipal Finances Self-Assessment

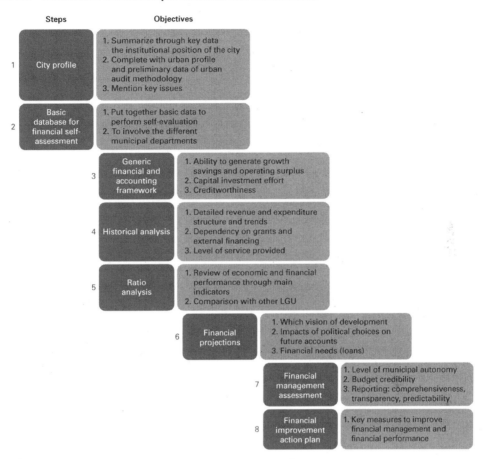

Note: LGU = Local Government Unit.

to borrow money, and ability to increase its capital investment.

- Financial governance and management quality, based on credibility of the budget and its comprehensiveness and transparency.

- Efficiency of service delivery, based on cost and tariff analysis, in addition to other ratios measuring physical performance.

Each step is explained in detail below with template tables to illustrate the process of filling out a MFSA with real data. Excel sheets are the best tool for an actual exercise. These illustrative template tables can be adjusted according to specific local context.

Step 1: City Profile

The City Profile is made of three components:

1. Institutional and territorial organization/ Demography/Economy of the City

2. Municipal organization

3. Main urban issues and challenges facing the city over the next three to five years.

1. Institutional Organization/City Map/Demography/Economy

Objective: To provide a general overview of the municipality's demographic and economic situation through a few summary indicators; and to clarify the make-up of the entity's territorial organization which can sometimes be quite complex (City, Municipality, Metropolitan area).

Insert a map of the city (A4) showing the municipality's administrative boundaries. For existing subdivisions (sub-city) or metropolitan entities, show the different levels of administration.

Insert short summaries on the three items—Territorial Organization, Demography, Economy—describing how they affect or are affected by the financial situation. For example, how the territorial organization has a direct effect on the distribution of the budget and the performance of public functions; how population increases, decreases, or composition affect the budget; or how the local tax system affects the local economy and vice versa.

2. Local finances and management

Objective: To provide a preliminary set of summary data describing the volume of local finance, utility management, numbers and composition of municipal staff, and so forth.

Insert a short descriptive summary on the different items.

Table 1   Summary Indicators of the Municipalities Demographic and Economic Situation

		One city level	City with sub-municipalities	City with inter-communal upper level	
I	**Territorial organization**				
	Number/Name of subnational/metropolitan entities				
	Sub-municipalities or metropolitan financed by the city level		*Yes/No*	*Yes/No*	
	City level financed by sub-municipality level and/or the metropolitan level		*Yes/No*	*Yes/No*	
	Area of the municipality and agglomeration in square kilometers				
		Year N-3	Year N-2	Year N-1	Year N
II	**Demography**				
	Country population				
	Total resident population				
	Annual growth				
	Rank in the country (in population)				
III	**Economy**				
	GDP per head (country level) - in USD or Euro				
	City GDP per head (if available) - in USD or Euro				
	Median disposable annual household income - in USD or Euro				
	Activity rate				
	Unemployment rate (% active population)				

	Year N-3	Year N-2	Year N-1	Year N
IV Total Municipal budget revenue				
Total revenue				
Revenue per capita				
Annual city capital investment				
Debt outstanding				

	Denomination	Annex to M budget (Yes/No)	Tariff (current)	
V Utilities management				
Water supply				
Wastewater				
Electricity				
Urban heating				
Other				

	Rate	Last increase	Fixed locally	
VI Tax policy				
Property tax				
Local business tax				
Tax 3				
Tax 4				

	Number	%		
VII Municipal staff (regular staff)				
Total		100%		
General administration				
Education				
Social services				
Technical service units				
Environment (including solid waste)				
Contractual workers total				

	Year N-3	Year N-2	Year N-1	Year N
VIII Financial reporting (Yes/No)				
Long-term investment program				
Annual budget				
Annual financial statement				
Audited accounts				

Timeframe: The timeframe for analysis could go back as far as three or four years to provide a better picture of trends.

Utilities: State if utility company budgets are reported on and annexed to the municipal budget reports.

Taxes: Fill in data for the property tax and local business tax line items and list the two other most important local taxes.

3. Urban issues and challenges

Objective and content: To explain and illustrate the municipality's development policy, using the following framework:

- *Is there a strategic vision for the development of the city?* If yes, outline the main components such as the *City Development Strategy and the long-term Development Plan,* and identify the levels of approval required such as the City Assembly or the central government.

- Present the main *components* of the Local Economic Development Plan needed to achieve the vision, including capital investments, institutional development, and so forth.

- *If one exists, outline the Capital Investment Plan* using the following rubric:

IX Capital Investment Plan			
Project name	Timeframe	Total costs	Source of financing

Provide a short summary of the multiyear development program approved by the city council. List all priority projects; add more lines if needed.

Step 2: Basic accounting and financial database

Objective and content: To collect the data and information on which to base historical analyses and projections and to calculate performance ratios and gaps. It consists of organizing data not in the usual accounting formats, which can vary from country to country or even among municipalities in the same country, but in a more generic financial format.

We suggest setting up a database (Excel sheets) with five main tables:

- Municipal/city budget + annex Public Utility Company (PUC) budgets

- Cash balance and arrears

- Indebtedness

- Capital investment

- Tax potential and performance

These five tables will each include three years of historical (actual data) and one year of planned data. Sources should be clearly identified, including document title and issuing entity, such as, for example: budget department, taxation department, economic department, entity other than the municipality, Ministry of Finance, and so forth.

General budget database:

- Because the accounting systems and classifications used are all different (functional classification, classification by category, and so forth), the budget database will have to be adjusted for consistency. Expenditures and revenues should be listed by type (tax revenue, grants, fees, loans, etc.) as well as how they will be used (payroll, operation and maintenance, debt service). Avoid simply making a long unorganized list of revenues and expenditures.

- *Actual data* are preferable to planned budget numbers. These can be cash accounting transactions (payment and receipt) or commitment accounting transactions (contract signed and receipts validated through an invoice or the equivalent).

- *Current and capital expenditures* should be clearly differentiated, even if the accounting format does not do so. Expenditures are normally considered to be *capital expenditures* when they contribute to expanding the municipality's public assets.

- *State-mandated expenditures* should be separated from the municipality's own expenditures. Similarly, revenues coming from the central State Government and earmarked for specific expenditures should be identified as such.

- The different *types of subsidies or intergovernmental transfers* should be included, distinguishing between transfers that *can* and *cannot be reallocated* by the municipality.

- The general budget should be analyzed separately from the independent *Public Utility Companies'* budgets. Consider only financial transactions between the city budget and the other budgets accounted for in the city budget. For example, subsidies from the general budget to the PUC's budget should be accounted for as expenditures in the city budget and as revenues in the PUC's budget; and similarly for dividends or cash coming from PUC budgets to the city budget. If possible, a consolidated budget should be set up subsequently.

Table 2   Step 2: Financial self-evaluation basic database

1. GENERAL BUDGET (simplified table)					
in millions of ...	Year N-3	Year N-2	Year N-1	Year N	Year N+1
	A	A	A	E	P

TOTAL REVENUES

I   STATE REVENUES (INTERGOVERNMENTAL)

1 Shared taxes	City share	
- VAT and sales taxes	... %	
- Personal income tax	... %	
- Corporate Income Tax (tax on company profit)	... %	
- Tax on the transfer of property rights	... %	
- Motor vehicle tax	... %	
- Others	... %	

2 Unconditional transfers
   - Operating transfer
   - Investment grant

                     Road rehabilitation
                           Education

  ...

3 Conditional transfers (path through)
   - for wages   from Ministry
                             ...

   - for social policy (poor households)   from Ministry
                             ...

   - ....   from Ministry
                             ...

(continued next page)

II LOCAL REVENUES

1 Local taxes and levies
- Property tax (regardless if centrally collected)
- Business taxes

2 Local fees
- Licenses
- Permits
- Local development fee
- Authorizations and issuance
- Others (fines ...)

3 Local asset proceeds
- Rents
- Sales
- Charges
- Levies on exploitation of natural resources (forest, mineral, water, etc.)
...other

4 Dividends, funds, or assets from PUCs

Utility 1
Utility 2
Utility 3

5 Donations
6 Loan proceeds
7 Municipal bond proceeds

Note: A = Actual; E = Estimated; P = Projection.

When filling in dividends, funds, or assets from the PUCs, please add the combined value of all wealth transferred from the PUCs to the municipality, if any occurred in the given year. This could include cash, land, or equipment.

Table 3 Total Expenditures

in million local currency...	Year N-3	Year N-2	Year N-1	Year N	Year N+1
	A	A	A	E	P

I EXPENSES ON DELEGATED FUNCTIONS

1 Preschool education

Wages
Operating
Maintenance
(Construction) Capital investment

2   Primary and secondary school

Wages

Operating

Maintenance

Capital investment

3   Healthcare

4   Social assistance and poverty alleviation

5   Public order and civil protection

Wages

Operating

Maintenance

Capital investment

6   Environment protection

Wastewater

Solid waste

7   Other

II OWN EXPENDITURES

1   Infrastructure and public services

- Current expenditures

Direct expenditures

Subcontracts

- Capital expenditures

Direct expenditures

Subcontracts

2   Social, cultural, recreational expenditures

3   Local economic development

4   Social housing

5   Urban development

6   Civil security

7   Transfer to local government entities

8   Support to PUC (subsidies, grants, or in-kind)

Utility 1

Utility 2

Utility 3

9   Loan repayment

10 Interest charges

11 Guarantees called (paid by the municipality)

For Support to PUC (subsidies, grants, or in-kind), enter the total combined value of all support provided to PUCs (by sectors or service) whether cash (grant, subsidy), equity, or in-kind asset (land, structures, or equipment) transferred by the municipality.

Cash balance and arrears:

- The objective is to complete the budgetary and accounting data picture by providing information on *cash transactions*. Provide a monthly summary.

- Identify the volume of arrears (expenses incurred but not paid) differentiating between public and private providers.

Table 4   2. Cash Balance, and Arrears

I   Cash Balance

	Cash receipts	Cash payments	Cumulative inflow	Cumulative outflow	Net change in the stock of cash
January					
February					
March					
April					
May					
June					
July					
August					
September					
October					
November					
December					

II   Arrears (overdue liabilities by the city or by its entities)

	Year N-3	Year N-2	Year N-1	Year N
Public stakeholders				
- Water supply PUC				
- Electricity PUC				
- Social welfare				
- …				
City dues to private contractors				
Labor arrears (wages, salaries)				

Indebtedness database:

- Put together useful data on *loans and bonds* launched and subscribed but not fully reimbursed.

- Differentiate between *Medium Long Term* (MLT) debt and Short Term (overdraft credit facility) debt.

- Complete the table with *amortization figures* for each loan, which can be used for further analysis and financial projections.

Table 5 3. Indebtedness Database

	Bank or institution	Year of the loan subscription	Initial amount	Duration	Currency	Maturity	Grace period	Interest Rate (fixed, variable)	Rate (%)
I MLT DEBT									
1 On-lending loan (from Central State)									
2 Direct loan									
- Commercial bank									
- State development bank									
3 Municipal bond									
II SHORT TERM DEBT									
1 Treasury facility from State									
2 Facility from commercial bank									

+ amortization figure for each MLT loan

Capital investment database:

- Provide a figure for capital investment expenditure *by year* (historical and projected) and *by sector* (sectors can be adjusted to reflect specific policy).

- Provide a simplified *tentative financing plan.*

Table 6   4. Capital Investment Database

	Year N-3	Year N-2	Year N-1	Year N	Year N+1	Year N+2	Year N+3	Year N+4
	A	A	A	E	P	P	P	P
Population								
Inflation rate (annual)								
I TOTAL INVESTMENT	100%							
% growth								
Delegated investments (from earmarked grants)	... %							
- Education								
- Healthcare								
- Housing								
- ...								
Municipal investment	... %							
- Roads rehabilitation								
- Street lighting								
- Solid waste equipment purchase								
- Urban renewal								
- ...								
Investment into PUC (assets, grants, or equity provided for PUC in cash or in-kind)	... %							
- Water supply								
- Wastewater								
- Transport								
- Urban heating								
- Other								
II TOTAL FINANCING								
- Earmarked grants	... %							
- Own budgetary revenue	... %							
- Loans or municipal bond	... %							
- Equity from PUC	... %							

Tax potential and Tax Performance:

- The objective is to put together relevant information from the tax administration about the city's tax potential.

- The items (property tax, business tax, ...) can be adjusted according to the local taxation

provisions: for example, the name of the tax and the related tax regulations.

- It is important to obtain information on the number of taxpayers and to distinguish between households and businesses, especially in the case of property taxes.

Table 7   Tax potential & Performance

	Year N-3		Year N-2		Year N-1		Year N	
	Number tax-payers	Amount	Number tax-payers	Amount	Number tax-payers	Amount	Number tax-payers	Amount
I PROPERTY TAX								
Tax base (taxable)								
Households								
Business								
Others								
Tax rate								
Households								
Business								
Others								
Exemption								
Households								
Business								
Others								
Tax collected								
Households								
Business								
Others								
II BUSINESS TAX								
Tax basis								
Rate								
Exemption								
Tax proceeds collected								
III Development fees (quasi taxes)...								

Step 3: Generic financial framework

Objective and content: Even if the database is different from one municipality to another, the generic financial framework should be the same. The purpose is to be able to evaluate the municipality's financial position at a glance and to assess the following:

- The ability to generate growth savings and operating surplus as a means of financing the capital investment budget: evaluate the operating margin or surplus and see how it contributes to the self-financing of the capital investment budget. This will show the municipality's financial ability, at the end of the year, to self-finance part of its capital investment budget, directly or through additional debt (borrowing).

- Creditworthiness: the level of debt service relative to the strength of the municipality's financial position.

- The level of capital investment compared with the operating budget.

- The degree of dependence on grants from the State Government.

- The general surplus at the end of the year: taking account of the general surplus or deficit from year N-1 in the actual budget of year N.

Figure 8.8 Structure of Current and Capital Budget

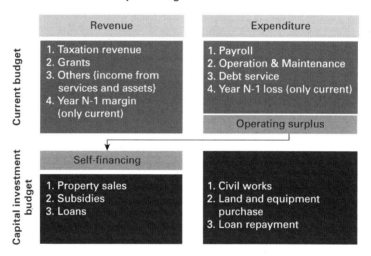

The figure should be complemented by a graph comparing the operating surplus or margin with the current revenue and capital investment expenditures.

Box 8.8 Main Definitions

- *Current or operating budget* should include the expenses and receipts used to provide for daily operation. They are often considered mandatory and are relatively predictable.

(continued next page)

Box 8.8 *(continued)*

- *Current revenues* include tax receipts, grants from the State or other levels of government, and resources recovered by the local authority in the form of prices, rates, fees, tariffs, and so forth, generated by the local assets owned by the municipality (land lease, public utilities and facilities, and so on).
- *Current expenditures* include mainly salaries (payroll including social insurance and other charges connected to staff management), running costs, operation and maintenance (often difficult to identify because subsidies paid by the local authority to assist other structures (associations, related budgets, and so on), and debt service incumbent on the local authority.
- *Capital revenues and expenditures* are operations that increase or reduce the assets of the local authority (acquisitions or sales, civil works). Most of the local public accounting systems are cash-based and thus do not include depreciation or physical amortization of the assets owned by the municipality.

These are administrative accounting systems. Consequently, the capital revenues and expenditures will be yearly operations.
- Usually, capital expenditures are implemented over more than one year (12 months) and have to be split over several fiscal years. The amounts can vary from one year to the next.
- *Debt service* should be split between the current budget–for loan interest, and the capital budget–for loan repayment. In a more prudential approach, all the debt service (including loan principal repayment) should be covered by the operating surplus, as a proof of debt servicing ability.
- *Total budget* or annual account can be balanced, positive, or in deficit (negative): net position.
- More precise budget analysis requires taking into account (including in or annexing to the budget report) expenditures that are not paid and that affect apparent surplus at the end of the year; likewise for revenues that are billed or levied but not recovered during the year.

Step 4: Historical analysis and summary table

Objective and content: To review the previous year's budget and identify trends and performance in the level of public services provided, taxation efficiency, and so forth.

The objective is to understand how the budget is structured and to identify the major trends and how they occur. The analysis is mainly based on gross self-financing (or savings) calculated as the positive difference between operating receipts and expenses. Self-financing makes it possible to pay for a portion of investments; it is a crucial indicator of the quality of management on the part of the local authority and features prominently in dialogues with financial partners: no financial partner wants to see its resources used to finance an operating deficit.

After self-financing, the analysis turns to the characteristics of debt already incurred by the local authority:

- Is the level of debt acceptable?

- Who are the lenders?

- What is the cost of the debt?

- How much time will be needed to pay it back, and so forth?

The capacity of the local authority to develop a summary table, such as the one recommended here, based on a transparent and easy-to-control methodology, reinforces the credibility of the municipality's financial management.

Main outputs: Ten tables should be produced:

- Table 1: Financial position
- Table 2: Main revenue sources
- Table 3: Tax potential and tax performance
- Table 4: Transfers Predictability and City Dependence
- Table 5: Main operating expenses line items by category
- Table 6: Municipal assets and maintenance expenditures
- Table 7: Indebtedness situation
- Table 8: Capital investment budget financing
- Table 9: Cash balance
- Table 10: Arrears

These tables and figures have to be set up from the database (five tables) prepared in Step 2. At this stage, links between both files have not been introduced because of the differences in accounting presentation among the various countries.

Table 1 1. Financial Position

	Items	Calculation	Year N-3 actual	Year N-2 actual	Year N-1 actual	Year N est.	Average annual growth	% structure
1	Total current revenues							
2	Balance N-1 (if surplus)							
3	Current revenues year N	(1 − 2)						
4	Operating expenditures							
5	Operating margin	(1 − 4)						
6	Debt repayment							
7	Net margin	(5 − 6)						
8	Capital expenditures							
9	Financing requirements	(8 − 7)						
10	- Own capital revenues							
11	- Investment grants							
12	- Loan	(9 − (10+11))						
13	Investment balance	(8 − (7+10+11+12))						
14	Overall closing balance	(1+10+11+12) − (4+6+8)						

Insert a short summary and comment on the main lessons learned from the financial position data (on the basis of ratios) included in ratio analysis—Step 5.

Table 2   2. Main Revenue Sources

Items	Calculation	Year N-3 actual	Year N-2 actual	Year N-1 actual	Year N est.	Average annual growth	% structure (total)
TOTAL CURRENT REVENUES							
1 State Transfers							
- Shared taxes							
- Unconditional transfers/grants	Refer to database						
- Conditional operating transfers							
2 Own revenues							
- Local taxes & levies							
- Local fees							
- Local asset proceeds							
3 Other revenues							
- Surplus Y-1							
- Revenues received from PUC							
TOTAL NON-RECURRENT REVENUES							
1 State transfers and grants							
- Unconditional development transfers							
- Conditional development grants	Refer to database						
2 Own revenues							
- Property sales							
- Long-term leases							
3 External revenues							
- Loans proceeds							
- Municipal bonds							
- Donations							
TOTAL REVENUES							
1 State Transfers	Refer to database						
2 Own revenues							
3 External revenues							

Insert a short summary and comment on the main lessons drawn from the revenue source data: analyze the principal sources of municipal financing (taxation, grants, local taxes, and so on); evaluate revenues and the potential of the local taxation system; and estimate revenues from commercial facilities.

Table 3   3. Tax Potential and Performance Analysis

	Items	Source	Year N-3 actual	Year N-2 actual	Year N-1 actual	Year N est.	Year N-3 to Year N-2 growth	Year N-2 to Year N-1 growth
1	**Property tax (housing)**							
	- Number of items							
	- Number of taxpayers							
	- Amount taxable							
	- Amount collected							
	- Collection rate							
2	**Property tax (commercial and business)**							
	- Number of items							
	- Number of taxpayers							
	- Amount taxable							
	- Amount collected							
	- Collection rate							
3	**Business tax**							
	- Number of items							
	- Number of taxpayers							
	- Amount taxable							
	- Amount collected							
	- Collection rate							
	Main tax payers							
	List of the 10 to 50 major taxpayers							

Insert a short summary and comment on the main lessons learned from the above data, analyzing the tax potential and pressure for land, property, and business taxes: (a) economic activity and tax potential: tax potential of the modern and informal sectors; (b) assessment rate; (c) collection rate overall and by category of tax paid (concentration).

Table 4   4. Transfers Predictability and City Dependence

Items	Allocation Criteria	Year N-3 actual	Year N-2 actual	Year N-1 actual	Year N plan	Average annual growth	% structure (total rev.)
1 **Unconditional transfers**							
- Transfer 1							
- Transfer 2							
- ...							
2 **Conditional transfers**							
- Transfer 1							
- Transfer 2							
- ...							

Insert a short summary and comment on the main lessons learned from the above data on predictability of transfers and the level of city dependence: percent of transfers compared to total revenues.

Provide information on allocation criteria for grants, and assess the degree to which local governments can affect the volume allocated to them (performance criteria, if any).

Table 5   5. Main Operating Expenses Line Items by Category (better than functional)

Items	Year N-3 actual	Year N-2 actual	Year N-1 actual	Year N plan	Average annual growth	% structure (total rev.)
CURRENT EXPENDITURES						
1 Payroll (including employees benefits and misc.)						
- Administrative staff						
- Technical department staff						
- Other staff (contractual workers)						
2 Operating costs						
- Office supplies						
- Electricity						
- Communication (telephone, etc.)						
- Fuel and gas						
- ...						
3 Maintenance costs						
...						
4 Of which maintain state assets						
Total						

Insert a short summary about the principal operating expenditure line items. Evaluate specific expenditures such as maintenance of infrastructure and facilities, and so forth.

Table 6   6. Municipal Assets and Maintenance Expenditures

Items	Tentative assets Inventory	Year N-3 actual	Year N-2 actual	Year N-1 actual	Year N plan	Average annual growth	Dominant implementation arrangement (1)
Roads, streets							
Artery roads km							
Residential streets km							
Paved roads total km							
Public lighting (number of lighting posts)							
Water, networks (km)							
Water treatment plants (number)							
Sewer network (km)							
Wastewater treatment plants (number)							
Solid waste management facilities trucks							
Solid waste (transfer stations, landfill total capacity ton per day)							
Other public infrastructure and equipment (parks, cemeteries, parking and garage, etc.) (m²)							
Educational facilities (number of classrooms or m²)							
Healthcare facilities (m²)							
Administrative facilities (m²)							
Cultural facilities (m²)							
Sport facilities (m²)							
Commercial facilities (m²)							
Environmental facilities							
Public housing (number of apartments and other units, m²)							
Cultural heritage							
Vacant municipal land (hectare)							

(1) direct by municipal staff, by contractors, by residents ...

Insert a short summary on the asset composition and management, particularly if there is public housing and land property. Provide a short description of how maintenance activities are carried out: directly by municipal staff, by municipal enterprises, by private contractors, and by the residents themselves.

No information is required on asset valuation because of the complexity of the calculation. If the municipality has already conducted an evaluation of its assets, provide the main results and analysis.

Table 7 7. Indebtedness Situation

Items	Donor/bank & conditions	Year N-3 actual	Year N-2 actual	Year N-1 actual	Year N plan
Loan 1					
- Outstanding loans					
- Loan repayment					
- Interest charge					
Loan 2					
- Outstanding loans					
- Loan repayment					
- Interest charge					
Loan 3					
- Outstanding loans					
- Loan repayment					
- Interest charge					
Municipal bond					
- Outstanding loans					
- Loan repayment					
- Interest charge					
Cash facility (short term)					
…Loan					
Overdraft					
Suppliers' credit					

Insert a short summary on the municipality's existing debt: (a) number of loans or other external financing, (b) profile of these loans, and (c) contribution to annual debt service. The amortization tables will be useful for making projections for the next 5 to 10 years.

Table 8   8. Capital Investment Financing

Items	Year N-3 actual	Year N-2 actual	Year N-1 actual	Year N plan	Average annual growth	% structure (total rev.)
Total capital investment costs						
- Civil works						
- Equipment purchase						
- Others						
Financing						
- Grants from state						
- Investment revenues (sales of assets, etc.)						
- Self-financing (Y1 or -1)						
- Loan						

Insert a short summary about the structure of the municipality's capital budget and its financing.

Table 9   9. Cash Balance

	Inflows	Cumulative	Outflows	Cumulative	Balance	
January						
February						
March						
April						
May						
June						Graph
July						
August						
September						
October						
November						
December						

Insert a short summary on both the cash balance at the end of the year and the monthly cash flow. Include possible difficulties faced during the year with fluctuations between monthly inflow rates (for example, the grants payment rate or the tax collection rate) and outflow rates. If applicable, mention any specific arrangements with the Treasury or the banks (cash facility).

Table 10   10. Arrears

Items	Calculation	Year N-3 actual	Year N-2 actual	Year N-1 actual	Year N plan	Average annual growth	% outflows current and capital inv.
CURRENT BUDGET							
Energy	-						
Material	-						
Salaries or other labor costs	-						
Social security dues							
CAPITAL BUDGET							
Public institutions	-						
Private entities	-						
TOTAL							

Insert a short summary regarding the municipality's unpaid invoices and commitment amounts, distinguishing between current and capital expenditures. The analysis can also differentiate between institutional debt or arrears and private contractors', arrears.

Step 5: Ratio analysis

Objective and content: The objective of the ratio analysis is to create municipal finance benchmarks for internal purposes (financial management dashboard) as well as for purposes of regional comparison.

The following ratios and benchmarks are based on international standards used in Western European countries and in the U.S.

Participating in the MFSA will help each municipality better understand its position relative to others in the region and in the world, and will also highlight its potentials and key gaps. The ratio analysis tables can be filled out by linking the relevant cells the historical analysis tables.

It is important to work closely with the Ministry of Finance to publish these ratios annually at the national level for all municipalities as a tool for comparison and self-improvement.

It is recommended that reference be made to ratios already used by the Ministry of Finance or the Ministry of Interior, or even to ratios calculated by regional associations of local governments.

Finally, ratios comparing local finance performance and GDP are not suggested at this stage but could be usefully added if data on local GDP were available. The following comparison is common at the national level: weight of local expenditures and local taxation/GDP.

Step 5. Ratio Analysis (Municipal Finance Dashboard)

Criteria	Indicator (definition)	Objective	Comparative index (benchmark)	City index			Graph with mention of the benchmark if possible
				YN-3	YN-2	YN-1	
STOCK RATIO							
Creditworthiness							
	Operating savings before interests/Current actual revenues	The LG has the capacity to borrow and to invest	> 0,3				Graph with mention of the benchmark if possible
	Net operating surplus (after debt service including capital repayment)/Current actual revenues	The LG has the capacity to borrow more	> 0,2				Graph with mention of the benchmark if possible
	Cash (end of the year)/current liabilities (divided by 365 days)	The LG ability to meet its short-term obligations	90 days				Graph with mention of the benchmark if possible
Indebtedness							
	Debt outstanding/Operating surplus (capacity to clear its debt)	The LG capacity to clear its debt with operating surplus	< 10 years				Graph with mention of the benchmark if possible
	Debt service/Total current revenues	The annual debt burden is correct regarding current revenue	< 10 %				Graph with mention of the benchmark if possible
Fiscal autonomy							
	Own tax receipts + unconditional grants/Current actual revenues	The LG has the ability to increase its revenue	> 80 %				Graph with mention of the benchmark if possible
	Tax pressure (Tax receipts/Tax potential)		< 70 %				

Capital investment effort			
Capital investment expenditures/Current actual revenues	The LG favors development expenditures	> 40 %	Graph with mention of the benchmark if possible
Capital investment expenditures delegated by state/Total investment expenditures	The LG functions are still weak	> 50 %	Graph with mention of the benchmark if possible
Level of service			
Maintenance works expenditures/Operating expenditures	The LG has important non-current assets to maintain and make it a priority	> 30 %	Graph with mention of the benchmark if possible
Others			
Total number of municipal employees/population	The LG has limited room for financing maintenance and capital investment	> 25 employees for 1,000 inhabitants	Graph with mention of the benchmark if possible
Salaries and wages/Operating actual expenses		> 40 %	
Actual revenues/Estimated revenues	The LG has a good visibility and budget is reliable	> 95 %	Graph with mention of the benchmark if possible
Arrears amount/Net cash (end of the year)	The LG accumulates short-term debt and reduces its credibility toward contractors	> 1	Graph with mention of the benchmark if possible

(continued next page)

Criteria	Indicator (definition)	Objective	Comparative index (benchmark)	City index YN-3	City index YN-2	City index YN-1	Graph with mention of the benchmark if possible
FLOW RATIO							
1	Margin ratio: Total financial resources (cash)/ total financial obligations (payment + arrears)	The city is living or not within its financial means	1,02				Graph with mention of the benchmark if possible
COMPARISON RATIO							
	Total revenues/capita Total expenditures/capita Current actual revenues/ capita Debt outstanding/capita Capital investment expenditures/capita	Comparison with LG of same size in the country or abroad (EU): list to establish					Graph with mention of the benchmark if possible

Insert a short summary about the lessons learned from the ratio analysis.

Step 6: Financial projections

Objective and content: The five-year financial projections serve to provide a review of the municipality's financial position with a focus on creditworthiness. The main objective is to demonstrate the impact of policy decisions (expenses, borrowing, tax pressure, and so on) and their underlying assumptions on the financial position of the municipality. Usually, several sets of assumptions and scenarios are tested: projections based on past trends and also taking significant changes into account. The methodology should be adjusted according to the size of the municipality and the issues it currently faces, such as specific future investment programs, specific indebtedness situations that need to be addressed, and so forth.

The following tables provide a preliminary and simplified framework for projections. Insert a short summary about the lessons learned from the preliminary results obtained.

Step 6. Five years of financial projections

In current currency											
Items	Trends for previous 3 years	Main assump-tions	Index	Specific calcula-tion	Year N-1	Year N	Year N+1	Year N+2	Year N+3	Year N+4	Year N+5
					Actual	Estimated	Projection	Projection	Projection	Projection	Projection

A TOTAL CURRENT REVENUES

Own tax revenues

- Property tax
- Business tax
- Others (development fee)

State transfers

- Shared tax
- Unconditional grants
- Conditional grants

Other revenues

- Asset rent, interest

B TOTAL OPERATING EXPENDITURES

Payroll (including employees' benefits and misc.)

- Administrative staff
- Technical department staff
- Other staff (specific ...)

Operating costs

- Office supplies
- Electricity
- Communication (telephone, etc.)
- Fuel and gas
- Maintenance costs
- Other

(continued next page)

Items	Trends for previous 3 years	Main assumptions	Index	Specific calculation	Year N-1 Actual	Year N Estimated	Year N+1 Projection	Year N+2 Projection	Year N+3 Projection	Year N+4 Projection	Year N+5 Projection
C GROSS OPERATING SAVINGS (A - B)											
D DEBT SERVICE											
Existing debt											
- Interest charge											
- Loan repayment											
New debt (loans >YN-1)											
- Interest charge											
- Loan repayment											
Total debt service											
- Interest charge											
- Loan repayment											
E NET SAVINGS (C - D)											
F CAPITAL EXPENDITURES											
G INVESTMENT FINANCING (F - E)											
Investment grants											
Own capital revenues excl. operation surplus											
Loans											
H OVERALL CLOSING BALANCE (CASHFLOW) (A+G) - (B+D+F)											

Step 7: Financial management assessment

Objective and content: The objective is to assess the strength of the municipality's financial management.

A municipality may have a good financial situation but weak financial management; likewise, a municipality may have poor financial capacity but a fair financial management system.

This section draws on the Public Expenditure and Financial Accountability (PEFA) methodology, also developed by the World Bank, and provides a checklist of six key indicators of sound financial management.

Insert comments on the different items and propose specific actions for improvement.

Financial Management Assessment

	Aggregate fiscal discipline	Strategic allocation of resources	Efficient service delivery
1. Credibility of the Budget	Overoptimistic revenue forecasts/ Underbudgeting of nondiscretionary/ Noncompliance in budget.	Revenue shortfalls/ Underestimation of the costs of the policy priorities/Noncompliance in the use of resources.	Efficiency of resources used at the service delivery level/A shift across expenditure categories, reflecting personal preferences rather than efficiency of service delivery.
2. Comprehensiveness and Transparency	Activities not managed and reported through adequate budget processes are unlikely to be subject to the same kind of scrutiny and controls (included from financial markets) as are operations included in the budget.	Extrabudgetary funds/ earmarking of some revenues to certain programs …/Limits the capacity of the legislature, civil society, and media to assess the extent to which the government is implementing its policy priorities.	Lack of comprehensiveness / increase waste of resources/ decrease the provision of services/limits competition in the review of the efficiency and effectiveness of the different programs and their inputs/ May facilitate the development of patronage or corrupt practices.
3. Policy-Based Budgeting	Weak planning process /no respect for the fiscal and macroeconomic framework/lead to unsustainable policies.	Process of allocation of the global resource envelop in line with LG priorities/annual budget too short to introduce significant changes in expenditure/ costs of new policy systematically under-estimated.	The lack of a multiyear perspective may contribute to inadequate planning of the recurrent costs of investment decisions and of the funding for multiyear procurement.
4. Predictability and Control in Budget Execution	Impact on fiscal management/ inadequate debt policy/ excess of expenditures.	Planned reallocations/ Authorized expenditures/ fraudulent payments.	Plan and use resources in a timely and efficient manner/ Competitive tendering process practices/control of payrolls.

(continued next page)

| 5. Accounting, Recording, Reporting | Allows for long-term fiscal sustainability and affordability of policies: timely and adequate information on revenue forecasting and collection/existing liquidity levels and expenditure flows/debt levels, guarantees/ contingent liability and forward costs of investment programs. | Regular information on budget execution allows monitoring the use of resources, but also facilitates identification of bottlenecks and problems that may lead to significant changes in the executed budget. | Inadequate information and records would reduce the availability of evidence that is required for effective audit and oversight of the use of funds and could provide the opportunity for leakages, corrupt procurement practices, or use of resources in an unintended manner. |
| 6. External Scrutiny and Audit | Consider long-term fiscal sustainability issues and respect its targets. | Pressure on LG to allocate and execute the budget in line with its stated policies. | LG is held accountable for efficient and rule-based management of resources, without which the value of services is likely to be diminished. The accounting and use of funds are subject to detailed review and verification. |

Step 7. Financial Management Assessment

Criteria	Indicator	Indicator
A. Credibility of the Budget		
	Aggregate expenditure out-turn compared to original approved budget	
	Composition of expenditure out-turn compared to original approved budget	
	Aggregate revenue out-turn compared to original approved budget	
	Stock and monitoring of expenditure payment arrears	
B. Comprehensiveness and Transparency		
	Classification of the budget	
	Comprehensiveness of information included in budget documentation	
	Extent of unreported government operations	
	Transparency of Inter-Governmental Fiscal Relations	
	Oversight of aggregate fiscal risk from other public sector entities	
	Public Access to key fiscal information	

C. Budget Cycle

Policy-Based Budgeting

Orderliness and participation in the annual budget process

Multiyear perspective in fiscal planning, expenditure policy, and budgeting

Predictability and Control in Budget Execution

Transparency of taxpayer obligations and liabilities

Effectiveness of measures for taxpayer registration and tax assessment

Effectiveness in collection of tax payments

Predictability in the availability of funds for commitment of expenditures

Recording and management of cash balances, debt, and guarantees

Effectiveness of payroll controls

Competition, value for money, and controls in procurement

Effectiveness of internal controls for non-salary expenditures

Effectiveness of internal audit

Accounting, Recording, and Reporting

Timeliness and regularity of accounts reconciliation

Availability of information on resources received by service delivery units

Quality and timeliness of in-year budget reports

Quality and timeliness of annual financial statements

External Scrutiny and Audit

Scope, nature, and follow-up of external audit

Scrutiny of the annual budget law by the City Council

Scrutiny of external audit reports by the City Council

D. Donor Practices

Predictability of direct budget support

Financial information provided by donors for budgeting and reporting on project and program aid

Proportion of aid that is managed by use of national procedures

Predictability of transfers from higher level of government

Step 8: Municipal Finances Improvement Plan

Objective and content: The objective is to translate the lessons learned from the different steps of the MFSA into a limited number of actions to improve the municipality's financial situation and financial management. The template below is a very preliminary and incomplete indication of what could be included and should be further developed based on the findings of the MFSA. The municipality is free to list any action it considers to be a priority. Actions that are not under the full control of the municipality can also be mentioned if they are part of State reforms currently under discussion or if they are included in the current agenda of National Associations of Local Governments. That is, they need to have some traction for actual implementation, and should include precisely what is expected from central government.

The Municipal Finances Improvement Plan can be divided into

– Short-term actions: 1 year

– Medium-term actions (1 to 3 years).

All of them should include a specific description of what needs to be done and why, quantified targets if appropriate, a timeline, and how and by whom the actions will be implemented. It should also indicate whether or not there is a cost.

Objective 1: Improve Financial Situation of the Municipality

Specific objective	Items	Priority action	Expected result	Schedule Short-term/ Long-term ST/LT	Cost estimate if any	Responsible entity/ person
Actions under the control of State						
Increase fiscal autonomy	*Replace conditional grants with unconditional grants or shared taxes*					
	Give more flexibility on local tax policy					
...						
Actions to be implemented at the LG level						
Increase fiscal autonomy	*Increase local tax collection*					
	Reconsider the rate of property tax for households					
...						

Objective 2: Improve Financial Management of the Municipality

Specific objective	Items	Priority action	Expected result	Schedule Short-term/ Long-term ST/LT	Cost estimate if any	Responsible entity/ person
Credibility of the budget	*Improve forecast reliability*					
Policy-based budgeting	*Improve cost analysis of main expenditure*					
Improve budget execution	*Improve expenditure control*	e.g., Competitive bidding, performance contacts				

Notes

1. Except for the property tax, most of the revenues of the local budgets come from tax proceeds distributed by the state or even by the national government as shared taxes or grants.

2. To get more information on the effectiveness of the performance measurement in the municipalities and counties in the United States, see the models of performance-measurement use in local governments. See also Melker and Willoughby 2005.

3. However, we note state and provincial initiative to fix some standards through a mandated municipal performance measurement program with the objective to standardize data collection and generate benchmarks and, potentially, comparisons. On this last development, there is a real caution because of the many outside factors that influence the results, including geography, population, community priorities, organizational forms, accounting and reporting practices, the age of the infrastructure, and so on.

4. The first measure taken by the decentralization reforms adopted in France, for example, was the repeal of the a priori control over the decisions taken by the municipal councils. However, the public finance accounts are consolidated (central and local governments) and contribute all together to the calculation of the economic performance ratios of the countries. Consequently, particular importance is given to the accounts balance and to the level of debt as the main risk indicators. In France, the calculation is supported both by the national treasury system and the principle of unity of cash transactions. Tax pressure is also generally determined on the basis of a consolidated analysis that brings together national and local taxation.

5. Municipal councils are free to decide on the use of the resources provided by the budget. This basic principle of municipal autonomy is reinforced by the financing system when more than 50 percent of the municipality's revenues are recovered locally through local taxes.

References

Abers, R. 2001. "Learning Democratic Practice: Distributing Government Resources through Popular Participation in Porto Alegre, Brazil." In *The Challenge of Urban Government: Policies and Practices,* edited by M. Freire and R. Stren, 129–43. Washington, DC: World Bank Institute.

ADM (l'Agence de Développement Municipal). 2008. *Guide de Ratios* 2008–2011. Senegal: l'Agence de Développement Municipal.

Agence Française de Notation. 2010. *Rapport de l'Observatoire des Finances Locales*. Paris: Agence Française de Notation.

Ammons, D. N. 2001. *Municipal Benchmarks: Assessing Local Performances and Establishing Community Standards*. Thousand Oaks, CA: Sage Publications Inc.

Boyle R. 2004. "Assessment of Performance Reports: A Comparative Perspective." In *Quality Matters: Seeking Confidence in Evaluation, Auditing and Performance Reporting*, edited by R. Schwartz and J. Mayne,. New Brunswick, N.J.: Transaction Publishers.

Epstein, P. D. 1984. *Using Performance Measurement in Local Government: A Guide to Improving Decisions, Performance and Accountability, with Case Examples Contributed by 23 Government Officials from across the Country*. Council on Municipal Performance Series. New York: Van Nostrand Reinhold.

Farvacque-Vitkovic C., A. Sinet, and L. Godin. *Municipal Self-Assessments, A Handbook for Local Governments*. World Bank publication (forthcoming).

Farvacque-Vitkovic C., A. Sinet, and S. Palmeuther, T. Nikolic, 2014. *Improving Local Governments Capacity, The Experience of Municipal Finances Self-Assessment (MFSA) in South East Europe*. World Bank publication.

Farvacque-Vitkovic C. and S. Palmeuther. 2014: *Improving Local Governments Capacity, City to City Dialogues on Municipal Finances, Urban Planning and Land Management in South East Europe*. World Bank publication (forthcoming).

GASB (Governmental Accounting Standards Board). 1997. "Analysis of State and Local Government Performance Measurement Applications." http://www.seagov.org.

Goldsmith, W.W., and C. B. Vainer. 2001. "Participatory Budgeting and Power Politics in Porto Alegre." *Land Lines* 13 (1):

Hatry, H., and D. Fisk. 1971. "Improving Productivity and Productivity Measurement." In *Local Governments*. Washington, DC: Urban Institute Press and National Commission on Productivity.

Hatry H., D. Fisk, M. D. Kimmel, and H. Blair. 1988. *Program Analysis for State and Local Governments*. 2nd ed. Lanham, MD: University Press of America.

International Centre for Local Credit. 2008. International Survey on the Impact of the Financial Crisis on the Public Finances (conducted October 2008–July 2009).

Josifov G., C. Pamfil, and R. Comsa. 2011. *Guidelines on Local Government Borrowing and Recent Developments in South East Europe*. Skopje, Macedonia: Network of Associations of Local Authorities of South-East Europe (NALAS).

Melker, S. J., and K. Willoughby. 2005. "Models of Performance-Measurement Use in Local Governments: Understanding Budgeting Communication and Lasting Effects." *Public Administration Review* 65 (2).

MIAC (Ministry of Internal Affairs and Communication). 2011. "White Paper on Local Public Finance." Tokyo: Ministry of Internal Affairs and Communication.

NALAS. 2011. Report on Fiscal Decentralization Indicators in South East Europe.

Paulais T. 2009. *Local Governments and the Financial Crisis: An Analysis*. Washington, DC: Cities Alliance and Agence Française de Développement.

Poister, H. T., and C. Streib. 1999. "Performance Measurement in Municipal Government: Assessing the State of the Practice." *Public Administration Review* 59: 325–35.

Ridley, Clarence E., and Simon A. Herbert. 1938. *Measuring Municipal Activities: A Survey of Suggested Criteria and Reporting Forms for Appraising Administration*. Chicago: International City Managers' Association.

Rubinoff D., A. Bellefleur, and M. Crisafulli. 2008. "Regional and Local Governments outside the US." Moody's International Public Finance. http://www.moodys.com.

Serageldin, M., D. Jones, F. Vigier, and E. Solloso. 2008. *Municipal Financing and Urban Development*. Human Settlements Global Dialogue Series 3. New York: UN-Habitat.

Williams, Daniel W. 2004. "Evolution of Performance Measurement until 1930." *Administration and Society* 36 (2): 131–65.

Additional Readings: Chapter 8

On Performance Measurement

All American City: History. 2004. http://www.ncl.org/aac/information/history
.html

Allecian, S., and Foucher, D. 1994. *Guide du Management dans le Service Public*.
Paris: Editions d'Organisations.

Allegre, H., and Mouterde, F. 1989. *Le Contrôle de Gestion dans les Collectivités
Locales: Méthodes, Outils, Tableaux de Bord*. Paris: Editions du Moniteur.

Ammons, D. N., C. Coe, and M. Lombardo. 2000. "Performance Comparison
Projects in Local Governments: Participants' Perspective." *Public
Administration Review* 61: 89–99.

Ammons, D. N. 1994. "The Role of Professional Associations in Establishing
and Promoting Performance Standards for Local Government." *Public
Productivity and Management Review* 17: 281–98.

Anthony, R. N. 1965. *Planning and Control System, A Framework for Analysis*.
Division or Research, Harvard Business School (180 p).

Arrow, K. J. 1997. *Choix collectifs et Préférences Individuelles (traduction française
de Social Choice and Individual Value, 1951)*. Diderot Editeur, Paris.

Bessire, D. 1999. "Définir la Performance." *Comptabilité Contrôle Audit* 5 (1):
416–24.

Bouquin, H. 1991. *Le Contrôle de Gestion*. Paris: PUF.

Bourguignon, A. 2000. "Performance et contrôle de gestion." In *Encyclopédie
comptabilité contrôle Audit*. 931–41. Paris: Economica.

Bruder, K. A., and Gray, E. M. 1994. "Public Sector Benchmarking: A Practical
Approach." *Public Management* 76: S9–S14.

Brule, J. 1997. "Contribution à l'Elaboration d'un Contrôle de Gestion dans les
Collectivités Locales." Thèse de Doctorat en Sciences de Gestion, CENAM,
Paris (344 p).

Carles, J. 1999. *Management Stratégique et Renouveau du Projet Politique*. La lettre
du cadre territorial (400 p).

Coe, C. 1999. "Local Government Benchmarking: Lessons from Two Major Multi-
Government Efforts." *Public Administration Review* 59: 110–23.

Crowel, A., and S. Sokol. 1993. "Playing in the Gray: Quality of Life and the
Municipal Bond Rating Game." *Public Management* 75: 2–6.

Demeestere, R. 2002. *Le Contrôle de Gestion dans le Secteur Public*. Paris LGDJ
(196 p).

Downs, A. 1957. *An Economic Theory of democracy*. New York: Harper.

Victor, D. A., and K. Kaiser. *Sub-National Performance Monitoring Systems –
Issues and options for higher levels of Government*.

Dupuis, F., and Thoening, J. C. 1985. *L'Administration en Miettes*. Paris Ed. Fayard (316 p).

Gibert, P. 1980. *Le Contrôle de Gestion dans les Organisations Publiques*. Editions d'organisations, Paris.

Grizzle, G. A. 1987. "Linking Performance to Funding Decisions: What is the Budgeter's Role." *Public Productivity Review* 10: 33–44.

Guenguant, A. 1995. "Equilibre Budgétaire et Diagnostic Financier Global." *In Analyse Financière des Collectivités Locales*. Paris: PUF.

Hofstede, G. 1981. "Management Control of Public and Not-For-Profit Activities." *Accounting, Organizations and society* 6(3): 193–211.

ICMA (International City/County Management Association). www.icma.org.

Jensen, M. C., and W. H. Meckling. 1976. "Theory of the Firm: Managerial Behavior, Agency Costs and Ownership Structure. *Journal of Financial Economics* 3 (October): 305–60.

Joncour, Y. 1993. "Moderniser la gestion et les financements publics: des priorités à contresens." *Pol et Management* 2 (June).

Morin, E. M., A. Savoie, and G. Beaudin. 1994. *L'Efficacité Organisationnelle: Théories, Représentations et Mesures*. Gaétan Morin Editeur, Québec.

Kaplan, R., and Norton, D. 1998. *Le tableau de bord prospectif*. Paris: les éditions d'organisations.

Kaplan, R., and Norton, D. 2004. *Strategy Maps: Converting Intangible Assets into Tangible Outcomes*. Harvard Business School Press.

Duff, R. L., and J.-C. Papillon. 1988. Gestion Publique. Editions d'organisations, Vuibert, Paris.

Lorino, P. 2003. *Méthodes et Pratiques de la Performance. Le Pilotage par les Processus et les Compétences*. Les Editions d'Organisations, Paris.

Meyssonier, F. 1992. *Stratégie et Style de Contrôle de Gestion dans les Communes*. 13ème Congrès de l'AFC Bordeaux mai (31 p).

Morin, E., M. Guindon, E. Boulianne. 1996. *Les Indicateurs de Performance*. Editeur Guérin Montréal.

Performance des Services Publics Locaux. 1989. *Colloque Paris IX 24 avril 1989*. Litec, Paris.

Poincelot, E., and Wegmann, G. 2007. "What Are the Motives of the Managers Using Non-Financial Indicators: An Empirical Study." Working Papers, FARGO (Research Center in Finance, Organizational Architecture and Network).

Poister, H. T. 2003. *Measuring Performance in Public and Nonprofit Organizations*. John Wiley & Sons–Jossey-Bass.

Rey, J. P. 1991. *Le Contrôle de Gestion des Services Publics Communaux*. Editions Dunod.

Roussarie, O. 1994. "Les Outils de Contrôle de Gestion Utilisés dans les Services Publics Urbains." Thèse de Doctorat Sciences de Gestion, Université de Poitiers.

Schmitt, D. 1988. "Le Contrôle Budgétaire Interne." *Politiques et Management 3* (September).

Thiebout, C. M. 1956. "A Pure Theory of Local Expenditures." *Journal of political Economy* 64 (October): 416–24.

UN-Habitat. 2009. *Guide To Municipal Finance*. UN-Habitat.

Self-Evaluation Handbooks

Almy, R. R., R. J. Gloudemans, and G. E. Thimgan. 1991. *Assessment Practices: Self-Evaluation Guide*. Chicago: International Association of Assessing Officers.

Shah, A. 2007. *Local Budgeting, Public Sector Governance and Accountability Series*. The World Bank. http://www.worldbankinfoshop.org/ecommerce/catalog /product?item_id=6355058

Fund for Moroccan Township Facilities and Infrastructure. (Fonds d'Equipement Communal du Maroc). 2008. *Handbook for Participatory Planning in Local Development*. DGCL, Ministry of Interior. www.fec.org.ma

Groupe de Travail Financement des Investissements des Collectivités Locales. 2005. Financer les Investissements des Villes en Développement—*Notes & Douments n°23*—Agence Française de Développement. http://www.afd.fr /jahia/webdav/site/myjahiasite/users/administrateur/public/publications /notesetdocuments/ND-24.pdf

Groves, S. M., and M. G. Valente. 2003. *Evaluating Financial Condition: A Handbook for Local Government*. Washington, DC: International City/County Management Association.

Hatry, H. P., D. Fisk, E. R. Winnie. 1973. *Practical Program Evaluation for State and Local Government Officials*. Urban Institute Press.

Partenariat Pour le Développement Municipal, L'Emprunt des Collectivités Locales D'Afrique Sub-Saharienne (PDM). 2008. *Revue Africaine des Finances Locales*. juin. http://www.pdm-net.org/PDM_final_130608_web.pdf

SNV Mali (Organisation Néerlandaise de Développement). 2004. *Outil d'Auto-évaluation des Performances des Collectivités Territoriales*. MATCL SNV Helvetas. http://www.snvmali.org/publications /outilautoeval.pdf

Southwestern Pennsylvania Regional Planning Commission. 1990. *Standards for Effective Local Governments: A Workbook for Performance Assessment*. Pittsburgh, PA.

The Way Forward

Catherine Farvacque-Vitkovic

The task of getting municipal finances right is daunting, but reachable. There is no doubt that the world is getting more complex. Municipal officials are not only dealing with the day-to-day business that comes with running a city, but they also increasingly have to address issues of social inclusion, local economic development, job creation, crime and violence, climate change, floods, droughts, and natural and man made disasters. They are also expected to welcome increasing numbers of urban dwellers, deal with an increasing number of informal settlements, and cover the costs of providing infrastructure and services in increasingly sprawling cities.

There are no quick solutions; no one size fits all. From the eight chapters of this book, however, readers can take away a greater understanding of what works and what does not:

Good Intergovernmental Relations Matter. A wave of decentralization policies has swept many parts of the world. That happened in part because of the recognition that local governments are closer to their constituents and thereby more responsive to their needs. The trend has not always been accompanied by good practices. Fiscal policies and transfer formulas have not always been as equitable as required. Thus, measuring the positive impacts of the devolution of functions and resources to the local level remained a challenge for policy makers and academia. This book helps share experiences on intergovernmental transfers. It promotes formula-based, as opposed to ad hoc, allocation of central government transfers and advocates incentive mechanisms to ensure that transfers do not crowd out, but rather stimulate, collection of local own-source revenues. Intergovernmental finance relations generate the governance framework, the playing field, and the underlying incentive mechanisms for the functioning of the systems to manage revenues, expenditures, assets, and external resources and for measuring performance.

Metropolitan finance matters. With continued urbanization around the world, cities become more and more economically interdependent with their surrounding settlements and hinterlands; thus, metropolitan areas compose a single economy and labor market, a community with common interests and joint actions. Such an area needs some areawide management, formed either from the bottom up by the local governments or as a top-down decision by a higher government. There is a great variety of metropolitan governance models and modalities, each with its merits and demerits. The range includes simple cooperation by local governments; regional authorities (or special purpose districts) organized voluntarily; metropolitan-level governments; and amalgamated local governments. The main areas of financial cooperation and benefits in metro regions include tax sharing to prevent tax competition and harmonize revenues; cost sharing or a common budget for metropolitan-level initiatives and services; coordinated revenue mobilization through user charges, property taxes, and earmarked taxes; and joint mobilization of funding sources for large infrastructure with areawide benefits. The main reasons for forming metropolitan governance include efficiency gains, economies of scale, addressing spillover effects and disparities, and improving services. However, often politics rather than efficiency and equity determines the formation of metropolitan governance and finance systems.

Financial management practices matter. Financial management concepts and techniques help local governments use their limited financial resources in an efficient and transparent manner and thereby enable them to function accountably. Budgeting, accounting, and financial reporting are the pillars of good financial management. Modern information technology, the introduction of computerized financial management systems, and use of other ICT instruments have accelerated information flows and data security. More importantly, they have shifted the functions of the three pillars from mere recording of data to daily strategic management of cities and timely informing of long-term strategic decisions. Financial management has myriad tools and techniques, but it is important to recognize that they are relevant only if local governments use them to fulfill their core mandate of providing services in an efficient, effective, and sustainable manner. Though all financial management concepts and tools are important, local government managers do better to adopt simple but fundamental tools and techniques first and gain proficiency in their practice before moving on to more sophisticated and complex tools and systems.

Revenues matter. Local governments have to learn to do more with less. In many countries, local revenues amount to less than 10 percent of public revenues, and many central governments are not inclined to empower the locals with additional sources of revenues or to pay much attention to the administration and collection of municipal fiscal revenues. Regardless of central policies, in many developing countries, local governments would be able to collect significantly larger revenues by improving revenue policies on taxes, fees, and charges and by focusing their efforts on a few key potential sources of revenues while paying attention to tax administration, revenue collection and tax base. A main message to take away is that improving local revenues depends on the local circumstances. But revenue opportunities always exist: expanding the basis of taxes and fees, rigorously collecting of market services fees, establishing a culture of taxing or charging beneficiaries of new infrastructure development, collecting land-based revenues, or using assets for strategic revenue generation and development. Introducing new revenue instruments or higher rates will be ineffective without establishing reliable databases and boosting revenue administration capacity. Collecting more revenues requires good communication with the citizens and informing them about how and where the revenues will be spent; it also requires instituting fair enforcement and remedies mechanisms.

Expenditures matter. Expenditure management should be seen as a cycle driven by the policies that the local government aims to achieve. After an agreement on the final policy agenda and strategies, it is essential to mobilize and allocate adequate resources and then proceed to implement the planned activities. The final steps in the cycle are monitoring and objectively evaluating the results to see whether the agreed-on outputs and outcomes are being achieved. The results of these evaluations will provide critical information to the next annual policy and program. There are a number of ways to analyze an activity in terms of both financial and operational performance, but an analysis of the variances between what was planned or budgeted and the actual result is arguably one of the best methods. Saving expenditures requires tight and daily control of operating expenditures (salaries and hiring staff), competitive procurement of bulk products and services (fuel, energy, maintenance, banking), competitive procurement in designing and implementing capital investment projects, and forceful contract management. Local governments in the developing world often try to avoid using competitive procurement because it is often a long and painful process. But with better expertise and human capacity, managing competitive procurement becomes faster and less complicated. Alignment between financial planning, expenditures planning and investments programming is key for expenditures management to be improved. This requires that a number of municipal departments which traditionally do not talk to each other start working together towards a same goal. It also implies that there should be more open debates to discuss key priorities and selection of investments.

Public asset management matters. Municipal governments everywhere control large portfolios of physical assets (land, buildings, infrastructure, and vehicles and equipment), which make up the lion's share of local public wealth. Good management of those assets is critical for quality and sustainability of local services (e.g., roads, water, schools); for local economic development (e.g., land for private production and business); and for citizens' quality of life. Good asset management generates multiple benefits: savings or additional revenues for the local budget, better quality of assets and services, and better trust between people and the government. The primary asset management tools and procedures include the following: inventorying assets; using transparent procedures for allocating assets for private use; aligning or classifying assets according to their role in delivering services; using the market value of assets for decision making; establishing a depreciation fund for financing asset replacement; monitoring key performance indicators such as costs and revenues; and planning ahead for operating and maintenance expenses when acquiring new capital assets. Finally, municipal staff need to gain expertise and pay attention to the regulatory framework, procedures and analytic tools, and real estate markets.

External funding matters. Local governments' investment needs are often much greater than their annual operating surplus can finance. Thus, they need external funding, which can be raised through borrowing, issuing bonds, private-public partnerships, and grants or philanthropic aid. Municipalities borrow funds directly from banks or indirectly through issuing bonds. The capacity of the municipality to borrow is a function of its creditworthiness, which depends on the economic and financial situation and guarantees or other enhancement tools. Creditworthiness analysis and credit ratings are valuable tools to demonstrate that the municipality has the capacity to repay a loan or bond on time. Prudent use of external resources is crucial because without it, the fiscal situation of a city may be jeopardized in the years ahead. External resources should be used to finance the priority projects identified in the city's capital improvement plan, and liabilities should never exceed the level of the expected revenue flows. Although project selection is always a political process, participatory dialogue and good feasibility studies supported by analytical techniques play an important role in ranking projects and supporting informed decisions.

Municipal finances performance measurement matters. Measuring municipal financial performance is important because it provides an opportunity to obtain a clear picture of the financial situation and supports dialogue with stakeholders (central government, financial partners, or citizens). It provides data and ratios that are useful in prioritizing investments. Finally it helps in evaluating how efficiently and effectively public funds are being used. In a democratic society where open government and open data have become accepted norms, an abundance of social media tools and instruments are ready to capture citizens' voices demanding accountability and transparency from their government. It is essential that local governments be prepared to present and articulate, as genuinely as possible, their current situation, their bottlenecks, and their perspectives for the future (projections). That will also help municipalities make their case to central governments regarding transfer allocation and guarantees; prepare well-packaged bankable projects; and be accountable to their constituents for the use of public funds. With these objectives in mind, the Municipal Finances Self-Assessment (MFSA) presents a unique opportunity to equip local governments with a tool that makes it easy for them to connect the dots among responsible fiscal and financial discipline, sound financial management, and capacity to finance recurrent and capital expenditures, as well as to attract private financing with a clear view of a path to reform.

Getting cities' finances in order should become our collective mantra. In an ever urbanizing world, cities and towns weigh heavily on national economies and on social prosperity and stability. The stakes are too high to leave room for complacency. What do we want the cities of tomorrow to look like? What is the legacy we want to pass on to the next generation and beyond? Municipal finance is at the core of the problems and at the crossroad of the solutions.

INDEX

Boxes and notes are indicated by b and n following the page numbers.

timeliness in, 119, 120
training and capacity development in, 120
types of, 110
weaknesses in standards and practices, 132
accounting equation, 114, 125
accrual-based accounting, 110, 117, 127, 144–45
action plan, in asset management, 289, 323
activity-based costing (ABC), 133
Addis Ababa, Ethiopia, financial accountability
assessment in, 255, 260
addresses, street
and asset inventory, 282
and tax systems, 184–85, 190–91, 191*b*, 208, 208*b*,
212*n6*
and user charge collection, 237, 238*b*
ad hoc scale economies, 58
ad hoc transfer mechanisms, 29
ADM. *See* Municipal Development Agency
administrative budgets, 95
administrative costs, 233
administrative decentralization, 5–6
adverse audit opinion, 142, 145
aerial photography, for property tax
information, 184
Afghanistan, informal settlements in, 91*n1*
Africa. *See also specific countries*
centralization in, 9, 10
local business taxes in, 173*b*, 174
metropolitan governance in, 51, 88–89
municipal bonds in, 341, 341*b*, 399–400
municipal contracts in, 30, 334
municipal development funds in, 362
performance measurement in, 394–95
property taxes in, 167, 190–91
public-private partnerships in, 372*b*, 373
revenue collection enforcement in, 186
urbanization in, 48
African Charter for Popular Participation
in Development and Transformation
(Arusha Declaration, 1990), 9
African Development Bank, 364
agency funds, 129*b*
agglomeration, urban, 42, 42*b*, 43–46
aggregate fiscal discipline, 220
Aguascalientes, Mexico, municipal bonds in, 341
Aguas de Tucuman, Argentina, public-private
partnership in, 372*b*
Ahmedabad Municipal Corporation (India), 341*b*

Alameda County, California, utility surcharges in,
177, 178*b*
Alaska, politics and expenditures in, 225*b*
allocation, 110–11, 111*b*, 220
allotments, from budget, 101
amalgamation of local governments, 51, 56, 82–86
Amman City, Jordan
fines and penalties in, revenue from, 179
tax authority in, 154–55
waste management in, 368
amortization, 350, 414
Amsterdam, Netherlands, metropolitan governance
in, 82, 90
analytical accounts, of assets, 282–84
Anchorage, Alaska, amalgamation of, 83
annexation, 51, 56, 82–86
annual account, 419*b*
annual rental value, for property taxation, 165–67
apportionment, in budget process, 101
appropriation, 110–11, 111*b*
appropriation accounting, 111
Aquino, Benigno, 11–12
area-based assessment, 164–65
Argentina
foreign currency borrowing in, 358, 358*b*
informal or exceptional borrowing practices in, 349
local business taxes in, 173*b*
metropolitan governance in, 50
municipal bonds in, 341, 342, 343
public-private partnership in, 372*b*
revenue intercepts in, 353
arithmetic mean growth rate, 198*b*
ARPEGIO, 59
Arusha Declaration (1990), 9
Asia. *See also specific countries*
financing needs in, 326
land development corporations in, 321–22
manual accounting in, 118–19*b*
metropolitan governance in, 50, 89–91
municipal bonds in, 341, 341*b*
municipal development funds in, 362–64
property tax assessment in, 167
public-private partnership in, 372*b*
special purpose vehicles in, 354–55, 355*b*
Asian Development Bank, 326, 364, 367
assessment
for local revenues, 183, 185
for property taxes, 155, 164–69

asset(s)
  in accounting equation, 114, 125
  capital, 276
  classification of, 276–77, 277b, 292–94, 314–15
  current revenue from, 179–80
  designated, 126
  as economic development resource, 280
  fixed, 129–32, 276
  functions of, 279–81
  grouping of, 289
  liabilities associated with, 280
  life cycle of, 278
  management of. *See* asset management
  as material base, 279
  net, 125–26, 127, 139
  nonphysical, 276
  permanently restricted (PR), 125–26
  physical, 276
  portfolio of, 274, 276
  as revenue source, 280, 296, 297. *See also*
    income-generating properties
  self-assessment (MFSA) of, 420, 424–25
  temporarily restricted (TR), 125–26
  undesignated, 126
  unrestricted (UR), 125–26
  valuation of, 296–99
  values beyond economic value, 280
  as wealth, 279–80
asset management, 274–325
  action plan for, 289, 323
  advanced, 320–22
  analytical accounting in, 282–84
  approaches in, 277–78
  balance sheet as tool in, 310–11
  challenges of, 287–89
  corruption potential in, 281
  in developing countries, 283–84
  employee incentives for improvements in, 307
  entities in charge of, 285–87, 287–89
  expertise in, 320, 324n5
  financial analysis in, 296, 301–7
  financial implications of, 296–310
  financial management and, 281, 282, 296
  financial planning in, 307–10
  financial principles and goals in, 293–94
  human (local) capacity for, 287
  importance of, 274–75, 446
  improvement of, 287–96

indicators for all types of properties in, 305–7
indicators for investment comparison in, 301–5
Initial Asset Management Model of, 285, 285b
inventorying of, 282, 283, 289–92
land, 312–22. *See also* land assets
life-cycle, 278, 279
multidisciplinary approach in, 281
municipal enterprises and, 286–87, 311–12
operating statements in, 299–301, 300b, 303
operation and maintenance costs in, 129–32, 280,
  299–301, 307–10, 420, 424–25
ownership of process in, 287
policy for, establishing, 294, 295
political cycle and, 287
portfolio management in, 277–78, 283, 284
public-private partnerships and, 287, 320–21
recommendations, 323
reform of, 287, 288b
sequencing of actions in, 287
shortcomings in, consequences of, 276
strategic, framework for, 281–85, 284b
strategic view in, 310–12
strategy and implementation in, 283, 284–85, 322–23
subsidies in, 306–7
task force on, 289, 322
transparency in, 294–96, 295b
asset management strategy (document), 322–23
auctions, for land disposition, 317
audit(s)
  compliance, 141, 143
  definition of, 101
  delayed, 143
  energy, 305
  financial, 141, 402. *See also* municipal finance
    self-assessment
  management or performance, 141–42
  municipal, 255–56
  types of, 141–42
  urban. *See* urban audit
audit committee, 270
audit conferences, 143–44
auditing, 93–94, 141–44, 145
  accounting and, 112, 120
  basic concepts and practices in, 141–42
  budget, 98, 101
  capacity shortage for, 143
  in expenditure management, 222–23, 225, 255–56,
    269–70

billing and collection
    for local revenues, 183, 185–86, 189, 212*n*7
    for property taxes, 169–71
Bio Carbon Fund, 368
blanket balance sheet subsidies, 237
block grants, 14
BNG (Netherlands), 339*b*
Bobo-Dioulasso, Burkina-Faso, street addressing
    initiative in, 190
Bogotá, Colombia
    metropolitan governance in, 51, 74
    municipal bonds in, 341*b*
    property taxes in, 159, 160–61*b*, 167, 169, 170
    public-private partnership in, 371–72
Bolivia
    informal or exceptional borrowing practices
      in, 349
    local expenditures in, 148
    local revenue in, 152, 153
    municipal development fund in, 362
    participatory budgeting in, 401
    waste management in, 368
Bologna, Italy, metropolitan governance in, 65, 89
bond banks, 354, 361, 361*b*
bond financing. *See* municipal bonds
bookkeeping, accounting *vs.*, 109–10
books of final entry, 113
books of original entry, 113
book value, 297–98
Boost (expenditure-tracking tool), 400–401
borrowing. *See* debt; external resources
borrowing capacity, 330–31, 356–59
Bosnia–Herzegovina, confederalism of, 8, 8*b*
BOT. *See* build-operate-transfer (BOT) arrangements
Botswana, local revenue in, 151–52, 153
bottom-up approach, in benchmarking, 267
Brazil. *See also specific cities*
    budgeting in, 102, 103*b*
    debt regulation in, 331, 347–48, 348*b*, 349*b*
    development bank/institution in, 360–61
    informal or exceptional borrowing practices in, 349
    local business taxes in, 174
    local revenue in, 151–52, 153, 154, 155
    metropolitan governance in, 50, 64, 66*b*, 90
    municipal bonds in, 341, 341*b*, 342
    municipal development fund in, 362, 363*b*
    participatory budgeting in, 102, 103*b*, 401, 402*b*

performance-based grants in, 398
revenue intercepts in, 353
sales taxes in, 171
targeted subsidies in, 210
tax authority in, 154
urban concessions in, 373*b*
break-even analysis, 134–35
"bridge to nowhere" (Alaska), 225*b*
Budapest, Hungary
    local capacity of, 9
    metropolitan governance in, 72, 89
budget(s)
    administrative, 95
    audits of, 98, 101
    balanced, 216–18
    capital, 97–98, 105–6, 229–32
    current or operating, 97, 418, 418*b*
    definition of, 94
    economic, 95
    execution of, 98, 101, 107–8, 194–95, 204
    expenditure side of, 105
    fixed, 96
    flexible, 96
    formulation of, 98–99
    functional, 96
    good, principles of, 95*b*
    as instruments of financial control, 95
    as instruments of planning, 94–95
    legislative approval of, 100–101, 194–95, 203–4
    line-item, 95, 96, 262–63
    monitoring of, 108–9, 194–95, 204, 205*b*
    multiyear, 229–32, 260–62
    operating, 97
    performance-based, 262–65, 394–95
    preparation of, 98–101, 104–6, 194–95
    program, 96–97
    responsibility accounting, 134
    revenue side of, 104–5
    self-assessment of, 404, 406, 410–17. *See also*
      municipal finance self-assessment
    standard structure of, 104
    supplementary or revised, 100–101, 107, 233
    total, 419*b*
    types of, 95–98
budget-actual variance analysis, 108–9
budgetary accounting, 111
budgetary reporting, 138–39

external resources for, 325–78, 446. *See also* bank
    credit (loans); debt; municipal bonds
land-based revenues for, 181–83, 184
metropolitan, 58–59, 60*b*
mobilization of, 326
pay-as-you-go, 326–28
pay-as-you-use, 326
ratio analysis of, 429
self-assessment (MFSA) of, 410, 416, 420, 426
capital investment plan (CIP), 105–6, 229–32, 307–10,
   329–35
  assessing financial need and capacity in, 330–31
  bridging long-term vision to annual budget in, 309
  citizen participation in, 334, 334*b*
  identification of needs and priorities in, 330, 333
  inclusion in city profile, 410
  information required for, 333, 376*n*
  local complications from central planning in, 230
  local financial capacity for, 230–32
  preparation of, 330, 332–34
  problems common in, 231–32
  public-private partnerships in, 230
  published document of, 330, 331
capital projects
  average accounting return of, 257
  cost-benefit analysis of, 257–59, 335–38, 337–38*b*
  database and assessment of, 410, 416, 420, 426
  environmental impact of, 333
  evaluation of, 257–58
  internal rate of return in, 257–59, 335, 337–38*b*
  lack of coordination on, 335, 335*b*
  net present value of, 257–59, 335, 337–38*b*
  payback rule for, 257
  planning for. *See* capital investment plan (CIP)
  politics and, 335
  selection of, tools for, 335–38
  sensitivity analysis of, 259–60
capital projects funds, 126, 129*b*
capital revenue, 155–56, 180–83, 419*b*
  current revenue *vs.*, 180
  donations and public contributions, 181, 328,
    374–75
  external, 181
  own-source, 180
  planning for, 196
  public-private partnerships, 181
  transfers and grants, 180–81, 327
capital subsidies, 239–40

Caracas, Venezuela, metropolitan governance in,
   51, 74
carbon credits/funds, 360, 365–68
cash balance and arrears, 410, 414, 420, 426–27
cash-based accounting, 110, 117, 127
cash book, 121–22
cash flow, 300*b*
cash flow analysis. *See also* internal rate of return;
   present value
  discounted, 303–5, 335–38
cash flow statement, 123, 145
cash forecast, 253–54
cash management, 251–54, 253*b*
cash payments, 234
cash transactions, 414
CBA. *See* cost-benefit analysis
CCB. *See* citizens community board
Central Asia. *See also specific countries*
  centralization in, 9
central city, in metropolitan area, 42
centralization
  arguments supporting, 8–10, 33
  clawback to, 10
  fulfillment of central functions in, 9
  lack of local capacity and, 8–9, 33
  legacy of, 9–10, 33
  macroeconomic record of, 12, 34
certified emissions reduction (CER), 367–68
CFO. *See* chief financial officer
Chad, municipal contracts in, 30
change orders, 250
charitable donations, 181, 328, 374–75
Charlotte, North Carolina, capital investment plan of,
   330, 331, 332, 334
chart of accounts, 113, 116
Chicago, Illinois, leasing of municipal land in, 318
chief financial officer (CFO), 99–100
Chile
  local borrowing prohibited in, 347
  local business taxes in, 173*b*
  metropolitan governance in, 90
  output-based transfers in, 20
  tariffs and subsidies in, 236
  tax authority in, 155
China. *See also specific cities*
  development promotion in, 182
  financing needs in, 326
  fiscal data in, 26

fiscal equalization in, 23, 24, 26
land tax in, history of, 159b
local borrowing prohibited in, 347
metropolitan governance in, 48, 50, 61, 62, 64b,
    85–87, 91
municipal bonds in, 341b
special purpose vehicles in, 350, 355, 360
unitary system and decentralization in, 7
Chiniot City, Pakistan, management information
    system in, 250, 251
CIP. *See* capital investment plan
Circonscription Urbaine (Benin), 208b
citizens
    accountability to, 400–402
    financial reporting for/by, 138b, 139
    information for. *See* transparency
    participation in budgeting process, 94–95, 101–4,
        401, 402b
    participation in capital investment planning,
        334, 334b
    participation in performance measurement,
        382–87, 384b, 388–89, 393–94, 400–402
    as users of financial reports, 136
citizens community board (CCB, Pakistan), 102
city council
    asset responsibilities of, 285, 323
    budget approval by, 100–101, 194–95, 203–4
    budget responsibilities of, 99, 285, 323
    capital planning responsibilities of, 332
    expenditure responsibilities of, 216
    oversight by, 269–70
city profile, 406–10
city-region. *See* metropolitan areas
city satisfaction indexes, 388–89
City to City (C2C) Dialogues, 403b
civic engagement, 400
Clean Development Mechanism, 366–67, 366–67b
closed-ended, matching transfers, 15–16
COG. *See* council of governments
Colombia
    bank lending in, 360
    betterment fees in, 314
    credit guarantees in, 354
    land-based revenues in, 182
    local business taxes in, 173b
    metropolitan governance in, 51, 74
    municipal bonds in, 341b
    municipal development fund in, 362

output-based transfers in, 20
property taxes in, 159, 160–61b, 167, 169, 170
public-private partnership in, 371–72
tax authority in, 154
colonialism and centralization, 9
commitments, financial, 110–11, 111b
communauté urbaine (UC), in France, 69–70
Communauté Urbaine of Marseille (CUM), 70
communes
    in Côte d'Ivoire, 77
    in France, 69
Community Development Carbon Fund, 368
community funds, 375
Community-Led Infrastructure Financing, 375
Community Mortgage Program (Philippines), 375
comparability, of financial reporting, 137
comparison ratio, 430
compensating errors, in accounting, 118
competitiveness of service provision, 388–89, 391–93
competitive tendering (bidding)
    in land disposition, 317
    in procurement process, 243–48, 246b, 257, 445
completeness, of financial reporting, 137
compliance audit, 141, 143
compound annual growth rate (CAGR), 198b
computer-aided, mass valuation systems (CAMA),
    159–62, 162b, 168–69, 168b
computerized accounting systems, 118–19, 145
Comunidad Autonoma de Madrid (CAM, Spain), 59,
    91n2
Conakry, Guinea, waste management in, 237, 238b
concessions, in public-private partnerships,
    370, 373b
conditional nonmatching transfers, 15–16, 17
conditional transfers, 14–17, 19–20, 26–32, 34–35
confederations, 8, 8b
confirmatory value, of financial reporting, 136
congestion (vehicle) taxes, 175, 211–12
construction permits, 178–79
contingent liability, 328
contracting
    among local governments, 54, 60–61, 62b
    in land disposition, 317
    in municipal enterprises, 311
    in procurement process, 247, 248–50, 249b
    in public-private partnerships, 248–49, 369–70
contract management, 248–50, 249b, 257
contracts, municipal. *See* municipal contracts

Dayton–Paris Agreement of 1995, 8b
DCA. *See* Development Credit Authority
debit(s), 114
debit side (Dr), of T-account, 114
Debrecen Holding (Hungary), 312
debt. *See also* bank credit (loans); municipal bonds
 amortization of, 350
 in capital investment financing, 58–59, 181
 conditions for incurring, 328–29
 default on and bankruptcy, 328, 329b, 347–48,
  351–54, 352b, 376n3
 deferred payments on, 349–50
 existing, 330
 financial feasibility and, 328, 329
 in fiscal decentralization, 2, 5, 12
 foreign currency, 357–58, 358b
 guarantees for, 328, 347–48, 352–54, 354b, 359
 institutional aid and support for, 359–65
 local capacity for, 330–31, 356–57
 log frame for, 359
 management of. *See* debt management
 medium long term (MLT) *vs.* short term, 414–15
 in metropolitan finance, 58–59
 need for, assessing, 330–31
 new instruments for, 360
 pooling of, 354, 361–64, 361b
 ratio analysis of, 428
 regulation of. *See* debt regulation
 self-assessment (MFSA) of, 410, 414–15, 420, 425
 special purpose vehicles for, 350, 354–55,
  355b, 360
debt crises, 347–52
debt limit, 348
debt management, 355–64
 borrowing capacity in, 330–31, 355–59
 comparing alternatives in, 357, 359
 objective and processes in, 357
 strategies for, 357–59
debt managers, checklist for, 350–52
debtor
 in accounting, 114–15
 in bond issue, 340
debt regulation, 331, 347–52, 348b, 349b
debt service, 348, 350, 351, 419b
debt service flow, 331
debt service fund, 126, 128b, 350, 357
debt stock, 331, 348, 350, 356–57
decentralization, 1–39

accounting effects of, 127
budgeting impact of, 106–8
centralization arguments *vs.*, 8–10
cycles and reversals in, 10
deconcentration in, 5–6, 6b, 33
delegation in, 5, 6–7, 33
devolution in, 5, 6, 33
economic efficiency in, 6, 10–11, 12, 33
economic growth in, 12, 34
fiscal, 2–7, 33. *See also* fiscal decentralization
fulfillment of central functions in, 9
globalization link to, 1, 10, 33
and infrastructure financing, 325
and intergovernmental relations, 443–44
intergovernmental transfers in, 2, 5, 12, 13–32, 34.
  See also intergovernmental transfers
legacy of centralization *vs.*, 9–10
lessons and results of, 12–13, 34
local capacity for, 8–9, 25, 33
local expenditure impact of, 218–19
local revenue impact of, 148–49
macroeconomic stability in, 12
matching principle in, 11
nation building in, 11–12, 11b, 33, 34
in Nepal, 3b
performance measurement in, 380–81, 390, 394–95
in Poland, 4b
political, 1, 33
public sector size in, 12
"reaction from below" and, 2, 10, 33
revenue mobilization efforts in, 208, 208b
subsidiary principle in, 2–4, 11
three D's of, 5–7, 33
top-down process of, 2
trend to, factors in, 10–12, 33
in unitary systems, 7
welfare gains in, 6, 10–11, 33
Decentralization Act of 1981–82 (Nepal), 3b
Decentralized City Management Program (Benin),
  208b
decision-making, management, 132–35
deconcentration, 5–6, 6b, 33
deferred maintenance, 305–6
deferred payment, 349–50
deficit(s)
 balanced budget *vs.*, 216–18
 budgetary weaknesses and, 107–8
deficit grants, 25

public-private partnerships for, 182. *See also* public-private partnerships

spatial plans for, 314–15

economic efficiency

in decentralization, 6, 10–11, 12, 33

in metropolitan governance, 49

economic growth

decentralization and, 12, 34

urbanization/megacities and, 47–48

economies of scale, in metropolitan finance, 49, 53, 58, 62, 87

economy, in city profile, 407–9

Ecuador

local business taxes in, 173*b*

metropolitan governance in, 50–51, 74, 90

education

expenditure management in, 223, 224

output-based transfers for, 20

as private *vs.* public good, 150

property taxes for, 170

effective gross income, 300*b*

effectiveness, as performance dimension, 379–80

efficiency

in municipal finance self-assessment, 404

in performance measurement, 379–80

Egypt. *See also* Cairo, Egypt

deconcentration in, 6*b*

electronic databases, for revenue collection, 207

emerging economies

credit guarantees in, 354

credit ratings in, 343, 343*b*

external resources for, 325

green financing in, 360

local government borrowing in, 339–40

employees

incentives for, 307

as users of financial reports, 136

encumbrances (commitments), financial, 110–11, 111*b*

energy audits, 305

energy-efficiency loans and credits, 360, 365–68, 366–67*b*

enforcement

good practices in, 187–88

in local revenue collection, 183, 185–88, 209

in property tax collection, 169–71, 212*n*4

enhancement programs, for local revenue, 191–94, 192*b*, 193*b*, 202

enhancements, credit, 352–54, 359

enterprise funds, 129*b*, 139

entries, accounting, 113

environmental impact, of projects, 333

environmental loans and credits, 365–68

EOIs. *See* expressions of interest

e-procurement, 248

equalization, fiscal, 22–24, 25–26, 397

equity

in accounting equation, 114, 125

in procurement, 247

Essen, Germany, water tariff in, 176*b*

Estonia, EU-EBRD financing in, 365

ethics. *See also* accountability; transparency

and procurement, 248

Ethiopia

financial accountability assessment in, 255, 260

inventorying of assets in, 292

public-private partnerships in, 374

Europe. *See also specific countries*

citizen satisfaction surveys in, 388–89

debt regulation in, 348

EU-EBRD financing in, 364–65

financial holding in, 312

local expenditures in, 218

local government borrowing in, 339, 339*b*, 340

metropolitan governance in, 50, 89

municipal bonds in, 341, 341*b*

municipal contracts in, 30

performance measurement in, 381, 387–89, 439*n*4

priority-setting by municipal councils in, 387, 439*n*5

property tax assessment in, 167

European Bank for Reconstruction and Development (EBRD), 364, 365

existing debt, 330

expenditure(s)

administrative, 233

authority to incur, 233

capital. *See* capital expenditures

control of, 222

current, 97–98, 226–29, 410, 419*b*

decentralization and, 218–19

management of. *See* expenditure management

mandatory (delegated), 411

miscellaneous, 226–29

mismatch with policy, 225, 226*b*

own, 226

projections of, 431–34

as share of total public expenditures, 148
expenditure assignment, 2–4, 12, 13–14. *See also* inter-
    governmental transfers
expenditure management, 215–74, 445
    accountability in, 224–25, 232–33, 254–55,
        400–401
    accounting in, 222, 250, 251
    auditing in, 222–23, 225, 255–56, 269–70
    balanced budget *vs.* fiscal deficit in, 216–18
    battle between finance and line departments in,
        219–20
    benchmarking in, 266–69
    big picture issues and challenges in, 216–17
    budgetary controls in, 232–34
    budget plans for, 226–32, 227–28*b*, 260–65
    capital, 229–32, 256–60
    cash management in, 251–54
    concept and principles of, 215–16
    cycle of, 221–24, 445
    definition of, 216
    in developing countries, 232
    donor-funded projects in, 229
    effective system of, 220–21
    entities involved in, 216
    feedback from, 269
    financial constraints and alternatives in, 224–25
    improvement or reform of, 222*b*
    internal control environment for, 250–51, 252*b*
    medium-term or multiyear, 229–32, 260–62
    monitoring and evaluation in, 220, 222–23, 225,
        265–69
    oversight in, 269–70
    payment systems in, 233–34
    performance-based budgets in, 262–65
    performance measurement in, 254–56, 380
    planning in, 221–22
    policy setting in, 221, 223–24
    politics and, 224, 225*b*, 270–72
    pressure from central government and, 271–72
    procurement and expenditure tracking in, 242–50
    resource allocation in, 222, 223*b*
    self-assessment in, 404, 410–13, 420, 423–25
    service cost comparisons in, 266, 269
    systems for, 250–56
    tools in, 216
    transparency in, 224–25, 232–33, 251, 269–70
    user charges (tariffs) and subsidies in, 231, 234–42
    variance analysis in, 265–66, 269

expenditure side, of municipal budget, 105, 404,
    410–13
expressions of interest (EOIs), 244
extended urban region. *See* metropolitan areas
external resources, 325–78, 446. *See also* bank credit
    (loans); municipal bonds
    combination of, choosing, 331–32
    conditions for obtaining, 328–29
    credit enhancement for, 352–54, 359
    definition of, 325
    energy-efficiency (green), 360, 366–67*b*
    feasibility studies on, 329
    guarantees for, 328, 347–48, 352–54, 354*b*, 359
    institutional aid and support for, 359–65
    intermediaries for, 349, 359–60
    key steps in securing, 376
    local credit and capital markets for, 327
    local government success and experience with,
        339–40, 339*b*
    mobilization of, need for, 326
    municipal development funds of, 59, 359,
        361–64, 363*b*
    need and capacity for, assessing, 330–31
    new instruments for, 360
    philanthropic and public contributions for, 181,
        328, 374–75
    pooling arrangements for, 354, 361–64, 361*b*
    private sector, 325, 327–28, 368–74. *See also*
        public-private partnerships
    special purpose vehicles for, 350, 354–55,
        355*b*, 360
    types of, 325

F
Fairfax County, Virginia
    education funding in, 170
    expenditure management in, 225–26
    transparency in, 233, 270
    utility surcharges in, 177, 178*b*
faithful representation, in financial reporting, 136–37
FASB. *See* Financial Accounting Standards Board
feasibility studies, 329, 372, 372*b*
federal systems, 7–8
fee(s), 157, 178–79. *See also* user charges
feedback, in performance measurement, 401
fee simple, 324*n*4
fiduciary funds, 129*b*, 139
Fifth Urban Project (Ghana), 207*b*

metropolitan governance in, 79, 90
municipal contracts in, 30
revenue sharing in, 18
tax authority in, 154
water tariff in, 176b
Ghana
citizen reporting in, 139
municipal contracts in, 32b
property tax reform in, 207b
GIS. *See* geographic information systems
GLA. *See* Greater London Authority
Glasgow, Scotland, water tariff in, 176b
globalization, 1, 10, 33
gmina (municipality), in Poland, 4b
going concern principle, 113
golden reserve, of land, 316
good disposition procedures, 317
governance systems, 7–8
Governmental Accounting Standards Board (GASB), 112, 139–41, 382
governorate, in Egypt, 6b
Grand Lyon, France, 69–70
grants. *See also* intergovernmental transfers
capital revenue from, 180–81, 327
general purpose (unconditional), 14, 15–16
performance-based, 19–20, 26–32, 34–35, 382, 397–98, 439n1
specific purpose (conditional), 14–17
Greater London Authority (GLA), 67–68, 76, 76b, 82
Greater Vancouver Regional District (GVRD), 68–69, 88
Greece, debt crisis in, 349–50
green financing, 360, 365–68, 366–67b
gross domestic product (GDP)
per capita, decentralization and, 12
property tax as percentage of, 159
ratios of local financial performance to, 427
gross potential income, 300b
gross receipts tax, 171
gross self-financing or savings. *See* operating surplus
growth rates, for revenue forecasting, 197, 198b
guarantees, 328, 347–48, 352–54, 354b, 359
Guatemala
local revenue in, 157
participatory budgeting in, 401
Guinea
municipal contracts in, 30
policy–expenditure mismatch in, 226b

street addressing and waste management in, 237, 238b
GVRD. *See* Greater Vancouver Regional District

H

The Hague, Netherlands, metropolitan governance in, 82, 90
Hanoi, Vietnam, public-private partnership in, 371–72
Harrisburg, Pennsylvania, bankruptcy of, 328, 329b, 347, 351, 353–54
Havana, Cuba, water tariff in, 176b
hay (district), in Egypt, 6b
hedonic price, 168
historical analysis, in municipal finance self-assessment, 406, 419–27
holding, for municipal enterprises, 312
Hong Kong, China
land leasing in, 319
municipal company in, 287
Honolulu, Hawaii, water tariff in, 176b
horizontal imbalance, 5, 13, 33
housing assistance, 375
human resource management, performance measures in, 385
Hungary
bankruptcy in, 376n3
centralization in, 9
EU-EBRD financing in, 365
expenditure assignment in, 14
financial holding in, 312
local business taxes in, 172, 173b, 174
local capacity in, 9
metropolitan governance in, 72, 89
municipal insolvency in, 351, 376n3
public *vs.* private domain in, 277b
revenue sharing in, 18–19
targeted subsidies in, 238
hurdle rate. *See* discount rate
hybrid financing, 355, 356b

I

IASB. *See* International Accounting Standards Board
IBRD. *See* International Bank for Reconstruction and Development
IBT. *See* increasing block tariff
IDA. *See* International Development Association
IEG. *See* Internal Evaluation Group
IFAC. *See* International Federation of Accountants

joint ventures, 370. *See also* public-private partnerships

Jordan
expenditure assignment in, 13–14
fines and penalties in, revenue from, 179
intergovernmental transfers in, 22
land-based revenues in, 181
local expenditures in, 218
municipal development fund in, 362
tax authority in, 154–55
waste management in, 368

journals, 113, 115, 120–21

judgmental forecasting, 203*b*

K

Kabul, Afghanistan, informal settlements in, 91*n1*

Kampala, Uganda
Financial Recovery Action Plan in, 192*b*, 193
informal settlements in, 91*n1*
political pressure and expenditures in, 272
tax authority in, 155

Karachi, Pakistan
asset management in, 283–84
water tariff in, 176*b*

Karnataka, India
energy-efficiency efforts in, 368
special purpose vehicle in, 360

Kathmandu, Nepal, asset management in, 287, 288*b*

Katowice, Poland, asset management in, 293

Kenya
community fund in, 375
expenditure management in, 401
local business taxes in, 173*b*, 174
local revenue in, 153
metropolitan governance in, 81–82, 89
property taxes in, 170
revenue mobilization strategy in, 205, 206*b*
tax authority in, 154

Kerala, India
fiscal data in, 29
intergovernmental transfers in, 22, 26, 29
participatory budgeting in, 102*b*

Kigali, Rwanda, municipal bonds in, 341*b*

Kommunalbanken (Denmark), 361

Korea, Republic of
guarantee fund in, 354, 359
land development corporations in, 321
metropolitan governance in, 50
municipal bonds in, 341*b*

Kosovo
expenditure management in, 401
property tax assessment in, 168–69

Kummunivest (Netherlands), 361

Kuwait City, Kuwait, management of land assets of, 313, 318, 319

Kyrgyzstan
asset management in, 284, 295*b*
public contributions in, 375

L

labor market, of metropolitan areas, 41–42

Lagos, Nigeria
growth of, 48
municipal bonds in, 400

Lahore, Pakistan
environmental (composting) project in, 366–67, 366–67*b*
expenditure budget of, 226
informal settlements of, 46
land corporation in, 321–22
public-private partnership in, 371–72
tariffs and subsidies in, 237

Lahore Development Authority, 321–22

land assets, 312–22
classification of, 314–15, 316
enhancing value of, 315–17
funding from. *See* land-based revenues
golden reserve of, 316
good disposition procedures and contracts for, 317
inventory of, 291–92
leasing or privatizing, 318–20
management and administration of, 314–18
percent needed for public use, 314
prepared site *vs.* "raw" land, 315
real estate brokers for disposition of, 318
risks and costs associated with, reducing, 317
sale of, 181–83, 211, 312–13, 319–20
valuation of, 296–99, 323*n2*

land-based revenues, 181–83, 211
instruments for, 184, 312–14
speculation reduction via, 183*b*
valorization for, 181–82, 182*b*

land-based taxes. *See* property taxes

land cadastre. *See* cadastre

land dedication, 314

land development corporations, 321–22

land development fees, 179, 314
land speculation, 183*b*, 321
land use planning and control, 313, 315, 316–17
land value-capture tax, 148, 181, 183*b*
land value increment tax, 182
Latin America. *See also specific countries*
    land-based revenues in, 181–82
    local business taxes in, 173*b*
    metropolitan governance in, 50–51
    municipal bonds in, 341, 341*b*
    participatory budgeting in, 102, 103*b*, 401, 402*b*
    property tax assessment in, 167
    public-private partnerships in, 371, 372*b*, 373
Latvia
    EU-EBRD financing in, 365
    municipal development fund in, 362
LDA. *See* London Development Agency
leapfrog development, 183*b*
leases, in public-private partnerships, 370
leasing, of municipal land, 318–20
    arguments for and benefits of, 318
    costs and risks of, 319
    policy implication of, 319–20
ledgers, 113, 115, 120–22
    cash book, 121–22
    trial balance and, 124, 125
legal department, role in asset management, 286
legislature
    asset responsibilities of, 285, 323
    budget approval by, 100–101, 194–95, 203–4
    budget responsibilities of, 99, 285, 323
    capital planning responsibilities of, 332
    expenditure responsibilities of, 216
    oversight by, 269–70
liabilities
    in accounting equation, 114, 125
    associated with assets, 280
license fees, 178–79
life-cycle asset management, 278, 279
life-cycle costing, 307–8, 309, 310
Lilongwe, Malawi, growth of, 48
Lima, Peru
    development rights in, 313
    revenue sharing in, 18
linear trend growth rate, 198*b*
line departments
    battle with finance department, 219–20
    budgetary responsibilities of, 99

    role in asset management, 286
    role in expenditure management, 216
line-item budgets, 95, 96, 262–63
Lithuania, EU-EBRD financing in, 365
Ljubljana, Slovenia, water tariff in, 176*b*
loans. *See* bank credit (loans)
local assets. *See* asset(s); asset management
local capacity
    borrowing, 330–31, 356–59
    for capital investment planning, 230–32
    development of, 9, 25
    lack of, and centralization, 8–9, 33
    for own-source revenue, 162, 188–89, 189*b*
local credit markets, 327
local expenditures. *See* expenditure(s); expenditure
    management
Local Governance Law of 1990 (Poland), 4*b*
Local Government Development Project (Ghana),
    207*b*
localization, 1. *See also* decentralization
local revenue. *See* revenue, local
Local Self-Governance Act of 1999 (LSGA, Nepal), 3*b*
Lomé, Togo, street addressing initiative in, 190
London, United Kingdom
    congestion (vehicle) taxes in, 175, 211–12
    cost-efficiency program in, 204, 205*b*
    metropolitan governance in, 48, 53, 67–68, 76, 76*b*,
        82, 89
London Development Agency (LDA), 67–68, 76*b*
Los Angeles, California
    assets as wealth of, 280
    energy-efficiency efforts in, 366
    metropolitan governance in, 61, 62*b*, 88
lowest evaluated bidder, 244, 247
LSGA. *See* Local Self-Governance Act of 1999
Lucerne, Switzerland, financial accountability assess-
    ment in, 255
Luxembourg, local business taxes in, 172
Lyon, France
    metropolitan finance in, 57*b*
    metropolitan governance in, 69–70, 89

M

Madagascar, municipal contracts in, 30
Madrid, Spain
    local revenue in, 153
    metropolitan finance in, 59, 91*n*2
Madurai Municipal Corporation (India), 342

maintenance, deferred, 305–6
maintenance and operations plan (MAP), 31*b*
maintenance and repair (M&R) costs, 308–10
maintenance costs, 129–32, 420, 424–25
maintenance pool fund, 133
Malawi, urbanization and economic growth in, 48
Malaysia, municipal bonds in, 341*b*
Mali
    municipal contracts in, 30, 256, 256*b*
    property taxes in, 190
management accounting, 110
management audit, 141–42
management discussion and analysis (MD&A),
    139–40
management information system (MIS), 108, 189, 250,
    251
management letter, from auditor, 143
Managing Municipal Services (USAID), 234
mandatory expenditures, 411
mandatory properties (assets), 292–93, 314–15
Manila, Philippines, metropolitan governance in, 79,
    81*b*, 90
manual accounting systems, 118–19, 118–19*b*, 145
manual cashbook, 234
MAP. *See* maintenance and operations plan
map, city, 408
Maputo, Mozambique, own-source revenues in, 189,
    189*b*
marginal cost pricing, 176
markaz, in Egypt, 6*b*
market-value
    of assets, 298–99, 323*n*2
    methods for estimating, 298, 298*b*
    of property, for taxation, 155, 164, 165, 166
Marseille, France
    metropolitan finance in, 57*b*
    metropolitan governance in, 70, 89
Maryland
    development promotion in, 182
    education funding in, 170
    employee incentives in, 307
    land-based financing in, 313
mass media, disclosure of information via, 296
matching principle, 11
matching provisions, of conditional transfers, 14–17, 34
material base, assets as, 279
materiality, of financial reporting, 137
maturity date, bond, 340

Mauritania, municipal contracts in, 30
Mauritius, local revenue in, 153
mayor
    asset responsibilities of, 285, 322
    budgetary responsibilities of, 99
    capital planning responsibilities of, 332
    expenditure responsibilities of, 216
MCPM. *See* Minimum Conditions Performance
    Measurement
MD&A. *See* management discussion and analysis
MDFs. *See* municipal development funds
MDQ. *See* Metropolitan District of Quito
Mechinagar, Nepal, expenditure budget of, 226–29,
    227–28*b*
medium-term expenditure framework, 260–62
megacities, 46–49
Melbourne, Australia, metropolitan governance in, 89
Mendoza, Argentina
    debt management in, 358*b*
    municipal bonds in, 343
Metro Manila (Philippines), 79, 81*b*, 90
metropolis, 42*b*
metropolitan areas
    corridor or belt, 42, 43, 45–46*b*
    definition of, 42
    economy and labor market of, 41–42
    emergence of, 41–48, 86
    finance of. *See* metropolitan finance
    governance of. *See* metropolitan governance
    informal settlements in, 43–46, 91*n*1
    megacities in, 46–49
    monocentric structure of, 43
    multipolar structure of, 43, 45
    one large municipality covering, 84–86
    polycentric structure of, 43, 44
    population of, 42
    radius of, 42
    socioeconomic cohesion of, 42
    spatial growth of, patterns of, 42–47
    sprawl of, 43, 44, 183*b*
    terms related to, 42*b*
metropolitan councils of government, 51, 55, 63–67,
    91*n*3
metropolitan development fund, 59
Metropolitan District of Quito (MDQ), 74, 90
metropolitan finance, 53–59, 87, 444
    amalgamation and, 83–84
    budget for metropolitan-level initiative in, 57*b*

cost sharing in, 49, 52*b*, 53–57
development funds in, 59
financing services and operations in, 53–58
funding of large infrastructure projects in, 58–59, 60*b*
funding of metropolitan-level entity in, 58
investment financing in, 58
pooling of resources in, 49
public-private partnerships in, 59
revenue mobilization in, 58*b*
scale economies in, 49, 53, 58, 62, 87
tax or fee policies in, 57–58*b*
metropolitan governance, 48–53, 60–87, 444
annexation or amalgamation for, 51, 56, 82–86
authority coinciding with representation in, 51
case-by-case joint initiatives by local governments for, 54, 60, 61
citizen accessibility in, 52*b*
committees and working groups for, 54, 61
contracting among local governments for, 54, 60–61, 62*b*
definition of, 48
disparities addressed in, 50
examples of, cities used as, 88–91. *See also specific cities*
financial reasons for, 57–58*b*
functions of, 48–49
good, examples of, 49–50
horizontal coordination among local governments for, 51, 54, 60–61
lack of, consequences of, 49, 49*b*
local context for, 50, 87
local government commitment to, 87
models of, 50–56
national context for, 50, 87
politics and choice of, 53, 87
questions for analyzing, 51–53, 52*b*
regional authorities for, 51, 55, 61–71
smaller (local) government units in, benefits of, 53
specialized services in, 49–50
spillovers (externalities) in, 49
stakeholders in selection or change of, 51–53
metropolitan-level government, 51, 56, 71–82
Metropolitan Montreal Community (MMC), 65–67
metropolitan planning and development agencies, 67–68
Metropolitan Washington Airports Authority (MWAA), 59, 60*b*

Metropolitan Washington Council of Governments, 63–64, 65, 65*b*, 88
Metropolitan Zone of the Valley of Mexico (ZMVM), 82, 88
Metro Vancouver/Greater Vancouver Regional Service District (GVRD), 68–69, 88
Mexico. *See also* Mexico City
credit ratings in, 346, 346*b*, 348
municipal bonds in, 341, 341*b*
performance-based grants in, 398
tax authority in, 154
water tariff in, 176*b*
Mexico City, Mexico
metropolitan governance in, 50, 82, 88
World Bank financing in, 365
MFSA. *See* municipal finance self-assessment
Middle East. *See also specific countries*
centralization in, 9–10
Milan, Italy, congestion (vehicle) taxes in, 175, 211–12
MILF. *See* Moro Islamic Liberation Front
Minimum Conditions Performance Measurement (MCPM), 26–27, 27*b*
Ministère des Finances et de l'Economie (Benin), 208*b*
Ministry of Nairobi Metropolitan Development (Kenya), 81–82, 89
Minneapolis–St. Paul, Minnesota
metropolitan finance in, 57–58*b*
metropolitan governance in, 70–71, 77, 80*b*, 88
MIPs. *See* Municipal Investment Plans
MIS. *See* management information system
miscellaneous expenditures, 226–29, 300*b*
MMC. *See* Metropolitan Montreal Community
modified accrual-based accounting, 117, 127
Moldova
expenditure management in, 401
property valuation/taxation in, 159–62
monocentric structure, 43
Montgomery County, Maryland, education funding in, 170
monthly cash forecast, 254
Montreal, Canada, metropolitan governance in, 65–67
Moody's Investors Service, 343–44, 398–99, 400*b*
Morocco
bank lending in, 360
local business taxes in, 173*b*
municipal bonds in, 400
municipal contracts in, 30
municipal development fund in, 362

performance measurement in, 391–93
tax authority in, 154
urban tax in, 190
waste management in, 368
Morocco Municipal Credit Institution, 391–93, 393
Moro Islamic Liberation Front (MILF), 11–12
mortgage principal payments, 300*b*
Moscow, Russia, municipal bonds in, 341*b*
motor vehicle taxes, 174–75, 211–12
motor vehicle violations, revenue from, 179
Mozambique
    own-source revenues in, 189, 189*b*
    public-private partnerships in, 374
Multan, Pakistan, budget of, 217–18
multipart tariffs, 177
multipolar structure, 43, 45
multiyear budgets, 229–32, 260–62
Mumbai, India
    energy/environmental program in, 367
    local revenue in, 153
    sales of public land in, 182
    World Bank financing in, 365
municipal audits, 255–56
municipal banks, 339, 339*b*, 340
municipal bonds, 339–47
    advantages of, 344
    bank credit *vs.*, 344–46, 345*b*, 359
    cost of issue, 346
    definition of, 340
    in developing and middle-income countries, 341,
        341*b*
    electronic issue of, 340
    general obligation, 339*b*, 342, 342*b*
    interest (coupon) of, 340
    investors in, characteristics of, 340
    legislation authorizing, 347
    maturity date of, 340
    performance measures for, 382, 397
    pooling of resources for, 354, 361, 361*b*
    reputation on bond market, 345*b*
    revenue or specific purpose, 339*b*, 342
    risks and credit ratings of, 343–44, 343*b*, 346,
        346*b*, 382, 398–400
    shortcomings of, 344–46
    short-term *vs.* long-term, 340
    standardization of, 345*b*
    structured, 343
    successful issue of, conditions for, 346–47

tax-free status in U.S., 340
    underwriting of, 340*b*
municipal contracts, 29–32, 30*b*, 31*b*, 35, 256, 256*b*, 334
Municipal Demarcation Board (South Africa),
    83, 91*n*6
Municipal Development Agency (ADM, Senegal), 393
municipal development funds (MDFs), 59, 359,
    361–64
municipal enterprises (companies), 286–87, 311–12
municipal finance improvement plan, 404, 406,
    438–39
Municipal Finance Management Act No. 56 of 2003
    (South Africa), 140*b*
municipal finance self-assessment (MFSA), 29, 31*b*,
    255–56, 381, 402–39, 447
    access to external funding in, 404
    accountability in, 404
    of assets and maintenance, 420, 424–25
    benchmarking in, 404
    of capital investment, 410, 416, 420, 426
    of cash balance and arrears, 410, 414, 420, 426–27
    city profile in, 406–10
    databases for, 410–17
    definitions in, 418–19*b*
    efficiency and transparency in, 404
    of expenditures, 404, 410–13, 423–25
    of financial management, 435–37
    of financial position, 420
    financial projections in, 404, 406, 431–34
    functions of, 404
    generic financial framework for, 418, 418–19*b*
    historical analysis and summary tables in, 406,
        419–27
    improvement plan in, 438–39
    of indebtedness, 410, 414–15, 420, 425
    innovations of, 404–5
    of intergovernmental transfers, 420, 423
    key findings from, 406–7
    modules of, 406–7
    for municipal contracts, 31*b*
    objective of, 402–4
    prioritization in, 404
    ratio analysis in, 427–30
    of revenue, 404, 410–13, 421
    South-East Europe experience with, 403*b*
    of tax potential and performance, 410, 417,
        420, 422
    template for, 406–39

performance measurement in, 380, 381, 382–87,
383*b*, 385*b*

North Carolina
capital plan in Charlotte, 330, 331, 332, 334
performance-based budgeting in, 264

Norway
debt regulation in, 349*b*
local income tax in, 172
water tariff in, 176*b*

Novi Sad, Serbia, municipal bonds in, 342*b*

NPV. *See* net present value

Nyiregyhaza, Hungary, targeted subsidies in, 238

O

OBA. *See* output-based aid

objectivity principle, 113

object-of-expenditure (line-item) budgets, 95, 96

obligations (commitments), financial, 110–11, 111*b*

obligations accounting, 111

observations, auditor's, 142

occupancy rate, 305

OECD countries
debt regulation in, 348
decentralization in, 34
local revenue in, 152, 159, 212*n*2
water tariffs in, 176*b*

"old ways" approach, 9–10, 33

one-stop shops, 207–8

Ontario, Canada. *See also* Toronto, Canada
performance measurement in, 385*b*, 386

OP. *See orcamento participativo*

open-ended, matching transfers, 15–16

open government, 400–401. *See also* accountability;
transparency

Open Society Institute, 374, 400

operating analysis, 305

operating (current) budget, 97, 418, 418*b*

operating expense(s), 300*b*, 420, 423–24

operating expense ratio, 303

operating income, net, 302

operating statements, 299–301, 300*b*, 303

operating surplus, 326–28, 420

operational efficiency, 215–16, 220. *See also* expenditure management

operation costs, 307–10

operation expenditures, and tariff setting, 235–36

operations of fixed assets, accounting for, 129–32

operation subsidies, 238–39, 240

Orange County, California, bankruptcy of, 347, 352*b*

orcamento participativo (OP), in Brazil, 102, 103*b*

Organisation for Economic Co-operation and
Development. *See* OECD countries

OSR. *See* own-source revenue

"other recurrent revenues," 180

Ouagadougou, Burkina Faso
expenditure management in, 401
hybrid financing in, 355, 356*b*
street addressing initiative in, 190

output-based aid (OBA), 371

output-based transfers, 14, 19–20, 26–32, 34–35

overhead costs, 299

oversight, 269–70

own expenditures, 226

own-source revenue (OSR), 4–5, 13, 105, 156–80
capital, 180
categories of, 157, 157*b*
definition of, 105, 148, 156
development level and, 151–52
local institutional capacity for, 162, 188–89, 189*b*
nontax sources of, 105, 157, 175–80. *See also specific
user charges and fees*
shared revenue *vs.*, 18, 155–56
as share of total revenue, 152, 157–58
size of municipality and, 151, 152
tax sources of, 105, 147–50, 155–71. *See also
specific taxes*

P

Pacioli, Luca, 112*b*

Pakistan. *See also specific cities*
balanced budgets *vs.* fiscal deficits in, 217–18
construction capacities in, 249–50
financial holding in, 312
informal settlements in, 46
intergovernmental transfers in, 22, 29
lack of coordinated planning in, 335*b*
land development corporations in, 321
local borrowing prohibited in, 347
local revenue in, 151
management information system in, 250, 251
manual accounting in, 118–19*b*
manual cashbook in, 234
municipal companies in, 287
natural resource sharing in, 29
participatory budgeting in, 102
property taxes, 165–67, 169

public-private partnership in, 371–72
tariffs and subsidies in, 237
user charges in, 175
vertical imbalances in, 13
water tariff in, 176*b*
Panama, municipal development fund in, 362
Parana State Urban Development Fund (FDU, Brazil), 362, 363*b*
Paris, France, metropolitan governance in, 48
participatory budgeting, 94–95, 101–4, 225, 401, 402*b*
benefits of, 103–4
examples of, 102, 102*b*, 103*b*
process of, 101–2
partners
financial, accountability to, 396–400
public–private. *See* public–private partnerships
pay-as-you-go financing, 326–28
pay-as-you-use financing, 326
payback rule, 257
payment systems, 233–34
PEFA. *See* Public Expenditure and Financial Accountability Assessment
penalties, revenue from, 179
Pennsylvania
annexation by Pittsburgh in, 83
bankruptcy by Harrisburg in, 328, 329*b*, 347, 351, 353–54
pension funds, 129*b*, 139
People's Plan Campaign for the Ninth Plan (PPC, India), 102*b*
percent change, 198*b*
performance audit, 141–42
performance-based budgets, 262–65, 264–65*b*, 394–95
performance-based grants, 19–20, 26–32, 34–35, 382, 397–98, 439*n*1
performance-based transfers, 396–98
performance measurement, 379–441
accountability in, 380, 394–402, 447
benchmarking in. *See* benchmarking
budgetary, 380, 394–95. *See also* performance-based budgets
citizen information and participation in, 393–94, 400–402
citizen participation in, 382–87, 384*b*, 388–89
comparisons in, 384
culture of, 380, 381
data for, 28–29, 391–93, 396

decentralization and, 390
in developing countries, 380, 390–93
dimensions of, 379–80
distortions in, 29
European approach to, 381, 387–89
in expenditure management, 254–56, 380
feedback in, 401
financial analysis in, 380–81
financial crisis and, 380, 388
financial partners and, 390–91, 396–400
formats for, 383–84
in grant process. *See* performance-based grants
in human resource management, 385
importance of, 446–47
indicators in, 384–87
internal financial monitoring in, 393, 394
lessons learned in, 381–93
methods and tools for, 393–402
in nonmarket economies, 381–82
objective of, 380
in public-private partnerships, 371
ratio analysis in, 394, 427–30
in revenue management, 204
risk analysis in, 393, 398, 399
self-assessment for. *See* municipal finance self-assessment
in service delivery, 385
standards for, caution on, 439*n*3
state (central government) supervision in, 393–98
third-party monitoring in, 401
too-ambitious system of, 387
U.S/Canadian system of, 380, 381, 382–87, 383*b*, 384*b*, 385*b*
performance reporting, 139, 140–41
periphery, of metropolitan area, 42
permanent funds, 129*b*
permanently restricted (PR) assets, 125–26
permit fees, 178–79
Peru
development rights in, 313
participatory budgeting in, 401
revenue sharing in, 18
philanthropic contributions, 181, 328, 374–75
Philippines
community fund in, 375
credit guarantees in, 353, 354*b*, 359
decentralization and nation building in, 11–12, 11*b*
fiscal equalization in, 23

property-related subsidies, 306–7
property taxes, 154b, 157–71
    appropriateness and usefulness of, 158–59
    assessment of tax base for, 155, 164–69, 185
    as benefit tax, 158, 212n3
    billing, delivery, collection, and enforcement of,
        169–71, 212n4
    cadastre for, 160–61b, 162–64, 191
    computer-aided, mass valuation systems (CAMA)
        for, 159–62, 162b, 168–69, 168b
    debate over, 170–71
    in developing countries, 159–62, 160–61b, 164–65
    development level and, 152
    disadvantages of, 159
    exemptions from, 210
    forecasting revenue from, 199–200
    as good local tax, 170, 211
    history of, 158, 159b
    local capacity for, 162
    as percentage of GDP, 159
    property identification for, 162–64, 184, 185,
        190–91, 191b
    property rights and, 159
    rates of, establishing, 169
    revenue enhancement programs and, 191–94
    revenue mobilization strategies for, 207, 207b
    split-rate, 183b
    street addressing system for, 184–85, 190–91, 191b,
        208, 208b, 212n6
proprietary funds, 129b
public contributions (donations), 181, 325, 368–74
public domain, 277, 277b
Public Expenditure and Financial Accountability
    Assessment (PEFA), 254–55, 260, 401, 435–37
public goods
    budget planning for, 94
    financing of, 147, 150
public land, sales of, 181–83
Public-Private Infrastructure Advisory Facility
    (PPIAF), 235, 324n6
public-private partnerships (PPPs), 59, 181, 327–28,
    368–74
    access to, performance measures and, 398–400
    asset management in, 287, 320–21
    benefits for the poor in, 373–74, 373b
    benefits of, 370–71
    build-operate-transfer arrangements in, 320, 370
    capital investment planning in, 230

    characteristics of, 369
    concessions in, 370, 373b
    contracting in, 248–49, 369–70
    cost savings in, 370
    failed or troubled, 371, 372–73
    feasibility studies for, 372, 372b
    forms of, 320, 369–70
    land-for-infrastructure approach in, 182, 211, 313
    lessons learned in, 371
    performance monitoring of, 371
    renegotiation or cancellation of, 371, 373
    risk sharing in, 370
    risks of, 371
    service delivery in, 209, 369, 371
    successful cases of, 371–72
    tariff (user charge) setting in, 235
Public Record of Operations and Finance (PROOF,
    India), 138b, 139
public sector accounting. See also accounting
    commercial accounting vs., 110
    key terms in, 110–11, 111b
public sector size, decentralization and, 12

Q

qariya (village), in Egypt, 6b
qualified audit opinion, 142, 145
qualitative revenue forecasts, 197, 202
quality-of-life measures, 391–93
quantitative revenue forecasts, 197, 198b
Quezon City Materials Recovery Facilities
    (Philippines), 371
Quito, Ecuador, metropolitan governance in, 50–51,
    74, 90

R

RAJUK. See Dhaka Capital Development Authority
Randstad (Netherlands), 82, 90
ratio analysis, 394, 427–30
"reaction from below," 2, 10, 33
reallocations, 233
recapitalization, 308
receipts and payment account, 123
recurrent revenue. See current revenue
reference rate. See discount rate
regional authorities, 51, 55, 61–71
regional development agency, 52b
regional (metropolitan-level) government, 51, 56,
    71–82

regional planning and service delivery authorities, 55, 63, 69–71

Regional Planning Association (RPA, New York City area), 67

regional planning authorities, 50, 51, 55, 63, 67

regional service delivery authorities, 55, 63, 68–69

registration, for local revenue collection, 183–84

registration fees, vehicle, 174

regressive tax, 171

relevance, of financial reports, 136

reliability, of revenue forecasts, 197–98

rent, as current revenue from assets, 179–80

rental value, for property taxation, 165–67

rent subsidies, 306–7

replacement cost, 298

residual land value, 298b

resource allocation, 222, 223b. See also expenditure management

responsibility accounting budgets, 134

responsibility accounting system, 133–34

restoration and modernization (R&M) costs, 308

results-based chain, 19–20

results benchmarking, 267

return on asset (RoA), 303

return on equity (RoE), 303

return on investment, 302–3

revenue, local, 147–214, 445

  accountability in collection, 158, 182–83, 194

  administration for, 183–94

    assessment functions in, 155, 164–69, 183, 185

    billing and collection functions in, 169–71, 183, 185–86, 189, 212n7

    enforcement functions in, 169–71, 183, 185–88, 209

    identification and registration functions in, 162–64, 183–84, 190–91, 190b, 191b

    local institutional capacity for, 162, 188–89, 189b

    street addressing systems in, 184–85, 190–91, 191b, 208, 208b, 212n6

  assets as source of, 280, 296, 297. See also income-generating properties

  authority to raise or collect, 153–55

  benefit principle and, 150, 151, 211

  budget approval of, 203–4

  budget debate over, 202–3

  budget execution of, 204

  budgeting of, 194–204

  capital, 155–56, 180–83, 419b

  vs. central government revenue, 154b

  classification of, 155–56

  current, 155–56, 419b

  decentralization and, 148–49

  development level and, 151–52

  enhancement of, programs for, 191–94, 192b, 193b, 202, 445

  estimation of, 155, 188b, 196–202. See also revenue forecasts

  incentives for collection, 189

  land-based, 181–84, 312–14

  management of, principles of, 150

  mobilization of. See revenue mobilization

  monitoring and evaluation of, 204, 205b

  municipal policy on, 208–11

  nontax sources of, 105, 154, 157, 175–80. See also specific user charges and fees

  outsourcing collection of, 209

  projected, 330, 431–34

  role of, 148–50

  self-assessment (MFSA) of, 404, 410–13, 421

  as share of total public revenue, 149, 445

  size of municipality and, 151, 152

  sources of, 147–48, 154b, 155–80

  structure of, 150–53, 155–56

  summary table of, 420, 421

  tax sources of, 105, 147–50, 155–71, 211–12. See also specific taxes

  from transfers. See intergovernmental transfers

revenue assignment, 2, 4–5, 12, 13–14. See also intergovernmental transfers

revenue bonds, 339b, 342

revenue budget cycle, 194–204

revenue collection sharing, 17–19

revenue forecasts, 196–202, 203b

revenue intercepts, 353

revenue mobilization

  decentralization and, 208, 208b

  improving collection efficiency for, 207–8

  linking revenue collection to service provision for, 205–7, 206b

  metropolitan, 58b

  strategies for, 204–8

revenue planning, 196

revenue sharing, 17–19, 34, 148

  derivation principle in, 18–19

  listing in financial documents, 18

  local reliance on, 152

competitiveness of, 388–89, 391–93
performance measurement of, 385
public-private partnership for, 209, 369, 371
ratio analysis of, 429
Service Efforts and Accomplishments reporting
(GASB), 140–41
settlements, informal, in metropolitan areas, 43–46,
91n1
SFCs. *See* state finance commissions
Shanghai, China
development promotion in, 182, 211
metropolitan governance in, 48, 61, 62, 64*b*,
85–86, 91
municipality and metropolitan area of, 85–86, 87
solid waste disposal system in, 62, 64*b*
special purpose vehicles in, 350, 355
World Bank financing in, 365
shared taxes. *See* tax sharing
Simon, Herbert, 383*b*
Singapore
congestion (vehicle) taxes in, 175, 211–12
land development corporations in, 321
single-entry accounting, 110, 114, 127
SKS Microfinance (India), 371
Slack, Enid, 91n5, 164
Slovak Republic, EU-EBRD financing in, 365
Slovenia
EU-EBRD financing in, 365
water tariff in, 176*b*
Slum Dwellers International, 375
slums, 46
social accountability, 400–402
social audits, 205–6, 212n9
Sofia, Bulgaria, municipal bonds in, 341*b*
solid waste. *See* waste management
Soros Foundation, 374
South Africa. *See also specific cities*
bank lending in, 360
fiscal data in, 26
intergovernmental transfers in, 14, 20–22, 21*b*, 26,
29, 398
local revenue in, 153
metropolitan governance in, 51, 53, 83, 84, 84*b*,
86*b*, 89, 91n6
municipal bonds in, 341*b*, 342, 342*b*, 361, 400
municipal development fund in, 361, 363*b*
municipal financial management in, 139, 140*b*
municipal insolvency in, 351

natural resource sharing in, 29
performance-based grants in, 398
philanthropic aid in, 374
property taxes in, 159, 168
water tariff in, 176*b*
South Asia
budget approval in, 90
land development corporations in, 321–22
metropolitan governance in, 50, 90
pooled-financing bonds in, 355*b*
South-East Europe
financial risk analysis in, 398, 399
municipal finance self-assessment in, 403*b*
revenue sharing in, 19
South Sudan, decentralization and nation building in,
11, 11*b*
Spain
debt regulation in, 349*b*
local business taxes in, 172
local government borrowing in, 339*b*
local revenue in, 153
metropolitan finance in, 59, 91n2
sales taxes in, 171
water tariff in, 176*b*
spatial development plan, 314–15
special interest groups, 270–71, 271*b*
special purpose districts. *See* regional authorities
special purpose vehicles (SPVs), 350, 354–55,
355*b*, 360
special revenue funds, 126, 128*b*, 139
specifications (terms of reference), 244, 246
specific purpose bonds, 339*b*, 342
specific purpose transfers, 14–17, 34. *See also* conditional transfers
speculation, land, 183*b*, 321
spillovers, in metropolitan governance, 49
spillovers, tax, 57
split-rate property tax, 183*b*
sprawl, 43, 44, 183*b*
SPVs. *See* special purpose vehicles
Sri Lanka, municipal development fund in, 362
Standard & Poor's, 343–44, 398–99
state finance commissions (SFCs, India), 22
statement of activities, 139, 145
statement of financial position. *See* balance sheet
statement of net assets, 139
statement of receipts and payments, 115, 123,
124–25, 126

state revolving funds, 360
state supervision, in performance measurement,
   393–98
stock-based business tax, 172–73
Stockholm, Sweden, congestion (vehicle) taxes in, 175
street addressing
   for collection of revenue (taxes), 184–85, 190–91,
      191b, 208, 208b, 212n6
   for collection of user charges, 237, 238b
   for inventory of assets, 282
structured bonds, 343
Stuttgart, Germany
   development rights in, 313
   metropolitan governance in, 79, 90
Sub-Saharan Africa. See also specific countries
   metropolitan governance in, 51
   municipal contracts in, 30
subsidiary principle, 2–3, 11
subsidies, 234–42
   allocation of, 240–42
   blanket balance sheet, 237
   capital, 239–40
   demand-side, 240
   in developing countries, 236–37, 237b
   fairness issues in, 234
   forms and implications of, 238–40
   management of, 237–42
   operation, 238–39, 240
   property-related (rent), 306–7
   self-assessment of, 411–13
   service delivery, to private sector, 371
   supply-side, 240
   targeted, 209–11, 238–42, 306
Sudan, decentralization and nation building in, 11, 11b
summary tables, in municipal finance self-
   assessment, 406, 419–27
Sunnyvale, California, performance-based budgeting
   in, 264–65, 264–65b
supplementary budget, 100–101, 107, 233
suppliers, as users of financial reports, 136
supply-side subsidies, 240
supreme audit institutions (SAIs), 120, 142–43
surcharges on utilities, 177–78, 178b, 212n5
surplus properties, 293–94, 314–16
surtax, 17
sustainability
   in intergovernmental transfers, 25
   in municipal finance self-assessment, 406

Sutton (London borough), United Kingdom, cost-efficiency program in, 204, 205b
Sweden
   local income tax in, 172
   local revenue in, 153
   municipal contracts in, 30
Switzerland
   financial accountability assessment in, 255
   philanthropic organizations in, 374
syndicats intercommunaux, in France, 69

T
T-accounts, 113–14, 121
Tamil Nadu, India
   municipal development fund in, 362, 363b
   special purpose vehicle in, 354, 355b, 360
tangible (physical) assets, 276. See also asset(s)
Tanzania
   development fund in, 59
   failure to pay taxes in, 187b
   informal settlements in, 91n1
   metropolitan governance in, 72, 73–74b, 89
   property valuation/taxation in, 159
   public-private partnerships in, 248–49, 373, 373b
   urbanization and economic growth in, 48
targeted subsidies, 209–11, 238–42, 306
tariffs. See user charges
task force, on asset management, 289, 322
tax(es)
   authority of local governments, 153–55
   billing and collection of, 169–71, 183, 185–86,
      189, 212n7
   in city profile, 409
   criteria for choosing best, 210b
   easy and convenient payments of, 186
   enforcement of, 169–71, 183, 186–88, 212n4
   failure to pay, reasons for, 186–87, 187b
   good, features of, 149–50, 150b, 155
   identifying payers of, 162–64, 183–85, 190–91,
      190b, 208, 208b
   impact analysis of, 209–11
   incentives for compliance, 189
   linking service provision to collection of, 205–7,
      206b
   local, 147–50, 155–75, 211–12. See also specific types
   potential and performance, self-assessment of,
      410, 417, 420, 422
   revenue enhancement programs and, 191–94

Ukraine
	local business taxes in, 173*b*, 174
	local revenue in, 153
unconditional (general purpose) transfers, 14, 15–16, 34
understandability, of financial reporting, 137
underwriting, 340*b*
undesignated assets, 126
unforeseen events, intergovernmental transfers for, 29
unfunded mandate, 7, 271–72
union parishads, in Bangladesh, 144*b*
unitary systems, 7
United Kingdom. *See also specific cities*
	betterment fees in, 314
	debt regulation in, 349*b*
	Department for International Development, 400
	metropolitan governance in, 48, 53, 67–68, 76, 76*b*, 82, 89
	municipal contracts in, 30
	performance measurement in, 380, 386
	property taxes in, 152, 157, 159
	public-private partnerships in, 320
	water tariff in, 176*b*
United Nations Carbon Authority, 366*b*
United States. *See also specific cities and states*
	accounting standards in, 112
	bond financing in, 339, 340, 354, 361
	financial reporting in, 139–41
	local business taxes in, 174
	local insolvency in, 328, 329*b*, 347, 351, 352*b*, 376*n*3
	performance measurement in, 380, 381, 382–87, 383*b*, 385*b*
	philanthropic aid from, 374
	property taxes in, 152, 164, 169, 170
	sales taxes in, 171
	surplus military properties in, 313
	utility surcharges in, 177, 178*b*
U.S. Agency for International Development (USAID), 328, 354, 364
U.S. Association of Contract Cities, 62*b*
Unit Guarantee Corporation (Philippines), 353, 354*b*, 359
unqualified audit opinion, 142, 145
unrestricted (UR) assets, 125–26
urban agglomeration, 42, 42*b*, 43–46
urban audit, 31*b*, 255–56, 289, 291*b*
	municipal finance self-assessment with, 403*b*, 404, 405*b*–406*b*
urban concessions, 373*b*

urbanization, 41–49, 86. *See also* metropolitan areas
Urban Renewal Authority of Hong Kong, 287
USAID. *See* U.S. Agency for International Development
user charges, 154*b*, 175–79, 176*b*, 234–42
	capital investment funds from, 231
	computing or setting of, 176–77
		average cost pricing for, 177
		average incremental pricing for, 177
		capital expenditures and, 235–36
		cost-plus pricing for, 234–35
		expenditure control in, 231, 234–37
		main steps in, 231*b*
		marginal cost pricing for, 176
		operation expenditures and, 235–36
		principles of, 236
		in public-private partnerships, 235
	cost recovery through, 175–77, 231, 236
	database assessment for, 185
	designing, 175
	in developing countries, 234, 236–37, 237*b*
	difficulties with, 177
	economic rationale for, 175
	free ridership *vs.*, 185, 185*b*
	impact analysis of, 209–11
	linking to service cost, 206–7, 209
	multipart, 177
	politics of, 175
	price regulation of, 209
	revenue mobilization strategy for, 206–7
	street addressing system for collecting, 237, 238*b*
	subsidies for, 209, 210–11, 234–42
utility budgets, 409, 411–13
utility surcharges, 177–78, 178*b*, 212*n*5
Utrecht, Netherlands, metropolitan governance in, 82, 90
Uzbekistan, procurement reform in, 246*b*
Uzgen, Kyrgyzstan, public contributions in, 375

V

validity, of revenue forecasts, 197–98
Vallejo, California, bankruptcy of, 329*b*
valorization, 181–82, 182*b*
valuation
	of assets, 296–99, 323*n*2
	of property, for taxation, 155, 164–69
value added tax (VAT), 154*b*, 171
value-based assessment, 164–69

value-capture technique, 148, 181, 183*b*

value for money (VfM), 204, 205*b*, 246, 247, 380

Vancouver, Canada

citizens and performance measurement in, 384*b*

metropolitan finance in, 58*b*

metropolitan governance in, 68–69, 88

variable costs, 134

variance analysis, 108–9, 265–66, 269

variation orders, 250

VAT. *See* value added tax

VDCs. *See* village development committees

vehicle taxes, 174–75, 211–12

vehicle violations, revenue from, 179

Venezuela, metropolitan governance in, 51, 74

Verband Stuttgart Region (Germany), 79

verifiability, of financial reporting, 137

vertical fiscal gap, 13

vertical imbalance, 5, 13, 18, 22, 33

VfM. *See* value for money

Vietnam

municipal development fund in, 362

performance-based grants in, 398

public-private partnership in, 371–72

special purpose vehicle in, 360

Village Act of 1956 (Nepal), 3*b*

Village Development Committee Act of 1991 (Nepal), 3*b*

village development committees (VDCs), in Nepal, 3*b*

Village Panchayat Act of 1962 (Nepal), 3*b*

virements, 233

Virginia. *See also* Fairfax County, Virginia

political pressure and expenditures in, 272

visibility, of public fund use, 404

voivodship (region), in Poland, 4*b*

volumetric tariff, 176*b*

W

Warsaw, Poland, assets as wealth of, 280

Washington, D.C.

bankruptcy of, 347

development promotion in, 182

metropolitan finance in, 59, 60*b*

metropolitan governance in, 63–64, 65, 65*b*, 88

Washington Metropolitan Area Transit Authority (WMATA), 59

waste management

comparative costs of, 266

environmental loans and credits for, 366–67*b*, 366–68, 371

inventorying assets for, 292

metropolitan governance and, 62, 64*b*

street addressing for, 237, 238*b*

Water and Sanitation Pooled Fund (India), 361, 361*b*

water tariffs and subsidies, 175, 176*b*, 236, 241–42, 241*b*

wealth, assets as, 279–80

weekly cash forecast, 254

welfare gains, in decentralization, 6, 10–11, 33

West Bank

property tax in, 170*b*

utility surcharges in, 177–78

WMATA. *See* Washington Metropolitan Area Transit Authority

World Bank

auditing initiatives of, 255–56

energy-efficiency programs of, 366

financial assessment tool of, 402–4. *See also* municipal finance self-assessment

financial assistance from, 364–65, 364*b*

general purpose (unconditional) transfers from, 14

municipal contracts supported/evaluated by, 30, 32, 32*b*

municipal development fund program of, 362

performance-based programs of, 26, 391

property tax programs of, 159–62, 167, 190–91, 207*b*

revenue enhancement programs of, 191–94, 192*b*

street addressing initiatives of, 190–91

urban audit framework of, 404

Wyoming, revenue authority in, 155

Z

Zimbabwe

municipal bonds in, 341*b*

municipal development funds in, 362

ZMVM. *See* Metropolitan Zone of the Valley of Mexico